T0335591

COMPUTER ARCHITECTURE

Digital Circuits to Microprocessors

COMPUTER ARCHITECTURE

Digital Circuits to Microprocessors

Guilherme Arroz • José Monteiro
Arlindo Oliveira

Instituto Superior Técnico, Portugal

World Scientific

NEW JERSEY • LONDON • SINGAPORE • BEIJING • SHANGHAI • HONG KONG • TAIPEI • CHENNAI • TOKYO

Published by

World Scientific Publishing Co. Pte. Ltd.

5 Toh Tuck Link, Singapore 596224

USA office: 27 Warren Street, Suite 401-402, Hackensack, NJ 07601

UK office: 57 Shelton Street, Covent Garden, London WC2H 9HE

Library of Congress Cataloging-in-Publication Data

Names: Arroz, Guilherme, author. | Monteiro, José, author. | Oliveira, Arlindo L., author.

Title: Computer architecture : digital circuits to microprocessors / by
  (author) Guilherme Arroz (Instituto Superior Técnico, Portugal),
  José Monteiro, (Instituto Superior Técnico, Portugal),
  Arlindo Oliveira, (Instituto Superior Técnico, Portugal).

Description: New Jersey : World Scientific, [2018] | Includes index.

Identifiers: LCCN 2018008587 | ISBN 9789813238336 (hc : alk. paper)

Subjects: LCSH: Computer architecture.

Classification: LCC QA76.9.C62 A77 2018 | DDC 004.2/2--dc23

LC record available at https://lccn.loc.gov/2018008587

British Library Cataloguing-in-Publication Data

A catalogue record for this book is available from the British Library.

Based on a translation from the Portuguese language edition:

Arquitectura de Computadores: dos Sistemas Digitais aso Microprocessadores by Guilherme Arroz, José Monteiro
and Arlindo Oliveira

Copyright © IST Press 2014, 2009, 2007 Instituto Superior Técnico

All Rights Reserved

Copyright © 2019 by José Monteiro, Arlindo Oliveira, and Guilherme Arroz

All rights reserved.

For any available supplementary material, please visit
https://www.worldscientific.com/worldscibooks/10.1142/10940#t=suppl

Desk Editor: Herbert Moses

Typeset by Stallion Press
Email: enquiries@stallionpress.com

Printed in Singapore

Preface

Until the last decades of the 20th century, the real world was viewed as a system described by continuous values. The perception that human beings had about the physical world, regarding sounds, images and other sensations, was one of inherently continuous phenomena. The same happened with models of physical systems, both inanimate and biological. To model and study various physical systems, analogue computers were developed during and immediately after the Second World War. These computers enabled the accurate modelling of those continuous physical values.

This vision suffered significant changes with the emergence of digital computers and, above all, with the popularisation of their use, boosted by technological advances resulting from integrated circuit technologies and magnetic and optical information storage.

It has thus become clear that magnitudes such as the intensity of light coming from a given direction or the pressure of air at a given point in time can be represented, with various advantages, by a numerical value digitally stored in a computer memory. Technology allowed the storage of these values (images and sounds, after suitable transformations from the analogue domain to the digital domain). Simultaneously the same technologies made possible the subsequent reproduction of the stored values (locally or remotely) on a computer monitor or a speaker, giving rise to a set of ever-present features of the modern society of today. These include, among others, telecommunications (telephones, computers and mobile phones) and various aspects of the entertainment industry (music, cinema, television and games) which are now based, in one way or another, on the digital encoding of information.

These applications, which already existed with different technologies before the appearance of digital computers, were joined by a set of applications made possible through computers and their use. Among those, information systems (databases, banking services, e-commerce) are of note, many of them boosted by the emergence of the Internet, the worldwide network connecting most of the world's computers. Mobile systems, all of them based on digital technologies, became ubiquitous in our lives and a fixture of today's daily life. Along with the rapid deployment of computers and digital technologies, it has also been found that, to a certain extent, biological systems are also encoded by nature in a manner comparable to that of digital technology. Genetic information is stored in a discrete manner in the DNA molecules which make up the chromosomes of organisms. As a result of large genome sequencing projects, there are now databases with complete information on the genome of numerous organisms, including humans. Likewise, the connection between these two areas has led to greater activity in the interface between biological systems and digital technology.

We are therefore living in an era in which all information is gradually becoming digital. In its simplest version, digital information is stored using some mechanism (electronic, magnetic or optical) which, at the lowest level, is physically supported by storing two possible values. The physical quantity used to represent each of these values may be an electrical voltage (in the case of a computer memory), reflectivity (in an optical disc) or a state of magnetisation (in a magnetic disk). In all cases, these different physical quantities always represent a discrete variable, which can typically take on the values 0 or 1. Since each of the variables involved has so little capacity to represent information, the effective use of digital systems implies the use of a very high number of variables of this type (bits) to represent useful information, from registers in databases to images, sounds or video.

The study of digital systems is thus essential not only for the professionals who directly design and operate computers but also for all those who wish to understand the foundations of the present-day society, deeply and systematically. The detailed way to encode films, music or communications is, obviously, outside the scope of an introductory book like this. These techniques, which have evolved over the last decades, represent a significant accumulated body of knowledge which it is not possible to address when first studying this material. However, all these matters depend on the knowledge of basic encoding techniques and digital information processing, which form the focus of the study of this book.

Therefore we will describe, in this book, the basic techniques of encoding information, and the fundamental concepts which form the basis of the computational systems that process and transform this information. The interested readers can then carry out a more in-depth study of these topics, both regarding encoding and information representation, as well as those related to computer system architectures.

There are numerous approaches to the topic of digital systems. At one extreme, there are the purely mathematical or algebraic approaches, which completely ignore the aspect of implementation. At the other extreme, there are those which start from electronic system technologies, giving special emphasis to the physical aspects related to the construction of digital systems.

This book has opted for an intermediate approach which, although not completely ignoring the physical aspects of the topic, essentially considers digital systems as abstract information processing elements which constitute the blocks of a computer.

From this perspective, this book has been designed as a support for an initial study of computer architectures, typically made in the context of two university-level semester courses. We anticipate that this book can be naturally used in the areas of Computer Science, Electronics and Electrical Engineering, but also in other technical areas, where there is interest in training students in digital systems, such as Mechanical Engineering, Physics Engineering or Aerospace Engineering.

A typical course will cover, in the first semester, the topics of digital systems that are the first part of the book, Chapters 1–8. The second semester typically covers the computer architecture components described in the second part of the book, made up of the remaining chapters.

It is also possible to consider the use of Chapters 9–11 and 13–15 as support for an introductory course on computer architecture, from a programmers point of view, for students who only have basic knowledge of digital systems. In this case, certain sections of these chapters will have to be covered in a necessarily superficial manner.

Chapter 1 describes the fundamental concepts related to the digital representation of information, the use of number systems using different bases, the arithmetic operations using these bases and conversions between representations with different bases.

Chapter 2 analyses logic functions and how they are manipulated, synthesised and optimised. Boolean logic is presented, in a systematic manner, but with a utilitarian perspective of describing the formulas used to manipulate logic expressions.

Chapter 3 deals, in a necessarily brief and synthetic way, with the technologies used to implement logic circuits and the limitations imposed by physical restrictions on the design of digital circuits.

Chapter 4 starts the process of integrating fundamental components, with the aim of constructing basic computer blocks. This chapter describes combinational modules of medium complexity, constructed using the logic gates previously studied.

Chapter 5 deals with the construction of arithmetic modules that allow the execution of basic arithmetic operations in base 2, and some aspects of the issues related to the performance of those modules.

Chapter 6 presents for the first time the concept of sequential behaviour and describes the circuits which preserve the state of the system (latches and flip-flops) and exhibit a behaviour that takes into account past history of the circuit.

Chapter 7 is dedicated to the design, analysis and optimisation of sequential circuits, which use the latches and flip-flops studied in the previous chapter as basic elements.

Chapter 8, which can be considered as the concluding chapter of the first part of the book, describes how the circuits of intermediate complexity studied in Chapters 4–6 may be interconnected, to process complex data when controlled by the systems studied in Chapter 7.

Chapter 9 represents a general introduction to computers, seen from a generalist perspective. It aims at providing the transition between the detailed analysis carried out in the first part of the book, dedicated to digital systems, and the high-level analysis which will gradually characterise the second part of the book, dedicated to computer architectures.

Chapter 10 presents the concepts of instruction and instruction set for a processor, and studies the way instructions are specified, executed and encoded. This chapter also introduces the P3 processor, the Petite Pedagogic Processor, which is the platform that will be used to practice the programming and architecture concepts which are the topics of the following two chapters.

Chapter 11 is dedicated to programming techniques in assembly language, using the P3 processor as a platform for the study and development of small programming projects.

Chapter 12 presents and analyses the internal structure of a processor, once again using the P3 as a case study. In this chapter, the P3 is used as a concrete example of how to design the internal circuits of a simple processor, including the datapath and the control circuit components.

The following three chapters cover, in a necessarily compact manner, architectural concepts which cannot be covered completely and systematically in an introductory book like this one. These chapters aim at describing the fundamental concepts involved in the use of memories, peripherals and more advanced pipelined architectures, without aspiring to cover these topics extensively.

Chapter 13 is dedicated to the study of memory systems and deals with basic concepts related to the organisation of memory maps, cache utilisation and virtual memory systems.

Chapter 14 deals with issues related to input/output operations and the use of peripherals in computer systems.

Finally, Chapter 15 provides a brief introduction to more advanced computer architectures, focusing on themes such as the use of pipelines and other alternatives which have been developed to exploit the parallelism present in computer programs. To focus this study, we use the P4 (Petite Pedagogic Processor with Pipeline) processor, which illustrates some of the concepts discussed.

Besides the text itself, and the series of problems included in the book, various resources have been created during the development of this work, which can be used to support training in this area. The concepts related to microprocessor architecture are studied in the lab using an implementation of a simple and didactic processor, the P3. To allow students to carry out work in labs on the same architecture studied in the lectures, the P3 has been described in VHDL and implemented in hardware on a board with an FPGA, external memory and a set of interface devices. At the same time, an assembler for P3 assembly and a simulator for this architecture were developed. Therefore, students can develop their programs in P3 assembly, generate the executable code, run the programs in the simulator and upload the executable to the board, through the parallel port of their computer. The simulator was intended to fully emulate the board, particularly regarding the peripherals available and their interface. On the one hand, the simulator allows students to run their programs anywhere and, on the other, it represents a precious tool for debugging their programs, since the debugging process in the board is much more complex. The fundamental limitation of the simulator is its speed of execution. On this board, the P3 has an operating frequency of 6.25 MHz. In addition to assembly level programming, both versions of the P3 allow the students to perform changes to the content of the control ROMs, which enables not only the alteration of the microprogram of the existing instructions but also the creation and micro-programming of new assembly instructions. These tools (assembler, simulator, implementation in VHDL) are freely available on the website of this book. Details of this implementation may be consulted in Appendix A.

A preface is never complete without the necessary acknowledgements section. Given the time this book took to be concluded, our initial thanks must go to our families who, for years, have uncomplainingly accepted the usual excuse for our systematic unavailability. To our wives, to whom this book is dedicated, as well as to our children, from whom we stole many hours to be able to finish it, here is a thank you from the bottom of our hearts.

Other thanks are due for more technical contributions. The reviewers, Pedro Diniz and João Cardoso, read preliminary versions of this work and contributed with many valuable suggestions to improve it. The students Jorge Santana, Nuno Barral and Fausto Ferreira, contributed to various aspects of the simulators and the implementation in hardware. The lecturers of the computer architecture courses at Técnico, Carlos Ribeiro, João Gonçalves, José Costa, Nuno Roma, Alberto Cunha and Nuno Horta, contributed with many comments, suggestions and various improvements. The editors and employees of IST Press, Joaquim Moura Ramos, Pedro Lourtie, Miguel Dionísio and Paulo Abreu, as well as the reviewers, provided valuable assistance during the editing and composition phase. The companies SAS Portugal and Novabase financially supported this publishing project, in the Portuguese original. The translation to English, a complex and lengthy process, was performed by David Hardisty. To all of you, our sincere thanks. Any typos, errors and omissions that remain, and there will surely be many, are entirely our responsibility. The authors José Monteiro and Arlindo Oliveira would also like to leave a very special thank you note to the third author, Guilherme Arroz, who performed the bulk of the work involved in creating the English version of this book.

Finally, the statement, obvious but indispensable, that all this has only been possible because of our parents.

Lisbon, December 2017

Arlindo Oliveira, José Monteiro
and Guilherme Arroz

Contents

Chapter 1

Digital Representation of Information

This chapter is focused on the ways computers represent information in digital format. In particular, it discusses the mechanisms used to represent various quantities in a digital computer. The digital electronic circuits that are commonly used in a digital computer can assume only one of two possible values, which implies that different quantities have to be represented in a format compatible with this restriction.

We will start by describing how integers are represented, both in the decimal number system, which is familiar to everybody and in other number systems more adequated to be manipulated by computers. In this chapter, this study is limited to non-negative integers and non-negative fractional numbers.

The chapter begins with Section 1.1, where we study binary, octal and hexadecimal number systems. Section 1.2 focuses on studying the foundations of binary arithmetic. Section 1.3 deals with the use of codes, both numeric (with emphasis on decimal codes) as well as alphanumeric (to represent other types of information). Section 1.4 concludes the chapter with some basic concepts on the organisation of binary representation of information.

1.1 Number Systems

This chapter deals with the representation of non-signed integer and fractional numbers. Later, in Chapter 5, this subject will be reconsidered to address the representation of signed integer and real numbers. The representation of numbers in digital systems has to be undertaken considering that they use devices which can represent only two possible values.

Given that the common representation of numbers is based on the utilisation of a decimal *number system*, using base-10, it is natural to consider that the representation of numbers in digital systems may be made using the binary system, using base-2. The *base* is the number of digits used to represent a number under a given number system.

1

The general case of representation using a generic base-b will be studied first, followed by the study of the base-2 case.

1.1.1   *Representation of Integers in Base-b*

The representation of a non-signed integer in base-10 is made using a sequence of digits. The number 435, for example, is represented by the sequence of digits 4, 3 and 5. The interpretation of the representation of a number results, firstly, from the digits used and, secondly, from their position within the sequence. As is evident, $435 \neq 354$, even though the digits used are the same.

The position of the digits indicates the *weight* for each digit. In the previous example, because the digit 4 is in the third position from the right, this means, in fact, four hundreds. The digit 3 represents three tens, and 5 represents five units. This system of representation of numbers is referred as *positional*.

This analysis can be stated more formally as follows:

$$435 = 400 + 30 + 5$$
$$= 4 \times 100 + 3 \times 10 + 5 \tag{1.1}$$

or, expressing the powers of 10 involved,

$$435 = 4 \times 10^2 + 3 \times 10^1 + 5 \times 10^0 \tag{1.2}$$

which is a more general way of representation, emphasising the powers of the base.

The number 435 is said to be represented in *base-10* since it results from the sum of consecutive powers of 10, each multiplied by the value of the corresponding digit as shown in Equation (1.2). To explicitly indicate that the number is represented in base-10, the following notation is used: 435_{10}. To represent a number in base-10, the weights of each power of 10 are indicated using digits from 0 to 9, using a total of 10 distinct digits.

There is nothing to prevent the use of another base to represent a number. Consider, for example, the sequence of digits 1161 in base-7, which is usually indicated by 1161_7. In this case, this representation has the following meaning:

$$1161_7 = 1 \times 7^3 + 1 \times 7^2 + 6 \times 7^1 + 1 \times 7^0$$
$$= 1 \times 343 + 1 \times 49 + 6 \times 7 + 1$$
$$= 435_{10}. \tag{1.3}$$

Therefore, 1161_7 is another way of representing the number 435_{10}.

Generally speaking, any integer N can be represented in any base-b with $b \geq 2$

$$N = p_{n-1} \times b^{n-1} + p_{n-2} \times b^{n-2} + \cdots + p_1 \times b^1 + p_0 \times b^0 \qquad (1.4)$$

or

$$N = \sum_{j=0}^{n-1} p_j \times b^j, \qquad (1.5)$$

where p_j is the digit which represents the weight of the jth power of the base. The number of digits necessary is b and it is usual that the digits are the integers between 0 and $b - 1$

$$p_j \in \{0, 1, \ldots, b - 1\}. \qquad (1.6)$$

Thus, to represent numbers in base-b, digits of a value equal to or greater than b cannot be used. For example, the representation of a number in base-7 cannot use the digit 7 nor any other digit greater than 7. The sequence of digits 1742_7 is therefore not a valid representation of a number.

The *conversion* of the representation of a number in base-b to a representation in base-10 is not difficult, as illustrated by Equation (1.3). The reverse, converting a number represented in base-10 to its representation in base-b requires a little more work, but it is also simple. One of the most common methods is the *method of successive divisions*. As an example, consider a number N represented in base-b, as shown in Equation (1.4). If the number is divided by b, this results in

$$\frac{N}{b} = (p_{n-1} \times b^{n-2} + p_{n-2} \times b^{n-3} + \cdots + p_1 \times b^0) + \frac{p_0 \times b^0}{b}$$

$$= (p_{n-1} \times b^{n-2} + p_{n-2} \times b^{n-3} + \cdots + p_1 \times b^0) + \frac{p_0}{b}, \qquad (1.7)$$

where p_0 is the rest of the division of N by b (remember that $p_0 < b$). In this way, the digit p_0 can be identified.

Repeating the previous procedure for the number $\frac{N}{b}$ will enable us to derive p_1 and through the successive application of the procedure, all the digits that represent the number.

As an example, consider obtaining the representation of the number 273_{10} in base-5

$$\frac{273}{5} = 54 + \frac{3}{5}. \qquad (1.8)$$

In the same way, the following can be obtained:

$$\frac{54}{5} = 10 + \frac{4}{5},$$
$$\frac{10}{5} = 2 + \frac{0}{5}, \tag{1.9}$$
$$\frac{2}{5} = 0 + \frac{2}{5}.$$

From Equations (1.8) and (1.9) it is easy to obtain $p_0 = 3$, $p_1 = 4$, $p_2 = 0$ e $p_3 = 2$. From which,

$$273_{10} = 2043_5. \tag{1.10}$$

1.1.2   *Representation of Non-signed Integers in Base-2*

The representation of numbers in *base-2* is important because, in computers and other digital systems, the representation of numbers has to be based on a set of two different values for some physical quantity. In digital computers, that physical quantity is usually the voltage between two points of an electronic circuit.

To represent an integer in base-2, two digits are required, usually designated by 0 and 1. Just as with other bases, an integer is, therefore, represented by a sequence of digits, in this case, *binary digits* or *bits*. Table 1.1 shows the integers from 0 to 15 represented in base-2.

For example, 110101_2 is a number represented in base-2 or, as it is also said, represented in *binary*.

The previous section presented a method to take a number in binary (or in any other base) and obtain the representation of the same number in base-10, the base we normally use.

Table 1.1   Representation of integers from 0 to 15 in base-2.

Base-10	Base-2	Base-10	Base-2
0	0	8	1000
1	1	9	1001
2	10	10	1010
3	11	11	1011
4	100	12	1100
5	101	13	1101
6	110	14	1110
7	111	15	1111

The technique used consisted in expressing the representation of the number in terms of weighted sums of the powers of the base and calculating the value of the number in base-10. This is a general technique, which can therefore also be applied for numbers represented in base-2. In the case of the number 110101_2 mentioned above, given that this is a 6 digit number, then

$$110101_2 = 1 \times 2^5 + 1 \times 2^4 + 0 \times 2^3 + 1 \times 2^2 + 0 \times 2^1 + 1 \times 2^0$$
$$= 32 + 16 + 4 + 1$$
$$= 53_{10}. \tag{1.11}$$

The inverse problem, the determination of the representation of a number in base-2 (or in any other base-b), given its representation in base-10 was also dealt with, by presenting the method of successive divisions. Now, using the number 23_{10} as an example, note that this number can be rewritten as

$$23 = 11 \times 2 + 1, \tag{1.12}$$

which makes explicit the quotient and the remainder of the division of the number by 2.

Now, the number 11 can be represented as $11 = 5 \times 2 + 1$, so that substituting this in Equation (1.12), the following is obtained:

$$23 = (5 \times 2 + 1) \times 2 + 1$$
$$= 5 \times 2^2 + 1 \times 2 + 1. \tag{1.13}$$

Now, given that $5 = 2 \times 2 + 1$, it is the case that

$$23 = (2 \times 2 + 1) \times 2^2 + 1 \times 2 + 1$$
$$= 2 \times 2^3 + 1 \times 2^2 + 1 \times 2 + 1. \tag{1.14}$$

And, as $2 = 1 \times 2 + 0$,

$$23 = (1 \times 2 + 0) \times 2^3 + 1 \times 2^2 + 1 \times 2 + 1$$
$$= 1 \times 2^4 + 0 \times 2^3 + 1 \times 2^2 + 1 \times 2 + 1. \tag{1.15}$$

Finally, writing out all the powers of 2, we obtain

$$23 = 1 \times 2^4 + 0 \times 2^3 + 1 \times 2^2 + 1 \times 2^1 + 1 \times 2^0. \tag{1.16}$$

It is now easy to see that the representation of number 23_{10} in base-2 is 10111_2.

The binary digits of the number are, as seen above, the successive remainders of the division by 2 of the initial number and the successive quotients. The most common (and fastest) way of carrying out the calculation, however, is the successive application of the usual algorithm for performing division and collecting the various remainders at the end.

2	23	Remainders	
2	11	1	Least significant bit
2	5	1	
2	2	1	
2	1	0	
	0	1	Most significant bit

The digit with the greatest weight corresponds to the remainder of the last division and so on until the digit with the least weight, which is the remainder of the first division.

1.1.3   *Representation of Fractional Numbers in Base-2*

The *representation of fractional numbers* in base-2 (or any other), does not present any problems, using the same method used for integers. A fractional number may have an integer part and a decimal part, that is, with a value less than 1. That decimal part, with n digits, is representable by the following expression:

$$N = p_{-1} \times b^{-1} + p_{-2} \times b^{-2} + \cdots + p_{-n} \times b^{-n}, \tag{1.17}$$

or

$$N = \sum_{i=-1}^{-n} p_i \times b^i. \tag{1.18}$$

Consider the number 0.1011010_2 as an example. The representation, as in the case of integer numbers, gives a direct method to convert the binary fractional number to decimal

$$0.1011010_2 = 1 \times 2^{-1} + 1 \times 2^{-3} + 1 \times 2^{-4} + 1 \times 2^{-6}$$

$$= 0.5 + 0.125 + 0.0625 + 0.015625$$

$$= 0.703125_{10}. \tag{1.19}$$

The conversion of a fractional number between base-b and base-10 is made, therefore, using the same algorithm used for integers, taking care not add more accuracy than was present in the original number through the conversion process, since this would have no meaning. Note that any non-integer number can have an infinitely long representation in a different base.

In fact, the number 0.1011010_2 is represented by 7 binary digits after the decimal point. This means that it is represented with a *precision* of 1 in 2^7 since, with these 7 digits, it is possible to represent 2^7 different numbers. The number obtained through base conversion represents the same measurable quantity and, thus, the number of digits must be such that the accuracy does not exceed the original representation. We will, therefore, have to choose a number p of digits, such that p is the largest integer verifying the equation

$$10^p \leq 2^7 \tag{1.20}$$

and, therefore,

$$p = \lfloor \log_{10} 2^7 \rfloor. \tag{1.21}$$

From Expression (1.21),[1] it can be seen that $p = 2$. Therefore, the correct representation in base-10 of the number 0.1011010_2 is 0.70_{10}, which is obtained by rounding the result of Expression (1.19).

The inverse problem of converting a fractional number represented in base-10 to any base, particularly base-2, uses, just as in the case of integers, a more sophisticated algorithm. The procedure used is shown below, using as an example the number 0.627_{10}. This number, when represented in base-2, will be

$$0.627_{10} = 0.p_{-1}p_{-2}p_{-3}p_{-4} \ldots p_{-n2}. \tag{1.22}$$

The objective is to obtain the value of the digits $p_{-1}, p_{-2}, p_{-3}, p_{-4} \ldots p_{-n}$. Multiplying both sides of Equation (1.22) by 2 gives

$$1.254_{10} = p_{-1}.p_{-2}p_{-3}p_{-4} \ldots p_{-n2}. \tag{1.23}$$

In fact, multiplying by 2 in base-2 results in moving all the digits one position to the left, like the multiplication by 10 in base-10. Analysing

---

[1]The function $\lfloor x \rfloor$ (floor) returns, for the real number x, the largest integer less or equal to x.

Equation (1.23) and noting that the integer parts of the two sides of the equation must be the same, as must the fractional parts, we obtain

$$p_{-1} = 1 \tag{1.24}$$

and

$$0.254_{10} = 0.p_{-2}p_{-3}p_{-4} \ldots p_{-n2}. \tag{1.25}$$

Equation (1.24) allows the identification of the digit p_{-1}. For the second digit, p_{-2}, the same algorithm is now applied to the resulting fractional number, represented in Expression (1.25). The successive use of multiplication by 2 gives the sequence of digits for the fractional part. It is clear that, just as in the inverse conversion, we should use the maximum number of digits, in the new base which does not increase the accuracy of the number compared to its original representation. In the above example, to not exceed the initial accuracy (1 in 10^3), 9 digits will be used to represent this in base-2 ($2^9 = 512$ and $2^{10} = 1\,024$). Completing the example

$$0.627_{10} = 0.101000001_2. \tag{1.26}$$

When the aim is to convert the representation of numbers with an integer and a fractional part between two bases, the conversion of the integer part and the fractional part is performed using the respective algorithms and the results added together at the end.

1.1.4   *Representation of Numbers in Bases Powers of 2*

The representation of numbers in base-2 is the one used by digital systems to represent numbers internally, but it has the major disadvantage of using relatively long sequences of digits. For example, 153.845_{10} is represented in base-2 by 10011001.110110001_2. These representations become difficult to remember and manipulate. Representation in base-10 does not have these drawbacks, but it cannot be used as the internal representation in digital systems. The solution to this dilemma is the use of condensed forms of binary representation, which become possible by representing numbers in *bases which are a power of* 2, that is, $4, 8, 16, \ldots$ Base-8 is commonly used or, even more frequently, base-16. As will be seen, these representations provide an abbreviated and readily convertible representation of binary numbers with many digits.

Base-8 uses digits from 0 to 7, and the conversion of numbers between base-8 and base-10, naturally, uses the procedures described above.

A number represented in base-8 is also said to be represented in *octal*. The representation of numbers in base-16, or in *hexadecimal*, as this type of representation is commonly designated, is similar to any other base, but it is necessary to take into account that there are 16 digits, from 0 to 15. For the digits which represent $10, 11, 12, 13, 14$ and 15, uppercase letters A to F are normally used. The 16 digits are listed in Table 1.2.

The number $4A6F_{16}$ is therefore represented in decimal as follows:

$$4A6F_{16} = 4 \times 16^3 + 10 \times 16^2 + 6 \times 16 + 15$$
$$= 4 \times 4096 + 10 \times 256 + 6 \times 16 + 15$$
$$= 19\,055_{10}. \tag{1.27}$$

Similarly, in base-8 the number 3605_8 is

$$3605_8 = 3 \times 8^3 + 6 \times 8^2 + 5$$
$$= 3 \times 512 + 6 \times 64 + 5$$
$$= 1\,925_{10}. \tag{1.28}$$

Conversion between bases in which one is a power of the other is carried out in an extremely easy way. Consider, in some detail, the conversion of the number 101101110101_2 to base-16. The first step is to represent the number, expressing it in terms of the powers of the base, similarly to what was carried out before

$$101101110101_2 = 1 \times 2^{11} + 0 \times 2^{10} + 1 \times 2^9 + 1 \times 2^8 + 0 \times 2^7$$
$$+ 1 \times 2^6 + 1 \times 2^5 + 1 \times 2^4 + 0 \times 2^3 + 1 \times 2^2$$
$$+ 0 \times 2^1 + 1 \times 2^0. \tag{1.29}$$

Table 1.2 Digits in base-16.

Value	Digit	Value	Digit
0	0	8	8
1	1	9	9
2	2	10	A
3	3	11	B
4	4	12	C
5	5	13	D
6	6	14	E
7	7	15	F

Then, the terms are put into groups of 4 starting from the least significant

$$101101110101_2 = (1 \times 2^{11} + 0 \times 2^{10} + 1 \times 2^9 + 1 \times 2^8)$$
$$+ (0 \times 2^7 + 1 \times 2^6 + 1 \times 2^5 + 1 \times 2^4)$$
$$+ (0 \times 2^3 + 1 \times 2^2 + 0 \times 2^1 + 1 \times 2^0). \qquad (1.30)$$

In each group, we factor out the powers of 2 necessary to have each group represented in terms of the weighted sum of the powers of order $0, 1, 2$ and 3.

$$101101110101_2 = (1 \times 2^3 + 0 \times 2^2 + 1 \times 2^1 + 1 \times 2^0) \times 2^8$$
$$+ (0 \times 2^3 + 1 \times 2^2 + 1 \times 2^1 + 1 \times 2^0) \times 2^4$$
$$+ (0 \times 2^3 + 1 \times 2^2 + 0 \times 2^1 + 1 \times 2^0) \times 2^0. \qquad (1.31)$$

However, $2^8 = 16^2, 2^4 = 16^1$ and $2^0 = 16^0$ are powers of 16. This can, therefore, be written,

$$101101110101_2 = 11 \times 16^2 + 7 \times 16^1 + 5 \times 16^0 \qquad (1.32)$$

and so, it is now easy to conclude that

$$101101110101_2 = B75_{16}. \qquad (1.33)$$

Note that each digit in base-16 was defined by the 4 binary digits which were initially grouped. So, if the equivalence between the digits of base-16 and its correspondence to a binary four-digit number is known, it is possible to directly determine the number in base-16 from the number in base-2. This correspondence can be easily obtained and is shown in Table 1.3.

Table 1.3   Correspondence between digits of base-16 and their representation in binary using 4 digits.

Binary	Digit	Binary	Digit
0000	0	1000	8
0001	1	1001	9
0010	2	1010	A
0011	3	1011	B
0100	4	1100	C
0101	5	1101	D
0110	6	1110	E
0111	7	1111	F

If the groups of four binary digits are isolated in the number $1011\ 0111\ 0101_2$, it can, therefore, be directly converted to base-16

$$1011 \Leftrightarrow B$$
$$0111 \Leftrightarrow 7$$
$$0101 \Leftrightarrow 5,$$

obtaining the number $B75_{16}$. It should be noted that the four-digit groups are formed from the least significant digit, i.e., from the right. This is a consequence of the way the algorithm was defined.

For a binary number with a number of bits that is not a multiple of 4, the method is applied in the same way. Take the number 1101011011_2. Separating the digits into groups of 4 from the least significant gives

$$1101011011_2 = 11\ 0101\ 1011_2$$
$$= 3\ 5\ B_{16}$$
$$= 35B_{16}. \tag{1.34}$$

For another base which is a power of 2, such as base-8, the method is similar, with a variation only in the number of digits to be grouped together. For base-8, the digits are grouped into groups of 3 ($2^3 = 8$). As an example

$$100101101010001_2 = 10\ 010\ 110\ 101\ 001_2$$
$$= 2\ 2\ 6\ 5\ 1_8$$
$$= 22651_8. \tag{1.35}$$

In the same way, going from a base which is a power of 2 to base-2 is carried out using the inverse process

$$7DA3F_{16} = 7\ D\ A\ 3\ F_{16}$$
$$= 0111\ 1101\ 1010\ 0011\ 1111_2$$
$$= 01111101101000111111_2. \tag{1.36}$$

A similar example may be considered for base-8

$$3461_8 = 3\ 4\ 6\ 1_8$$
$$= 011\ 100\ 110\ 001_2$$
$$= 11100110001_2. \tag{1.37}$$

An alternative way, which is often used, of signalling that a number is represented in base-16 consists in ending the number with the letter h.

Therefore, writing 4871_{16} is the same as writing 4871h, for example. In the same way, it is usual to use the letters b, o and d to indicate that the number is represented in binary, octal or decimal, respectively. For example, 1110101_2 may be represented by 1110101b. This form of representation will, from now on, be the preferred way when it is necessary to indicate the base in which a number is represented.

Representing numbers in bases which are powers of 2, particularly base-8 and base-16, thus offers a compact representation of binary numbers with many digits. In addition, as has been seen, there is a very simple way of converting numbers between base-2 and those bases, which is practically independent in complexity, of the number of digits of the representation of the numbers. Finally, this allows for partial conversions of sections of the number which may be of interest. It is easy to discover, for example, the least or most significant binary digits of a number represented in these bases without the need for its complete conversion. For example, in the number A23Bh, it is easy to see that the five most significant binary digits are 10100.

The conversion of numbers with a fractional part between base-2 and bases that are powers of 2 is carried out in the same manner, taking care to group the binary digits starting at the decimal point. Take, for example, the number 1001010.101100111111b

$$1001010.101100111111b = 100\ 1010\ .\ 1011\ 0011\ 1111b$$

$$= 4\ A\ .\ B\ 3\ Fh$$

$$= 4A.B3Fh. \tag{1.38}$$

In the same way, the conversion from a base which is a power of 2 to base-2 does not present any difficulty for numbers with a fractional part

$$5271.3527o = 5\ 2\ 7\ 1\ .\ 3\ 5\ 2\ 7o$$

$$= 101\ 010\ 111\ 001\ .\ 011\ 101\ 010\ 111b$$

$$= 101010111001.011101010111b. \tag{1.39}$$

1.2 Arithmetic Operations in Base-2, Base-8 and Base-16

This section briefly deals with simple *arithmetic operations* in base-2, base-8 and base-16. The scope is limited to the sums and products of positive integers. The study of arithmetic involving negative integers will be dealt with later, in Chapter 5, where subtraction will also be considered.

Table 1.4   Table of addition in base-2.

$X + Y$	Y	
	0	1
X 0	0	1
1	1	10

1.2.1   *Sums in Base-2*

The *sum in base-2*, as with any other base, is not fundamentally different from a sum in base-10. The procedure adopted is based on the existence of a table of addition and a method of adding numbers digit by digit. The sum is carried out by adding, for each digit starting with the least significant digit, the digits of the numbers to be added to the *carry* of the previous digit. The sum should also create the carry to the next digit. The table of addition in base-2 (Table 1.4) is particularly simple.

It should be noted that, in the sum $1 + 1$, the result cannot be represented by a single digit, and it is necessary to use two digits. This means that, in the sum algorithm, there will be in this case a carry of 1. In the other cases of the table, the carry is always 0.

As an example, take the sum of 10001111_2 and 1011010_2. In the least significant digits, in the rightmost column, the sum does not have to consider the carry from the previous column. The sum of 1 and 0, according to Table 1.4, is 1, and the carry, 0 (Figure 1.1(a)).

In the second column, the sum of 1 and 1 is 10 (that is, 2_{10}). As the carry from the previous column is 0, the sum does not change. However, since 10 is a two-digit number, in this column, the result of the sum is 0, and the carry is 1 (Figure 1.1(b)).

In the next column, adding 1 and 0 gives 1. As the carry is 1, it is also necessary to add this 1, which gives 10. Therefore, the sum is 0, and the carry is 1 (Figure 1.1(c)).

```
  10001111            10001111             10001111
 +1011010            +1011010             +1011010
 ─────────           ─────────            ─────────
        1                  01                   001
       0   carry          10   carry           110   carry

      (a)                 (b)                  (c)
```

Fig. 1.1   Process for executing a sum.

$$
\begin{array}{r}
10001111 \\
+1011010 \\
\hline
1001 \\
1110 \quad \text{carry}
\end{array}
\qquad\qquad
\begin{array}{r}
10001111 \\
+1011010 \\
\hline
11101001 \\
00011110 \quad \text{carry}
\end{array}
$$

(a)   (b)

Fig. 1.2 Process for executing a sum (continuation of Figure 1.1).

Table 1.5 Multiplication table in base-2.

$X \times Y$		Y	
		0	1
X	0	0	0
	1	0	1

In the fourth column from the right, there is the sum of 1 and 1, which gives 10, and also a carry of 1, which gives 11. In this case, the sum is 1, and the carry is also 1 (Figure 1.2(a)).

Continuing this reasoning, the final result is shown in Figure 1.2(b).

It is, of course, possible to sum more than two numbers The only aspect to be taken into consideration is that the carry may not be just one digit. Take the sum of the 4 numbers given below.

In the first column, the sum is 100_2. Here, the sum is, of course, 0, and the carry, 10. Taking this aspect into consideration, the final result will be:

$$
\begin{array}{r}
10011101 \\
101011 \\
11001 \\
+ \ 1011011 \\
\hline
100111100
\end{array}
$$

In digital systems, sums are normally made between two numbers, with the sums of more than two numbers made by successive sums of the various terms to be summed.

1.2.2 *Multiplications in Base-2*

Just as with addition, *multiplication in base-2* follows the same methods for multiplication in base-10. The multiplication table is shown in Table 1.5.

Each digit of the multiplier is multiplied by the multiplicand to generate a partial product. The sum of all the partial products is the product of the two numbers. In fact, the product $M \times N$ may be expressed by representing the multiplier N as the sum of the powers of the base weighed by the correspondent digits (the same can be done for any base) using Equation (1.40).

$$
\begin{aligned}
M \times N &= M \times (p_{n-1} \times 2^{n-1} + p_{n-2} \times 2^{n-2} + \cdots + p_1 \times 2^1 + p_0 \times 2^0) \\
&= M \times p_{n-1} \times 2^{n-1} + M \times p_{n-2} \times 2^{n-2} + \cdots + M \times p_1 \times 2^1 \\
&\quad + M \times p_0 \times 2^0.
\end{aligned}
\tag{1.40}
$$

For example, when multiplying $M = 10001111\mathrm{b}$ by $N = 1010\mathrm{b}$, the product is obtained by adding the four partial products

$$
\begin{aligned}
&10001111 \times 1000 \\
&10001111 \times 0 \\
&10001111 \times 10 \\
&10001111 \times 0,
\end{aligned}
$$

corresponding to the four digits of the multiplier.

In the usual algorithm, it is, therefore, essential to place the various partial products aligned with the respective digit of the multiplier.

$$
\begin{array}{r}
10001111 \\
\times\ 1010 \\
\hline
00000000 \quad (= 10001111 \times 0) \\
10001111 \quad (= 10001111 \times 10) \\
00000000 \quad (= 10001111 \times 0) \\
10001111 \quad (= 10001111 \times 1000). \\
\hline
10110010110
\end{array}
$$

Naturally, just as in the case of multiplication in base-10, the results of the product of the multiplicand by digits of the multiplier that are 0 can be omitted

$$
\begin{array}{r}
10001111 \\
\times\ 1010 \\
\hline
10001111 \\
10001111 \\
\hline
10110010110
\end{array}
\cdot
$$

It should be noted that, in base-2, there are only two hypotheses for the partial products: either the multiplier digit is 0, and the partial product is 0, or that digit is 1, and the partial product is equal to the multiplicand with the displacement corresponding to the weighting of the digit. It will be seen later that this characteristic is important when digital systems carry out this operation.

1.2.3   *Arithmetic Operations in Other Bases*

Performing arithmetic operations between numbers represented on other bases do not raise any problems besides knowing the tables of operations for those bases. Using as an example the *sum in base-16*, the table of sums can be constructed (Table 1.6).

This table can be constructed in various ways. One possibility is to consider the value of the digits for each sum, sum them in decimal and transfer the result to hexadecimal. As an example, the sum 5h + Dh, is the sum of 5d and 13d (the decimal value of digit Dh). The result of this sum is 18d or, in hexadecimal, 12h, which is the value to be placed in the table.

As an example, take the sum of 1F3A5h and A542h:

$$
\begin{array}{r}
1F3A5 \\
+A542 \\
\hline
298E7 \\
01000 \quad \text{carry.}
\end{array}
$$

Multiplication is also easy to carry out. This will be shown using the *multiplication table in base-8* (Table 1.7) and the product of two numbers in that base.

Table 1.6   Table of the sum in base-16.

$X+Y$		Y														
		0	1	2	3	4	5	6	7	8	9	A	B	C	D	E	F
X	0	0	1	2	3	4	5	6	7	8	9	A	B	C	D	E	F
	1	1	2	3	4	5	6	7	8	9	A	B	C	D	E	F	10
	2	2	3	4	5	6	7	8	9	A	B	C	D	E	F	10	11
	3	3	4	5	6	7	8	9	A	B	C	D	E	F	10	11	12
	4	4	5	6	7	8	9	A	B	C	D	E	F	10	11	12	13
	5	5	6	7	8	9	A	B	C	D	E	F	10	11	12	13	14
	6	6	7	8	9	A	B	C	D	E	F	10	11	12	13	14	15
	7	7	8	9	A	B	C	D	E	F	10	11	12	13	14	15	16
	8	8	9	A	B	C	D	E	F	10	11	12	13	14	15	16	17
	9	9	A	B	C	D	E	F	10	11	12	13	14	15	16	17	18
	A	A	B	C	D	E	F	10	11	12	13	14	15	16	17	18	19
	B	B	C	D	E	F	10	11	12	13	14	15	16	17	18	19	1A
	C	C	D	E	F	10	11	12	13	14	15	16	17	18	19	1A	1B
	D	D	E	F	10	11	12	13	14	15	16	17	18	19	1A	1B	1C
	E	E	F	10	11	12	13	14	15	16	17	18	19	1A	1B	1C	1D
	F	F	10	11	12	13	14	15	16	17	18	19	1A	1B	1C	1D	1E

Table 1.7 Table of multiplication in base-8.

$X \times Y$		Y						
		0	1	2	3	4	5	6	7
	0	0	0	0	0	0	0	0	0
	1	0	1	2	3	4	5	6	7
	2	0	2	4	6	10	12	14	16
	3	0	3	6	11	14	17	22	25
X	4	0	4	10	14	20	24	30	34
	5	0	5	12	17	24	31	36	43
	6	0	6	14	22	30	36	44	52
	7	0	7	16	25	34	43	52	61

The product of 1537o and 314o is

$$
\begin{array}{r}
1537 \\
\times\ 314 \\
\hline
6574 \\
1537 \\
5035 \\
\hline
527664
\end{array}
$$

The multiplication operation in base-b, although not conceptually different from the operation in base-10, requires a good knowledge of the respective multiplication table, which, in general, is unavailable. In these circumstances, it is clear that carrying out multiplications directly in these bases is a difficult task and is not frequent. The sum, however, is very useful, as will be seen later, in the context of computer architecture and programming.

1.3 Codes

Representation in base-2 allows for the representation of numbers in digital systems. However, not all information is numeric. There are many other types of data that need to be stored and processed. Text is an obvious example, but it is far from being the only one. This section will analyse the methods to represent information using codes. Particular emphasis will be given to binary codes, BCD and alphanumeric codes. The representation of other types of information is outside the scope of this book.

1.3.1 *Coding*

The *representation of information in digital systems* is based on the fact that systems of this type are supported in quantities that can only assume two values: 0 and 1. As is the case with binary digits, an entity which can take on two values is called a bit. If there is an entity which generates information and that information is created in sequences of symbols with several possible values, the solution for the representation of those values in a digital system is to *encode* them. This means that each possible value is made to correspond to a specified combination of bits which then represent that value. Take as an example an elevator in a building with six floors: two basements, the ground floor and another three floors. If the goal is to register the floor where the elevator is in a digital system, or where it is heading if moving, there is the need to codify that information, i.e., make each floor correspond to a particular bit pattern. The number of bits to be used will be at least those necessary to produce six combinations. Three bits are enough for that code. A coding example is shown in Table 1.8.

The correspondence between the entities to be represented and their coding is called *code*. In this way, the previous table sets out a code. Each of the configurations is referred as a *code word*. If the number of bits for the code words is equal for all configurations, it is known as the *code length*. This code is, therefore, a code of length 3. Obviously, this is not the only possible code for this application. Table 1.9 shows another possibility.

The only restriction for a valid code is that it does not have repeated encodings, which means that two different entities may not be encoded with the same code word.

Table 1.8   Sample code.

Floor	Coding
2nd basement	000
1st basement	001
Ground floor	010
1st floor	011
2nd floor	100
3rd floor	101

Table 1.9   Alternative sample code.

Floor	Coding
2nd basement	110
1st basement	111
Main floor	000
1st floor	001
2nd floor	010
3rd floor	011

Table 1.10   Sample code with restrictions.

Floor	Coding
2nd basement	0011
1st basement	0101
Main floor	1001
1st floor	0110
2nd floor	1010
3rd floor	1100

Either of this codings is acceptable. The two codes shown have no feature which significantly distinguishes them from one another. However, codes can be designed with some particular characteristics. For example, using words of 4 bits to represent the various floors, it is possible to design a code that represents each floor as a sequence of 2 bits with the value 0 and 2 bits with value 1, as shown in Table 1.10.

A possible use for codes of this type is to *detect errors* which could happen in the coding process or as a consequence of a malfunction of a system. If at any given time, the system has registered that the elevator is on a floor represented by the word 0010, it is immediately clear there was an error, since the word 0010 does not belong to the code.

1.3.2   *Numeric Codes*

Although numbers are generally stored and processed using their representation in base-2 (and, in a way, this also corresponds to a code), it is often necessary to use codes to represent numbers, particularly integers. These codes are known as *numeric codes*. The easiest way to represent integers by a code is to have each number represented by a code word which is its binary representation. Table 1.11 shows a code of this type with words of constant length.

It should be noted that all the code words have the same length. For example, the number 3 is represented by 00011 and not by 11, which would be its normal representation in base-2. This type of code in which each number is coded by its representation in base-2 with a fixed number of bits, is known as *natural binary code*. Obviously, there are natural binary codes for any number of bits.

A very common situation of a different kind is the need to encode decimal digits. It is sometimes convenient to represent a number not by its natural binary code, but rather by the binary coding of each of its digits in base-10. An obvious situation is that of the display of a calculator which represents a number in decimal for easy reading by the user, but which, internally, is

Table 1.11   Natural binary code with 5 bits.

Number	Coding	Number	Coding
0	00000	16	10000
1	00001	17	10001
2	00010	18	10010
3	00011	19	10011
4	00100	20	10100
5	00101	21	10101
6	00110	22	10110
7	00111	23	10111
8	01000	24	11000
9	01001	25	11001
10	01010	26	11010
11	01011	27	11011
12	01100	28	11100
13	01101	29	11101
14	01110	30	11110
15	01111	31	11111

Table 1.12   BCD code.

Digit	Coding
0	0000
1	0001
2	0010
3	0011
4	0100
5	0101
6	0110
7	0111
8	1000
9	1001

represented in binary. The classic solution is to represent each decimal digit of the number using its binary representation and a fixed length, as shown in Table 1.12.

This code is called *BCD code*. BCD stands for *Binary Coded Decimal*. It should be noted that the BCD code for each digit has the same representation as the natural binary code representation with 4 bits. However, not all the configurations have a meaning. The indication that a number is represented in BCD is made by writing BCD in subscript. For example, 7_{10} is represented by 0111_{BCD} in BCD.

The representation of a number in BCD code is made by representing each decimal digit by its binary representation, as shown in the representation of the number 2 719 in BCD

$$2\,719_{10} = 0010011100011001_{BCD}, \tag{1.41}$$

in which 0010 corresponds to the digit 2_{10}; 0111, to 7_{10}; 0001, to 1_{10}; and 1001, to 9_{10}.

It should be noted that not every sequence of bits may correspond to a coding using BCD code. For example, the sequence 10110101 is not a number encoded in BCD, since the 4 bits on the left (1011) do not correspond to any digit, as can be seen in Table 1.12.

In the same way, it is important to mention that a representation of a number in BCD code is not a representation of this number in binary. Returning to the previous example,

$$0010011100011001_{BCD} = 2\,719_{10}, \tag{1.42}$$

although the same sequence of bits interpreted as a number in base-2 has another meaning

$$0010011100011001_2 = 10\,009_{10}, \tag{1.43}$$

which, clearly, does not correspond to the same number.

1.3.3 *Reflected Codes*

A particularly important type of numeric codes are the *reflected codes* (sometimes referred to as *Gray code*). The fundamental characteristic of these codes is that two words which code consecutive numbers differ in only one bit. This feature is important, as will become clear in Chapter 2.

Table 1.13 shows a three-bit reflected code. It should be noted that with 3 bits, it is possible to encode 8 different numbers.

As can be easily seen, in this code each number is not, except in some cases, represented by its binary representation. It is possible to verify that between each two successive numbers only one bit of its representation is

Table 1.13   Three-bit reflected code.

Number	Coding
0	000
1	001
2	011
3	010
4	110
5	111
6	101
7	100

Table 1.14 Construction of 4 bit reflected code. (a) Reflection and (b) additional bit.

	Number	Coding
000	0	0000
001	1	0001
011	2	0011
010	3	0010
110	4	0110
111	5	0111
101	6	0101
100	7	0100
100	8	1100
101	9	1101
111	10	1111
110	11	1110
010	12	1010
011	13	1011
001	14	1001
000	15	1000

(a)   (b)

altered. This is also true with the representations of 0 and 7, the two extremes represented.

The most direct way to build an n bit reflected code is to start from a $n - 1$ bit code. Start with 2^{n-1} configurations of the $n - 1$ bit code and repeat them in an inverse manner, i.e., as if reflected in an imaginary mirror (hence the name reflected code), as shown in Table 1.14(a).

The fourth bit of the coding is then added, making it equal to 0, in the initial positions, and equal to 1, in the "reflected" positions, as shown in Table 1.14(b), where the code is represented.

A suggested exercise would be to obtain the reflected codes of 2 and 3 bits, from the one-bit code. Clearly, the latter does not differ from 1 bit natural binary code.

1.3.4 *Alphanumeric Codes*

One type of information that it is important to represent in digital systems is text. Therefore, it is essential to use a code to represent all the possible characters in a text. These codes are called *alphanumeric codes*. Throughout the evolution of digital systems, various codes with this purpose have been utilised. The code most commonly used is the *ASCII code* (American Standard Code for Information Interchange), which originated in

Table 1.15 ASCII code.

$b_6b_5b_4$	000	001	010	011	100	101	110	111
$b_3b_2b_1b_0$								
0000	NUL	DLE	SP	0	@	P	'	p
0001	STH	DC1	!	1	A	Q	a	q
0010	STX	DC2	"	2	B	R	b	r
0011	ETX	DC3	#	3	C	S	c	s
0100	EOT	DC4	$	4	D	T	d	t
0101	ENQ	NAK	%	5	E	U	e	u
0110	ACK	SYN	&	6	F	V	f	v
0111	BEL	ETB	'	7	G	W	g	w
1000	BS	CAN	(	8	H	X	h	x
1001	HT	EM	)	9	I	Y	i	y
1010	LF	SUB	*	:	J	Z	j	z
1011	VT	ESC	+	;	K	[	k	{
1100	FF	FS	,	<	L	\	l		
1101	CR	GS	−	=	M	]	m	}
1110	SO	RS	.	>	N	^	n	~
1111	SI	US	/	?	O	_	o	DEL

the United States, quickly became a universally accepted code. A code of this type has to encode the 26 letters of the alphabet, both uppercase and lowercase, the 10 digits, all punctuation signs and some special characters. The code has words of 7 bits, the number of bits necessary to encode all the characters. It is usual to represent the code word with the bits ordered from 1 to 7 in the following way: $b_6b_5b_4b_3b_2b_1b_0$. The code is shown in Table 1.15.

The character «SP» is the space.

The characters in the first two columns and the «DEL» in the last position of the table are *control characters*. The meaning of the control characters is mostly connected to the applications of the code in transmitting information between devices. In many cases, these characters are not used anymore due to the evolution of communication protocols.

The representation of a text in ASCII is done by indicating the succession of codes of the text characters. For example, the text «Digital Systems» is encoded in ASCII as 1000100b 1101001b 1100111b 1101001b 1110100b 1100001b 1101100b 0100000b 1010011b 1111001b 1110011b 1110100b 1100101b 1101101b 1110011b .

It is more convenient to represent the ASCII code configurations in hexadecimal. In this case, the text above would, therefore, be codified as: 44h 69h 67h 69h 74h 61h 6Ch 20h 53h 79h 73h 74h 65h 6Dh 73h.

The ASCII sequence 44h 69h 67h 69h 74h 61h 6Ch 20h 73h 79h 73h 74h 65h 6Dh73h 20h 75h 73h 65h 20h 41h 53h 43h 49h 49h 20h 74h 6Fh 20h

72h 65h 70h 72h 65h 73h 65h 6Eh 74h 20h 63h 68h 61h 72h 61h 63h 74h 65h 72h 73h 2Eh codifies the following phrase: «Digital systems use ASCII to represent characters.»

Sometimes the designation of the characters in ASCII code is carried out in decimal instead of hexadecimal. For example, the letter «A», which has the hexadecimal code 41h, has the decimal code 65d.

ASCII code enables representing a text, but with some limitations. In one hand, it does not allow the special characters of a specific language to be represented, for example, «ç» in Portuguese, «ø» in Swedish or «ß» in German. Furthermore, it does not code accentuated characters nor can it represent other alphabets. As such, various extensions have been developed to represent specific characters and accentuated characters. The extension is done by changing the code to an eight-bit code, while keeping it compatible with the basic ASCII. Unfortunately, there are currently several mutually incompatible codes. In all of them, however, the representation of the 00h to 7Fh values are the same as in classic ASCII, to maintain compatibility between these extensions and ASCII. For example, the *ISO-8859-1 code*, the ISO (International Standard Organisation) standardised extension for Western European alphabets, has the correspondence for characters coded from 80h to FFh shown in Table 1.16.

Table 1.16   Code ISO-8859-1 (with $b_7 = 1$).

$b_7b_6b_5b_4$	1000	1001	1010	1011	1100	1101	1110	1111
$b_3b_2b_1b_0$								
0000			nbsp	°	À	Ð	à	ð
0001			¡	±	Á	Ñ	á	ñ
0010			¢	²	Â	Ò	â	ò
0011			£	³	Ã	Ó	ã	ó
0100			€	´	Ä	Ô	ä	ô
0101			¥	µ	Å	Õ	å	õ
0110			¦	¶	Æ	Ö	œ	ö
0111			§	·		×		÷
1000			¨	¸	È	Ø	è	ø
1001			©	¹	É	Ù	é	ù
1010					Ê	Ú	ê	ú
1011			«	»	Ë	Û	ë	û
1100			¬	¼	Ì	Ü	ì	ü
1101			-	½	Í	Ý	í	ý
1110			®	¾	Î	Þ	î	þ
1111			-	¿	Ï	ß	ï	ÿ

The «nbsp» character is a special character preventing the breaking up of a line of text by a word processor or a browser.

The ISO-8859 standard contains other substandards which define codes for characters for other areas or linguistic groups.

UNICODE has since appeared, which seeks to code all the characters of every language. Each code word has 16 bits and, if necessary, uses a 20-bit extension. Normal ASCII and the ISO-8859-1 extension shown above are compatible with UNICODE. This code is recommended as a support for future Internet protocols.

1.4 Units of Information

From an abstract point of view, digital information can be represented using two values, usually designated by 0 and 1. As has already been mentioned, an entity of this type is called a bit. As is evident, a bit — which can only have one of two values — cannot, by itself, support the type of information mentioned above. To represent information it is usual to arrange the bits into larger capacity entities.

If we consider, for example, alphanumeric information represented using the ISO-8859-1 code (Table 1.16), each character, which is the minimum useful information unit, occupies 8 bits. Those 8 bits are a primary unit of information, if processing text, and should be processed, transferred or stored together. A set of 8 bits is called a *byte*, or *octet*.

A byte has this designation, independently of the meaning attributed to the information it carries. It is immaterial whether the byte represents a character, two digits codified in BCD, the colour of a pixel from the image on a computer monitor, or any other type of information. The concept of a byte is linked to the set of 8 bits interpreted as a coherent entity.

In the same way, a *nibble* is defined as a set of 4 bits, which is interpreted as a coherent unit. A BCD coded digit, for example, is represented by a nibble. The basic unit of information in an Intel 4004, one of the first microprocessors, which processed sets of 4 bits, was also a nibble.

Clearly, a set of two nibbles, if regarded as one unit, is a byte.

Another entity to consider at this stage is the *word*. A word is the smallest unit processed or stored in a system. For example, the Intel 4004 mentioned above is a processor with words of 4 bits. The Intel 8080 or the Motorola 6800, which process bytes, have words of 8 bits. The Intel 8086 or the Motorola

68000 or the P3 processor, presented later in this book, process words of 16 bits. Current computers use words of larger sizes. Unlike the concepts of byte or nibble, the concept of word is not linked to a fixed size. The number of bits of a word depends on the context being considered. However, it is common to consider a size of 16 bits when referring to a word, unless another size is explicitly specified.

No non-trivial amount of text, image, film or sound can be represented by a byte or a word. Useful digital systems applications, in the overwhelming majority of cases, need to store large quantities of information in sets of bytes or words.

When considering large amounts of objects or abstract entities, it is usual to refer to hundreds, thousands or millions of units. That reference assumes that the reference basis of the numbers utilised is base-10, where concepts such as thousand and million are natural since they are powers of the base. In digital systems, however, the normal base to represent numbers is base-2. In base-2, the sizes used are also usually powers of the base.

In base-10, as used in units of measurement systems, the representation of large numbers can be achieved using multiples of the units. For example, instead of speaking of 1 000 m, it is natural to talk about 1 km. The «k» here represents 1 000×.

In base-2, 1 000d= 1111101000b. The philosophy at the basis of representation of multiples in base-10 may be applied to any base, but with different values. These values must be, just as in base-10, powers of the base. But it is convenient to have "useful" multiples in base-2, that is, multiples not too different from those which are useful in base-10 to maintain the intuition associated with the use of multiples.

The power of 2 closest to 1 000d is

$$2^{10} = 10000000000b = 1\,024d. \tag{1.44}$$

Therefore, it is conventional that in digital systems of all types (including computers), $1K = 2^{10} = 1\,024d$. Thus, 1 Kbyte (or KB) means exactly 1 024 bytes,[2] but, if you are willing to admit a small error, it may be considered as 1 thousand bytes.

The *multiples* normally used in digital systems are described in Table 1.17.

---

[2]Note that in this context the letters used are uppercase.

Table 1.17   Multiples in base-2.

Multiple	Power	Relation with lower multiple	Representation in base-10	Denomination
1 K	2^{10}		1 024d	Kilo
1 M	2^{20}	$= 2^{10}$ K	1 048 576d	Mega
1 G	2^{30}	$= 2^{10}$ M	1 073 741 824d	Giga
1 T	2^{40}	$= 2^{10}$ G	1 099 511 627 776d	Tera
1 P	2^{50}	$= 2^{10}$ T	1 125 899 906 842 624d	Peta

1.5   Summary

This chapter presents various ways of representing information in digital systems.

The first aspect dealt with is the binary representation of non-negative integers and fractional numbers, describing the conversion processes between the representation in binary and the representation in decimal. To facilitate the representation and manipulation of binary numbers with a large number of digits, octal and hexadecimal representations were also studied.

The chapter also described the use of the normal arithmetic rules for performing operations directly in binary, octal or hexadecimal.

The representation of non-numeric information content is also considered, with the introduction of the use of codes. Besides numeric and alphanumeric codes, reflected codes are also introduced. These codes are of great importance in the study of methods to simplify logic functions presented in the next chapter.

The chapter ends with some definitions related to basic aspects of information representation.

Exercises

1.1 Represent the following numbers in base-2:

   (a) 33_{10}

   (b) 162_{10}.

1.2 Consider the following numbers and represent them in base-2, taking care not to exceed the precision represented in the original numbers:

   (a) 28.54_{10}

   (b) 28.540_{10}

   (c) 143.7_{10}

   (d) 143.70_{10}.

1.3 Represent the following numbers in base-8, base-10 and base-16:

    (a) 10101101011_2

    (b) 110000001.1101_2

    (c) 11111000.0011_2.

1.4 Represent the following numbers in base-2 and base-8:

    (a) $A57D_{16}$

    (b) $CAFE_{16}$

    (c) $17D.A8_{16}$.

1.5 Consider the number 35_x. It is known that this number is less than 64_{10}. Which values can x assume?

1.6 Numbers are usually represented in base-n, with n being positive. However, that is not strictly necessary. Take, for example, base-(-2). Nothing prevents the representation of numbers in that base. Represent the first 16 integers in base-(-2). Note that the number of bits necessary may be greater than four, the minimum number of bits necessary to represent 16 configurations.

1.7 Carry out the following operations in the bases indicated:

    (a) $1001.11011_2 + 0.10101_2$

    (b) $10010.11_2 \times 10.01_2$

    (c) $2314.21_5 + 12.413_5$

    (d) $24.1_5 \times 3.2_5$.

1.8 Suggest the algorithm for the subtraction in base-2.

1.9 Construct the addition and multiplication tables in base-16. Use them to carry out the following operations:

    (a) $A57D_{16} + CAFE_{16}$

    (b) $A57D_{16} \times 37_{16}$

    (c) $35A.7E_{16} + 2D.1A6_{16}$

    (d) $35A.7E_{16} \times 7.F_{16}$.

1.10 The conversion of numbers from one base-b to base-10, is, as has been seen, easy to carry out, by describing the number as a weighted sum (by its digits) of powers of the base and carrying out the operations thus made explicit. The operations are carried out in base-10. In the opposite way, conversion from base-10 to base-b, a different algorithm was presented. However, the situation is perfectly symmetrical, and the number in base-10 may be described as a weighted sum of powers of 10, with all the intervening numbers expressed in base-b. Carrying out the operations in base-b the representation of the number in that base can be obtained. Try using this method to represent in base-2 and base-5 the numbers 35_{10} and 572_{10} and confirm these by using the usual algorithms. Does the method also work with fractional numbers?

1.11 Starting from the usual algorithms for decimal division, obtain the algorithm for division in binary, carry it out and validate it (using the inverse operation), for the division of 1010110_2 by 101_2.

1.12 Consider the following sequence of bits: 100001110011

(a) If the sequence is a number in binary, what is the number represented?

(b) If the sequence is the representation of a number in BCD, what is the number represented?

(c) If the sequence is a number in base-3, what is the number represented?

1.13 Consider the numbers in Problem 1.1.

(a) Represent them in BCD code.

(b) Represent them in ASCII code.

(c) Represent them in ISO-Latin code (ISO-8859-1).

1.14 What is the phrase represented by the sequence of bytes in the ISO-8859-1 code represented below?
45h, 6Eh, 67h, 6Ch, 69h, 73h, 68h, 20h, 6Ch, 61h, 6Eh, 67h, 75h, 61h, 67h, 65h, 20h, 64h, 6Fh, 65h, 73h, 20h, 6Eh, 6Fh, 74h, 20h, 68h, 61h, 76h, 65h, 20h, 63h, 68h, 61h, 72h, 61h, 63h, 74h, 65h, 72h, 73h, 20h, 61h, 73h, 20h, C3h, A7h, 2Ch, 20h, C3h, A5h, 2Ch, 20h, C3h, 98h, 20h, 61h, 6Eh, 64h, 20h, C2h, A4h, 2Eh.

1.15 The names of airports are encoded by sequences of three capital letters. For example, the Changi Airport in Singapore has the code SIN, the El Prat Airport in Barcelona has the code BCN, and the John Kennedy Airport in New York has the code JFK.

(a) How many airports can be encoded in this way?

(b) How many bits will be necessary in ASCII code to code the airport codes in binary? And can a more efficient code be used to make it possible to encode only uppercase letters?

(c) How many bits would be necessary if a single binary code was attributed to each airport with a minimum number of bits?

1.16 A weighted code is a numerical code in which each bit of the code has a weight, and the encoded number is obtained by adding the weights multiplied by the value of the bit in each respective position. Natural binary code and BCD code are weighted codes with weights 8, 4, 2 and 1. Represent the ten decimal digits in the following weighted codes:

(a) 2, 4, 2, 1

(b) 5, 4, 2, 1

(c) 8, −4, 2, 1.

Chapter 2

Logic Functions

Digital systems, as previously mentioned, are based on the use of electronic circuits that can, at any moment, be in one of two states. In Chapter 1, we learned how it is possible to represent various types of information using binary quantities.

The design and analysis of circuits of the kind used in digital systems need theoretical tools that support this kind of work. In many cases, basic electronic circuits must perform a particular logic function. Take the example of a fire alarm system that should be activated when the temperature rises above a certain threshold and one of two smoke sensors is activated. Designing this system involves an analysis and specification phase, followed by a possible simplification and implementation of the result.

The functionality of the system is typically specified using mathematical formalisms, the most important of which is Boolean algebra. From the mathematical point of view, binary Boolean algebra is the theory upon which many practical tools currently used in digital systems are based. Binary Boolean algebra is presented in Section 2.1.

This algebra enables the use of Boolean functions, also known as logic functions, which are essential for the methods normally employed to analyse and synthesise circuits. Logic function representation techniques are presented in Section 2.2.

A central aspect of the design of digital circuits is the minimisation of logic functions, to reduce the complexity of expressions and, implicitly, the complexity of the circuits used to support these functions in digital systems. This issue is studied in Section 2.3.

2.1 Binary Boolean Algebra

There are several ways of approaching *Boolean algebra*. From the algebraic point of view, the most appropriate approach is the axiomatic definition of an abstract Boolean algebra, followed by the derivation of the structure. To be useful in digital systems, the structure obtained would be refined to the case of *binary Boolean algebra*, i.e., with two values. From this, all the interesting properties in the context of digital systems would follow.

The approach used in this book is different. The structure will be constructed from a set of two elements and the operations that can be defined over the elements of the set. Boolean algebra will appear *a posteriori*.

As mentioned already, and will be seen in a little more detail in Chapter 3, the electronic circuits that form the basis of digital systems may at any moment have a voltage value in one of two possible intervals. This situation may be instantiated at a higher level of abstraction by a quantity which can take two values. These values are usually referred to as 0 and 1. It should be noted that this quantity has no numerical significance and the two values 0 and 1 are not numbers. It should also be noted that, instead of 0 and 1, any other set of two different designations may be used. Common alternative designations are F and T (False and True) or L and H (Low and High), for example.

A quantity which can take one of two values is represented by a *binary variable*, *logic variable*, *bit* or, even, *Boolean variable*. In the same way, the values 0 and 1 which the Boolean variable may take may be called *binary values*, *logic values* or *Boolean values*.

2.1.1   *One-variable Logic Functions*

Consider the set $\mathbb{B} = \{0, 1\}$. It is a finite set of two elements, which leads to a very simple algebraic approach.

Functions known as *logic functions*, *binary functions* or *Boolean functions* may be defined over the elements of this set. As there are only two elements in the set, the number of functions with a certain number of variables is finite. The number of functions of one variable $f(x)$, for example, corresponds to the various forms of matching elements of the set $\mathbb{B}$ to each of the two elements of that set. The number of different one-variable functions is, as it is easy to see, four. They are described in Table 2.1.

Table 2.1   One-variable logic functions.

x	$x = 0$	$x = 1$	Function Expression	Function Name
$f(x)$	0	0	$f_0(x) = 0$	constant 0
	0	1	$f_1(x) = x$	identity
	1	0	$f_2(x) = \overline{x}$	inversion or NOT
	1	1	$f_3(x) = 1$	constant 1

In contrast to what happens with the set $\mathbb{R}$ of the real numbers or even with the set $\mathbb{N}$ of the integers, in this set $\mathbb{B}$, the functions $f(x)$ may be defined by the complete indication of their values for each of the two possible values of the variable x. The number of these values, two, is not only finite but also small. It is, therefore, possible to define a one-variable function by the indication in a table of its value for each value of the independent variable. This type of table is called *truth table* or *function table*.

This happens, for example, with the function $f_2(x)$ which matches each value x of $\mathbb{B}$ to the other value of the same set. $f_2(x)$ is an important function, and it is called *inversion*, *complement* and, most frequently, NOT. Figure 2.1(a) is the truth table for function NOT.

The designation of this function results from Boole's initial work, that studied *propositional algebra* in which the inversion function transformed a *false* statement into a *true* one and vice versa. The values *false* and *true* make up the set of two values, homologous to the set $\mathbb{B}$.

Of the four one-variable functions, NOT is, as we will see, the most relevant one. In fact, $f_0(x)$ and $f_3(x)$ are the two possible constants, $f_0(x) = 0$ and $f_3(x) = 1$, and the function $f_1(x) = x$ is also trivial.

These functions may also be represented by their *logic expression*, as was done for the three trivial functions in the previous paragraph. Inversion or NOT is represented by Expression (2.1).

$$f_2(x) = \overline{x}. \tag{2.1}$$

Logic functions may also be represented graphically. The NOT function is graphically represented by one of the symbols in Figure 2.1(b).

The fact that their truth table can define logic functions makes it possible to consider, in the formal algebraisation process, the hypothesis of demonstrating theorems by complete induction. It is evident that methods to carry out these demonstrations through deduction using a set of axioms are also valid, but the fact that the alternative mentioned exists is, in itself, an important fact with various consequences.

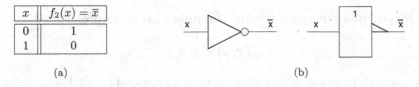

x	$f_2(x) = \overline{x}$
0	1
1	0

(a)   (b)

Fig. 2.1 Function NOT: (a) Truth table and (b) graphical representation.

Table 2.2   Proof of the double inversion theorem.

x	$\bar{x}$	$\bar{\bar{x}}$
0	1	0
1	0	1

What has been stated can be shown for an important theorem, the *double inversion theorem*:

$$\bar{\bar{x}} = x. \tag{2.2}$$

Proof by complete induction arises from the fact that there are only two possible values for x. If it is found that, for each of the values of x, the Expression (2.2) is true, then the theorem has been proved.

Table 2.2 provides the organisation to verify this. In fact, it is true that, for the two values of x, column x is equal to column $\bar{\bar{x}}$, which proves the double inversion theorem by complete induction.

2.1.2   *Two-variable Logic Functions*

Two-variable logic functions $f(x,y)$ are also limited in number, of course, more numerous than one-variable functions. In fact, a two-variable table has $2^2 = 4$ rows, or, in more abstract terms, the number of possible configurations for two binary variables is $2^2 = 4$; therefore, the number of functions will be $2^4 = 16$, since there is a different sequence of four binary quantities for each function. The 16 functions are shown in Table 2.3.

2.1.3   *The Functions AND and OR*

Some of the functions indicated in Table 2.3 are more important than others for applications related to digital systems. The conjunction, or AND, and the disjunction, or OR, are, in particular, of the greatest importance.

2.1.4   *Conjunction or AND Function*

The *conjunction* function, or AND, is represented by Expression (2.3).

$$f(x,y) = x \wedge y, \tag{2.3}$$

In general, however, where there is no possibility of confusion between the AND and the numeric multiplication, Expression (2.4) is used emphasising

Table 2.3 Two-variable logic functions.

x	0	0	1	1	Expression of Function	Name of the Function
y	0	1	0	1		
	0	0	0	0	$f_0(x,y) = 0$	constant 0
	0	0	0	1	$f_1(x,y) = x \wedge y$	conjunction or AND
	0	0	1	0	$f_2(x,y) = \overline{x} \Rightarrow \overline{y}$	inverted implication
	0	0	1	1	$f_3(x,y) = x$	identity
	0	1	0	0	$f_4(x,y) = \overline{x} \Leftarrow \overline{y}$	inverted implication
	0	1	0	1	$f_5(x,y) = y$	identity
	0	1	1	0	$f_6(x,y) = x \oplus y$	exclusive disjunction or XOR
$f(x,y)$	0	1	1	1	$f_7(x,y) = x \vee y$	disjunction or OR
	1	0	0	0	$f_8(x,y) = \overline{x \vee y}$	NOR
	1	0	0	1	$f_9(x,y) = x \Leftrightarrow y$	equivalence
	1	0	1	0	$f_{10}(x,y) = \overline{y}$	inversion or NOT
	1	0	1	1	$f_{11}(x,y) = x \Leftarrow y$	implication
	1	1	0	0	$f_{12}(x,y) = \overline{x}$	inversion or NOT
	1	1	0	1	$f_{13}(x,y) = x \Rightarrow y$	implication
	1	1	1	0	$f_{14}(x,y) = \overline{x \wedge y}$	NAND
	1	1	1	1	$f_{15}(x,y) = 1$	constant 1

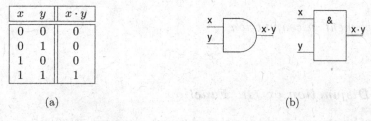

x	y	$x \cdot y$
0	0	0
0	1	0
1	0	0
1	1	1

(a)   (b)

Fig. 2.2 Two-variable AND function: (a) Truth table and (b) graphical representation.

the fact that the AND is a function with the algebraic character of a product.

$$f(x,y) = x \cdot y. \tag{2.4}$$

Often, to further simplify, the «·» is removed, where this will not cause confusion, as shown in Expression (2.5).

$$f(x,y) = x \; y. \tag{2.5}$$

The truth table for AND is shown in Figure 2.2(a).

The function AND, a more current designation then conjunction, is a function that derives its name from the fact that, as can be seen in the table, the function is 1 only when $x = 1$ **and** $y = 1$. It is also common to designate the AND as *logic product*.

The AND function is graphically represented by one of the symbols in Figure 2.2(b).

There are several theorems[1] involving the conjunction that are important. Some of them are listed below:

Commutativity of conjunction

$$x \cdot y = y \cdot x. \tag{2.6}$$

Associativity of conjunction

$$(x \cdot y) \cdot z = x \cdot (y \cdot z). \tag{2.7}$$

Idempotency of conjunction

$$x \cdot x = x. \tag{2.8}$$

Neutral element of conjunction

$$x \cdot 1 = x. \tag{2.9}$$

Absorbent element of conjunction

$$x \cdot 0 = 0. \tag{2.10}$$

Complement in conjunction

$$x \cdot \overline{x} = 0. \tag{2.11}$$

2.1.5 *Disjunction or* OR *Function*

The other function already mentioned, which along with the AND is, as will be seen in Section 2.1.9, important, in the formal definition of Boolean algebra, is the OR or *disjunction*. The logic expression of the function OR is shown in Expression (2.12):

$$f(x, y) = x \vee y. \tag{2.12}$$

In general, however, where there is no possibility of confusion between the OR and the numeric sum, the representation in Expression (2.13), is used, which emphasises the fact that OR is a function with the algebraic character of a sum.

$$f(x, y) = x + y. \tag{2.13}$$

The truth table for the OR is shown in Figure 2.3(a).

---

[1] In Section 2.1.9, it will be discussed, in a more formal way, the context in which some of these theorems are real theorems or defining axioms of the algebra.

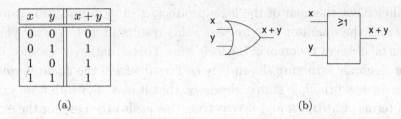

x	y	$x+y$
0	0	0
0	1	1
1	0	1
1	1	1

(a)   (b)

Fig. 2.3 Two-variable OR function: (a) Truth table and (b) graphical representation.

The disjunction, or OR, is a function that derives its name from the fact that the function is 1 when $x = 1$ **or** $y = 1$. It is also common to designate the disjunction as *logic sum*.

The OR is graphically represented by one of the symbols in Figure 2.3(b).

As with conjunction, there are several theorems relating to disjunction that are important:

Commutativity of disjunction

$$x + y = y + x. \tag{2.14}$$

Associativity of disjunction

$$(x + y) + z = x + (y + z). \tag{2.15}$$

Idempotency of disjunction

$$x + x = x. \tag{2.16}$$

Neutral element of disjunction

$$x + 0 = x. \tag{2.17}$$

Absorbent element of disjunction

$$x + 1 = 1. \tag{2.18}$$

Complement in disjunction

$$x + \overline{x} = 1. \tag{2.19}$$

2.1.6 Duality Principle

As can be seen in the two sets of theorems shown for AND and OR, for each valid expression in one of the sets, there is an expression in the other which is obtained from the first, by exchanging the pair of values 0 and 1 between them as well as the operators AND and OR. For example, if you take the neutral element theorem of the logic product, $x \cdot 1 = x$, and substitute the 1 by 0 and the operator «·» by «+», this results in $x + 0 = x$, which is the neutral element theorem of the logic sum. This situation is common in the type of algebraic structure shown here and results from the *duality principle*.

The duality principle states, precisely, that if it is shown that an expression in terms of AND, OR and NOT is true, this is also the case for the expression obtained through exchanging all operators AND by OR, all operators OR by AND, all 0 values by 1 and all 1 values by 0.

The duality principle results from a certain symmetry between AND and OR operations, which is evident in their respective tables. Indeed, AND is a function where the result is 1 only when both variables are 1. Symmetrically, OR, only results in 0 only when the two variables are 0.

Throughout this book, this symmetry, which is the basis for the duality principle, will frequently appear, giving us the opportunity to observe the same reality through two symmetrical perspectives systematically.

2.1.7 *Operation Priority*

When there are logic expressions involving more than one operation, it is necessary to know what is the *priority in carrying out the operations*. For example, in the expression $f(x, y, z) = x + y \cdot z$, the order in which the operations are performed is important. Table 2.4 shows what happens when the AND, or the OR, are carried out first.

Using parentheses eliminates the ambiguity. Therefore, if it is intended first to conduct the logic product of y and z, this is indicated by $x + (y \cdot z)$, while if it is intended first to carry out the sum of x and y, this should be represented by $(x + y) \cdot z$. To simplify expressions, however, it is assumed

Table 2.4   Truth table showing the ambiguity of the expression $f(x, y, z) = x + y \cdot z$.

x	y	z	$f(x, y, z) = x + y \cdot z$	
			Priority to OR	Priority to AND
0	0	0	0	0
0	0	1	0	0
0	1	0	0	0
0	1	1	1	1
1	0	0	0	1
1	0	1	1	1
1	1	0	0	1
1	1	1	1	1

that the product has priority over the sum (as is usual in classical algebra) and, therefore, in the first case shown the parentheses can be removed.

2.1.8 *Theorems Involving* AND *and* OR

Two of the fundamental theorems simultaneously involving AND and OR are the pair relating to *distributivity*. These two theorems are the theorem of the distributivity of the product over the sum (Expression (2.20)),

$$x \cdot (y + z) = x \cdot y + x \cdot z \tag{2.20}$$

and the theorem of the distributivity of the sum over the product (Expression (2.21)).

$$x + y \cdot z = (x + y) \cdot (x + z). \tag{2.21}$$

The existence of two theorems of distributivity, with one being the sum over the product, and the other, the product over the sum, is compatible with the principle of duality.

These two equalities are important since in the axiomatic approach to Boolean algebra they are defining postulates of the algebraic structure, as Section 2.1.9 will show.

Any of the theorems presented in this section may be proved by complete induction, similarly to what was carried out for the double inversion theorem. Table 2.5 illustrates the proof by complete induction for Theorem 2.21.

Other important theorems involving both AND and OR are the following:

Absorption

$$x + x \cdot y = x, \tag{2.22}$$
$$x \cdot (x + y) = x. \tag{2.23}$$

Table 2.5 Proof of the theorem of the distributivity of the sum over the product.

x	y	z	$x + y$	$x + z$	$(x + y) \cdot (x + z)$	$y \cdot z$	$x + y \cdot z$
0	0	0	0	0	0	0	0
0	0	1	0	1	0	0	0
0	1	0	1	0	0	0	0
0	1	1	1	1	1	1	1
1	0	0	1	1	1	0	1
1	0	1	1	1	1	0	1
1	1	0	1	1	1	0	1
1	1	1	1	1	1	1	1

Redundancy

$$x + \overline{x} \cdot y = x + y, \tag{2.24}$$

$$x \cdot (\overline{x} + y) = x \cdot y. \tag{2.25}$$

Consensus

$$x \cdot y + y \cdot z + \overline{x} \cdot z = x \cdot y + \overline{x} \cdot z, \tag{2.26}$$

$$(x + y) \cdot (y + z) \cdot (\overline{x} + z) = (x + y) \cdot (\overline{x} + z). \tag{2.27}$$

De Morgan's Laws

$$\overline{x + y} = \overline{x} \cdot \overline{y}, \tag{2.28}$$

$$\overline{x \cdot y} = \overline{x} + \overline{y}. \tag{2.29}$$

De Morgan's laws, in particular, are extremely important, since they enable expressions in terms of sums to be transformed into expressions in terms of products, with an added inversion, as is shown, for example in Expression (2.30), and vice-versa.

$$\begin{aligned}
x \cdot \overline{y} + \overline{z} \cdot w &= \overline{\overline{x \cdot \overline{y} + \overline{z} \cdot w}} \\
&= \overline{\overline{x \cdot \overline{y}} \cdot \overline{\overline{z} \cdot w}} \\
&= \overline{(\overline{x} + y) \cdot (z + \overline{w})}. \tag{2.30}
\end{aligned}$$

Graphically, the change in structure is clearer. Figure 2.4 shows the same example.

The graphical representation of a function, such as that given in the previous example, is called the *logic diagram* of the function. The logic diagram of a function is, therefore, one of the ways of representing a function.

2.1.9   *Formal Definition of Boolean Algebra*

Throughout this chapter, an algebraic structure was constructed in a natural way from a set $\mathbb{B}$ of two elements and some of the functions that can be defined over it. This structure is one of a set of structures called Boolean algebras.

Within the perspective which has been followed, all of the above listed properties are theorems. They can be demonstrated from the definition of the functions over the elements of set $\mathbb{B}$ using the complete induction method.

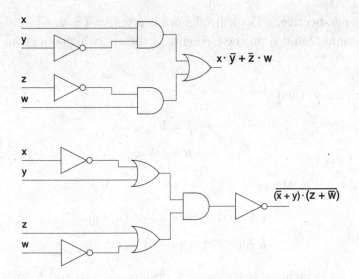

Fig. 2.4   Sample application from one of de Morgan's laws.

The theorems, however, are not independent of each other and some are deductible from others. The following example shows how deduction can prove the theorem shown in Expression (2.31).

$$x + \overline{x} \cdot y = x + y. \tag{2.31}$$

In fact, using distributivity,

$$x + \overline{x} \cdot y = (x + \overline{x}) \cdot (x + y). \tag{2.32}$$

But, given that $x + \overline{x} = 1$, we can obtain

$$x + \overline{x} \cdot y = 1 \cdot (x + y) \tag{2.33}$$

and using commutativity,

$$x + \overline{x} \cdot y = (x + y) \cdot 1. \tag{2.34}$$

From the neutral element theorem of the logic product, we conclude with Expression (2.35) which proves the theorem.

$$x + \overline{x} \cdot y = x + y. \tag{2.35}$$

Another way of looking at the definition of a Boolean algebra is the definition of a set of postulates for the algebraic structure, and, from them, deducing a set of theorems that characterise the structure.

In this perspective, a Boolean algebra is a triplet $\{\mathbb{B}, \vee, \wedge\}$ of a set $\mathbb{B}$ and two operations $\vee$ and $\wedge$ on the elements of the set, which obey the following postulates:

- P1: If $a, b \in \mathbb{B}$, then

$$a \vee b = b \vee a, \tag{2.36}$$

$$a \wedge b = b \wedge a. \tag{2.37}$$

- P2: If $a, b, c \in \mathbb{B}$, then

$$a \vee (b \wedge c) = (a \vee b) \wedge (a \vee c), \tag{2.38}$$

$$a \wedge (b \vee c) = (a \wedge b) \vee (a \wedge c). \tag{2.39}$$

- P3: The set $\mathbb{B}$ includes two elements, designated as 0 and 1, such that, for each $a \in \mathbb{B}$,

$$0 \vee a = a \vee 0 = a, \tag{2.40}$$

$$1 \wedge a = a \wedge 1 = a. \tag{2.41}$$

- P4: For each $a \in \mathbb{B}$, there is an element $\bar{a} \in \mathbb{B}$ designated by the complement of a, such that

$$a \vee \bar{a} = 1, \tag{2.42}$$

$$a \wedge \bar{a} = 0. \tag{2.43}$$

Provided an algebraic structure obeys the above postulates, it is a Boolean algebra. The set of subsets of a set and the operations union ($\cup$) and intersection ($\cap$), for example, constitute a Boolean algebra.

Two-element Boolean algebras are a particular case. The algebra defined above is, as can be seen, a Boolean algebra. From this point of view, all the theorems that have been presented can be deduced from the stated postulates.

2.1.10   *N*AND *and* N*OR* *Functions*

In addition to the essential functions of Boolean algebra (AND, OR and NOT), Section 2.1.2 lists a number of other two-variable functions over the binary set $\mathbb{B}$. Two other important functions are NAND (the inversion of AND) and NOR (the inversion of OR).

The algebraic expressions of NAND and NOR are Expressions (2.44) and (2.45), respectively.

$$f(x, y) = \overline{x \cdot y}, \qquad (2.44)$$

$$f(x, y) = \overline{x + y}. \qquad (2.45)$$

NAND can be represented more simply by (Expression (2.46)).

$$f(x, y) = \overline{x \ y}. \qquad (2.46)$$

For convenience, Figure 2.5(a) provides a repetition of the truth table for both functions.

Figures 2.5(a) and 2.5(b) show respectively the graphical representation of NAND and NOR functions.

These functions are commutative but do not have the properties of associativity or distributivity. Their importance is made clear a little further on.

2.1.11 *XOR Function*

The last two-variable function that deserves a special mention is the *exclusive disjunction* function, or XOR (from, *eXclusive OR*).

Figure 2.6(a) repeats the truth table for XOR for convenience.

The exclusive disjunction function has this designation because it takes the value 1 only when one, and only one, of the variables, is 1. The logic expression of XOR is Expression (2.47).

$$f(x, y) = x \oplus y. \qquad (2.47)$$

x	y	$\overline{x \ y}$	$\overline{x + y}$
0	0	1	1
0	1	1	0
1	0	1	0
1	1	0	0

(a)

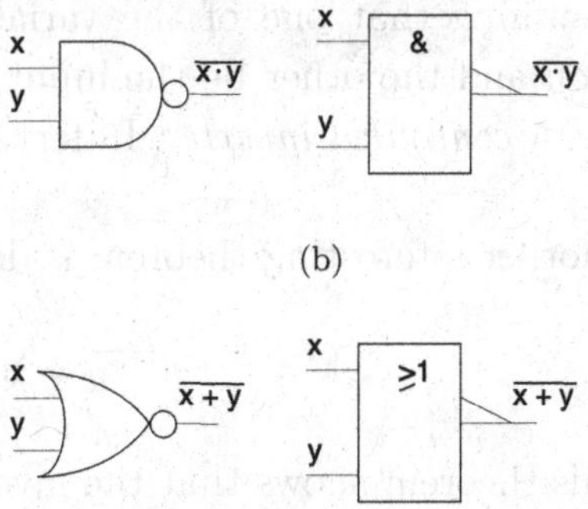

Fig. 2.5   NAND and NOR functions: (a) Truth tables; (b) graphical representation of NAND and (c) graphical representation of NOR.

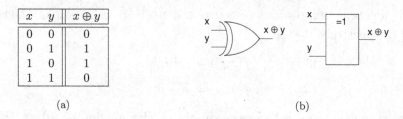

x	y	$x \oplus y$
0	0	0
0	1	1
1	0	1
1	1	0

(a)   (b)

Fig. 2.6   Two-variable XOR function: (a) Truth table and (b) graphical representation.

The graphical representation of XOR is illustrated in Figure 2.6(b).

The exclusive disjunction is a commutative and associative function. More specific theorems which are of significant practical interest are shown in the Expressions (2.48) and (2.49).

$$x \oplus y = \overline{x} \cdot y + x \cdot \overline{y}, \tag{2.48}$$

$$x \oplus y = (x + y) \cdot (\overline{x} + \overline{y}). \tag{2.49}$$

These two theorems provide a relation between XOR and AND, OR and NOT and can be used to represent XOR in terms of these functions.

The two theorems illustrated in Expressions (2.50) and (2.51) provide a new perspective of XOR which is very relevant, as we will see, both in arithmetic circuits and computer architectures.

$$x \oplus 0 = x, \tag{2.50}$$

$$x \oplus 1 = \overline{x}. \tag{2.51}$$

Assuming that one of the variables may be used to control the function (c), and the other be the input variable (x), the XOR $y = x \oplus c$ can be seen as a *controlled inverter*. In fact, if, $c = 0$, then $y = x$, and if $c = 1$, then $y = \overline{x}$.

Another interesting theorem is defined in Expression (2.52).

$$\overline{x \oplus y} = \overline{x} \oplus y = x \oplus \overline{y}. \tag{2.52}$$

This theorem shows that the inversion of XOR is equal to the XOR of one of the variables inverted, with the other variable. The obvious consequence is the theorem shown in Expression (2.53).

$$\overline{x} \oplus \overline{y} = x \oplus y. \tag{2.53}$$

2.1.12 *N-variable Logic Functions*

The previous sections studied logic functions of one and two variables and outlined Boolean algebra, a mathematical structure that supports its use and manipulation. Using Boolean algebra it is possible to generalise the concepts presented, to functions with more than two variables. Some of the listed functions are easily generalisable as is the case of the functions AND and OR. The three-input AND function is defined by Expression (2.54), using associativity.

$$x \cdot y \cdot z = (x \cdot y) \cdot z = x \cdot (y \cdot z). \qquad (2.54)$$

The generalisation for n variables is immediate.
Similarly, for the OR function, the definition is made by Expression (2.55).

$$x + y + z = (x + y) + z = x + (y + z). \qquad (2.55)$$

In other cases, it is necessary to proceed with more caution. NAND and NOR, for example, are not associative functions. The process starts from the fact that AND and OR functions are associative functions. The definition is shown in the Expressions (2.56) and (2.57).

$$\overline{x \cdot y \cdot z} = \overline{(x \cdot y) \cdot z} = \overline{x \cdot (y \cdot z)}, \qquad (2.56)$$

$$\overline{x + y + z} = \overline{(x + y) + z} = \overline{x + (y + z)}. \qquad (2.57)$$

It is now possible to define functions with n variables, using the previous functions. For example, the function represented by Expression (2.58) is a four-variable function defined through a logic expression.

$$f(x, y, z, w) = x \cdot y + \overline{x} \cdot y \cdot z + \overline{(x \cdot \overline{y} + w)} + (x \cdot y \oplus z). \qquad (2.58)$$

In logic expressions involving XOR, the function AND takes priority over XOR, so there is no ambiguity in the last term of Expression (2.58). No order of priority is defined between OR and XOR, which makes the use of parentheses necessary in such cases.

Functions of n variables can of course also be represented by their table or a logic diagram. Figure 2.7 and Table 2.6 are two other representations of the function defined by Expression (2.58). The OR symbol used in the figure, which is commonly used when the number of inputs requires this, should be noted. Similarly, the AND symbol can be modified to accommodate a larger number of entries, as illustrated for the case of five variables in Figure 2.8.

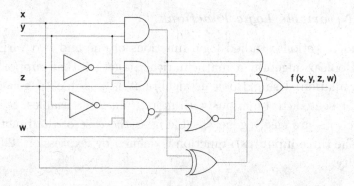

Fig. 2.7   Graphical representation of the function defined by Expression (2.58).

Table 2.6   Table for the function defined by Expression (2.58).

x	y	z	w	$f(x, y, z, w)$
0	0	0	0	0
0	0	0	1	0
0	0	1	0	1
0	0	1	1	1
0	1	0	0	0
0	1	0	1	0
0	1	1	0	1
0	1	1	1	1
1	0	0	0	1
1	0	0	1	0
1	0	1	0	1
1	0	1	1	1
1	1	0	0	1
1	1	0	1	1
1	1	1	0	1
1	1	1	1	1

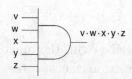

Fig. 2.8   Symbol for a five-input AND function.

2.1.13   *Handling of Logic Expressions*

The set of theorems presented in the previous sections enables us to perform the *algebraic manipulation of logic expressions*, both to simplify them and to obtain equivalent expressions which meet certain criteria. Examples of two types of manipulation will be presented in this section.

As mentioned previously, the function AND can be represented by three different logic expressions. The AND of two variables x and y may be represented by $x \wedge y$, or more generally by $x \cdot y$ and even, when there is no possibility of confusion, by $x\,y$. From this section onwards, unless it is necessary to do otherwise, the third form, most common, will be systematically used to represent the function AND.

The issue of simplification of expressions is of great interest since, as discussed below, the implementation of circuits which instantiate logic functions leads to structures with a larger or smaller number of components, according to the complexity of the expressions which represent the functions.

Take, for example, the simplification of Expression (2.59) a three-variable logic function.

$$f(a,b,c) = \bar{a}\,\bar{b}\,c + b\,c + a\,c. \tag{2.59}$$

Use of commutativity, gives

$$f(a,b,c) = c\,\bar{a}\,\bar{b} + c\,b + c\,a \tag{2.60}$$

or, taking into consideration the distributivity of the product over the sum

$$f(a,b,c) = c\,(\bar{a}\,\bar{b} + b) + c\,a. \tag{2.61}$$

From commutativity and Theorem 2.24, we obtain Expression (2.62).

$$f(a,b,c) = c\,(\bar{a} + b) + c\,a. \tag{2.62}$$

Applying again the distributivity of the product over the sum we arrive at

$$f(a,b,c) = c\,(\bar{a} + b + a) \tag{2.63}$$

and taking under consideration, once again, the commutativity and, also, Theorem 2.19, we obtain

$$f(a,b,c) = c\,(1 + b) \tag{2.64}$$

and, therefore (Expressions (2.6), (2.18) and (2.9)), we obtain finally Expression (2.65).

$$f(a,b,c) = c. \tag{2.65}$$

In this case the simplification has shown that the initial function with three variables is only nominally so, since it has been simplified to the trivial function of Expression (2.65).

Another example is the simplification of the expression of the function used as an example in the previous section (Expression (2.58)). This time, identifying the various theorems used is left as an exercise.

$$
\begin{aligned}
f(x, y, z, w) &= x\,y + \overline{x}\,y\,z + \overline{(x\,\overline{y} + w)} + (x\,y \oplus z)\\
&= (x + \overline{x}\,z)\,y + \overline{(\overline{x} + y + w)} + x\,y\,\overline{z} + \overline{x}\,\overline{y}\,z\\
&= x\,y + y\,z + x\,\overline{y}\,\overline{w} + x\,y\,\overline{z} + \overline{x}\,\overline{y}\,z\\
&= x\,y + y\,z + x\,\overline{w} + \overline{x}\,\overline{y}\,z\\
&= x\,y + y\,z + x\,\overline{w} + z\\
&= x\,y + x\,\overline{w} + z. \qquad (2.66)
\end{aligned}
$$

As is easy to see, the manipulation of the expression resulted in a much simpler expression, which is also reflected in the logic diagram in Figure 2.9, with much fewer operators and with a complexity inferior to the one in Figure 2.7.

As has already been mentioned, sometimes manipulating logic expressions has the purpose of obtaining certain forms rather than their simplification. As an example, consider the manipulation of Expression (2.67) to obtain an expression using only operators with two input variables and operators NOT:

$$
f(a, b, c, d) = \overline{a}\,\overline{b}\,d + \overline{a}\,\overline{c}\,d + a\,c\,d + a\,\overline{b}\,\overline{d}. \qquad (2.67)
$$

Applying the distributivity theorem of the product to the sum, it is easy to obtain Expression (2.68).

$$
f(a, b, c, d) = \overline{a}\,(\overline{b}\,d + \overline{c}\,d) + a\,(c\,d + \overline{b}\,\overline{d}). \qquad (2.68)
$$

This expression only uses two-input operators, as well as NOTs. This structure is perhaps clearer in Figure 2.10.

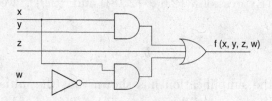

Fig. 2.9   Graphical representation of the function defined by Expression (2.66).

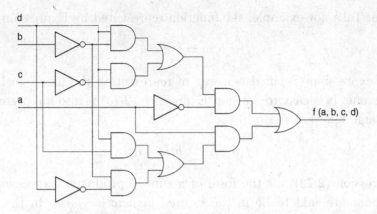

Fig. 2.10 Graphical representation of the function defined by Expression (2.68).

Another example is the manipulation of Expression (2.69) to obtain an expression of the same function, using only NAND and NOT operators.

$$f(a,b,c,d) = (a \oplus b)\ c + b\ \bar{c}\ d + \bar{a}\ \bar{c}\ (b+d). \tag{2.69}$$

Applying Theorem 2.48 and the distributivity of the product over the sum (Expression (2.20)), it is easy to obtain Expression (2.70).

$$f(a,b,c,d) = (a \oplus b)\ c + b\ \bar{c}\ d + \bar{a}\ \bar{c}\ (b+d)$$
$$= (a\ \bar{b} + \bar{a}\ b)\ c + b\ \bar{c}\ d + \bar{a}\ \bar{c}\ (b+d)$$
$$= a\ \bar{b}\ c + \bar{a}\ b\ c + b\ \bar{c}\ d + \bar{a}\ \bar{c}\ b + \bar{a}\ \bar{c}\ d. \tag{2.70}$$

Through the application of the double inversion theorem (Expression (2.2)) and one of de Morgan laws (Expression (2.28)), Expression (2.71) is obtained, which is the desired expression.

$$f(a,b,c,d) = a\ \bar{b}\ c + \bar{a}\ b\ c + b\ \bar{c}\ d + \bar{a}\ \bar{c}\ b + \bar{a}\ \bar{c}\ d$$
$$= \overline{\overline{a\ \bar{b}\ c + \bar{a}\ b\ c + b\ \bar{c}\ d + \bar{a}\ \bar{c}\ b + \bar{a}\ \bar{c}\ d}}$$
$$= \overline{\overline{a\ \bar{b}\ c}\ \overline{\bar{a}\ b\ c}\ \overline{b\ \bar{c}\ d}\ \overline{\bar{a}\ \bar{c}\ b}\ \overline{\bar{a}\ \bar{c}\ d}}. \tag{2.71}$$

2.2 Representation of Logic Functions

As we saw, there are various ways of *representation of logic functions*, namely through their logic expression, through their table or through their logic diagram. Take, for example, the function represented by Expression (2.72).

$$f(a, b, c) = b\ \overline{c} + a\ b. \tag{2.72}$$

The expression specified is a way of representing the function. It is not the only one. It is easy to see that Expression (2.73) is also a representation of the same function $f(a, b, c)$.

$$f(a, b, c) = b\ (\overline{c} + a). \tag{2.73}$$

Expression (2.72) has the form of a sum of products. Expressions with this format are said to be in the *normal disjunctive form*. In the normal disjunctive form, one or more of the products may be reduced to a variable which may be inverted. Expression (2.73) has the form of a product of sums (one of the products is reduced to the variable b). This format is called *normal conjunctive form*. As in the previous case, one or more of the products may be reduced to one variable, inverted or not.

Another way of representing the function is through its table. Obtaining the table of a function from its expression is relatively easy. Tables are obtained for parts of the expression of the function which correspond to simple operators and, from that, the final table is constructed, operating on the partial tables. In the case of the function under study, the table of $\overline{c}$, can, for example, be obtained and, from this, the construction of the table for $b\ \overline{c}$ and, in parallel, the table for $a\ b$. Finally, the table for the sum of the two products may be obtained, which is the desired table. The method detailed here is illustrated in Table 2.7.

The table of a function, unlike the expression, is, as can easily be understood, unique.

A third way of representing a function is its logic diagram. As the logic diagram corresponds to a graphical representation of a logic expression, there

Table 2.7   Construction of the table of function $f(a, b, c) = b\ \overline{c} + a\ b$.

a	b	c	$\overline{c}$	$b\ \overline{c}$	$a\ b$	$f(a, b, c)$
0	0	0	1	0	0	0
0	0	1	0	0	0	0
0	1	0	1	1	0	1
0	1	1	0	0	0	0
1	0	0	1	0	0	0
1	0	1	0	0	0	0
1	1	0	1	1	1	1
1	1	1	0	0	1	1

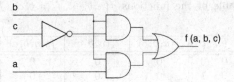

Fig. 2.11   Graphical representation of the function defined by Expression (2.72).

is no single logic diagram to represent a function. In the case of the function under study, there will be a logic diagram for every possible expression of the function. The logic diagram corresponding to Expression (2.72) is represented in Figure 2.11.

All the ways of representing a given function represent the same information. It is therefore possible to go from each one of them to all the others. If, for example, an expression of a function is the starting point, obtaining the other two forms, as has been seen, is easy. In the same way, going from a logic diagram to an expression and then to a table does not present any difficulties. However, obtaining the expression of a function from its table is not so immediate. In the following subsections, this problem will be analysed.

2.2.1   *Standard Sum of Products Form*

Consider, once again, Table 2.7. Looking at the table, it is easy to conclude that the represented function has the value 1 in three positions in the table and the value 0 in the other five positions. It can be concluded from this that the represented function $f(a, b, c)$ can be considered as the sum of three functions $f_x(a, b, c)$, $f_y(a, b, c)$ and $f_z(a, b, c)$. Each of these functions is represented by a table with only one row with value 1. Table 2.8 illustrates these three functions and also function $f(a, b, c)$.

The rows of the table are numbered from 0 to 7 to aid identification. It should be noted that the numbering of each row corresponds to the interpretation as a binary number of the configurations of the values of the three logic variables a, b and c of the respective row.

It is easy to understand that function $f(a, b, c)$ is the logic sum of $f_x(a, b, c)$, $f_y(a, b, c)$ and $f_z(a, b, c)$ as Expression (2.74) shows.

$$f(a, b, c) = f_x(a, b, c) + f_y(a, b, c) + f_z(a, b, c). \qquad (2.74)$$

The identification of the expressions of the functions $f_x(a, b, c)$, $f_y(a, b, c)$ and $f_z(a, b, c)$ is not so immediate. But, if the function $f_z(a, b, c)$ is

Table 2.8   Table of the functions $f(a,b,c)$, $f_x(a,b,c)$, $f_y(a,b,c)$ and $f_z(a,b,c)$.

Row	a	b	c	$f(a,b,c)$	$f_x(a,b,c)$	$f_y(a,b,c)$	$f_z(a,b,c)$
0	0	0	0	0	0	0	0
1	0	0	1	0	0	0	0
2	0	1	0	1	1	0	0
3	0	1	1	0	0	0	0
4	1	0	0	0	0	0	0
5	1	0	1	0	0	0	0
6	1	1	0	1	0	1	0
7	1	1	1	1	0	0	1

considered, it is easy to verify that it involves a three-input AND (Expression (2.75)).

$$f_z(a,b,c) = a\ b\ c. \tag{2.75}$$

It is also possible to verify that $f_y(a,b,c)$ is a function that takes the value 1, only when $a = 1$, $b = 1$ and $c = 0$, that is, when $a = 1$, $b = 1$ and $\bar{c} = 1$. Therefore, it is defined by Expression (2.76).

$$f_y(a,b,c) = a\ b\ \bar{c}. \tag{2.76}$$

In the same way, it is possible to conclude Expression (2.77).

$$f_x(a,b,c) = \bar{a}\ b\ \bar{c}. \tag{2.77}$$

From the Expressions (2.74)–(2.77) it is easy to obtain the Expression (2.78) for the function $f(a,b,c)$:

$$f(a,b,c) = a\ b\ c + a\ b\ \bar{c} + \bar{a}\ b\ \bar{c}. \tag{2.78}$$

The method is general and enables us to obtain a logic expression of a function from its truth table. The expression obtained is not usually the most simple expression. It does, however, have a very important feature: it is a sum of products form in which, all the products involve all the variables of the function, even though some variables may be inverted. These variables, which may be inverted or not, are called *literals*.

Products of this kind are called *minterms*. The expression in the form of a sum of minterms is unique. In fact, as the table of a function is unique and this expression reflects, in its structure, the structure of the table, it is also unique. This expression is called *first canonical form, first standard form, standard disjunctive normal form* or *standard sum of products form*, designation used preferentially in the rest of this text.

In the standard sum of products form of a function, each minterm corresponds to a row of the table, in which the function takes the value 1.

Once again, it should be noted that each minterm corresponds to one of the values 1 for the function in its table. For example, the minterm $a\ b\ c$ corresponds to the 1 of the last row of the table. It is usual to number the rows of the table, as was done for Table 2.8. Each of the minterms can then be referred to by the number of the respective row number. For example, the minterm $a\ b\ c$ may be designated as m_7.

And, in this way, we may shorten Expression (2.78) to Expression (2.79),

$$f(a,b,c) = m_2 + m_6 + m_7 \qquad (2.79)$$

or, in a further abbreviated form, to Expression (2.80).

$$f(a,b,c) = \sum m(2,6,7). \qquad (2.80)$$

Clearly, this convention requires that a certain order of the variables in the function table is assumed. In the examples above, the variable a is the variable corresponding to the bit with the greatest weight, and the variable c, to the bit with the smallest weight in the numbering of the rows.

The expression of a minterm from its number is obtained by making the correspondence of the number in binary with the various variables or its inversions. The minterm m_2, for example, corresponds to the row 2 of the table, i.e., the row where $a = 0$, $b = 1$ and $c = 0$ (binary 010 configuration). It follows that $m_2 = \bar{a}\ b\ \bar{c}$. Conversely, if the expression of a minterm of a function is known, e.g., $a\ \bar{b}\ \bar{c}$, it is easy to conclude that the expression only takes the value 1 when $a = 1$, $b = 0$ and $c = 0$. This configuration corresponds to 100 in binary and to row 4 of the table. This is, therefore, the minterm m_4.

In conclusion, it is not difficult to obtain the standard sum of products form of a function represented by its truth table. However, this is not generally the simplest expression of the function.

The standard sum of products form of a function corresponds, of course, to a logic diagram. In the case of the function being considered, the corresponding logic diagram is shown in Figure 2.12. Considering what is said about the structure of the standard sum of products form, it is now possible to conclude that, in the logic diagram corresponding to this form, each AND operator also corresponds to one of the rows of the table of the function, where it takes on the value 1.

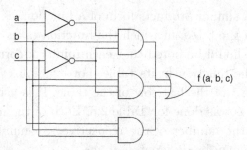

Fig. 2.12   Logic diagram corresponding to the standard sum of products form of $f(a, b, c)$.

Table 2.9   Table for the function $f(a, b, c)$ and its maxterms.

Row	a	b	c	$f(a,b,c)$	M_0	M_1	M_3	M_4	M_5
0	0	0	0	0	0	1	1	1	1
1	0	0	1	0	1	0	1	1	1
2	0	1	0	1	1	1	1	1	1
3	0	1	1	0	1	1	0	1	1
4	1	0	0	0	1	1	1	0	1
5	1	0	1	0	1	1	1	1	0
6	1	1	0	1	1	1	1	1	1
7	1	1	1	1	1	1	1	1	1

It is easy to understand, both from the expression of the standard sum of products form and from the observation of the corresponding logic diagram, that the function is represented, if we do not take into account the inversions, by two levels of operators. There are ANDs in the first level and one OR in the second. This type of representation is usually called *two-level representation*. As we will see, this type of representation is extremely relevant. Not considering the inversions as a third level results from the fact that, in practice, variables are often available, both in the non-inverted and inverted forms and as such it is not necessary to explicitly consider NOT operators.

2.2.2   *Standard Product of Sums Form*

In Section 2.2.1, a process of obtaining an expression from a function, the sum of products form, was presented, using its table. As was seen, the expression is the sum of its minterms, with these corresponding to the positions in the table in which the function takes the value 1. The duality principle, however, implies that an entirely similar method is possible, starting now from the configuration of variables in which the function has the value 0. In fact, repeating the table of the function, now isolating the values 0, Table 2.9 is obtained.

Each one of the functions M_i is designated a *maxterm*. Each maxterm M_i has just one 0 in its table, which corresponds to one of the possible configurations of variables. For example, the maxterm M_0 has the value 0, only for the configuration $a = b = c = 0$ and, as it is easy to see, corresponds to the OR of the three variables (Expression (2.81)).

$$M_0 = a + b + c. \tag{2.81}$$

In the same way, Expressions (2.82) define other maxterms.

$$\begin{aligned} M_1 &= a + b + \bar{c}, \\ M_3 &= a + \bar{b} + \bar{c}, \\ M_4 &= \bar{a} + b + c, \\ M_5 &= \bar{a} + b + \bar{c}. \end{aligned} \tag{2.82}$$

Maxterms are logic sums in which all the input variables of the function are represented, possibly inverted.

Obtaining the expression of the maxterm from its number is similar to what happens in the case of minterms, but here with the alterations imposed by the duality principle. Thus, for example, maxterm M_3 is the maxterm which only takes the value 0 when $a = 0$, $b = 1$ and $c = 1$. This corresponds to the binary configuration 011. The function M_3, therefore, takes on the value 1 when $a = 1$ or $b = 0$ or $c = 0$. Hence $M_3 = a + \bar{b} + \bar{c}$.

The expression of the function can be obtained by the product of the different maxterms

$$f(a, b, c) = (a + b + c)\,(a + b + \bar{c})\,(a + \bar{b} + \bar{c})\,(\bar{a} + b + c)\,(\bar{a} + b + \bar{c}). \tag{2.83}$$

This expression, in terms of products of maxterms, has the name of *second standard form*, *standard conjunctive normal form* or *standard product of sums form* and, as is the case with the standard sum of products form, is unique. In the standard product of sums form of a function, each maxterm corresponds to a row of the table in which the function takes the value 0.

Figure 2.13 shows the logic diagram corresponding to the standard product of sums form of the function as described in Expression (2.83).

Just as in the case of the standard sum of products form, it is possible to specify the expression in an abbreviated way specifying the maxterms involved in the product as in Expression (2.84).

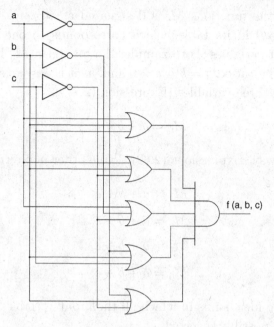

Fig. 2.13   Logic diagram corresponding to the standard product of sums form of $f(a, b, c)$.

$$f(a, b, c) = M_0 \, M_1 \, M_3 \, M_4 \, M_5. \tag{2.84}$$

A further abbreviated form is

$$f(a, b, c) = \prod M(0, 1, 3, 4, 5). \tag{2.85}$$

Just as in the case of the sum of products form, this representation is a two-level representation.

It should be noted that, for any function, in each row of the table there is either a 0 or a 1. This means that if this row corresponds to a minterm of the function, it cannot correspond to a maxterm, and vice versa. Just as in the table, if all the rows at 1 are known, implicitly all the rows with 0 are known; if the standard sum of products form of a function is known, then the standard product of sums form is known, and vice versa.

For example, for the function $f(a, b, c) = \sum m(0, 3, 6)$, it can immediately be concluded that $f(a, b, c) = \Pi M(1, 2, 4, 5, 7)$. It is, therefore, possible to directly obtain the expression for the standard product of sums form (Expression (2.83)) from the standard sum of products form (Expression (2.77)). The reverse procedure is analogous.

2.2.3 Representation of Functions Using a Single Operator Type

The two previous sections showed the procedures to obtain the logic expression of a function from its table. The method used, to obtain the standard sum of products and product of sums forms, leads to expressions which use only the AND, OR and NOT operators. As no restriction on the possible type of functions has been made, any function of any number of variables may be submitted to the procedure presented, which is, therefore, a general one. An obvious consequence of great importance is that any logic function may be represented by an expression using only operators of the type indicated, that is, AND, OR and NOT.

A set of functions which, when used in logic functions, enables any other function to be represented is called a *complete set*. The set {AND, OR, NOT} is, therefore, a complete set.

There are various other complete sets, including two subsets of the previous set: the set {AND, NOT} and the set {OR, NOT}.

Two other complete sets are, however, of great importance. These are the set consisting only of the function NAND and the set consisting only of the function NOR.

If it is possible to represent any of the three operators — AND, OR and NOT — only by NAND or NOR operators, given that an expression using those three operators can represent any function, then any function may be represented using only the operators NAND or NOR. This is easy to prove. It will be shown for the case of NAND (the case for NOR is similar).

Take the NOT function. Using the idempotency theorem (Expression (2.8)) it is easy to verify Expression (2.86).

$$\overline{x} = \overline{x\ x}. \tag{2.86}$$

But $\overline{x\ x}$ is the function NAND (with the same value in the two inputs).

Using, now, the double inversion Theorem (Expression (2.2)) and Expression (2.86), it is possible to verify that the AND may easily be represented using only the operator NAND Expression (2.87).

$$x\ y = \overline{\overline{x\ y}}$$
$$= \overline{\overline{x\ y}\ \overline{x\ y}}. \tag{2.87}$$

To represent OR, the double inversion theorem is once again used, as well as one of the de Morgan's law (Expression (2.28)), as shown in

Expression (2.88).

$$x + y = \overline{\overline{x + y}}$$
$$= \overline{\overline{x}\ \overline{y}}$$
$$= \overline{\overline{x}\ \overline{x}\ \overline{y}\ \overline{y}}. \tag{2.88}$$

Representation using logic diagrams is clearer, as can be seen in Figure 2.14.

It is, therefore, possible to represent any function by a logic expression, using only NAND or NOR operators. The way to do this may lead to very complex expressions if we do this from another expression, substituting each AND, OR and NOT by NAND or NOR, according to the given rules. There are, however, in some cases, easier and more structured ways of obtaining such expressions.

If a function is represented by the sum of products form, the application of the double inversion theorem and, then, one of de Morgan's laws leads directly to the expression in terms of NAND. Take, as an example, the function previously studied, represented by Expression (2.72). The method proposed above is illustrated in Expression (2.89).

$$f(a, b, c) = b\,\overline{c} + a\,b$$
$$= \overline{\overline{b\,\overline{c} + a\,b}}$$
$$= \overline{\overline{b\,\overline{c}\,\overline{c}}\ \overline{a\,b}}. \tag{2.89}$$

Through the manipulation of Expression (2.72) it is easy to obtain Expression (2.90), which represents the same function in the product of sums form.

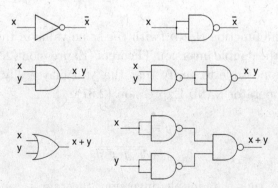

Fig. 2.14   Representation of the functions NOT, AND and OR with NANDs.

$$f(a, b, c) = (a + \bar{c})\ b. \tag{2.90}$$

From this expression it is easy to obtain an expression using only NOR operators, as illustrated in Expression (2.91).

$$f(a, b, c) = (a + \bar{c})\ b$$
$$= \overline{\overline{(a + \bar{c})\ b}}$$
$$= \overline{\overline{a + c} + \overline{c} + \overline{b} + b}. \tag{2.91}$$

The function NOT may be considered as a particular case of NAND and NOR. It would be the NAND and the NOR of one variable. Hence, when it is intended to represent functions in logic expressions with only one of those operators, expressions which do not transform NOTs are often used. Therefore, the Expressions (2.89) and (2.91) will, in that case, be represented, respectively, by the Expressions (2.92) and (2.93).

$$f(a, b, c) = \overline{\overline{b\ \bar{c}}\ \overline{a\ b}} \tag{2.92}$$
$$f(a, b, c) = \overline{\overline{a + \bar{c}} + \bar{b}} \tag{2.93}$$

Of course, this method may be applied to an expression in the standard forms. If starting from a standard sum of products form, an expression in terms of NAND is obtained, which is called the *third standard form*. If starting, on the other hand, from a standard product of sums form, an expression using only operators NOR is obtained, which is called the *fourth standard form*. Expressions (2.94) and (2.95) are, respectively, the third and fourth standard form of the function $f(a, b, c) = b\ \bar{c} + a\ b$, which this section has been considering.

$$f(a, b, c) = \overline{\overline{a\ b\ c}\ \overline{a\ b\ \bar{c}}\ \overline{\bar{a}\ b\ \bar{c}}}, \tag{2.94}$$

$$f(a, b, c) = \overline{\overline{(a + b + c)} + \overline{(a + b + \bar{c})} + \overline{(a + \bar{b} + \bar{c})} + \overline{(\bar{a} + b + c)} + \overline{(\bar{a} + b + \bar{c})}}. \tag{2.95}$$

2.3 Minimising Logic Expressions

Section 2.1.13 showed that it is possible to use the rules of Boolean algebra, to obtain simplified expressions of logic functions. This simplification is necessary since, as will be seen, the various circuits in digital systems are implemented from logic expressions of functions, and simpler expressions lead to simpler circuits. The goal is to get the minimum expressions of functions. This process is known as *minimisation of logic functions*. For complex cases of functions with many variables, this can be extremely difficult or even impossible, and sub-optimal solutions are acceptable. For functions with a reduced number of variables, however, the determination of a simplified expression is relatively easy. As, sometimes, there are various expressions with the same complexity which cannot be simplified, the designation *minimal expression* is used instead of the minimum expression to designate these forms.

There are several degrees of freedom in obtaining expressions of functions, as we saw. Thus, an expression which appears to be minimal when using a certain type of structure may be simplified opting for other structures. The methods initially presented are applied to obtain normal forms (sums of products or products of sums). This type of expression, as has already been mentioned in Section 2.2.1, is designated as a two-level expression. Some techniques obtain solutions with more than two levels, although they are not covered in this book.

An obvious approach to simplify an expression consists, of course, in applying Boolean algebra theorems to reduce its complexity. However, it is not always easy to ensure that an expression is minimal. Achieving this goal depends greatly on the experience and expertise of the individual carrying out this minimisation process. Let us take, for example, the function represented by Expression (2.96).

$$f(a,b,c,d) = b\ (a \oplus c) + a\ b\ d + b\ c\ (a \oplus d) + \overline{a}\ c\ d + \overline{a}\ c\ \overline{d}. \qquad (2.96)$$

For any expression there are, in general, many ways to proceed. The following will demonstrate one of these ways. By applying Theorem 2.48, Expression (2.97) is obtained

$$f(a,b,c,d) = a\ b\ \overline{c} + \overline{a}\ b\ c + a\ b\ d + \overline{a}\ b\ c\ d$$
$$+ a\ b\ c\ \overline{d} + \overline{a}\ c\ d + \overline{a}\ c\ \overline{d}. \qquad (2.97)$$

Now considering the distributivity of the product over the sum, Expression (2.98) is obtained.

$$f(a,b,c,d) = a\ b\ (\overline{c} + d + c\ \overline{d}) + \overline{a}\ b\ c + \overline{a}\ c\ (b\ d + d + \overline{d}). \qquad (2.98)$$

Taking under consideration Expressions (2.18), (2.19) and (2.24), we simplify to Expression (2.99).

$$f(a, b, c, d) = a\ b + \bar{a}\ b\ c + \bar{a}\ c. \tag{2.99}$$

And finally (Expressions (2.20) and (2.24)) we arrive to Expression (2.100).

$$f(a, b, c, d) = a\ b + b\ c + \bar{a}\ c. \tag{2.100}$$

Expression (2.100) may appear to be a minimal expression of the logic function under consideration. However, if the consensus theorem is used (Expression (2.26)), it can be seen that the expression can be simplified a little more, to obtain Expression (2.101)

$$f(a, b, c, d) = a\ b + \bar{a}\ c, \tag{2.101}$$

which is in fact a minimal expression of the function.

This simple example shows that although the algebraic manipulation of the expressions allows simplifying them, it would be more interesting to have available a method to obtain, in a systematic way, a minimal expression. The following section will study a first method to achieve this objective.

2.3.1 *Karnaugh Method*

2.3.1.1 *Motivation for the Karnaugh method*

Let us reconsider the example of the function $f(a, b, c) = b\ \bar{c} + a\ b$. As was seen in Section 2.2.1, Table 2.7 represents the truth table of that function, the essential part of which is repeated here in Table 2.10.

Table 2.10 Table for the function $f(a, b, c) = b\ \bar{c} + a\ b$.

Row	a	b	c	$f(a, b, c)$
0	0	0	0	0
1	0	0	1	0
2	0	1	0	1
3	0	1	1	0
4	1	0	0	0
5	1	0	1	0
6	1	1	0	1
7	1	1	1	1

As has been seen, reading the table leads to Expression (2.102) in a standard sum of products form.

$$f(a, b, c) = \bar{a}\ b\ \bar{c} + a\ b\ \bar{c} + a\ b\ c. \qquad (2.102)$$

It is possible to simplify this expression to obtain the most simplified expression already known. We may follow the procedure in Expressions (2.103).

$$\begin{aligned}
f(a, b, c) &= \bar{a}\ b\ \bar{c} + a\ b\ \bar{c} + a\ b\ c \\
&= \bar{a}\ b\ \bar{c} + a\ b\ \bar{c} + a\ b\ \bar{c} + a\ b\ c \\
&= (\bar{a} + a)\ b\ \bar{c} + a\ b\ (\bar{c} + c) \\
&= b\ \bar{c} + a\ b.
\end{aligned} \qquad (2.103)$$

In the same way that the representation of functions can be done indifferently in a tabular form or as a logic expression, the very process of simplification can be done in both ways. Consider how the term $a\ b$ in Expression (2.103) was obtained. It results from the junction of the minterms $a\ b\ \bar{c}$ and $a\ b\ c$, minterms 6 and 7 which correspond to rows 6 and 7 of the table.

However, the table shows that these rows have a particularity: in both, the function has the value 1 and, also, they are the only two rows of the table in which a and b are simultaneously 1. The difference between the two lies in the variable c. Therefore, in this function, it suffices that a and b are 1 for the function to assume the value 1. Hence it can be concluded that $f(a, b, c) = a\ b + \cdots$ The same reasoning can be applied to the other product. However, here, the rows in question are 2 and 6. It is easy to see that it is sufficient that b is 1 and c is 0 to conclude that the function has the value 1.

In conclusion, it is possible to simplify the function by observing the table, associating rows in which the function takes the value 1 and which only differ in one variable. In the first product, lines 6 and 7 are associated, and they differ only in the variable c, and in the second, 2 and 6 are associated, which differ only in the variable a. *Adjacent rows* are defined as rows which differ by only one variable. Therefore, simplification is made identifying, in the table of the function, adjacent rows with the same value for the function.

2.3.1.2   *Three-variable Karnaugh map*

When simplifying a function by observing its truth table, it is clear that reading the expression from the table would be easier if the logic adjacent

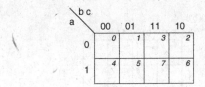

Fig. 2.15   Three-variable Karnaugh Map.

rows were physically adjacent. However, for three-variable functions, each position always has three adjacent positions, and this makes it impossible, in a table with the structure of Table 2.10, for all adjacencies to be contiguous. The solution is to change the structure of the table so that these requirements are satisfied. The objective is that each cell of the table is adjacent to the three cells that differ only in the value of one variable. This new type of table is the *Karnaugh map*. One possible structure of a Karnaugh map for three-variable functions a, b and c is shown in Figure 2.15.

The Karnaugh map is a two-input table, in which the coding of the different variables in each of the two dimensions for the inputs is done according to the reflected code. This leads directly to each position in the table always having logic adjacent positions physically juxtaposed, both horizontally and vertically. The counterpart is a greater complexity in the numbering of the table positions. The map shown in Figure 2.15 indicates, for each position, the number of the corresponding row of the truth table.

It can now be noted that each position has the three adjacent positions juxtaposed. For example, if we consider the minterm $m_5 = a \, \bar{b} \, c$, corresponding to position 5 in the table and the Karnaugh map, there are three adjacent positions. Minterm $m_1 = \bar{a} \, \bar{b} \, c$ is located on the map at the position immediately above m_5, $m_7 = a \, b \, c$ is located at the position immediately to the right, and $m_4 = a \, \bar{b} \, \bar{c}$ is located at the position immediately to the left on the map.

On the Karnaugh map, everything happens as if the lateral positions were against each other, which would be achieved with the map drawn on a vertical axis cylinder. For example, the minterm m_0 corresponding to position 0 of the map, where the adjacent positions are position 4, immediately below, position 1, immediately to the right and position 2, which would be to the left, but actually lies on the other extremity of the row of the map. Another way of visualising the adjacencies on the Karnaugh map is to relate them to the axes of symmetry corresponding to the position of the "mirrors" in the reflected code. Figure 2.16 shows the map of Figure 2.15, highlighting the axes of symmetry.

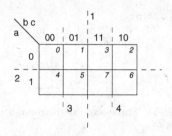

Fig. 2.16   Three-variable Karnaugh map showing the axes of symmetry.

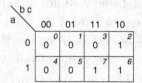

Fig. 2.17   Karnaugh Map of the function $f(a, b, c)$.

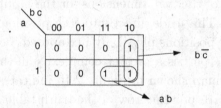

Fig. 2.18   Reading of the Karnaugh map for function $f(a, b, c)$.

Axis 1 shows the symmetry between the positions indicated in the following pairs: $(0, 2)$, $(1, 3)$, $(4, 6)$ and $(5, 7)$. Axis 2 shows the symmetry between the positions grouped in pairs $(0, 4)$, $(1, 5)$, $(3, 7)$ and $(2, 6)$. Axis 3 is linked to pairs $(0, 1)$ and $(4, 5)$, and axis 4, to the pairs $(2, 3)$ and $(6, 7)$.

The function that is being considered is shown on the map represented in Figure 2.17.

It is now possible to observe the adjacencies in the map and group them using *rectangles* (usually drawn with round corners for clarity) or, as we will refer to them in this text, *loops* which are shown in Figure 2.18. This figure also indicates the reading of the simplified product corresponding to each loop.

The expression of each product results from observing which variables remain constant in the positions selected in the loops. For example, in the group read as $a\ b$, it is easy to observe that the variables a and b take the value 1 in both positions. The variable c, on the contrary, takes the value 0, in position 6, and 1 in position 7. It can be concluded that the value of the product is not sensitive to variable c and that it only takes the value 1 when $a = 1$ and $b = 1$ simultaneously, that is, when $a\ b = 1$ and, therefore, corresponds to the product $a\ b$. In the same way, it is easy to verify that the other loop takes the value 1, only when $b = 1$ and $c = 0$, and is insensitive to the value of a, which, therefore, corresponds to the product $b\ \bar{c}$. Therefore, Expression (2.104) can be directly read from the map.

$$f(a, b, c) = b\ \bar{c} + a\ b. \tag{2.104}$$

It is, therefore, possible to read the simplified expression of a function directly from its Karnaugh map.

All loops which group two adjacent positions, not only in the formal sense of the term but also in their symmetrical location on the map, are valid.

The Karnaugh map does not need to have the variables distributed in the way shown in Figure 2.15, nor the format shown in the same figure. First, the variables may be arranged in another way, provided that reflected binary code is used. In addition, the map may be represented with 4 rows of 2 positions or even other configurations. Some alternative examples for representing the Karnaugh map for three-variable functions are shown in Figure 2.19. Naturally, the correspondence between map positions and the rows of the truth table is also changed and the same figure shows this correspondence.

Take another example, representing on a Karnaugh map the function $g(a, b, c) = \sum m(0, 2, 4, 5, 6)$. Figure 2.20 shows the respective map.

In the map, it is easy to read Expression (2.105).

$$g(a, b, c) = a\ \bar{b} + \bar{b}\ \bar{c} + b\ \bar{c}. \tag{2.105}$$

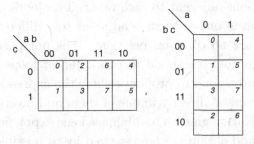

Fig. 2.19 Variations in representing a three-variable Karnaugh map.

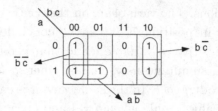

Fig. 2.20   Karnaugh map of the function $g(a, b, c)$.

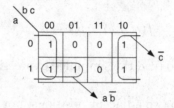

Fig. 2.21   Second reading of the Karnaugh map function $g(a, b, c)$.

Clearly, however, the final two terms can be associated, producing $\bar{c}$, to obtain Expression (2.106) which is now simpler than before.

$$g(a, b, c) = a\,\bar{b} + \bar{c}. \tag{2.106}$$

But, that is readable directly on the Karnaugh Map. Indeed, the two groups of two 1s at the extremes of the map are adjacent and may be joined to give the map shown in Figure 2.21, where it is now easy to read the most simplified expression.

It should be noted that the reading of the product corresponding to the loop involving four positions follows the same reasoning as the two positions case with the necessary extensions. Indeed, the only variable which is constant in the four positions is the variable c with the value 0. In this way, the product is reduced to $\bar{c}$.

In a Karnaugh map, a loop involving four positions is equivalent to two loops of two positions adjacent to each other. Two loops are *adjacent loops* when each position in one of them is adjacent to a different position of the other, and there are no common positions. It is not possible to link four positions which do not correspond to two adjacent loops. The loops to be connected must correspond to products where the expression only differs by one variable represented directly in one of them and inverted in the other.

When using a Karnaugh map to minimise logic expressions, it is therefore of interest to try and obtain the largest sized loops possible. But, as we will see ahead, this is not an absolute criterion.

It is easy to generalise this procedure to connect adjacent groups of four positions to form groups of eight positions. In maps corresponding to functions with a greater number of variables it is possible to group loops of eight positions to obtain loops of 16 positions, and so on. It should be noted that, since only loops with the same number of positions are grouped together, this always gives loops with a size which is a power of 2.

Figure 2.22 shows some of the illegal connections on the Karnaugh map.

There are two loops of two positions in (a), but the two groups are not adjacent. Position 1 of one of the groups is adjacent to position 3 of the other, but the other positions are not (position 2 is not adjacent to position 5). In (b) the situation is similar. Thus, position 4 of the left loop is adjacent to position 5 of the right loop, just as position 5 of the left is adjacent to position 7 of the right loop, but they overlap since position 5 is shared by both loops. Finally, (c) shows a connection of two loops with different sizes.

Until now, only examples for the use of a Karnaugh map to obtain expressions in a sum of products form have been shown, connecting 1s in the map that represent minterms of the function. The duality principle (Section 2.1.6) suggests, however, that maxterms can be connected to obtain expressions in the product of sums form. The Karnaugh map for the function studied can be considered once again, this time looking to group positions with the value 0. This gives the map shown in Figure 2.23.

It is now possible to read Expression (2.107).

$$g(a, b, c) = (a + \bar{c})\,(\bar{b} + \bar{c}). \tag{2.107}$$

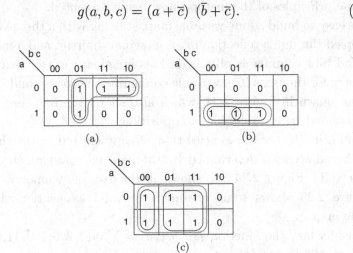

Fig. 2.22   Illegal connections on the Karnaugh map.

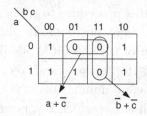

Fig. 2.23   Karnaugh map for the function $g(a, b, c)$ connecting the maxterms.

It should be noted that, in this reading, as was the case previously in Section 2.2.2, sums are now being read (connections of maxterms), and the variables, when they are 0, are read not inverted and, when they are 1, are read inverted.

Expression (2.107) is a minimal expression in the product of sums form. Clearly, for each function, two types of minimal expressions can be obtained: a sum of products or a product of sums. The function being discussed has a minimal expression, as a sum of products (Expression (2.106)), and another minimal expression, as a product of sums (Expression (2.107)).

2.3.1.3   *Four-variable Karnaugh map*

We introduced the Karnaugh map for three-variable functions, but it can, in theory, be used for any number of variables. In practice, when there are more than six variables, it becomes harder to use, and there are better methods. In Section 2.3.5, another method will be studied which, however, is based on the same principles of the method now being presented.

It is easy to build a four-variable map: starting with a three-variable map, it is copied through a reflection in an imaginary mirror, and a map with four rows and four columns is obtained. This imaginary mirror is a new axis of symmetry for the map. The variable configurations correspond to a reflected code, as shown in Figure 2.24, which also shows the row corresponding to the associated truth table, for each position.

In addition to the adjacencies that already existed in the three-variable map, the adjacencies determined by the new axis of symmetry introduced become valid. Figure 2.24 also shows all the axes of symmetry.

Figure 2.25 shows some examples of valid associations in the four-variable map.

Consider now the function $f(a, b, c, d) = \sum m(2, 3, 5, 7, 9, 11, 14, 15)$. Figure 2.26 illustrates the corresponding Karnaugh map.

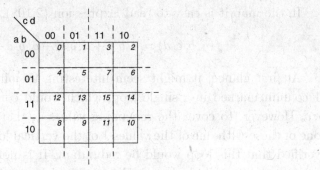

Fig. 2.24 Four-variable Karnaugh map.

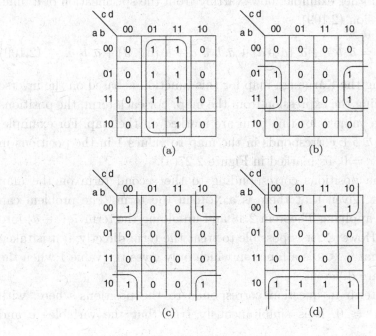

Fig. 2.25 Examples of valid associations in the Karnaugh map.

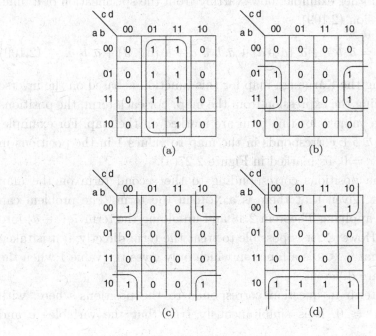

Fig. 2.26 Karnaugh Map of the function $f(a, b, c, d)$.

In the map it is easy to read Expression (2.108).

$$f(a,b,c,d) = \bar{a}\,\bar{b}\,c + \bar{a}\,b\,d + a\,b\,c + a\,\bar{b}\,d. \qquad (2.108)$$

At first glance, it might seem interesting to join the four values of the 1 column marked in a single loop, which would correspond to the product $c\,d$. However, to cover the remaining values 1, there is a need to join each one of these with one of the values 1 of the vertical loop. It can, therefore, be verified that this loop would be redundant. It is not true, therefore, in this minimisation method, that the largest-sized loops should always be chosen. This issue will be reconsidered later.

Consider another example, now starting from the specification of a function by Expression (2.109).

$$f(a,b,c,d) = \bar{a}\,\bar{b}\,\bar{c} + \bar{a}\,(c \oplus d) + \bar{a}\,b\,\bar{c}\,\bar{d} + \bar{b}\,(c \oplus d) + a\,\bar{b}\,c. \qquad (2.109)$$

Constructing the Karnaugh map for this function is based on the inverse process of reading the expression from the map. For each term, the positions which have the value 1 for this term are marked on the map. For example, the first term $\bar{a}\,\bar{b}\,\bar{c}$ corresponds in the map to values 1 in the positions in which $a = b = c = 0$, as marked in Figure 2.27(a).

Marking the positions corresponding to the second term on the map appears harder, given that there is a XOR in the term. The problem can be resolved by applying Theorem 2.48 and unfolding the term $\bar{a}\,(c \oplus d)$ into two products. However, it is possible to treat the term directly, if it is taken into account that a XOR is a function which only gives the value 1 when the two variables are different.

Thus, the term in question corresponds to the positions where, with the variable $a = 0$, it is simultaneously true that the variables c and

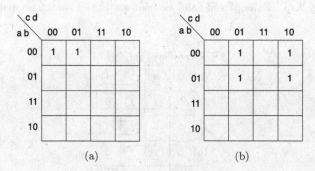

(a)   (b)

Fig. 2.27   Karnaugh Map with two terms marked: (a) $\bar{a}\,\bar{b}\,\bar{c}$; (b) $\bar{a}\,(c \oplus d)$.

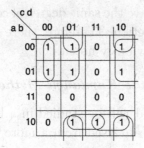

Fig. 2.28 Karnaugh map representing the function under study.

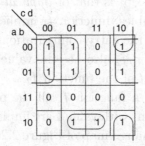

Fig. 2.29 Alternative Karnaugh map representing the function under study.

d are different. This corresponds to the positions marked in the map of Figure 2.27(b).

It is, therefore, easy to construct the Karnaugh map which represents the function being studied, which is shown in Figure 2.28.

The map has a set of loops marked in black enabling Expression (2.110) to be read, which is a minimal expression. There are other possible loops, marked in grey, that are not needed to build this expression.

$$f(a, b, c, d) = \bar{a}\,\bar{c} + \bar{a}\,\bar{d} + a\,\bar{b}\,d + a\,\bar{b}\,c. \tag{2.110}$$

The expression obtained is a minimal expression, but it is not unique. Indeed, if instead of linking the minterm m_{10} with m_{11}, it is linked with m_2, as shown in Figure 2.29, a new expression for the function is obtained, the Expression (2.111).

$$f(a, b, c, d) = \bar{a}\,\bar{c} + \bar{a}\,\bar{d} + a\,\bar{b}\,d + \bar{b}\,c\,\bar{d}. \tag{2.111}$$

There is also a third variant with Expression (2.112), as can easily be verified.

$$f(a, b, c, d) = \bar{a}\,\bar{c} + \bar{a}\,\bar{d} + \bar{b}\,\bar{c}\,d + a\,\bar{b}\,c. \tag{2.112}$$

The three expressions have the same degree of complexity and are all minimal expressions of the function. Therefore, there are functions with several minimal expressions as previously noted.

2.3.2   *Foundations of the Karnaugh Method*

Now, the Karnaugh method will be studied in a little more depth, and the questions left open will be analysed from a more integrated perspective. A better understanding of the mechanisms presented will enable procedures to be more appropriately defined so as to minimise logic expressions.

The first important concept is that of *implication between functions*. For functions of the same variables, function f_1 implies f_2, with the representation $f_1 \Rightarrow f_2$, when, for all the entry configurations in which the function f_1 has the value 1, the function f_2 also has the value 1. When f_1 is a product, it is said to be an *implicant* of the function f_2.

In a Karnaugh map, of a function f, all the products corresponding to valid associations of positions with value 1 are implicants. For example, in the function shown in the Karnaugh map of Figure 2.26, repeated in Figure 2.30 for convenience, the product $a\ b\ c$ is an implicant of the function $f(a,b,c,d)$, which can be indicated by $a\ b\ c \Rightarrow f(a,b,c,d)$. In the same way, the product $c\ d$ is an implicant of the function. It should be noted that the product $a\ c\ d$, not represented by a loop on the map, is also an implicant of the function $f(a,b,c,d)$. In the same way, it can be seen that $a\ c\ d \Rightarrow c\ d$. Furthermore, it should be noted that all the minterms of the function are implicants of that function. The implication has *transitivity*, that is, if $f_1 \Rightarrow f_2$ and $f_2 \Rightarrow f_3$, then $f_1 \Rightarrow f_3$.

The minterm $m_3 = \bar{a}\ \bar{b}\ c\ d$ is one of the implicants of the product $\bar{a}\ \bar{b}\ c$ and the function $f(a,b,c,d)$. That is, $m_3 \Rightarrow \bar{a}\ \bar{b}\ c \Rightarrow f(a,b,c,d)$.

An implicant which does not imply any other implicants is called a *prime implicant* or *main implicant*. In the example being used, the implicant $\bar{a}\ \bar{b}\ c$

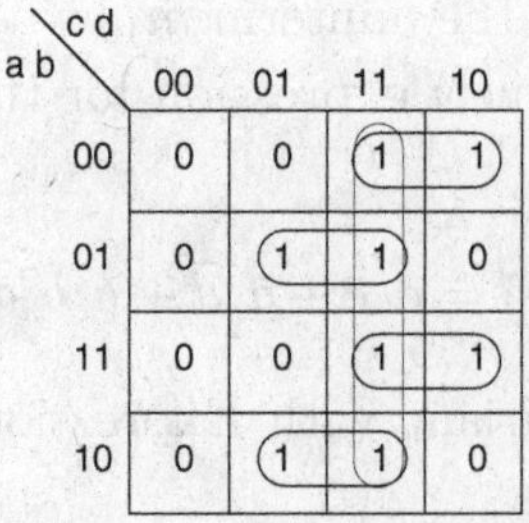

Fig. 2.30   Karnaugh Map of the function $f(a,b,c,d)$.

is a prime implicant, just as is the implicant $c\,d$. On the other hand, the implicant $a\,c\,d$ is not a prime implicant, since $a\,c\,d \Rightarrow c\,d$. The importance of prime implicants results from the fact that on a Karnaugh map they correspond to the largest associations, which cannot be expanded. It so happens that these are exactly the groups that are of interest for minimisations. Hence the minimised algebraic expression of a function expressed in the sum of products form is always a sum of prime implicants.

In the map of the function which has been used as an example, all the prime implicants of the function are marked. However, as has been seen, not all the prime implicants of the function were used in the minimised expression. Only the implicants necessary to include all the minterms of the function were used or, in terms of the Karnaugh map, the associations necessary to include all the 1s of the map. The implicants used were the following four: $\bar{a}\,\bar{b}\,c$, $\bar{a}\,b\,d$, $a\,b\,c$ and $a\,\bar{b}\,d$.

It should be noted that each one of the implicants used has an important feature: the prime implicant $\bar{a}\,\bar{b}\,c$, for example, is the only one which includes the minterm m_2. In the same way, each one of the other prime implicants includes a minterm which cannot be combined in another way. On the other hand, the prime implicant $c\,d$ (which ended up not being used) includes only minterms that can be combined in another way. The prime implicants which combine at least one minterm that cannot be combined in prime implicants in another way are called *essential prime implicants*. In the example that is being used, the four products used in the logic expression of the function (Expression (2.113)) are, therefore, essential prime implicants.

$$f(a,b,c,d) = \bar{a}\,\bar{b}\,c + \bar{a}\,b\,d + a\,b\,c + a\,\bar{b}\,d. \qquad (2.113)$$

As we saw, the algebraic expression of a function in terms of the sum of products is a sum of prime implicants. But not all of the prime implicants of the function have to be used. However, all the essential prime implicants have to be present in the expression. If an essential prime implicant is not present in the expression of the function, this means that at least one minterm is not included, and the function represented by the expression would differ from the function to be represented at least in the configuration of the input variables corresponding to that or those minterm(s).

It should be noted that, although in this example the only prime implicants used are essential prime implicants, this is not a rule. Let us now consider the function represented by the Karnaugh map of Figure 2.28 here repeated for convenience as Figure 2.31.

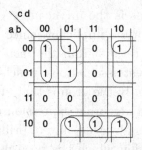

Fig. 2.31　Karnaugh map representing the function under study.

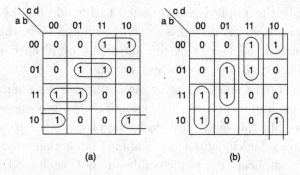

(a)　　　　　　　　　　　(b)

Fig. 2.32　Example of a function without essential prime implicants.

The essential prime implicants of this function are: $\overline{a}\,\overline{d}$, which is the only prime implicant to include the minterm m_6 and $\overline{a}\,\overline{c}$, which is the only prime implicant to include m_5. The function also has four non-essential prime implicants: $a\,\overline{b}\,d$, $a\,\overline{b}\,c$, $\overline{b}\,\overline{c}\,d$ and $\overline{b}\,c\,\overline{d}$. The three possible minimal expressions of the function, Expressions (2.114), include the essential prime implicants, and each one of them includes two of the non-essential prime implicants.

$$f(a,b,c,d) = \overline{a}\,\overline{c} + \overline{a}\,\overline{d} + a\,\overline{b}\,d + a\,\overline{b}\,c,$$
$$f(a,b,c,d) = \overline{a}\,\overline{c} + \overline{a}\,\overline{d} + a\,\overline{b}\,d + \overline{b}\,c\,\overline{d}, \qquad (2.114)$$
$$f(a,b,c,d) = \overline{a}\,\overline{c} + \overline{a}\,\overline{d} + \overline{b}\,\overline{c}\,d + a\,\overline{b}\,c.$$

Attention should also be drawn to the fact that there can be functions without essential prime implicants. Let us take the example of the function with two different sets of loops in the Karnaugh maps represented in Figure 2.32. The function represented has two possible minimal expressions: Expression (2.115) for the map in Figure 2.32(a) and Expression (2.116) for the map in Figure 2.32(b). The function has no essential prime implicants.

$$f(a, b, c, d) = \overline{a} \ \overline{b} \ c + \overline{a} \ b \ d + a \ b \ \overline{c} + a \ \overline{b} \ \overline{d}, \qquad (2.115)$$

$$f(a, b, c, d) = a \ \overline{c} \ \overline{d} + b \ \overline{c} \ d + \overline{a} \ c \ d + \overline{b} \ c \ \overline{d}. \qquad (2.116)$$

The duality principle provides support for the development of a dual vision of what has been exposed in terms of the utilisation of the 0s of the function, *implicate functions*, maxterms, *implicates*, *prime implicates* and *essential prime implicates*. As an exercise, repeat the analysis for the previous two examples in this new context.

2.3.3 *Karnaugh Method for Incompletely Specified Functions*

It sometimes happens that, in a logic function, there are some input configurations that never occur. It is possible to take advantage of this fact, in many cases, to additionally simplify the algebraic expression of the function. The functions in those circumstances are referred as *incompletely specified functions*. An example will be studied, throughout which the methodology to be used is presented.

Let us consider obtaining a function where the input variables are the 4 bits of a representation in BCD code and which should have output 1, only when the number represented is a positive multiple of 3. There are four input variables, A_3, A_2, A_1 and A_0 which represent the 4 bits of the BCD code, with the indices of the variables representing the weight of the respective bits. Table 2.11 specifies the intended function.

It should be noted that there are three different situations:

- BCD digits which are positive multiples of 3 ($f = 1$);
- BCD digits which are not positive multiples of 3 ($f = 0$);
- configurations which are not a BCD digit.

In the latter case, it is not important to consider the value of the function, since the respective input configurations never occur because they are not BCD digits, and therefore the value that the function would have in that situation is indifferent. It is usual to refer to the value taken by the function in these cases as *don't-care*. Initially, this will not be taken into account, and the minimal expression of the function will be obtained with values of 0 in those positions (the most conservative option). The corresponding Karnaugh map is shown in Figure 2.33.

Table 2.11   Table for the function holding multiples of 3 in BCD.

BCD	A_3	A_2	A_1	A_0	f	Comments
0	0	0	0	0	0	It is not a positive multiple of 3
1	0	0	0	1	0	It is not a positive multiple of 3
2	0	0	1	0	0	It is not a positive multiple of 3
3	0	0	1	1	1	It is a positive multiple of 3
4	0	1	0	0	0	It is not a positive multiple of 3
5	0	1	0	1	0	It is not a positive multiple of 3
6	0	1	1	0	1	It is a positive multiple of 3
7	0	1	1	1	0	It is not a positive multiple of 3
8	1	0	0	0	0	It is not a positive multiple of 3
9	1	0	0	1	1	It is a positive multiple of 3
—	1	0	1	0	—	It is not a BCD digit
—	1	0	1	1	—	It is not a BCD digit
—	1	1	0	0	—	It is not a BCD digit
—	1	1	0	1	—	It is not a BCD digit
—	1	1	1	0	—	It is not a BCD digit
—	1	1	1	1	—	It is not a BCD digit

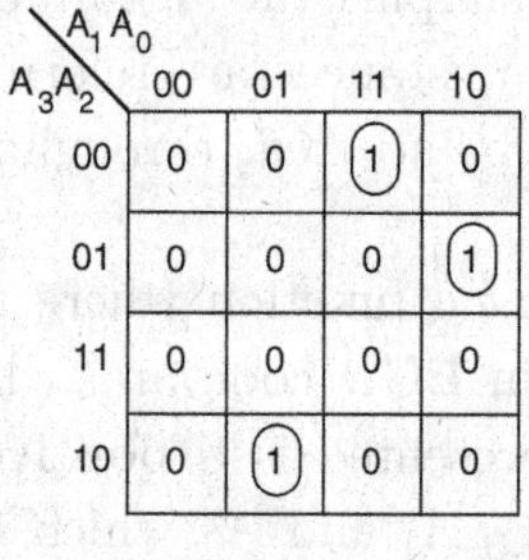

Fig. 2.33   Karnaugh map of the detector function for multiples of 3 in BCD.

It can be seen that there are no possible associations on the map and that all the minterms are, at the same time, essential prime implicants. The minimal expression for the function is, therefore, its sum of products form shown in Expression (2.117).

$$f(A_3, A_2, A_1, A_0) = \overline{A_3}\ \overline{A_2}\ A_1\ A_0 + \overline{A_3}\ A_2\ A_1\ \overline{A_0}$$
$$+ A_3\ \overline{A_2}\ \overline{A_1}\ A_0. \tag{2.117}$$

But now, let us postpone the attribution of values to the function in the configurations not corresponding to the BCD. A Karnaugh map is obtained in which, in addition to the positions with values 0 and 1, the don't-care positions will be marked, represented, for example, by an X. The map so constructed is shown in Figure 2.34.

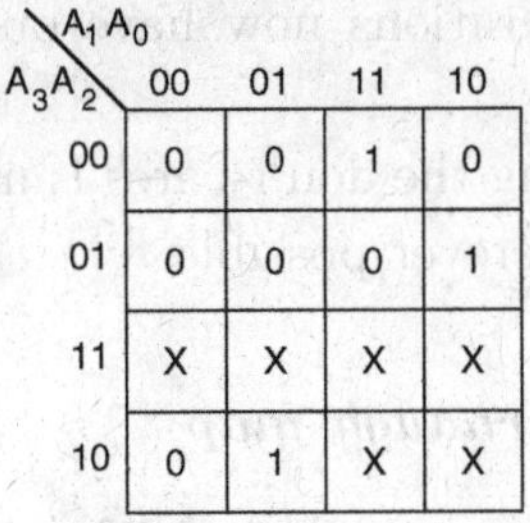

Fig. 2.34 Karnaugh map of the detector function for multiples of 3 in BCD with the don't-cares marked.

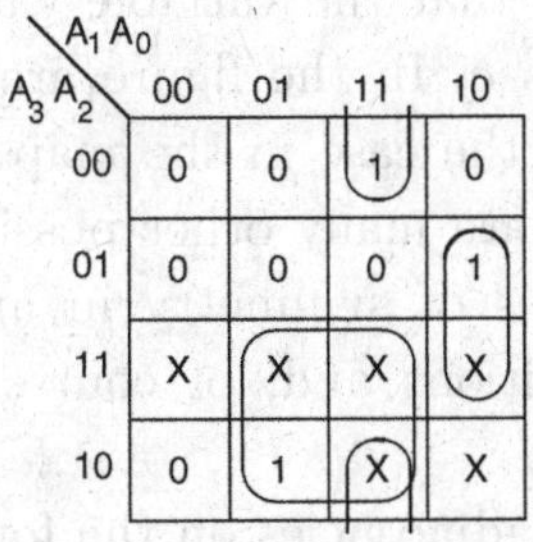

Fig. 2.35 Karnaugh map of the detector function for multiples of 3 in BCD with the don't-cares utilised.

Let us now consider the minterm m_9. If, in positions 11, 13 and 15, corresponding to the don't-cares, the value of the function was 1, the four respective minterms could be combined, which would considerably simplify the expression. But since, in fact, as the value which the function takes in these positions is indifferent, it is possible to place there the values that are most convenient for simplification, without changing the intended functionality. The same happens for other positions on the map.

Minimisation based on the groups shown in the map of Figure 2.35 can then be carried out, to obtain Expression (2.118).

$$f(A_3, A_2, A_1, A_0) = A_3\, A_0 + A_2\, A_1\, \overline{A_0} + \overline{A_2}\, A_1\, A_0. \qquad (2.118)$$

As can be seen, the expression obtained using the flexibility offered by having don't-care positions is simpler than the one previously obtained. It should be taken into account the fact that the function described in Expression (2.118) ceased to have non-defined positions. The configurations of input variables corresponding to the don't-cares which were combined with minterms of the function now have output 1 for the function.

The non-associated configurations now have output 0, since they were in fact processed as 0.

This technique of utilising the don't-cares is used to minimise the expressions of logic functions, wherever possible.

2.3.4   *Five-variable Karnaugh map*

Obtaining five-variable Karnaugh maps is done from a four-variable map, in the same way that this one was obtained from a three-variable map. Figure 2.36 shows a five-variable map, including the numbering of the positions, with the assumption that the variable with the greatest weight is a and that of least weight is e. In the figure are marked the axes of symmetry of the map. As was the case in the maps of functions with a lower number of variables, there are many other possibilities of constructing the map by using the new axis of symmetry in another position or placing the variables in other positions and, of course, numbering the positions consistently.

In addition to the valid adjacencies on the four-variable map (in each of the "halves" of the map), there are now adjacencies between symmetrical positions in relation to the new axis of symmetry.

As the number of variables increases, the complexity of the map increases in the same way, but, above all, it increases the difficulty in finding the appropriate groupings to minimise the function. Take, then, an example, using the Karnaugh map to minimise the function given by Expression (2.119) in terms of the sum of minterms.

$$f(a,b,c,d,e) = \sum m(1,3,5,6,7,8,9,12,15,20,21,22,29,30,31). \quad (2.119)$$

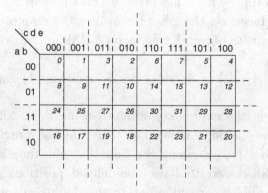

Fig. 2.36   Five-variable Karnaugh Map.

It should further be considered that the function has don't-cares for the input conditions corresponding to the positions $10, 17, 24, 25$ and 27. This is often indicated in the expression of the function by a sum of terms designated by md.[2] In this representation hypothesis, the function in question will be represented by Expression (2.120).

$$f(a, b, c, d, e) = \sum m(1, 3, 5, 6, 7, 8, 9, 12, 15, 20, 21, 22, 29, 30, 31)$$

$$+ \sum md(10, 17, 24, 25, 27). \tag{2.120}$$

The Karnaugh map corresponding to this function is shown in Figure 2.37.

The best strategy to tackle the problem of finding the appropriate groups is, of course, by starting to look for the essential prime implicants. If present, they have to be considered and, in addition, several of the minterms of the function will be covered by them. Analysing the map, it is possible to verify that almost all the minterms can be grouped at least in two ways into prime implicants. There are two exceptions, which are marked in Figure 2.38 with a grey background. The minterm m_3 can only be grouped in the prime implicant $\bar{a}\,\bar{b}\,e$, marked with the reference «1» in the figure. In turn, the minterm m_{12} may only be grouped in the prime implicant $\bar{a}\,b\,\bar{d}\,\bar{e}$ (reference «2»). It should be noted that the essential prime implicants, in this example, do not group don't-cares, but that is not the general case.

Minimisation continues with the determination of a minimum set of prime implicants, corresponding to groupings of the largest possible size, covering all the minterms. This search may lead to the map in Figure 2.39.

In the figure, the prime implicants are numbered, to facilitate their identification. Expression (2.121) shows the minimal expression of the function.

ab＼cde	000	001	011	010	110	111	101	100
00	0	1	1	0	1	1	1	0
01	1	1	0	X	0	1	0	1
11	X	X	X	0	1	1	1	0
10	0	X	0	0	1	0	1	1

Fig. 2.37   Karnaugh map of a five-variable function.

---

[2]In this context "d" stands for *don't-care*.

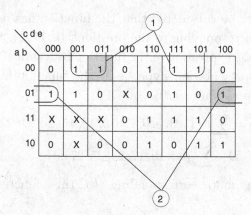

Fig. 2.38   Karnaugh map of a five-variable function with the essential prime implicants marked.

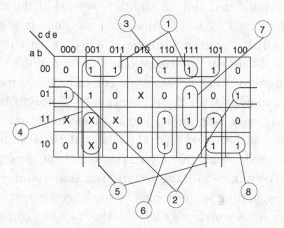

Fig. 2.39   Karnaugh map of a five-variable function with a minimum set of prime implicants marked.

For clarity, the products in the expression are in the same order as the loops in the map.

$$f(a, b, c, d, e) = \overline{a}\,\overline{b}\,e + \overline{a}\,b\,\overline{d}\,\overline{e} + \overline{a}\,\overline{b}\,c\,d + \overline{c}\,\overline{d}\,e + a\,\overline{d}\,e$$

$$+\, a\,c\,d\,\overline{e} + b\,c\,d\,e + a\,\overline{b}\,c\,\overline{d}. \qquad (2.121)$$

A metric of the *complexity of an expression* may be obtained, in a simplified manner, through the number of implicants involved and by the number of variables involved in each of them. This criterion may be summed up as the total number of inputs in all AND and OR functions of the expression. From that point of view, this expression has eight prime implicants, of which three are three-variable products, and the remaining five are four-variable

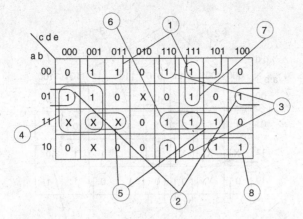

Fig. 2.40 Alternative minimisation of the function represented in the Karnaugh map of Figure 2.39.

products. The complexity C is, therefore, given by $C = 8 + 3 \times 3 + 5 \times 4 = 37$. As we saw, sometimes there are several different minimal expressions for the same function with, of course, the same complexity. In Figure 2.40, a different set of associations on the Karnaugh map leads to Expression (2.122), which has the same complexity as the previous expression, as can easily be verified. This function, in fact, has a large number of minimal expressions, as can be seen as exercise.

$$f(a, b, c, d, e) = \overline{a}\,\overline{b}\,e + \overline{a}\,b\,\overline{d}\,\overline{e} + \overline{b}\,c\,d\,\overline{e} + b\,\overline{c}\,\overline{d} + a\,b\,e + a\,b\,c\,d$$
$$+ \overline{a}\,c\,d\,e + a\,\overline{b}\,c\,\overline{d}. \tag{2.122}$$

Until now, the function being used as an example was used to obtain expressions in the form of sum of products. It is, of course, possible to obtain minimal expressions in the form of product of sums, if one works with the 0s of the function, maxterms, implicates, etc. Figure 2.41 shows, for the same function, the groupings chosen in the Karnaugh map. It should be noted that all the prime implicates marked are essential with the exception of the $(b + c + e)$. The maxterm responsible for its essentiality is marked for each of the essential primes implicates.

Expression (2.123) is the minimal expression read from the Karnaugh map.

$$f(a, b, c, d, e) = (a + b + d + e) \cdot (\overline{b} + c + \overline{d}) \cdot (a + \overline{b} + \overline{d} + e)$$
$$\times (a + \overline{b} + \overline{c} + d + \overline{e}) \cdot (\overline{a} + \overline{b} + d + e)$$
$$\times (\overline{a} + b + \overline{d} + \overline{e}) \cdot (b + c + e). \tag{2.123}$$

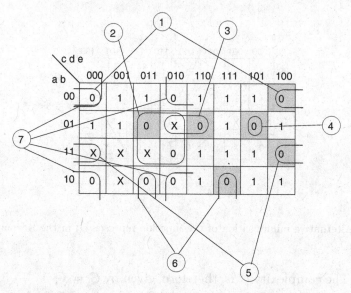

Fig. 2.41   Alternative minimisation of the function represented in the Karnaugh map of Figure 2.39, using maxterms.

The expression obtained has a similar level of complexity, albeit a little lower ($C = 34$) then that obtained with the minimisations in terms of the sum of products form. It should be noted that, despite this expression having a non-essential prime implicate, it is not possible to obtain another minimal expression in terms of the product of sums.

The various expressions obtained correspond to functions where, as already mentioned, don't-cares are no longer present. In fact, each don't-care was chosen, in the Karnaugh map, as assuming the value 0 or the value 1 to carry out the groupings that led to the minimal expressions. It is important to emphasise that, although each expression is a minimal expression, the various expressions correspond to different functions. Hence, for example, as can be seen on the corresponding map, Expression (2.121) corresponds to a function that takes value 0, for the configuration corresponding to the minterm m_{24}, and value 1, for the configuration corresponding to the minterm m_{17}, while Expression (2.122) corresponds to a function in which $m_{24} = 1$ and $m_{17} = 0$. There are more differences, but these are sufficient to show that the two functions — and not only the expressions — are different. It should, however, be noted that where the original function has specified values, all functions corresponding to the minimal expressions assume the same values.

2.3.5 *Quine–McCluskey Method*

The minimisation method using the Karnaugh map has limitations because it is difficult to use for functions with a high number of variables. Even for maps with seven or eight variables, it is practically impossible to identify the adjacencies between positions. However, the fundamental aspects of the technique used — determining prime implicants (or implicates) and essential primes, with a choice of a minimum set of implicants (or implicates) — are general and can be used for any function.

A different method, which consists in processing tables instead of observing adjacency graphic patterns, is the basis of the *Quine–McCluskey method*, which will be analysed below. This method enables us to work with functions with a much greater number of variables, thus considerably extending the practical limits of optimal minimisation. The Quine–McCluskey method is well adapted to build computer applications to simplify functions with a large number of variables.

The study of this method will only consider the variant corresponding to the use of implicants to obtain expressions in the form of a sum of products. The use of implicates to build the product of sums form is suggested as an exercise.

The Quine–McCluskey method starts by obtaining all the prime implicants. Then, the essential prime implicants are selected. If these are not enough to represent the function, then a sufficient and minimum number of non-essential prime implicants are selected.

To obtain a list of prime implicants, we start by obtaining the implicants corresponding to the association of two minterms, which will be designated as *level 1 implicants*. If there are minterms which could not be associated, they are prime implicants. Then, all the possible pairs of implicants of level 1 are associated to obtain *level 2 implicants* (implicants resulting from the association of implicants of level 1). Non-associated implicants of level 1 are, of course, prime implicants. The procedure continues, recursively, until there can be no more association of implicants, finding the complete list of prime implicants.

The following example illustrates the method. Let us take the function given by Expression (2.124):

$$f(a, b, c, d, e) = \sum m(0, 1, 2, 3, 8, 11, 13, 15, 17, 18, 21, 23, 25, 27, 29, 31).$$
$$(2.124)$$

To obtain the initial association of minterms in prime implicants of level 1, the various minterms have to be represented, and the possibility of each one of them being associated with all the others tested. Three measures may be taken to simplify the process: first, instead of representing the minterms by their expression, they will be represented by the configuration of variables for which they assume the value 1. The minterm m_{11}, for example, will be represented by 01011 instead of $\bar{a}\ b\ \bar{c}\ d\ e$.

The second measure is the result of understanding that, since only minterms that differ in just one variable can be associated, this means that we can associate only pairs of minterms in which one of them has n ones in its representation and the other $n + 1$ ones in its representation. For example, minterm m_3, represented by 00011, and m_{11}, represented by 01011, only differ in the position corresponding to the variable b and have, respectively, two and three ones in their representation. From this results the fact that the minterms should be grouped into sets of minterms with the same number of ones in the representation and that it is only worth testing pairs of minterms corresponding to successive sets in terms of the number of ones.

Finally, the third verification is that it is not worth comparing the minterm m_y with the minterm m_x, if the minterm m_x has already been compared to m_y.

Now, we can organise a table with a structure reflecting the considerations previously made. Thus, for this example, a *table of minterms* can be built with the structure shown in Table 2.12. This table groups the minterms by the number of ones.

The first column of the table indicates the number of the respective minterm.

The comparison of the minterms of contiguous groups will be made, as a second table is being built, a table of the implicants of level 1. Therefore, the minterm m_0 differs from the minterm m_1, only in the position corresponding to the e variable. An entry in the new table is created, where this association is registered and, at the same time, the two minterms are marked as already associated, using, for example, the symbol $\sqrt{}$. This process is shown in Table 2.13(a). In this way, the *table of implicants of level 1* is built.

In the first column of the table with the associated minterms, for each association (in this case the minterms 0 and 1) the associated minterms are indicated (Table 2.13(b)). The variable which was reduced in the implicants (in this case the variable e) is marked with the symbol «X».

Table 2.12   Table of minterms of the function used as an example.

	abcde
(0)	00000
(1)	00001
(2)	00010
(8)	01000
(3)	00011
(17)	10001
(18)	10010
(11)	01011
(13)	01101
(21)	10101
(25)	11001
(15)	01111
(23)	10111
(27)	11011
(29)	11101
(31)	11111

Table 2.13   Start of Quine–McCluskey method; (a) level 1 implicants and (b) associated minterms.

	abcde	
(0)	00000	√
(1)	00001	√
(2)	00010	
...	...	

(a)

	abcde
(0, 1)	0000X
...	...

(b)

Continuing the process until all possible associations have been exhausted, gives Tables 2.14. It should be noted that, in this table, all the minterms were associated and, therefore, none of them is a prime implicant.

Given the way these tables are constructed, the new groups obtained have an increasing number of ones. Horizontal lines separate groups with the same number of ones, as was the case with the table for the minterms.

The next phase tries to associate pairs of implicants of this level to obtain implicants of level 2. Of course, only pairs with the symbol X in the same position can be associated. In Table 2.15, the implicants of level 2 are listed and, once again, the implicants of level 1, now marking the associated implicants.

Table 2.15 shows that not all the implicants of level 1 were associated between themselves to produce implicants of level 2. Those not associated are prime implicants. These are the implicants listed in Table 2.16(a).

Table 2.14   Complete table (a) of the minterms and (b) of the prime implicants of level 1 of the function used as an example.

	abcde	
(0)	00000	√
(1)	00001	√
(2)	00010	√
(8)	01000	√
(3)	00011	√
(17)	10001	√
(18)	10010	√
(11)	01011	√
(13)	01101	√
(21)	10101	√
(25)	11001	√
(15)	01111	√
(23)	10111	√
(27)	11011	√
(29)	11101	√
(31)	11111	√

(a)

	abcde
(0, 1)	0000X
(0, 2)	000X0
(0, 8)	0X000
(1, 3)	000X1
(1, 17)	X0001
(2, 3)	0001X
(2, 18)	X0010
(3, 11)	0X011
(17, 21)	10X01
(17, 25)	1X001
(11, 15)	01X11
(11, 27)	X1011
(13, 15)	011X1
(13, 29)	X1101
(21, 23)	101X1
(21, 29)	1X101
(25, 27)	110X1
(25, 29)	11X01
(15, 31)	X1111
(23, 31)	1X111
(27, 31)	11X11
(29, 31)	1111X

(b)

As there are no longer two pairs with «X» in the same position, it is not possible to associate any pairs of implicants of level 2 to obtain implicants of level 3, implying that all the implicants of Table 2.15(b) are prime implicants. These are the implicants listed in Table 2.16(b).

We know all the prime implicants in this point of the algorithm. The next step is to identify, from these, which ones are the essential prime implicants. It is now necessary to construct the *table of prime implicants*, which allows us to verify, for each minterm, the prime implicants that cover it. Table 2.17 has that information.

Analysing Table 2.17, we see that the only prime implicant which covers minterm m_8 is the prime implicant designated by $(0, 8)$, which is, therefore, an essential prime implicant. Similarly, it is easy to check that the prime implicant $(2, 18)$ is essential because of the minterm m_{18}, that $(13, 15, 29, 31)$ is essential because of the minterm m_{13}, and that, finally $(21, 23, 29, 31)$ is essential because of the minterm m_{23}. Table 2.18 lists all essential prime implicants.

Table 2.15 Table of the (a) implicants of level 1 associated and (b) implicants of level 2 of the function used as an example.

	abcde	
(0, 1)	0000X	√
(0, 2)	000X0	√
(0, 8)	0X000	
(1, 3)	000X1	√
(1, 17)	X0001	
(2, 3)	0001X	√
(2, 18)	X0010	
(3, 11)	0X011	
(17, 21)	10X01	√
(17, 25)	1X001	√
(11, 15)	01X11	√
(11, 27)	X1011	√
(13, 15)	011X1	√
(13, 29)	X1101	√
(21, 23)	101X1	√
(21, 29)	1X101	√
(25, 27)	110X1	√
(25, 29)	11X01	√
(15, 31)	X1111	√
(23, 31)	1X111	√
(27, 31)	11X11	√
(29, 31)	111X1	√

(a)

	abcde
(0, 1, 2, 3)	000XX
(17, 21, 25, 29)	1XX01
(11, 15, 27, 31)	X1X11
(13, 15, 29, 31)	X11X1
(21, 23, 29, 31)	1X1X1
(25, 27, 29, 31)	11XX1

(b)

Table 2.16 (a) Prime implicants of level 1 (a) and of level 2 (b) of the function used as an example.

Designation	Expression
(0, 8)	$\bar{a}\,\bar{c}\,\bar{d}\,\bar{e}$
(1, 17)	$\bar{b}\,\bar{c}\,\bar{d}\,e$
(2, 18)	$\bar{b}\,\bar{c}\,d\,\bar{e}$
(3, 11)	$\bar{a}\,\bar{c}\,d\,e$

(a)

Designation	Expression
(0, 1, 2, 3)	$\bar{a}\,\bar{b}\,\bar{c}$
(17, 21, 25, 29)	$a\,\bar{d}\,e$
(11, 15, 27, 31)	$b\,d\,e$
(13, 15, 29, 31)	$b\,c\,e$
(21, 23, 29, 31)	$a\,c\,e$
(25, 27, 29, 31)	$a\,b\,e$

(b)

In this way, the essential prime implicants of the function are found. It is easy to see that this set of essential prime implicants covers many of the minterms of the function — the minterms $m(0, 2, 8, 13, 15, 18, 21, 23, 29, 31)$ — but there are still minterms of the function not covered: $m(1, 3, 11, 17, 25, 27)$. The following stage of the process consists in reducing the table of the prime implicants, taking into consideration only

Table 2.17   Table of the prime implicants of the function used as an example.

	0	1	2	3	8	11	13	15	17	18	21	23	25	27	29	31
(0, 8)	√				√											
(1, 17)		√							√							
(2, 18)			√							√						
(3, 11)				√		√										
(0, 1, 2, 3)	√	√	√	√												
(17, 21, 25, 29)									√		√		√		√	
(11, 15, 27, 31)						√		√						√		√
(13, 15, 29, 31)							√	√							√	√
(21, 23, 29, 31)											√	√			√	√
(25, 27, 29, 31)													√	√	√	√

Table 2.18   Essential prime implicants of the function used as an example.

Designation	Expression
(0, 8)	$\bar{a}\,\bar{c}\,\bar{d}\,\bar{e}$
(2, 18)	$\bar{b}\,\bar{c}\,d\,\bar{e}$
(13, 15, 29, 31)	$b\,c\,e$
(21, 23, 29, 31)	$a\,c\,e$

Table 2.19   Reduced table for the prime implicants of the function used as an example.

		1	3	11	17	25	27
A	(1, 17)	√			√		
B	(3, 11)		√	√			
C	(0, 1, 2, 3)	√	√				
D	(17, 21, 25, 29)				√	√	
E	(11, 15, 27, 31)			√			√
F	(25, 27, 29, 31)					√	√

the non-covered minterms and removing the essential prime implicants from the table that have already been selected. This leads to Table 2.19.

This table may lead to the definition of new prime implicants which, in the present circumstances, may be necessary to cover some of the minterms not yet covered. This is a typical situation, but it is not the case for this function. What is obtained here, is a table which indicates that, for each minterm, there are two prime implicants which can be chosen. In these circumstances, the problem becomes that of selecting a minimum set of prime implicants which cover the totality of the minterms. This can be done heuristically by observing the table. The prime implicants were, in this new table, designated by a set of letters from A to F. If the implicants A and B are chosen, the first four minterms are covered and, clearly, the implicant C is no longer needed. The last two minterms were not covered, which could have been done by choosing the implicants D and E or, better yet, the implicant F. Another possibility is choosing the implicants C, D and E. In both cases three implicants cover the remaining minterms. It is not possible to resolve the problem with fewer implicants, as is easy to conclude by analysing the table. The sets of implicants A, B and F or C, D and E may, therefore, be used. The choice is not, however, indifferent. In fact, A and B are four-variable products, while all the others are three-variable products, and as such the expression which includes C, D and E, is simpler.

The result of all this process is Expression (2.125) as the minimal expression (as a sum of products) of the function under study. The four first terms correspond to the essential prime implicants found (Table 2.18), and the remaining three, to the prime implicants additionally selected to obtain this expression.

$$f(a,b,c,d,e) = \bar{a}\,\bar{c}\,\bar{d}\,\bar{e} + \bar{b}\,\bar{c}\,d\,\bar{e} + b\,c\,e + a\,c\,e$$
$$+ \bar{a}\,\bar{b}\,\bar{c} + a\,\bar{d}\,e + b\,d\,e. \qquad (2.125)$$

The process of selecting additional prime implicants, after obtaining the essential prime implicants, is based on a heuristic analysis, which was only possible to carry out because the table was relatively simple. There is, however, a systematic way of obtaining the minimum set of non-essential prime implicants using the *function of prime implicants* or *function-p*. Function-p determines which are the prime implicants necessary in the expression of the function and uses as variables the designations of the prime implicants still present in the table of prime implicants. It is easy to understand that, in the final expression, there has to be at least one implicant which covers each one of the minterms of the function. For example, implicant A or C have to be present to cover m_1, the implicant B or C to cover m_3 and so on. It follows that function-p has Expression (2.126).

$$p = (A + C)\,(B + C)\,(B + E)\,(A + D)\,(D + F)\,(E + F). \qquad (2.126)$$

Expression (2.126) is manipulated algebraically to obtain the sum of products form, and Expression (2.127) is obtained.

$$p = A\,B\,D\,E + A\,B\,F + B\,C\,D\,E$$
$$+ B\,C\,D\,F + C\,D\,E + A\,C\,E\,F. \qquad (2.127)$$

Understanding the meaning of this expression is easy: for the minimal expression of the function it is necessary to use the prime implicants A and B and D and E or the implicants A and B and F, and so on. It is, now, obvious that the minimum number of implicants to use is three and that it is possible to opt for the set A, B and F, or C, D and E.

The Quine–McCluskey method is a replica of the Karnaugh method, using the manipulation of tables and, when the function-p is necessary, of expressions, instead of pattern recognition on the map. It is more laborious than the Karnaugh method but, by being more systematic, it has the advantage of being more easily implementable by a computer programme. The use of a computer programme enables the minimisation of expressions of functions with a much larger number of variables.

2.3.6 *Quine–McCluskey Method for Incompletely Specified Functions*

It is not necessary to make big alterations to the Quine–McKluskey method when functions are incompletely specified. The positions where there are don't-cares are considered as minterms to obtain the prime implicants, but they are omitted in the table of prime implicants to select the implicants necessary in the expression of the function. The method is exemplified using the function that detects BCD digits multiples of 3 specified in Table 2.11, which was used to introduce this topic in the presentation of the Karnaugh method for incompletely specified functions. The table is repeated for convenience in Table 2.20.

The function has the minterms m_3, m_6 and m_9 and has don't-cares in the positions 10 to 15. Tables 2.21 and 2.22(a) show the various tables of minterms and implicants of levels 1 and 2 (there are no implicants of level 3). Note that, for convenience, a new column is added to the minterms table, with the information if the row is present because the function has a 1 or an «X» in that position.

The table of prime implicants of this function, represented in Table 2.22b, only has three minterms. Of the prime implicants obtained in the previous step, two of them, $(10, 11, 14, 15)$ and $(12, 13, 14, 15)$, do not cover any minterm (they are there just because of the don't-cares). Therefore, they are not included in the table.

Table 2.20 Table for the function holding multiples of 3 in BCD.

BCD	A_3	A_2	A_1	A_0	f
0	0	0	0	0	0
1	0	0	0	1	0
2	0	0	1	0	0
3	0	0	1	1	1
4	0	1	0	0	0
5	0	1	0	1	0
6	0	1	1	0	1
7	0	1	1	1	0
8	1	0	0	0	0
9	1	0	0	1	1
—	1	0	1	0	X
—	1	0	1	1	X
—	1	1	0	0	X
—	1	1	0	1	X
—	1	1	1	0	X
—	1	1	1	1	X

Table 2.21 Tables of (a) minterms and (b) implicants of level 1 of the function being studied.

	$A_3A_2A_1A_0$		
3	0011	1	√
6	0101	1	√
9	1001	1	√
10	1010	X	√
12	1100	X	√
11	1011	X	√
13	1101	X	√
14	1110	X	√
15	1111	X	√

(a)

	$A_3A_2A_1A_0$	
(3, 11)	X011	
(6, 13)	X101	
(9, 11)	10X1	√
(9, 13)	1X01	√
(10, 11)	101X	√
(10, 14)	1X10	√
(12, 13)	110X	√
(12, 14)	11X0	√
(11, 15)	1X11	√
(13, 15)	11X1	√
(14, 15)	111X	√

(b)

Table 2.22 Tables of implicants of level 2 (a) and prime implicants (b) of the function being studied.

	$A_3A_2A_1A_0$
(9, 11, 13, 15)	1XX1
(10, 11, 14, 15)	1X1X
(12, 13, 14, 15)	11XX

(a)

	3	6	9
(3, 11)	√		
(6, 13)		√	
(9, 11, 13, 15)			√

(b)

From this table, it is easy to conclude that the three prime implicants are essential and are also sufficient to represent the function. Expression (2.128) is, therefore, the minimal expression of the function under study, according, in fact, with the results already obtained in Expression (2.118).

$$f(A_3, A_2, A_1, A_0) = A_3\ A_0 + A_2\ \overline{A_1}\ A_0 + \overline{A_2}\ A_1\ A_0. \qquad (2.128)$$

2.3.7   *Comparison between Karnaugh and Quine–McCluskey Methods*

The final example corresponds to the function already minimised by the Karnaugh method, previously defined by Expression (2.120), repeated here (Expression (2.129)). In addition to the intrinsic interest of this example, it will allow an interesting comparison between the two methods studied: Karnaugh's and Quine–McCluskey's.

$$f(a, b, c, d, e) = \sum m(1, 3, 5, 6, 7, 8, 9, 12, 15, 20, 21, 22, 29, 30, 31)$$

$$+ \sum md(10, 17, 24, 25, 27). \qquad (2.129)$$

Table 2.23 shows the minterms and implicants of the function.

From the previous tables, it is easy to build the table of prime implicants, which, as before, will only include the minterms and the prime implicants which combine minterms — all in this case — with no need to add don't-cares. Table 2.24 is the table of prime implicants.

In this table, it can be seen that the prime implicant $(8, 10)$, since the position 10 corresponds to a don't-care, only covers the minterm m_8, which is also covered by the prime implicant $(8, 12)$. It is thus possible to do without this prime implicant. Observing the table it is possible to conclude that there are only two essential prime implicants: $(8, 12)$, the only one which covers the minterm m_{12}, and $(1, 3, 5, 7)$, the only prime implicant which covers minterm m_3. The expression of the function will, therefore, include these two implicants, but it is not limited to them since there are still several non-covered minterms. The table can, therefore, be restructured, removing the minterms already covered, to obtain the new Table 2.25.

In this new table, it is easy to see that there are some prime implicants that only cover minterms included in other prime implicants. This is the case of the prime implicants represented by $(6, 7)$, $(7, 15)$ and $(1, 5, 17, 21)$, which will therefore not be considered. Similarly, the prime implicants $(1, 9, 17, 25)$ and $(8, 9, 24, 25)$ only cover minterm m_9 in this table which has already been reduced. It is, therefore, possible to do without one of them. From the table, the choice of the prime implicants is naturally $(6, 22)$, $(15, 31)$ and $(1, 9, 17, 25)$.

Table 2.23   Tables of (a) minterms, (b) implicants of level 1 and (c) implicants of level 2 of the function under study.

	a,b,c,d,e		
1	00001	1	✓
8	01000	1	✓
3	00011	1	✓
5	00101	1	✓
6	00101	1	✓
9	01001	1	✓
10′	01010	X	✓
12	01100	1	✓
17	10001	X	✓
20	10100	1	✓
24	11000	X	✓
7	00111	1	✓
21	10101	1	✓
22	10110	1	✓
25	11001	X	✓
15	01111	1	✓
27	11011	X	✓
29	11101	1	✓
30	11110	1	✓
31	11111	1	✓

(a)

	a,b,c,d,e	
(1,3)	000X1	✓
(1,5)	00X01	✓
(1,9)	0X001	✓
(1,17)	X0001	✓
(8,9)	0100X	✓
(8,10)	010X0	
(8,12)	01X00	
(8,24)	X1000	✓
(3,7)	00X11	✓
(5,7)	001X1	✓
(5,21)	X0101	✓
(6,7)	0011X	
(6,22)	X0110	
(9,25)	X1001	✓
(17,21)	10X01	✓
(17,25)	1X001	✓
(20,21)	1010X	
(20,22)	101X0	
(24,25)	1100X	✓
(7,15)	0X111	
(21,29)	1X101	✓
(22,30)	1X110	
(25,27)	110X1	✓
(25,29)	11X01	✓
(15,31)	X1111	
(27,31)	11X11	✓
(29,31)	111X1	✓
(30,31)	1111X	

(b)

	a,b,c,d,e	
(1,3,5,7)	00XX1	
(1,5,17,21)	X0X01	
(1,9,17,25)	XX001	
(8,9,24,25)	X100X	
(17,21,25,29)	1XX01	
(25,27,29,31)	11XX1	

(c)

Since there are still non-covered minterms, it is necessary to move forward to the new, more reduced version of the table, now shown in Table 2.26.

For similar reasons to those previously mentioned, it is now possible to do without the prime implicants $(20, 22)$ and $(25, 27, 29, 31)$ and also one of the pair $(22, 30)$ and $(30, 31)$. It is possible to select the prime implicants $(20, 21)$, $(30, 31)$ and $(17, 21, 25, 29)$. The function can, therefore, be represented by Expression (2.130).

$$f(a,b,c,d,e) = \bar{a}\,b\,\bar{d}\,\bar{e} + \bar{a}\,\bar{b}\,e + \bar{b}\,c\,d\,\bar{e} + b\,c\,d\,e$$

$$+\,\bar{c}\,\bar{d}\,e + a\,\bar{b}\,c\,\bar{d} + a\,b\,c\,d + a\,\bar{d}\,e. \qquad (2.130)$$

Table 2.24   Table of the prime implicants of the function under study.

	1	3	5	6	7	8	9	12	15	20	21	22	29	30	31
(8, 10)						√									
(8, 12)						√		√							
(6, 7)				√	√										
(6, 22)				√								√			
(20, 21)										√	√				
(20, 22)										√		√			
(7, 15)					√				√						
(22, 30)												√		√	
(15, 31)									√						√
(30, 31)														√	√
(1, 3, 5, 7)	√	√	√		√										
(1, 5, 17, 21)	√		√								√				
(1, 9, 17, 25)	√						√								
(8, 9, 24, 25)						√	√								
(17, 21, 25, 29)											√		√		
(25, 27, 29, 31)													√		√

Table 2.25   Modified table for the prime implicants of the function under study.

	6	9	15	20	21	22	29	30	31
(6, 7)	√								
(6, 22)	√					√			
(20, 21)				√	√				
(20, 22)				√		√			
(7, 15)			√						
(22, 30)						√		√	
(15, 31)			√						√
(30, 31)								√	√
(1, 5, 17, 21)					√				
(1, 9, 17, 25)		√							
(8, 9, 24, 25)		√							
(17, 21, 25, 29)					√		√		
(25, 27, 29, 31)							√		√

It should be noted that, in this case, it was not necessary to resort to function-p to determine the non-essential prime implicants. It was possible, through successive analysis of the tables of prime implicants, to select the minimal expression of the function. Another interesting point is, in this case, the comparison between the Karnaugh and the Quine–McCluskey method for the same function. In the Karnaugh method, it had been verified that there were many possible minimal expressions, while, using the Quine–McCluskey method, an expression was obtained where there were

Table 2.26   New modified table for the prime implicants of the function under study.

	20	21	29	30
(20, 21)	√	√		
(20, 22)	√			
(22, 30)				√
(30, 31)				√
(17, 21, 25, 29)		√	√	
(25, 27, 29, 31)			√	

apparently few options. This resulted from the way in which the table of prime implicants had evolved, which hid possible options to obtain the final expression. For example, in the final table, the prime implicant $(20, 22)$ was not used, since $(20, 21)$ covered the minterm m_{20}, only covered by the first prime implicant. However, this was not necessary. If the implicant $(20, 22)$ had been chosen, this would have been a valid option, since the minterm m_{21} is also covered by the prime implicant $(17, 21, 25, 29)$, which was also selected. Many other such situations occur in this example. If the function-p had been applied to the first table of prime implicants, it would have been possible to obtain an expression in which all the minimisation options of the expression of this function would have explicitly been listed.

2.4   Summary

This chapter studies the various aspects of functions which formally describe digital systems, commonly known as logic functions. We present Boolean algebra, which is the mathematical support tool for the study of digital circuits. Although it is possible to define Boolean algebras with more than two elements, in the case that is of interest here, the study is restricted to binary Boolean algebra.

Based on Boolean algebra, we describe the various ways of representing logic functions, with emphasis on equivalence and complementarity, for the different forms of representation. The particular aspect of minimisation of expressions which represent logic functions is discussed in great detail for the case where two-level expressions are considered. In this context, we presented the Karnaugh and Quine–McCluskey methods as well as aspects linked to the minimisation of expressions corresponding to incompletely specified functions.

Exercises

2.1 Draw up the truth tables for the following logic functions:

  (a) $f(A, B, C) = A\ B + \overline{A}\ \overline{B}\ \overline{C}$

  (b) $f(A, B, C, D) = A\ B\ (\overline{C} \oplus D) + A\ B\ C + \overline{A}\ \overline{C}\ D + \overline{B}\ C\ D$

  (c) $f(A, B, C) = \overline{A}\ B\ C + A\ \overline{B} + C$

2.2 Algebraically minimise the following functions:

  (a) $f(A, B, C, D) = A\ B\ (\overline{C} \oplus D) + A\ B\ C + \overline{A}\ \overline{C}\ D + \overline{B}\ C\ D$

  (b) $f(A, B, C, D) = A\ B\ C + A\ \overline{B}\ (C + D) + \overline{A + B + \overline{D}}$

2.3 Obtain the expression, in the form of the sum of products, of the three-variable majority function. The majority function is a logic function which takes the value 1 when the number of input variables at 1 is greater than the number of input variables at 0. Repeat for the majority functions of four and five input variables.

2.4 Consider the following function: $f(A, B, C) = (A \oplus B)\ C + \overline{A}\ (B \oplus C)$:

  (a) Minimise algebraically the function to obtain a product of sums.

  (b) Minimise algebraically the function to obtain a sum of products.

  (c) Obtain the standard sum of products form.

  (d) Obtain the standard product of sums form.

2.5 Obtain the expression of a logic function which specifies if a certain configuration of 4 bits is a BCD encoded word.

2.6 Consider the following logic diagram: Determine an algebraic expression for the function F, minimise it and design the corresponding logic diagram for the resulting expression.

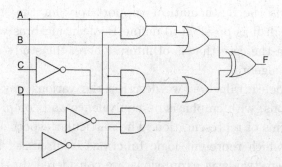

2.7 Construct the logic diagram for a set of three-variable functions which calculate the factorial of the binary number represented by the three input variables.

2.8 Determine a set of logic functions which carry out the multiplication of two 2-digit binary numbers.

2.9 Determine a set of logic functions which can obtain the integer value of the square root of a five-digit binary number.

2.10 Minimise the following logic functions, using Karnaugh's method. For each case use, both sums of products and products of sums, and conclude which produces the simplest expression:

(a) $f(A, B, C, D, E) = \sum m(1, 3, 5, 8, 10, 12, 14, 21, 23, 24, 26, 31)$ with don't-cares in positions 0, 4, 7, 15, 17, 18, 27 and 28;

(b) $f(A, B, C, D, E) = \Pi M(0, 2, 5, 7, 9, 10, 11, 20, 22, 23, 27, 30)$ with don't-cares in positions 1, 8, 12, 15, 16, 25 and 31;

(c) $f(A, B, C, D, E) = \sum m(3, 4, 6, 7, 10, 13, 19, 23, 28, 29, 31)$ with don't-cares in positions 5, 12, 15, 21, 22 and 25;

(d) $f(A, B, C, D, E) = \sum m(1, 3, 5, 6, 7, 8, 9, 12, 15, 20, 21, 22, 29, 30, 31)$ with don't-cares in positions 10, 17, 24, 25 and 27;

(e) $f(A, B, C, D) = \overline{A} \, (\overline{C} \oplus D) + A \, \overline{D} + \overline{A} \, \overline{C} \, D + \overline{A} \, C \, \overline{D}$ with don't-cares in positions 1, 7, 11 and 13.

2.11 For the logic functions of the previous problem determine all the prime implicants/implicates and, if they exist, the essential prime implicants/implicates.

2.12 Repeat Problem 2.10, using the Quine–McCluskey method.

2.13 Consider the function $f(A, B, C, D) = \sum m(0, 1, 3, 4, 7, 9, 10, 12)$ with don't-cares in positions 2, 5, 14 and 15. Obtain all the minimal expressions of the function, both by using sums of products and by using products of sums. Make sure, using truth tables constructed for each of the expressions obtained, that the various expressions do not correspond to the same function. Justify this fact.

2.14 Consider the following function: $f(A, B, C, D, E) = \Pi M(1, 7, 9, 12, 14, 18, 19, 21, 22, 25, 28, 30, 31)$ with don't-cares in positions 4, 15, 16, 17 and 20.

(a) Minimise it using Karnaugh's method.

(b) Using the function $f(A, B, C, D, E)$ as a basic block and without altering it, design a function $g(A, B, C, D, E)$ with a similar table, taking as the only difference that there is an output 1 in positions 1, 4 and 21. Use the minimum additional logic possible.

2.15 Manipulate the logic expressions obtained in Problem (2.10) to obtain:

(a) expressions using only NAND operators up to four inputs;

(b) expressions using only AND and OR operators with two input variables and NOT operators;

(c) when possible, expressions which are simpler, with more than two layers.

Chapter 3

Physical Implementation of Logic Circuits

This chapter presents some of the techniques used to build logic circuits that support the implementation of logic functions, i.e., electric circuits whose behaviour can be described by those functions.

Section 3.1 describes some of the integrated circuit techniques used to build logic circuits. Some useful devices to design systems are also considered, which do not directly implement functions such as those defined in the previous chapter.

The use of the described devices to implement circuits, and the associated methodologies are discussed in Section 3.2.

Section 3.4 analyses the aspects relating to the fact that electronic circuits need time to operate and the consequences for digital circuits.

An alternative method of implementing circuits directly from their formal specification, using programmable logic devices is presented in Section 3.5.

3.1 Digital Integrated Circuits

Logic functions are useful because they can be used to describe and specify the intended actions and processes of a piece of equipment. At the same time, there are methods that provide a smooth transition from a description in terms of logic functions to the implementation of electronic circuits with a behaviour specified by these functions, as will be seen throughout this chapter.

3.1.1 *Logic Families*

A possible implementation of digital circuits is based on electronic devices which behave similarly to some of the logic functions described in Chapter 2, such as the operators AND, OR, NOT or others. These devices are usually called *gates*. Logic gates are included in *integrated circuits*.

Integrated circuit technology has been responsible for the enormous development of digital systems, since it has enabled the construction of very complex digital electronic circuits, at extremely reduced costs, while occupying very tiny spaces.

An integrated circuit is a small silicon crystal (there are other technologies, but silicon is widely used) which have impurities in certain areas resulting in transistors, diodes, resistors and other interconnected electronic components, in such a way as to form electronic circuits of greater or lesser complexity. Digital integrated circuits are easy to design and have relatively low manufacturing costs.

Each integrated circuit may have between a few gates and a few billion gates. For example, one of the simplest integrated circuits available on the market is a circuit with AND gates, which has four independent two-input AND gates which can be used separately. A circuit such as a counter has dozens of gates that are connected to form the counter. Current processors have now hundreds of millions, or even billions, of gates.

The complexity of integrated circuits is usually classified as described in Table 3.1. Current microprocessors are reaching several billions of transistors per circuit.

There are various technologies used for manufacturing integrated digital circuits, of which the most important are currently *TTL, CMOS* and *ECL*:

- **TTL:** A technology that has for many years been by far the most used and, in practice, established a reference for architectures, criteria and standards, with consequences for the development of other families. It uses *bipolar transistors* operating in cutoff mode (the device behaves as an open switch) or in saturation mode (the device acts as a closed switch), two of the modes of operation of this type of device. It has an average performance regarding speed and consumption. TTL has several subfamilies with different characteristics, all compatible with each other. Since it became very popular, other technologies have circuits with inputs and

Table 3.1   Classification of the complexity of integrated circuits.

Complexity	Number of Transistors	Number of Gates
SSI — Small Scale Integration	<100	<10
MSI — Medium Scale Integration	<500	<100
LSI — Large Scale Integration	500 to 20 000	100 to 10 000
VLSI — Very Large Scale Integration	20 000 to 1 000 000	10 000 to 300 000
ULSI — Ultra High Scale Integration	>1 000 000	>300 000

outputs which are TTL-compatible. It is a technology that, today, lost most of its market to CMOS. The acronym TTL stands for *Transistor-Transistor Logic*, which highlights the internal structure of these gates, built with two levels of bipolar transistors.

- **CMOS:** CMOS is currently the most widely used technology, becoming more popular than TTL at the end of the 1980s. It uses *MOSFET transistors*. Initially, it was a technology slower than TTL, but had the advantage of consuming less power. Today, with the development of integrated circuit technology, the operating frequencies obtained are very high, although partially at the expense of power consumption. The speed gains from CMOS technology, combined with the large integration capacity, make it the most important technology in the design and manufacture of integrated circuits today. There are also some subfamilies within this technology. The acronym CMOS derives from the initials of *Complementary Metal Oxide Semiconductor*, a designation referring to the technology used, which uses n-type and p-type transistors in the same gate.

- **ECL:** This is a technology that enables very fast circuits to be built, although at the cost of very high power consumption. It has very limited niche markets, including military applications. It uses bipolar transistors in the active zone. While the previous technologies permit circuit designs using existing devices, particularly gates, requiring little expertise in electronics and propagation of signals in transmission lines, ECL technology requires this knowledge to obtain correct circuit designs with good performance. The acronym ECL results from the first letters of *Emitter Coupled Logic*, a reference to the type of electronic circuit structure used.

Physically, an integrated circuit can have several package formats, the most common in the introductory laboratory being the *DIL* from *Dual In-Line*. This package consists of a plastic or ceramic parallelepiped box, with two rows of *terminals* along the larger sides of the package. These terminals are usually called *pins*. Figure 3.1 shows an integrated circuit with 14 pins.

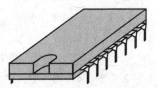

Fig. 3.1 Integrated circuit in a DIL package.

It is important to note, however, that at present, most of the integrated circuits available on the market use different packages, which provide for *surface mounting*, a technology that enables a much higher area and volume reduction and the use of circuits with a much larger number of pins.

Manufacturers produce series of integrated circuits with similar electrical characteristics, labelled with strings of digits and letters with the same structure. Often, several manufacturers agree to use the same names for similar products. On digital circuits LSI and MSI, the *74nn series* is still widely used today, although the trend, as will be discussed in Section 3.5, is to use either programmable circuits or those designed especially for certain applications, in both cases with a very high number of gates. An integrated circuit example is the 7408, of which there are versions in both the TTL and the CMOS families. This integrated circuit has four two-input AND gates. When looking at the circuit from above, the layout is the one shown in Figure 3.2. The pin distribution is known as *pin-out*.

It should be noted that the numbering of the terminals starts at the lower left-hand corner and continues in a counterclockwise manner until the upper left-hand corner. The mark in one of the smaller sides of the circuit (to the left in the figure) makes it possible to tell the orientation of the device. Terminals 14 and 7 are the terminals that provide electrical power to the circuit. In the TTL family, they have, respectively, the designation V_{CC} and *GND*. The V_{CC} terminal is connected to a positive voltage of 5 V and the *GND* (Ground), to 0 V.

Integrated circuit catalogues contain the distribution of terminals for all integrated circuits of any family. For example, Table 3.2 includes references to a few integrated circuits that make available several logic gates.

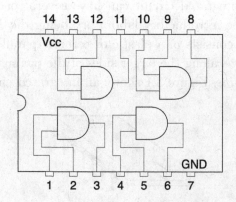

Fig. 3.2   Pin-out for the 7408 integrated circuit.

Table 3.2   Description of some digital integrated circuits.

Reference	Description
7400	Four 2-input NAND gates
7402	Four 2-input NOR gates
7404	Six NOT gates
7408	Four 2-input AND gates
7410	Three 3-input NAND gates
7411	Three 3-input AND gates
7420	Two 4-input NAND gates
7421	Two 4-input AND gates
7430	One 8-input NAND gate
7432	Four 2-input OR gates
7486	Four 2-input XOR gates

These references are valid for the TTL family and various CMOS sub-families.

As noted earlier, there are various *TTL subfamilies* with different specifications. The subfamily is indicated by putting the reference letters for the integrated circuit after the digits 74. For example, a 74LS00 is a TTL circuit of the LS (*Low-power Schottky*) subfamily. No letter means that it is a normal series TTL, the use of which is very restricted nowadays, as it is technologically obsolete. Manufacturer catalogues indicate the characteristics of each subfamily. CMOS subfamilies are designated in the same way as TTL. For example, there are currently two very popular CMOS subfamilies, the 74HC and the 74HCT (the latter, while accepting the levels of the CMOS family, maintains compatibility at the electrical level with the TTL family). The 74HC08 and 74HCT08 have the same pin-out as the 7408 and the 74LS08.

3.1.2   *Basic Gates*

This book will not analyse the internal structure of the TTL gates, as this would introduce some complexity and would not contribute significantly to the objectives of this book.

However, it is easy to understand the structure and functioning of *CMOS gates*. CMOS gates use n-channel and p-channel MOSFET transistors in the same circuit, hence their designation, where C stands for Complementary, since complementary type transistors are used. Figure 3.3(a) shows the symbol of a p-channel transistor and its functional equivalent at the level of abstraction which is of interest in the context of this book. The transistor acts as a switch that, while the gate voltage is below a threshold V_l, is kept

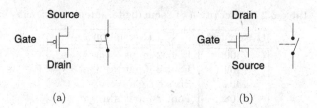

Fig. 3.3 Symbols of MOSFET transistors: (a) p-channel transistor and (b) n-channel transistor.

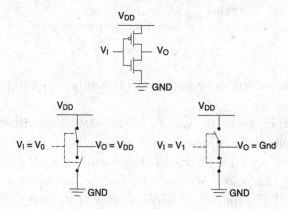

Fig. 3.4 Structure of a CMOS NOT gate.

closed, creating a connection between the source and drain terminals. If the gate voltage goes over another threshold V_h, the transistor breaks the connection between the source and the drain. Figure 3.3(b) represents an n-channel transistor and, equally, its functional equivalent. In this transistor, the drain is only connected to the source when a gate voltage is applied beyond the threshold V_h, keeping the circuit open if the gate voltage is less than V_l. The operation of the transistors between the values of the two thresholds is irrelevant in the case of digital circuits.

Figure 3.4 shows the structure of a NOT gate in CMOS technology and, in a simplified manner, the relationship between input and output signals. The index I is short for Input and the index O is short for Output. Besides the gate structure, this figure shows its equivalent electric circuit. Keeping at the level of abstraction we are working, it can be seen that for an input at a level less than V_l, the gate responds with a voltage V_O approximately equal to V_{DD}, the usual designation of the supply voltage in CMOS technology, which is greater than the threshold V_h. For an input with a level greater than V_h, it responds with an output V_O at a level lower than V_l. If a level

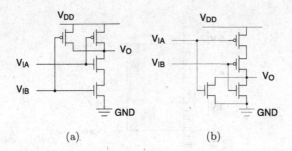

Fig. 3.5   Structure of CMOS gates: (a) NAND gate and (b) NOR gate.

less than V_l is made to correspond to a 0 and a level greater than V_h to a 1, the circuit does in fact operate as an inverter.

Figure 3.5 shows the structure of CMOS NAND and NOR gates. The analysis of these circuits using the assumptions used in the NOT case is left as an exercise to the reader.

3.1.3   *Logic Levels and Voltage Levels*

The electronic circuits which implement the logic functions studied in Chapter 2 assume some *voltage levels* at their inputs and produce other levels at their outputs. Logic circuit manufacturers do not guarantee fixed voltage values to represent logic values. What they guarantee is an interval of values such that if the output of a gate is within that interval, it is considered to represent a particular logic value.

In the case of the TTL family, the power supplied is a stable voltage of $V_{CC} = 5\,\text{V} \pm 5\%$. The manufacturers guarantee that, except for the moments when there is a transition at the output of the gate as a result of a change in the inputs, the voltage level will either be at the level *High*, also designated as H, or at the level *Low*, also designated as L. Level H corresponds to a value within the range $2.4\,\text{V}$ to $5\,\text{V}$, and level L corresponds to a value within the range $0\,\text{V}$ to $0.4\,\text{V}$. Figure 3.6 illustrates the two levels. The minimum value of the output voltage for the gate, which also corresponds to H, is designated by V_{OHmin}, *minimum output high voltage*. The maximum value of the output voltage for the gate, which still corresponds to L, is designated by V_{OLmax}, *maximum output low voltage*. The definitions for TTL are shown in Equation (3.2).

$$V_{\text{OHmin}} = 2.4\,\text{V},$$
$$V_{\text{OLmax}} = 0.4\,\text{V}.$$

$$(3.1)$$

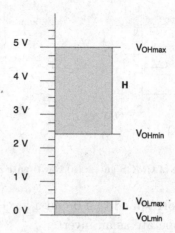

Fig. 3.6   Definition of output voltage levels for a TTL circuit.

The natural tendency is to associate the High (H) voltage range to the logic value 1 and the Low (L) voltage range to the logic value 0. We will return to this issue later in Section 3.2.

The operation of the circuits is affected by electrical noise which is no more than the influence of all the electromagnetic fields that exist in the area where the circuit is (radio, TV and mobile phone emissions, interference from electric engines, electromagnetic radiation from other connections of the same circuit, etc.). Thus, it is possible that there is a valid voltage value at a gate output (e.g., 0.3 V) and a gate input to which it is connected has an invalid value (e.g., 0.5 V).

To take into account that this may occur and still be be tolerated, gate inputs, including for TTL, have a slightly wider specification, with values between 2 V and 5 V considered H, and values between 0 V and 0.8 V considered L, as Equation (3.3) specify. V_{IHmin} corresponds to *minimum input high voltage*, and V_{ILmax} to *maximum input low voltage*.

$$V_{IHmin} = 2\,V,$$
$$V_{ILmax} = 0.8\,V. \tag{3.2}$$

Figure 3.7 summarises the relations between input and output levels for TTL circuits.

The interval of 0.4 V between the specified extreme values for the output and input is called the *noise margin*.

In the case of the 74HC CMOS family, the supply voltages are more flexible than for TTL and may take values between 2 V and 6 V. The reference

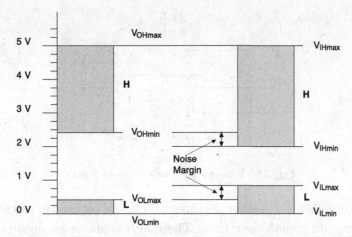

Fig. 3.7 Definition of voltage levels for the TTL family for the input and output of a gate.

values for the voltage levels corresponding to H and L vary according to the supply voltage. The specified values, for example, by Philips, for the supply voltage of 4.5 V at a temperature of 25°C, are listed in Equation (3.4).

$$V_{IHmin} = 3.15\,V,$$

$$V_{ILmax} = 1.35\,V,$$

$$V_{OHmin} = 4.32\,V,$$ \hspace{1cm} (3.3)

$$V_{OLmax} = 0.26\,V.$$

In these conditions, the noise margin is about 1.15 V, which is higher than the value for TTL.

In the case of the CMOS families, the 74HC subfamily has references and distribution of terminals compatible with the TTL families. It is, however, not electrically compatible, as can be seen from Equations (3.2)–(3.4). The 74HCT family is an HC variant with logic levels compatible with the TTL family.

3.1.4 *Delays*

Since integrated circuits are physical devices, they do not react instantly to changes in their inputs. This means that delays can be observed between changes imposed to the inputs of a gate and any resulting changes in its output. Figure 3.8 analyses an example of a gate AND in a 7408 circuit.

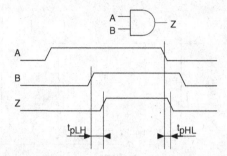

Fig. 3.8   Example of delays in an AND gate.

The figure shows a *timing diagram* which is a schematic representation of the change in signals over time. The diagram shows an evolution of the input and output signals of an AND gate. The signals do not change instantly, and the representation of this is an inclined line at the transition. In reality, the transition is more complex, but this form of representation is sufficient at the level of abstraction at which this analysis is made. Timing diagrams sometimes omit the representation of a non-instantaneous transition when this helps to make them clearer, and vertical lines represent the changes.

In the gate the first change of input A produces no effect on the output, given that input B stays at 0, keeping the output at 0. This is a clear case where an alteration in an input does not affect the output and in which, therefore, one cannot speak of a delay.

The transition of input B from 0 to 1 causes the output to change to 1. However, the response of output Z to the change in B occurs only after a certain time, represented in the figure by t_{pLH}. This time, called *delay time* or *propagation time*, is a result of the physical phenomena necessary to implement the switching of the gate. The index pLH in the designation above of the delay time indicates that this is an L to H output transition. The delay times for transitions from L to H are not necessarily the same as the delay time of the inverse transitions from H to L. The figure shows a representation where t_{pLH} is different from t_{pHL}. We will return to the theme of delays later, in more detail, in Section 3.4.

The value of these delay times is typically in the order of 10 ns for the subfamily 74HC $(1\,\text{ns} = 10^{-9}\,\text{s})$.

3.1.5   *Power*

Operating electronic circuits requires *power consumption*. That power dissipates, heating the circuits. This poses two problems. On the one hand, it is necessary to ensure that the circuits have the power needed for their operation. Besides, there is a need to have cooling mechanisms that keep the temperature of a circuit stable to prevent the components from degrading. With the current trend towards the development of portable products, these issues have become increasingly more important.

TTL, and especially ECL gates, are devices with relatively high power consumption due to their structure. CMOS gates, however, are characterised by dissipating less power because CMOS gates spend most of their power only during the time in which they are switching between levels. If a CMOS gate keeps the output level stable for some time, it practically does not consume power. However, power consumption grows with the number of transitions per time unit, i.e., with the level of activity. The power dissipation due to switching, the most important component, is given by Expression (3.4).

$$P_d = C_L V_{DD}^2 \alpha. \tag{3.4}$$

In this expression, P_d is the dissipated power, C_L is the capacity seen from the gate output, V_{DD} the supply voltage and α the activity level of the gate, that is, the average number of transitions per unit of time.

Decreasing the supply voltage has recently been used by manufacturers to reduce consumption in logic circuits, despite the increase in their operating frequency and therefore the activity level of the gates. This solution which, considering Expression (3.4), seems obvious, has the drawback of reducing the noise margin and the speed of the circuits, leading to the need to find a balance between power and speed.

3.1.6 *Special Devices*

In addition to basic gates, in digital systems, it is common to use other devices, which are important to ensure a particular type of functionality. Due to their importance, we will analyse *tri-state buffers* and *transmission gates*.

3.1.6.1 *Tri-state buffers*

A tri-state buffer is a device with an input and output for data and a control input. When the control input is H, the output value is equal to the value present at the data input. When, on the other hand, the control input is L, the output is in a high impedance state, i.e., is disconnected from any voltage. Table 3.3 summarises the operation of this device, while Figure 3.9 shows

Table 3.3   Table for a tri-state buffer.

C	I	O
L	X	no voltage
H	L	L
H	H	H

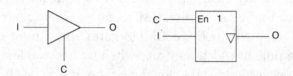

Fig. 3.9   Tri-state buffer symbols.

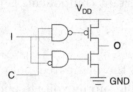

Fig. 3.10   Internal structure of a tri-state buffer using CMOS technology.

two versions of the symbol used for this circuit. In the version at the right, the triangle is the indication of a tri-state output.

Figure 3.10 shows the internal structure of a tri-state buffer. The gates represented aim to simplify the circuit, so as to make its structure easier to understand, but, as is evident, they are, in turn, implemented using a set of transistors.

When line C is at L, both output transistors are in the cutoff mode, that is, the equivalent switches are open, and there is no connection between the output and, neither the V_{DD} nor the GND. The output is, as intended, disconnected from any voltage source. When the C input is active, that is, at H, the output reproduces the input voltage level.

There are two essential applications for tri-state buffers. Firstly, they make possible the use of bidirectional lines. Secondly, they make it possible to connect several signals to a single line.

Consider the logic diagram in Figure 3.11. In this logic diagram, it is possible to see that two lines connect two entities, one to the right and the other to the left of the logic diagram.

If the line DIR is at level H, then the tri-state buffer at the right is inhibited and, as a result, it acts as if it was not there. On the other hand,

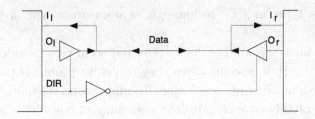

Fig. 3.11 Bidirectional line.

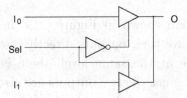

Fig. 3.12 Use of tri-state buffers to select signals.

the left buffer is active, and the data line transmits the information present on O_l to the right part, where input I_r can read it. If the *DIR* line is at *L*, the opposite happens. *Data* is, therefore, a bidirectional line, i.e., which transmits information in two directions (one at a time, of course). Clearly, it is possible to have multiple data lines connecting the two entities. A line *DIR* controls this set of lines, which is commonly called a *Bus*. As we will see, this type of application is crucial, in computer architecture.

Let us now consider the second application of tri-state buffers, the interconnection of several signals on a given line. Consider the logic diagram in Figure 3.12.

Assume that the *Sel* line is at level *L*. In these circumstances, the lower buffer is disabled and the upper one is active, placing the value of line I_0 on the output line *O*. Conversely, if *Sel* is at level *H*, it will be the lower buffer that will be active and the upper one disabled, making *O* assume the value of I_1. The structure shown allows the value in one of the input lines to be selected and placed in the output. Generalising this configuration to more than two input lines is easy. This functionality will be found again in Chapter 4, when analysing the multiplexers.

3.1.6.2 *Incomplete devices*

Another type of device that is interesting to consider are gates whose output only sets one of the voltage levels. These are gates with outputs of the *open-collector* type, in TTL technology, or *open-drain* type in CMOS technology.

At first glance, this kind of device does not seem very useful. However, as we will see, in certain specific cases they can solve problems that otherwise would require a more complex solution. To understand the motivation for the development of this type of gate it is necessary to consider a technological limitation of classic gates. In fact, with normal gates, it is not possible to directly interconnect outputs of gates, whether working with TTL or with CMOS.

Consider the situation shown in Figure 3.13, in which two NOT gates in CMOS technology have their outputs directly interconnected. If the two inputs V_{I0} and V_{I1} are at the same level, there is no problem with the operation of the circuit, since the two outputs are also at the same level, and V_O shows the value that either of the two outputs would show independently. However, if the input values are different, then there is a problem at the output. In these circumstances, what happens is that one of the gates turns on the upper transistor while the other turns on the lower one. There is then a direct path between the power V_{DD} and the ground of the circuit (GND) with a very low electrical resistance, causing a very high electrical current which may damage both transistors. It is true that the circuit shown does not, in itself, at first glance, appear particularly interesting, and it is not even clear which logic function it is intended to perform.

However, analysing the same structure with open-drain gates which do not have the upper transistor, as shown in Figure 3.14, a new application will be found. Figure 3.14(a) shows a NOT gate with an open-drain (this name derives from the fact that the drain of the lower transistor is open

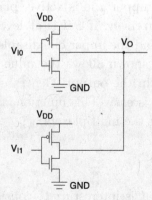

Fig. 3.13   Circuit with two NOT gates with their outputs interconnected.

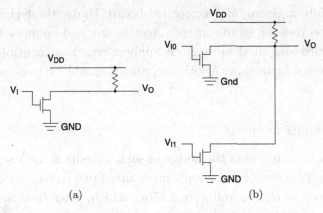

(a) (b)

Fig. 3.14   (a) NOT gate with open-drain and (b) interconnection of two gates of this type.

without any connection). The resistor shown is not part of the gate and is added externally. Since the only transistor in each gate is the lower one, it manages to establish a L level at the output of each gate. However, it is impossible to set the output to H without connecting it to V_{DD} through the resistor, since there is no other connection to positive voltage V_{DD}. When the lower transistor of the gate is not setting a L level, the resistor enables the output of the gate to be connected to the positive voltage, and assume level H.

Accordingly, the structure in Figure 3.14(b), which for gates of this type replicates the circuit in the Figure 3.13, no longer has any problem in the operation of the gates, since it is never possible to obtain a low-resistance path between V_{DD} and GND. It is now possible to understand the logic function achieved by the direct connection of the outputs of the gates. Whenever one of the gates seeks to set its output to L, there is a transistor which interconnects V_O and GND, setting the output at level L. Only if neither of the gates wants to set its output to L does the connection through the resistor set output V_O to level H. It is, therefore, easy to see that this is a virtual AND, although there is no gate. This type of connection is called *wired-and*.

The idea that the use of connections of this type allows you to use fewer gates, and therefore should be common and recommended, is not true. There are several reasons for this. One is that it is easier to use circuits with greater levels of integration that enable the internal interconnection of many more gates. Another is that this type of connection is comparatively slow.

However, there are circumstances where the use of open-drain connections (or open-collector in TTL) is particularly useful. A typical situation is where each of the gates is on a separate board, which may be inserted, through connectors, into a global interconnection board. Under these circumstances, just place the resistor in the interconnect board and connect the number of circuit boards required for a given application, thus ensuring operation, whatever the configuration. Another application will be presented later in Section 3.5.

3.1.6.3 *Transmission gates*

One type of device useful in the design of some circuits is the so-called *transmission gate*. This device is a circuit made up of two connected complementary transistors, as shown in Figure 3.15(a), which, when both are activated, enables the passage of signals throughout the voltage range between the ground and the supply voltage, allowing the transmission of signals inside or outside the CMOS range of digital levels. When the two transistors are disabled, the output of the gate is isolated from the input and, therefore, disconnected from any voltage. We will see the usefulness of these devices further ahead.

Figure 3.15(b) shows the symbol for these devices.

Transmission gates are often used with connections configured as shown in Figure 3.16(a). That configuration is represented by the symbol in Figure 3.16(b).

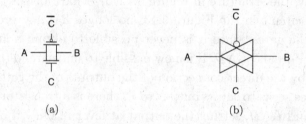

Fig. 3.15   Transmission gate: (a) circuit and (b) symbol.

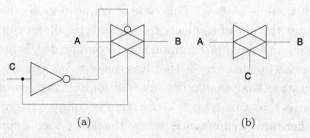

Fig. 3.16   (a) Typical application configuration of a transmission gate. (b) Usual symbol for the previous configuration.

The operation of this type of device and that of a tri-state buffer are frequently compatible. In fact, if the output of a logic gate includes a transmission gate, the overall behaviour obtained is similar to the inclusion of a tri-state buffer. The two devices do, however, have different characteristics. For example, a transmission gate is bidirectional, which is not the case with a tri-state buffer. A transmission gate is not a purely digital device thus making the transmission of analogue signals possible.

3.2 Positive, Negative and Polarity Logic

The logic functions NOT, OR, NOR, etc., studied in Chapter 2, may, of course, be implemented using logic gates of the type that has been presented. There are, however, certain conventions which are needed to carry this out in an unambiguous manner.

As we saw in Section 3.1.3, a gate has a binary operation, taking one of two ranges of voltage, both for its inputs and for its output. A NOT, for example, produces an H level at its output, whenever there is an L at its input. The use of circuits of this type to provide support for logic functions results from the fact that, in both contexts, logic circuits and logic functions use sets of two elements. As has already been mentioned, it is natural to associate the high H level to the logic value 1 and the low L level to the logic value 0. Table 3.4(a) shows this correspondence.

This convention is called *positive logic* and is widely used, perhaps because it is very intuitive. Let us analyse this concept a little more deeply.

An AND gate of a 74HC08 circuit, for example, has the operation specified by the circuit manufacturers, described in Table 3.4(b), where A and B are inputs and Z the output. Manufacturers specify the operation of the gate in voltage levels since that is what they can, in fact, guarantee.

Applying the correspondence given in Table 3.4(a), the classic table for the logic function AND is obtained, as can be seen in Table 3.4(c).

Table 3.4 (a) Positive logic correspondence; (b) table for a 74HC08 gate and (c) table for a 74HC08 gate interpreted in positive logic.

Logic Value	Voltage Level
0	L
1	H

A	B	Z
L	L	L
L	H	L
H	L	L
H	H	H

A	B	Z
0	0	0
0	1	0
1	0	0
1	1	1

(a) (b) (c)

Clearly, positive logic is not the only possible convention. The alternative is the *negative logic* described in Table 3.5(a).

Using negative logic, the interpretation of the operation of logic circuits is different from the one using positive logic. Interpreting Table 3.4(b), which, as we saw, describes the electrical operation of 74HC08, using the negative logic convention, gives Table 3.5(b).

This table corresponds to the function OR. So, using negative logic, the gates included in the 74HC08 are interpreted as OR circuits. It is obvious that the electronic circuit always operates in the same way. The interpretation of its operation is what is different.

Due to all this, it is natural that the name given by the product manufacturers to the gates included in the 74HC08 is POSITIVE AND GATE, showing that the interpretation of the circuit as an AND is associated with the assumption that positive logic is being used. Negative logic is much less used than positive logic.

There is another possibility that is called *polarity logic* or *mixed logic*. Using this convention, each gate terminal (input or output) and each variable can be in positive or negative logic, accordingly to what is more convenient to show the functionality of the circuit. Obviously, each element must reveal which kind of logic is being used. An example will clarify this methodology.

Consider the circuit shown if Figure 3.17.

Note that the variables have now a suffix L or H. X_H means that the variable X is represented in positive logic. Z_L means that the variable Z

Table 3.5   (a) Negative logic correspondence and (b) table for a 74HC08 gate interpreted in negative logic.

Logic Value	Voltage Level
0	H
1	L

A	B	Z
1	1	1
1	0	1
0	1	1
0	0	0

(a)   (b)

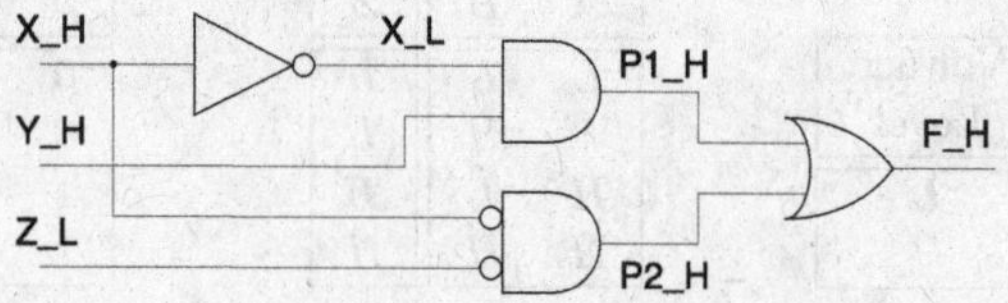

Fig. 3.17   Example of circuit using polarity logic.

is represented in negative logic. The terminals of the upper AND gate are all represented in positive logic because they don't have any small circle. The input lines of the operator that produces $P2\_H$ are in negative logic as they have the small circle representing an inversion. The output of the same operator is in positive logic.

Consider, now the variable X. When we consider the role of the inverter, we can assume the classical view that the inverter is a NOT and that the upper AND gate has the function $P1 = \overline{X} \, Y$. Another way to interpret the inverter is as an inverter of the polarity of the variable X that is active (i.e., assuming the logic value 1) when H in the NOT input and when L at the output. As the upper input of the upper gate is in positive logic (active when H) there is a logic inversion between X_L and the input of the AND gate. The result is the same, but the analysis is different.

Finally, when considering the lower gate that generates $P2\_H$ we may assume, in a classic view, that it is an AND with its inputs inverted and, consequently, a NOR. As an option, accordingly to the perspective of polarity logic, we may assume that the gate is an AND with the inputs in negative logic, i.e., active when L.

Whatever the perspective that is adopted, the function F is represented by Expression (3.5).

$$F = P1 + P2 = \overline{X} \, Y + \overline{X} \, Z. \tag{3.5}$$

This methodology, which may initially seem a little confusing, makes the design of diagrams much clearer, since they include all the actual electrical information, but keep the underlying logic information. On the other hand, all the ambiguity is eliminated concerning the relation between the logic state of the variables and the inputs and outputs of the various gates.

In the rest of this book, positive logic will be assumed unless otherwise specified.

3.3 Circuit Wiring Diagrams

We discussed until now, the design of logic functions to materialise the solution of problems, and some aspects of the devices used to implement circuits that implement these logic functions. In this section, we are going to illustrate the conversion of a logic diagram into a *wiring diagram* of a circuit.

A wiring diagram, in this context, is a conventional representation of a digital electronic circuit, showing the components and their interconnections.

A logic diagram is a basis for the design of a wiring diagram. We will illustrate the process of designing a wiring diagram, with an example.

Let us suppose that we need to build an alarm for a car that signals, by activating a buzzer, that the car is moving with an open door or that it is parked with the lights on. Obtaining a logic function that supports the desired behaviour is easy.

If the car has four doors, we define four variables, $D1$ to $D4$, each one representing the status of a door. Each of these variables will be at 1 when the respective door is open. It is easy now to verify that Expression (3.6) corresponds to a function that indicates when it assumes the value 1, that there is at least one door open.

$$D = D1 + D2 + D3 + D4. \tag{3.6}$$

In the same way, we define the variable L, that takes the value 1 when the lights are on and the variable I that is 1 when the ignition key is turned on. It is easy to see that function A, with Expression (3.7), describes the desired alarm.

$$A = I\,D + \overline{I}\,L. \tag{3.7}$$

Substituting D for the expression in terms of the variables Di, leads to Expression (3.8).

$$A = I\,(D1 + D2 + D3 + D4) + \overline{I}\,L. \tag{3.8}$$

The function A can be represented by the logic diagram of Figure 3.18.

We assume that the variables $D1$ to $D4$, I and L are accessible, as well as an input A in the alarm buzzer. If all variables are implemented using positive logic, the logic diagram may correspond more or less directly to a circuit that implements the alarm system.

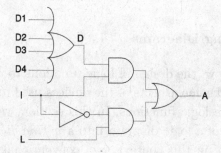

Fig. 3.18   Logic diagram of the function A.

For the circuit to be implemented in positive logic, however, we need signals to materialise the variables that are H when the variables are 1, and L, when they are 0. It turns out, however, that this is not always possible and that it is common for certain variables to be represented in negative logic.

For example, consider that, when a car door is open, the wire that provides physical support to the respective variable Di assumes the L level for reasons related to the electric circuit of the car. Similarly, assume that the same happens with variable I. When looking at the situation in positive logic, it means that what we have access to are, in fact, these negated variables. The logic diagram will have to be adjusted accordingly, originating the diagram shown in Figure 3.19.

However, this logic diagram is too complex to implement directly and it can be altered to make it simpler and use fewer integrated circuits:

- The OR with the inversions may be reconverted into a four-input NAND by applying one of Morgan's laws.
- A NAND-NAND structure may substitute the final AND-OR structure by once again applying Morgan's laws.
- As, after previous alterations, this lower part of the circuit uses only three NAND gates in an integrated circuit which has four, the NOT may be substituted by this fourth NAND, and an integrated circuit with NOT gates is thus avoided.

Figure 3.20 shows the simplified logic diagram, with an indication of the integrated circuits involved and all the terminals and their connections, and is, therefore, a wiring diagram.

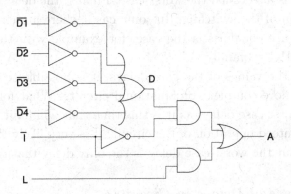

Fig. 3.19   Logic diagram adapted for function A, using positive logic.

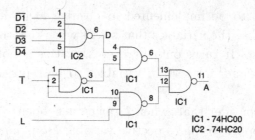

Fig. 3.20   Wiring diagram of the circuit implementing the function A.

3.4   Timing Characteristics

Section 3.1.4 has already mentioned that the operation of the physical devices used in digital circuits is not instantaneous, and therefore, is subject to delays.

The delay times under consideration are specified for each integrated circuit in its data sheet. In the issue of timing, we will consider devices of the 74LS TTL subfamily to show certain aspects less present in CMOS circuits. For example, Table 3.6 shows the delay times specified in the Texas Instruments catalogue for 74LS08. Recall that, for instance, t_{pLH} corresponds to the delay between a change in the inputs of the gate and the occurrence of a transition from L to H in its output.

There are some comments which can be made about Table 3.6. The values of the delays specified in the table are small, but gate delays in current microprocessors are even smaller, typically below 1 ns. For technological reasons, manufacturers usually don't specify the minimum delay values. The typical value is only an indicative value. The manufacturer does not guarantee this, and the user cannot trust this. Only the maximum value can be trusted, which is also called the worst-case. Finally, the delay values depend on the direction of the switching. In some cases, there are circuits in which the two times are equal, as is the case, for example with the 74LS00 and most of the 74HC subfamily.

If we know the values of the gate delays, it is possible to determine the delay time of more complex combinational circuits. What follows will only consider the worst case delays as it is this time that will limit the maximum speed of guaranteed operation of the circuit. It is very likely that the circuit works faster, but the worst-case delay is the only delay that can be trusted.

3.4.1   *Analysis of Delays in Circuits*

Let us consider the circuit in Figure 3.21.

Table 3.6   Timing specifications for the 74HC08.

Parameter	Minimum Value	Typical Value	Maximum Value
t_{pLH}		8 ns	15 ns
t_{pHL}		10 ns	20 ns

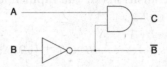

Fig. 3.21   Example of simple combinational circuit.

In a circuit with various inputs and various outputs, as is the case here, two types of significant delays may be specified:

- the delay between a given input and a given output;
- the longest delay between any input and any output.

The sequence of nodes involved in the second type of delay is called *critical path*. There are techniques and sophisticated algorithms to determine those values for complex circuits. Within the context of this book, only an introductory approach to the subject will be made.

In the circuit shown in Figure 3.21, consider the delay between the B input and the C output. The first aspect to consider is whether the B input influences the C output. There is, in fact, a path between these lines through the $\overline{B}$ node.

However, the variations in B only affect C if line A assumes the level H. Otherwise, since 0 is the absorbent element of the logic product, the output C would be at L, independently of the value of B. This is a second aspect to consider: what are the conditions that, for a defined input–output pair, enable a variation in the input to cause a change in the output. The action of establishing these conditions in the circuit is given the name *path sensitisation*.

Once the path has been sensitised, the third aspect to be taken into consideration is the transition in the input which causes the greatest delay in the circuit. Table 3.6 lists the delays for the 74LS08 circuit. The equivalent table for the 74LS04 is shown in Table 3.7.

Assume initially that A is at level H and that B has a transition from L to H. Line $\overline{B}$ changes from H to L and line C also goes from H to L. The

Table 3.7   Timing specifications for the 74LS04.

Parameter	Minimum Value	Typical Value	Maximum Value
t_{pLH}		9 ns	15 ns
t_{pHL}		10 ns	15 ns

delay time between the transitions in the input and the output is given by Expression (3.9).

$$t_{pHL\,B \to C} = t_{pHL\,\mathrm{NOT}} + t_{pHL\,\mathrm{AND}}$$

$$= 15\,\mathrm{ns} + 20\,\mathrm{ns}$$

$$= 35\,\mathrm{ns}. \tag{3.9}$$

Conversely, if B changes from H to L with the path sensitised, then $\overline{B}$ and C go from L to H, and the delay time is calculated by Expression (3.10).

$$t_{pLH\,B \to C} = t_{pLH\,\mathrm{NOT}} + t_{pLH\,\mathrm{AND}}$$

$$= 15\,\mathrm{ns} + 15\,\mathrm{ns}$$

$$= 30\,\mathrm{ns}. \tag{3.10}$$

The maximum delay will be the maximum of the two calculated delays. In this case, it will have the value $t_{p\mathrm{MAX}\,B \to C} = 35\,\mathrm{ns}$. This example illustrates the general procedure for this type of problem.

Consider now the delay of the logic block with n inputs and m outputs. A possible solution to determine the maximum delay is to test all the possible pairs and choose the greatest delay.

Clearly, there are more suitable procedures, which is particularly important in complex circuits. In the circuit used as an example, it is not worth considering the pairs with output in $\overline{B}$. The modifications in B will also influence C and, therefore, any delay between a given input and $\overline{B}$ is less than the delay between that same input and C.

In the same way, any delay between A and C is less than another delay between B and C, given that the AND is common to the two paths, and the second has yet another gate between the input and output. In the example given, therefore, the delay between B and C is the greatest delay for the circuit considered and corresponds to its critical path.

Let us now examine an example which is a little more complex based on the circuit in Figure 3.22.

In this case, there is influence from all the input variables on the output variable F. It is easy to understand, given a certain regularity in the circuit,

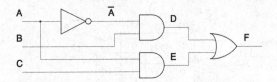

Fig. 3.22   Combinational circuit to exemplify the calculation of delays.

Table 3.8   Timing specifications for the 74LS32.

Parameter	Minimum Value	Typical Value	Maximum Value
t_{pLH}		14 ns	22 ns
t_{pHL}		14 ns	22 ns

that the greatest delay between a transition in an input and the consequent alteration in its output corresponds to transitions on the line A.

We assume that the AND gate which generates the E signal has the same characteristics as the one which generates D. Therefore, the delay time of the path which includes the NOT and AND gates is always greater than the delay in the path which only includes an AND gate. There are two paths which connect input A to output F. When there is more than one path causing an input signal to influence the value of an output signal, these paths take the name *reconvergent paths*.

Table 3.8 describes the delays for the circuit 74LS32 that implements the OR circuit.

Upon analysing all the delay times in question, it is clear that the delay times of type $H \to L$ and $L \to H$, are identical, both for the NOT and for the OR. It is, therefore, the AND that defines the direction of the transition in the inputs which leads to the worst case delay. As $t_{pHL\,AND} > t_{pLH\,AND}$, this transition is a transition from L to H.

After the NOT, both the input and the output of the AND have a transition from H to L. The worst case delay time of the circuit will, therefore, be given by Expression (3.11).

$$t_{pA \to F\mathrm{MAX}} = t_{pHL\,\mathrm{NOT}} + t_{pHL\,\mathrm{AND}} + t_{pHL\,\mathrm{OR}}$$

$$= 15\,\mathrm{ns} + 20\,\mathrm{ns} + 22\,\mathrm{ns}$$

$$= 57\,\mathrm{ns}. \tag{3.11}$$

As to determining which are the values in the inputs that sensitise the path between the chosen input and the output, a method for relatively simple circuits and which is based on the use of a Karnaugh map is presented.

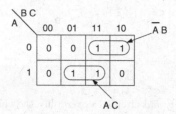

Fig. 3.23   Karnaugh map of the combinational circuit under study.

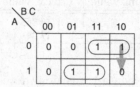

Fig. 3.24   Karnaugh map of the combinational circuit with the transition under study marked.

The Karnaugh map for the function corresponding to this circuit is shown in Figure 3.23.

As we saw, the necessary transition in A is a transition from L to H, which, in the variable, means a transition from 0 to 1. And this transition has to correspond, in its operation and, therefore, on the map, to a transition from 1 to 0. The only position in which this happens is marked in Figure 3.24.

For this transition to take place, it is easy to read the conditions in the map: $B = 1$ and $C = 0$, values which correspond to the column where the transition occurs. Therefore, B must be set to H and C set to L to sensitise the worst case path.

3.4.2   *Spurious Transitions in Combinational Circuits*

Another important aspect of the correct design or analysis of combinational circuits which considers gate delays is the problem of *spurious transitions*, also known as *hazards*. Let us return to the previous example to explain what the problem is.

Let us assume that A, B and C are at H. The output F has the value H given that the lower AND gate has its output active. If A transitions from H to L, given that the output of the upper AND gate is active, the output takes on the value H. This is in accordance with the Karnaugh map, given that, in the two positions of the map corresponding to the situations described, the function has the value 1.

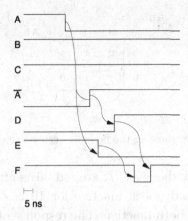

Fig. 3.25   Timing diagram showing spurious transitions.

Now consider a detailed timing diagram, showing this transition, including the transitions in the intermediate nodes of the circuit. The timing diagram is created using the delay times described above and the progression of time is analysed for each line. Figure 3.25 shows the timing diagram.

As can be seen, there is a small interval of time of around 10 ns in which the output, contrary to what is predicted, takes on the value L. This event is called a spurious transition or hazard, a momentary excursion to a unwanted value in the signal which is otherwise constant. These situations may or may not be important, depending on the use of the F line. If the F line is intended only to mark its state through a LED, for example, the hazard is harmless and is not even seen, due to its brevity. If the line activates a device where a transition can trigger some event, things change completely and the situation is not acceptable.

This type of hazard in which a signal assumes only momentarily a level contrary of the intended level is a *static hazard*. When the signal should remain at H and has a small change to L before setting again to H this is called a *Static-H* or *Static-1* hazard. In the inverse situation we have a *Static-L* or *Static-0* hazard. A *dynamic hazard* happens in different situations with more complex logic structures when there is a change of level but with instabilities.

Fortunately, in the case of static hazards it is easy to solve the problem, eliminating the hazard. Let us analyse what happened more carefully. Initially, the lower AND is active and the upper one is inactive. When line A goes to L, the upper input of the lower AND immediately goes to L and the AND responds 20 ns later, lowering its output. However, the upper AND feels the rise of $\overline{A}$ only 15 ns after A has lowered. And it takes another 15 ns to

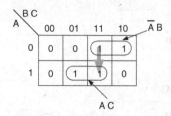

Fig. 3.26   Karnaugh map showing the possible occurrence of a spurious transition.

react. It is, therefore, at the level H, around 30 ns after the fall of A, while the other AND has already been inactive for 10 ns. The result is that, for 10 ns the OR inputs are both inactive. The response of the OR is to make its output inactive for a period of 10 ns, 22 ns later.[1]

Let us once again consider the Karnaugh map. From this perspective, what happened was the transition marked in Figure 3.26.

In this transition, the prime implicant $\overline{A}\,B$ is no longer active and the prime implicant $A\,C$ becomes the active prime implicant. What went wrong was that no prime implicant, in temporal terms, could guarantee maintaining the function at 1. In the transition from the upper to the lower group, there was no evidence that the value of the function would remain at 1. The solution to the problem is to use a new redundant prime implicant which, though not algebraically necessary for determining the expression of the function, holds the output in 1 during the transition caused by the change in A. The map, therefore, gets another implicant, as shown in Figure 3.27.

The function is then represented by Expression (3.12).

$$F = \overline{A}\,B + A\,C + B\,C. \tag{3.12}$$

Now, constructing the circuit from this expression, as shown in Figure 3.28, the problem is solved.

For simple cases, this type of solution can address this kind of problem. Of course, for functions with many variables, in which a Karnaugh map is not

---

[1]In reality the situation is much more complicated for two reasons: in the first place, because the various gates normally show actual delays that are neither worst case nor predictable; secondly, because the internal structure of the OR, with the internal delays involved, may sometimes cause the hazard not to happen. It is, therefore, not possible in most cases, to predict for all the circumstances of the operation of the circuit whether there will be an occurrence of the hazard and with what duration. But it is possible to predict the possibility of such event and act in conformity with the cases in which its possible occurrence has disastrous consequences.

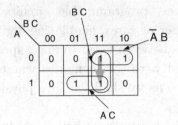

Fig. 3.27 Karnaugh map showing a redundant implicant to avoid the possible occurrence of a spurious transition.

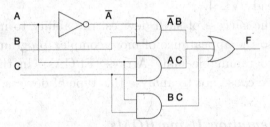

Fig. 3.28 Alteration of the combinational circuit in Figure 3.22 to avoid spurious transitions.

acceptable, other tools have to be used. It is also necessary to recall that, throughout this analysis, only one input variable is altered, which is not, in any way, a current situation. Therefore, in practice, for highly complex circuits, it may be preferable to ensure that the operation of the circuit which receives signals generated by a combinational circuit with this type of problem, is not affected by the presence of hazards. This issue will be considered later in Chapter 6.

3.5   Direct Implementation

So far, in this book, the construction of logic circuits has been made based on integrated circuits SSI that are limited to a few simple gates.

In the following chapters, we will present combinational modules and, later, sequential modules of greater complexity. Since these circuits are of general use there are MSI integrated circuits, of greater complexity, that implement them.

As integration capacity grew, manufacturers encountered a problem: In addition to microprocessors and memories that naturally took advantage of this ability to manufacture very complex circuits, there are no other modules of high complexity for general use.

In such circumstances, programmable circuits have emerged which, including a higher number of gates, enable the digital systems designer to program the connections between them to make specific circuits.

The first devices used were the memories where it is possible to store function tables and, thus, as we shall see, give physical support to complex logic functions.

In the sequence, new architectures have already been specifically built with the concern of facilitating the implementation of complex circuits. In this class of circuits, we will study the programmable logic arrays, still circuits MSI or already VLSI.

Considering the success of such devices, the ability to implement VLSI circuits has led to the appearance of more complex programmable circuits, namely Field Programmable Gate Arrays (FPGAs). In this introductory book, however, we chose not to analyse this type of devices.

3.5.1 *Implementation Using ROMs*

A *Read-Only Memory*, known by the acronym ROM, is a device where it is possible, at the manufacturing stage, to record information in a permanent manner. ROMs are sometimes considered sequential circuits, a type of circuit which will be studied later, but, in reality, they are combinational circuits. The ROM has the structure shown in Figure 3.29 for an example of an eight-word four-bit ROM. The small square where two lines cross means that this connection may or may not be made, and the decision as to which connections will be done is taken when recording the information on the ROM. The structure shown does not, in fact, correspond to the way the ROM is implemented, but it is sufficiently illustrative of its operating principles.

In reality, the structure of the ROM is slightly different, with the or implemented by an open-drain type connection, using, therefore, just one line which may or may not be connected to the output of each AND. Figure 3.30 shows the structure using this technology.

The operation of a ROM is simple to understand. The set of lines A_i constitutes what is designated by the *address*. As can be seen, for each address placed in the ROM input, the output line of the AND gate corresponding to that address is set at 1. The output lines which have an input connected to that line will be set to 1. The rest will have the value 0. The set of output bits is designated as a *word*. The ROM may, therefore, be seen as a set of stored words. The address present in the input lines selects one of these words which is placed at the output.

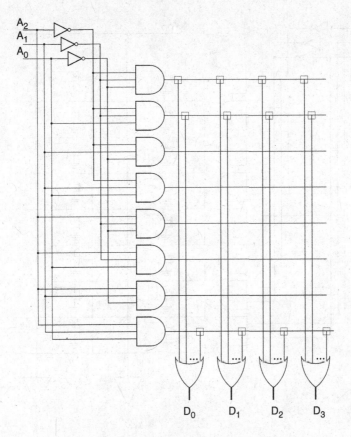

Fig. 3.29 Internal operating structure of a ROM.

As an example, Figure 3.31 shows the content of a ROM already programmed, with a preset content. We will use, from now on, two conventions. Firstly, instead of designing the internal structure as it is, which would make this type of schematic representation complex, the internal connection is represented as if there were OR output gates, but collapsing all the lines into only one. On the other hand, the connections at the and gates output are indicated by a cross. For example, the output D_0 is connected to the outputs of the AND gates $P2$, $P3$, $P5$ and $P7$.

The connections between the vertical and horizontal lines in the figure would give rise, if they were just as described above, to a short circuit between all the lines. For example, in the case which illustrates the detail of the previous ROM programming, all the lines would be short-circuited and, therefore, their operation would not be as intended. In fact, in the place where lines cross, there are small devices, diodes, to be more precise,

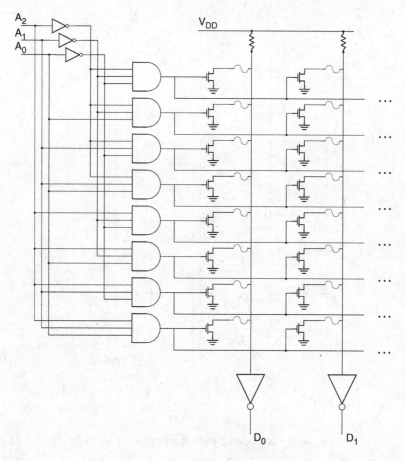

Fig. 3.30   Internal structure of a ROM.

to prevent such a situation to arise. For clarity, those devices will not be shown.

The content of a ROM can be specified by a table which indicates, for each address, the corresponding data word. For example, the ROM shown in Figure 3.31 can, in a more compact form, be described by Table 3.9.

The graphical manner of representing a ROM in a logic diagram is much more compact than that shown in the previous figures, which only serve to illustrate the concept and an example of the internal structure of a device of this type. Figure 3.32 shows the symbol for the ROM used previously as an example.

There are several types of read-only memories. Actual ROMs are integrated circuits designed from scratch with the intended content. They are not programmed by the user and are not alterable. Programmable ROM

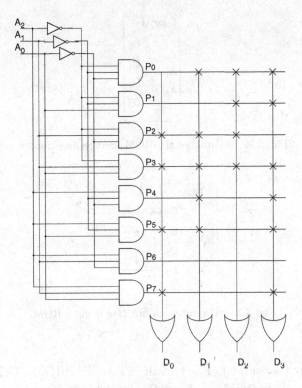

Fig. 3.31   Example of a programmed ROM.

Table 3.9   Specification of the contents of the ROM under study.

A_2	A_1	A_0	D_3	D_2	D_1	D_0
\multicolumn{3}{Address}	\multicolumn{4}{Data}

Address			Data			
A_2	A_1	A_0	D_3	D_2	D_1	D_0
0	0	0	1	1	1	0
0	0	1	1	1	0	0
0	1	0	0	1	1	1
0	1	1	1	1	1	1
1	0	0	1	0	1	0
1	0	1	1	0	1	1
1	1	0	0	0	0	0
1	1	1	1	0	0	1

(PROM), devices, more common than ROMs, are devices which can be programmed, destroying small fuses inside the integrated circuit. They are bought virgin, programmed by the users and are not alterable after that. Should it be necessary to alter the programming, a new device has to be programmed. Erasable PROM (EPROM) are devices which may be programmed and which may be erased (usually through bathing them for some minutes in ultraviolet radiation). EPROMs can be rewritten a number of

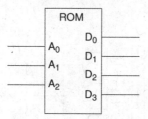

Fig. 3.32   Symbol of the ROM used as an example.

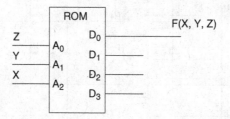

Fig. 3.33   Circuit for a function using a ROM.

times (tens to thousands). Electrically Erasable PROMs (EEPROM) are electrically alterable ROMs without the need to remove them from the circuit to which they belong. In the same way, they can be altered a limited number of times.

ROMs can have a variety of applications:

- support for programs in embedded systems which will not be altered (ROM or PROM use) or which can be updated a limited number of times;
- memorisation of tables;
- logic implementation of functions.

This latter application, the single one of interest in this context, needs further explanation. The description of the ROM is made by specifying its physical structure (number of address and data lines) and by its content table, as was seen above.

We use the ROM indicated above as an example and consider, in particular, the data line D_0. We will view data column D_0 as a table of a three-variable logic function with inputs A_2, A_1 and A_0. Hence, if this ROM is to be used with this content in a circuit, it will implement the logic function described by the table and, in most cases, it will use less material. The circuit is therefore reduced to the ROM, as shown in Figure 3.33. The function implemented is $F(X, Y, Z)$ with X corresponding to A_2, Y to A_1 and Z to A_0 and with Expression (3.13) as it is easy to see.

$$F = Y\,\overline{Z} + X\,Z. \tag{3.13}$$

In the previous example, the ROM could offer support for other functions. For example, it would be possible to use the ROM to provide support for four three-variable functions, provided that the input variables were the same.

This implementation method uses, as a basis, function tables instead of logic expressions, as in the case of the implementation with logic gates. This is an interesting observation because it brings to the level of the implementation of a circuit, the duality of representation of logic functions with tables or expressions that we saw in Chapter 2.

Commercial ROM circuits have many more address lines and, possibly, data lines, thus making it possible to implement various functions with a high number of inputs. For example, an 8K × 8 bit ROM may implement up to 8 logic functions of up to 13 variables ($8K = 2^{13}$). Obviously, some of these functions may not depend on all the input variables.

Implementation of functions using ROM circuits has some significant advantages. On the one hand, the number of integrated circuits used is drastically reduced, especially for systems with a high degree of complexity, with a corresponding reduction in the weight and volume of the equipment and, up to a certain point, in power consumed. On the other hand, any alteration of the intended functionality is resolved by using a new ROM or reprogramming an existing one (in the case of EPROMs) without changing the rest of the implemented circuit. Finally, the use of ROM circuits makes it difficult for third parties to analyse the developed circuit, protecting the confidentiality of a design to a certain extent.

3.5.2 *Implementation Using Programmable Logic Arrays*

A ROM uses much of its area in the integrated circuit to implement the AND gates connected to the address lines. For example, the 8K ROM mentioned above would have eight 8,192 13-input AND gates.[2] For applications that save information in the ROM (programs or tables), there is no alternative. However, to generate logic functions, most of the AND gates are often not necessary. Therefore, it is more advantageous to have fewer AND gates with a greater number of inputs than the contrary, to implement functions with

---

[2] In Section 4.2 this aspect will be treated further.

more inputs in integrated circuits not too complex. This idea led to the design of different programmable devices. Those devices, as happens in ROMs have a number of AND gates and a number of OR gates. The connections between the inputs and the AND gates on the one hand, and between the ANDs and the ORs, on the other hand, can be programmed. These structures and others are known as *programmable logic arrays*.

As a very simple example, consider the circuit in Figure 3.34. In this figure, the symbol for Figure 3.35(a) is the abbreviated representation of what is shown in Figure 3.35(b). It should be noted that the device shown has four inputs. If a ROM was built, it would have as its input 16 AND gates. In the circuit shown, there are only five, and the number could, of course, have been any other.

As an example, consider the implementation of the functions described in Table 3.10 using the previous array. If the implementation was carried out

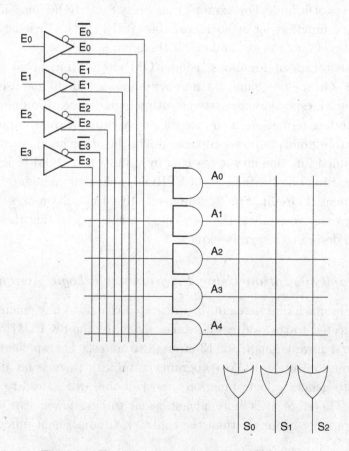

Fig. 3.34   Example of a programmable logic array.

(a)   (b)

Fig. 3.35   Double buffer representation: (a) symbol and (b) structure.

Table 3.10   Functions used as an example.

$ABCD$	$f_x(A,B,C,D)$	$f_y(A,B,C,D)$
0000	0	0
0001	1	1
0010	0	0
0011	1	1
0100	0	0
0101	1	1
0110	0	0
0111	1	1
1000	1	1
1001	0	1
1010	1	1
1011	1	0
1100	0	0
1101	0	1
1110	0	0
1111	1	1

based on a ROM, the simple recording of the table in ROM, with at least 16 words and two data lines, would solve the problem. The use of programmable logic arrays, however, requires the algebraic expressions of the functions. There are computer applications that do this translation of formats.

In the case under analysis, using the methods described in Chapter 2, it is possible to obtain the Expressions (3.15).

$$f_x(A,B,C,D) = \overline{A}\,D + C\,D + A\,\overline{B}\,\overline{D},$$

$$f_y(A,B,C,D) = \overline{A}\,D + \overline{C}\,D + B\,D + A\,\overline{B}\,\overline{D}.$$

(3.14)

The programming of the programmable logic array is shown schematically in Figure 3.36, in which the connections are marked by the symbol «×» in the crossing of the lines to interconnect. This type of programmable logic array is usually abbreviated and designated as PLA.

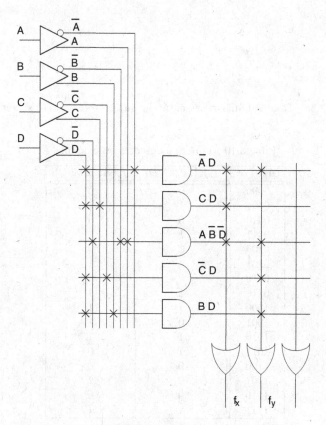

Fig. 3.36   Example of programming of a PLA.

3.5.3   *Implementation Using Programmable Array Logic*

In the case of the ROMs, as we saw, the connections between the inputs and the AND gates are fixed, and it is possible to program the ones between the AND and the OR gates. With PLAs, we can program both types of connections. It can be seen that the most interesting possibilities stem from the ability to program the input connections of the AND gates. Thus, a new type of programmable array was developed in which the connections between the AND and the OR gates are fixed and it is only possible to program the AND connections to the inputs. This option is not limiting, and it has the advantage of optimising the architecture of the device, placing the only programmable area, in the zone where it promotes greater flexibility.

This structure is designated as *programmable array logic*, with the abbreviation *PAL*. An example of a possible PAL, is that of Figure 3.37. In this

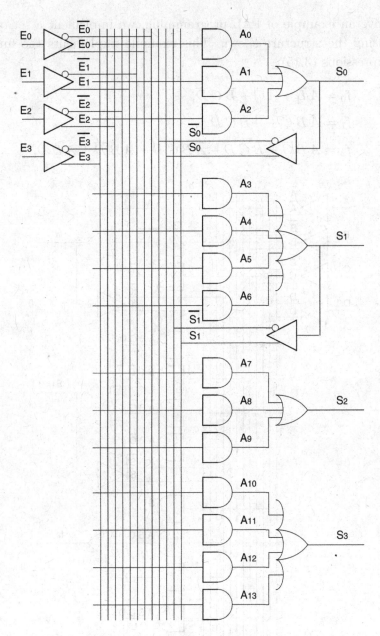

Fig. 3.37   Example of a programmable array of the PAL type.

type of array, it is often the case that some of the outputs are fed back as if they were inputs, enabling, in this way, to enlarge the number of AND gates connected to an OR operator. In the example given this is the case for the output S_0 and S_1.

To give an example of PAL programming, we implement a set of functions, using the structure shown. This example implements the functions with Expressions (3.15).

$$f_0 = A\overline{B} + \overline{A}\,\overline{C} + \overline{B}\,C\,\overline{D},$$

$$f_1 = A\,B\,\overline{C} + \overline{A}\,\overline{B}\,C\,\overline{D}, \tag{3.15}$$

$$f_2 = \overline{A}\,\overline{B}\,\overline{C} + \overline{B}\,C\,\overline{D} + \overline{A}\,B\,C\,D + A\,B\,\overline{D} + A\,\overline{B}\,D.$$

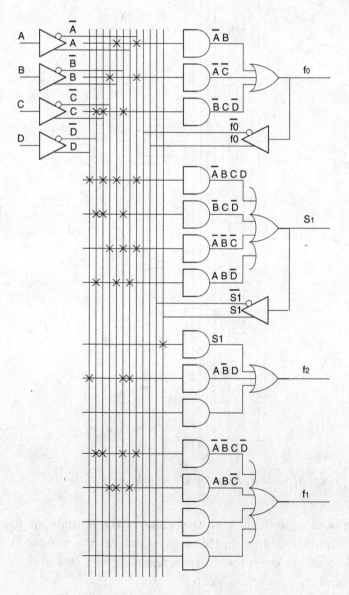

Fig. 3.38   Example of programming a PAL.

The programming of the PAL is shown in Figure 3.38. In this example, the function f_2 used two of the structures AND-OR and the feedback line S_1.

The use of programmable logic arrays has advantages similar to the utilisation of ROM circuits, with some additional aspects. On the one hand, the programmable arrays allow for an improvement in the usage of the programmable area, enabling more entries for the same level of internal complexity of the device. On the other, the employment of programmable logic arrays enables functions to be implemented eliminating spurious transitions, as Section 3.4.2 details, which is not possible in the case of ROMs.

The programming of this type of devices is, generally, undertaken with the help of suitable software. These tools enable the introduction of the specification of the functions to be programmed in the most convenient form for the user and produce a file with the necessary data for the equipment programming the device to implement the programming physically.

The use of ROM circuits and *programmable logic devices*, as has just been described, allows the implementation of logic functions, that is, combinational circuits. Later chapters will study sequential circuits. The use of programmable logic arrays can be extended to such circuits provided memory elements are included in the array structure, which is common.

3.6   Summary

This chapter considers aspects related to the implementation of logic circuits specified by logic functions and deals with their most important physical characteristics. It starts with a description of the building blocks for logic circuits, that is, digital integrated circuits, including their underlying technology and electronic behaviour. The chapter continues with a description of the methods associated with constructing circuits using basic gates from a description of a logic function. Aspects connected to the timing characteristics of the circuits are also described in some detail, including the generation of spurious transitions. The chapter ends with an analysis of the use of ROM and programmable logic to implement combinational digital circuits.

Exercises

3.1 Find on Internet the datasheets for circuits with the same reference, in TTL for the sub-families LS and AS, and in CMOS, both for the

HC and HCT sub-families. Consider, for example, the circuits 7400 in several versions.

(a) Check, by referring to the parameters for the input and output voltage values, that the HCT family is compatible with the LS one regarding voltage levels, but that, in the case of the HC and LS and AS sub-families, this is not true.

(b) Check what the typical delays of these three sub-families are and compare these from that point of view.

3.2 For each of the following functions, build a diagram of a circuit that implements them, using the minimum number of integrated circuits (see online catalogues):

(a) $f(A, B, C) = A\ B + \overline{A}\ \overline{B}\ \overline{C}$
(b) $f(A, B, C, D) = A\ B\ (\overline{C} \oplus D) + A\ B\ C + \overline{A}\ \overline{C}\ D + \overline{B}\ C\ D$
(c) $f(A, B, C) = \overline{A}\ B\ C + A\ \overline{B} + C.$

3.3 Consider the following circuit:

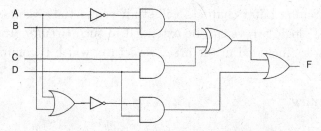

Obtain, from an online catalogue, the timing characteristics of the gates involved, assuming the use of the 74LS sub-family.

(a) What is the critical path of this circuit?

(b) Is there a transition direction from the input variable of the critical path leading to a delay time higher than the transition in the opposite direction?

(c) What/which configuration(s) of the input variables sensitise the critical path?

3.4 Consider the following circuit:

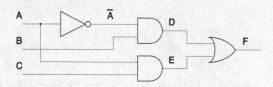

(a) Indicate near each gate the integrated circuit used assuming positive logic.

(b) Repeat using negative logic.

3.5 Using a ROM with a capacity that you specify, construct a combinational circuit which calculates n^3, with n being a four-bit binary number.

3.6 Program the PAL in Figure 3.37 to implement the following set of logic functions:

$$f(A, B, C, D) = \overline{A}\ \overline{C} + \overline{B}\ \overline{C}\ D + A\ B\ C + \overline{A}\ \overline{B}\ D$$

$$f(A, B, C, D) = \overline{A}\ B + A\ D + \overline{A}\ B\ \overline{C} + \overline{A}\ \overline{C}\ \overline{D}$$

$$f(A, B, C, D) = \overline{C}\ D + A\ D + \overline{A}\ \overline{B}\ \overline{C} + \overline{A}\ B\ \overline{C} + \overline{A}\ B\ C\ \overline{D}$$

$$f(A, B, C, D) = \overline{C}\ D + \overline{A}\ B\ \overline{C} + \overline{A}\ B\ C\ \overline{D}$$

3.7 Consider the following circuit:

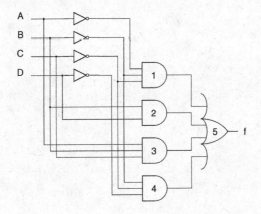

(a) Construct the corresponding Karnaugh map.

(b) This circuit may have spurious transitions when a particular variable is changed. Under what circumstances?

(c) Alter the previous circuit, so as to eliminate the aforementioned spurious transitions.

Chapter 4

Combinational Modules of Medium Complexity

Previous chapters presented methods for designing simple functions as well as their respective combinational circuits. Naturally, most circuits which are necessary for current applications display a complexity which is not compatible with such a simple approach.

This chapter will analyse a method to design complex combinational circuits from simpler models and describe the structure of most typical simple modules.

The issue of modular design is developed in Section 4.1, which shows how complex circuits are designed from simpler circuits. The concept of levels of abstraction is also introduced to deal with the problem of developing complex systems.

The three following sections are dedicated to three types of modules which are very frequently used. Section 4.2 analyses decoders, Section 4.3 deals with encoders and Section 4.4 presents multiplexers.

As this topic is practically and educationally relevant, Section 4.5 describes how to implement simple logic functions based on some of the modules previously discussed, particularly decoders and multiplexers, to complement the techniques presented in Chapter 3.

The chapter finishes with Section 4.6, which refers to the design of iterative circuits. The design of a comparator circuit for two n-bit numbers illustrates the concept.

4.1 Modularity

The design of a combinational circuit always starts with a circuit specification connecting a set of outputs with a set of inputs. The circuit specification level takes place in an abstract manner, where the internal structure is still not known. The circuit is, therefore, a black box, with its interior unknown. Only its input and output terminals and its behavioural specification are known. A circuit with n inputs, I_0 to I_{n-1} and m outputs, O_0 to O_{m-1}, can

Fig. 4.1   Functional block for a combinational circuit with n inputs and m outputs.

be graphically described as shown in Figure 4.1. This representation of the circuit is called *functional block*.

When the modules are at a lower *level of abstraction* and correspond to an integrated circuit or a standard block in modern implementation strategies, we use *symbols* of the circuit describing its functionality.

The specification of the system is the first step in the design. The circuit is specified at a high *level of abstraction* without any concern for the implementation details. After, we refine the analysis and obtain new descriptions of the system successively closer to the physical implementation. The design begins, therefore with a *functional description* at a very abstract level and concludes with a *structural description* at the implementation level, specifying the wiring diagram of the modules of the system. The succession of levels of abstraction enables the use of an approach based on *modularity concepts*, addressed in this section.

Once the functional block for a circuit has been defined, its implementation can be based on the methods used in Chapters 2 and 3 to build m functions of n variables.

As an example, take a circuit which converts BCD coded words into words of the *2-out-of-5* code, which has words of 5 bits with 2 bits at 1 and 3 bits at 0 for each valid configuration. Table 4.1 shows the 2-out-of-5 code and, at the same time, the correspondence between it and the BCD code words. The corresponding functional block is shown in Figure 4.2.

Table 4.1, besides representing the correspondence between the words of two codes, may also be seen as a set of five truth tables for the logic functions $P(A, B, C, D)$, $Q(A, B, C, D)$, $R(A, B, C, D)$, $S(A, B, C, D)$ and $T(A, B, C, D)$. The circuit may now be implemented using the methods previously presented.

Out of curiosity, there are several theoretically possible 2-out-of-5 codes. The one shown is the Dennison variation in the coding with weights $P = 7$, $Q = 4$, $R = 2$, $S = 1$ and $T = 0$.

As in other variations of the 2-out-of-5 code with weights associated with the various columns, the encoding of 0 is an invalid combination (in this case corresponding to 11).

Table 4.1 Correspondence between the BCD code and the 2-out-of-5 code.

Number	Code BCD $ABCD$	Code 2-out-of-5 $PQRST$
0	0 0 0 0	1 1 0 0 0
1	0 0 0 1	0 0 0 1 1
2	0 0 1 0	0 0 1 0 1
3	0 0 1 1	0 0 1 1 0
4	0 1 0 0	0 1 0 0 1
5	0 1 0 1	0 1 0 1 0
6	0 1 1 0	0 1 1 0 0
7	0 1 1 1	1 0 0 0 1
8	1 0 0 0	1 0 0 1 0
9	1 0 0 1	1 0 1 0 0

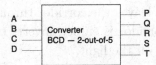

Fig. 4.2 Functional block for a combinational circuit which converts BCD code into 2-out-of-5 code.

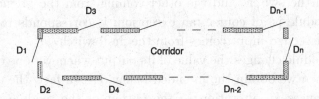

Fig. 4.3 Schematic representation of the example of light control of the corridor.

However, it is common to design circuits that have levels of complexity which hinder or make many direct implementation methods not possible since they involve a large number of inputs and outputs. In such circumstances, it is preferable to adopt an approach based on modular structures. This type of method analyses the specifications of a circuit to try and find some internal structure for the design of a set of modules that when interconnected, can implement the intended specification.

As an example, take the following problem. There is a long corridor with a series of doors to rooms and an access door to the outside, D_1, as shown in Figure 4.3. Close to each door, there is a switch. Whenever someone enters the corridor, and it is not lit, they reverse the position of this switch, and the

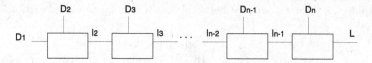

Fig. 4.4   Modular representation of the control circuit of the corridor lighting.

Table 4.2   XOR function.

x	y	$x \oplus y$
0	0	0
0	1	1
1	0	1
1	1	0

light turns on. If someone leaves the corridor through one of the doors, and after verifying that the corridor is empty, inverts the position of the switch close to that door to turn off the light.

The circuit with the structure shown in Figure 4.4 represents the control of the illumination of the corridor. It exhibits a modular structure in which each module is placed alongside each door. Each module has two inputs, one coming from the switch, and the other coming from the previous module. The first module is, of course, an exception: it corresponds to the second door and the second input comes from the first switch.

If each module changes the value of its output whenever one of the inputs is altered, then we obtain the intended behaviour. In fact, the alteration of any input causes an alteration to the output of the module and, with a domino-like effect, a change in the successive modules. The output of the last module controls the lighting of the corridor. The problem now comes down to designing one of the modules, which, since they are all the same, corresponds to the complete design of the circuit.

To solve this problem, it is useful to remember that the exclusive-or function has an important characteristic: if one of the inputs inverts its value, the output also inverts its output, whatever is in the other input, provided that it is constant. Table 4.2, reproduced here, allows you to check that property. It is easy to see that each model is simply made up of a XOR gate, as shown in Figure 4.5 for the case of module i.

Modular design is not always based on the use of modules which are all the same. An alternative is the design of a circuit involving functionally different modules, but which interact to correspond to the intended circuit.

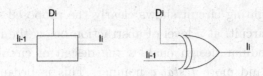

Fig. 4.5   Circuit corresponding to each module of the control circuit for the corridor lighting.

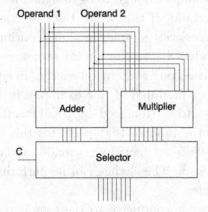

Fig. 4.6   Circuit enabling the addition or multiplication of two four-bit binary numbers.

For example, consider a circuit which adds or multiplies four-bit binary numbers under the command of a control signal C.

A possible design for this circuit has a module which carries out the addition of two numbers, a second module which calculates the product of those numbers and a third module which allows the choice of which of the results obtained by the modules above should be used as the final result for the circuit. Figure 4.6 shows this solution.

In this example note that the result of the sum of two binary numbers of 4 (n) bits can be a binary number of 5 $(n + 1)$ bits and that the product is a number of 8 $(2n)$ bits. We will study this further in Chapter 5.

Now, of course, each of the modules has to be designed. These may, in turn, be divided into modules of lesser complexity or, alternatively, be directly constructed.

The design of circuits in this way offers several advantages:

• This modular design enables you to start from the functional description of the circuit, ignoring the details of its structure. By successively refining the abstract vision, the process brings us closer to the structural vision of the circuit and, therefore, to its physical design. The functional block of the corridor lighting circuit shows clearly the proposed structure for the design of the circuit, at a level of abstraction below the initial one.

- In general, modular design enables the design of circuits in a quicker, more elegant and more *testable* manner. This is because it is possible to divide the problem into simpler problems, designing the circuit as a set of interconnected modules of lesser complexity. Then, each module is analysed and, if it is simple enough to be designed with the available tools, that design is carried out. If this is not the case, the process of dividing the design into progressively simpler modules continues.

- A *hierarchy* is introduced into the circuit structure which enables local alterations to be carried out without interfering in either the overall hierarchy or in the other modules. If, for example, in the adder/multiplier circuit, the sum was to be replaced by a subtraction operation, action is only required on the module that performs this operation. The same happens if a more efficient algorithm is made available to carry out the multiplication operation. The change can be performed by changing only the respective module.

- Designing in this way is conducive to the easy expansion of the desired functionality. In the corridor lighting circuit, if it is necessary to extend the corridor, it is only necessary to add more modules which have already been designed. In the adder/multiplier circuit, if any new operations are required, then it is only necessary to create the new modules and resize the selector circuit or, even more simply, to use several cascaded selector circuits (if the added delays are tolerable).

- Another advantage of this way of designing is that the various modules can always be reused in other systems. If for example, you want to design an adder circuit for 16-bit numbers, it is possible to design it from an existing four-bit adder by juxtaposing identical modules, as we will see in Chapter 5.

- A final advantage of considerable importance is that it becomes more economical to produce circuits. They are based on relatively less complex modules which, as they are often reusable, enables their manufacture in larger quantities. In this type of industry, increasing the amounts produced lowers the unit production cost considerably.

Clearly, there are also disadvantages to this approach. However, these are clearly minor and, in most cases, the modular approach is indeed used. The most significant inconvenience of a modular approach is that when a design is made directly from the truth table of the circuits, it is practicable to build a circuit with two layers of gates between the inputs and the outputs (not counting any possible inversions, which may represent a third layer). The circuit delay time is therefore known and limited to the time delay of three gates at most. In a modular approach, the delays are much higher, since each module may have a higher degree of complexity and with the module interconnection, it is very likely that this results in a slower circuit than would be possible through direct implementation. The designer has, for each case, to weigh up the pros and cons of each of the options. This issue will be taken up in later chapters.

Ideally, the design should be carried out using a *top-down approach*, starting from the upper level of abstraction of the logic circuit through successively lower levels in the hierarchy, down to the simpler modules, followed by the circuit design of those modules. However, there are often constraints concerning the modules already available for use at lower levels, for example, due to the reuse of previously designed modules. This means that often the top-down strategy is combined, or even replaced, with a *bottom-up approach*, which starts with knowledge of the modules available for the design of a more complex circuit. A child using LEGO^{TM} to carry out a construction knows this reality from experience. Although a construction plan for implementation is made in complex constructions, this does not ignore the shape and functionality of the parts that are available.

In the design of digital circuits, the use of certain types of modules which represent relatively common functionalities or that allow the implementation of logic functions, in an alternative and, in some cases, advantageous way, is recurrent. In the following sections, some of these modules will be studied.

4.2 Decoders

The *decoder* is a circuit that obtains, from a set of bits coding a word of a code, the identification of that word. For this, the decoder has as many outputs as the number of code words and activates, at each moment, only one of the many outputs corresponding to the word present in the inputs.

4.2.1 *Binary Decoders*

A three-input *binary decoder*, usually called *3-line-to-8-line decoder* or *1-out-of-8 decoder* accepts words of three-bit binary code in its inputs, that is, configurations between 000 and 111, and has eight outputs numbered from 0 to 7. The symbol for a decoder of this type is shown in Figure 4.7. It is

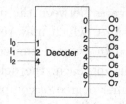

Fig. 4.7   Symbol for a 3-line-to-8-line decoder.

Table 4.3   Table for a 3-line-to-8-line binary decoder.

Binary Encoding	Outputs							
$I_2\,I_1\,I_0$	$O7$	$O6$	$O5$	$O4$	$O3$	$O2$	$O1$	$O0$
0 0 0	0	0	0	0	0	0	0	1
0 0 1	0	0	0	0	0	0	1	0
0 1 0	0	0	0	0	0	1	0	0
0 1 1	0	0	0	0	1	0	0	0
1 0 0	0	0	0	1	0	0	0	0
1 0 1	0	0	1	0	0	0	0	0
1 1 0	0	1	0	0	0	0	0	0
1 1 1	1	0	0	0	0	0	0	0

important to note that in the symbol it should be clear what is the weight of each of the input lines. Each of the outputs should also be clearly identified.

Table 4.3 describes the intended operation, in which Oi is the output corresponding to word i of the binary code.

The possible internal structure of a decoder is easy to define. In fact, each output represents one of the possible binary configurations of the inputs. For example, if the inputs I_2 and I_1 are active (at logic level 1) and I_0 is not active (at logic level 0), the output $O6$ should be active, that is, at 1, and all the remaining outputs at 0. It is easy to conclude that the output $O6$ has the Expression (4.1).

$$O6 = \overline{I_0}\ I_1\ I_2. \tag{4.1}$$

Continuing this reasoning, we find that Figure 4.8 represents the internal structure of a 3-line-to-8-line binary decoder.

The example shown for a 3-line-to-8-line binary decoder may, of course, be extended to binary decoders with any number of input bits.

In addition to this type of decoder (n-to-2^n), there are specific decoders for certain codes, such as the *BCD decoder*. This type, in particular, has four inputs and 10 outputs, which go from $O0$ to $O9$. Clearly, the configurations for the inputs that do not correspond to BCD words leave all outputs

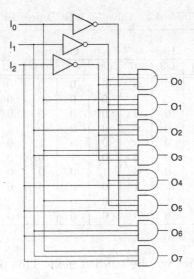

Fig. 4.8   Possible internal structure for the 3-line-to-8-line binary decoder.

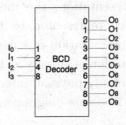

Fig. 4.9   Symbol for a BCD decoder.

inactive. Other designations for this decoder are *4-line-to-10-line decoder* and *1-of-10 decoder.*

Figure 4.9 shows the symbol for a decoder of this type. In terms of the desired operation described above, this can be specified by Table 4.4.

It is very common for the decoders to have their outputs active at 0. In these circumstances, the internal circuit is organised around NAND gates instead of ANDs, and the active output of the module becomes the one set at 0, with the inactive ones remaining at 1. There are strong technological reasons for this solution. One of these reasons is that the NAND gates are faster than the AND gates, which allows faster decoders to be constructed using NAND gates. Furthermore, in TTL, the value 0 in a line consumes more power than the value 1 because the structure of the internal circuit means that the currents involved in maintaining a 0 are almost three orders of magnitude larger than those necessary to maintain a 1. The same applies

Table 4.4 Table for a BCD decoder.

BCD Encoding $I_3\,I_2\,I_1\,I_0$	Outputs									
	O9	O8	O7	O6	O5	O4	O3	O2	O1	O0
0 0 0 0	0	0	0	0	0	0	0	0	0	1
0 0 0 1	0	0	0	0	0	0	0	0	1	0
0 0 1 0	0	0	0	0	0	0	0	1	0	0
0 0 1 1	0	0	0	0	0	0	1	0	0	0
0 1 0 0	0	0	0	0	0	1	0	0	0	0
0 1 0 1	0	0	0	0	1	0	0	0	0	0
0 1 1 0	0	0	0	1	0	0	0	0	0	0
0 1 1 1	0	0	1	0	0	0	0	0	0	0
1 0 0 0	0	1	0	0	0	0	0	0	0	0
1 0 0 1	1	0	0	0	0	0	0	0	0	0

to the enable inputs that will be studied next. This power issue is not valid in CMOS circuits, but, as we already discussed, circuit architecture of the CMOS circuits has reproduced the one in TTL circuits.

Regarding symbolic representation, the modules, as is the case with the binary decoder, are often represented by their symbol, perhaps with some variations, and this representation is sometimes referred to as a *block diagram*. When the representation is already at the component level and the interconnections represent already physical interconnections between terminals of the components, the resulting diagram is called a *wiring diagram* as presented in Section 3.3.

4.2.2 *Decoder Expansion*

Often the decoder modules available don't have the number of inputs (and outputs) necessary for decoding a certain encoding. There is, therefore, a need to undertake an *expansion of the decoding capacity*. Many decoders have a decoder *enable* input. When active, this input enables the decoder to function normally. When not enabled, all the outputs remain inactive. The operation of a 2-line-to-4-line decoder with an enable input is described in Table 4.5.

The enable input, usually present in commercially available decoders, has other uses beyond the simple expansion of the decoding capacity. A possible internal structure of a 2-line-to-4-line decoder with enable input is shown in Figure 4.10.

Decoders with many outputs can be built with smaller decoders with less outputs, used as building blocks. The construction of a 4-line-to-16-line

Table 4.5   Table for a 2-line-to-4-line decoder with enable.

Binary Encoding	Enable	Output			
$I_1\ I_0$	En	$S0$	$S1$	$S2$	$S3$
0 0	0	0	0	0	0
0 0	1	1	0	0	0
0 1	0	0	0	0	0
0 1	1	0	1	0	0
1 0	0	0	0	0	0
1 0	1	0	0	1	0
1 1	0	0	0	0	0
1 1	1	0	0	0	1

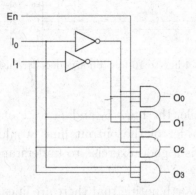

Fig. 4.10   Internal structure of a 2-line-to-4-line binary decoder with enable input.

binary decoder using 2-line-to-4-line binary decoders is given as an example in Figure 4.11.

In the example used it can be seen that there is a final layer of decoders sufficient in number, four, in this case, to create the total number of necessary outputs, in this case, 16. All these decoders share the same input lines, such that they decode the same subset of the input lines, in this case, I_0 and I_1. There is an additional decoder, which decodes the remaining lines of the input code, in this case, I_2 and I_3, and controls through the enable lines which of the decoders of the output layer is active. In this way, there is always just one active line in the output. In this example, one decoder is sufficient for this task. In more general situations it may be necessary to use various layers of decoders to obtain the appropriate decoder.

Another important observation is that the final marking of the outputs depends on the way the lines of the input encoding are distributed by the

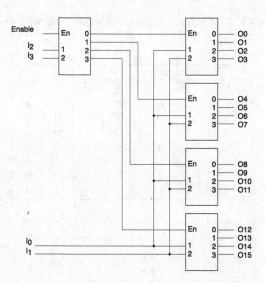

Fig. 4.11   Example of a 4-line-to-16-line binary decoder, using 2-line-to-4-line binary decoders.

decoders. If for example, the lines I_0 and I_2 were exchanged, such as lines I_1 and I_3, then the order of the output lines would be entirely changed. Finding this marking is a good exercise to understand the operation of the circuit.

In Figure 4.11 it is worth noting that there are lines which have an internal meaning from the point of view of the decoders, and an external one from the point of view of the overall circuit. For example, line $O4$, which is the line that decodes the word 4 of the four-bit code, has that meaning in the global circuit under analysis. However, taking the point of view of the module that generates the signal, the same line is the output line 0 of that module, meaning that, for this 2-line-to-4-line decoder, that is the active line when the inputs represent the word 0 of the two-bit binary code.

4.3 Encoders

The *encoder* is a circuit which, in a certain way, has an inverse operation to that of the decoder. In the encoder, the inputs are a set of lines that correspond to of the words of a code, and the outputs express the bits of the code word. Figure 4.12 shows the symbol of an encoder for a three-bit binary code, also called *8-line-to-3-line encoder*.

This section will only analyse encoders for natural binary codes but, clearly, encoders can be implemented for any code.

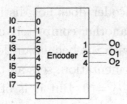

Fig. 4.12 Symbol of an 8-line-to-3-line encoder.

Table 4.6 Table of the 8-line-to-3-line binary encoder.

Active Input								Encoding
$I7$	$I6$	$I5$	$I4$	$I3$	$I2$	$I1$	$I0$	$O_2\,O_1\,O_0$
0	0	0	0	0	0	0	1	0 0 0
0	0	0	0	0	0	1	0	0 0 1
0	0	0	0	0	1	0	0	0 1 0
0	0	0	0	1	0	0	0	0 1 1
0	0	0	1	0	0	0	0	1 0 0
0	0	1	0	0	0	0	0	1 0 1
0	1	0	0	0	0	0	0	1 1 0
1	0	0	0	0	0	0	0	1 1 1

4.3.1 *Binary Encoders*

In its simplest version, an 8-line-to-3-line binary encoder, for example, can be designed from the specification in Table 4.6.

Note that the table does not list all the configurations of input variables, but only those corresponding to the cases of interest. Obtaining the functions O_i from the variables Ij is impractical using the Karnaugh method, for example. However, by observing the table, it is relatively easy to conclude that, if one considers all other input combinations as don't cares, each function O_i may be obtained from the logic sum of the input variables, which places O_i at 1 in every one of the output configurations. In this way, the functions described by the Expressions (4.2) are obtained.

$$O_0 = I1 + I3 + I5 + I7,$$
$$O_1 = I2 + I3 + I6 + I7, \tag{4.2}$$
$$O_2 = I4 + I5 + I6 + I7.$$

This encoder circuit may be easily built using three four-input OR gates.

It turns out, however, that this encoder would have a very limited spectrum of use. There are two aspects which would cause problems in the utilisation of this encoder.

In the first place, the encoder does not distinguish the situation where only input $I0$ is active from another completely different situation, where no input is active. The circuit with the behaviour described by the table above, and with the proposed implementation, sets all the outputs inactive in both cases, that is, $O_2 = O_1 = O_0 = 0$. But it is of interest to distinguish the two situations. A way of doing that is to add a supplementary output which indicates if the encoding present in the other outputs is valid. This output will be active whenever there is at least one active input and will remain inactive when there is none.

The second aspect has a more complex solution. The problem is the hypothesis of more than one input being active, which, in our previous solution, we considered as don't cares. If such a combination occurs, the circuit, which is not designed for this eventuality, will respond either by ignoring one of the inputs or supplying a configuration in the output which does not correspond to any of the active inputs. For example, if inputs $I1$ and $I3$ are active, the circuit will respond with the output configuration 011 corresponding to the input $I3$. In the case of the active inputs being, for example, $I3$ and $I6$, the response will be 111, corresponding to the input $I7$, which is not active.

The solution to this problem involves clarifying the behaviour that the circuit should have, when more than one input is active, and design the circuit accordingly. There are two solutions. One of them corresponds to only validating the output when there is only one active input. This is an extension of the answer to the previous problem.

A more useful solution with greater potential regarding applications is, however, that of introducing an order of priorities in the inputs, in such a way that the input actually encoded in the output will be that which has the highest priority. The order usually chosen corresponds to the attribution of highest priority to input $I7$ and the lowest to input $I0$, with successively lower priorities for the intermediate ones. The inverse order can also be used.

Table 4.7 shows the specification of an encoder with a validation output and with priority in its inputs, with $I7$ as the highest priority input. This circuit is called a *priority encoder*.

Note that, keeping a very compact formulation, thanks to the use of indifferences, the table is now a complete table with the implicit representation of the 256 possible configurations of the input variables. Obtaining the output functions is easy if the more classical methods are not used and if a more

Table 4.7   Complete table of the 8-line-to-3-line priority encoder.

Input Configuration								Encoding	Data Valid
$I7$	$I6$	$I5$	$I4$	$I3$	$I2$	$I1$	$I0$	$O_2\,O_1\,O_0$	DVAL
0	0	0	0	0	0	0	0	0 0 0	0
0	0	0	0	0	0	0	1	0 0 0	1
0	0	0	0	0	0	1	X	0 0 1	1
0	0	0	0	0	1	X	X	0 1 0	1
0	0	0	0	1	X	X	X	0 1 1	1
0	0	0	1	X	X	X	X	1 0 0	1
0	0	1	X	X	X	X	X	1 0 1	1
0	1	X	X	X	X	X	X	1 1 0	1
1	X	X	X	X	X	X	X	1 1 1	1

heuristic approach is taken. For example, the function referring to the valid data, which is designated by DV, will be given by Equation (4.3).

$$DV = I0 + I1 + I2 + I3 + I4 + I5 + I6 + I7. \qquad (4.3)$$

As for the functions O_i it is not difficult, through direct reading of the table, to extract Equations (4.4).

$$O_0 = I1\ \overline{I2}\ \overline{I3}\ \overline{I4}\ \overline{I5}\ \overline{I6}\ \overline{I7} + I3\ \overline{I4}\ \overline{I5}\ \overline{I6}\ \overline{I7} + I5\ \overline{I6}\ \overline{I7} + I7,$$
$$O_1 = I2\ \overline{I3}\ \overline{I4}\ \overline{I5}\ \overline{I6}\ \overline{I7} + I3\ \overline{I4}\ \overline{I5}\ \overline{I6}\ \overline{I7} + I6\ \overline{I7} + I7, \qquad (4.4)$$
$$O_2 = I4\ \overline{I5}\ \overline{I6}\ \overline{I7} + I5\ \overline{I6}\ \overline{I7} + I6\ \overline{I7} + I7.$$

Using algebraic techniques described in Chapter 2 to manipulate the functions leads to Equations (4.5), which are considerably simpler.

$$O_0 = I1\ \overline{I2}\ \overline{I4}\ \overline{I6} + I3\ \overline{I4}\ \overline{I6} + I5\ \overline{I6} + I7,$$
$$O_1 = I2\ \overline{I4}\ \overline{I5} + I3\ \overline{I4}\ \overline{I5} + I6 + I7, \qquad (4.5)$$
$$O_2 = I4 + I5 + I6 + I7.$$

4.4   Multiplexers

The *multiplexer* is a very common circuit in digital systems. A multiplexer is a circuit which selects one of its inputs and outputs its value. Therefore, the multiplexer has data inputs, from which it selects one, and control or selection inputs, which enable it to choose which of the data inputs is placed at the output. A four-input data multiplexer, for example, will have the symbol shown in Figure 4.13. For ease and clarity, the word

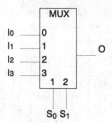

Fig. 4.13   Symbol for a four-input multiplexer.

Table 4.8   Condensed table of the operation of a multiplexer.

S_1	S_0	O
0	0	$I0$
0	1	$I1$
1	0	$I2$
1	1	$I3$

Table 4.9   Expanded table of the functioning of a multiplexer.

Data Inputs				Selection Inputs		Output
$I3$	$I2$	$I1$	$I0$	S_1	S_0	O
X	X	X	0	0	0	0
X	X	X	1	0	0	1
X	X	0	X	0	1	0
X	X	1	X	0	1	1
X	0	X	X	1	0	0
X	1	X	X	1	0	1
0	X	X	X	1	1	0
1	X	X	X	1	1	1

"Multiplexer" is substituted by the abbreviation "MUX" in this type of representation.

Inputs I_i are the *data inputs*, and S_i are *selection inputs*. The binary number placed in the pair S_1 S_0 determines which input value is placed at the output. The functional description of the behaviour described is shown in Table 4.8. This table is not a classical truth table for the output function O of the multiplexer as a function of the input variables. In fact, it is a very condensed representation of that table. However, it does have the advantage of being much more readable and clear.

The same functional description in a classical truth table, even if simplified through the use of indifferences, is much less clear, as can be seen in Table 4.9.

4.4.1 *Implementation of Multiplexers*

The internal structure of the multiplexer is easy to understand and a simple version is shown in Figure 4.14.

The decoder has the multiplex selection lines as inputs and activates only one output line at any given time. If for example, we have the configuration $S_1S_0 = 10$, only the output line 2 of the decoder is active. Consequently, all the AND gates, except the one connected to the active line of the decoder (2, in the example), have an input at 0 and, therefore, the output at 0. The output O of the multiplexer will, therefore, be equal to the line Ii selected by this process (in the example, $I2$).

An alternative implementation of the same circuit, which does not require the explicit decoder, and which has fewer layers of gates and, therefore, is faster, is shown in Figure 4.15, and should now be easy to understand.

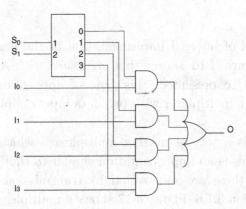

Fig. 4.14 Possible implementation of a multiplexer with four data inputs.

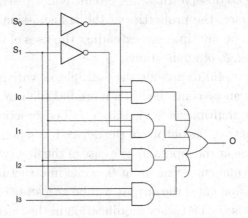

Fig. 4.15 Alternative implementation of a multiplexer with four data inputs.

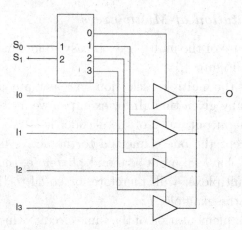

Fig. 4.16   Implementation of a multiplexer with four data inputs using tri-state buffers.

The third form of internal implementation of the multiplexer uses tri-state buffers. Figure 4.16 shows this structure. In Section 3.1.6, when tri-state buffers were presented, this type of application was mentioned. Figure 3.12 shows a multiplexer with two data inputs implemented with this approach.

Finally, there is a way of making multiplexers which do not use only digital circuits. This is an implementation similar to that based on tri-state buffers, in which these are substituted by transmission gates, as already mentioned in Section 3.1.6. Figure 4.17 shows a multiplexer built using that approach.

It is interesting to observe that this circuit is not restricted to multiplex digital signals. In fact, the properties of the transmission gates also enable analogue signals to be multiplexed, extending the uses of this type of circuit to a much wider range of applications.

Sometimes it is useful to provide the multiplexer with an enable input so that its operation can be controlled in a more flexible way. An active enable signal provides the multiplexer with the described functionality. When the enable signal is inactive, the output of the device is not active, independently of what is happening at the inputs. In the case of the first two examples given, the output will permanently remain at 0, while in structures using tri-state buffers or transmission gates the output will be at a state of high impedance.

Figure 4.18 shows the necessary modification in the third structure shown above, as an example, to include the enable line.

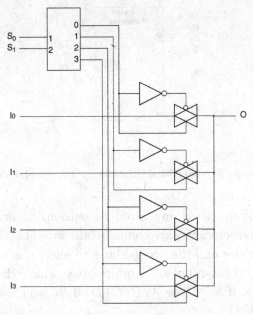

Fig. 4.17 Implementation of a multiplexer with four data inputs using transmission gates.

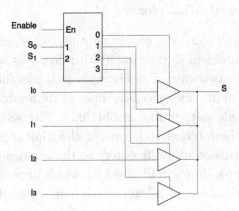

Fig. 4.18 Implementation of the multiplexer four data inputs using tri-state buffers, with enable input.

4.4.2 Types of Multiplexers

The multiplexers studied until now are circuits that place at its "1"-bit output, one of several input bits, selected by the selection lines. Through a simple combined use of several multiplexers, there is nothing to prevent the construction of circuits which provide for the selection, not of isolated

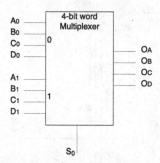

Fig. 4.19   Symbol of a multiplexer for two four-bit words.

bits, but rather of words of any given dimension. Several integrated circuits with these characteristics are commercially available. Multiplexers with words of moderate size and the needed lines to select one word are common. Figure 4.19 shows the symbol of a multiplexer which chooses one of two words ($A_0\, B_0\, C_0\, D_0$ if $S_0 = 0$ or $A_1\, B_1\, C_1\, D_1$ if $S_1 = 1$), and places it at the outputs, $O_A\, O_B\, O_C\, O_D$.

4.4.3   *Expansion of Multiplexers*

The *expansion of multiplexers* to obtain multiplexers with a larger number of inputs is a similar problem to that found with decoders, studied before, and can be carried out in two ways. The first approach uses the actual concept of the multiplexer to multiplex successive lines of data into a smaller number of lines until a single output line is obtained. The second approach uses the knowledge of the internal structure of the multiplexers to reduce the problem of the expansion of multiplexers to the expansion of their internal decoders. The example shown in Figure 4.20, which implements a multiplexer with sixteen inputs using multiplexers with four inputs, illustrates the first option.

Note that, once again, for larger systems, the solution is to use successive layers of devices until the required depth is reached. This solution does not require the multiplexers to have enable inputs. If it is necessary for the set to have an enable line, this can be present in just the multiplexer in the last layer.

The variant of the same system using expansion through decoders is illustrated in Figure 4.21. Note that this type of solution requires the multiplexers to have an enable input. It should also be noted that the OR gate at the output is not necessary if working with multiplexers with tri-state outputs.

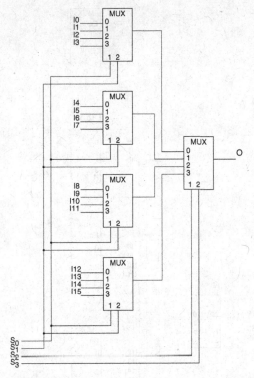

Fig. 4.20 Construction of a multiplexer with sixteen inputs using multiplexers of four inputs.

4.4.4 *Multiplexing and Demultiplexing*

The main application of multiplexers is that of implementing *multiplexing* and *demultiplexing* for a set of signals. The goal is to transfer one of several input signals through a single line, placing the signal transmitted on the reception side in one of several possible output lines. Also, in a more local type of application, it is important to be able to select, among several signals, the one that, at each moment, must be chosen to be processed by another given circuit.

Demultiplexing should be carried out by a *demultiplexer*. This circuit must have a data input and several outputs. Data received in the input line is placed in one of the outputs, selected through a set of selection lines. Figure 4.22 shows the symbol of a circuit of this type. Note that the abbreviated designation "DEMUX", can substitute the longer name "demultiplexer". The demultiplexer circuit will have the function specified by Table 4.10.

A brief comparative analysis of Table 4.10 with Table 4.5 enables us to conclude that, although the application of a demultiplexer is conceptually

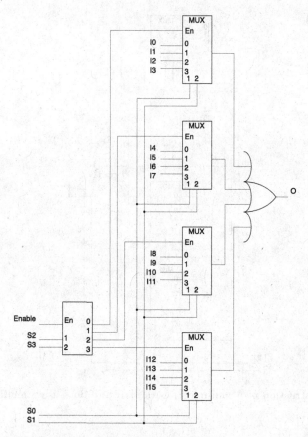

Fig. 4.21 Alternative structure for a multiplexer with sixteen inputs using multiplexers of four inputs.

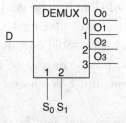

Fig. 4.22 Symbol for a demultiplexer.

different from that of a decoder, the desired operation of these modules is the same, implying that the same circuit does indeed have two applications. It is the interpretation of the operation that is different.

Figure 4.23 shows a circuit which enables four lines to be multiplexed into a single line and later recovered. Note that, if the input selection variables

Table 4.10   Table for a demultiplexer.

Selection inputs		Data input	Outputs			
S_1	S_0	D	$O0$	$O1$	$O2$	$O3$
0	0	0	0	0	0	0
0	0	1	1	0	0	0
0	1	0	0	0	0	0
0	1	1	0	1	0	0
1	0	0	0	0	0	0
1	0	1	0	0	1	0
1	1	0	0	0	0	0
1	1	1	0	0	0	1

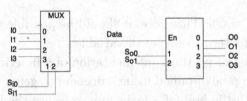

Fig. 4.23   Use of the multiplexer and a decoder for four-line multiplexing and demultiplexing.

S_{i0} and S_{i1} have a configuration identical to the output selection variables S_{o0} and S_{o1}, the value present in the line selected is delivered in the corresponding line at the output. If the configurations are different, it is possible to implement signal switching, thereby adding a new functionality to this circuit.

4.5   Implementation of Logic Functions with Modules of Medium Complexity

The various modules presented in this chapter should be seen by designers as building blocks with a particular functionality, but with potential for other uses in addition to those initially shown. One of the most common options is to use these modules as usable *logic blocks to implement logic functions*. Some cases will be studied below.

4.5.1   *Implementation with Decoders*

The binary decoder implements all the minterms of the input variables in its outputs. In fact, each output of a decoder is a product of literals, which are always all the input variables, inverted or not. For example, the output

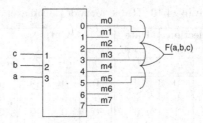

Fig. 4.24   Implementation of the function $F(a, b, c) = \sum m(0, 2, 3, 5)$ using a decoder.

S_3 of the decoder of Figure 4.8 is given by Expression (4.6).

$$O3 = \overline{I_2} \, I_1 \, I_0. \tag{4.6}$$

Hence, clearly, $m_3 = O3$. Therefore, it should be possible to use the decoder to obtain all the minterms of a set of variables.

In these circumstances, the implementation of a function in the form of a sum of minterms can be obtained using a decoder to generate all the possible minterms and, with the help of a logic sum, produce the intended function. Figure 4.24 shows a circuit, which uses this principle, and which implements the logic function. $F(a, b, c) = \sum m(0, 2, 3, 5)$.

4.5.2   *Implementation with Multiplexers*

As was the case with decoders, it is possible to use multiplexers to implement logic functions. This application is possible because, internally, the multiplexer generates a sum of products of all combinations of values of the selection variables, i.e., a sum of the minterms of these variables. Consider the multiplexer illustrated in Figure 4.25. The output of the circuit has Expression (4.7).

$$O = \overline{S_1} \, \overline{S_0} \, I_0 + \overline{S_1} \, S_0 \, I_1 + S_1 \, \overline{S_0} \, I_2 + S_1 \, S_0 \, I_3. \tag{4.7}$$

The variables I_i can be viewed as programming lines that enable minterms m_i to be present in the expression of O. Depending on the values of the variables I_i different sums of products of variables S_i, i.e., different functions of these variables are chosen.

Let us, for example, take the function described in Table 4.11.

Using a multiplexer with two selection lines and four data lines (as many as the rows of the table), let us start by connecting the variables of the function to the selection lines of the multiplexer and, respecting the weight order as shown in Figure 4.26.

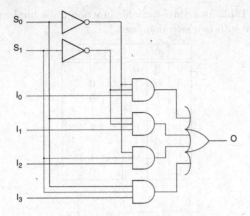

Fig. 4.25   Multiplexer with four data inputs.

Table 4.11   Table of a function being implemented using a multiplexer.

a	b	$f(a,b)$
0	0	0
0	1	1
1	0	1
1	1	0

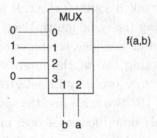

Fig. 4.26   Implementation of the function $f(a,b)$ using a multiplexer.

When $a = 0$ and $b = 0$, the multiplexer selects the value in data line 0 for its output. With that configuration of the input variables, the function has the value 0 (first row of the table). If the logic value 0 is connected to the 0 input of the multiplexer, when $a = b = 0$, it will show the value of the function for that configuration at its output. If we do the same for the rest of the multiplexer inputs and the respective rows of the table, the multiplexer will implement the whole function. This methodology enables the construction of any function of n variables when using a multiplexer with n selection variables.

Table 4.12   Table for a three-variable function to be implemented using a multiplexer with two selection lines.

a	b	c	$f(a,b,c)$
0	0	0	0
0	0	1	0
0	1	0	0
0	1	1	1
1	0	0	1
1	0	1	1
1	1	0	1
1	1	1	0

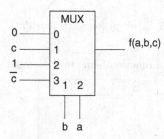

Fig. 4.27   Implementation of the function $f(a,b,c)$ using a multiplexer.

But this process can be taken a step further. It is possible to implement a three-variable function using the same multiplexer with two selection inputs in a relatively easy way. Let us consider, the function described in Table 4.12.

Let us start by connecting two of the input variables to the selection inputs of the multiplexer. Any two may be selected, but the technique will be easier to understand if the two with greater weight are chosen, a and b. Connect them as previously described, as shown in Figure 4.27.

Note what happens now when $a = 0$ and $b = 0$. The multiplexer selects the data input 0. The function has two rows, in the table in which $a = 0$ and $b = 0$, which only differ in the value of the variable c. For both, the value of the function is 0. Therefore, as in the previous case, the connection of that input to the logic value 0 enables the output of the multiplexer to correspond to the value of the function for these two configurations. In the following situation, $a = 0$ and $b = 1$, the function does not have the same value for the two rows. Indeed, in this case, the function is 0 when $c = 0$ and is 1 when $c = 1$. That is, in this *slice* of the table, the function is c. Therefore, the data input 1 of the multiplexer connects to c. The function table can be restructured by showing its behaviour in the various slices, as shown in Table 4.13. Therefore the circuit represented in Figure 4.27, illustrates

Table 4.13   Table modified for the function under consideration.

a	b	c	$f(a,b,c)$	
0	0	0	0	$f = 0$
0	0	1	0	
0	1	0	0	$f = c$
0	1	1	1	
1	0	0	1	$f = 1$
1	0	1	1	
1	1	0	1	$f = \bar{c}$
1	1	1	0	

the implementation of the function under consideration. Note that in the example chosen all the possible configurations of variable c are present in the slices of the table. Therefore, it is always feasible to use this technique to represent a function of $n + 1$ variables using a multiplexer with n selection variables and, possibly, a gate NOT. There are only four possible functions of the variable $n + 1$: the constants 0 and 1, the variable itself and the negated variable. Any of these functions can be used as input to the multiplexer, leading to a flexible and economic way to implement functions of $n + 1$ variables.

This idea may be extended to implement functions of $n + m$ variables with multiplexers with n selection variables and functions with m variables in the data inputs of the multiplexer.

4.6   Iterative Circuits

In the various types of modules previously described in this chapter, it was always more or less explicitly assumed that their design was carried out globally. However, in certain types of circuits, it is preferable to deal with the problem in a different way seeking, as was the case with the first example regarding the lighting of a corridor, to find a structure based on a juxtaposition of a set of equal modules. *Iterative circuits* are circuits made up of a sequence of equal circuits or *cells* interconnected in a regular manner. This section will provide more details of this concept and a comparator circuit for binary numbers will be designed using this technique.

We use iterative circuits when there is a significant number of inputs, and it is possible to organise the circuit into a sequence of modules. These modules consider the value of some *primary inputs*, as well as aggregated information from the set of inputs processed by previous modules in the sequence called *cascading inputs*. Each module calculates its direct *primary*

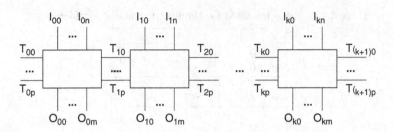

Fig. 4.28   Structure of an iterative circuit.

outputs and, also, a set of outputs which encapsulate the relevant information to pass to the next module in the sequence, the *cascading outputs*. The use of this type of circuit enables the design of combinational modules, which are regular, in a simple way. Instead of designing a circuit with a large number of inputs, it is, therefore, possible to divide the circuit into a certain number of equal cells with a much smaller number of inputs.

An iterative circuit will, therefore, have the structured illustrated in Figure 4.28. Cell i receives primary inputs of the circuit (I_{ij}), and also cascading inputs coming from the previous cell (T_{il}), and produces primary outputs (O_{ip}) and cascading outputs destined for the next cell $(T_{(i+1)l})$. Although in principle, the circulation of information between cells is unidirectional, it is possible to design iterative circuits with bidirectional information transmitted between cells if the possibility of unstable situations is prevented.

To illustrate the design of this type of circuit, let us consider a typical example of a *comparator circuit*. The comparator has as entries two n bits binary numbers A and B and indicates if they are the same or different and, in the latter case, which one is larger. It is possible to design a circuit as a set of functions of $2n$ input variables, but, for a value of n minimally interesting, the number of variables makes the use of classical methods for their synthesis not viable.

We begin by dividing the circuit into cells which deal with only one bit of each of the numbers. Cell i, therefore, has bits A_i and B_i, as primary inputs. The previous cell provides information about the analysis of the number up to the previous bit, and the following cell receives information about the analysis up to bit i. In this organisation, the order in which the bits are analysed has to be defined. It is possible to use either of two possible orders, that is, with the cells which analyse the most significant bits passing information to the corresponding cells of the least significant bits, or in the inverse order. In the example, we assume that the order of analysis starts with the most significant bit down to the least significant bit. As will be seen, in this circuit there are no primary outputs of the cells, there are final outputs.

An interesting point is the definition of the information necessary between cells. In the case of the comparator, the first cell will compare the most significant bits of the two numbers. If they are equal, the information to be transmitted is that, until that bit, the numbers do not differ. If on the contrary, they are different, either $A > B$ or $A < B$ will have to be indicated. Note that, if the most significant bit of one of the numbers is 1, and the other is 0, the first number is greater than the second. If on the contrary, they are the same, nothing can be concluded, and the following bits will have to be considered.

The architecture of the circuit is, therefore, that which is illustrated in Figure 4.29. The cascading outputs of the last cell will be the final outputs of the circuit. Note that 2 bits would be enough to pass information between the cells since there are only three different types of information that have to be encoded. However, the use of three line simplifies the interpretation of the circuit and does not make it more complex.

The internal structure of each cell can now be determined in two possible ways: either the table of output functions is defined, or the expression of the output functions is directly determined, by analysing the expected behaviour. Using this latter method, let us consider cell i. This cell has the variables A_i and B_i as its primary inputs and $(A > B)_i$, $(A = B)_i$ and $(A < B)i$ as inputs from the previous cell.

Consider the function $(A > B)_{i-1}$. This cell considers that $A > B$ under two conditions: the previous cell has already concluded that, or, in the case of the previous cell indicating that, until then, $A = B$, if $A_i = 1$ and $B_i = 0$ in this cell. It is then easier to define Expression (4.8).

$$(A > B)_{i-1} = (A > B)_i + (A = B)_i A_i \overline{B_i}. \tag{4.8}$$

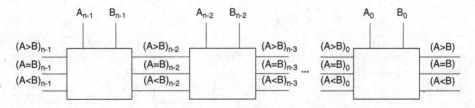

Fig. 4.29   Structure of an iterative comparator.

In the same way, the Expressions (4.9) and (4.10) can be defined.

$$(A = B)_{i-1} = (A = B)_i \, A_i \, B_i + (A = B)_i \, \overline{A_i} \, \overline{B_i}, \qquad (4.9)$$

$$(A < B)_{i-1} = (A < B)_i + (A = B)_i \, \overline{A_i} \, B_i. \qquad (4.10)$$

The circuit of the cell will, therefore, be the one shown in Figure 4.30.

The interconnection of n cells of this type, with the structure shown in Figure 4.29, leads to a comparator with numbers of n bits. Figure 4.31 shows a comparator for four-bit numbers. The inputs to the cell corresponding to the most significant bits should be placed at values which enable the first cell to decide non-conditionally, that is, this should be $(A > B)_3 = (A < B)_3 = 0$ and $(A = B_3) = 1$. If the comparator is considered for the numbers $A = 12$ and $B = 10$, for example, the sequence of signals is shown in the same figure, given that $12_{10} = 1100_2$ and $10_{10} = 1010_2$.

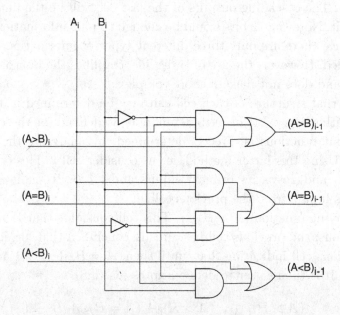

Fig. 4.30   An iterative comparator cell.

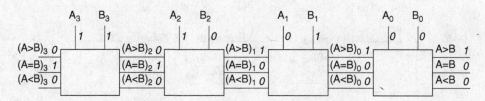

Fig. 4.31   Illustration of the functioning of an iterative comparator with four bit numbers.

An important aspect, which should be considered when connecting modules in the systematic manner that is described in this section, is the possible circuit operation speed. As we saw above, the sum of the delays of the logic gates throughout the critical path determines the reaction time for the circuit and, as a result, the maximum speed at which it can be operated when included in a system.

As an example, take the comparator in Figure 4.29, implemented with the cells of Figure 4.30. Each cell will impose, between the inputs receiving the previous module, and the outputs sent to the following module, a delay of two logic gates. A composition of N cells, to implement an N-bit comparator, will thus show a total delay equivalent to that of $2N$ logic gates.

For a comparator of 32 bits, this means a delay of 64 gates, which can be too much for many applications. With other implementations of the same comparator, it will be possible to obtain significantly faster response times.

In many cases, circuits which can be implemented in an iterative manner, such as comparators, adders and multipliers are exactly those which limit digital circuit performance. To avoid the severe limitations imposed by the use of simple iterative circuits, such as those described in this section, techniques have been developed to construct faster circuits, based on more complex interconnection schemes. Some of these techniques will be considered in later chapters.

4.7 Summary

This chapter addresses the design of digital systems based on modules of medium complexity. It begins by introducing the concept of modularity and an approach to design using the division of circuits into simpler modules. Three types of logic modules are studied, with a focus on their architectures, as well as their typical applications and expansion methods: decoders, encoders and multiplexers. Methods for the use of modules of this type to implement logic functions are also described. The chapter ends with a discussion of the use of iterative circuits for the design of modules that have words as input instead of simple configurations of bits.

Exercises

4.1 Design the logic diagram for a BCD/decimal decoder.

4.2 Design a transcoder that accepts in its inputs a BCD digit, and supplies in its outputs the required code to light a display of seven segments representing the input digit. The seven segments code is a way of representing digits through seven line segments with an arrangement shown in the following figure:

4.3 Using only binary decoders with two inputs, construct a binary decoder with six inputs.

4.4 Using only two binary decoders with two data inputs and 2-input AND gates, construct a binary decoder with four inputs.
Suggestion: consider the hypothesis of combining the outputs of the two decoders.

4.5 Using a BCD/decimal decoder as the base element,

(a) Implement the function $f(A, B, C, D) = \sum m(0, 1, 2, 4, 8)$.
(b) With a decoder of this type, all the functions of four variables cannot be implemented. Why?
(c) It can therefore be considered that the function $f(A, B, C, D) = \sum m(0, 8, 10, 11, 13)$ is one of those which cannot be implemented. However, it can be implemented. How?

4.6 Consider the priority encoder shown in Section 4.3. Starting from this design, add an enable line. Using this encoder as a basic block, construct a priority encoder for 32 inputs.

4.7 Using a binary decoder with three input variables as a base element, and any additional logic considered necessary, construct the four functions described in the following table:

x	y	z	$f_0(x, y, z)$	$f_1(x, y, z)$	$f_2(x, y, z)$	$f_3(x, y, z)$
0	0	0	0	1	0	0
0	0	1	0	0	1	0
0	1	0	0	0	1	0
0	1	1	1	0	1	1
1	0	0	0	1	0	0
1	0	1	1	1	0	0
1	1	0	0	1	0	0
1	1	1	1	0	1	0

4.8 Using tri-state buffers and minimal additional logic considered necessary, construct a multiplexer with eight data inputs.

4.9 Consider that multiplexers with three selection variables and tri-state output controlled by an enable input are available. Design a multiplexer of 64 inputs with an architecture that takes advantage of the tri-state outputs.

4.10 As we saw in Section 3.4.2 spurious transitions may occur in a combinational circuit if concrete measures are not taken. Is it possible to carry out these types of care in a function implemented based on a multiplexer? Why?

4.11 Consider the circuit in the following figure.

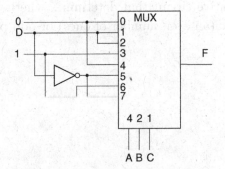

What is the logic function implemented by the circuit?

4.12 Consider the circuit represented in the following figure which implements the logic function F. Implement the same function using a multiplexer with three selection variables. Repeat, using a multiplexer with two selection variables as a base.

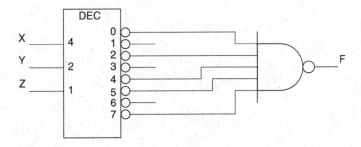

4.13 Consider the logic function

$$f(A, B, C, D, E) = B\ C\ \overline{D} + \overline{B}\ D\ E + \overline{A}\ B\ C$$
$$+ C\ E + \overline{A}\ B\ \overline{C}\ D\ \overline{E}.$$

Implement it using a multiplexer with three selection variables and any logic considered necessary.

Tip: when a multiplexer with n selection variables is used to implement functions of $n + 1$ variables, functions of one variable are used in the data inputs of the multiplexer.

4.14 Based on a comparator circuit, construct a circuit that, having received two binary numbers of 8 bits, places the largest one in its output. In the solution adopted, what happens when the two numbers are equal?

4.15 Design an iterative circuit that determines whether a sequence of bits has even parity (an even number of ones) or odd parity.

Chapter 5

Arithmetic Circuits

This chapter studies an important class of combinational circuits, the arithmetic circuits. For these type of circuits, the set of inputs (operands) and outputs (result) bits uses a numeric encoding. As with nearly all existing systems, this text assumes that the operands and result use the natural binary code notation, which we studied in Section 1.1, or one of its variations to enable the representation of negative values, which we will examine in this chapter. Thus, each combination of input bits is interpreted as a base-2 numeric value, and the output represents the result of a given arithmetic operation on the numeric input values.

Given their characteristics, the techniques for designing iterative circuits are generally used, as presented in Section 4.6. In this way, arithmetic modules are developed such that they operate on the same order bit of each operand, with the arithmetic operation on operands of n bits achieved through the integration of n of these modules. This approach enables us to implement logic circuits for operands with a large number of bits, which would be impractical using the synthesis techniques described in Chapter 2.

Section 5.1 starts by analysing the adder circuit, since it is the simplest operation. Before going on to analyse the functioning of a subtractor, in Section 5.2.6, new numerical encodings are defined in Section 5.2 which enable the representation of negative integers. Section 5.3 then considers multiplication and division circuits.

In many applications, numeric values are not integers but fractional values. This chapter presents two ways of representing fractions: fixed-point representation and floating-point representation. Fixed-point representation, studied in Section 5.4, allows the arithmetic circuits studied up to there to be used almost directly. However, for many applications, the range of possible values using this representation is too limited. Section 5.5 introduces the floating-point representation, which greatly increases this range, but involves more complex arithmetic circuits.

5.1   Adders

This section analyses the *adder circuit* with two operands in natural binary code. At the level of block diagrams, this circuit can have the representation shown in Figure 5.1. This representation just indicates that the output S of the circuit will have a binary value which corresponds to the sum of the two operands A and B and does not say anything about the implementation of the adder. Indeed, there are many possible implementations of an adder, some of which we will study in this section.

In Figure 5.1, the block diagram of the adder has only two input lines, one for each operand. However, note that these lines have a thicker form, indicating that there are n bits being input for each operand. Such a group of lines together as a set is given the name *bus*. To better illustrate this representation, Figure 5.2 shows a bus four bits wide. The term *bus-width* is often used to indicate the number of bits in a bus. As such, Figure 5.2 shows a bus with a four-bit width.

Note that in the case of an adder circuit, the output value uses $n+1$ bits, to take into account the possible carry of the sum of the most significant bit of the operands, as mentioned in Section 1.2.1.

5.1.1   *Half-Adder*

The simplest way to implement an adder circuit is to follow the algebraic procedure. Section 1.2.1 introduced the binary sum operation. To recall, let

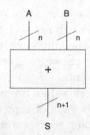

Fig. 5.1   Representation of an adder in a block diagram.

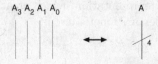

Fig. 5.2   Example of a four-bit bus representation.

us consider the example of the sum of the four-bit values $A = 1011b$ and $B = 1110b$, the result of which is $S = 11001b$ and in which the carry bits, C, are explicitly represented:

$$
\begin{array}{rccccc}
A & & 1 & 0 & 1 & 1 \\
B & + & 1 & 1 & 1 & 0 \\
\hline
S & 1 & 1 & 0 & 0 & 1 \\
C & & 1 & 1 & 1 & 0 & \text{carry}
\end{array}
$$

The bits of the result are generated from the least significant (on the right) to the most significant (on the left). Therefore, to generate the least significant bit of the result, S_0, only the least significant bit of each of the operands, A_0 and B_0, are of interest. We can list all the possible combinations of the input values with the corresponding values for the result and carry, as given in Table 5.1.

A quick look at this table enables us to conclude that the least significant bit of the sum is the XOR function of the least significant bits of the input operands, while the carry bit is an AND of the two. Figure 5.3 shows the corresponding logic circuit.

This circuit is called a *half-adder*. By not accounting for an incoming carry bit, a half-adder circuit may only be used to implement the sum of the bit with least weight.

Table 5.1 Result and carry bit for the sum of the least significant bit.

A_0	B_0	C_0	S_0
0	0	0	0
0	1	0	1
1	0	0	1
1	1	1	0

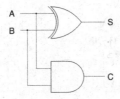

Fig. 5.3 Logic circuit for a half-adder.

5.1.2   *Full-Adder*

To calculate the bit of order i of the result, S_i, it is necessary to account for not only the respective bits of the operands, A_i and B_i but also the carry bit generated by the sum of the bits with the immediately lower order, C_{i-1}. Table 5.2 shows the truth table for this case which is obtained by simple binary calculation of the different possibilities. The first observation is that the three inputs are equivalent. If the three are 0, then the result will be 0, that is, $C_i = S_i = 0$. If only one of them is 1, then the result is 1, there is no carry, $C_i = 0$, and the result is 1, $S_i = 1$. If two of them are 1, then there will be a carry, $C_i = 1$, but the result is 0, $S_i = 0$. If the three are 1, then $C_i = S_i = 1$.

We cannot readily obtain the logic functions from this table by simple inspection. The Karnaugh maps for the two outputs are represented in Figure 5.4.

From these maps, and with the marked loops, we obtain the following logic functions:

$$C_i = A_i\, B_i + A_i\, C_{i-1} + B_i\, C_{i-1} \tag{5.1}$$

and

$$S_i = \overline{A_i}\, \overline{B_i}\, C_{i-1} + \overline{A_i}\, B_i\, \overline{C_{i-1}} + A_i\, B_i\, C_{i-1} + A_i\, \overline{B_i}\, \overline{C_{i-1}}. \tag{5.2}$$

Table 5.2   Result and carry bit for the sum taking into account the previous carry bit.

A_i	B_i	C_{i-1}	C_i	S_i
0	0	0	0	0
0	0	1	0	1
0	1	0	0	1
0	1	1	1	0
1	0	0	0	1
1	0	1	1	0
1	1	0	1	0
1	1	1	1	1

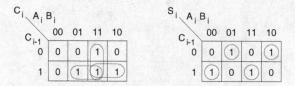

Fig. 5.4   Karnaugh map for the one-bit full-adder.

Through algebraic manipulation, it is possible to simplify this last expression, writing it using only XOR gates:

$$S_i = \overline{A_i}\,\overline{B_i}\,C_{i-1} + \overline{A_i}\,B_i\,\overline{C_{i-1}} + A_i\,B_i\,C_{i-1} + A_i\,\overline{B_i}\,\overline{C_{i-1}}$$

$$= \overline{A_i}\,(\overline{B_i}\,C_{i-1} + B_i\,\overline{C_{i-1}}) + A_i\,(B_i\,C_{i-1} + \overline{B_i}\,\overline{C_{i-1}})$$

$$= \overline{A_i}\,(B_i \oplus C_{i-1}) + A_i\,(\overline{B_i \oplus C_{i-1}})$$

$$= A_i \oplus B_i \oplus C_{i-1}. \tag{5.3}$$

Moreover, using some of the techniques of Chapter 2, the Expression (5.1) may be organised to reuse part of the logic of the generating function for S_i:

$$C_i = A_i\,B_i + A_i\,C_{i-1} + B_i\,C_{i-1}$$

$$= A_i\,B_i + C_{i-1}\,(A_i + B_i)$$

$$= A_i\,B_i + C_{i-1}\,((A_i \oplus B_i) + A_i\,B_i)$$

$$= A_i\,B_i + C_{i-1}\,A_i\,B_i + C_{i-1}\,(A_i \oplus B_i)$$

$$= A_i\,B_i + C_{i-1}\,(A_i \oplus B_i). \tag{5.4}$$

The logic circuit constructed with the simplified expressions for C_i and S_i calculated above is given the name *full-adder*, and is presented in Figure 5.5. Observe that it is possible to organise the logic gates so that the one-bit adder circuit is made up of two half-adder circuits and one OR gate. This solution makes sense because we are adding another bit, the carry bit C_{i-1}, to the sum of A_i and B_i.

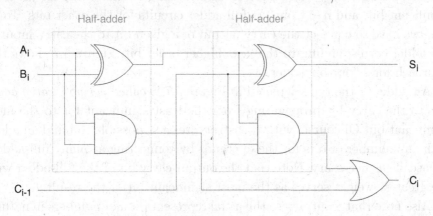

Fig. 5.5 Logic circuit for a one-bit full-adder.

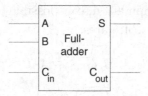

Fig. 5.6   Terminal model for a one-bit full-adder with input C_{in} and output C_{out}.

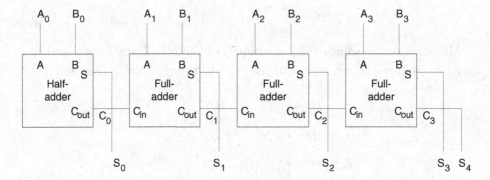

Fig. 5.7   Example of a four-bit ripple carry adder.

Generally, in a full-adder, the input carry bit is given the name C_{in} and the output carry bit the name C_{out}. A one-bit full-adder may, therefore, be represented as shown in Figure 5.6.

5.1.3   *N-bit Adder*

Following the methodology outlined in the previous chapter for iterative circuits, we can easily build an n-bit adder, using an half-adder for the least significant bit, and $n - 1$ one-bit full-adder circuits for the other bits. To do this, we have to connect the carry output of a given bit to the carry input of the adder corresponding to the next higher order bit. Figure 5.7 shows this approach for a four-bit adder.

An adder of the type depicted in Figure 5.7 is called a *ripple carry adder* due to the carry bit propagating from the least significant bit to the most significant bit. Of course, with this structure, it is possible to build an adder with any number of bits for the operands by connecting as many full-adders in cascade as necessary. Note that the output carry bit of the full-adder with the greatest weight serves as the most significant bit of the result.

Also note that, contrary to the usual representation of numbers in natural binary, in the circuit in Figure 5.7 the bit of least weight is to be found on the left side. This inversion is related to the convention that signals propagate from left to right in logic diagrams. Therefore, it is convenient to represent full-adder circuits of least weight to the left, since these generate the carry bits for the adders of greatest weight, without complicating the figure too much.

A variation of this circuit in cascade allows us to take this reasoning a little further. Figure 5.8 shows the same four-bit adder, with the difference that a full-adder is used for the lower order bit instead of a half-adder. This alteration adds one input carry to the adder, C_{in}, enabling adder modules of n bits to have the same type of cascade connection used for one-bit adders.

Figure 5.9 shows an example of an eight-bit adder built using a cascade connection of four-bit adder modules such as the one in Figure 5.8. The output C_{out} of the four-bit adder of least weight, bits 0 to 3, is used as the input carry bit for the input C_{in} of the four-bit adder of greatest weight, bits 4 to 7. In turn, the output C_{out} of the adder of 4 bits of greatest weight serves as the most significant bit of the result, S_8. Note that the input carry bit in the first adder is set to 0.

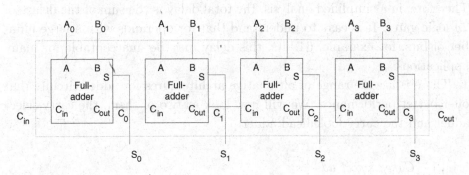

Fig. 5.8   Four-bit ripple carry adder considering an input carry bit C_{in}.

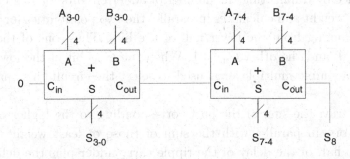

Fig. 5.9   Eight-bit adder using four-bit adders in cascade.

Therefore, through the interconnection of output carry bits, C_{out}, to input carry bits, C_{in}, it is possible to construct adders for operands with an arbitrary number of bits through the composition of smaller sized adder circuits.

5.1.4   *Fast Adders*

The ripple carry adders in cascade presented above are the simplest and most economical adders regarding hardware. However, they are also the slowest. The critical path of the circuit, as we saw in Section 3.4.1, is defined by the propagation of the carry signal from bit to bit across the connected modules. The total delay is then the sum of the delays of all the gates between the least significant bit of one of the operands (A_0 or B_0) and the most significant bit of the output (S_n). For an adder of n bits in cascade, the maximum delay corresponds to the sum of the delay of $n - 1$ AND gates plus $n - 1$ OR gates (for the propagation of the carry bit through the $n - 1$ levels), plus an AND gate and an OR gate from the first level (for the generation of C_1 from A_0 and B_0 – assuming a full-adder on the first level). Therefore, in a simplified analysis, the total delay is the sum of the delays of $2n$ logic gates. It is easy to understand that for operands with a large number of bits, for example, 64 bits, this delay may be unacceptable for many applications.

There is a wide range of alternative architectures for adder circuits that offer better performance. We will now look at two of them, the carry-select adder and the carry-lookahead adder.

5.1.4.1   *Carry-select adders*

Figure 5.10 shows an eight-bit *carry-select adder*. This architecture increases performance by duplicating the number of adder circuits for half of the bits of greatest weight and calculates in parallel the two possibilities for the carry bit value coming from the lower half of the bits. Thus, one of the circuits has $C_{in} = 0$, and the other $C_{in} = 1$. When the C_{out} bit of the lower half is available, a simple multiplexer is used to select the circuit that matches its value.

In this way, the sum of the part corresponding to the higher order bits is carried out in parallel with the sum of those of least weight. Delay is reduced to half of the delay of the ripple carry adder plus the delay added by the multiplexer. The penalty to pay is, of course, the amount of extra

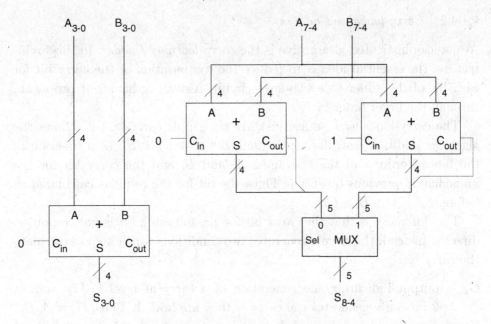

Fig. 5.10   Eight-bit carry-select adder.

hardware, the second adder circuit for the higher half and the multiplexer, which represents more than 50% of additional hardware when compared to an equivalent ripple carry adder.

Note that, assuming an average delay time of 1 ns per gate, an eight-bit adder constructed as shown in Figure 5.9 would have a total delay time of 17 ns. In comparison, the circuit shown in Figure 5.10 has a delay time of 12 ns, corresponding to 9 ns of delay for the adders (working in parallel) and 3 ns for the three gates the multiplexer has on its critical path. Of course, for larger sized adders, the difference tends to increase, making the advantage more evident. In an adder with 64 bits, for example, the two approaches result in delays of 129 ns and 68 ns, respectively.

We should mention that this technique can be applied recursively, to each of the halves: the lower half adder and the two adders for the higher half. Theoretically, for each additional level, the delay would be reduced by approximately half. Therefore, applying this technique to one more level, the delay will become roughly a quarter of the original ripple carry adder, then to an eighth, etc. However, in addition to the significant increase in hardware, the delays in the multiplexers selecting each level would quickly start to dominate the overall delay, undermining the predicted performance increase.

5.1.4.2   *Carry-lookahead adders*

A more sophisticated alternative is the *carry-lookahead adder*. In this architecture, the essential idea is to reduce the computation of the carry bit for each bit of the adder to a two-level circuit, instead of having it propagate through the lower order bits.

The carry-lookahead adder, just like the ripple carry adder, follows the algebraic addition, calculating the sum bit of order i, S_i, as a function of the bits of order i of the operands, A_i and B_i and the carry bit for the immediately previous bit, C_{i-1}. Thus, the bit for the result is calculated as before, $S_i = A_i \oplus B_i \oplus C_{i-1}$.

The difference is that the carry bit for the following bit is not computed directly. Instead, the circuit generates two conditions which help to calculate the carry bit:

G_i — output indicating the generation of a carry at level i. The sum of
2 bits only generates the carry is they are both 1. Thus, $G_i = A_i B_i$.
P_i — output which indicates that a carry coming from the previous level
propagates to the next level. It is easy to see that this situation occurs
when one of the 2 bits of the input operands is 1, that is, $P_i = A_i \oplus B_i$.

This is known as a *partial full-adder* and Figure 5.11 shows this circuit.

A carry-lookahead adder of n bits is not made up simply from the interconnection of the partial full-adder circuits. Some logic is necessary to generate the input carry bit from the generating and propagating conditions at each level. Generally, for the bit of order i, the carry bit can be calculated by

$$C_i = G_i + P_i\, C_{i-1}, \tag{5.5}$$

which is the solution used by the ripple carry adder. As we saw, the disadvantage is the generation of C_i from C_{i-1}, leading to a high propagation time. To reduce this delay, in the carry-lookahead adder the bit C_i is generated directly from the bits of the input operands.

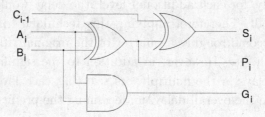

Fig. 5.11   Partial full-adder circuit.

For the least significant bit, this is simply

$$C_0 = G_0 + P_0\, C_{\text{in}}. \tag{5.6}$$

For the order 1 bit,

$$C_1 = G_1 + P_1\, C_0. \tag{5.7}$$

Substituting in this the expression of C_0, we obtain

$$C_1 = G_1 + P_1\, (G_0 + P_0\, C_{\text{in}})$$
$$= G_1 + P_1\, G_0 + P_1\, P_0\, C_{\text{in}}. \tag{5.8}$$

Using this approach for the order 2 bit we obtain:

$$C_2 = G_2 + P_2\, C_1$$
$$= G_2 + P_2\, (G_1 + P_1\, G_0 + P_1\, P_0\, C_{\text{in}})$$
$$= G_2 + P_2\, G_1 + P_2\, P_1\, G_0 + P_2\, P_1\, P_0\, C_{\text{in}}. \tag{5.9}$$

Using this logic, we can derive the four-bit carry-lookahead adder shown in Figure 5.12. Note that, as we saw above, the carry bit C_{in} at each level only serves as an input for the result S, with the outputs P and G determined directly from the bits of the operands.

The advantage of this architecture, as we saw above, is the reduced number of logic gates in the path from the inputs to the generation of the carry bit for any order bit, although at the cost of a considerable increase in the total number of gates in the circuit. The maximum delay corresponds to an

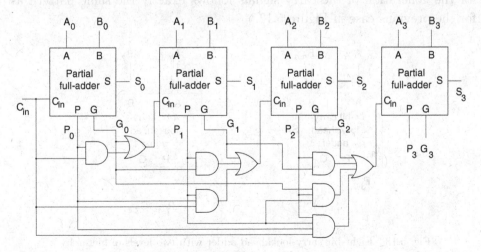

Fig. 5.12   Four-bit carry-lookahead adder.

XOR gate, generating the carry bit, plus an AND gate and another OR gate, regardless of the size of the adder.

There is a problem with this architecture, however. The logic for the generation of the carry bit becomes increasingly complicated for the most significant bits, requiring logic gates with many inputs, which, for technological reasons, makes them slower.

The solution once again is to use a hierarchical approach, in which, for instance, the four-bit adder circuit of Figure 5.12 becomes a module for a larger size adder. For the second level of the hierarchy to use the technique of carry-lookahead adders, the four-bit adder module must provide bits indicating the generating and the propagating conditions for the carry bit by this group of 4 bits. The condition for a carry bit at the input of the four-bit adder, C_{in}, to be propagated by the group of 4 bits is simply a combination of the propagation conditions:

$$P_{3-0} = P_3 P_2 P_1 P_0. \tag{5.10}$$

The generating condition will be a logic sum of the generation at each bit, along with the condition that this is propagated until the last bit of the group of 4 bits:

$$G_{3-0} = G_3 + G_2 P_3 + G_1 P_3 P_2 + G_0 P_3 P_2 P_1. \tag{5.11}$$

Figure 5.13 shows the construction of an eight-bit adder using the carry-lookahead technique with two levels of hierarchy. Note that the external logic for the generation of the carry signals follows exactly the same pattern as for the previous case in Figure 5.12.

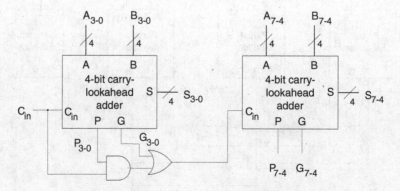

Fig. 5.13   Eight-bit carry-lookahead adder with two levels of hierarchy.

The price for each hierarchical level in a carry-lookahead adder are the two levels of logic gates, an AND and another OR. For comparison, and using a simple analysis, for an adder with $n = 8$ bits, the ripple carry adder in Figure 5.9 has a critical path with 17 logic gates. This value for the carry-select adder in Figure 5.10 is 11 logic gates (assuming 2 for the multiplexer). For the carry-lookahead adder in Figure 5.13, the critical path will be just 5 logic gates.[1]

5.2 Signed Numbers

The study of subtractors would be the next natural part of this text. However, the subtraction operation raises the problem of representing negative values. In the development of the previous adder circuits, the natural binary code was used as the numerical code, which does not consider the representation of the sign, and can only represent unsigned numbers. We will discuss alternative codes to represent negative numbers in this section.

5.2.1 *Sign and Magnitude Encoding*

There are different encodings used in digital systems to represent negative numbers. We will now look at two of these.

As a first approach for encoding negative numbers, let us consider representing the number with sign and magnitude. The most obvious way to represent the sign is to reserve one bit for the sign and define that, for instance, if this bit is 0, the number is positive, and negative if it is 1. Typically, the most significant bit is the sign bit. For the magnitude, the other bits use the natural binary code, just as above. This is called the *sign-magnitude numbers* representation.

For example, operands of 4 bits can be represented by the values shown in Table 5.3.

This representation of integers is perhaps the simplest. It does, however, have certain drawbacks.

First, note that there are two representations for the number 0, which may lead to problems, such as the need for circuits to realise that they are dealing with the same value.

---

[1]Note that the carry-select adder in Figure 5.10 can also be implemented using carry-lookahead modules instead of a ripple carry, reducing its critical path to the same 5 logic gates.

Table 5.3 Range of possible values represented in 4 bits in the sign-magnitude notation.

Representation	Number
0000	0
0001	+1
0010	+2
0011	+3
0100	+4
0101	+5
0110	+6
0111	+7
1000	0
1001	−1
1010	−2
1011	−3
1100	−4
1101	−5
1110	−6
1111	−7

Second, to carry out operations on numbers represented in this way, it is necessary to process the sign and magnitude separately. Even worse, it is necessary to choose the operation to be carried out based on the intended operation and the sign of the numbers. For example, to perform the operation $(+5) + (-3)$ what is necessary is to carry out the subtraction $5 - 3$, with the sign remaining positive. If the problem is to implement $(-5) + (+3)$, then a subtraction has also to be carried out, but the magnitude of the negative number is lower than the positive number, with the need to convert the result into a negative number.

Obviously, this makes the circuits that carry out the addition and subtraction operations much more complicated.

5.2.2   *2's Complement Encoding*

The *2's complement* of a number x with n bits is defined as the result of the operation $2^n - x$. This representation has the great advantage of enabling addition and subtraction operations to be carried out in the same way, regardless if the operands are positive or negative numbers.

For example, the 2's complement of the four-bit number 0101 is

$$
\begin{array}{rcccc}
  & 1 & 0 & 0 & 0 & 0 \\
- &   & 0 & 1 & 0 & 1 \\
\hline
  &   & 1 & 0 & 1 & 1 \\
  &   & 1 & 1 & 1 & 1 \\
\end{array}
$$

        2's complement

        carry

The number 1011 is, therefore, the 2's complement of 0101. Note that if the number x has n bits, its 2's complement is always represented by n bits.

It is trivial to verify that the 2's complement of the 2's complement of a number x is x:

$$2^n - (2^n - x) = x. \tag{5.12}$$

Thus, the 2's complement of 1011 is, as we can verify, 0101.

An expeditious way of determining the 2's complement for a number x is inverting all the bits of the number (which is called *1's complement* of x) and adding 1. Again using the number 0101, its 2's complement can be obtained by

(1) taking its 1's complement (bitwise complement): 1010;
(2) and add 1: $1010 + 1 = 1011$;

which is the same result obtained above.

Based on the 2's complement operation, we can define the *2's complement representation* of a number. In 2's complement representation

- A positive number is represented in the same way as in natural binary encoding and sign and magnitude encoding. For example, the representation in 2's complement notation with 4 bits of the number $+6$ is 0110.
- A negative number in 2's complement notation is represented by the 2's complement of its magnitude. For example, the number -5 is represented by the 2's complement of 0101, that is, by 1011. Note that the computation of the 2's complement for a positive number leaves the sign bit at 1, indicating a negative number.
- The zero is represented with n bits at 0 (note that the 2's complement of 0000 is 0000).[2]

As a result, in 2's complement notation, the numbers are also represented in such a way that one of the bits (the most significant) represents the sign. Just as in the sign-magnitude representation, that bit at 0 indicates that the number is positive or zero, and at 1 indicates the number is negative.

Table 5.4 shows the 16 possible numbers that can be represented in this notation with 4 bits.

---

[2]In fact, $2^n - 0 = 2^n \neq 0$, but we are considering n-bit numbers and the bit at 1 is in position $n + 1$, being discarded.

Table 5.4 Range of possible values represented in 4 bits in the 2's complement notation.

Representation	Number
0000	0
0001	+1
0010	+2
0011	+3
0100	+4
0101	+5
0110	+6
0111	+7
1000	−8
1001	−7
1010	−6
1011	−5
1100	−4
1101	−3
1110	−2
1111	−1

The number of values represented with n bits is of course 2^n. We can observe from Table 5.4 that the interval that can be represented in 2's complement notation for an n-bit number is $[-2^{n-1}, +2^{n-1} - 1]$, which for the particular case of $n = 4$ bits is $[-8, +7]$. The reason for the asymmetry between the number of positive and negative values lies in the need to represent 0, with a single representation with all the bits at zero. This value occupies one combination with the sign bit at 0, so in the 2's complement notation there is one more negative value than the positive values.

In sign-magnitude representation, this interval is $[-2^{n-1} + 1, +2^{n-1} - 1]$ (for $n = 4$ bits, $[-7, +7]$), since in this representation there are two different encodings for the value 0 (as shown in Table 5.3).

Finally, note that the representation of a number in 2's complement notation does not mean having to carry out the 2's complement of that number. If the number is positive, its representation in 2's complement will be the same as its unsigned representation.

5.2.3 *Sign Extension*

In natural binary encoding, which can only represent unsigned numbers, the conversion of a number represented with n bits to the same value in m bits, with $m > n$, is trivial. As with a decimal base, this operation may be carried out by simply adding $m - n$ zeros to the left of the number of n bits. For example, the four-bit number 0101 converted to 8 bits will be 00000101.

The conversion to a representation with fewer bits, $m < n$, is only possible if the value is also representable with m bits, that is, if the most significant $n - m$ bits are all 0. The conversion is carried out by removing those zeros. Thus, 0101 represented with 3 bits will be 101, and it will not be possible to represent this number with a lesser number of bits.

However, for the encodings presented in the previous section, the conversion to a different number of bits cannot be so direct since, in both encodings, the most significant bit represents the sign. We can easily see this. In either of the two representations, sign-magnitude and 2's complement, the four-bit number 1011 represents a negative value. If the conversion to 8 bits was done simply adding four zeros to the left the number would become 00001011, which would represent a positive value in both encodings, and would, therefore, be incorrect.

The way of carrying out this conversion for the sign-magnitude notation is to first remove the sign bit, add or remove zeros to the left and then place back the sign bit. Taking the previous example with 4 bits, 1011, which in sign-magnitude notation represents the value -3, its conversion to 8 bits needs to:

(1) remove the sign bit, 1, remaining the magnitude value, 011;
(2) add the four zeros, 0000011;
(3) place back the sign bit, to obtain the final value, 10000011.

The result represents the same numerical value in sign-magnitude with 8 bits.

In 2's complement notation, this same operation has the name *sign extension*. The reason for this name is that, instead of adding $m - n$ (or removing $n - m$) zeros to the left, as in binary encoding, under this notation, we add $m - n$ (or remove $n - m$) bits to the left with the same value as the sign bit. If the number is positive, we insert $m - n$ zeros. If the number is negative, we insert $m - n$ ones.

Removal is similar, but bearing in mind that for positive numbers the conversion is only valid provided that the bits to be removed left are all zeros and, in the end, the most significant bit is also zero. In a similar way for negative numbers, the conversion is only valid provided that the bits to be removed to the left are all ones and, at the end, the most significant bit is still one.

Consider, once again, the previous four-bit example, 1011, which in 2's complement notation represents the value -5. Its conversion to 8 bits implies the insertion to the left of 4 bits at 1, becoming 11111011, which also represents -5 in 2's complement, but now with 8 bits. The value 1011 cannot be represented using 3 bits, because the removal of the bit 1 to the left would leave the most significant bit with a zero, violating the above rule (the negative number -5 would change to the positive number $+3$).

5.2.4   *Operations with Numbers in 2's Complement*

As mentioned, operations on values under 2's complement representation can be performed without any particular care related to their sign. To show this, we will now consider some examples of additions involving four-bit operands:

- Sum of two positive numbers, $(+2) + (+5) = 7$:

$$
\begin{array}{r}
0\ \ 0\ \ 1\ \ 0 \\
+\ \ 0\ \ 1\ \ 0\ \ 1 \\
\hline
0\ \ 1\ \ 1\ \ 1
\end{array}
$$

The two numbers are represented in the 2's complement notation, and so is their sum. Nothing is surprising up to here since two positive numbers in this notation are represented in the same way as they are in natural binary encoding.

- Sum of two negative numbers, $(-2) + (-5) = -7$. The sum is carried out normally, adding the numbers bitwise:

$$
\begin{array}{r}
1\ \ 1\ \ 1\ \ 0 \\
+\ \ 1\ \ 0\ \ 1\ \ 1 \\
\hline
1|\ \ 1\ \ 0\ \ 0\ \ 1
\end{array}
$$

The result has a carry which is not considered because it extends beyond the n bits (4 in this case) of the representation. The result is correct, -7 in 2's complement notation.

In general, two negative numbers, x and y, with n bits, represented in 2's complement notation by $2^n - x$ and $2^n - y$, respectively, when added will have the result $(2^n - x) + (2^n - y) = 2^n + (2^n - (x + y))$. The first 2^n is the carry bit, which is discarded as it is outside the n bits of the representation. $2^n - (x + y)$ is the 2's complement for $x + y$, representing, therefore, $-x - y$.

- Sum of a positive number with a negative number having a positive result,
$(+5) + (-3) = +2$

$$
\begin{array}{r}
0 \;\; 1 \;\; 0 \;\; 1 \\
+ \;\; 1 \;\; 1 \;\; 0 \;\; 1 \;. \\
\hline
1 \mid 0 \;\; 0 \;\; 1 \;\; 0
\end{array}
$$

Once again, the last carry is dropped since it is outside the representational capacity. The result is correct.

We can make a similar analysis of the general case of a positive number, x, and a negative number, y, with n bits and $|x| > |y|$. The representation in 2's complement notation will be, respectively, x and $2^n - y$. The result of the addition is $x + (2^n - y) = 2^n + (x - y)$. The 2^n is the carry bit which is ignored because it goes outside the n bits used to represent the number. $x - y$ is a positive value and the correct result of the sum.

- Sum of a positive number with a negative number with a negative result,
$(+2) + (-5) = -3$

$$
\begin{array}{r}
0 \;\; 0 \;\; 1 \;\; 0 \\
+ \;\; 1 \;\; 0 \;\; 1 \;\; 1 \;. \\
\hline
0 \mid 1 \;\; 1 \;\; 0 \;\; 1
\end{array}
$$

We can see the result is correct, obtaining -3 in 2's complement notation.

Consider the general case, with a positive number, x, and a negative number, y, of n bits, but where $|x| < |y|$. The two numbers are represented in 2's complement notation by x and $2^n - y$, respectively. The result of the addition will be $x + (2^n - y) = 2^n - (y - x)$. This expression represents the 2's complement of the value $-(y - x)$.

These four cases cover all the possible combinations of the input and output signs, showing that the addition of operands in 2's complement generates the correct result in this notation, as long as it can be represented with the number of bits available.

5.2.5 Overflow

One possibility still not considered is the addition of two numbers of the same sign with a result that cannot be represented with the number of bits available. For example, for the addition $4 + 5 = 9$, the value 9 cannot be represented with 4 bits in 2's complement notation. So, the result is incoherent:

$$
\begin{array}{cccccc}
 & 0 & 1 & 0 & 0 & \\
+ & 0 & 1 & 0 & 1 & \\
\hline
0\,| & 1 & 0 & 0 & 1 & \text{result} \\
 & 0 & 1 & 0 & 0 & \text{carry}
\end{array}
$$

According to the 2's complement notation, 1001 represents the value -7, which is clearly wrong. In this situation, we say there was an *overflow*. Whenever the result of the addition of two positive values gives a negative number or vice versa, it means an overflow situation has occurred.

Figure 5.14 illustrates what happens in an addition operation. This figure shows the four-bit values in 2's complement notation laid out in a ring. The previous sum of 2 and 5 corresponds to the clockwise rotation of the ring 5 positions from position 2. The sum of 4 and 5 starts from 4 and rotates 5 positions. Note that, when the rotation crosses the line separating the positive from the negative numbers, the representation limit is passed and we have gone through that limit to an invalid representation.

Note that an overflow situation never occurs when adding numbers with different signs, because in this case, the magnitude of the result will always be less than the magnitude of the largest of the operands.

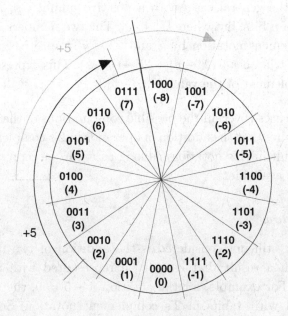

Fig. 5.14   Graphic representation of an overflow situation in an addition.

It is easy to see that overflow situations always occur when the carry for the last bit, C_{n-1}, is different from the carry of the previous bit, C_{n-2}:

- Sum of positive numbers: in this case, we always have $C_{n-1} = 0$, since the most significant bits of the operands are 0. If $C_{n-2} = 1$, this means that the sign bit of the result will be 1 and, therefore, an overflow has occurred. This is the case with the example given above.
- Sum of negative numbers: in a similar way, in this case, we always have $C_{n-1} = 1$, since the most significant bits of the operands are 1. If $C_{n-2} = 0$, this means that the sign bit of the result will be 0 and, therefore, there is an overflow. An example of this situation is

$$
\begin{array}{r}
1\ 0\ 0\ 0 \\
+\quad 1\ 0\ 0\ 1 \\
\hline
1\mid 0\ 0\ 0\ 1 \quad \text{result} \\
1\ 0\ 0\ 0 \quad \text{carry}
\end{array}
$$

in which the sum of -8 and -7 gives the result $+1$.

- Sum of numbers with different signs: in this case, the sign bits of the operands have different values. Thus, it is easy to see that we always have $C_{n-1} = C_{n-2}$, since this will only be carried from the last bit if, and only if, there has been a carry from the previous bit: $C_{n-2} = 0 \Rightarrow C_{n-1} = 0$ and $C_{n-2} = 1 \Rightarrow C_{n-1} = 1$. For example:

$$
\begin{array}{r}
1\ 0\ 0\ 0 \\
+\quad 0\ 0\ 0\ 1 \\
\hline
0\mid 1\ 0\ 0\ 1 \quad \text{result} \\
0\ 0\ 0\ 0 \quad \text{carry}
\end{array}
$$

or

$$
\begin{array}{r}
1\ 1\ 0\ 0 \\
+\quad 0\ 1\ 0\ 1 \\
\hline
1\mid 0\ 0\ 0\ 1 \quad \text{result} \\
1\ 1\ 0\ 0 \quad \text{carry}
\end{array}
$$

so, in this case, there is never an overflow.

Therefore, the condition $\overline{C_{n-1}}C_{n-2}$ is only true in the sum of two positive numbers which generate an overflow, and the condition $C_{n-1}\overline{C_{n-2}}$ is only true in the sum of two negative numbers which generate an overflow. We can test these two situations by simply calculating $C_{n-1} \oplus C_{n-2}$. This condition is easier to implement in hardware than the coherence test for the signs of the operands and results, and for this reason, it is used in practice to *detect overflow.*

It is important to discuss here the parallel between the situation in which the most significant carry bit is at 1 and when there is overflow. In fact, both indicate that the capacity to represent the value using the number of bits available has been exceeded, but in different situations. The carry bit indicates an overflow in operations with values with unsigned representation. In this representation, the overflow condition as defined in the previous paragraph has no meaning. In turn, in operations using 2's complement notation, the carry bit does not have any meaning in itself and, as we saw in the previous section, is ignored in operations which use this notation. It is, however, used as an auxiliary in calculating the overflow bit, as analysed above.

Again note that the sums presented here would be substantially more difficult to implement in hardware with a sign-magnitude representation. This option would require testing the signed bits of the operands to determine if an addition or subtraction should be carried out, and, in the latter case, define which number is the subtrahend and which the subtractor.

Finally, we should remember that an encoding attributes a meaning to a combination of bits. So a given combination of bits in itself does not mean anything and may mean different things depending on the encoding used to interpret it. For example, the four-bit combination 1001 does not have any special meaning. However, assuming it is a value in natural binary encoding, then it corresponds to the value 9 in the decimal base. If instead, we consider it to be in sign-magnitude notation, then it will have the meaning -1. The same combination of bits interpreted as being in 2's complement notation would correspond to the value -7.

5.2.6 *Subtractors*

We can implement *subtractors* using logic circuits in the same way as that for adders, following the procedures of algebraic operation. This, in turn, is carried out in binary just as in decimal by asking for a *borrow bit* whenever attempting to subtract 1 from 0. For example, the operation $S = A - B$, with $A = 0101$ and $B = 0010$, is carried out in the following manner:

$$
\begin{array}{lccccl}
A &   & 0 & 1 & 0 & 1 \\
B & - & 0 & 0 & 1 & 0 \\
\hline
S &   & 0 & 0 & 1 & 1 \\
C &   & 0 & 0 & 1 & 0 & \text{borrow}
\end{array}
$$

The borrow bit, for which we continue to use the letter C, is a value removed from the following bit.

5.2.7 *Subtractor Circuit*

Following the same procedure as for the adder, it is easy to obtain the truth table for a *half-subtractor*, that is, the circuit that computes the least significant bit of the result, as shown in Table 5.5.

As we can see, this logic is very simple. To generate the least significant bit of the result we have

$$S_0 = A_0 \oplus B_0 \tag{5.13}$$

and, for the borrow bit,

$$C_0 = \overline{A_0}\, B_0. \tag{5.14}$$

Similarly, Table 5.6 shows the truth table for a full-subtractor, the circuit for the subtraction of 1 bit taking into account the previous borrow bit.

From this table, we obtain the Karnaugh maps for each of the output bits shown in Figure 5.15.

We can observe by comparing the maps in Figures 5.4 and 5.15 that the logic behind a full-subtractor circuit is very similar to that of the full-adder.

Table 5.5 Result and carry bit of the subtraction of the least significant bit.

A_0	B_0	C_0	S_0
0	0	0	0
0	1	1	1
1	0	0	1
1	1	0	0

Table 5.6 Result and borrow bit for the subtraction taking into account the previous borrow.

A_i	B_i	C_{i-1}	C_i	S_i
0	0	0	0	0
0	0	1	1	1
0	1	0	1	1
0	1	1	1	0
1	0	0	0	1
1	0	1	0	0
1	1	0	0	0
1	1	1	1	1

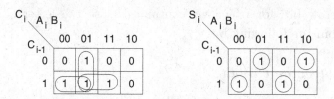

Fig. 5.15   Karnaugh map for the one-bit full-subtractor circuit.

For the result bit, S_i, it is actually the same logic

$$S_i = A_i \oplus B_i \oplus C_{i-1}. \tag{5.15}$$

For the borrow bit, an extra inverter is necessary to complement the input A_i

$$C_i = \overline{A_i}\, B_i + \overline{A_i}\, C_{i-1} + B_i\, C_{i-1}. \tag{5.16}$$

From these elementary one-bit circuits, subtractor circuits can be implemented for operands of n bits using the same architectures described in Section 5.1 for the adders.

Also in an analogous manner to the case of adders, it is easy to carry out an analysis of the subtraction operations on operands with 2's complement notation to verify that the result will always be correct. Just as in the case of adders, this result is achieved without any specific concern in the design of the subtractor circuits.

A limitation of subtractor circuits is they do not operate with the most negative value of a number with n bits, -2^{n-1}. This limitation is inherent to the 2's complement notation since the the representation of this value in 2's complement is not valid with n bits. For example, for $n = 4$, the most negative value that it is possible to represent is -8, but in positive numbers the maximum is 7. The operation $0 - (-8)$ does not, therefore, have a result representable in 4 bits (the result presented by the subtractor circuit will be -8). To ensure the correct functioning of the system, we must avoid operations on the extreme negative value for n bits. If this is a value necessary to take into consideration, then a subtractor with $n + 1$ bits is needed.

5.2.8   *Subtraction Using Adders*

Although the design complexity of a subtractor circuit is similar to that of an adder circuit, in practice it is very common to find subtractors implemented using just adder circuits. In fact, the use of numbers represented in

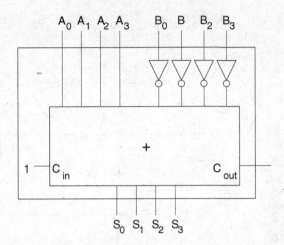

Fig. 5.16   Subtraction circuit using an adder.

2's complement notation enables subtractions to be carried out very simply with an adder circuit. As we know, computing the subtraction $A - B$ is the same as computing the addition $A + (-B)$. Furthermore, changing the sign of a number represented in 2's complement notation simply means making the 2's complement of the number. Thus, using the expeditious rule of 2's complement for a number, to compute the subtraction $A - B$ we can simply add A to the complement value of B and then add 1. We can easily do this increment by setting the carry bit sign of the adder input, C_{in}, to 1. A subtractor constructed using this approach is shown in Figure 5.16.

5.2.9   *Adder/Subtractor Circuit*

Extending this technique of constructing subtractors a little further, it is easy with just an adder circuit to build a module that can compute an addition or a subtraction in a controlled way. This circuit is known as an *adder/subtractor circuit*.

To this end, we resort to the properties of an EXCLUSIVE-OR gate. As we saw in Section 2.1.11, we can consider one of the inputs to an XOR gate as a control input. This defines whether the XOR gate behaves to the other input as an inverter, if this first input is at 1, or not, if that input is at 0, a situation where the second input is simply copied to the output.

Using this property of *controlled inverter* of the XOR gate, we can easily construct an adder/subtractor circuit, as shown in Figure 5.17. The input F

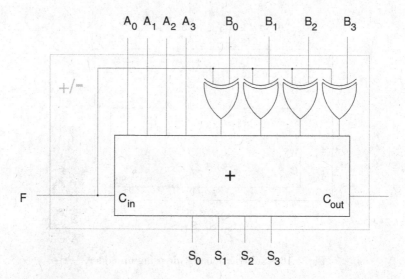

Fig. 5.17   Adder/subtractor circuit: adder with $F = 0$, subtractor with $F = 1$.

is the signal which defines which of the two operations is carried out on the inputs A and B. If $F = 0$, the operand B enters without being altered into the adder, and the input C_{in} has the value 0, hence the operation carried out is an addition, $S = A + B$. If $F = 1$, the bits of the operand B are all inverted and the input C_{in} has the value 1. Therefore, we have the same situation as in Figure 5.16 in which the 2's complement for the operand B is obtained, and the operation implemented is $S = A + (-B) = A - B$.

5.3   Multipliers and Dividers

We considered the algebraic operation of multiplication in binary in Section 1.2.2. Let us consider the multiplication of two binary numbers of 4 bits, $A = 1101b$ and $B = 1010b$, $M = A \times B$. Therefore, and just like a multiplication in base-10, each digit of the multiplier is multiplied by the multiplicand, generating a *partial product*. The result is the sum of the partial products, moved a number of places to the left equal to the position of the corresponding digit of the multiplier. Note that the result of the multiplication is a value which, to be correctly represented, needs a number of bits which is the sum of the number of significant bits of the two operands. In the case of operands with the same fixed number of bits n, the result will be a value with $2n$ bits.

A				1	1	0	1		Multiplicand
B		$\times$		1	0	1	0		Multiplier
			0	0	0	0			Partial product
			1	1	0	1			Partial product
		0	0	0	0				Partial product
	1	1	0	1					Partial product
M	1	0	0	0	0	0	1	0	Result.

5.3.1 *Multiplication of Unsigned Numbers: Array Multiplier*

Just as with adders and subtractors, the simplest multiplier circuit maps the structure of the algorithm for the algebraic operation to the logic circuit. This section will analyse the *multiplication of unsigned numbers*.

One first note is that, when generating each partial product for base-2 values, both the digit of the multiplier used to multiply the multiplicand and the digit of the multiplicand, are either 0 or 1. The second note is that the product of two digits in base-2 has the same table as the logic conjunction of 2 bits, as we can see in Tables 1.5 and 2.2(b). The generation of each partial product in the multiplication will therefore just consist in a conjunction of each bit of the multiplicand with the bit of the multiplier corresponding to this partial product. This circuit is shown in Figure 5.18 for operands with 4 bits, with the partial product obtained with the least significant bit of the multiplier, B_0.

The next step is to add the partial products, taking into account the shift to the left of each one. However, adder circuits with more than two inputs are not usual. Typically, the sum of more than two operands is carried out with a set of two-input adders, such as those presented in previous sections. For an n-bit number multiplication, n partial products

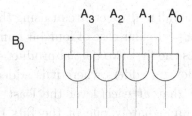

Fig. 5.18   Circuit that generates one partial product in a four-bit array multiplier.

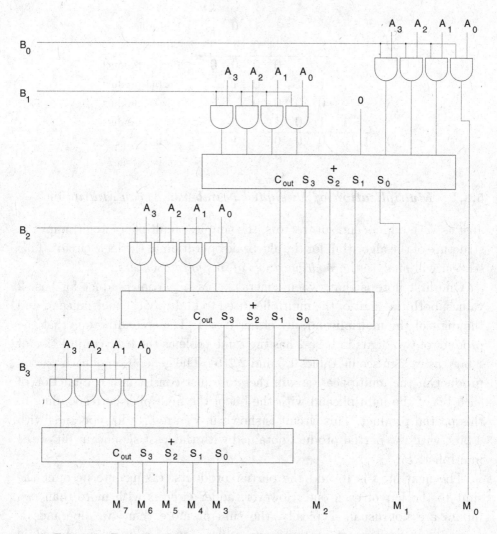

Fig. 5.19   Example of an array multiplier circuit for operands with 4 bits.

are generated. The sum of these n partial products is implemented using $n-1$ adders.

Figure 5.19 shows the full multiplier circuit using this approach, known as *array multiplier*, for the particular case of four-bit numbers. We can see that the upper adder receives the first two partial products, and the accumulated result passes to the following adders where it is added to each of the other partial products. Note that at each level the least significant bit of this accumulated result is immediately one of the bits of the result, and the other bits are used for the following sum.

5.3.2 *Analysis of the Array Multiplier Circuit*

As we can observe, the multiplication operation is significantly more complex than addition or subtraction. Note that for operands with n bits, $n-1$ adders of n bits each are necessary, besides n AND gates for each of the n partial products, giving a total of n^2 AND gates. Hence, a single multiplier has a complexity equivalent to n adder circuits. For operands of, for example, $n = 32$ bits, the hardware of a multiplier circuit is comparable to that of 32 adder circuits.

In addition to the necessary hardware, multipliers are also costly in terms of their computation delay and energy consumption. Note that the critical path of an array multiplier circuit corresponds to the propagation of the carry bit for the sum of the least significant bits of the two first partial products, $A_1 B_0 + A_0 B_1$, which have to propagate through all the adders of the multiplier. This delay corresponds to double the delay of an adder approximately.

More than power consumption increase due to the amount of hardware, array multipliers exhibit a high power consumption due to the generated spurious transitions. These are due to a large number of logic levels and reconvergent paths, that characterise this type of multiplier circuits.

For these reasons, there are many alternative architectures for the implementation of multiplier circuits, the study of which is outside the scope of this text.

In some cases, multiplier circuits are even avoided. Instead of a direct implementation, multiplication is carried out through' an appropriate sequence of shifts and adds, a matter we will address ahead, after studying sequential circuits. We save in hardware and increase the system performance by not including what would probably be the slowest element of the circuit. The penalty is that each complete multiplication becomes slower. However, in most applications, multiplication is much less used than the other operations, particularly addition operations. Therefore, the penalty of slow multiplications is amply compensated by the speed gain in the other operations. We will discuss this issue in Chapter 15 in the context of improving performance in advanced processors.

5.3.3 *Multiplication of Signed Numbers*

In contrast to addition and subtraction operations, where the same circuit operates correctly for unsigned numbers and numbers in 2's complement notation, the array multiplier can only be used for unsigned numbers.

Let us once again take the previous example. Assuming unsigned values for the operands, $A = 1101b = 13d$ and $B = 1010b = 10d$, and for the result, this is interpreted as $M = A \times B = 10000010b = 130d$ which is correct. It is easy to see that, if these operands were considered signed numbers, whether sign-magnitude or 2's complement, the result would be wrong since, to start with, the multiplication of two negative values would have to give a positive value.

5.3.4 *Multiplication of Numbers in Sign-Magnitude Representation*

The adaptation of the array multiplier to implement *multiplications of numbers in sign-magnitude* representation is straightforward. We just need to use the algebraic operation rules: the magnitude of the result is the product of the magnitudes; the sign of the result is positive if the operands have the same sign. Otherwise it is negative.

For a logic circuit adapted to this methodology, it is thus sufficient to use the array multiplier on the part of the magnitude of the operands (involving all the bits, except the most significant) to generate the magnitude of the result. For the sign bit, we simply use an XOR gate.

Consider once again multiplying $A = 1101$ and $B = 1010$, but now assuming two four-bit values in sign-magnitude notation, representing, therefore, -5 and -2, respectively. $M = A \times B$ is obtained by multiplying the bits from the magnitude part:

			1	0	1		Multiplicand
$|A|$							
$|B|$	$\times$		0	1	0		Multiplier
			0	0	0		Partial product
		1	0	1			Partial product
	0	0	0				Partial product
$|M|$	0	0	1	0	1	0	Result.

The sign bit will be $A_3 \oplus B_3 = 1 \oplus 1 = 0$, giving the result $M = 00001010$, which represents the value 10d, hence the correct result.

Note that when multiplying values using sign-magnitude, the most significant bit of the magnitude field is always 0. The reason for this is that, as we saw before, the magnitude of a number with n bits in sign-magnitude representation has the maximum value of $2^{n-1} - 1$. The product of two of these values is, thus, $(2^{n-1} - 1) \times (2^{n-1} - 1) = 2^{2n-2} - 2^n + 1$. This value is always lower than 2^{2n-2}, the value corresponding to having the most significant bit

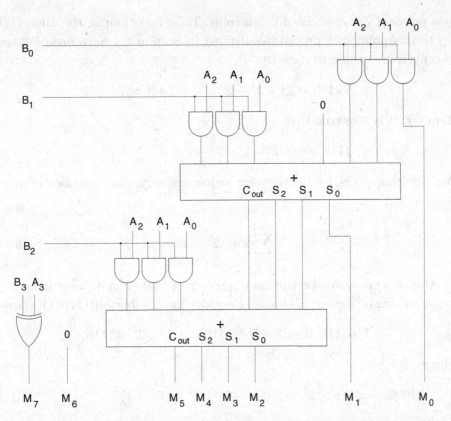

Fig. 5.20 Example of a multiplier circuit for four-bit operands in sign-magnitude representation.

of the magnitude of the result, of order $2n - 2$, at 1. In the previous case, with $n = 4$, the maximum value for the magnitude is 7, and $7 \times 7 = 49$ a value less than $1000000b = 2^6 = 64d$.

The logic circuit for a multiplier with operands in sign-magnitude notation for $n = 4$ bits is shown in Figure 5.20.

5.3.5 *Multiplication of Numbers in 2's Complement Notation*

The multiplier circuit most used for the *multiplication of numbers in 2's complement notation* is the *Booth multiplier*. This multiplier is based on the *Booth's algorithm*, which defines how a numeric value for a number in 2's complement may be obtained by the sum of powers of 2, alternating the sign in each term.

Booth's algorithm results from a set of observations. The first is that, for unsigned numbers, we can verify that any sequence of ones may be replaced by a power of 2 decremented by one unit. Take, for example, the value 111b. Up to this point, the procedures defined in Section 1.1 have been followed to convert this value to base 10

$$111b = 2^2 + 2^1 + 2^0 = 4 + 2 + 1 = 7d.$$

However, it is also true that

$$111b = 1000b - 1 = 2^3 - 1 = 8 - 1 = 7d.$$

We can show this to be true for sequences with any number of ones. Generally,

$$\sum_{i=0}^{n-1} 2^i = 2^n - 1. \tag{5.17}$$

Also, it is easy to see that any number in binary may be written as a weighted sum of sequences of ones. Consider the number 110111b. Of course,

$$110111b = 110000b + 111b = 11b \times 2^4 + 111b,$$

where

$$110000b = 11b \times 2^4 = (100b - 1) \times 2^4 = (2^2 - 1) \times 2^4 = 2^6 - 2^4$$

and, as seen above,

$$111b = 1000b - 1 = 2^3 - 2^0.$$

Hence,

$$110111b = 2^6 - 2^4 + 2^3 - 2^0 = 64 - 16 + 8 - 1 = 55d.$$

The third and final observation is related to the handling of the sign bit in 2's complement notation. For a number with n bits in this notation, its numerical value x is determined by

$$x = \begin{cases} \sum_{i=0}^{n-2} b_i 2^i, & \text{if } b_{n-1} = 0 \\ \\ \sum_{i=0}^{n-2} b_i 2^i - 2^{n-1}, & \text{if } b_{n-1} = 1. \end{cases} \tag{5.18}$$

The way that Booth's algorithm deals with the sign bit is very elegant. If the number is positive, the sign bit is zero, therefore, the sequence of ones of higher order is surrounded by zeros and the number is processed as an unsigned number, as presented above. For example, for a number in 2's complement notation with $n = 5$ bits,

$$00111b = 01000b - 1 = 2^3 - 2^0 = 7.$$

If the number is negative, the sign bit is 1 and it is as if the sequence of ones of the higher order had not terminated. In this case, we do not add the positive component of Expression (5.17), since this cancels out the negative component of the calculation of the 2's complement of Expression (5.18). For example,

$$11111b = (2^4 - 2^0) - 2^4 = -2^0 = -1$$

or

$$
\begin{aligned}
11011b &= 1011b - 10000b \\
&= (1000b + 11b) - 10000b \\
&= ((1)2^3 + (2^2 - 2^0)) - 2^4 \\
&= ((2^1 - 2^0)2^3 + (2^2 - 2^0)) - 2^4 \\
&= 2^4 - 2^3 + 2^2 - 2^0 - 2^4 \\
&= -2^3 + 2^2 - 2^0 \\
&= -8 + 4 - 1 \\
&= -5.
\end{aligned}
$$

The algorithm to implement Booth's calculation is very simple. The number is processed from right to left, examining each bit i taking into account the previous bit $i - 1$ (for the least significant bit, it is assumed there is a 0 to the right). Table 5.7 is used to determine the operation to be carried out for each possible situation.

Table 5.7 Table to calculate Booth's algorithm.

b_i	b_{i-1}	Operation
0	0	nothing to add
0	1	add 2^i
1	0	subtract 2^i
1	1	nothing to add

Considering a new example with only 4 bits, 1101

$$
\begin{array}{ll}
11\underline{01}(0) & -2^0 \\
110\underline{1} & +2^1 \\
1\underline{10}1 & -2^2 \\
\underline{1}101 & 0 \\
\hline
& -3.
\end{array}
$$

Booth's multiplier directly uses Booth's decomposition of the operands in 2's complement notation. Let us consider two numbers with $n = 4$ bits in this representation, A and B, with $B = 1101$, as above. It is easy to see that $A \times B = -2^2 A + 2^1 A - 2^0 A$.

Just as in the array multiplier, in Booth's multiplier n partial products are generated for numbers of n bits. However, in generating each partial product, 2 bits of the multiplier are used, interpreted in accordance with Table 5.7.

To illustrate this operation, consider the example $M = A \times B$, with the values $A = 0101$ and $B = 1101$:

A					0	1	0	1		Multiplicand
B				$\times$	1	1	0	1		Multiplier
	(1)	(1)	(1)	1	0	1	1			Partial product $(10 \Rightarrow -2^0 A)$
	(0)	(0)	0	1	0	1				Partial product $(01 \Rightarrow +2^1 A)$
	(1)	1	0	1	1					Partial product $(10 \Rightarrow -2^2 A)$
	0	0	0	0						Partial product $(11 \Rightarrow 0)$
M	1	1	1	1	0	0	0	1		Result.

Depending on the 2 bits of the multiplier under analysis, for the generation of each partial product, this could be zero, A or $-A$. Only the value of A and $-A$ is necessary since the power of 2 involved comes from shifting the partial product to the left. $-A$ is calculated through the sum of 1 to the bitwise complement of A. Obviously, this value is obtained only once and then shared by the different partial products.

As the partial products are values in 2's complement notation, to correctly implement their sum it is necessary to carry out the sign extension, as mentioned in Section 5.2.3. The bits in this situation were represented above in brackets.

The operation of multiplication using Booth's algorithm presented above may be mapped directly onto a logic circuit. Figure 5.21 shows the circuit for a four-bit Booth multiplier.

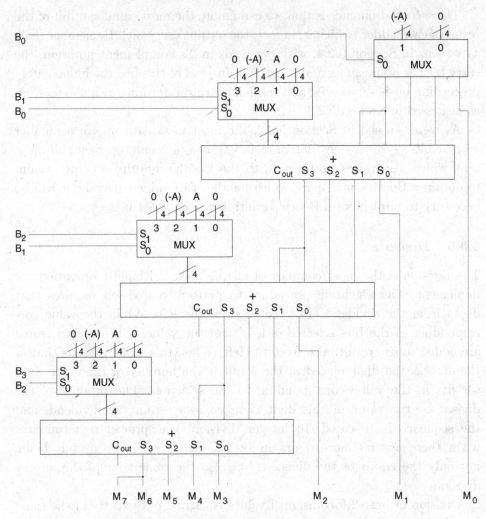

Fig. 5.21 Example of a Booth multiplier circuit for operands with 4 bits in 2's complement notation.

We can see the structure is very similar to that of an array multiplier, with two essential differences. One is that the partial products, instead of simple AND gates, are obtained through multiplexers, which implement Table 5.7. For each level, the control inputs of these multiplexers are two of the bits of the multiplier operand. The exception is the first level, in which, following Booth's algorithm, a zero is always assumed in the initial position, which simplifies the multiplexer at this level.

The second difference is that we can ignore the most significant bit of the result of each adder (which is, in fact, the output carry bit). Remember that, as we saw in Section 5.2.4, with operands in 2's complement notation, the carry bit has no meaning and is ignored. Instead of this bit, the immediately proceeding bit is duplicated and takes its turn, performing a sign extension, as discussed in Section 5.2.3.

As we discussed in Section 5.2.7, the most negative value of a number with n bits, -2^{n-1}, does not have its 2's complement representable in n bits, which also raises problems with the Booth's multiplier. Once again, to obtain a Booth's multiplier which handles this value correctly, it will be necessary to implement a Booth's multiplier with $n + 1$ bits.

5.3.6   *Divisors*

The *division* is the most complex of all the basic arithmetic operations to implement. The algebraic procedure to perform a division requires that digits from the dividend are selected from the left. While the value corresponding to the bits selected is less than the value of the divisor, zeros are added to the result, also from the left. When this value exceeds that of the divisor, the digit placed in the result is the number of times the divisor fits in the value corresponding to the selection. The product of the divisor by the value of this digit is taken away from the dividend, and the sequence is repeated. In integer division, this procedure terminates when there are no more digits in the dividend, with the output being not only the result of the division, but also the remainder of the integer division.

Division in base-2 for unsigned values is carried out exactly in the same way. Below, as an example, is the division of $A = 10010011b = 147d$ by $B = 0101b = 5d$. Here, it is necessary to select the 4 first bits of the dividend until the selection has a value greater than the divisor

```
            Divisor B
                           1
      0  1  0  1   │  1  0  0  1  0  0  1  1      Dividend A.
                   │- 0  1  0  1
                      ─────────────
                      0  1  0  0
```

The value of the divisor is subtracted from the selected 4 bits. This sequence continues with the successive selection of more bits of the dividend.

```
        Divisor B
                        1   1   1   0   1                        Result D
        0   1   0   1 │   1   0   0   1   0   0   1   1          Dividend A
                      −   0   1   0   1
                      ─────────────────
                          0   1   0   0   0
                      −   0   1   0   1
                      ─────────────────
                              0   0   1   1   0
                          −   0   1   0   1
                          ─────────────────
                                  0   0   0   1   1   1
                              −   0   1   0   1
                              ─────────────────
                                      0   0   1   0          Remainder R,
```

obtaining the result 00011101b = 29d and remainder 0010b = 2d.

In contrast with previous arithmetic operations, the division does not have a fixed sequence of basic operations. The number of bits of the dividend selected each time varies for different operands, and so the subtraction operation will be carried out on a different set of bits. This variation makes it very complicated to directly translate the algebraic operation to a logic circuit, as this would have to predict all the different subtraction possibilities.

Division operations are very rare when compared to other basic arithmetic operations. This reason, along with the complexity of its implementation, means that it is not common to find purely combinational logic circuits for the division. Instead, divisions are typically carried out through a sequence of simpler hardware operations. This type of approach will be the subject of study in Chapter 8, following the study of the design of sequential circuits.

5.4   Fixed-Point

Until now we have assumed that the operands for the different operations are integers. However, in many situations, it is necessary to implement calculations over fractional values. One of the simplest ways of representing fractional values is to assume that the point is in a fixed position.

5.4.1   *Fixed-Point Representation*

As the name indicates, in *fixed-point representation* for fractional numbers, the point is always located at the same position. Therefore, out of the n bits of the operand, the i bits of the left side represent the integer part and the j bits on the right side, the decimal part, with i and j constant and $i + j = n$.

For example, let us consider, for operands with 8 bits ($n = 8$) in 2's complement, that it is set that $i = 5$ and $j = 3$. Then the set of bits 01101011 is interpreted as

$$\underbrace{01101}_{5\text{ bits}} \cdot \underbrace{011}_{3\text{ bits}}.$$

The numerical value represented by this set of bits can be calculated[3] by the methods of Chapter 1, 01101.011b = 13.375d. For negative values, everything is analogous to the integer case: the magnitude of the value can be obtained by bitwise complementation followed by the sum of one unit, after which the point is placed. Using the previous representation, the set of bits 10000100 corresponds to the numerical value 10000.100b = −15.5d.

In a system using a different position for the point, for example, with $i = 2$ and $j = 6$, the sets of bits considered above, 01101011 and 10000100, will, respectively, represent the values 01.101011b = 1.671875d and 10.000100b = −1.9375d.

At the limit, it is possible to consider systems in which all the bits are located in the decimal part, that is, $i = 0$ and $j = n$. Once again using the examples above, the set of bits 01101011 then represents .01101011b = 0.41796875d and 10000100 represents .10000100b = −0.484375d.

The other extreme is to consider that all the bits are in the integer part, $i = n$ and $j = 0$: 01101011.b = 107.0d and 10000100.b = −124.0d. This is, of course, the situation for the representation of integers which we previously assumed in this chapter. In fact, the representation of integers is nothing more than a particular case of fixed-point representation.

5.4.2   *Operations Under Fixed-Point Using Integer Units*

Fixed-point addition and subtraction operations may be carried out with integer operators without modifications. For example, take the following addition operation:

$$
\begin{array}{r}
0\ \ 0\ \ 1\ \ 0 \\
+\ \ 0\ \ 1\ \ 0\ \ 1 \\
\hline
0\ \ 1\ \ 1\ \ 1
\end{array}
$$

---

[3]This equality is valid in purely mathematical terms. However, as discussed in Chapter 1, the three decimal places of the binary value do not allow the indicated accuracy level for the decimal part.

Table 5.8   Interpretation of the result of the fixed point addition based on the position of the point, for unsigned numbers.

i	j	Operation
4	0	$2.0 + 5.0 = 7.0$
3	1	$1.0 + 2.5 = 3.5$
2	2	$0.5 + 1.25 = 1.75$
1	3	$0.25 + 0.625 = 0.875$
0	4	$0.125 + 0.3125 = 0.4375$

Table 5.9   Interpretation of the result of the fixed point addition based on the position of the point, for 2's complement numbers.

i	j	Operation
4	0	$(-7.0) + (+3.0) = -4.0$
3	1	$(-3.5) + (+1.5) = -2.0$
2	2	$(-1.75) + (+0.75) = -1.0$
1	3	$(-0.875) + (+0.375) = -0.5$
0	4	$(-0.4375) + (+0.1875) = -0.25$

In the analysis of the previous sections we assumed this set of bits represented integers and, in which case, this addition represents $2+5 = 7$. Note, however, that the result of this operation is valid for any position considered for the point, as shown in Table 5.8.

Although the interpretation of the numerical value of the operands and results varies according to the position considered for the point, the operation is always the same and is, therefore, applicable in the same way to all cases.

This result is valid with unsigned numbers or with 2's complement numbers. For example, the result presented by an adder circuit for the following two input operands is

$$
\begin{array}{r}
1\ 0\ 0\ 1 \\
+\ 0\ 0\ 1\ 1 \\
\hline
1\ 1\ 0\ 0
\end{array}
$$

If the operands are interpreted as unsigned integers, the sum carried out is $9 + 3 = 12$. Also with integers, but in 2's complement, the operation will be $(-7) + (+3) = -4$.

Considering fixed-point values, the result of this addition for the different possibilities regarding the positioning of the point may be interpreted as shown in Table 5.9.

Integer multiplication and division operators can also be used directly, carefully adjusting the number of bits on the decimal part in the result. As we saw above, the multiplication of two integer operands with n bits generates a result with $2n$ bits. Assuming fixed-point operands with i bits in the integer part and j bits in the decimal part, the result will have $2i$ bits in the integer part and $2j$ bits in the decimal part. Therefore, to keep the result with n bits and the point in the same position, we need to shift it j positions to the right, thus losing the j low order fractional bits of the result. For example

$$
\begin{array}{r}
0\ 1\ 1\ 0 \\
\times\ \ 0\ 1\ 1\ 0 \\
\hline
0\ 0\ 0\ 0 \\
0\ 1\ 1\ 0 \\
0\ 1\ 1\ 0 \\
0\ 0\ 0\ 0 \\
\hline
0\ 0\ 1\ 0\ 0\ 1\ 0\ 0.
\end{array}
$$

In an integer representation, the operation carried out is $6 \times 6 = 36$. If a fixed-point representation with $i = j = 2$ is considered, the result should be interpreted as $00|\underline{10.01}|00$. Therefore, the operation carried out is $1.5 \times 1.5 = 2.25$. For $i = 1$ and $j = 3$, the interpretation of results will be $0|\underline{0.100}|100$, therefore $0.75 \times 0.75 = 0.5$. Note that in this case the result is not exact, since 1 bit of the decimal part has been lost. Another possible situation happens when $i = 3$ and $j = 1$, where we have $001|\underline{001.0}|0$. Therefore, the operation carried out is $3.0 \times 3.0 = 1$. This value is incorrect, because the value has exceeded the representational capacity, and there is a high order bit outside the valid range.

This problem also occurs in the representation of integers, as it is a particular case of fixed-point representation. The result of the operation often has $2n$ bits so we can see if it fits in n bits and take the appropriate action.

Note that in operations with fractional numbers, whether fixed-point or floating-point, it is possible to multiply two numbers different from zero with the result being zero. This condition, in which the result is so small that it is not possible to represent it in the format utilised, is named *underflow* (in contrast to *overflow*, in which the value is too large to be representable). For example, also with $n = 4$ bits and $i = j = 2$, multiplication

00.11b × 00.01b = 0.75d × 0.25d is given by

$$
\begin{array}{r}
0\ 0\ 1\ 1 \\
\times\ 0\ 0\ 0\ 1 \\
\hline
0\ 0\ 1\ 1 \\
0\ 0\ 0\ 0 \\
0\ 0\ 0\ 0 \\
0\ 0\ 0\ 0 \\
\hline
0\ 0\ 0\ 0\ 0\ 0\ 1\ 1.
\end{array}
$$

The result is interpreted as $00|\underline{00.00}|11$, therefore, zero.

In fixed-point representation, division is carried out by an inverse process to that of multiplication: the dividend should first be shifted j bits to the left, to have $2j$ decimal bits, so that the result will have j decimal bits. As an example, let us divide 01.11 by 01.10, that is, a fixed-point representation with $i = j = 2$. Thus, shifting the dividend two positions to the left, the division will be carried out over the values 011100 and 0110:

$$
\begin{array}{r}
1\ 0\ 0 \\
0\ 1\ 1\ 0\ \overline{\left|\ 0\ 1\ 1\ 1\ 0\ 0\right.} \\
-\ 0\ 1\ 1\ 0 \\
\hline
0\ 0\ 0\ 1\ 0\ 0.
\end{array}
$$

Thus, this operation is interpreted as involving integer operations and corresponds to the division of 28 by 6, the result of which is 4 and the remainder is also 4. In fixed-point, with $i = j = 2$, the operation will be the division of 1.75 by 1.5, with the result being 1.0 (because the dividend has been shifted j positions to the left, the result has j bits in its decimal part, 01.00) and remainder 0.25 (the result has $2j$ decimal positions, so it has to be shifted j positions to the right, 00.01).

5.4.3   *Limitations of Fixed-Point Representation*

Although simple to implement, operations in fixed-point greatly limit the range of representable real values. Considering unsigned numbers, the largest number that can be represented is $2^i - 2^{-j}$, and the lowest positive is 2^{-j}. In 2's complement numbers, the largest positive number will be $2^{i-1} - 2^{-j}$, and the lowest negative number -2^{i-1}. In either case, the minimum resolution is 2^{-j}.

In many situations, particularly in scientific calculations, it is necessary to represent operands with very large or very small magnitudes. For example, when designing VLSI integrated circuits, it is required to work with transistor sizes which, nowadays, have values in the order of nanometres, that is, 10^{-9} m. To manage this resolution in binary, as mentioned in Section 1.1.3, what is needed is $j > 9 \times \log_2 10 \approx 30$ bits. Furthermore, the number of transistors per integrated circuits nowadays has gone beyond 1 billion, that is, 10^9. This implies that $i > 9 \times \log_2 10 \approx 30$ bits. Therefore, a computer used in the design of VLSI circuits functioning in fixed-point needs words of at least $n = i + j = 60$ bits.

Although this value is in itself high, making fixed-point operations less attractive, there are many situations in which it is necessary to manipulate much larger quantities. For example, in chemistry, a value often used to measure the quantity of material is the mole, which represents, approximately, 6.02×10^{23} atoms. Other situations require even greater resolutions (for example, Planck's constant, the constant of proportionality between the energy of a photon and its frequency, has the approximate value of 6.6×10^{-34} Js). In these cases, the use of fixed-point is completely impractical.

In a given system, although very high and very low values may coexist, in practice operations normally use operands of a similar order of magnitude. The ideal solution would then be to not define the same position for the point for all operands, but rather adapt its position on a case-by-case basis depending on the magnitude of the value represented. Therefore, with numbers with greater magnitude, a larger number of bits in the integer part should be used, which implies a lower resolution since there are fewer bits in the decimal part. For lower magnitude values fewer bits can be used in the integer part, which allows a greater number of bits in the decimal part. Floating point representation, which we will discuss next, develops this idea.

5.5   Floating-Point Representations

As the name suggests, in *floating-point representation* the position of the point is not fixed and varies from operand to operand. As is easy to realise, this representation introduces some additional complexity. To start with, it is necessary to associate extra information to each operand to indicate the position of the point. Then, operations between operands using floating-point become more complicated, since the calculation of the result will have to bear in mind the position of the point for each operand.

Due to its complexity, this text will not deal with implementation in terms of the logic circuit for floating-point operators, and will only discuss the representation and manipulation of operands in this format.

5.5.1 *Mantissa and Exponent*

The format of floating-point numbers requires two fields: the *fraction* or *mantissa*, which contains the value itself, usually represented by the letter F; and the *exponent* which represents a scale factor (essentially, defining the position of the point in the operand), normally represented by the letter E. In addition to these fields, there is also a sign bit S, since the sign-magnitude representation is more common in floating-point. The exponent may be negative, and some encoding is used for the field E, as we will see ahead.

Thus, the n bits used to represent a given value are organised into the following fields:

S	E	F

The size of fields E and F may vary but will be fixed for each system. A given set of bits in this format will, therefore, represent the value $(-1)^S \times F \times 2^E$.

Note that a given value does not have a unique representation in this format. For example, the value 12 may be represented as 3×2^2 or 6×2^1. Assuming that the fields E and F have 3 and 4 bits, respectively, the value 12 will be represented in binary as

0	0	1	0	0	0	1	1

or

0	0	0	1	0	1	1	0

In the reverse direction, this ambiguity does not exist. The pattern of bits

1	1	0	1	1	0	0	1

represents, in the previous format, the value $(-1)^1 \times 9 \times 2^5 = -288$.

5.5.2 *Floating-Point Operations*

In floating-point representation, and contrary to fixed-point representation, the easiest operations to carry out are multiplication and division. A *floating-point multiplication* is carried out by multiplying the fractions, adding the exponents and performing an exclusive-or on the sign bit. It is similar for the division: the fractions are divided, the exponents are subtracted and an exclusive-or is carried out on the sign bit.

To illustrate these operations, consider two operands: $Op1 = (-1)^{S_1} \times F_1 \times 2^{E_1}$ and $Op2 = (-1)^{S_2} \times F_2 \times 2^{E_2}$. Then,

$$Op1 \times Op2 = (-1)^{S_1 \oplus S_2} \times (F_1 \times F_2) \times 2^{E_1 + E_2} \qquad (5.19)$$

and

$$Op1/Op2 = (-1)^{S_1 \oplus S_2} \times (F_1/F_2) \times 2^{E_1 - E_2}. \qquad (5.20)$$

The additions and subtractions are more complicated than multiplications and divisions since they involve adjusting the exponents. If the first operand has an exponent E_1 and the second operand an exponent E_2, the operation between fractions is only possible if $E_1 = E_2$. If the exponents are different, it is necessary to match them up, and so there are two options: either increase the exponent of the smaller operand, so it is the same as the larger one, shifting the mantissa to the right so as to keep its value; or reduce the exponent of a larger one, shifting its mantissa to the left.

The shifting of the mantissa may lead to the loss of some of its bits. Therefore, it is always preferable to carry out the shifting of the mantissa to the right, since if bits are lost, these will be the least significant. The error caused by the shifting will necessarily be less than that caused by the loss of the most significant bit caused by a shifting to the left. Therefore, for two operands in which $E_1 \neq E_2$, the adjustment will be made in the direction of the larger exponent. For example, if $E_1 > E_2$, then the mantissa of the second operand will be shifted $E_1 - E_2$ positions to the right. Once this operation has been carried out, the mantissas can be added or subtracted, in accordance with the signs of the two operands and the operation being carried out.

Consider once again the operands $Op1$ and $Op2$, with $Op1 = (-1)^{S_1} \times F_1 \times 2^{E_1}$, $Op2 = (-1)^{S_2} \times F_2 \times 2^{E_2}$, and with $E_1 > E_2$. Therefore, for $Op1 + Op2$, with $S_1 = S_2$, or $Op1 - Op2$, with $S_1 \neq S_2$, the operation is a sum and the result is given by[4]

$$(-1)^{S_1} \times (F_1 + (F_2 \gg (E_1 - E_2))) \times 2^{E_1}. \qquad (5.21)$$

---

[4]The formulation "$\gg (n)$" represents the shift of n bits to the right.

For $Op1 - Op2$, with $S_1 = S_2$, or $Op1 + Op2$, with $S_1 \neq S_2$, the operation is a subtraction. If $Op1 \geq Op2$, the result is given by

$$(-1)^{S_1} \times (F_1 - (F_2 \gg (E_1 - E_2))) \times 2^{E_1} \qquad (5.22)$$

and if $Op1 < Op2$ the result will be

$$(-1)^{S_2} \times ((F_2 \gg (E_1 - E_2) - F_1)) \times 2^{E_1}. \qquad (5.23)$$

5.5.3 *IEEE-754 Standard*

As we saw, the number of bits to be used for the mantissa and the exponent may vary from computer to computer. To enable easy portability of applications between systems, the *IEEE*[5] proposed a recommendation which almost all computers follow, which is known as the *IEEE format*. This standard defines the two formats supported by most processors: the *single precision* format and the *double precision* format. In single precision, the operands are 32 bits, 8 of which are for the exponent and 23 for the mantissa (the remaining bit is the sign bit). In double precision, the operands are 64 bits, 11 for the exponent and 52 for the mantissa.

In IEEE format, the interpretation of the mantissa and the exponent is slightly different from that mentioned above. For the mantissa, it is assumed that a 1 is always implicit in the highest order position, with the point immediately on its right. This restriction implies that the representation of operands in this format is unique. Besides this, as this 1 is always in this position, it does not need to be represented, and so one bit is gained.

In turn, the exponent is always represented by a *biased exponent*, which enables it to have negative exponents to represent small fractional values. In single precision, this shift is 127, and in double precision, this shift is 1023. This means that the real exponent is calculated by $E - 127$ or $E - 1023$, respectively. Thus, the values represented in the IEEE format are given, with single precision, by $(-1)^S \times (1.F) \times 2^{E-127}$ and, with double precision, by $(-1)^S \times (1.F) \times 2^{E-1023}$.

Specifically, the following bit pattern written in single precision $11000000101100000000000000000000\text{b} = \text{C0B00000h}$

1	10000001	01100000000000000000000

represents the value $-1.011\text{b} \times 2^{(129\text{d}-127\text{d})} = -1.375\text{d} \times 4\text{d} = -5.5\text{d}$.

---

[5]Institute of Electrical and Electronic Engineers, today the world's largest association of technical professionals.

In the opposite direction, to represent the value 35.875d with single precision, its representation in binary is first obtained and then this value is shifted until the point is at the right of the most significant bit. Therefore, $35.875d = 100011.111b = 1.00011111 \times 2^5$. Hence, in the IEEE format, this value is represented by $S = 0$, $E = 127 + 5 = 132d = 10000100b$ and $F = 00011111000000000000000$, that is, 01000010000011111000000000000000b = 420F8000h.

As we will see below, this standard defines particular exponent values, namely all ones and all zeros, as special cases. Thus, eliminating those cases, the maximum magnitude and the minimum resolution that this format can represent using single precision and double precision are those values presented in Table 5.10.

A difficulty that this format raises is that of not allowing direct representation of the zero value since it always implicitly assumes one bit at 1! The standard resolves this problem by treating the zero value as a special case. Due to this, the recommendation specifies that the extreme values of the exponent (that is, all the bits at 0, $E = 0$, and all those at 1, $E = 255$ or $E = 1\,023$, for single or double precision, respectively) must not be interpreted in the general format, but have special meanings as indicated in Table 5.11.

The first observation is that these special cases define the all zeros pattern for the value 0, which is the most common representation of this value in most numeric encodings.

Table 5.10   Range of representable values in single and double precision provided for by the standard IEEE format.

	Precision	E	F	Value
Max	Single	254	all 1's	$2^{254-127} \times (1 - 2^{-23}) \approx 1.7014 \times 10^{38}$
	Double	2 046	all 1's	$2^{2\,046-1\,023} \times (1 - 2^{-52}) \approx 8.9885 \times 10^{307}$
Min	Single	1	all 0's	$2^{1-127} \times (1.0) \approx 1.1755 \times 10^{-38}$
	Double	1	all 0's	$2^{1-1\,023} \times (1.0) \approx 2.2251 \times 10^{-308}$

Table 5.11   Special cases of the IEEE format.

E	F	Meaning
255/1023	$= 0$	$\pm\infty$
	$\neq 0$	Invalid number (NaN)
0	$= 0$	Zero value
	$\neq 0$	Denormalised number

The other cases are used to cover situations which fall outside the range of values covered by the general format of the recommendation. The case where E takes on the maximum value and $F = 0$ is used in situations in which the result of an operation has exceeded the maximum value in magnitude, either for positive of for negative numbers. Another case in which E takes on the maximum value, but $F \neq 0$, serves to indicate that the result of the operation is not a real number. For example, the calculation of a square root for -1 should return NaN, *Not-a-Number*.

These two cases require the definition of rules for operations between these values. In general, an operation which involves a NaN value returns a NaN. The case of the infinities ($\pm\infty$) should be considered with greater care. For example, a multiplication where one of the operands is infinity should return infinity, with the corresponding sign. The same for the sum of infinities of the same sign. A sum of infinities with a different sign, a division between infinities or a multiplication between an infinity and zero should return the value NaN.

The final special case, $E = 0$ and $F \neq 0$, is used to represent a value so small, in magnitude, that a 1 in the position to the left of the point cannot be assumed. A simple solution would be to immediately assume some under-flow numeric error and save the value as 0. Instead, the recommendation provides for the representation of this value in a denormalised format. For this combination of E and F, the point remains to the left of the mantissa but assuming a zero at its left. The denormalised format thus has the meaning $(-1)^S \times (0.F) \times 2^{-126}$, in single precision, and $(-1)^S \times (0.F) \times 2^{-1022}$, in double precision.

Although carrying out arithmetic operations is complicated, the format used in the IEEE standard greatly facilitates comparison between values in this representation. The first observation is that it does not make much sense to carry out equality comparisons between values in floating-point. The exception is the comparison with zero, which, as we saw, means testing if all the bits are zero. For greater or lesser comparisons, the sign bits should be dealt with first of all. If they are different, the response is immediate. If the sign bit is equal, it is necessary to compare the exponents. By using an exponent with shift, the greater magnitudes always correspond to a greater binary value in the exponent field. By having this field in a higher weight position in the IEEE format, a higher binary value corresponds to a higher magnitude of the floating point value. Note that if the exponents are equal, then the mantissas will determine the relative value of the magnitudes. This observation enables the relative comparison between two values in the IEEE format to be carried out with a simple integer comparison unit!

5.6   Summary

This chapter presents circuits used to perform arithmetic operations. It starts by analysing addition, the simplest operation between integer values. The first adder analysed, the ripple carry adder, uses a structure similar to that used in the algebraic operation, first adding the bits of least weight, taking into account the carry that comes from the immediately previous weight bit. This implementation has the disadvantage of being slow since, potentially, it may be necessary for the carry bit to propagate throughout all the bits of the adder. Carry-select and carry-lookahead adders are two faster alternatives.

Before discussing subtractors, the sign-magnitude and 2's complement encodings are introduced, as a mechanism to represent negative values. 2's complement encoding is shown to have the advantage that it can be used in binary adders and subtractors and, for this reason, it is the most used in practice. The subtractor circuit may be designed either by a process totally similar to the design of an adder or by the use of an adder in which the 2's complement is carried out for one of the operands, inverting all its bits and adding 1 through the input carry signal of the adder.

For multiplication, the array multiplication circuit is presented for unsigned operands and Booth's multiplier for operands in 2's complement. In this text, we do not study a circuit for the division operation, due to its relative complexity and low usage in practice. We present only a brief discussion of the main points to take into account when implementing the divider circuit.

These circuits are developed for operands with integer values. The use of the fixed-point format to represent fractional values makes it possible to use the same circuits, introducing the proper adjustments after the multiplication and division operations. Finally, the floating-point format is introduced as a way of increasing both the precision and the range of fractional values that are possible to represent in the fixed-point format. Hardware implementation of operations in this format is much more complex, and only the elementary operations implied for each arithmetic operation for floating-point operands are discussed. The IEEE format is presented, in its single and double precision formats, as the standard for floating-point numbers used in practice by most computer systems.

Exercises

5.1 Applying the same methodology used to design a one-bit full-adder, design a one-bit full-subtractor. In addition, design a circuit with an input S which, when $S = 0$, behaves as a one-bit full-adder and, when $S = 1$, behaves as a one-bit full-subtractor.

5.2 Design a two-bit full-adder. Discuss the advantages and disadvantages of using the circuit you have now designed to implement adders of n bits, when compared with the use of one-bit adder circuits.

5.3 Consider the various architectures studied for building a 64-bit adder. Supposing that the gates used have a delay-time of 100 ps, compare the performance of the different alternatives.

5.4 Consider implementing a circuit to sum numbers represented in 2's complement with 32 bits using adders of 8 bits, which have as an output the sum, the carry bit and the overflow bit. How do you interconnect the adders to implement this circuit?

5.5 Consider the following numbers represented in 2's complement:
$A = 01011011$
$B = 11110100$
$C = 10000011$
$D = 01111111$

(a) Represent the numbers in decimal.
(b) Represent the numbers in 2's complement using 12 bits.
(c) Represent the numbers in sign-magnitude with 8 bits.
(d) Compute the following operations directly in binary and determine whether there is an overflow in the result: $A + B$; $A - B$; $C + D$; $C - D$; $D - C$.

5.6 Just as it is possible to represent signed numbers in 2's complement notation in base-2, it is possible to represent signed numbers in 10's complement notation in base 10.

(a) With four decimal digits, what is the range of numbers that can be represented?
(b) Calculate the ten's complement for the number 0371.

(c) How is a negative number identified in ten's complement?

(d) Represent the numbers $4\,503$, $-6\,335$, $4\,999$ and $-4\,999$ in ten's complement using four digits.

(e) Determine the rule to conclude if there is overflow in the result of an operation.

5.7 Design a circuit which adds or subtracts four-bit numbers represented in sign-magnitude. When the result of the operation is 0, the representation used should be only 0000.

5.8 Using a four-bit comparator, a four-bit adder and any necessary complementary logic, design a circuit which receives two four-bit numbers A and B and computes $\max(A, B) - \min(A, B)$.

5.9 Design a circuit which calculates the integer part of the average of two numbers.

5.10 Consider an array multiplier circuit for eight-bit numbers. Using gates with a delay time of 100 ps, determine the total delay time of the circuit, using ripple carry adders without any modification. Recalculate this time assuming eight-bit carry-lookahead adders.

5.11 Calculate, using Booth's algorithm, the value in decimal for the binary values 01111111b and 01010101b.

5.12 Represent in fixed point notation, assuming eight-bit numbers with 3 bits for the fractional part, the numbers: 4.24, 12.3 and 12.375. Some cases do not have an exact representation, give the best approximate one.

5.13 Obtain the most accurate representation of the following numbers in floating point with an eight-bit mantissa and a seven-bit exponent:

(a) 35.67

(b) 261.9

(c) −35.67

(d) −261.9

(e) 0.00023

(f) 2 300.

5.14 Represent the numbers in the previous problem in single precision IEEE-754 format.

Chapter 6

Basic Sequential Circuits

The logic circuits presented in the previous chapters all belong to the class of combinational circuits. They are so named because each combination of values in the circuit inputs determines a unique combination of values in their outputs.

This chapter analyses new elemental logic devices, which enable the controlled storage of information about logic values which have previously occurred. These elements are known as *memory elements*, and the logic circuits that include them are called *sequential circuits*. As the name indicates, sequential circuits react to the occurrence of sequences in their inputs. They consider previous values at the inputs, while combinational circuits are only able to identify, at any time, combinations of inputs present at that time. Section 6.1 analyses the different behaviour of these two types of circuits.

It is important for digital circuits to be able to store events and internal states under certain circumstances. The behaviour of circuits of this type implies that they take into consideration not only the current situation of their environment, as set by the values presented at their inputs, but also knowledge obtained in the past. This knowledge is necessary to provide suitable reactions in complex applications.

Sequential circuits are divided into two classes, *synchronous sequential circuits* and *asynchronous sequential circuits*. The distinction between these two types of sequential circuits is determined by whether there is a global control signal, known as the *clock signal*, which regulates the updating of the different memory elements of the circuit. Section 6.3 discusses the desirable features of a clock signal.

The most basic memory elements enable the storage of one bit of information at a time. The simpler ones are called *latches* and are analysed in Section 6.2. The more sophisticated memory elements, controlled by a clock signal, are called *flip-flops* and are discussed in Section 6.4.

Building up on these basic elements, Section 6.5 analyses the construction of modules which enable the organised storage of sets of bits (words) which constitute a unit of information. These modules are called *registers*. Registers may have different architectures, and this section includes also the description of *shift registers*. Another type of specialised registers, *counters*, are analysed in more depth in Section 6.6.

Finally, modules which store a larger quantity of information are described. Section 6.7 presents ways of interconnecting registers and organising sets of registers, so as to form a *register file*. Section 6.8 introduces the functioning and organisation of large *memory circuits*, which typically have a much greater storage capacity than register files.

6.1 Sequential Behaviour of Circuits

Combinational circuits have many applications, as was demonstrated by the different modules studied in previous chapters, and constitute a significant part of the modules in complex digital systems. An example of a combinational circuit is an adder, such as studied in Section 5.1. If the objective is to carry out an addition, it is of course enough to have the values of the operands in the inputs at a given moment to determine the result in the output.

However, this class of logic circuits has an significant limitation: it cannot store information and, therefore, it cannot operate on previous input values which are not available anymore to the circuit. There are many situations in which it is necessary to take into account the history of the circuit. For example, if we want to identify if an input signal has changed from 0 to 1, it is necessary to have information not only about its current level but also about its previous condition. Or, returning to the case of addition, if we want to add a third value to the result of the previous addition, it will be necessary to store the result of that addition in some way so that it can be added to the new value.

As we mentioned before, a combination of input values from a combinational circuit specifies one and only one combination of possible values of the outputs. This is not the case with sequential circuits, since the outputs of these circuits, in addition to depending on current inputs, also depend on prior values, which are stored in memory elements. This characteristic makes it possible to identify, under certain conditions, the type of logic circuit at hand, by observing the input evolution and the behaviour of the outputs.

Consider the timing diagrams in Figure 6.1 which show the evolution over time of circuits with two input signals, $i1$ and $i2$ and an output signal, f. The timing diagram (a) may correspond to a combinational circuit since each combination of inputs always generates the same output. However, timing diagram (b) must necessarily correspond to a sequential circuit, since there

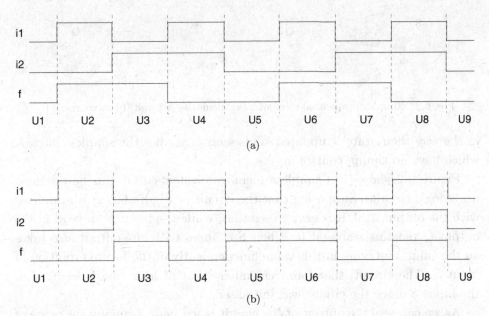

Fig. 6.1 The timing diagrams may enable the identification of the type of logic circuit: (a) the circuit has a combinational behaviour, but could be a sequential circuit and (b) the circuit is necessarily a sequential circuit.

are different time instances in which, when there is the same configuration of values in the inputs, a different value appears in the output, for example, the intervals $U3$ and $U7$. This behaviour implies the existence of information stored internally in the circuit by memory elements.

It is not possible to be certain that the circuit which corresponds to the diagram in Figure 6.1(a) is indeed a combinational circuit. In fact, there may be memory elements in this circuit whose presence that sequence of inputs cannot identify. In this case, what can be stated is that it is possible to design a purely combinational circuit with the behaviour shown in this timing diagram.

6.2 Latches

The most basic memory elements can store only one bit of information at a time and are called *latches*. The value stored in the latch is called *state*. Typically, the state of the latch is observable in one of its outputs, which is usually given the name Q. The updating of the state is done by activating one of the latch control signals. There are different types of latches, varying

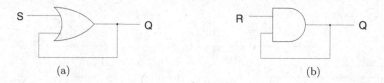

Fig. 6.2   Simplest sequential elements: (a) memorise a 1 and (b) memorise a 0.

in the way their state is updated. This section studies the simplest latches, which have no timing control inputs.

Figure 6.2 shows the simplest memory elements that can be designed using logic circuits. Supposing that the circuit in Figure 6.2(a) is initialised with the output at 0, it is easy to see that, while the input S stays at 0, the output Q remains stable at 0. When S changes to 1, the output also takes on the value 1, staying in this value independently of the future evolution of input S. The circuit, therefore, remembers that at least one 1 occurred in the input S since the circuit was initialised.

As we can see, the output of the circuit is fed back, bringing the value of the output to one of the OR gate inputs and thus ensuring that this value is taken into account in the immediate future when calculating new outputs. It is this feedback that gives support to the state of the latch. However, as can be understood, the usefulness of the circuit is reduced, since once it has changed to 1, there is no way of making it return to 0.

The circuit in Figure 6.2(b) has a similar behaviour, but stores the occurrence of the value 0 at the input. These two circuits show a fundamental issue about memory elements in general: the existence of the feedback line in the circuit. It is this line that causes the output not to depend exclusively on the inputs, but also on the current state value which, in the case of these particular circuits, is also the output itself.

6.2.1   SR Latch

A useful memory element should be able to maintain its state or change it to 0 or 1 in a controlled manner. This behaviour can be achieved through two signals, S (Set) and R (Reset), with the set signal S, when active, setting the value of the state to 1, and the R signal, resetting the value of the state to 0. The state of the latch is maintained when neither of these signals is active. This specification may be described in a truth table, as shown in Figure 6.3(a), in which $Q(n-1)$ is the current value of the state of the

S	R	Q(n − 1)	Q(n)
0	0	0	0
0	0	1	1
0	1	X	0
1	0	X	1
1	1	X	X

(a)

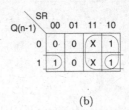

(b)

Fig. 6.3   Specification of a basic set/reset memory element: (a) Truth table; (b) Karnaugh map.

memory element, and $Q(n)$ the new value for the state. The output of the latch coincides with its state Q. Note that there is no definition of the value of the state when both signals S and R are active since this situation configures contradictory requests.

We can obtain the logic function of this circuit by simplifying the Karnaugh map in Figure 6.3(b). The Q output is then given by Expression (6.1).

$$Q(n) = S + \overline{R} \cdot Q(n-1). \tag{6.1}$$

The logic circuit corresponding to this latch, known as a *level-sensitive SR latch* or just *SR latch*, is shown in Figure 6.4(a). We can see that if $S = R = 0$ both the AND gate and the OR gate have their neutral element in these inputs, such that the output is just fed back, therefore keeping it constant. If $S = 1$, the output takes on the value 1, regardless of the other signals. When this input changes to 0, the output is maintained at 1. If $R = 1$ and $S = 0$, Q goes to 0 and this will be the new value stored in the latch. In this implementation, with $S = R = 1$, the latch state is set to 1, a consequence of the way the indifferences were used when minimising the Karnaugh map in Figure 6.3(b). As we can see, both remain inside a loop. Although it does not correspond to a specified behaviour, this is, however, a predictable behaviour for this latch, when implemented in this way.

Figure 6.4 also shows the *transition table* for the *SR* latch. The transition table has a role similar to that of the truth table used with combinational circuits, enabling the description of the evolution of the sequential circuit according to its inputs and previous state. As we can see, the current state of the circuit does not appear in the input columns. The output column, in

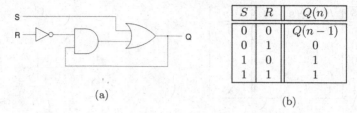

S	R	$Q(n)$
0	0	$Q(n-1)$
0	1	0
1	0	1
1	1	1

(a)   (b)

Fig. 6.4   Level-sensitive SR latch: (a) logic circuit with AND-OR gates and (b) transition table.

SR

$Q(n-1)$	00	01	11	10
0	0	0	X	1
1	1	0	X	1

Fig. 6.5   Minimising the Karnaugh map of the SR latch by connecting maxterms.

addition to showing the values 0 and 1, may show the current value of the state or, as will be seen below in other devices, its complement.

It is easy to obtain implementations of the SR latch using just one of the universal logic gates, NOR or NAND. Applying de Morgan's Law to Expression (6.1) we get an implementation with NAND gates as shown in Expression (6.2) and Figure 6.6(a). This implementation is far more popular than the one presented in Figure 6.4.

$$Q(n) = S + \overline{R} \cdot Q(n-1)$$
$$= \overline{\overline{S + \overline{R} \cdot Q(n-1)}}$$
$$= \overline{\overline{S} \cdot (\overline{\overline{R} \cdot Q(n-1)})}. \tag{6.2}$$

In the case of an implementation with NOR gates, it is convenient to simplify the Karnaugh map in Figure 6.3(b) using groupings of zeros, as shown in Figure 6.5.

In this way, the expression obtained is $Q(n) = (S+Q(n-1)) \cdot \overline{R}$. Applying de Morgan's law to this expression results in Expression (6.3).

$$Q(n) = (S + Q(n-1)) \cdot \overline{R}$$
$$= \overline{\overline{(S + Q(n-1)) \cdot \overline{R}}}$$
$$= \overline{\overline{(S + Q(n-1))} + R}. \tag{6.3}$$

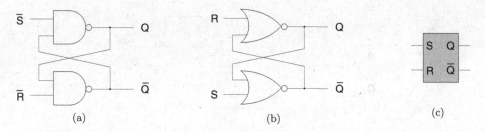

Fig. 6.6 Level-sensitive *SR* latches implemented with logic gates of the same type: (a) NAND-NAND latch; (b) NOR-NOR latch and (c) symbol.

Figure 6.6 shows these circuits. Besides the advantage of using a single type of logic gates to enable a more optimised implementation in terms of hardware (as discussed in Section 2.2.3), these versions offer an output without additional cost which, in normal conditions, represents the complement of the state. For these reasons, in practice, one of the implementations in Figure 6.6 is usually used, instead of the circuit in Figure 6.4(a).

The symbol used for the *SR* latch in this text is shown in Figure 6.6(c). To make the logic diagrams clearer, this book adopts the convention that the sequential elements are represented with a dark background, as is the case with this symbol.

Two details which characterise each of these circuits should be highlighted. In the NOR-NOR version, Figure 6.6(b), the combination of inputs $S = R = 1$, for which the behaviour of the latch was not specified (Figure 6.3), sets the state of the latch to 0, unlike the previous two implementations. On the other hand, in the NAND-NAND version, Figure 6.6(a), the inputs $\overline{S}$ and $\overline{R}$ are both active at 0. Also note that in both circuits, the combination of inputs $S = R = 1$ $(\overline{S} = \overline{R} = 0)$ places the output $\overline{Q}$ equal to Q. The designation of the output $\overline{Q}$ is incorrect but, usual in the literature and general documentation.

Figure 6.7 shows the behaviour of the level-sensitive *SR* latch, NOR-NOR version, over time, subject to a certain sequence of input signals. At the interval $U1$, both inputs are inactive, and the circuit maintains its prior state, which in this case is assumed to be 0. At the start of $U2$, the signal S becomes active, setting the state of the circuit to 1. This state is maintained independently of whether S rises or falls. In $U3$ it is the R signal which becomes active, leading to the latch state once again becoming 0. The period $U4$ corresponds to the situation in which both signals S and R are active. In this situation, the outputs Q and $\overline{Q}$ remain equal, in the NOR-NOR case,

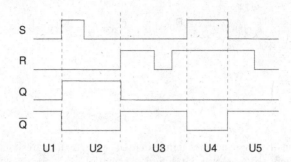

Fig. 6.7 Time diagram for an *SR* NOR-NOR latch.

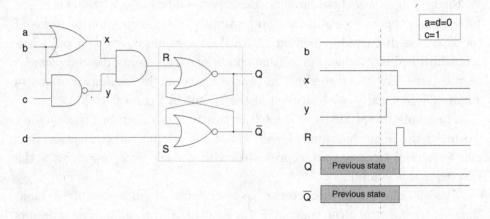

Fig. 6.8 Example of the effect of a hazard in the inputs that causes the loss of information stored in the latch.

both with the value 0. In $U5$, the signal S changes to 0 and, therefore, the active R signal resets the latch state to 0.

6.2.2 *SR Latches with an Enable Signal*

In the SR latches shown, the activation of either of the inputs, if it causes an alteration in the state of the latch, has an immediate effect. In the design of logic circuits, this approach is potentially dangerous, because any hazard (see Section 3.4.2) in the signals S or R can cause the loss of the state stored in the latch. Figure 6.8 shows this situation.

In this figure, the logic function of the combinational circuit which generates the signal R is given by $R = (a + b) \cdot \overline{bc} = a\overline{b} + a\overline{c} + b\overline{c}$. So if, $a = 0$ and $c = 1$, then $R = 0$, independently of the value of b. However, when implementing the circuit, it can happen that the gate OR is slower than the NAND gate (as discussed in Section 3.1.4). In this case, the transition of the signal b from 1 to 0 causes a hazard at 1 in the signal R.[1] The hazard which may arise in signal R places the state of the latch at 0, erasing the value which was previously stored and making its recovery impossible. Thus, the type of latches shown in the previous section should only be used when it is possible to guarantee that the input signals are free of hazards.

The SR latch can be modified in such a way that it can only be updated when an *Enable* signal is found at 1, as shown in Figure 6.9(a). The *Enable* input is often designated by c (from control). The already known circuit of the SR latch is located within the line in grey. Two NAND gates were added. When the c signal has value 0, these gates keep the inputs $\overline{S'}$ and $\overline{R'}$ at 1, thus ensuring that the state of the latch remains unaltered. With c at 1, the NAND gates behave as inverters for the signals S and R. In this situation, the SR latch functions as shown in the previous section, although with the inputs active at 1. In a similar manner, NOR gates may be used for the construction of this type of latches, with all the signals (S, R and c) in this case active at 0. Figure 6.9(c) shows the *transition table* for this latch.

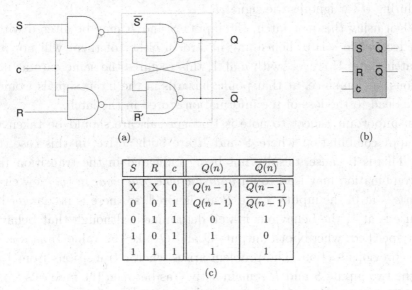

S	R	c	$Q(n)$	$\overline{Q(n)}$
X	X	0	$Q(n-1)$	$\overline{Q(n-1)}$
0	0	1	$Q(n-1)$	$\overline{Q(n-1)}$
0	1	1	0	1
1	0	1	1	0
1	1	1	1	1

(c)

Fig. 6.9 SR latch with *Enable* signal: (a) logic circuit; (b) symbol and (c) transition table.

---

[1]The delay time of a logic gate greatly depends on the manufacturing process of the circuit, which can make it difficult to know at the outset exactly which is the slowest gate. Due to the difficulty of controlling this parameter, it is necessary to arrange mechanisms to ensure the operation of the circuits, independently of variations in the delay times of the logic gates.

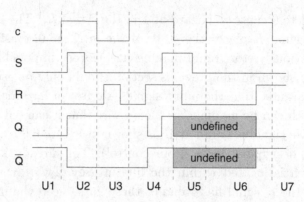

Fig. 6.10 Timing diagram illustrating the operation of the *SR* latch with an *Enable* signal.

Figure 6.10 shows the operation of this latch. We can see that, in the intervals in which $c = 0$, the signals S and R are ignored as the enable signal is at 0. For example, in the interval $U2$, the latch responds to the signal S, but during $U3$ it ignores the signal R.

When using this new latch, the inputs S and R may be altered without any effect while c is 0, hence any hazard in either of them will not affect the latch state. However, with c at 1, this requires the same care as in the previous section since, at that point, hazards in the input signals would, as before, lead to the loss of the information stored in the latch.

An important aspect to note is that special care should be taken with the input combination where S and R are both active, in this case, both at 1. This is because, despite not being indicated in the transition table, this combination may lead to an *unpredictable behaviour* in the new circuit. When c is at 0, the inputs S and R are ignored, so there is no danger here. When c is at 1, the behaviour is well determined, although that behaviour is not specified, where both outputs Q and $\overline{Q}$ take the value 1, as was seen in the previous section. The problem arises when c transitions from 1 to 0 and the two inputs S and R remain active (as between the intervals $U4$ and $U5$ of Figure 6.10). In this situation, the signals $\overline{S'}$ and $\overline{R'}$ simultaneously go from $\overline{S'} = \overline{R'} = 1$ to $\overline{S'} = \overline{R'} = 0$. With $\overline{S'} = \overline{R'} = 0$, the latch maintains its previous state, but in this case what is the previous state? Both outputs Q and $\overline{Q}$ are at 1! In that case, what will be the next state of the latch? The answer is that this is not known at the outset, and it may be either one. The final value depends on which of the NAND gates feedback is the fastest (which in turn may be related to the manufacture of the circuit).

This problem is called a *race*. The race arises when two (or more) signals alter their value, simultaneously or with time intervals clearly below the delay times of the circuits involved. It is often impossible to predict what will happen to some signals dependent on them. It is even possible that the latch remains with a voltage value at the output that does not correspond to a valid logic value, a situation known as *metastability*. The conclusion is that, for the correct and deterministic operation of this latch, the inputs S and R can never be both active when c has a transition to 0.

6.2.3 *D Latch*

The previous SR latch stores one bit of information, with the value determined by the inputs S and R while the enable signal c is active. What is often required is to store the value of a given signal in a memory element. The mode of operation of the SR latch is not the most appropriate for this purpose because the values of the two signals S and R suitable to store the intended value have to be determined.

A simple variation of this latch is the *D-type latch*, shown in Figure 6.11. The only alteration is the addition of an inverter between inputs S and R. This inverter makes these two signals complementary, which implies that this circuit always forces a *set* or a *reset* of the latch, depending on the input signal. Thus, when c is active, the latch output takes the value of D.

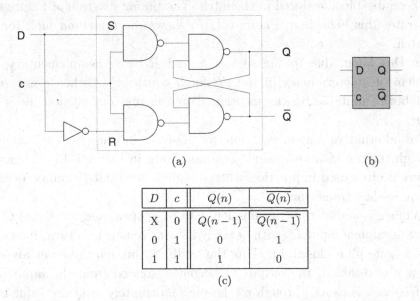

D	c	$Q(n)$	$\overline{Q(n)}$
X	0	$Q(n-1)$	$\overline{Q(n-1)}$
0	1	0	1
1	1	1	0

(c)

Fig. 6.11 D type latch: (a) logic circuit; (b) symbol and (c) transition table.

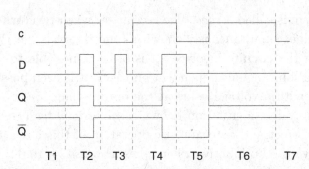

Fig. 6.12   Timing diagram illustrating the operation of the D latch.

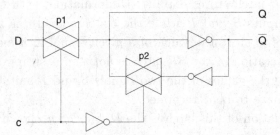

Fig. 6.13   Implementation of a D-type latch using transition gates.

When that signal is disabled, the last value present in the D input, before c has been disabled, is stored in the latch. The timing diagram of Figure 6.12 illustrates this behaviour. Figure 6.11(c) shows the *transition table* for the D latch.

In this latch, due to the signals S and R being complementary, the problem of indeterminacy in the SR latch which arises when c goes to 0 with both inputs active, as mentioned in the previous section, does not occur.

An alternative implementation for D-type latches can be achieved through the use of transmission gates, as shown in Figure 6.13. This architecture is often used in practice, when designing integrated circuits, because it requires less transistors.

While c is active, the transmission gate **p1** is open, and the signal Q follows the value of input D (with $\overline{Q}$ being its complement). In turn, the transmission gate **p2** is closed, breaking the feedback through the lower inverter. When c is disabled, the output Q becomes isolated from the input, and the feedback is closed through **p2**, keeping indefinitely in Q the value of D present immediately before disabling c.

Of course, the implementation of Figure 6.13 corresponds to the same symbol, Figure 6.11(b), the same transition table, Figure 6.11(c), and the same timing behaviour of Figure 6.12.

6.3 Clock Signal

Hazards in logic signals are very common in the implementation of combinational circuits (see Section 3.4.2). The hazards represent wrong values, of short duration, which are quickly replaced by the value defined in the circuit design. Although it is often possible to eliminate them by using additional logic gates, generally such care is not necessary in the design of combinational circuits. Instead of increasing the complexity of the circuit with the addition of extra logic for the sole purpose of eliminating the hazards, what is done in practice is to ensure that the outputs are used only after a period sufficiently long for all the hazards to have passed and for the signals to be stable.

However, the consequences of these hazards in sequential circuits can be disastrous. As we saw above, a hazard in one of the input signals can cause a permanent change in a memory element. In this case, there is no way to recover the previously stored value, leading to malfunction of the circuit.

6.3.1 *Global Synchronisation Signal*

Sequential circuits may be classified as synchronous sequential circuits or asynchronous sequential circuits. The difference is that in synchronous sequential circuits there is a global control signal that determines the updating of the memory elements of the circuit, the clock signal, often represented by *CLK*, or by *CP* (*clock pulse*). The advantage of this signal is to set phases in the operation of the sequential circuit, one phase calculating the signals to update the different memory elements and another phase in which these are updated. This way, the hazards which arise in the logic when generating input signals are ignored by the memory elements. In addition to this advantage, the clock signal guarantees that the memory elements keep the same value during the phase calculating the following values, and that they change synchronously when there is a transition in the clock signal, thus creating conditions to define the *state of a sequential circuit*. Hence the name synchronous given to this type of circuits. The design of synchronous circuits will be studied in the following chapter.

In contrast, asynchronous sequential circuits do not have a clock signal and, therefore, it is necessary to be extra careful in their design with respect to the existence of hazards in the input signals. Additionally, each memory element may be updated at any time, making the design of this type of circuit more complicated. On the other hand, there is an advantage for asynchronous circuits. Given that there is no clock signal controlling the loading of the memory elements, each of them operates at its maximum speed, making asynchronous circuits faster than synchronous circuits. Still, synchronous sequential circuits are those which are almost always used in practice, due to the greater complexity of the design and difficulty in testing asynchronous sequential circuits. For these reasons, this book does not cover the design of asynchronous sequential circuits.

6.3.2   *Characteristics of the Clock Signal*

As we have mentioned, synchronous sequential circuits have a particular signal, the clock signal, which synchronises the updating of the memory elements of the circuit. An essential characteristic of this signal is that it is a *clean* signal, that is, it does not have hazards. The clock signal, CLK, is a periodic signal in the form of a rectangular wave, as shown in Figure 6.14. In this figure, T is the *period of the clock signal*, that is, the time between two *rising edges* (or between two *falling edges*) of the clock.

In a clock signal period (also called *clock cycle*) there is one and only one *rising transition*, also referred to as rising edge, and one and only one *falling transition* (or falling edge), marked in the Figure 6.14 by t_1 and t_2, respectively. The clock signal has two *phases* in which the level is constant. Each phase corresponds to the time between two successive transitions. The length of each phase of the clock signal, at level 1 or level 0, may or may not be equal, varying from circuit to circuit. *Duty cycle* is defined as the fraction of the period of the clock signal in phase 1. In the discussion which follows, the value of the duty circle is not very important, but to simplify it

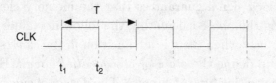

Fig. 6.14   Typical waveform of a clock signal.

is assumed that the clock spends half of the time in each phase, that is, that the duty cycle is 0.5.

The *frequency of the clock signal*, represented by the letter f, is the number of clock periods per second and is the inverse of the clock period, $f = 1/T$. The fundamental unit of measurement for frequency is s^{-1}, or *hertz* (Hz), with $1 \text{ s}^{-1} = 1 \text{ Hz} = 1$ cycle per second. For example, if the clock period is 100 ns, $T = 100$ ns, then the clock frequency will be $f = 10$ MHz as Expression (6.4) shows.

$$f = \frac{1}{T} = \frac{1}{100 \text{ ns}} = \frac{1}{10^{-7} \text{ s}} = 10^7 \text{ Hz} = 10 \text{ MHz} \qquad (6.4)$$

In some situations, it can be useful for the circuit to have more than one clock signal, for example, when a part of the circuit must operate at a higher frequency than another. These circuits pose some synchronisation problems, the discussion of which is outside the scope of this book. In the context of this book, we always assume that there is a single clock signal.

6.4 Flip-Flops

If in the latches presented in Section 6.2, the *Enable* (or c) input is connected to the clock signal, the output (which represents the latch state) is continuously being updated during the active phase of the clock, and the inputs must remain stable during this time interval. Therefore, it is only in the opposite clock phase that it is possible to generate new values for the inputs, without risking the generation of hazards which may inadvertently cause the loss of information stored in the latch. Furthermore, it is not possible to ensure that the states are stable during the phase in which the clock signal is active, therefore losing the notion of synchronous transition of the state in a complex circuit.

This section analyses a new type of memory element, *edge-sensitive memory elements*, in which the output is only updated in a *transition of the clock signal*. This mode of operation enables, firstly, that almost all the clock period is used for updating the inputs and, in addition, ensures that the state of the memory element is only altered once every clock period. This second characteristic is essential in the design of synchronous sequential circuits, as we will see below. Memory elements of this type are also called *flip-flops*. In the rest of this book, we will use the designation flip-flop.

Even so, level-sensitive latches have their own applications because having the output immediately reflect the inputs during one of the phases of the clock makes it possible to create faster sequential circuits. This characteristic is called transparency since the changes which have taken place in the inputs when the c line is active are immediately visible in the outputs. There are specific applications which require the behaviour offered by a level-sensitive latch. Furthermore, as we will see, flip-flops are more complex.

6.4.1 *Types of Sampling*

Although the state of the flip-flops is updated in a clock edge, there are several variants as to when the input signals which define the state of the flip-flop are sampled. This section analyses the operation of two of the most common types of sampling: *Master–Slave* and *Edge-Triggered*.

6.4.1.1 *Master–slave flip-flops*

Figure 6.15(a) shows a master–slave SR flip-flop. The basic operation of this flip-flop is the same as the SR latch, with the same response behaviour to the two signals S and R, as shown in the transition table in Figure 6.15(c). The difference lies only in the fact that the updating of the output is carried

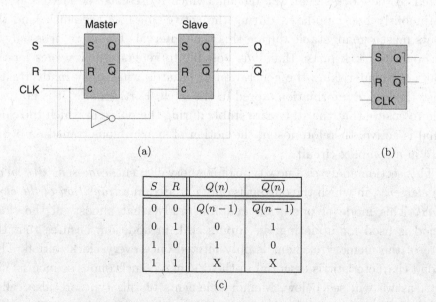

(a)   (b)

S	R	$Q(n)$	$\overline{Q(n)}$
0	0	$Q(n-1)$	$\overline{Q(n-1)}$
0	1	0	1
1	0	1	0
1	1	X	X

(c)

Fig. 6.15   Master–slave SR flip-flops: (a) logic circuit; (b) symbol and (c) transition table.

out at one of the edges of the clock (in the case of the flip-flop shown, at the falling edge).

This flip-flop is made up of two *SR* latches, but with the *Enable* lines active at different levels. The first of these latches is the master and responds directly to the input signals. The second is the slave and follows the state of the master in the inverse phase of the clock cycle. The state of the slave defines the state of the master–slave flip-flop.

It is easy to see that the state of the master–slave flip-flop is kept stable throughout almost all of the clock period. While the clock is at its inactive phase for the slave, the latter ignores its inputs, and its state does not change. In the opposite phase, it is the master which is inactive, therefore, although the slave is active, its inputs are constant since the state of the master does not change. The alteration of the state of the master–slave flip-flop only takes place at the edge of the clock, which disables the master and enables the slave.

Figure 6.15(b) shows the symbol used in this text for an *SR* master–slave flip-flop. The symbol alongside the output indicates that the outputs are enabled only at the falling edge of the clock. If the enabling takes place at the rising edge, that is indicated by a circle (representing inversion) in the clock input.

The timing diagram of Figure 6.16 shows the behaviour of this type of flip-flop. The master latch has the operation described in Section 6.2.2, responding to the inputs while the clock level is 1 and ignoring those inputs during the opposite phase of the clock. The slave latch reads the value of the master latch from the moment in which the clock transitions to 0, and it is only at the moment of that transition that its state can change. Note that the problem of *unpredictable behaviour* in the output remains in the case of this flip-flop, when the S and R signals are both active at the moment when the clock signal makes a falling transition. The situation is shown in Figure 6.16 between the clock cycles $T6$ and $T7$. Upon falling, the clock signal leads the master flip-flop to take on an unpredictable value, and this indefinition is propagated to the slave.

Some master–slave flip-flops, including the master–slave *SR*, are also called *ones-catching*. The reason for this name is shown in the cycles $T2$ and $T4$ in Figure 6.16. The master flip-flop follows the value of the inputs, but the state that is recorded corresponds to the last input that was at 1 before the clock edge.

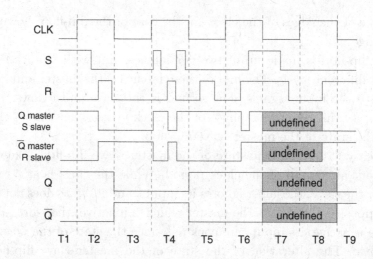

Fig. 6.16   Timing diagram showing the operation of the SR master–slave flip-flop.

Master–slave flip-flops are relatively simple to construct and achieve the objective of maintaining the output constant during a clock period, a very useful characteristic in designing state machines as will be seen in the next chapter. However, they are still sensitive to hazards in the input signals. The characteristic of ones-catching means that, if a hazard in one of the inputs is the last active event in the input signals, the master keeps the wrong value and that value is transmitted to the slave.

6.4.1.2   *Edge-triggered flip-flops*

One solution to solve the problem of hazards in the inputs is to sample the input signals only at an edge and, of course, at the same clock edge in which the state of the flip-flop is updated.[2] Figure 6.17 shows a flip-flop, in this case a D-type flip-flop, triggered by the rising edge of the clock. Figure 6.17(a) shows the logic circuit of this flip-flop. Analysis of the internal operation is a little more complicated, and a more careful analysis is left for the more interested readers. The symbol for the D-type flip-flop triggered in the rising edge is shown in Figure 6.17(b). The edge-triggered behaviour is identified by the triangle in the clock input. If the triggering was on the falling edge, there would be a circle at the clock input.

---

[2]There is another type of flip-flop with the sampling of the inputs done on the opposite edge of the one that triggers the update of the flip-flop state. However, that architecture is obsolete and will not be considered in this text.

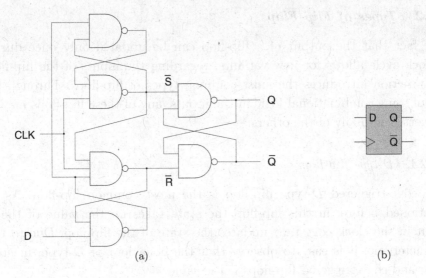

Fig. 6.17   Edge-triggered *D*-type flip-flop: (a) logic circuit and (b) symbol.

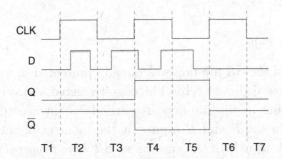

Fig. 6.18   Timing diagram showing the operation of the edge-triggered *D* flip-flop.

This type of flip-flop is called an edge-triggered flip-flop. This is a little misleading, since the master–slave flip-flops are also triggered in an edge of the clock. However this is the usual name in the literature and in all the technical documentation and, as such, it is the name that we will use in this book.

This circuit keeps the state Q stable while the clock signal is constant at 0, constant at 1 or makes a transition from 1 to 0. Its state is only updated at the rising edge of the clock signal, assuming the value of input D at that same instance. This behaviour is shown in Figure 6.18. The clock edge which enables the flip-flop is referred to as the *active edge* of the clock signal. Sometimes the term *clock pulse* is used, with the same meaning as active edge.

6.4.2　Types of Flip-Flops

The fact that the output of a flip-flop can be updated only once during a clock cycle allows for new variants, regarding the inputs of the flip-flop. This section introduces the most common types of flip-flops. Through the use of some combinational logic in the inputs, any of these flip-flops may be converted into any of the others.

6.4.2.1　D-type flip-flops

The edge-triggered D-type flip-flop is the most common flip-flop. As we mentioned before, in this flip-flop the state takes on the value of the D input in the clock edge that updates the state of the flip-flop. Due to this characteristic, it is easy to observe that the behaviour of D-type, master–slave and edge-triggered flip-flops is the same.

The edge-triggered D-type flip-flop was described above in Figures 6.17 and 6.18.

6.4.2.2　SR flip-flops

The operation of the SR flip-flop was already presented in the master–slave version in Figures 6.15 and 6.16. The edge-triggered version differs only in that the updating of the flip-flops is carried out in accordance with the values present in the S and R inputs at the moment of the active transition of the clock signal. In the case of an SR *edge-triggered flip-flop* active at the falling edge, the difference of behaviour for the master–slave flip-flop in Figure 6.16 will only occur between cycles $T3$ and $T4$, as we can see, for the same input sequence in Figure 6.19. At the falling edge at the start of $T3$, both the S and R inputs are inactive, and, therefore, the edge-triggered flip-flop maintains its state. Then, during the cycles $T3$ and $T4$, the flip-flop has the value 1 at the output. In this way, the consequences of the possible occurrence of hazards in the input signals are eliminated, but the unpredictability of the operation of the flip-flop is maintained if, at the moment of the active clock edge, the two inputs S and R both have the value 1.

6.4.2.3　JK flip-flops

JK flip-flops are an extension of SR flip-flops, in which the input J is equivalent to S and the input K is equivalent to R, exploiting the invalid

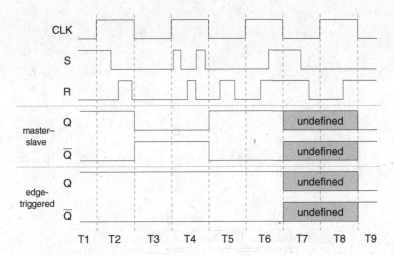

Fig. 6.19   Timing diagram showing the difference in operation between a master–slave and an edge-triggered *SR* flip-flops.

combination of the inputs ($S = R = 1$) in a useful way. For the other combinations of inputs, the behaviour of the *JK* flip-flop is equal to that of the *SR* flip-flops. The difference is that with $J = K = 1$ the next state of this flip-flop is defined as being the complement of the current state. Figure 6.20(c) shows the transition table which defines the behaviour of the *JK* flip-flop.

Figure 6.20(b) shows the symbol of a master–slave *JK* flip-flop, above, and an edge-triggered *JK* flip-flop, below. The symbols show the master–slave flip-flop active in the falling edge of the clock signal and the edge-triggered flip-flop active in the rising edge of the clock signal. The active versions on the opposite edges are represented using a circle in the clock input.

As we can see in Figure 6.20(a), only one of the S or R signals can be at 1, since one of the and gates has Q as an input, and the other, $\overline{Q}$, and one and only one of these will be at 1. For example, if the current state is 1, the value present in input J will be ignored, due to the fact that $\overline{Q} = 0$. In these circumstances, only the signal $R = K$ can become 1. The consequence is that, independently of the value of J, if $K = 1$, then the next state will be 0. This behaviour agrees with the specification of the *JK* flip-flop: if $J = 0$ and $K = 1$, then the flip-flop is reset, and the next state will be 0; if $J = 1$ and $K = 1$, the state is complemented, with the next state taking the value 0. A similar reasoning can be made for the case of the current state being at 0.

Figure 6.21 shows the operation of the *JK* flip-flop triggered at the falling edge of the clock, in the master–slave and edge-triggered versions. In the transition between cycles $T2$ and $T3$, the master–slave flip-flop changes state,

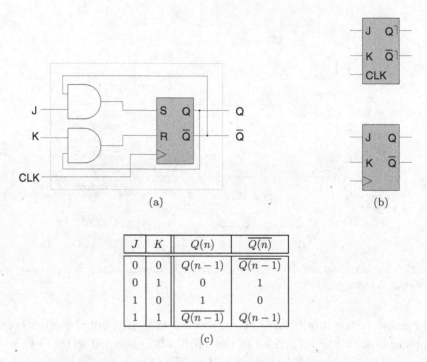

J	K	$Q(n)$	$\overline{Q(n)}$
0	0	$Q(n-1)$	$\overline{Q(n-1)}$
0	1	0	1
1	0	1	0
1	1	$\overline{Q(n-1)}$	$Q(n-1)$

(c)

Fig. 6.20   *JK* flip-flop: (a) logic circuit; (b) symbols and (c) transition table.

because during the active phase of the master the input J has taken the value 1.[3] On the other hand, the edge-triggered version reacts only to the values of the inputs in the rising transition, where $J = K = 0$, thus maintaining its state.

The *JK* configuration presupposes the use of flip-flops, i.e., with the updating of states in an edge of the clock signal. With level-sensitive latches, the combination $J = K = 1$ would cause an oscillation in its state during the active phase of the control signal and once again this would lead to the impossibility to determine the value of the latch when the control signal becomes inactive.

---

[3] As has been seen, the input K has no influence when the state is 0. However, taking into account the ones-catching characteristic of this flip-flop, the fact that K has also taken the value 1, means this transition may be interpreted as the complement of the state because $J = K = 1$.

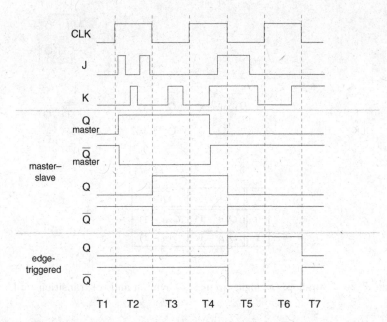

Fig. 6.21   Timing diagram showing the operation of the JK flip-flop updated in the falling edge, both in the master–slave and edge-triggered versions.

6.4.2.4 T flip-flops

Another type of very common flip-flop is the T *flip-flop* (from *toggle*), shown in Figure 6.22. These flip-flops have only one input, T, in addition to the clock signal. If T is 0, the flip-flop maintains its state. If T is 1, the flip-flop switches to the complementary state. Figure 6.22(a) shows how a T-type edge-triggered flip-flop can easily be constructed from a D-type flip-flop. Another simple way of obtaining a T flip-flop is from a JK flip-flop, by making $T = J = K$.

As is the case with the other flip-flops, the T-type flip-flop may be master–slave or edge-triggered. Figure 6.22(b) shows the symbols. The upper model is a master–slave T flip-flop active in the falling edge of the clock signal, and, the lower model, is an edge-triggered T flip-flop active in the rising edge of the clock signal. The difference in behaviour between the master–slave and edge-triggered versions is shown in Figure 6.23. In the case of the master–slave flip-flop, with T assuming the value 1 during the previous clock cycle, the flip-flop complements its state. Note that the fact that T rises twice in a given clock cycle (cycle $T4$) does not cause the complement of the output twice, which would be equivalent to maintaining it constant. The characteristic of ones-catching indicates only that this input has risen at

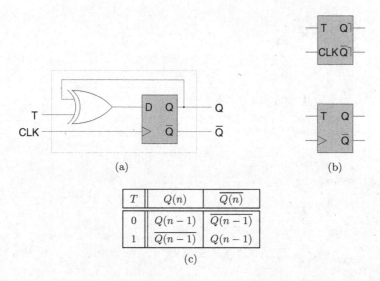

(a)   (b)

T	$Q(n)$	$\overline{Q(n)}$
0	$Q(n-1)$	$\overline{Q(n-1)}$
1	$\overline{Q(n-1)}$	$Q(n-1)$

(c)

Fig. 6.22 T flip-flop: (a) logic circuit; (b) symbol and (c) transition table.

least once, and is only counted as one rise. In the edge-triggered case, there is only one change of state in the flip-flops, since the only active transition of the clock where T is at 1 is the rising edge between the cycles $T3$ and $T4$.

In some situations, such as, for example, in the design of counters, to be studied below, flip-flops which have an output transition in all clock cycles are necessary. This behaviour is obtained through T-type flip-flops with their input fixed at 1. This simple case is shown in Figure 6.24. As we can see, in the timing diagram of the figure, this flip-flop in practice operates as a *frequency divider*. The output is a signal with double the period (or half the frequency) of the clock signal.

6.4.3   *Direct Inputs*

The input signals for the flip-flops, whether master–slave or edge-triggered, only have effect when the next active edge of the clock signal occurs. Similarly, in the case of the level-sensitive latches, during the interval of time in which the *Enable* signal is inactive, the input signals do not have an effect on the state. Although, as we will see in the next chapter, this is the desired behaviour for the design of sequential circuits, there are situations in which it is necessary to break this dependency. To this end, flip-flops may have control signals with immediate effect available, known as *direct inputs* or *asynchronous inputs*.

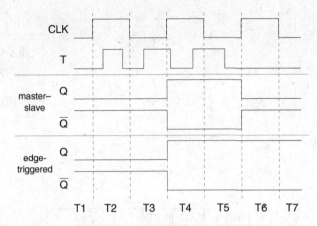

Fig. 6.23 Timing diagram showing the operation of T flip-flops enabled in the rising edge, both the master–slave and edge-triggered versions.

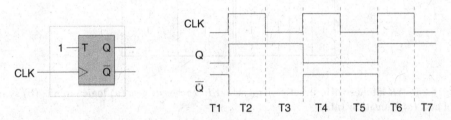

Fig. 6.24 T-type flip-flop with input fixed at 1 and timing diagram showing its operation.

Figure 6.25 shows an SR latch with an immediate control signal, RD (from Reset Direct). As we can see by the circuit in Figure 6.25(a), when RD is inactive ($\overline{RD} = 1$), the latch functions as previously defined by Figure 6.9. When RD is active, $\overline{RD} = 0$, this signal simultaneously determines that $\overline{S'} = 1$ and $\overline{Q} = 1$, such that the state of the latch immediately assumes the value $Q = 0$, independently of the other input signals. This behaviour is shown in Figure 6.26.

The direct control signal for set, $\overline{SD}$, may be constructed in an equivalent way and may be made available in a latch as an alternative, or together with the $\overline{RD}$ signal. We assume that the signals are active at 0, as this is typically the convention (for historical and technological reasons). The behaviour of immediate control signals in the other types of latches and flip-flops is similar.

Figure 6.27 shows a master–slave SR flip-flop with $\overline{SD}$ and $\overline{RD}$ direct control signals. The timing diagram in Figure 6.28 illustrates the operation of this flip-flop. While the immediate control signals are inactive, $\overline{SD} = \overline{RD} = 1$, the flip-flop has a behaviour equal to that shown in Figure 6.16.

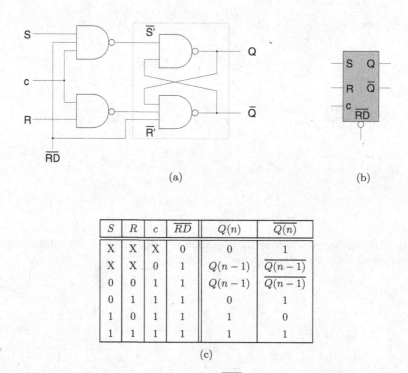

(a)   (b)

S	R	c	$\overline{RD}$	$Q(n)$	$\overline{Q(n)}$
X	X	X	0	0	1
X	X	0	1	$Q(n-1)$	$\overline{Q(n-1)}$
0	0	1	1	$Q(n-1)$	$\overline{Q(n-1)}$
0	1	1	1	0	1
1	0	1	1	1	0
1	1	1	1	1	1

(c)

Fig. 6.25   *SR* latches with direct control signal $\overline{RD}$ reset direct: (a) logic circuit; (b) symbol and (c) transition table.

In the clock cycle $T2$, the $\overline{RD}$ signal at 0 both prevents the master latch from going to 1 when S goes to 1 and also causes the slave latch to take the value 0 immediately. In the cycle $T3$, as soon as $\overline{SD}$ goes to 0, both the master and the slave latches assume the value 1. Finally, in the cycle $T5$, the $\overline{RD}$ signal going to 0 resolves the indefinite situation of the latches, setting both to 0.

An *SR* flip-flop triggered in the falling edge of the clock signal, with *SD* and *RD* direct control signals, will have the same behaviour for the particular case of the timing diagram in Figure 6.28.

6.4.4   *Timing Parameters of Flip-Flops*

In the case of combinational logic elements, the important timing parameter, as was studied in Section 3.1.4, is the propagation delay caused by the gate, that is, how long it takes for the change of a logic signal in one of the inputs to take effect in the output. In the case of sequential elements, the propagation delay is also an important parameter. In flip-flops, it indicates how long it takes for the output to change after the active transition of the clock signal.

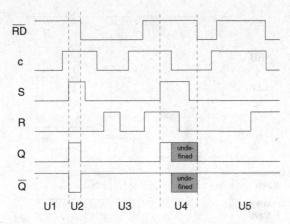

Fig. 6.26 Timing diagram showing the operation of the level-sensitive SR latch with a direct $\overline{RD}$ control signal.

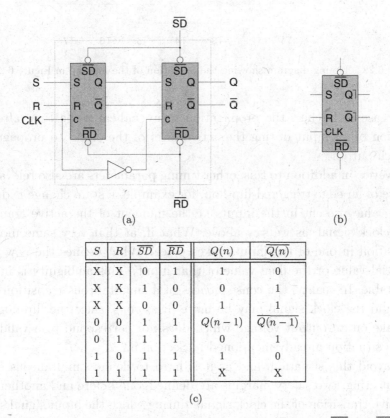

S	R	$\overline{SD}$	$\overline{RD}$	$Q(n)$	$\overline{Q(n)}$
X	X	0	1	1	0
X	X	1	0	0	1
X	X	0	0	1	1
0	0	1	1	$Q(n-1)$	$\overline{Q(n-1)}$
0	1	1	1	0	1
1	0	1	1	1	0
1	1	1	1	X	X

(c)

Fig. 6.27 SR master–slave flip-flop enabled in the falling edge with $\overline{SD}$ and $\overline{RD}$ direct control signals: (a) logic circuit; (b) symbol and (c) transition table. This table assumes that the SR flip-flops are built with NAND gates.

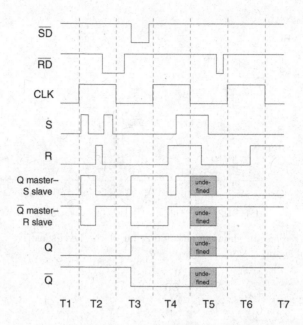

Fig. 6.28   Timing diagram showing the operation of the flip-flop in Figure 6.27.

In the case of latches, the propagation delay indicates the time after the transition of an input during the active level of the clock, to propagate to the latch output.

However, in addition to this, other timing parameters are also relevant. In the case of an edge-triggered flip-flop, for example, a state change is defined by the value present in the inputs at the moment of the active transition of the clock signal, as we saw above. What if, at that very same moment, a transition in one of the inputs takes place? What defines the new state: the initial value or the final value of that input? This ambiguity is in itself undesirable. In reality, the consequences of a simultaneous transition of an input and the clock signal may be more disastrous, since the flip-flop may even take on an output voltage which does not correspond to a valid logic state, a situation already mentioned in Section 6.2.2.

To avoid this situation, and as it is hard to define simultaneous events in engineering, two safety margins are defined, one before and another after the active transition of the clock signal, during which the input signal should remain stable to ensure the correct operation of the flip-flops. Therefore, the *setup time*, t_{setup}, is defined as the time interval before the active transition of the clock signal in which the inputs should not be altered, so as to be correctly interpreted. *Hold time*, t_{hold}, is defined as the time interval after

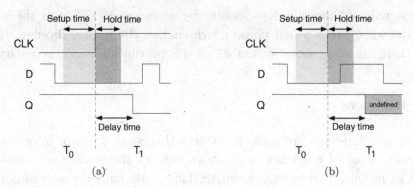

Fig. 6.29 Timing diagram indicating the setup times and hold times: (a) correct operation and (b) violation of the timing.

the active transition of the clock signal in which the inputs should also remain constant, so as to guarantee that these are correctly interpreted. The hold time, in certain devices and technologies, may be negative.

Figure 6.29 shows a timing diagram for an edge-triggered D flip-flop, updated in the rising edge of the clock signal, which shows the setup and hold times. In the situation illustrated in Figure 6.29(a), both times are respected, and the flip-flop operates normally. In the case of Figure 6.29(b), the input D has a transition during the hold interval, causing an indefinite state (and output) of this flip-flop in the subsequent clock period.

Another parameter used to characterise the flip-flops is the *maximum frequency* of operation. As the name indicates, the correct functioning of the flip-flop is only guaranteed if a clock signal is used with a frequency lower than or equal to the maximum frequency of that flip-flop.

Setup, hold and delay times, as well as the maximum frequency of operation, are specifications supplied by the manufacturer of the flip-flops. As we mentioned above, due to the manufacturing process, there may be a significant variation in the characteristics of logic elements. Therefore, the values indicated by the manufacturer correspond to the worst case. The manufacturer ensures that, if these values are respected, the logic elements operate in accordance with the specifications. Therefore, although a violation of these values does not necessarily imply erroneous behaviour of the circuit, the guarantee of correct operation is lost, which is equivalent to a wrong design.

Strictly speaking, the setup and hold times, such as those shown here, apply to edge-triggered flip-flops. In the case of master–slave flip-flops, these could have different timing parameters, depending on the design in which they are being used. For example, to resolve the problem of hazards in the input signals of these flip-flops, it may be necessary to define as the setup time the whole clock signal phase which enables the master flip-flop. However, there are other situations in which this precaution is not necessary.

6.5 Registers

Latches and flip-flops are memory devices that store 1 bit of information. Naturally, a set of n latches or flip-flops enables the storage of n bits. In many situations, particularly when working with numeric information or codes (Chapter 1), several bits are necessary to represent an item of data with meaning, such as a code word or a numerical value. Thus, it is this set of bits which has an elementary meaning and that, in general, is intended to be processed as a whole. *Registers* are used to store a set of bits which form a given entity.

6.5.1 *Basic Registers*

In its simplest form, a register of n bits is nothing more than a set of n flip-flops or latches, as shown in Figure 6.30 for the particular case of $n = 4$ bits. In the case of the register in this figure, on each rising edge of the clock cycle, the value present in the input A is stored in the register and placed in its output. This behaviour depends, as expected, on the type of flip-flop used. The register in Figure 6.30 uses D-type flip-flops with its inputs sampled and its states updated in the rising edge of the clock signal. D-type flip-flops are undoubtedly the most used to construct registers, since they are most naturally suitable for the most common use, which is storing the value present at the inputs. However, there is nothing to prevent the construction of registers with flip-flops of types SR, JK, T or other, with the necessary adaptations.

Although edge-triggered flip-flops are the most commonly used to build registers, in many situations registers using latches are used. These have the property of being transparent while the clock signal is in its active phase, and therefore, during this time, the signals at the input of the register are propagated directly to the outputs. When the clock shifts to its inactive phase, this type of register keeps the last value present in the input in the active phase, filtering further alterations in the inputs.

A register is always made up of the same type of memory elements. From now on, unless otherwise stated, we will always assume that the registers

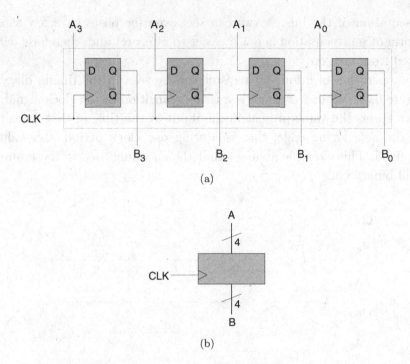

Fig. 6.30   Simple register: (a) internal structure and (b) symbol.

used are made up of D-type edge-triggered flip-flops updated in the rising edge of the clock signal.

As we mentioned before, the bits stored in a register are, in general, related in some way, representing one word of a code, a numerical value or another coherent information entity. Each bit has a position in this code or numerical value, and there is, therefore, an underlying order organising these bits. The index i in the inputs A_i and the outputs B_i in Figure 6.30(a) represents that order. In Figure 6.30(b), the input and the output of the register are represented as a bus, a concept briefly referred in Section 3.1.6 and further analysed in Section 5.1.

This representation, a thick line crossed by another line with a number below it, indicates not only that there are four signals, but also that the signals are related, logically forming a unit. The details of the logic circuit, as presented in Figure 6.30(a), show what is behind the bus A, that is, the four signals $A_3 A_2 A_1 A_0$. The same applies for the bus B, with the additional assumption that the signals with the same index are connected to the same flip-flops, that is, the output B_0 corresponds to the input A_0 and so on. In Figure 6.30(b) the signals which form the bus are collapsed into the representation of the bus. As we can see, even for buses with few signals, this form of representation is much easier to interpret and, therefore, will be adopted from now on.

The operation of a four-bit register can be seen in the timing diagrams in Figure 6.31. Whenever there is a rising transition in the clock signal, the register stores the value present in the input at the time of that transition. Until the next rising edge, that is, during one clock period, this value is maintained. This example assumes that the encoding used in these buses is natural binary code.

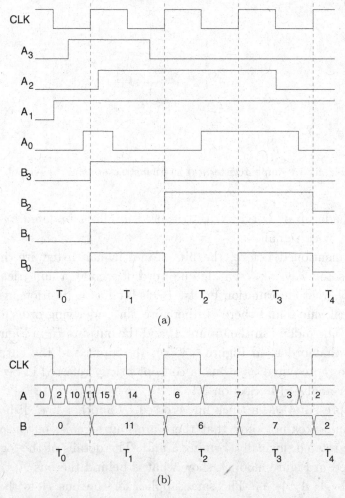

Fig. 6.31   Timing diagram representing the operation of a simple four-bit register, assuming an initial state at 0 for the flip-flops: (a) individual signals and (b) bus level.

6.5.2 *Register Control Signals*

The simple register shown above has the serious limitation that the value stored in the register is modified at each rising edge of the clock signal. A more useful register is shown in Figure 6.32.

The register of this figure has a *Load signal* with the acronym *Ld*, which determines when it is intended or not to store a new value in the register. When this signal is at 0, the register state remains unchanged. This signal should be maintained at 1 during the active transition of the clock signal to store a new value in the register. Figure 6.33 shows this behaviour.

Another very common control signal in registers is a signal which *clears* the content of the register, that is, that places the state of the register with all the bits at zero. This signal is also known by its acronym *Cl*. An example of a four-bit register with this control signal is shown in Figure 6.34. Figure 6.35 illustrates the behaviour of a register of this kind. We can see that when the control signal $\overline{Cl} = 1$, the behaviour is equal to that of a simple register, such as that in Figure 6.31. When the clock pulse occurs with $\overline{Cl} = 0$, the

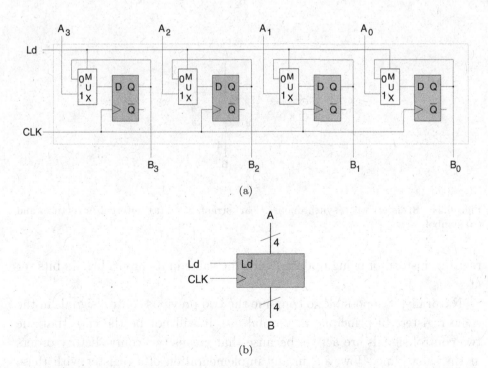

Fig. 6.32 Register with load signal *Ld*: (a) internal structure and (b) symbol.

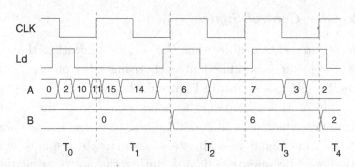

Fig. 6.33   Timing diagram representing the operation of a four-bit register with load signal, Ld, assuming that the initial register state is 0.

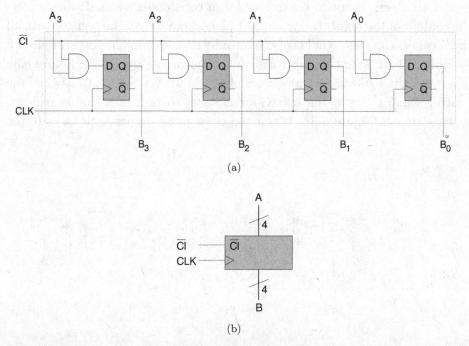

Fig. 6.34   Register with synchronous clear signal, $\overline{Cl}$: (a) internal structure and (b) symbol.

register, instead of being updated with the value in its input, has its bits set at zero.

Naturally, it is possible to combine the two previous control signals in the same register. In principle, in normal use, it will not be the case that the two control signals are active, because that means two contradictory orders at the same time. However, in any implementation of a register with these two control signals, it is defined at the outset which of the signals will have

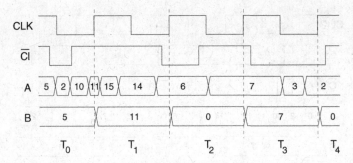

Fig. 6.35 Timing diagram representing the operation of a four-bit register with synchronous clear control signal, $\overline{Cl}$, assuming that the initial register state is 0.

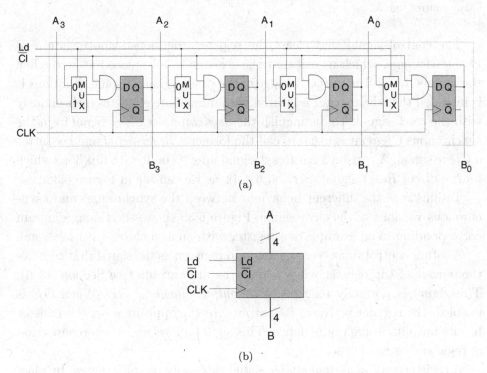

Fig. 6.36 Register with load and clear signals, Ld and $\overline{Cl}$: (a) internal structure and (b) symbol.

precedence in a situation in which they are both active at the active edge of the clock. Figure 6.36 shows an example of a four-bit register with *Load* and *Clear* signals, Ld and $\overline{Cl}$, where the latter has precedence, which means that the register is cleared if both are active. Figure 6.37 also shows a timing diagram for this circuit illustrating its behaviour.

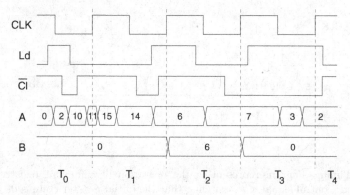

Fig. 6.37   Timing diagram representing the operation of a four-bit register with *Load* and *Clear* control signals.

The control signal that clears the register, mentioned above, is a *synchronous signal*, which means that the register is only placed at zero when the signal $\overline{Cl}$ is at 0 at the active edge of the clock signal. In some situations it is intended that the register is cleared with immediate effect, asynchronously with the clock signal. To distinguish the *asynchronous Clear signal* from the synchronous *Clear*, it is usual to call the former a *Reset* signal and the latter a *Clear* signal. A register with *Reset* signal may be built with flip-flops which have a direct *Reset* signal (Section 6.4.3), as we can see in Figure 6.38.

To illustrate the different behaviour between the synchronous and asynchronous versions of the clear signal, Figure 6.39 shows the timing diagram corresponding to an example of a register with an asynchronous clear signal.

Another control signal very common in registers is the signal that controls the output of the register when it has tri-state outputs (see Section 3.1.6). This signal is normally referred to as *output enable* or *OE*. When *OE* is enabled, the register activates its outputs. In the opposite case, the register has its outputs in high impedance. This signal allows easier interconnection of registers, as we will see.

A register with an *output enable* signal can easily be constructed, by placing tri-state buffers in the outputs of the flip-flops, as shown in Figure 6.40.

6.5.3   *Shift Registers*

A very important type of register is the *shift register*, which differs from the previous registers in the way the values are loaded into the register. The registers studied up to now receive all the bits simultaneously from an input

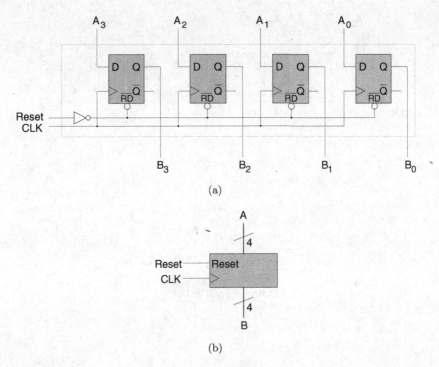

(a)

(b)

Fig. 6.38 Register with asynchronous clear signal, *Reset*: (a) internal structure and (b) symbol.

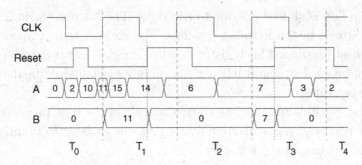

Fig. 6.39 Timing diagram representing the operation of a four-bit register with asynchronous *Reset* control signal.

bus, a loading mode known as *parallel input*. A shift register, in its simplest version, is a register in which the loading of data is carried out in series, that is, bit by bit, by a *serial input*.

The basic circuit is very simple to design. A four-bit right shift register is shown in Figure 6.41. At each active edge of the clock signal, the content

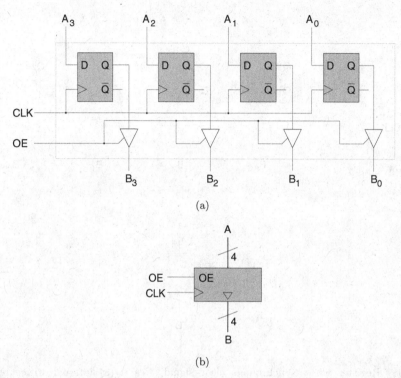

Fig. 6.40   Register with output enable signal, OE: (a) internal structure and (b) symbol.

of each flip-flop is shifted one bit to the right. The bit present in SI (Serial Input) is stored in the leftmost flip-flop. The register loses the contents of the rightmost flip-flop. This register is called a right shift register. The same circuit can be used as a shift left register merely by changing the designation of the output lines.

It is also possible to associate control signals of the type presented above with shift registers, particularly *Clear* to set the register to 0 and *Load* to control the loading of the register.

It is also possible to construct registers which are a combination of a normal register, with parallel loading, and a shift register, with serial loading. A special case is the so-called *universal register*, which has the following features, selected by control signals:

(1) maintain the content (despite the occurrence of active clock edges);
(2) shift the content to the left;
(3) shift the content to the right;
(4) parallel load.

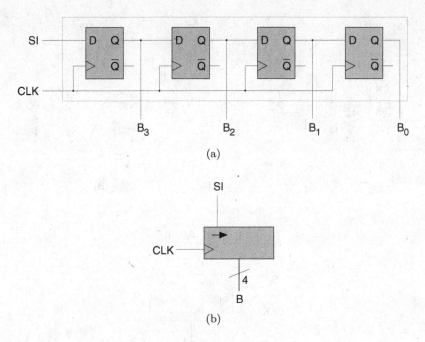

(a)

(b)

Fig. 6.41   Right shift register: (a) internal structure and (b) symbol.

Figure 6.42 shows a four-bit universal register. While the figure is complex due to the number of lines, the construction of this register is very simple. There is a multiplexer at the input of each flip-flop which selects, based on the two control signals S_1 and S_0, what is loaded in that flip-flop. In the example shown in the figure, the correspondence between the configuration of the selection bits and the mode of operation of the register is as follows:

$S_1S_0 = 00$: Each flip-flop loads its own output, therefore its state is maintained.

$S_1S_0 = 01$: Each flip-flop receives the value of the flip-flop immediately to its right. Therefore a shift to the left is implemented. Note that the rightmost flip-flop receives the series input bit, RI (right input), and that the value of the leftmost flip-flop is lost.

$S_1S_0 = 10$: This situation is symmetrical to the previous one. Each flip-flop receives the value of the flip-flop immediately to its left. Therefore a shift to the right is implemented. Note that the leftmost flip-flop receives the series input bit, LI

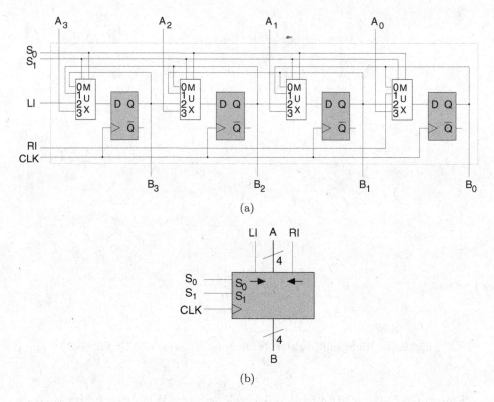

Fig. 6.42   Universal register: (a) internal structure and (b) symbol.

(left input), and that the value of the rightmost flip-flop is lost.

$S_1 S_0 = 11$: With this combination, each flip-flop receives the respective parallel input bit, A_i, therefore loading the value A into the register. This combination is equivalent to the Ld signal in a parallel load register.

6.5.4   *Status Signals in Registers*

In addition to the data output signals, registers may supply auxiliary *status output signals*, whose function is to provide some useful indication of the value stored in the register. Normally, the signals correspond to conditions which are often useful in circuits described at the level of transference between registers, as we will analyse in Chapter 8. We refer the signals Z

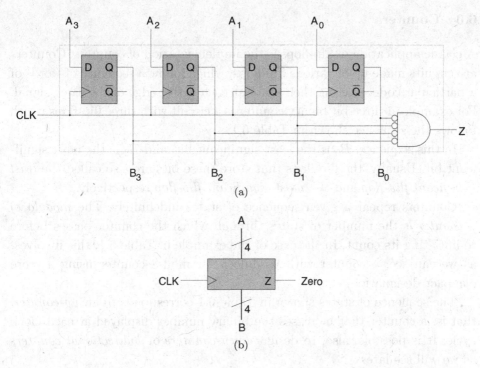

Fig. 6.43 Simple register with status Z signal: (a) internal structure and (b) symbol.

and N, although there is a large set of other possible status signals. As we will see ahead, when integrated in computer architectures, the status signals are called *flags*.

Perhaps the most common status signal is the signal Z, which, when active, indicates that the value stored in the register is the value zero. The implementation of a simple register with the state signal Z is shown in Figure 6.43. As we can see, this simply implies the use of a NOR gate which has as input all the outputs of the flip-flops of the register (in the figure, represented as an AND gate with inverted inputs).

Another very common example of a status signal is the negative status signal, N, which is active when the value stored in the register is negative. In the cases in which the register is used in systems that use values in *2's complement representation* or *sign and magnitude*, the generation of this signal is trivial since it is equal to the value of the most significant bit, as concluded from Section 5.2.

6.6   Counters

A classic application of flip-flops is the implementation of counters. Counters are circuits made up of various flip-flops, which follow a sequence of words of a particular code, altering their state at each active edge of the clock signal. For example, a three-bit binary counter is a circuit with three flip-flops which follows the sequence shown in Table 6.1.

In this sequence, B_0 is the least significant bit, and B_2 is the most significant bit. Usually, the flip-flops that store these bits are also called the *least significant flip-flop* and the *most significant flip-flop* respectively.

Counters repeat a given sequence of states indefinitely. The *modulo of a counter* is the number of states through which the counter passes before re-initiating its count. In the case of the example in Table 6.1, this involves, as we can see, a counter with modulo 8, or mod-8 counter using a more compact designation.

The sequence of states shown in Table 6.1 corresponds to an *up-counter*, that is, a counter that increases the binary number displayed at each clock cycle. It is possible, also, to design *down-counters* or *bidirectional counters* as we will see later.

There are essentially two types of counters: synchronous and asynchronous, that are analysed below. This chapter uses a heuristic approach to the construction of counters. The following chapter studies design methods for sequential circuits which may equally be applied to the particular case of counters.

Table 6.1   Count sequence for a three-bit binary counter.

T	Configuration			Counter Value
	B_2	B_1	B_0	
0	0	0	0	0
1	0	0	1	1
2	0	1	0	2
3	0	1	1	3
4	1	0	0	4
5	1	0	1	5
6	1	1	0	6
7	1	1	1	7
8	0	0	0	0
9	0	0	1	1
10	0	1	0	2
11	0	1	1	3
⋮				

6.6.1 Asynchronous Counters

It is easy to see in Table 6.1 that the flip-flop which has the output designated as B_0 changes state whenever the counter receives a clock pulse. A T flip-flop with the input T set at 1 has this behaviour. In Table 6.1, we can observe that the flip-flop B_1 changes state whenever the B_0 bit transitions from 1 to 0. That dependence happens in the transitions $001 \rightarrow 010$, $011 \rightarrow 100$, etc. By selecting flip-flops which react to the falling edge of the clock, it is possible to use the transition at B_0 to generate clock impulses for B_1. The T input of the flip-flop B_1 will also have to be at 1 so that the flip-flop changes state whenever there is a falling transition in B_0.[4]

In the same way, the third flip-flop, B_2 should change state when the second flip-flop, B_1, changes from 1 to 0. And this will successively be the case for counters with a larger number of bits. Figure 6.44 illustrates the complete circuit for a three-bit asynchronous counter.

In this counter, the flip-flops never react simultaneously. It is the change in one that can cause the change in another. In this sense, there is no synchronism between the various flip-flops. Therefore the counter is said to be an *asynchronous counter*. We should note that it is important that the edge of the clock in which the flip-flops react is the falling edge since it is the transition $1 \rightarrow 0$ of the bit of lower significance that causes the alteration in the flip-flop with a significance immediately above.

This counter with three flip-flops counts using a sequence of eight (2^3) states, and so is designated as a mod-8 counter. When the counter reaches the last count state, a new clock pulse will return the counter to the first state and, therefore, restarts counting.

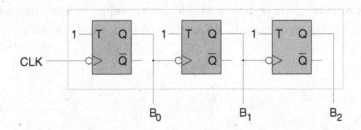

Fig. 6.44 Circuit for a three-bit asynchronous counter.

---

[4]The choice between edge-triggered and master–slave flip-flops is irrelevant.

6.6.1.1 *Timing diagram*

The evolution of the states in asynchronous counters has the particularity of the state transitions of each flip-flop occur as a consequence of a change in another flip-flop. The timing diagram in Figure 6.45 shows the operation of a three-bit asynchronous counter. The arrows show cause-effect relationships between transitions. This figure illustrates the evolution of the states of the counter. However, we can also see that there are intermediate states, which are *transient states*, which correspond to transition phases between two stable states. These transient states are a direct consequence of the switching mechanism of the flip-flops. Their duration is in the order of magnitude of the propagation times for the flip-flops, and the sequence is entirely predictable.

6.6.1.2 *Maximum operating frequency*

An important parameter in the design of sequential circuits in general and counters, in particular, is the maximum operating frequency. In the case of simple asynchronous counters, as the one shown, the limitation for the maximum operating frequency is determined by the characteristics of the least significant flip-flop, since, as was seen, the other flip-flops operate at a clock frequency which is successively divided by 2 in each stage. Therefore, for this type of counter, the maximum operating frequency is simply equal to the maximum operating frequency of the least significant flip-flop.

This maximum value only guarantees that each flip-flop will individually have the predicted behaviour. In general, the objective of the counter is that the value represented by the set of flip-flops follows the intended sequence count. Considering Figure 6.45, it can be seen that the time interval in which an asynchronous counter has a stable count value is less than the clock period, due to the propagation delay time of each flip-flop. As the clock for

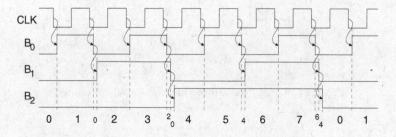

Fig. 6.45 Timing diagram for a three-bit asynchronous counter.

a flip-flop is the output of the flip-flop with immediately lower significance, this delay is cumulative. Therefore, the worst case happens when all flip-flops change state. With a counter of n bits, the total delay time for the bit of greatest significance is $n \times t_p$, where t_p is the delay time for each flip-flop, assuming they are all equal.

The designer must specify the minimum time interval, $t_{\min}$, acceptable for each count value to be stable. From this value, the propagation delay time of the flip-flops, t_p, and the number of bits of the counter, n, it is easy to determine Expression (6.5), which defines the minimum period, $T_{\min}$, of the clock signal.

$$T_{\min} > n \times t_p + t_{\min}. \tag{6.5}$$

To give a concrete example in numerical values, let us consider a modulo 256 counter, that is, $n = 8$, and flip-flops with a delay time of $t_p = 100$ ps. Let us define $t_{\min} = 400$ ps as the minimum time for a stable count value. For this case, the minimum period of the clock signal will be $T_{\min} = 1.2$ ns. The maximum frequency will be the inverse of that value, that is, $f_{\min} = 833$ MHz.

6.6.1.3 *Asynchronous counter with a generic modulo*

It is easy to design an asynchronous counter to count in any module that is a power of 2. Each flip-flop added to an asynchronous counter doubles its count modulo. However, counters which count in other modulos are often necessary. A mod-n counter counts cyclically from 0 to $n - 1$. The classic solution is to use a counter with a modulo power of 2 higher than the desired value and use the *Reset* control signal of the flip-flops to return the counter value to zero after the last desired state of the counter, $n - 1$.

The signal connected to the *Reset* input of the flip-flops is generated decoding the count n. This state is used and not the one corresponding to $n - 1$ because this state must be stable until the occurrence of the clock pulse which should cause the transition to 0. Thus, for example, to implement a mod-6 counter, with the count sequence from 0 to 5, it will be necessary to use a mod-8 counter. A circuit that decodes the configuration 6 activates the Reset signal of the flip-flops. Figure 6.46 shows this solution.

Note that, to decode state 6, it is only necessary to take into consideration the bits at 1, in this case, $B_2 = 1$ and $B_1 = 1$. This possibility results from the fact that, for any value in an increasing binary sequence, the set of the bits at 1 for a number occurs simultaneously at 1 for the first time in that

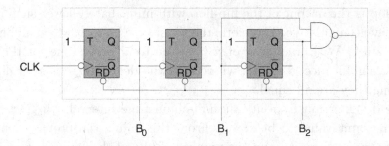

Fig. 6.46   Circuit for a mod-6 asynchronous counter.

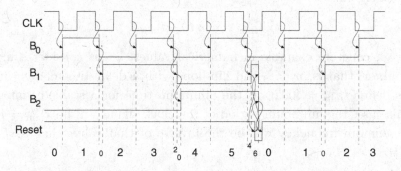

Fig. 6.47   Timing diagram for a mod-6 asynchronous counter.

value. Hence, it is not worth taking the zeros into consideration. Indeed, 110 is the first number which has the two most significant bits at 1. The other number in this situation is 111, which only would occur after the 110 if the *Reset* had not occurred. Figure 6.47 shows the timing diagram for this mod-6 counter.

The methodology presented created another transient state corresponding to the count 6, which only exists due to the time that the flip-flops take to carry out the *Reset*. We should also note that there is no danger that a transient state in the normal sequence of the counter triggers the *Reset* because none of the standard transient states in the count is the state 6. All transient states correspond always to a value less than the actual value of the counter. In fact, the transition states arise through a flip-flop of lower weight changing from 1 to 0, which triggers a transition in the flip-flop of immediately higher significance but only after its propagation time. The transition $1 \rightarrow 0$ of the flip-flop of lower weight will always firstly lead to a decrease in the count, and, therefore, the transition states always correspond to the values of the count below that of the previous stable state.

Finally, it is important to note that, for a correct operation of this type of counter, it must be considered that the delay times of the devices used must be such that it ensures that all the flip-flops are set to 0 before disabling the *Reset* signal. This limitation exists because when the *Reset* signal action in the flip-flop updates its output this causes the same *Reset* signal to become inactive. At this time, it is necessary that this signal has already taken effect on the other flip-flops. We also need to consider that the calculation of the maximum count frequency is now affected by the presence of the detection of a state and the implementation of the asynchronous *Reset* of the counter.

6.6.2 *Synchronous Counters*

Synchronous counters are, as the name suggests, synchronous sequential circuits capable of carrying out a count on a given code. The various flip-flops share, therefore, the same clock signal and are triggered by the same edge of that signal. Just like asynchronous counters, the counters count clock pulses, that is, the evolution through the sequence of states of a count sequence is caused by the transition of the set of states of the flip-flops.

The design of a synchronous counter can be carried out by applying the concepts of sequential circuit synthesis, which will be presented in Chapter 7, starting from a state table or diagram which reflects the intended count sequence. In certain cases, however, it is possible to implement a more pragmatic design.

Let us once again take the example of a three-bit binary counter, which counts according to the binary sequence in Table 6.1. Once again, three flip-flops will be necessary. We will use T flip-flops as we did to implement an asynchronous counter. We should note, as in the case of the asynchronous counter, that the least significant flip-flop, B_0, changes its state in all the clock pulses (which is natural, since the behaviour is the same of the asynchronous counter). This is achieved by setting the T input signal of that flip-flop always at 1. In the case of the second flip-flop, B_1, it must change state, as we saw, whenever in the least significant bit there is the transition $1 \rightarrow 0$. In the synchronous counter, it is not possible to connect B_0 to the clock input of flip-flop B_1, as in the asynchronous case, because the clocks of all flip-flops are interconnected. The only control point available is the T signal. Furthermore, by inspecting Table 6.1, it can be concluded that B_1 changes state when the least significant bit is at 1, which is translated making $T_1 = B_0$. In this way, the level of signals, and not transitions, are used to determine the changes of state.

The control of the third flip-flop, B_2 is more complicated. The immediate idea which could arise, that its input should be connected to B_1, is wrong. In fact, it is not enough that $B_1 = 1$ for B_2 to change state. For example, in $B_2\,B_1\,B_0 = 010$, the following count state is 011 and, therefore, B_2 is not altered. Analysing Table 6.1, we conclude that for B_2 to be altered, both B_1 and B_0 must be 1. Thus $T_2 = B_0\,B_1$. The circuit for a three-bit binary synchronous counter is shown in Figure 6.48. Figure 6.49 shows a timing diagram for the three-bit counter.

We should note that, in the case of synchronous counters, the active clock edge is irrelevant to define the counting sequence. The fact that the control of the change in the flip-flops is carried out by the input, and not by the clock, leads to its active edge losing relevance to the definition of the operation (except to define the moment at which the change occurs).

For counting in natural binary code, it is easy to generalise that, for a larger number of bits, the function of the input T of flip-flop n will be $T_n = B_0\,B_1 \cdots B_{n-1}$. This product may be implemented in two ways:

- Using at each flip-flop i one AND gate with i inputs, B_0 to B_{i-1}. For a counter of n bits, $n - 2$ AND gates are necessary (the first two flip-flops do not need these gates). The disadvantage of this approach is that each gate must have i inputs each, in which i corresponds to the flip-flop order, $i = 2, 3, \ldots, n-1$ and, for n significative the AND gates are very complex. The advantage is that the generation of the T input of each flip-flop is very fast;
- reusing the logic of the previous level to generate the T input of each level, that is, for level i, make $T_i = T_{i-1}\,B_{i-1}$. In this case, for a counter of n bits, $n - 2$ AND gates will also be necessary, but now all with only two inputs. However, the circuit becomes slower, since the changes in the

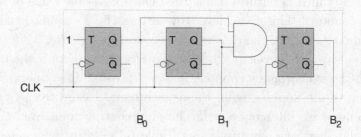

Fig. 6.48   Circuit for a three-bit synchronous counter.

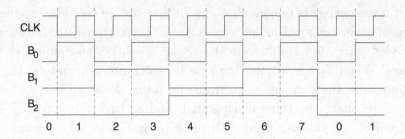

Fig. 6.49   Timing diagram for a three-bit synchronous counter.

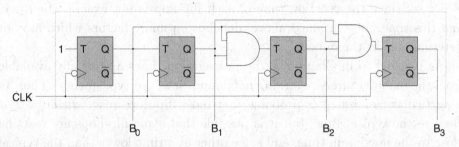

Fig. 6.50   Circuit for a mod-16 synchronous counter, using one three-input AND gate to generate the control of the most significant flip-flop.

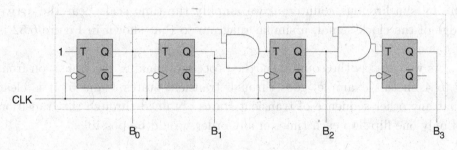

Fig. 6.51   Circuit for a mod-16 synchronous counter, using two two-input AND gates in series to generate the control of the most significant flip-flop.

outputs of the flip-flops have, in the worst case, to be propagated by those $n - 2$ gates, until all the inputs have stabilised.

These two alternatives are illustrated, respectively, in Figures 6.50 and 6.51, for a mod-16 synchronous counter.

6.6.2.1   *Transient states in synchronous counters*

When asynchronous counters were studied, we considered carefully the existence of transient states which result from the behaviour of those structures, since it is the change of one bit that may or may not, in cascade, produce the change of other bit(s) of higher significance. These transient states cannot be avoided since they result from the actual operating mechanism of those counters. When first analysing the case of synchronous counters, the false idea may arise that, in this case, transient states do not occur. Indeed, as all flip-flops share the same clock signal, and as each flip-flop only has a maximum of one transition for each pulse (either changing or maintaining the state), it may be tempting to take an additional step and suppose that all the flip-flops which change state do so at the same time. In reality, this is not so, since the reaction time of each flip-flop is not exactly the same, and this time, as mentioned above, depends on many factors which are not determinable at the outset.

As referred to in Chapter 3, the propagation times are usually available from the manufacturers regarding maximum time and typical time. Thus, in a particular counter, it is probable that most flip-flops react within a time close to the typical time, but it is possible that some flip-flops are reacting close to the maximum time, and some other at a time lower than the typical time. All this leads to the appearance of transient states. Indeed, Figure 6.49 shows a portion of an ideal timing diagram for a synchronous counter. In any synchronous counter, if we amplify the time scale near the active edge of the clock signal, a similar diagram to that shown in Figure 6.52 is obtained.

As we can see, the counter, in the process of making the transition from 3 to 4, in this example, goes through transient states 1 and 5. It is clear that any other sequence of transient states obtained through the transition of only one flip-flop each time, in any order, would be possible.

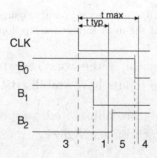

Fig. 6.52 Timing diagram for a synchronous counter with an amplified time scale around the active edge of the clock signal, so as to show transient states.

There are also, therefore, transient states in synchronous counters. However, there are differences in relation to transient states in asynchronous counters:

Length: The transient states in synchronous counters have lengths close to the difference between propagation times, while in asynchronous counters this length is of the order of the actual propagation times. In practice, this means that the transient states in synchronous counters have a much lower duration.

Predictability: In asynchronous counters, the exact sequence of transient states may is predictable, since this sequence is a consequence of the counting mechanism. In the case of synchronous counters, it is not possible at the outset to determine what the transition states are or the order in which they appear.

Type of states: In asynchronous up-counters, the transient states always correspond to values lower than the starting state. For example, in the transition from 7 to 8, the transient states are 6, 4 and 0, in this order. In the case of synchronous counters, transient states, as we can see in the previous example, may correspond to counts higher or lower than the starting state.

6.6.2.2 *Maximum operating frequency*

Calculating the maximum operating frequency in synchronous counters is substantially different from the asynchronous case. In the synchronous case, there are no transitions in cascade, with all flip-flop updates starting simultaneously. What has to be ensured in this case (and this is similar to a generic synchronous sequential circuit, to be analysed in the following chapter) is that, at each active edge of the clock, all inputs are stable, so as to respect the timing parameters of the flip-flops. When an active edge occurs, the output is updated, but only after the propagation time of the flip-flops, t_p. In the case of synchronous counters, some logic is necessary to generate the input values of the flip-flops, as we can see, for example, in Figures 6.50 and 6.51. Then, after updating the outputs of the flip-flops, there will be a delay corresponding to this logic, $t_{\log}$, until the inputs of the flip-flops have stabilised with the next logic value. This stabilisation must happen, at least before the setup time of the flip-flop, t_{setup}, as mentioned in Section 6.4.4. Hence, the minimum period of the clock cycle is given by Expression (6.6).

$$T_{min} > t_p + t_{log} + t_{setup}. \tag{6.6}$$

Note that now a minimum time interval for the stable presence of the count values at the output of the counter, t_{min}, has not been defined, as in the case of asynchronous counters in the previous section. If we need to comply with a value for t_{min}, the following analysis must be considered. In the synchronous case, the count value is maintained stable immediately after the propagation delay time of the flip-flops. Therefore, at least, during the time interval $t_{log} + t_{setup}$, the count is stable. If $t_{min} < t_{log} + t_{setup}$, then Expression (6.6) is sufficient. Otherwise, the minimum period of the clock signal will be defined by Expression (6.7).

$$T_{min} > t_p + t_{min}. \tag{6.7}$$

The values t_p and t_{setup} are parameters characteristic of the flip-flops used. The value t_{log} deserves some discussion. Of course, the limitation will be the slowest critical path between the combinational circuits to generate all the input bits for the flip-flops (as discussed in Section 3.4.1). In the examples used, the most complex circuit is the logic at the input of the most significant flip-flop, in Figure 6.51, where there is a delay of $n - 2$ AND gates with two inputs, $t_{log} = (n - 2) \times t_{pAND2}$.

Examining a concrete example, let us consider a mod-256 counter ($n = 8$) and flip-flops with a delay time of $t_p = 100$ ps and setup time $t_{setup} = 40$ ps. Furthermore, let us consider that the delay times for the AND gate with two inputs and the AND gate with seven inputs are, respectively, $t_{pAND2} = 50$ ps and $t_{pAND7} = 75$ ps. For the case of the implementation in Figure 6.50, the critical path is defined by the delay of the AND gate with seven inputs, $t_{log} = 75$ ps. Therefore the minimum period for the clock signal is $T_{min} = 215$ ps ($f_{max} = 4.7$ GHz). For the case of the implementation in Figure 6.51, the critical path is defined by the sum of the delays of the $n - 2$ AND gates with two inputs in series, $t_{log} = 6 \times 50 = 300$ ps, therefore the minimum period for the clock signal is $T_{min} = 440$ ps ($f_{max} = 2.3$ GHz). We assume that in these two cases the maximum operating frequency of the flip-flops is greater than the value f_{max} obtained, which is often true.

This analysis has never referred to the hold time parameter, t_{hold}, that defines a time interval in which the inputs of the flip-flops have to remain stable after the active transition of the clock signal. As the inputs of the flip-flops only change after $t_p + t_{log}$ and, usually, $t_p > t_{hold}$, it is assured from the outset that this parameter is respected.

6.6.2.3 *Count control signal*

It is often necessary to build counters with a *Count* or *Inc* (from Increment) signal, that is, with an input that controls if the circuit counts when it receives a clock pulse or, conversely, that if it maintains its state without alteration. This feature is easy to implement by altering the T input logic a little, as shown in Figure 6.53. In this book we will use preferably the designation *Increment*.

Note that, if the input *Inc* is 1, the operation of the counter is that described above. On the contrary, while *Inc* is at 0, all the T inputs remain at 0, the flip-flops do not change state, and the counter is therefore blocked. Figure 6.54 shows this behaviour.

In this counter, as it is a synchronous circuit, it is the value of the *Inc* signal at the active edge of the clock that determines the evolution of the circuit.

6.6.2.4 *Counters as registers*

Besides the control signal which determines if the counter counts, there are other possible useful control signals. One of them is one that sets the counter

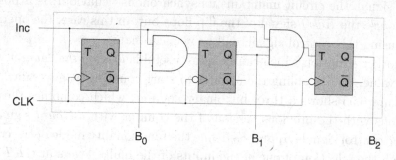

Fig. 6.53   Circuit for a three-bit synchronous counter with *Increment* signal.

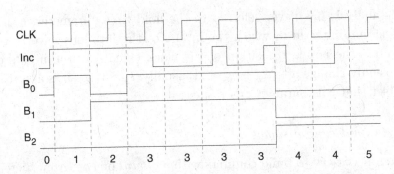

Fig. 6.54   Timing diagram for a three-bit synchronous counter with *Inc* signal.

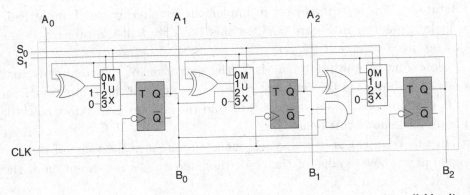

Fig. 6.55   Circuit for a three-bit synchronous counter with count, clear and parallel loading capability.

to zero at any time. In the case of a binary counter, this would correspond to clearing all the flip-flops of the counter. If the flip-flops have a synchronous *Clear* signal, the circuit maintains its synchronous behaviour. Is is possible, also, to use the *Reset* signal of the flip-flops but, in this case, the operation, when using this control signal, will be asynchronous.

Another situation which can be quite useful is *loading the counter* with a given value, thus enabling the counter to start counting at any value.

Figure 6.55 shows a three-bit binary counter, which combines these two functions with the previous version of the counter with a *Count* signal.

The control signals S_1 and S_0 define the functionality mode of the counter through the selection of one of the inputs of the multiplexers at the T input of each flip-flop. As we can see in the figure, if:

$S_1 S_0 = 00$: $T_i = B_i$, therefore, if $B_i = 0$, the flip-flop maintains its state, and if $B_i = 1$, the flip-flop changes state. In either of the two hypothesis, the result will be that the flip-flop will set its state at 0. Thus, this combination of the control inputs leads to the clearing of the counter.

$S_1 S_0 = 01$: $T_i = B_i \oplus A_i$, therefore, if $B_i = A_i$ then $T_i = 0$, and the flip-flop maintains its state, otherwise, the state of the flip-flop is complemented. In either of the two situations, the result will be that the flip-flop sets its state equal to the input A_i. Thus, this combination of the control inputs leads to the parallel loading of the counter.

$S_1 S_0 = 10$: In this case, the same logic of the simple counter in Figure 6.48 is selected for each flip-flop, $T_0 = 1$, $T_1 = B_0$ and $T_2 = B_1 B_0$. Therefore, with this combination of control inputs, the circuit operates as a binary counter.

$S_1 S_0 = 11$: $T_i = 0$ and, therefore, the counter maintains its state.

It is possible to look at the counter in Figure 6.55 as a register, in the sense that it is an element that allows the storage of a set of bits which together have a meaning. Indeed, counters are nothing more than registers which have an *Inc* control signal, at the same level of the control signals presented in Section 6.5.2, which enables it to increment (or decrement in a down-counter mode) its content.

A possible representation for a counter is shown in Figure 6.56. The control signal *Ld* allows the loading of the value in input A to the register, and the control signal *Inc* causes an increment in the value stored in the register. Usually, unless otherwise indicated, it is assumed a increasing counting sequence. Of course, in this case, it is necessary to guarantee that either the *Ld* and *Inc* signals are not active simultaneously, or define, at the circuit

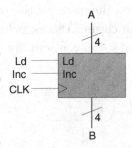

Fig. 6.56 Representation for a register with a counting mode.

level, which of these two signals has priority. Note that, if a structure similar to Figure 6.55 is chosen for the register in Figure 6.56, it is necessary to have some additional logic to translate the control signals Ld and Inc into the internal control signals S_0 and S_1.

It is also possible to design counters which alternatively enable *increasing* or *decreasing the count. Down* normally indicates the control signal for decrementing a count. The enabling of this signal leads to the counter carrying out an inverted counting sequence. In counters with the two modes, called bidirectional counters, there is usually a signal that controls in which direction the counter counts. This signal is usually referred as $Up/\overline{Down}$.

6.6.2.5   *Synchronous counters with an arbitrary modulo*

When a counter has a *Clear* control signal available which functions synchronously, it is simple to design a synchronous counter in natural binary code for an arbitrary modulo. To do this, all we have to do is to add logic which enables the final value of the sequence of states to be decoded and at that time carry out the synchronous clearing of the counter, thus resulting in its re-initialisation. Figure 6.57 shows a mod-6 counter using this approach.

To design a mod-6 counter (counting from 0 to 5), we decode state 5 to activate the *Clear* signal so that at the next active edge the counter transitions to state 0, instead of continuing to state 6. As in the case of the asynchronous counter, the logic only needs to use the bits at 1 for the state we intend to decode since this always corresponds to the first time this combination appears in the count sequence. However, note that the state to be decoded by counters of the same modulo is different in the case of asynchronous and synchronous counters.

Figure 6.58 shows a timing diagram for the mod-6 synchronous counter. Note that, as opposed to the case of the asynchronous counter, in a mod-n synchronous counter, the state n never actually occurs.

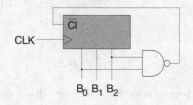

Fig. 6.57   Mod-6 synchronous counter.

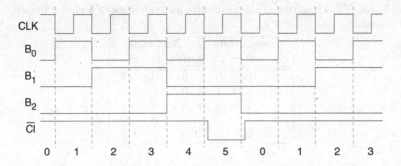

Fig. 6.58   Timing diagram for the mod-6 synchronous counter.

Table 6.2   Definition of the next state for each state of a mod-8 binary counter.

Current state			Next state		
B_2	B_1	B_0	B_2	B_1	B_0
0	0	0	0	0	1
0	0	1	0	1	0
0	1	0	0	1	1
0	1	1	1	0	0
1	0	0	1	0	1
1	0	1	1	1	0
1	1	0	1	1	1
1	1	1	0	0	0

6.6.2.6   *Synchronous counters with an arbitrary sequence*

The design of any synchronous counter may be made using a systematic procedure of synthesis. The first step is to define the sequence of states, i.e., define, for each possible state of the counter, which is the state that follows it. For example, for a mod-8 counter in natural binary, such as that analysed up to here, this definition will be that in Table 6.2.

If we need a counter with a generic modulo n, it is easy to see that the only alteration necessary is to define the initial state as the state following state $n - 1$. For example, to design a mod-5 counter, the definition of the next states will be that given in Table 6.3.

Indeed, this procedure for the design of counters offers almost complete freedom in defining the next state. The restrictions are, that for a counter, the sequence is unique, therefore:

- All the states which appear in the next state column have to appear in the current state column, that is, it is necessary to define the next states for all the states that the counter can reach.

Table 6.3 Definition of the next state for each state of a mod-5 binary counter.

Current state			Next state		
B_2	B_1	B_0	B_2	B_1	B_0
0	0	0	0	0	1
0	0	1	0	1	0
0	1	0	0	1	1
0	1	1	1	0	0
1	0	0	0	0	0

Table 6.4 Definition of the next state for each state of a mod-8 counter in Gray's code.

Current state			Next state		
B_2	B_1	B_0	B_2	B_1	B_0
0	0	0	0	0	1
0	0	1	0	1	1
0	1	1	0	1	0
0	1	0	1	1	0
1	1	0	1	1	1
1	1	1	1	0	1
1	0	1	1	0	0
1	0	0	0	0	0

- A state may only appear once as a next state. If not, the counter would count only a subset of the defined present states. For example, if in Table 6.3 the state 000 was to appear repeated in another line, the states defined in the lines below that one would never occur in the count sequence.

This approach allows the definition of very generic sequences of counting. For example, if what is intended is a mod-8 counter in Gray's code (as described in Section 1.3.3), the definition table for the next states will be that given in Table 6.4.

Tables like the ones shown in this section are the starting point for the synthesis procedure of synchronous sequential circuits in general. The following steps of this procedure will be studied in the following chapter, and we will postpone, for now, the synthesis of the counters discussed here.

There are also specific procedures for a similar approach in the design of asynchronous counters, although more complex. This material will not be covered in this book.

6.6.3 *Interconnection of Counters*

It is often necessary to *interconnect counters* to increase the count modulo. An obvious solution is to interconnect them in such a way that one of the counters is the least significant, and the subsequent ones only count when the first turns over from the last count state to the first state.

In the case of asynchronous counters, this interconnection is trivial. We follow the same philosophy that is used to connect the flip-flops inside the counter, that is, use the most significant bit of the counter as a clock signal for next counter. For example, a mod-64 asynchronous counter is built by interconnecting two three-bit asynchronous counters (such as that in Figure 6.44), as shown in Figure 6.59.

In the case of synchronous counters, to maintain the synchronous nature of the whole, the solution involves interconnecting the counters in such a way that the clock is common to all connected counters. The *Inc* signal for the most significant counter is connected to logic that decodes the last count state of the least significant counter. An example of this type of connection is shown in Figure 6.60, which presents a mod-64 synchronous counter built using two mod-8 synchronous counters.

As we can see, the *Inc* signal of the most significant counter only remains active during the clock cycle in which the counter with least weight is at its maximum count state, in this case, state 7. In this situation, the following clock pulse will, at the same time, cause the counter with least weight to return to 0, and the counter with greatest weight to increment one unit. During the remaining state transitions in the counter with least weight, the most significant counter will maintain its state. Many counters have the logic necessary for the detection of the last count state already integrated within them. It is usual to call this output *Terminal Count* or *Tc*.

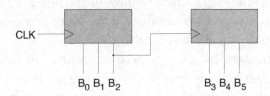

Fig. 6.59 Mod-64 asynchronous counter using two three-bit asynchronous counters.

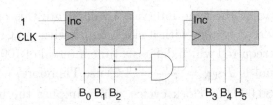

Fig. 6.60 Mod-64 synchronous counter using two three-bit synchronous counters.

6.6.4 *Applications of Counters*

In addition to counting events, counters have two main applications: as *frequency divider circuits* and *timer circuits*.

Consider the timing diagram of a counter with a modulo which is a power of 2 (see, for example, Figures 6.45 or 6.49). Each output shows a square wave with a frequency that is half of the preceding output. The frequency of the least significant bit is half of the clock frequency. Therefore, the frequency of the signal in flip-flop i in a counter is given by Expression (6.8).

$$f_i = \frac{f_{\text{CLK}}}{2^{i+1}}. \tag{6.8}$$

In systems in which it is necessary that parts of the circuit operate at a lower frequency than the frequency of the system clock, counters may be used to generate that lower frequency clock signal. The counter should be designed to have a count modulo so that it is possible to obtain the desired frequency. For example, if the system clock is $f_{\text{CLK}} = 800\,\text{MHz}$ and we want to generate a clock signal of $f'_{\text{CLK}} = 25\,\text{MHz}$, we must use a counter with modulo 32, that is, with $n = 5$ bits as Expression (6.9) shows.

$$\frac{f_{\text{CLK}}}{f'_{\text{CLK}}} = \frac{800\ \text{MHz}}{25\ \text{MHz}} = 32 = 2^5. \tag{6.9}$$

Counters can also be used as timers, elements which enable the specification of a given time interval in a system. There are many situations in which it is necessary to generate a waiting period between two events. This time interval may have any length, from timings in the order of microseconds, for subsystem synchronisation, up to values in the order of seconds, for example, typically in modules which interact with the user.

The use of counters for this purpose is natural. In their most general operation, a counter is incremented (or decremented) at each clock cycle. Knowing the period of the clock signal, it is sufficient to determine how many clock cycles make up the desired time interval. Therefore, the counter should be initialised and set counting until it reaches the intended count, indicating the end of the time interval. To illustrate this operation, let us once again consider a system with a clock signal with $f_{\text{CLK}} = 800\,\text{MHz}$ and where a signal is required which defines a time interval of 100 ms. The period of this clock signal is $T_{\text{CLK}} = \frac{1}{f_{\text{CLK}}} = 1.25\,\text{ns}$. Therefore, it is necessary to count $\frac{100\ \text{ms}}{1.25\ \text{ns}} = 80{,}000{,}000$ clock cycles, which implies the use of a counter with a count modulo of, at least, 128 M$=2^{27}$.

6.7 Register Transfers

In a digital system, the registers are typically the elements which store the information to process. The way *register interconnection* is designed, which will define what direct data transfers are possible in the system, is one of the most important decisions in defining the architecture of a digital system.

This section discusses the two main alternatives for interconnecting registers. These two options represent the extreme possibilities: the use of as many buses as the number of registers and the use of a single global bus in the system. In complex systems, these approaches can coexist in different parts of the system, as well as some intermediate configurations.

The examples presented only consider the direct transfer of values between registers. In general, the data transferred will undergo some form of processing before being stored again in registers. Chapter 8 will analyse these issues.

6.7.1 *Interconnection Using Multiplexers*

One way of selecting the value to be loaded into one of a set of interconnected registers is to use a multiplexer at the input of each register, as shown in Figure 6.61. This approach corresponds to a situation in which there is one bus per register.

This option is the most flexible way of transferring values from a given register to any other register, since, through the enabling of the respective signals Si and Li, it allows the loading of any register (Li signals) with the value stored in any other register (Si). For example, to transfer a value from R0 to R2, the $L2$ signal must be active, so that R2 is updated, and the $S2$ signal must be at 1 so as to select R0 as the input source for R2. Note that

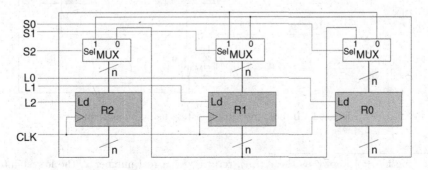

Fig. 6.61 Interconnecting registers using multiplexers.

it is possible to load any of the other registers simultaneously with the same value or with a different value, meaning that there is total flexibility.

However, this approach requires a multiplexer at the input of each one of the registers and, therefore, for r registers, r multiplexers are necessary. Also, each of these multiplexers has $r-1$ inputs. Of course, when the number of registers r is high, this approach is not very attractive due to:

- The significant amount of hardware necessary to implement the r multiplexers with $r - 1$ inputs of n bits.
- The large number of control signals that is necessary. As each multiplexer has $\lceil \log_2(r-1) \rceil$ selection inputs,[5] and assuming independent control lines for the multiplexers, this requires a total of $r \times \lceil \log_2(r - 1) \rceil$ lines (for example, for $r = 16$, there are $16 \times 3 = 48$ control lines).
- The large number of lines required by the buses which, potentially, have to reach all the points of the circuit, occupy on its own a lot of physical space. For n bits, the total number of lines for the buses is $r \times n$.

6.7.2 *Interconnection Using a Single Bus*

A more economic alternative consists in using a single bus in the system, as we can see in Figure 6.62. This approach requires much less hardware and control signals, since only one multiplexer is necessary. However, as the input for all the registers is common, it is impossible to carry out simultaneous transfers having different origins. For example, it is not possible to simultaneously move the content of R0 to R1 and of R1 to R2, because

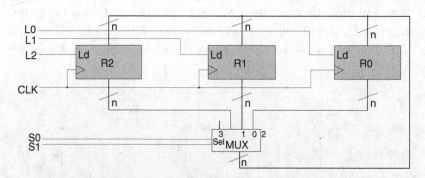

Fig. 6.62   Interconnecting registers using a single bus.

---

[5]The function $\lceil x \rceil$ known as the *ceiling*, returns, for a real number x, the lowest integer greater than or equal to x.

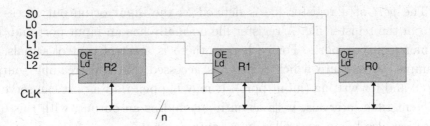

Fig. 6.63 Interconnection of registers with tri-state output using a single bus.

the bus either contains the content of R0 or R1. Simultaneous transfers continue to be possible provided the origin is common. For example, it is possible to transfer the value of R0 simultaneously to R1 and R2, being sufficient to select the multiplexer at input 0 and activate the signals $L1$ and $L2$.

This type of interconnection of registers can be greatly simplified if registers with tri-state outputs are used, controlled by the OE signal, as studied in Section 6.5.2. Using this type of register, and provided that at each moment only one of them has its output active, they can all be connected to the same bus, therefore completely avoiding the use of multiplexers. This solution of interconnection with a single bus and registers with tri-state outputs is shown in Figure 6.63.

In addition to reducing the hardware needs, this type of architecture is very flexible, since it is possible to add any number of registers to the bus, provided that only one of them has an active output. Due to this characteristic, this approach is frequently used, despite its limitation of having each transfer a single source.

As was stated, there are possible intermediate solutions between this single bus architecture and that of the previous section, in which there is a different bus at the input of each register. For example, two buses in the system may be considered, making it necessary to define at the outset which registers connect to each bus.

6.7.3 Register Files

Often, when registers are intended for general use, instead of using isolated devices, these are grouped into a block, which is called a *register file*. The number of registers in the register file can vary greatly, although it is typically a value which is a power of 2. In general, each register in the register file is referenced by an index.

The *port* of a register file is defined as the input or output access for data in the register file. A register file normally has an input port and one, or more, output ports. For each port there is a set of control signals, for example, to indicate which register is accessed, both for reading (output port), and for writing (input port). It may happen that a port can serve, at different time intervals, both as an input and as an output, with this data direction also being controlled by a control signal.

Figure 6.64 shows an example of a register file. The number of registers in this file is 8, and these are normally referenced by the names R0 to R7. This register file has a write port, port D, and two read ports, ports A and B. In each clock cycle, the control signals $SelA$ and $SelB$ specify the index of the registers which are the source of the values at the output of ports A and B, respectively. Signals $SelD$ choose the register that will be written to with the value at the input of port D. Additionally, there is a control signal *Write* which can enable or disable writing in the register file. This signal makes possible the existence of clock cycles in which none of the registers is altered.

Internally, this register file may have the structure shown in Figure 6.65. As we can see, port D is connected in parallel to the inputs of all the bank registers. The control signal SelD enters the decoder circuit which, as was described in Section 4.2, activates only one of its outputs, the one that corresponds to the binary value of the input. In this way, only one of the registers has an active load signal, and the value of bus D is written to that, and only that, register. A decoder with an *Enable* signal is used in that register file (in agreement with Table 4.5). This *Enable* signal sets all

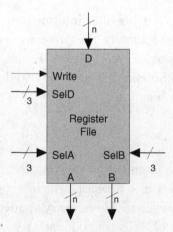

Fig. 6.64　Example of a register file with 8 registers — Symbol.

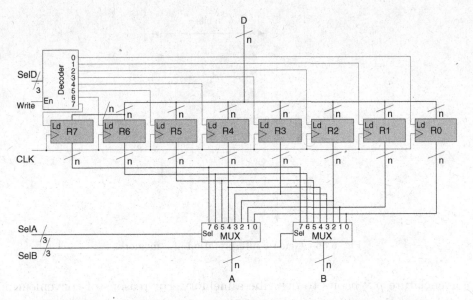

Fig. 6.65 Example of a register file with 8 registers — Internal structure.

outputs to zero if it is disabled. In this situation, all the load signals are disabled, and so, no register is altered. As described above, the operation of the *Enable* signal is that intended for the *Write* control signal.

Selecting the registers present in output buses, *A* and *B*, simply involves two multiplexers, independently controlled by the control signals *SelA* and *SelB*.

The width of the word stored in each of the registers was not defined at the outset for this register file. In Figures 6.64 and 6.65, this is indicated by the variable n in the width of the input and output buses. Of course, all analysis made are valid for any value of n. Each of the registers of this file will have the internal structure shown in Figure 6.32. Therefore, a register file with r registers for words of n bits will use a total of $r \times n$ flip-flops.

6.8 Memories

In many situations, it is necessary to store a vast set of words simultaneously. A relevant example is processor-based systems, which will be studied in this text from Chapter 9 onwards. In these cases, *memory circuits* are used, which are nothing more than specialised circuits used to store a large amount of information.

A memory circuit is simply a circuit capable of storing a set of p words, each with n bits, as shown in Figure 6.66. It is common to use the

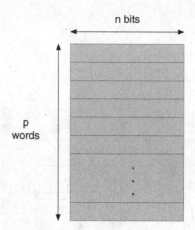

Fig. 6.66   Generic interpretation of a memory.

nomenclature $p \times n$ bits to describe a memory. For reasons of convenience, p and n are almost always powers of 2.

There are different ways of organising and accessing information stored in a memory circuit. Some of the most common variants will be analysed below.

6.8.1   *Random Access Memories*

The functionality usually associated with a memory circuit is the same as that described for a register file: each word stored in the memory circuit has an index, usually called an address. To access a memory position, we specify what the address of that position is and what is the operation intended, reading the stored word or writing a new word in that position. This type of operation corresponds to a *direct access* memory, also known as *RAM* (from Random Access Memory).

6.8.1.1   *Random access memory operation*

Figure 6.67 shows the symbol for a random access memory circuit. We can see that there are two buses connected to the memory circuit. One of them is only for input and serves to specify the memory position to be accessed. The most common term to designate this specification is *memory address*, with this bus known as the *address bus*. For a memory circuit with p memory locations, the width of the address bus, m, is the smallest value such that $2^m \geq p$, or $m = \lceil \log_2 p \rceil$.

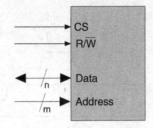

Fig. 6.67   Symbol for a random access memory circuit.

The second bus is bidirectional, and it is through this bus that the information is stored in the memory or read from it. This bus is known as the *data bus*. In a memory read, the direction of the data on the bus is from within the memory to outside, and in a memory write, it is from outside into the memory.

Besides these two buses, there are two control signals for the memory circuit. The $R/\overline{W}$ signal indicates if the operation is a read if it is at 1, or a write if it is at 0. This signal is sometimes referred as $Read/\overline{Write}$. Finally, the CS signal (from *chip select* — sometimes also called *chip enable*, CE) can enable or disable the memory circuit. When the signal is active ($CS = 1$), the circuit operates as described above. When inactive ($CS = 0$), the data bus is placed in the high impedance state and, therefore, the memory circuit is isolated from the rest of the system. The situation is useful in the construction of memory systems, as will be analysed in Section 13.1.

Note that the clock signal is not an input to the memory circuits, since these circuits, in general, operate in asynchronous mode and behave like a register file made up of latches instead of flip-flops. Thus, to use a given memory circuit, it is necessary to consult the specifications of that circuit and adhere to the times indicated for each operation.

Reading of words stored in a particular memory address is achieved by placing the value of the address on the address bus, enabling the memory circuit with $CS = 1$ and setting the $R/\overline{W}$ to 1 to indicate a read operation. The intended word will be available on the data bus, after the time interval necessary for the read operation, according to the timing specifications of the circuit. Note that this procedure is almost entirely identical to that described in Section 3.5.1 for access to a ROM. The only difference is that the latter does not have an $R/\overline{W}$ control signal. Figure 6.68 shows an example of the timing diagram for a read operation from memory.

The write operation is similar, although it requires some additional care regarding the sequence in which the control signals of the memory are

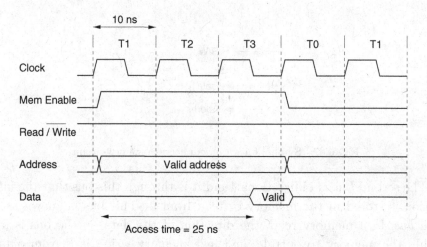

Fig. 6.68   Example of waveforms for a memory read operation.

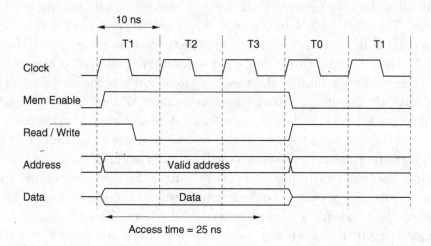

Fig. 6.69   Example of waveforms for a memory write operation.

activated so as not to alter values stored in other memory addresses. The procedure starts by placing the address of the position to be modified in the address bus and the value to be written at that address on the data bus. As with the read operation, the CS signal should be at 1. Finally, the $R/\overline{W}$ signal should be set at 0, but only when the other inputs have been defined and are stable. These signals should be kept stable during the time required for a write operation. In particular, it is important not to alter the value in the address bus when $R/\overline{W} = 0$ to ensure that other memory locations are not written too. Figure 6.69 shows an example of a timing diagram for the write operation in memory.

6.8.1.2   *Comparison with a register file*

The fundamental difference between a random-access memory and a register file lies in the storage capacity. This difference immediately translates into a larger number of bits necessary to specify a memory position than to select a register in a register file. For example, a register file typically does not have more than 128 registers, needing only 7 selection bits. In the case of a memory with 256 Mwords, for example, the address bus will have 28 bits.

As a consequence, in general, memory circuits only provide one port (connected to the data bus), which, by being unique, requires that it is bidirectional, to enable both read and write operations. The reason for this limitation is that each port needs its address bus, which in the case of memory circuits, as mentioned, implies a very high number of input signals. In comparison, reconsider the example of the register file in Figure 6.64, which easily offers three ports, one for input and two for output.

On the other hand, a greater storage capacity in the memory circuits compared with register files implies a considerably higher number of logic elements for their implementation. Naturally, this fact is reflected in the greater size of memory circuits. However, a more serious consequence is that the operating speed of the memory circuits is significantly lower than that of a register file. In designing a register file, an important objective is that the read or write operations can be carried out within a clock period. This objective is not generally possible for memory circuits. To illustrate the relative speeds, operations on a register file can be implemented in 1 ns or less. A random access memory has difficulty in responding in less than 5 ns (that is, in the case of static memories, since dynamic ones are significantly slower, currently with access times in the order of 60 ns).

Another fundamental difference is that register files are synchronous elements, therefore operating at the rhythm of a clock signal, and may be implemented using edge-triggered flip-flops. Memory circuits are asynchronous devices and are implemented using the functionality of level-sensitive latches.

6.8.1.3   *Internal structure*

A problem which occurs in the design of a memory circuit is the considerable complexity of the decoder for such a large number of lines in the address bus. The solution commonly adopted consists in laying out the basic memory elements (known as *memory cells*) in an array. Figure 6.70 shows an example

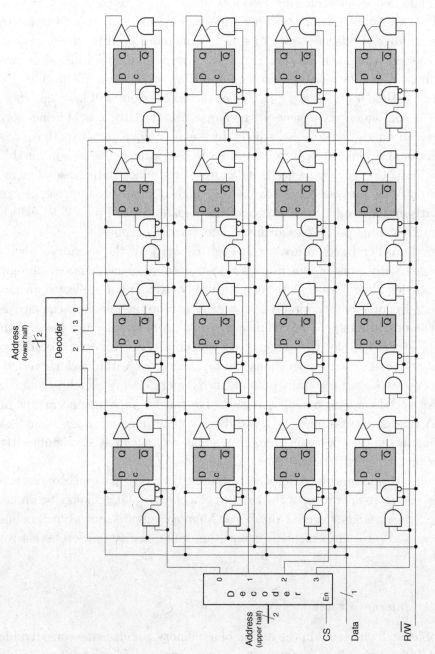

Fig. 6.70   Array structure for a memory circuit with 16×1 bits.

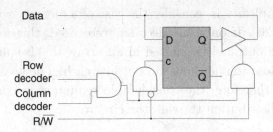

Fig. 6.71   Cell from a static memory circuit.

for a small memory circuit of 16×1 bits (therefore, 16 memory locations with 1 bit each). A single memory cell is shown isolated in Figure 6.71.[6]

Figure 6.71 shows that, in this case where each memory position only stores 1 bit, the cell is basically made up of a D-type latch. For the general case of memory locations of n bits, each cell will have n latches, all controlled by the same control signals, with each one connected to a different bit of the data bus. The enable signal c is only active if the lines of both the row and column decoders are active and the $R/\overline{W}$ signal is at 0 (indicating a write operation). In this situation, the bit in the data line is stored in the latch. In turn, the tri-state buffer at the output only places the value of the latch in the data line if the same lines of the decoders are active and the $R/\overline{W}$ signal is at 1 (read operation).

Returning to Figure 6.70, we can see that the 16 memory cells are arranged in a 4 by 4 array. The address bus is divided into two smaller buses, and each of these is separately decoded. Therefore, the decoder on the top has as inputs the least weighted half of the address bits, and the output of this decoder selects one of the array columns. This decoder is called the column decoder. The other half of the address enters into the decoder on the left, the row decoder, which will select a row. Only the memory cell corresponding to the activated row and column is selected to be read or written. Note that the data bus and the $R/\overline{W}$ signal connect to all the memory cells. The CS signal only enters into the *Enable* input of the row decoder. If this signal is disabled, no array line is active, meaning that all the memory cells have been disabled.

This organisation enables a decoder of n inputs and 2^n outputs to be substituted by two decoders of $n/2$ inputs and $\sqrt{2^n}$ outputs as well as 2^n AND gates (one for each memory cell). To underline how significant this

---

[6] Figure 6.71 shows a conceptual diagram. The technological reality may be very different.

reduction in complexity is, consider the case of a memory with 1 M memory locations ($n = 20$). If only one decoder were used, this would have more than one million outputs! Organised in an array, this is substituted by two decoders with close to one thousand outputs each. The great impact of this organisation is, therefore, the considerable reduction in control lines, thus simplifying its distribution through the circuit.

6.8.2   *Dynamic Memories*

Figure 6.72 shows an alternative structure to the memory cell in Figure 6.71. These two architectures are called *dynamic memory* and *static memory*, respectively. Dynamic random access memories are often designated as *DRAM*. The fundamental difference is the substitution of the latch in the static RAM by a *capacitor* in the dynamic RAM. This capacitor has one of the terminals connected to the input and output line and the other to ground (which corresponds to the low logic level). A capacitor is an electric element which can store electric charges and, in this way, maintain a voltage value at its terminals. Therefore, to store a *High* value in this memory cell the capacitor is charged with the corresponding voltage value through a write transmission gate. To store a *Low* value, simply discharge the capacitor through that same gate.

The implementation of Figure 6.72 has the significant advantage that a capacitor is an element much smaller in size than a latch, which is made up of approximately six transistors (as in Figure 6.13). This fact means that the density (that is, the number of memory cells per unit of physical space) of dynamic memories may be much greater than the density of static memories. Therefore, it is possible to manufacture dynamic memories with a larger capacity and with a much lower cost than static memories.

Unfortunately, this cost reduction entails a significant number of disadvantages, all related to the fact that the logic value is preserved by electric charges stored in a capacitor. Real capacitors have leaks, that is, the charge stored is slowly discharged through *parasitic resistances*. Although

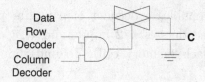

Fig. 6.72   Cell from a dynamic memory circuit.

techniques are used to minimise such losses, it is not possible to completely avoid this.

As a consequence, dynamic memories must be periodically *refreshed*, a process which consists in going through all the memory locations reading and rewriting the value stored there. Naturally, this process has to be carried out at an interval which ensures that it is still possible to determine all the memory values, to preserve them. For present-day dynamic memory circuits, a typical value for the *refresh period* is 100 ms. There are specific control circuits to facilitate the management of this process. It should be mentioned that this problem does not occur with static memories, since the feedback that exists in the latches (as shown in Figure 6.11) reinforces the signal stored there, thus preserving this value indefinitely (while the device remains connected to the circuit power supply).

A second problem which arises in dynamic memories is that the read operation is *destructive* since, the reading of the value stored in the capacitor discharges partially, at least, the capacitor. To solve this problem, each read operation triggers a write so as to restore the logic value in that memory position; a process managed internally by the memory circuit. The negative impact is that the memory remains unavailable during the period the read value is rewritten, possibly delaying future accesses to that memory.

Another disadvantage is the lower performance of dynamic memories. The electrical charge stored in the capacitor for one of these memory cells is necessarily very low. To determine the logic value stored there, electronic circuits which are very sensitive are used to measure that charge. These circuits are inherently slow in carrying out that operation, making read operations significantly slower than in the case of static memories (around ten times slower, nowadays).

Despite these disadvantages, the cost factor is decisive in favour of dynamic memory. Dynamic memories make computers economically viable and are the memory circuits used as primary memory (except in special cases where the performance factor is more important than the cost factor).

6.8.3   FIFO Memories

Although RAMs are the most common type of memory, there are some other types of memory circuits. This section will present the operation of *FIFO* memories (from *First-In First-Out*), perhaps the most common after RAM and ROM memories. Another example of a different type of memory is the *associative memory*, analysed in Section 13.3.1.

The fundamental difference between a random access memory and a FIFO memory is that in the latter it is not necessary to specify the location in which a given value is being written or read. As the name indicates, the data in a FIFO memory (or simply, in a FIFO) is read in the same order as it was written, and the memory circuit is responsible for ensuring that that happens.

From an external point of view, a FIFO does not, therefore, have an address bus, but typically has two data buses, one for writing and another for reading, as shown in Figure 6.73(a). The control signals R and W indicate, respectively, when it is intended to read a value from the FIFO or to store a value in the FIFO. These two operations are independent, do not use the same signals and even can take place simultaneously. The status bits *Empty* and *Full* indicate situations in which, respectively, the memory is empty (there are no data to be read) or the memory is full (new writes are ignored).

Figure 6.73(b) represents, in a schematic way, a possible internal organization of a FIFO memory. Data is stored in a RAM. The addresses of the memory locations to be accessed are maintained by two internal counters, one for read operations and the other for write operations. A logic module controls the inner functioning of the FIFO. For example, when the W signal is activated, this logic should, firstly, enable the w signal to write the value present on the write data bus in the location defined by the write counter and then increment this counter. Read is carried out in a similar manner. First, the position addressed by the read counter is placed on the read data

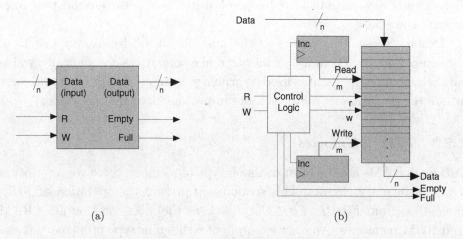

(a)   (b)

Fig. 6.73   FIFO memories: (a) symbol and (b) possible internal structure.

bus by activating the r signal and then this counter is incremented. Note that, if the value of the counters is equal, this means that the FIFO is either empty or full (since the write counter has turned over and is once again in the first written position that has still not been read). The logic module has mechanisms to identify the situation in question to be identified and activate the corresponding output bit, *Empty* or *Full*. There are other possible organisations based on asynchronous modules that we will not consider.

FIFO memories are often used as buffers in communication channels, with the write bus being controlled by the sender, and the read bus controlled by the receiver. Their use enables the sender to write and the receiver to read data, each at their own pace. Of course, if the receiver is much quicker than the sender, the FIFO will almost always be empty. If the sender is much faster, it will almost always be full. In either case, for its correct use, before each operation, each will have to test, respectively, the signals *Empty* and *Full*.

There are also *LIFO memories* (Last-In First-Out), with different operation and implementation, but with less practical applications. In these memories, we can write words until the memory is full. When we read a word, it is always the last one that was written. Note, however, that the stack, a very simple data structure used in most of the computers to be studied in Section 10.3.5, has a LIFO type operation, although implemented in a random access memory.

6.9   Summary

This chapter analyses the elements which allow the memorisation of values of logic signals. It starts with latches and flip-flops, which can store one bit of information each time. Next, it describes registers, which have the capacity to store a word, followed by register files, which contain a set of registers and, then, memory circuits, which can store a large quantity of data words in an organised manner.

Different types of latches and flip-flops are presented, differing in the way the control signals enable the storage of information. Among the control signals, the clock signal is analysed in detail. The clock, as we will see in the following chapters, functions as an overall control signal marking the rhythm of operation of sequential circuits.

Besides the operation of basic registers, the definition of register control signals is generalised, to enable operations of some sophistication on the values stored. Shift registers and counters are presented as particular cases of registers.

Finally, the operation of memory circuits is studied, at the level of the address bus, data bus, and the way they operate during read and write cycles.

Exercises

6.1 Design:

   (a) a combinational circuit with the behaviour shown in the diagram of Figure 6.1(a);

   (b) a sequential circuit with the behaviour illustrated in the diagram of Figure 6.1(a);

   (c) a sequential circuit with the behaviour illustrated in the diagram of Figure 6.1(b).

6.2 Design a level-sensitive SR latch with enable signal, similar to Figure 6.9, based on a latch with NOR-NOR gates, such as Figure 6.6(a). Produce the transition table for this latch.

6.3 Based on a T flip-flop and the necessary additional logic, design:

   (a) a D-type flip-flop;

   (b) a JK flip-flop.

6.4 For the version with NOR-NOR gates, construct the transition table for a level-sensitive SR latch with an *Enable* signal and a direct control signal for *Reset*, as shown in Figure 6.25.

6.5 Calculate the maximum operating frequency for the following counters, assuming that the flip-flops have a setup time of $t_{setup} = 0.5$ ns, hold time $t_{hold} = 0.3$ ns and delay time $t_{p\text{-}FF} = 1$ ns, and the logic gates a propagation time $t_{p\text{-}gate} = 1.5$ ns.

   (a) Counter in Figure 6.50.

   (b) Counter in Figure 6.51.

6.6 Using D flip-flops and the needed additional logic, construct a four-bit register which has the following operating modes:

   • parallel load
   • asynchronous *Reset*
   • shift right
   • rotation to the right.

Rotation is a shift in which the bit which is to be lost is reintroduced in the series input.

6.7 Using an integrated universal register (with parallel loading and bidirectional shifting), construct, using any material deemed useful, a register with the same features and also an additional counting mode.

6.8 Using an integrated mod-16 synchronous counter, with parallel loading and synchronous *Reset*, design a counter with the following count sequence: $\ldots 0, 1, 2, 3, 4, 5, 9, 10, 11, 12, 0, \ldots$.

6.9 Using a 4-bit binary counter with synchronous parallel loading, along with any supplementary material considered necessary (registers, comparators, multiplexers, gates, flip-flops, etc.), design a circuit with the following characteristics. After receiving n clock pulses, the circuit activates a *FINISH* signal which remains active until a *START* variable is activated. At that time the process is restarted. The number n, which is a 4-bit number, should be able to be programmed using a bus and the variable *LOAD*.

Chapter 7

Analysis and Design of Sequential Circuits

As we saw in previous chapters, combinational circuits compute a value at their output that depends only on the value present in the inputs at that moment. They are different from sequential circuits, whose output values depend on a sequence of values in the inputs.

The use of memory elements, such as those studied in Chapter 6, enables the referred behaviour of sequential circuits. In a circuit which uses memory elements, its response depends on its prior history and the values stored in the memory elements represent the relevant part of this history.

Most digital circuits which carry out functions of any complexity (such as a calculator) show values in their outputs which depend on inputs at previous moments in time.

More complex systems, such as computers, personal assistants and smartphones are also sequential circuits. However, the complexity of these systems is so high that it is more convenient to analyse them as systems made up of components viewed at a greater level of abstraction, such as memories, processors and input/output controllers. Each of these elements is, typically, still too complex to be analysed at the level of logic gates, latches and flip-flops. Each of them is, in fact, made up of a set of simpler modules that, in some cases, can already be described at the level of logic gates, latches and flip-flops, as was seen for combinational circuits, in Chapter 4. If we analyse each of these modules, we can see that, usually, they are sequential circuits, the behaviour of which depends on the history of the system.

This chapter studies methods for the design and analysis of sequential circuits. The examples studied are necessarily simple, but it is indispensable to understand the operation of the simple systems in detail, before going on to analyse more complex circuits. Complex circuits may always be broken down to the level of a subcircuit simple enough to be described and analysed by the formalisms presented: state diagrams and flowcharts.

7.1   Synchronous and Asynchronous Sequential Circuits

Chapter 6 studied various circuits which could maintain their state, independently of the values in some of their inputs. For example, a D-type edge-sensitive flip-flop keeps its internal state between two clock transitions, regardless of the value of its input D during this interval.

We also mentioned that sequential circuits have two major classes: synchronous and asynchronous. Synchronous circuits include a clock signal, which synchronises all of the circuit activity. This clock signal acts on flip-flops, which store the state of the circuit and change state only when there is an active edge of the clock signal. In this way, the state of the circuit changes only when there is an active edge of the clock signal. Asynchronous circuits do not use the clock signal and can, therefore, have state transitions whenever there is a change in the circuit inputs.

Figure 7.1 shows a representation of an asynchronous sequential circuit.

Since there is feedback from outputs to the inputs, the circuit can exhibit behaviour that does not depend only on the values of the inputs, but also on the values of the variables fed back, which are known as *state variables*. For example, the SR latch in Figure 7.2 (already studied in Section 6.2.1) may change its internal state in response to alterations in the level of the signal S

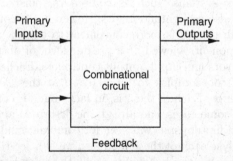

Fig. 7.1   General structure of an asynchronous sequential circuit.

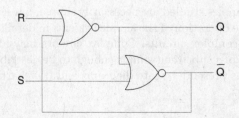

Fig. 7.2   Asynchronous circuit model for the SR NOR-NOR latch.

or the signal R. This circuit is asynchronous because there is no clock signal to synchronise the changes of the internal state that occur as a response to the variations in the input signals. Figure 7.2 shows the latch according to the model in Figure 7.1. This figure enables us to verify that the sequential behaviour of this latch is due to the presence of a state variable, Q.

In principle, there is nothing to prevent sequential circuits of small, medium and large complexity from being designed as asynchronous circuits, through the use of state variables which correspond to the feedback from the outputs to the inputs. In practice, the design of circuits of this type is extremely complex. It is necessary to predict which way the circuit may evolve in response to all the possible transitions in the inputs, taking into account that these do not change at the same time and that the order in which they change is, often, arbitrary. If it is not possible to design an asynchronous circuit which functions correctly for all the possible sequences of transitions in the inputs, it is necessary to impose restrictions in the way these changes may occur, which makes the design of the overall system more complex and difficult to verify. For example, in the SR latch in Figure 7.2, the final state of the circuit is undefined when both of the input signals simultaneously transit from 1 to 0. This type of limitation means that, in practice, the overwhelming majority of circuits currently designed are synchronous circuits. In these circuits, the change of state of the circuit may only occur when there is a transition in the clock signal.

A synchronous sequential circuit has the structure shown in Figure 7.3. As we can see, there are two components: a purely combinational logic block and a set of memory elements controlled by a clock signal.

The combinational logic block is used to implement the functions necessary to make the circuit exhibit the intended behaviour. The set of memory elements is made up of a variable number of flip-flops triggered at one of

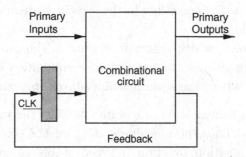

Fig. 7.3 General structure of a synchronous sequential circuit.

the clock edges, and maintains the state of the circuit over time, giving it its sequential behaviour. These elements may be sensitive to the falling edge or the rising edge, but all of them should, to a first analysis, respond to the same edge.

As we have seen, in a synchronous circuit, the values present in the outputs fed back from the combinational logic block output to define the next state must be stable when there is an active clock transition. Therefore a synchronous circuit is much easier to analyse than an asynchronous circuit, both from the theoretical and the practical point of view, since the order in which the signals change is no longer relevant.

From a practical point of view, the insensitivity of the memory elements to spurious transitions (hazards) in their inputs, which occur when the clock is stable, means that these circuits are much easier to develop and test than asynchronous circuits.

This text will only deal with methodologies for the design of synchronous sequential circuits. Indeed, although the design of asynchronous sequential circuits has been taking on a greater interest in some areas, the techniques used are significantly more complex and more difficult to use without the appropriate support tools. For this reason, all the methods that will be studied are applicable only to synchronous sequential circuits.

7.2 Mealy and Moore Machines

From a formal point of view, a synchronous sequential circuit corresponds to a *state machine*. A state machine is defined by the following components:

- the inputs of the state machine;
- the outputs generated by the state machine;
- the set of machine *states*;
- the *state transition function*, which determines the way the machine evolves between states, according to the present state and the combination of values in the inputs;
- the *output function*, which determines what is the output generated by the machine for a given state and a given combination of inputs;
- the *initial state*, where the state machine starts operating.

In a physical implementation of a state machine, the values stored in the memory elements defines the machine state, and the combinational circuit implements the transition function between states as well as the output function. The initial state may be imposed in various ways, but it is typically

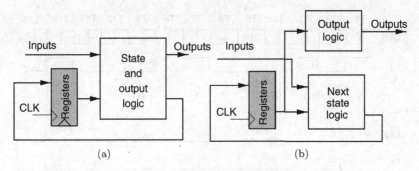

Fig. 7.4   Models for Mealy (a) and Moore (b) machines.

controlled by an asynchronous control variable, which brings all the flip-flops to a given state, independently of the clock signal.

Although the diagram in Figure 7.3, represents all the synchronous sequential circuits, it is useful to consider two distinct models, known as *Mealy* and *Moore machines*, which are distinguished only by the way the outputs are generated. Figure 7.4 represents the general structure of each of these types of models. In a Mealy machine, the value of the outputs is a function of the value of the state variables and the current input values. In a Moore machine, the output configuration is based solely on the values of the state variables.

The choice of a Mealy or Moore machine to implement a certain circuit depends on various factors. First, it is necessary to analyse the problem in question and understand if it is necessary for the outputs to immediately change in response to an alteration in the inputs, or if, on the contrary, it is possible to wait for the next active clock edge before altering the value of the outputs. In many cases, the frequency of the clock is so high, when compared with the frequency with which the input values are altered, that it is perfectly possible to wait for the next clock edge. In other applications, this may not be the case, because the clock frequency is not as high, or because there are other constraints, which vary from problem to problem.

Furthermore, some implementation techniques may restrict the type of machine which may be used. For example, when microprogramming is used to implement a state machine (Section 7.5.3), the architecture of the control unit may prevent a Mealy machine from being used.

The choice of a Mealy or Moore machine, therefore, depends on numerous factors, and one or the other may be adopted. It is, therefore, important to clearly understand the difference in the behaviour of these two machines.

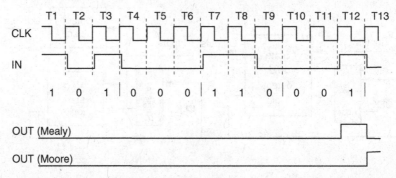

Fig. 7.5 Example of serial data transmission showing the limits of the three-bit groups and the *OUT* line for Mealy and Moore machines.

To illustrate this difference, take the following example. Suppose we want to send data through a line, in three-bit groups. This line is subject to noise, and, in some cases, this noise may be such that it prevents the correct recognition of one bit. For this reason, we will use a specific protocol to ensure that each three-bit group has an even number of bits at 1.[1]

Let us design a sequential system that processes the input data and marks a transmission error in its output, when there is an odd number of bits in a three-bit group. Figure 7.5 shows the data line over time, for a communication which follows the protocol described. This figure illustrates the transmission of four three-bit groups. In the final group, the parity is wrong, which means that there was a communication error and one of the bits is incorrect. At time $T12$, the sequential system to be designed should show the value 1 in its output OUT, indicating that there has been a transmission error.

To understand why this system must be implemented as a Mealy machine, it is necessary to carry out a detailed examination of the operation of the synchronous circuit to be designed. Firstly, note that the value of the input data line is sampled at the rising edge of the clock. At the rising edge of the clock, the line has the value transmitted according to the protocol. When there is

---

[1]Indeed, this example represents an extreme simplification of the protocol used in serial communication. In this protocol, a parity bit is added after a group of 7 or 8 bits (depending on the configuration), in such a way that there is always the transmission of an even (or odd) number of 1s, but the clock is not sent separately, rather recovered from the transitions observed in the data line. This matter will be discussed in more detail in Chapter 14.

a clock transition at the beginning of the period $T12$, corresponding to the last bit of a group, the value of that bit is still not known.

Therefore, the wrong value of this bit may only cause a change of state at the end of the clock period $T12$. This means that a Moore machine can only indicate an error in the interval $T13$. A Mealy machine can signal the existence of an incorrect bit as soon as the input takes the value of the last bit and the parity is found wrong.

In many situations, both operating modes will be acceptable. In others, it may be necessary to adopt a Mealy or a Moore machine, according to the desired operation.

Note that the Moore machine is, in fact, a particular case of the Mealy machine, with the output functions implemented by the combinational block not dependent on the current input variables. However, this particular case is important, since it guarantees that the outputs of the circuit are only altered when there is a clock transition.

7.3 Design of Synchronous Sequential Circuits

Just as with combinational circuits, there are design methods for synchronous sequential circuits which start the development of the system from the intended functional specification. There are four stages to the design of a sequential circuit:

- *formal specification* using state machines, flowcharts, tables, diagrams or microprograms;
- *simplification of the specification*;
- state assignment;
- determination of the output and next state functions.

The following sections will provide more details about each of these phases.

7.3.1 *State Diagrams*

As mentioned before, each synchronous sequential circuit corresponds to a state machine, characterised by three main components: the set of its states, the transition function and the output function.

The set of states corresponds to the set of configurations that the memory elements of the sequential system can take. The transition function specifies what is the value of the next state of the circuit, for each possible value of the present state and each logic configuration in the inputs. The output function specifies the value that the outputs should take, as a function of the present state and the values in the inputs. In the case of Moore machines, the output function only depends on the state, and not on the value of the circuit inputs.

A natural way of representing these three components is the *state diagram*. This diagram graphically represents each state as a circle and each transition as an arrow. Each combination of state and value of the inputs has an associated arrow which points to the state to which the machine moves as a result of that combination. Each of these transitions is labelled with the input combination which corresponds to it and, in the case of Mealy machines, with the value of the output shown by the circuit. In the case of Moore machines, the output is directly associated to the state, as it does not depend on the current input values.

For example, Figure 7.6 shows a two-state machine, which, as we will see, corresponds to the sequential circuit in Figure 7.7.

In this machine, state $S0$ is the initial state and corresponds to the state in which the flip-flop has its output at 0. Each state in the state diagram corresponds to a configuration of the output values of the flip-flops. In this example, the two states of the diagram correspond to the two states of the flip-flop.

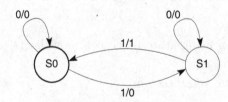

Fig. 7.6   Example of a state diagram for a Mealy machine.

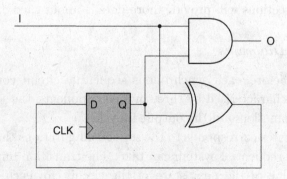

Fig. 7.7   Sequential circuit corresponding to the state diagram in Figure 7.6.

For a simple state diagram, it is easy to determine the behaviour of the state machine to which it corresponds by inspecting it. In the present case, the machine is initialised at the $S0$ state and maintains the $S0$ state, until the input signal is at 1. When this happens, the machine moves (in the next active clock edge) to the state $S1$, which is maintained while the input is 0. When the input returns to 1 (or if it is maintained at 1 until the next active clock edge), the machine will assume once again the $S0$ state, returning to the original situation.

As we mentioned before, in a sequential circuit, the value of the output depends on the previous history of the inputs. The waveforms in Figure 7.8 show a possible behaviour of the circuit. It is possible to understand that the internal state (value of the output Q of the flip-flop) will switch when the input takes the value 1. The circuit output will be active (at 1) when the internal state of the circuit is 1, and the input is also at 1. In this state diagram, as with all those that we will use in this text, the *initial state of the system* ($S0$) is drawn with a thicker outline. Also, when looking at it, and by comparison with Figure 7.4, we can see that the circuit in Figure 7.7 is a Mealy machine since the output depends both on the state variables and the current inputs. This dependence means that the value of the output can immediately change when there is a change in the input value, as we can see in the clock period $T3$ in Figure 7.8. For this reason, in the state diagram of a Mealy machine, the representation of the value of the outputs is associated with the state/input pair configuration.

In a state diagram, when there is more than one input, each transition is labelled with the possible combinations of the input variables, as shown in Figure 7.9(a). In some cases, it is useful to mark the transitions for a machine in a more compact way, using the symbol «-» to represent all the possible values for one or more inputs, as shown in the state diagram in

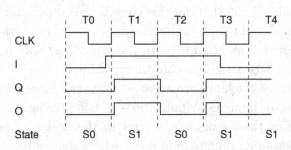

Fig. 7.8 Waveforms generated by the sequential circuit in Figure 7.7.

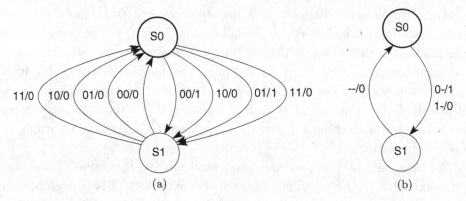

Fig. 7.9   State diagram for a system with two inputs and one output: (a) original and (b) described in a compact form.

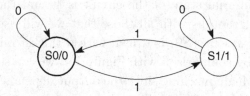

Fig. 7.10   Example of a state diagram for a Moore machine.

Figure 7.9(b). In the same way, it is also useful to use various labels for an arc between the same pair of states.

In a Moore machine, such as, for example, that shown in Figure 7.10, the value of the outputs only depends on the state of the circuit, and, therefore, can only change when there is a clock transition.

For this reason, in the state diagram represented in Figure 7.10, which corresponds to the circuit in Figure 7.11, the value of the outputs is associated with the states and not the transitions.

Figure 7.12 also shows that, for this circuit, the output only changes when there are transitions in the clock signal, and, consequently, when the state of the circuit changes. Any alterations in the inputs can only affect the result of the outputs indirectly, by altering the machine state.

Although Mealy machines are more generic than Moore machines, as we have mentioned, in numerous applications it is advantageous to use Moore machines. One of these examples occurs in the design of state machines which use a microprogramming approach, where the additional flexibility of the Mealy machines does not bring any advantages and, on the contrary, has

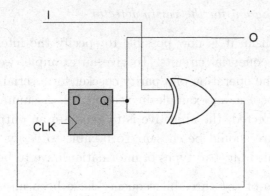

Fig. 7.11   Sequential circuit corresponding to the state diagram in Figure 7.10.

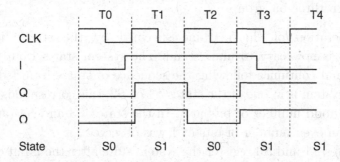

Fig. 7.12   Waveforms generated by the sequential circuit in Figure 7.11.

significant costs. Section 7.5.3 studies this type of sequential circuit implementation.

The state diagram is a natural way of specifying the behaviour of a sequential system, since it explains, in a clear, understandable and non-ambiguous manner, the evolution of the circuit. In simple systems, it is generally possible to literally interpret each state as a machine state summarising its previous history. Indeed, simple sequential circuits are used to interact with the external world in more complex situations than it is possible to achieve with a combinational circuit. To do this, it is necessary to maintain a register of the history of past events, i.e., preserve the *state* of the system.

The state of the system, therefore, represents two things: a particular configuration of values in the flip-flops and a summary of the history of the values of the inputs. This double, but coincidental, interpretation of the meaning of "state" in a sequential system is simple to understand by using concrete examples, which will be studied below.

7.3.1.1 *State diagram for the parity detector*

With this formalism, it is now possible to specify the intended behaviour of synchronous sequential circuits. To give an example, we will study the specification of the operation of a parity checker for a serial communication line which we used as an example in Section 7.2. Assuming that, as soon as an error is detected, the objective is to generate an output at 1, then a Mealy architecture should be chosen. To be able to verify the parity after receiving each third bit, two types of information have to be kept:

- how many bits of the three-bit sequence have been already seen at the input;
- what is the number of bits at 1 that we have already seen since the first bit of each three-bit group.

The operation of the machine specified by the state diagram in Figure 7.13 is now easy to understand. The system starts from the initial state, $S0$, and continues following the sequence of states from left to right. When the system is in one of the states $S1$ or $S2$, this corresponds to having observed an odd number of bits at 1. In the states $S3$ and $S4$ (and also in state $S0$), an even number of bits at 1 was observed.

The states $S1$ and $S3$ register the system state after the input of the first bit, and the states $S2$ and $S4$ register the state after the second bit.

7.3.1.2 *State diagram for an alarm detector*

As another example, let us consider the design of an electronic system which only has one input (besides the system clock), A. Let us assume that input

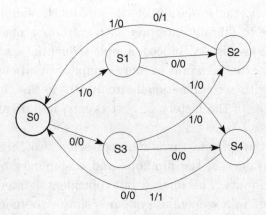

Fig. 7.13 State diagram for the Mealy machine which generates the waveforms in Figure 7.5.

A detects an anomalous situation (for example, a temperature which is too high in the reactor of a nuclear power station). An alarm (signal B, the output) needs to be activated (permanently) if the temperature stays too high for three consecutive clock periods.

There are many ways to deal with this problem,[2] but it should be obvious to the reader that a combinational circuit is not enough. Indeed, it is not sufficient to look at the value of variable A at a given moment of time. It is necessary to know how many periods this variable has been at 1, and cause the alarm to sound only when it has stayed at 1 for three consecutive clock edges.

The first analysis of the problem shows that the system should be capable of recording four different situations (or states):

- $S0$: signal A has not yet gone to 1;
- $S1$: signal A was at 1 for one clock period;
- $S2$: signal A was at 1 for two consecutive clock periods;
- $S3$: signal A was at 1 for three or more consecutive clock periods.

In the last of these situations, an alarm should be permanently sounded, by activating signal B.

From this first analysis, we can immediately conclude that the state diagram of the system should show four states, which correspond to the symbolic names of $S0$, $S1$, $S2$ and $S3$. A first version of the state diagram can also be immediately designed. Indeed, the system should move from state $S0$ to state $S1$ when there is a 1 in input A. In the same way, a 1 in that input should cause a transition from state $S1$ to state $S2$ and from state $S2$ to state $S3$. Finally, we know that after observing line A at 1 three times (state $S3$), the output should be set at 1, and should remain at this level independently of the value of A from that moment. In this way, we achieve the partial state diagram shown in Figure 7.14.

Note, however, that the state diagram shown is not complete since it is necessary to fill in various transitions which are not specified. The complete diagram in Figure 7.15 is progressively built with the following analysis. When signal A is at 0 in state $S0$, the system should naturally remain in state $S0$, noting that the variable has still not shown the value 1.

---

[2] A natural way would be to use a counter, as studied in the previous chapter. However, not every problem can be resolved with a counter, and the method that we describe in this chapter is sufficiently general for all problems.

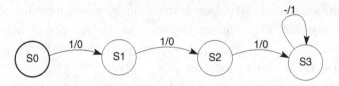

Fig. 7.14   State diagram for the alarm system, with transitions partially completed.

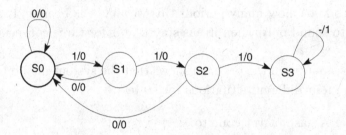

Fig. 7.15   Complete state diagram for the alarm system.

The transition which should occur when the system is in the state $S1$ and variable A takes the value 0 should be analysed with a little more care. Firstly, this situation appears to be different than that represented by state $S0$, until now used to mark the fact that the variable A has never taken the value 1. However, a closer look at the statement of the problem makes it clear that the fact that the variable A has gone to 1 one or more times non-consecutively does not require any special treatment. Indeed, the system we want to design should only distinguish the case in which the variable stays at 1 for three consecutive clock periods. If the variable A is sampled at 1 on a clock edge and then returns to 0, the system should restart counting from zero and wait until the variable goes to 1 for three consecutive clock edges. From this analysis, it is clear that when the input variable is 0 and the state is $S1$, the system should move to state $S0$. The same analysis applies to the transition from state $S2$ when the input variable is 0.

Additionally, let us comment on the two possible transitions from the state $S3$. The observation that state $S3$ indicates that the variable A has already been observed at 1 for three consecutive clock periods immediately leads to the conclusion that these transitions should have as next state the same state $S3$, and that the corresponding output value should be 1.

Finally, it is necessary to define the initial state of the system, that is, the state in which a sequential system should be initialised, when the circuit is connected. While for a combinational system it is not necessary to take any special care with the initial configuration of values in the lines of the circuit, this is not true for a sequential circuit. In a sequential circuit, each flip-flop can take on the value 0 or the value 1 when the circuit is connected. This means that the sequential circuit will start its execution in a given state, which depends on the initial, unpredictable, configuration of the flip-flops. In general, the correct operation of the circuit depends on the state in which the operation starts. Thus, it is necessary to ensure that the flip-flops are initialised, using the direct inputs (Section 6.4.3), with the correct values, which corresponds to the configuration of the initial state.

This initialisation is generally achieved by setting the asynchronous signals *Set* and *Reset* with the appropriate values. In some cases, the use of asynchronous signals can be avoided, if it is possible to ensure that the circuit becomes stable, with the desired behaviour, either in an independent manner or through some synchronous control signal.

In this case, this circuit will operate very badly if its operation starts in state $S3$, given that this would permanently set off an alarm for a situation which has not occurred. In this case, the intended initial state is state $S0$, marked with a thicker line in the state diagram in Figure 7.15. This figure shows the complete state diagram for the proposed system.

The state diagram in Figure 7.15 shows the simplest state diagram which corresponds to a solution for the system. However, there are other state diagrams, with more states, which also describe the correct functionality, although they do not correspond to the simplest diagram.

For example, when we analysed the transition from state $S1$ with $A = 0$, we could have concluded that the destination should be a fifth state, $S4$, with different characteristics than the already existing state $S0$. This could lead to the state diagram in Figure 7.16, which has five states but continues to operate as specified. In this case, the information contained in state $S4$ is that there have previously been sequences of 1 or 2 bits at 1, which is irrelevant to the problem in question. The reader can verify that the outputs generated by both state diagrams are the same, for any sequence of inputs.

The next section describes an algorithm which, from any state diagram, derives the simplest diagram, that is, the diagram with the smaller possible number of states with an operation equivalent to that of the original. Thus, obtaining the simplest state diagram in the design stage is not critical to either the success or the efficiency of the resulting system. However, the designer should always carefully look for possible redundancies in the state

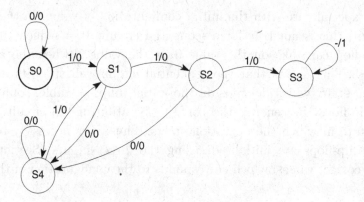

Fig. 7.16   Alternative state diagram for the alarm system.

diagrams derived from specifications, since these redundancies are frequently the result of less careful, or even wrong, analysis of the system specifications.

7.3.2   *Elimination of Redundant States*

As mentioned, there may exist different state diagrams which generate an identical behaviour in a sequential system. For example, the systems which correspond to the diagrams in Figures 7.15 and 7.16 generate the same output sequences for any sequence presented in their inputs. In the case of these two state diagrams, it is easy to understand the reason why this happens.

If we analyse states $S4$ and $S0$ in Figure 7.16, we can see that:

- when the input is 1, the output is equal for both states (0);
- when the input is 0, the output is also equal for both states (0);
- when the input is 1, the next state is the same for both states ($S1$);
- when the input is 0, the next state is the current state in both cases.

These four conditions imply that the function carried out by the states $S0$ and $S4$ is the same. Indeed, they show the same output for all possible inputs, and they move (for all the possible input values) to states which are equal or which have been shown to be equivalent. These considerations mean that the states $S0$ and $S4$ are equivalent and can be merged into one state, as shown schematically in Figure 7.17. The state diagram that results from the merger of states $S0$ and $S4$ is that of Figure 7.15. In this case, to obtain the new state diagram, it is sufficient to remove state $S4$ and alter the transitions from states $S1$ and $S2$ to $S4$ to have a new destination, state $S0$.

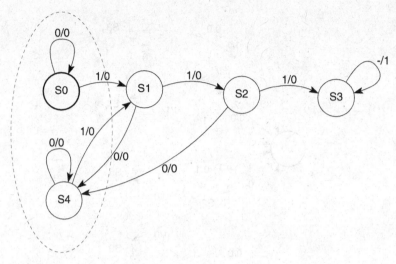

Fig. 7.17 Illustration of the process of merging states $S0$ and $S4$ in the state diagram of Figure 7.16.

The method to eliminate redundant states in an arbitrary state diagram is based exactly on identifying the groups of states that can be merged because their behaviour is equivalent, both regarding the outputs that they generate as well as regarding the states to which a transition occurs.

Two states are said to be *equivalent* or *redundant* if, and only if, for each possible combination of inputs, they generate the same output and transition to the same state or to states which are also equivalent.

Although there are different methods to eliminate redundant states, the method based on an implication table is the easiest to use when the simplification operation is carried out manually.

To illustrate the method, we will use the sequential system which detects a parity error in each three-bit group, studied in Section 7.2. We should remember that this system should issue a 1 in its output whenever a three-bit group shows an odd number of 1s.

The direct construction of the state diagram with the smallest number of states fulfilling this specification was carried out in Section 7.3.1.1. However, it may not be simple, for those who do not have significant experience of designing sequential systems, to directly obtain this state diagram.

In compensation, the construction of the state diagram in Figure 7.18 can easily be carried out from the definition of the problem. In this case, list all the possible combinations of inputs which may occur from the initial state ($S0$), and generate the value 1 in the output when the number of 1s which

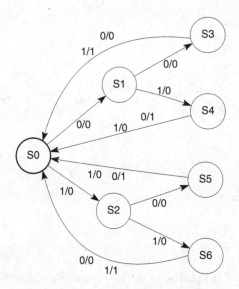

Fig. 7.18   State diagram of a detector of an odd number of 1 bits in each three-bit group.

has occurred is odd, returning to the state $S0$ to process the next three-bit sequence.

Looking at the state diagram of Figure 7.18, it is not immediately obvious which are the pairs of equivalent states. For example, states $S1$ and $S2$ have the same outputs, but may or may not be equivalent, since, for each input, they have different next states.

A simple way of structuring the information we need is to use a matrix, which has one row and one column per state, and use it to record which pairs of states are equivalent. The matrix for the diagram in Figure 7.18, our current example, is shown in Figure 7.19(a). Each entry will be used to store information about the possible equivalence between each pair of states.

For example, the entry corresponding to the pair of states $(S1, S2)$ will contain information about which are the states that have to be equivalent so that states $S1$ and $S2$ are equivalent. From the definition of equivalent states, we can deduce that, for this example, states $S1$ and $S2$ are equivalent if, and only if, state $S3$ is equivalent to state $S5$ and state $S4$ is equivalent to state $S6$ (see Figure 7.20(b)).

For some pairs of states, it can immediately be clear that they are not equivalent. For example, states $S0$ and $S6$ are necessarily not equivalent because they generate different outputs when the input is 1. In this case, that entry for the matrix will be marked with a cross, to show that those states are not equivalent.

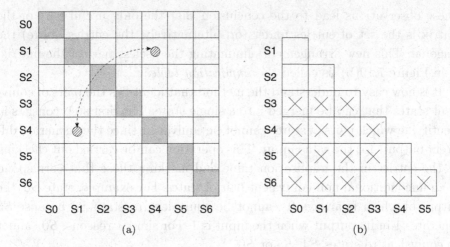

Fig. 7.19 (a) Equivalence matrix between states and (b) the component lower than the diagonal (implication table).

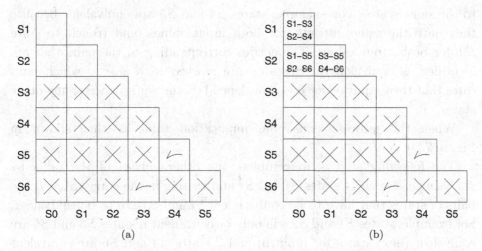

Fig. 7.20 Implication table for the sequence detecting machine (a) with indication of the states which are not equivalent and the states which are unconditionally equivalent (b) with the conditions necessary for equivalence filled in.

A more careful observation reveals, however, that many of the entries in the matrix are redundant due to two reasons:

- a state is always equivalent to itself (which means that the information in the diagonal of the matrix is useless);
- when state A is equivalent to state B, then state B is also equivalent to state A (the equivalence is commutative), which means that the matrix is symmetrical.

These observations lead to the conclusion that the only useful part of the matrix is the set of entries under (or, alternatively, the entries above) the diagonal. This new arrangement eliminating the useless part of the matrix, as in Figure 7.19(b), is called the *implication table*.

It is now easy to understand the method that identifies the pairs of equivalent states that can be merged into a single state. The first step consists in identifying which pairs of states cannot be equivalent since they generate different outputs for the same input. This operation can be carried out checking all the entries in the implication table and marking those that correspond to an unconditional non-equivalent pair of states. For example, state $S0$, the output of which is always 0, cannot be equivalent to state $S3$ because $S3$ generates 1 in its output when the input is 1. For similar reasons, $S0$ cannot be equivalent to states $S4$, $S5$ or $S6$.

The following step consists in identifying which pairs of states are directly identifiable as equivalent because they generate the same outputs and move to the same states. For example, states $S4$ and $S5$ are equivalent, because they have the same outputs, for both input values, and transit to state $S0$, for both input values. The entries corresponding to the pairs that are identified as equivalent in this step are marked with a ✓, which indicates that their equivalence does not depend on the equivalence of any other states.

When this process ends, the implication table is that shown in Figure 7.20(a).

The following step is to complete the other entries of the table by analysing each pair of states Si and Sj and writing in the entry (Si, Sj) the pairs of states that have to be equivalent if Si and Sj are to be equivalent. For example, states $S1$ and $S2$ will only be equivalent if states $S3$ and $S5$ are equivalent (next states for input 0) and if states $S4$ and $S6$ are equivalent (next states for the input 1). Thus, the implication table entry corresponding to the pair $(S1, S2)$ will be filled in with the pairs $(S3, S5)$ and $(S4, S6)$. Through an analogous procedure, the entries $(S0, S1)$ and $(S0, S2)$ are filled in. Figure 7.20(b) shows the implication table resulting from this process.

It is now necessary to eliminate, using successive passes through the implication table, the state pairs which cannot be equivalent, since their equivalence depends on the equivalence of non-equivalent states. In this case, it is only necessary to analyse the entries corresponding to the pairs $(S0, S1)$, $(S0, S2)$ and $(S1, S2)$. It is easy to see that, in this case, none of these pairs of states can be equivalent. The pair $(S0, S1)$ cannot be equivalent

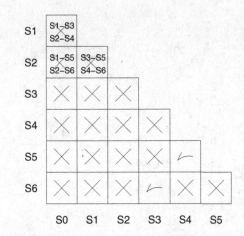

Fig. 7.21 Final implication table for the machine under study. The equivalent states are the pairs $(S3, S6)$ and $(S4, S5)$.

because it depends on the pair $(S1, S3)$ of non-equivalent states. The same happens with the pair $(S0, S2)$, because of the pair $(S1, S5)$ and with the pair $(S1, S2)$ because of the pair $(S3, S5)$.

The final implication table is that shown in Figure 7.21. It indicates that state $S3$ is equivalent to state $S6$ and that state $S4$ is equivalent to state $S5$.

This simple example does not illustrate all the possibilities that may occur. It may, for instance, happen that three or more states are all equivalent between them, two by two. In this case, all of them are in the same equivalence class and may be merged.

Knowing the states which are equivalent to each other, it is now easy to generate the simplified state diagram, in two steps.

The first step consists in choosing one of the states for each equivalence class as representative of the class. In the example in consideration, there are two equivalence classes, each one with two states: $(S3, S6)$ and $(S4, S5)$. Figure 7.22 shows these equivalence classes. It will be necessary to keep only one state for each one of these equivalence classes since all the states in each of them perform the same function. Arbitrarily, it could be decided to maintain state $S3$ (for the $S3$, $S6$ class) and state $S4$ (for the $S4$, $S5$ class).

The second step consists in substituting the transitions which occur from and to each state of a given equivalence class by transitions from and to the state which is representative of the class.

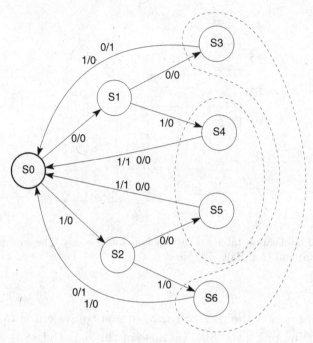

Fig. 7.22   Equivalence classes for the problem under study. States $S3$ and $S6$ are in one equivalence class, and states $S4$ and $S5$ in another equivalence class.

Considering the example we are studying, the arrows, representing transitions, which enter and leave state $S6$ will be considered first. The transition which, with input 1, causes the system to go from state $S2$ to state $S6$, now makes the system change from state $S2$ to state $S3$, which is the representative of the equivalence class ($S3$, $S6$). The two transitions which cause the circuit to go from state $S6$ to state $S0$ will be substituted by transitions from state $S3$ to state $S0$. However, careful observation of the diagram shows that these transitions already exist between state $S3$ and state $S0$, and so it is not necessary to add them.

After removing state $S6$, and altering the transitions involving this state, we consider state $S5$. In this case, the transition between state $S2$ and state $S5$ changes to a transition between state $S2$ and state $S4$, which is the representative of the equivalence class ($S4$, $S5$).

Figure 7.23 represents the state diagram which results from these alterations. The functionality of the original state diagram (Figure 7.18), with seven states, is the same as the reduced state diagram, with only five states. The reader can verify that all input sequences generate the same output sequences when applied to the diagrams in Figures (7.18) and (7.23).

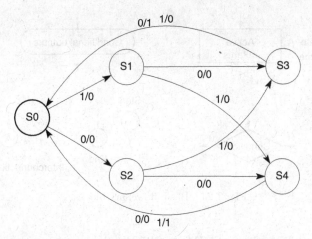

Fig. 7.23 State diagram of the detector of an odd number of 1 bits in each three-bit group after reducing the number of states.

7.3.3 Specification Using Flowcharts

Although the specification of a sequential system using state diagrams is always possible, there are various situations in which this is not the most appropriate representation. One of these situations occurs when specifying one type of state machine used for controlling systems and called *control unit*. A control unit is nothing more than a sequential circuit that accepts inputs coming from another digital system (the controlled circuit) and generates outputs that *control* that system. These units typically show the following characteristics:

- a large number of inputs;
- a large number of outputs;
- in each state, there is only a small fraction of inputs which affect system behaviour;
- in each state, there is only a small fraction of outputs which are active.

An alternative way of specifying the behaviour of a sequential system, which is particularly advantageous for this type of system, is based on the use of flowcharts. A *flowchart* is made up of the interconnection of various blocks, each of which has a specific meaning, as shown in Figure 7.24.

There are essentially three types of blocks in a flowchart used to specify a control unit: *states*, *tests* and *conditional outputs*. Indeed, a flowchart is a much more general representation than this. The particular case of a flowchart with the characteristics presented here has the name *Algorithmic*

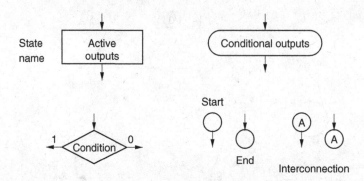

Fig. 7.24   Basic flowchart blocks.

State Machine diagram or *ASM*. In this book, however, the generic term flowchart is used to model state machines.

A block in the form of a rectangle represents a state. Inside the rectangle are indicated the active outputs and next to it is the state name. A diamond-shaped object denotes a test for a Boolean condition, and has two outputs, according to the value of the condition tested. This condition may represent a test for a single variable or a test for a Boolean expression with several variables. The rounded corner rectangle is used to denote conditional outputs, that is, outputs which are active only when a given condition is true. A conditional output block may only be used after a test block. The use of conditional output blocks is only necessary when the state machine to be designed is a Mealy machine. In the case of a Moore machine, the outputs only depend on the states (and not on the values present in the inputs) and the conditional blocks are not necessary. In addition to these main blocks, there also are circles which are used to interconnect distant parts of complex flowcharts.

Figure 7.25 shows the flowchart which corresponds to the state diagram in Figure 7.15. When analysing the two specifications, it is easy to understand the direct correspondence between a state in the state diagram (represented by a circle) and a state in the flowchart (represented by a rectangle).

In this state machine, in which there is only one input variable and one output variable, the representation using the flowchart is not much clearer than the one using state diagrams. However, when the number of inputs and outputs increases, the situation is significantly altered.

Let us take a slightly more complicated example which corresponds to a control system for a hypothetical railroad crossing for a single-track line, shown in Figure 7.26.

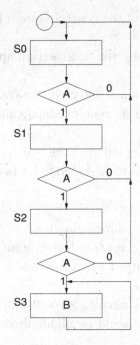

Fig. 7.25   Flowchart equivalent to the state diagram in Figure 7.15.

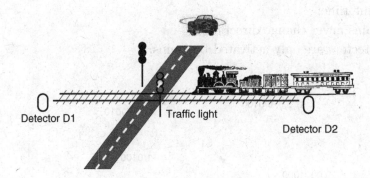

Detector D1   Traffic light

Detector D2

Fig. 7.26   Railroad crossing with two detectors to detect the presence of the train and traffic lights to control traffic.

The control system should enable the activation of the traffic lights so that the cars do not cross the railroad line while the train is approaching. To do this, the control system has access to two detectors ($D1$ and $D2$) which are active when the train is in the respective position. This example assumes that the detectors are sufficiently distant from the railroad crossing so that it is possible to control the traffic lights in adequate time. It also assumes that the distance between the detectors and the crossing is much greater than the size of the train.

The intended operation of the control system is as follows:

- the traffic lights should be green until a train approaches, thereby activating one of the detectors;
- when the approach of a train is detected, the traffic lights should change to yellow and stay yellow for a predetermined time, after which they should change to red;
- the traffic lights should stay red until the train activates the detector on the opposite side to that which was activated when it approached, changing to green at this time.

To control the time that the traffic lights remain yellow, the control unit has access to a counter, which accepts a Reset input (*StartTimer*) and which generates a value 1 in its output when the time intended for the duration of the yellow signal has passed.

In designing the control circuit, we will assume a few simplifications, among which the following should be highlighted:

- as it is a single-track line, trains in both directions will never appear at the same time;
- the trains never change direction;
- the detectors are only activated by trains.

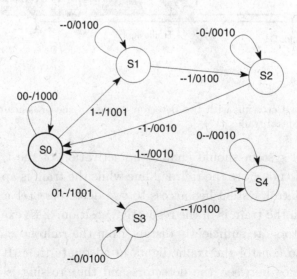

Fig. 7.27   State diagram for the railroad crossing control unit.

The control system to be designed has the following inputs and outputs:

Inputs: $D1$, $D2$ and $Timer$;
Outputs: $Green$, $Yellow$, Red and $StartTimer$.

Given the specifications, it is possible to represent the sequential behaviour of the circuit, using the state diagram in Figure 7.27, in which the inputs/outputs are in the following order $D1$ $D2$ $Timer/Green$ $Yellow$ Red $StartTimer$. However, although this state diagram correctly describes the behaviour of the system, it does not transmit the operation of the state machine in a very intuitive manner.

First, although there is only a small number of active outputs in each state, this fact is obscured by the need to represent the value of each output at each state explicitly.

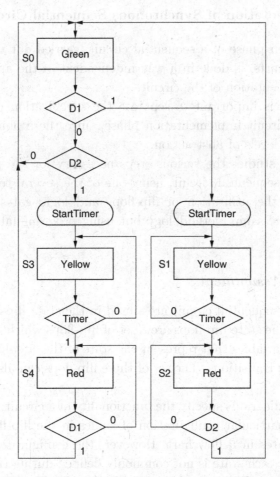

Fig. 7.28 Flowchart for the sequential system in Figure 7.27.

Second, there are various structures, which are repeated many times in control circuits and that are not clearly shown in their representation in state diagrams. For example, in state $S1$ the system waits for the signal to indicate the end of the waiting time counted by the timer (*Timer* having reached 1). After that, the machine moves to state $S2$. However, only attentive observation of the state diagram identifies this characteristic of that state.

The representation of the sequential system in Figure 7.27 in the form of a flowchart, illustrated in Figure 7.28, is much easier to understand than the state diagram referred. The analysis of this flowchart provides a much simpler understanding of what the intended function of the sequential system is since, for each state, it only shows the variables which influence the behaviour of the system in that state.

7.4   Implementation of Synchronous Sequential Circuits

The specification phase of a sequential circuit, carried out using state diagrams or flowcharts, is done in a way independent of the approach for the physical implementation of the circuit.

Moreover, it is important to separate the specification phase from the encoding and circuit implementation phase, since these phases use significantly different levels of abstraction.

This section studies the various steps necessary for the physical implementation of a sequential circuit, using one of the several techniques available based on the utilisation of flip-flops and logic gates. Obviously, a variant using the same methodology but using programmable logic is also possible.

7.4.1   *State Assignment*

The states of a sequential circuit are stored in the state flip-flops, as shown in Figure 7.3. The state flip-flops are a set of flip-flops which store a configuration of logic variables that represent the state of the circuit between every two active clock transitions. The set of these flip-flops can also be called the state register.

When state diagrams specify the functionality of a circuit, each state corresponds to a particular configuration of values in the flip-flops. The same happens for states in a flowchart. However, the configuration of values in the registers for each state is not commonly defined during the specification stage. This option enables the state diagram (or flowchart) to be designed, altered and redesigned, if necessary, using symbolic names for the states before any concerns with the implementation phase are taken into consideration.

However, to define the structure of the circuit at the level of the interconnection of logic gates and memory elements, it is necessary to choose an encoding for each of the system states. This action is known as *state assignment*.

The only required constraint for each circuit to function correctly is that the encoding for each state is unique, that is, that the code word attributed to a state is distinct from the code word assigned to any other state. The problem of choosing the best encoding for the states regarding the complexity or the performance of the final circuit is a complex problem which is seldom solvable in an optimal manner, even using powerful circuit design tools. It is, therefore, necessary to define, in a necessarily non-optimal way, a particular encoding for the states.

In some cases, an experienced designer may analyse the state diagram or the flowchart and define encodings that lead to a final implementation of the circuit more compact than others. However, this type of analysis requires considerable experience and intuition, and is not an approach within reach of the novice designer.

Fortunately, it is possible to use simple methods to encode states which, in general, lead to satisfactory results regarding the complexity of the resulting circuit.

In this text, we present two state assignment methods: encoding using binary code and encoding using one flip-flop per state.

7.4.1.1 *State assignment using binary code*

When state encoding is carried out using binary code, the assignment of code words to the states is made using the smallest number of flip-flops possible. The rationale underlying this choice is that the utilisation of a minimum number of flip-flops minimises the number of functions to synthesise and the number of variables on which they depend, thereby reducing, besides the flip-flops, the total number of logic gates which will be necessary.

Note that this reasoning is not foolproof, since the number of logic gates necessary to synthesise a logic function varies widely with the complexity of the function to be implemented, and a smaller number of functions does not necessarily mean a smaller overall complexity for the circuit as a whole.

Assuming that the states in the state diagram (or in the flowchart) are named $S0$, $S1$, ..., Sn, the encoding using binary code will use a number of flip-flops equal to $k = \lceil \log_2(n+1) \rceil$. The reason for this formula is easier to understand if we analyse the particular case in which $n+1$, the number of states, is a power of 2. In this case, $k = \log_2(n+1)$, and, since k flip-flops allow for the representation of 2^k different combinations, the choice of $k = \log_2(n+1)$ makes possible to represent the $n+1$ combinations necessary to encode each one of the $n+1$ states. In the general case, where the number of states is not a power of 2, it is necessary to round up the value of $\log_2(n+1)$ to the next integer value. For example, on a machine with five states it is necessary to use three flip-flops, using only five of the eight possible combinations of values.

For the alarm system with the state diagram shown in Figure 7.15, the use of the binary coding method means that the assignment of codes can be carried out according to Table 7.1.

Note that, although this encoding is, in some way, natural, it would be possible to encode the states using many other ways, using only 2 bits. However, and as there are no strong reasons to prefer alternative encodings, the choice shown is simple and intuitive.

7.4.1.2 *Encoding with one flip-flop per state*

An alternative method of encoding consists in using as many flip-flops as states, and choosing a code in which, for each state, only one of the flip-flops is set to 1 (this method of encoding is also known as *one-hot encoding*). The fact that it is necessary to have as many flip-flops as the number of states in the system requires a greater number of functions to be synthesised. However, it is legitimate to expect that each one of these functions is simpler to implement and that the outputs are also easy to implement from the values in the state registers. Furthermore, with this type of encoding, it is possible to synthesise the logic functions in an expeditious manner, by

Table 7.1   Encoding of the states for the alarm system using the binary coding method.

State	Encoding	
	Q_1	Q_0
$S0$	0	0
$S1$	0	1
$S2$	1	0
$S3$	1	1

simple inspection of the state diagram or the flowchart, as we will see in the implementation stage.

Using this method, we obtain Table 7.2, for example, which lists the encoding of the states of the state diagram in Figure 7.16 (or the flowchart in Figure 7.25).

7.4.2 State Transition Table

After the state assignment, the elaboration of the *state transition table* is carried out by analysing the state diagram, or the flowchart, taking into consideration the codes assigned to each state. This table summarises the information in the state diagram and the choices made for the state assignment.

This table has a row for each possible combination of values of the primary inputs of the circuit and the state register. Each row indicates the values of the state variables in the next clock cycle and the values that the outputs take in the current clock period, as a function of the values of the state variables and the primary inputs.

Considering once again the example of the alarm system and assuming the use of the encoding in Table 7.1, we obtain the state transition table shown in Table 7.3.

Table 7.2   Encoding of the states of the alarm system using one flip-flop per state.

State	Encoding			
	Q_3	Q_2	Q_1	Q_0
S0	0	0	0	1
S1	0	0	1	0
S2	0	1	0	0
S3	1	0	0	0

Table 7.3   State transition table for the example of the alarm system.

Input	Present state		Next state		Output
A	$Q_1(n-1)$	$Q_0(n-1)$	$Q_1(n)$	$Q_0(n)$	B
0	0	0	0	0	0
1	0	0	0	1	0
0	0	1	0	0	0
1	0	1	1	0	0
0	1	0	0	0	0
1	1	0	1	1	0
0	1	1	1	1	1
1	1	1	1	1	1

7.4.3   *Circuit Synthesis*

From this point, the synthesis process depends on the type of flip-flops. If the designer chooses D-type flip-flops, the circuit synthesis may proceed directly from the state transition table. Since, in a D-type flip-flop, the input value in the flip-flop specifies the intended value for the next state, the state transition table directly specifies the functionality of the combinational circuit which generates the input variables in the flip-flops.

When flip-flops of another type are used, such as, for example, JK flip-flops, the procedure is somewhat different. In this case, which is studied next, it is necessary to determine what are the appropriate values to place in the input of the flip-flops so that the flip-flop goes to the specified next state.

7.4.3.1   *Synthesis using D-type flip-flops*

When D-type flip-flops are used, the state transition table contains the information necessary to carry out the synthesis process for the sequential circuit, in a way similar to what we used for the combinational circuit design described in Chapter 2. Indeed, each of the columns on the right side of the table corresponds to a truth table of a logic function of the combinational circuit, which should be synthesised using one of the methods described in Chapter 2.

In the example used so far, and making use of binary encoding defined in Table 7.1, we obtain the Karnaugh maps in Figure 7.29.

Expressions (7.1) can be directly obtained from the Karnaugh maps

$$D_1 = Q_0A + Q_1A + Q_1Q_0,$$
$$D_0 = Q_1Q_0 + \overline{Q_0}A, \tag{7.1}$$
$$B = Q_1Q_0,$$

which leads to the circuit in Figure 7.30.

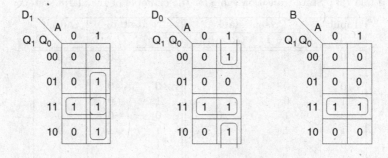

Fig. 7.29   Karnaugh maps for the state and output variables for the alarm circuit.

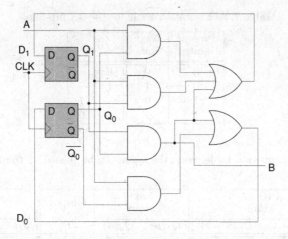

Fig. 7.30 Sequential circuit for the alarm system, implemented with D-type flip-flops.

The synthesis with one flip-flop per state using D-type flip-flops and using the encoding in Table 7.2 may, formally, follow an identical process. However, the specific way in which each state is encoded makes the use of Karnaugh tables useless for the synthesis of the state variables, as it is possible to write the equations directly. This procedure will be studied further ahead.

7.4.3.2 *Circuit synthesis using JK flip-flops*

If we want to use flip-flops other than D, the synthesis process should take into account the flip-flops excitation table, to obtain the intended transition in the state variables of the circuit. The excitation table shows, for each desired state transition of the flip-flop, the values that shall be present on its input lines.

The most used flip-flops, besides D-type flip-flops, are JK flip-flops. Indeed, the excitation table for JK flip-flops often enables simpler functions for the input lines of the flip-flop to be obtained, which leads to logic circuits with fewer logic gates.

This happens because JK flip-flops show significant flexibility regarding the values that should be present in their inputs for a given transition to be obtained. Let us consider, for example, that a JK flip-flop is in state 1 and we want to alter its state to state 0. Analysing Figure 6.20, we can see that there are two combinations of the inputs that cause the desired result: $JK = 01$ and $JK = 11$. The first combination indicates that the flip-flop should go to state 0, and the second combination indicates that it should switch state. Both will cause the next state of the flip-flop to be 0.

Table 7.4   Excitation table for the JK flip-flop.

Present state	Next state	J	K
0	0	0	—
0	1	1	—
1	0	—	1
1	1	—	0

Table 7.5   State transition table, with the values to be placed at the inputs of the JK flip-flops.

Input	Present state		Next state		Output	Flip-flop inputs			
A	$Q_1(n-1)$	$Q_0(n-1)$	$Q_1(n)$	$Q_0(n)$	B	J_1	K_1	J_0	K_0
0	0	0	0	0	0	0	X	0	X
1	0	0	0	1	0	0	X	1	X
0	0	1	0	0	0	0	X	X	1
1	0	1	1	0	0	1	X	X	1
0	1	0	0	0	0	X	1	0	X
1	1	0	1	1	0	X	0	1	X
0	1	1	1	1	1	X	0	X	0
1	1	1	1	1	1	X	0	X	0

A similar analysis can be carried out for other transitions we want to produce on the flip-flop. Table 7.4, the excitation table of the JK flip-flop, synthesises the results of that analysis, indicating the combinations necessary to have in the input to achieve a given transition in the state of the flip-flop.

Reusing the example of the alarm circuit, and taking into consideration the combinations that should be placed in the inputs to achieve a given transition, we obtain the state transition table shown in Table 7.5. For example, in the first row of the table, keeping of the state variable Q_1 in the value 0 may be obtained with two combinations of the variables J_0 and K_0, $(0,0)$ and $(0,1)$, by Table 7.4. In this way, it is possible to specify that the variable J_0 should take the value 0 and the variable K_0 may take the value 0 or 1, what is represented by the symbol «X».

The construction of the Karnaugh maps (Figure 7.31) for the input variables of the flip-flops leads, in this case, to Expressions (7.2)

$$J_1 = Q_0 A,$$
$$K_1 = \overline{Q_0}\,\overline{A},$$
$$J_0 = A,$$
$$K_0 = \overline{Q_1}, \tag{7.2}$$

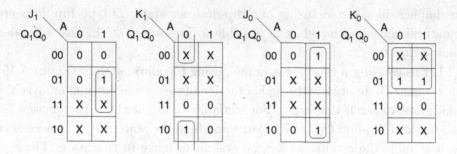

Fig. 7.31 Karnaugh maps for the state variables of the circuit.

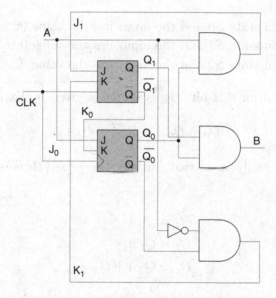

Fig. 7.32 Sequential circuit for the alarm system, implemented with JK flip-flops.

which lead to the sequential circuit for the alarm system, implemented with JK flip-flops, in Figure 7.32. As we can see, the logic required for the synthesis of the state variables is simpler than the implementation with D-type flip-flops. The logic which implements the output variables is the same because it does not depend on the flip-flop type.

7.4.3.3 *Synthesis using one flip-flop per state*

When we use a D-type flip-flop per state (Table 7.2), it is possible to directly synthesise the circuit, without resorting to Karnaugh maps, defining logic functions through simple inspection of the state diagram (or flowchart), avoiding the construction of the transition table. For these reasons, when we implement a circuit using one flip-flop per state, D-type flip-flops are a natural choice, although it is possible to use others at the cost of added complexity.

Let us consider a concrete example, using the alarm system (Figure 7.15) once again. To determine the logic function of each state bit, just analyse the conditions to reach that state. For example, to define the logic function for the input of flip-flop Q_0 (which corresponds to the state $S0$), it is necessary to determine the conditions for the system to move to this state. Through analysis of the state diagram, we can see that there is a transition to the state $S0$ when:

- the system is in state $S0$ and the input has the value 0;
- the system is in state $S1$ and the input has the value 0;
- the system is in state $S2$ and the input has the value 0.

The logic function for this bit, D_0, is therefore given by Expression (7.3).

$$D_0 = Q_0\overline{A} + Q_1\overline{A} + Q_2\overline{A}. \tag{7.3}$$

An identical analysis carried out for the other three states leads to Expressions (7.4).

$$
\begin{aligned}
D_1 &= Q_0 A, \\
D_2 &= Q_1 A, \\
D_3 &= Q_2 A + Q_3.
\end{aligned}
\tag{7.4}
$$

We can also see easily, by inspection, that output B is given by Expression (7.5) since it is only active in state $S3$.

$$B = Q_3. \tag{7.5}$$

The circuit diagram can be obtained directly from the equations as Figure 7.33 illustrates. In this case, the complexity of the circuit is comparable (although a little larger) to that of the circuit implemented with D flip-flops and binary encoding. However, for systems with a large number of states, the approach using binary encoding is not normally so economical.

The use of one flip-flop per state makes it possible to obtain the circuit diagram much more directly from the fluxogram. To design the circuit, just convert each element of the flowchart into a circuit element, using the following rules as illustrated in the figures:

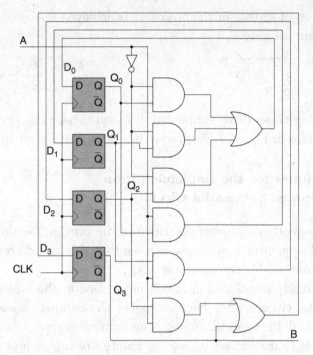

Fig. 7.33 Sequential circuit for the alarm system, implemented using one D flip-flop per state.

- Use one flip-flop for each state, connecting the input and output signals as the correspondent origin and destination in the flowchart. The outputs active in this state connect to the output of this flip-flop.

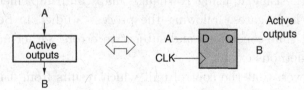

- For each test use a one-bit decoder with enable. The conditional outputs connect to the output corresponding to the decoder.

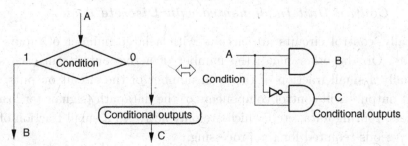

- The junction of signals in the flowchart is achieved in the circuit through the use of an OR gate.

It is easy using these three simple rules, to synthesise the circuit specified by the flowchart in Figure 7.25 directly to obtain the circuit in Figure 7.33.

7.5   Techniques for the Implementation of Complex Sequential Circuits

Although the synthesis process described in the previous sections applies to every type of sequential system, we can see that this is not always the most appropriate method for complex systems.

As was already mentioned, and will be studied in the following chapter, complex digital circuits often have two parts: the *datapath*, sometimes called *data circuit* and the *control circuit*. The control circuit, often called also *control unit*, is characterised by a large number of inputs and outputs, and by not having a regular structure. Although simple, the railroad crossing control unit in Figure 7.27 is an example of this type of system.

Given that a control unit may be very complex, it is not always feasible to synthesise it using the techniques described above. In fact, it is always possible to specify a synchronous control unit using state diagrams or flowcharts. However, synthesising it using Karnaugh maps and implementing it with flip-flops and logic gates, following the process studied in Section 7.3, is often difficult, time-consuming and subject to errors. Other more powerful and scalable methods exist.

Note, however, that the control unit which results from using the alternative methods described in this section continues to be a sequential circuit, represented by a state machine with the structure of Figure 7.3.

7.5.1   *Control Unit Implemented with Discrete Logic*

Typically, control circuits are circuits with a large number of inputs and outputs. On the other hand, the number of active outputs in each state is usually a small fraction of the total number of the circuit outputs. The circuit outputs will control components of the datapath (signals for loading registers, routing data, etc.) which are only active in a small fraction of the clock periods required for the processing.

These characteristics mean that it is more natural to use flowcharts to specify the operation of a control circuit than a state diagram. In fact, as we saw in Section 7.3.3, a flowchart for a circuit with many inputs and many outputs is significantly more readable than the equivalent state diagram.

When the control circuit has few states and is represented by a relatively simple flowchart, the direct synthesis of the circuit using Karnaugh maps and discrete logic is entirely feasible. It may be carried out without significant difficulties. However, the process rapidly becomes more complicated when the size of the problem increases.

Let us consider, for example, the flowchart for the control circuit of the railroad crossing in Figure 7.28, which is equivalent to the state diagram in Figure 7.27. If we use the state assignment in Table 7.6, we get the Karnaugh map for the output variable *Red* in Figure 7.34. In this simple case, it is enough to note that the variable *Red* is active in the states

Table 7.6   Binary encoding of the states for the railroad crossing control system.

State	Encoding		
	Q_2	Q_1	Q_0
$S0$	0	0	0
$S1$	0	0	1
$S2$	0	1	0
$S3$	0	1	1
$S4$	1	0	0

Red

$D_1 D_2$ Temp

$Q_0 Q_1 Q_2$	000	001	011	010	110	111	101	100
000	0	0	0	0	0	0	0	0
001	0	0	0	0	0	0	0	0
011	0	0	0	0	0	0	0	0
010	1	1	1	1	1	1	1	1
110	X	X	X	X	X	X	X	X
111	X	X	X	X	X	X	X	X
101	X	X	X	X	X	X	X	X
100	1	1	1	1	1	1	1	1

Fig. 7.34   Karnaugh map for the variable *Red* in the flowchart in Figure 7.28.

$S2$ and $S4$, which are the fourth and eighth rows of the Karnaugh map, respectively.

It is possible to synthesise the combinational circuit for this output variable, as well as for the other three variables, from the Karnaugh maps. However, it is clear that the synthesis of complex control units using this method cannot usually be carried out in an efficient way. This consideration is even more evident if the number of input variables is large.

Note that, even for a very simple flowchart, the specification of the combinational circuit is complicated. Implementation of these equations using simple logic gates, although possible, quickly reaches levels of considerable complexity. Without suitable support tools, this complexity would lead to an unsustainable implementation effort. Indeed, it is unreasonable to think that it is possible to use discrete logic to synthesise control circuits with tens or hundreds of states and variables.

Fortunately, there are alternatives to structure the synthesis process which lead to the possibility of designing complex control units even without the help of sophisticated tools. The most powerful and flexible method for the synthesis of control units uses microprogramming. This methodology will be dealt with in detail in Section 7.5.3. However, it is useful to firstly analyse the way in which the use of modules of medium complexity (counters, decoders and multiplexers) makes possible the synthesis of control units with a more regular and more understandable structure.

7.5.2 *Counter-based Control Units*

A common characteristic of many control units is the existence of somewhat regular sequences of states in the flowchart describing their behaviour. Considering that feature, the railroad crossing control unit in Figure 7.35 may be implemented, in a very intuitive manner, using a counter and a decoder. The flowchart contains sequences of states linked to tests on variables which map in a relatively natural way for a counter.

Figure 7.36 represents an implementation of this control units, using a counter, a decoder and some discrete logic. Although the circuit may appear complicated, it may be designed directly by simple inspection of the flowchart in Figure 7.35.

First, we should understand the operation of the counter, which has three control inputs, Cl, Ld and Inc, with the functionality described in Chapter 6.

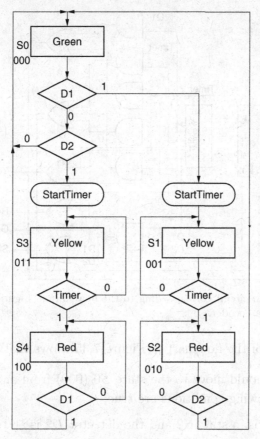

Fig. 7.35 Flowchart for the railroad crossing control unit, with the encodings for the states, according to Table 7.6.

All of these act synchronously, respectively causing the following:

Cl the counter assumes the state 000;
Ld the counter loads in parallel the bits present in its parallel input;
Inc the counter counts, proceeding to the next state in the counting sequence.

If none of the inputs is enabled, the counter maintains its current state. We assume that Cl has priority over the other two control signals and that Ld has priority over Inc, although this detail is irrelevant in this case.

The implementation carried out uses the fact that the counter can be directly loaded with the value 000 (using the signal Cl) or with the value of the parallel input (using signal Ld).

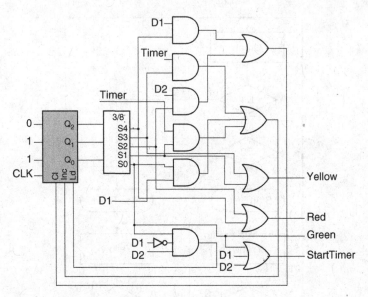

Fig. 7.36   Sequential circuit corresponding to the flowchart in Figure 7.28, implemented with a counter and a decoder.

The analysis of the flowchart in Figure 7.35 shows that:

- The counter should move to the state $S0$ (000) from another state when one of the following conditions are true:
  - the system is in state $S2$ and the detector $D2$ is at 1;
  - the system is in state $S4$ and the detector $D1$ is at 1.
- The counter should jump directly to the state $S3$ (011) when the system is in state $S0$, the value of $D1$ is 0 and the value of $D2$ is 1.
- The counter should count when one of the following conditions is true:
  - the system is in state $S0$ and the detector $D1$ is at 1;
  - the system is in state $S1$ and the detector $Timer$ is at 1;
  - the system is in state $S3$ and the detector $Timer$ is at 1.

These observations show that it is relatively easy, through inspection, to design the logic circuits which control the signals Cl, Ld and Inc for the counter. For example, the AND gate which generates the signal Ld detects a situation in which the system is in state $S0$ and the values of $D1$ and $D2$ are respectively 0 and 1.

The Cl signal requires a slightly more complicated logic when detecting the two conditions set out above in which the state of the system should change to $S0$.

Finally, the outputs of the circuit are immediately obtained, also by inspection. As an example, the variable *Red* should be active in the states *S*2 and *S*4, while the variable *StartTimer* should be active only in the state *S*0 and when one of the two detectors *D*1 and *D*2 is at 1.

7.5.3 *Microprogrammed Control Unit*

Although the procedure described in the previous section applies to any control unit, it rapidly becomes tough to generate, in a structured and organised manner, the circuits which are necessary to load the counter and produce the outputs, in complex controllers.

Microprogrammed control units deal with this problem in a more structured manner. Let us suppose that, from the specification of the control units, it has the following characteristics:

- the outputs only depend on the state, with no conditional outputs, meaning that the control unit is a Moore machine;
- in each state, only one input variable is tested;
- as a result of each test on an input variable, the control unit may jump to an arbitrary state (if the test is true) or move to the following state in a sequence (if the test is false).

All control units which satisfy these restrictions may be implemented by the structure in Figure 7.37. This structure, simple and regular, enables the implementation of any control unit that follows the constraints described above. To achieve the expected operation, just determine the number of

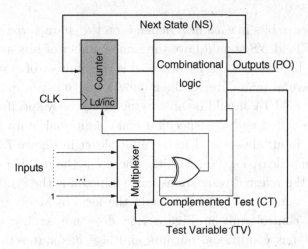

Fig. 7.37 Generic diagram for a simple microprogrammed control unit.

bits of the counter and the size of the multiplexer and, finally, design the combinational block according to the intended functionality.

Up to this point, the procedure is not very dissimilar to that carried out in the two previous sections. The motivation to use microprogrammed control unit results from the possibility to implement the combinational block using a ROM. This ROM must have a number of words equal to the number of states and with so many outputs as necessary to generate the output variables of the combinational block, as shown in Chapter 4.

The counter that keeps the present state and where the address bus of the ROM connects is called the *Control Address Register* (CAR).

The specification of the combinational circuit, which is the only complicated part of the procedure, is carried out by specifying the content of the ROM positions, to perform the specified operation.

Each word of the ROM has four *fields*:

- a field *NS* which specifies the next state to which the control unit should jump if the test carried out has a positive result (abbreviation for Next State);
- a field *PO* which contains the intended values for the output variables (abbreviation for Primary Output);
- a field *TV* which indicates what is the variable which should be tested (abbreviation for Test Variable);
- a field *CT*, of one single bit, which indicates if the jump should occur when the test variable is at 1 or when the variable is at 0 (abbreviation for Complement Test).

The number of bits in each field depends on the characteristics of the control unit. The field *NS* should have the same number of bits as the counter, which cannot be less than $\log_2 n$, where n is the number of states. The field *PO* should have as many bits as the number of output variables of the control unit. The field *TV* should be able to unambiguously specify which is the variable to be tested and also specify a non-conditional jump (which corresponds to the input always at 1 in the multiplexer in Figure 7.37). As such, it should have at least $\log_2(I + 1)$ bits, where I is the number of inputs.

Note that the referred restrictions make impossible the synthesis of some control units, namely all control units in the form of Mealy machines. For example, the control unit in Figure 7.35 does not satisfy these restrictions, since it has conditional outputs and also has states that test more than one variable. However, a modified version of the flowchart, shown in Figure 7.38, presents an almost similar behaviour, and is amenable for microprogramming.

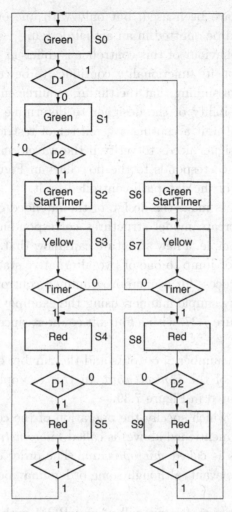

Fig. 7.38 Flowchart of the railroad crossing controller, altered so as not to need conditional outputs and only test one variable at a time.

In this flowchart, it was necessary to split the state $S0$ in Figure 7.28, which tested two variables. It was also essential to create two additional states, to eliminate the conditional outputs in the original flowchart. Finally, it was necessary to create two states ($S5$ and $S9$, in Figure 7.38) which could carry out an unconditional jump to the state $S0$. Note that the states $S2$ and $S4$ of the flowchart in Figure 7.28 do not meet the condition to make a transition to the next state in the sequence of the counter or to jump to another state. In this flowchart, two unconditional jumps are also shown, both for the state $S0$. To make it clear that these are unconditional jumps, which use the same mechanism used for conditional jumps, the symbols for conditional jump have been used, but only with one output. In practice, these symbols would be omitted in an actual design.

Although the behaviour of this controller is different from what is specified in the flowchart, its functionality continues to be compatible with the initial specification assuming that the timing requirements are still met.

It is the responsibility of the designer to determine if it is possible to implement a control unit accepting a given set of restrictions. In this particular case, the designer needs to verify if the waveforms generated by the control unit, which corresponds to the flowchart in Figure 7.38, satisfy or not the restrictions of the datapath controlled by it.

If these constraints make the design of the intended control unit impossible, we need to create model structures corresponding to other sets of restrictions. For example, a new structure can allow that, for each state, the counter may count or jump to one of two alternative states.

The synthesis process for a microprogrammed control unit may now be exemplified in a very simple manner, using the example in Figure 7.38 and the structure of Figure 7.37, with a four-bit counter, since the flowchart now has ten states.

By analysing the number of outputs and the number of inputs, we determine the structure of the *control word*. In this example, we will use the control word illustrated in Figure 7.39.

The set of fields which specify the operation of the control unit (in this case, the four fields mentioned above) is called *microinstruction*, and the set of microinstructions is called *microprogram*. The order of the fields in the memory word is irrelevant, although some orders may be more legible than others.

Since there are ten states, we will need a ROM with 16 positions, with 11 bits each.[3] The content of the ROM, described as a symbolic program, is now simple to define, by simple inspection of the flowchart.

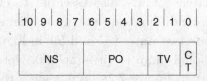

Fig. 7.39   Format of the microinstruction for the flowchart in Figure 7.38.

---

[3] Typically, the number of words of a ROM is a power of 2. As we need ten words, it is necessary to use a ROM with 2^4 positions.

Table 7.7 Symbolic microprogram for the control unit in Figure 7.38.

Address	Value				
	NS	PO		TV	CT
S0	S6	Green		D1	Non-inverted
S1	S0	Green		D2	Inverted
S2	XX	Green, Start Timer		1	Inverted
S3	S3	Yellow		Timer	Inverted
S4	S4	Red		D1	Inverted
S5	S0	Red		1	Non-inverted
S6	XX	Green, Start Timer		1	Inverted
S7	S7	Yellow		Timer	Inverted
S8	S8	Red		D2	Inverted
S9	S0	Red		1	Non-inverted

Table 7.8 Binary encoding of the states for the flowchart in Figure 7.38.

State	Encoding
S0	0000
S1	0001
S2	0010
S3	0011
S4	0100
S5	0101
S6	0110
S7	0111
S8	1000
S9	1001

Table 7.7 describes symbolically, the content of the ROM required to obtain the expected operation. For example, in state $S0$, the output *Green* should be activated, and the variable $D1$ tested. If this variable is active, in its non-inverted form, the next state should be the state $S6$. Otherwise, the counter will count to the next state, which, in this case, is the state $S1$. The other lines of the table result from a similar reasoning.

To fill in the bits for each field, just define an encoding for the states and a given order for the input and output variables. Choosing binary encoding as in Table 7.8 and with the input and output variables in the same order as in Figure 7.27, that is, $D1\ D2\ Timer - Green\ Yellow\ Red\ StartTimer$, we immediately obtain Table 7.9, which lists the content for each position of the ROM.

In many control units, there may be various states in which the value of one or more of the bits in the control word do not matter. In these cases, it will be necessary to arbitrate a value for these variables in those states, since we must choose a single value (0 or 1) for each bit of the memory words.

Table 7.9   Microprogram for the control unit in Figure 7.38.

Address	NS	PO	TV	CT
0000	0110	1000	00	0
0001	0000	1000	01	1
0010	0000	1001	11	1
0011	0011	0100	10	1
0100	0100	0010	00	1
0101	0000	0010	11	0
0110	0000	1001	11	1
0111	0111	0100	10	1
1000	1000	0010	01	1
1001	0000	0010	11	0

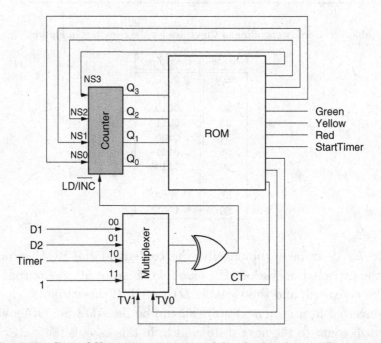

Fig. 7.40   Control Unit microprogrammed for the flowchart in Figure 7.38.

Figure 7.40 shows the circuit which results for this example from this synthesis process.

It is important to note that, given the general structure of the control unit, the synthesis process consists in filling the positions of the micropro-gram memory and suitably interconnecting the memory, the counter and the multiplexer.

This process, while long and slow, is much simpler and less subject to errors than other methods for synthesising control units, implemented either with discrete logic, using Karnaugh maps, or carried out with counters and discrete logic, such as in the example in Figure 7.36. It also has the advantage of making it possible to change the operation of the control unit simply by reprogramming the content of the ROM.

In Chapter 12, this technique will be used to synthesise a control unit for a much more complex digital system, the processor P3.

7.6 Summary

This chapter studies methods to carry out the synthesis of synchronous sequential circuits, applicable both to Mealy and Moore machines.

The synthesis process studied consists of four stages: specification of the operation, simplification of the specification, encoding of the states and, finally, synthesis of the combinational logic of the control unit.

The chapter studies state diagrams and flowcharts as the specification formalisms, and analyses the advantages and disadvantages of each of these formalisms.

Binary encoding and encoding using one flip-flop per state are considered as mechanisms for state assignment.

Finally, we study three ways of carrying out the synthesis of the combinational block of control units: using discrete logic, with both type D or JK flip-flops; using counters and, finally, using microprogramming.

Exercises

7.1 Consider the following state diagram, of a machine which counts the number of bits at 1 received in its input, and sets the value 1 at the output when the number of bits at 1 received is a multiple of 3.

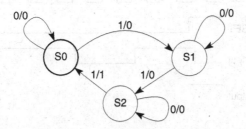

(a) Why is it possible to affirm that this state diagram corresponds to a Mealy machine?

(b) Propose a Moore machine which has an equivalent functionality, that is, which generates the value 1 in its output, whenever it has seen a number of bits at 1 which is a multiple of 3 in its input.

(c) Make a sketch of the waveforms in the output for the two machines when the input sequence 0110100111 is presented, assuming that the input changes in a manner approximately synchronised with the active edge of the clock.

7.2 Find the state diagram of a synchronous sequential circuit with two inputs, X and Y, and an output Z. The circuit is the sequence detector for sequences at the input Y. If $X = 0$, the sequence 1001 is the one to detected. If $X = 1$, the sequence to detect is 1101. In both cases, Z should take the value 1 only when the sequence is detected. When X changes value we assume that a new sequence test has started, with the value of Y interpreted as the first bit of a new possible sequence.

7.3 Consider the following state diagram:

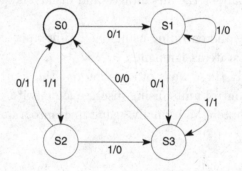

Supposing the circuit described by the state diagram uses flip-flops triggered at the rising edge of the clock, complete the following timing diagram:

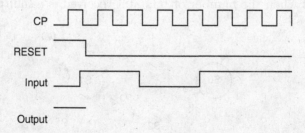

7.4 Determine the state diagram of a synchronous sequential circuit with one input and one output. The objective is for the output to always be (0) except in the case of having entered exactly (and only) two equal bits, followed by other two equal bits, but inverted in relation to the previous ones. When this happens, the output is 1 during one clock period. This means that sequences of the type $\cdots 01100$ should be recognised, but sequences such as $\cdots 00011$ should not be recognised. The sequence $\cdots 10011$ should be recognised, but the sequence $\cdots 100111$ should not. Obtain the state diagram, both for the case in which it accepts overlapping sequences and for the case in which it does not.

7.5 Determine the state diagram of a synchronous sequential circuit with two inputs and one output, with the following operation: the output should normally be at 0, except when in three successive clock pulses there are equal bits in both inputs. In this case, the circuit generates the sequence 1010 in the output. During the generation of the output sequence, the circuit is not aware of the values present in the inputs.

7.6 Consider the following state diagram:

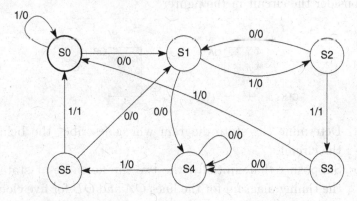

Simplify this state diagram, obtaining a state diagram with an equivalent operation, but with a minimum number of states.

7.7 Draw the state diagram or the flowchart for a synchronous sequential circuit with one input and three outputs which receive successive four-bit sequences and interprets them as BCD digits with the most significant bit in first place. The circuit should show in the two outputs, at the same time as the last bit which enters, the result of the integer division of the digit by 3. If the input sequence is not a BCD digit, the third circuit output should take on the value 1 also at the same time as the last entered bit. In all other circumstances, the three outputs should take on the value 0. The input sequences should be considered as non-overlapping successive independent groups of 4 bits.

7.8 Consider the following state diagram:

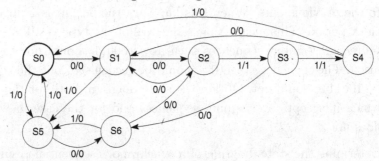

(a) Simplify this state diagram, obtaining a new diagram with an equivalent operation, but with a minimum number of states.

(b) Explain, in plain language, the operation of the state diagram obtained in the previous paragraph and interpret the equivalences between states obtained through the state reduction algorithm.

7.9 Consider the circuit in the figure:

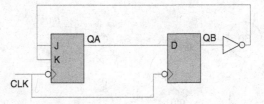

(a) Determine the state diagram which describes the behaviour of the circuit.

(b) Supposing that, initially, the two flip-flops are at state 0, draw the timing diagram for the lines QA and QB for five clock pulses.

(c) Obtain an expression which defines the maximum operating frequency of the circuit as a function of the timing parameters which are considered relevant.

7.10 Design, according to the classic method of sequential circuit synthesis, using your choice of flip-flops, a synchronous counter with the following table:

Present state	Next state	
	$x = 0$	$x = 1$
$Q_1\ Q_0$	$Q_1\ Q_0$	$Q_1\ Q_0$
00	01	01
01	10	11
10	11	00
11	00	10

7.11 Consider the state diagram used for problem 7.6.

(a) Write the state transition table for this state diagram.
(b) Using *JK* flip-flops, design the sequential circuit which implements this state diagram.

7.12 Consider the state diagram obtained in problem 7.7.

(a) Write the state transition table for this state diagram.
(b) Using *JK* flip-flops, design the sequential circuit which implements this state diagram.

7.13 Consider the state machine which results from the simplification of the diagram for the problem 7.8.

(a) Write the state transition table for this state diagram.
(b) Design, using *D* flip-flops, the sequential circuit which implements this state machine.

7.14 Consider the following flowchart which specifies a synchronous sequential circuit:

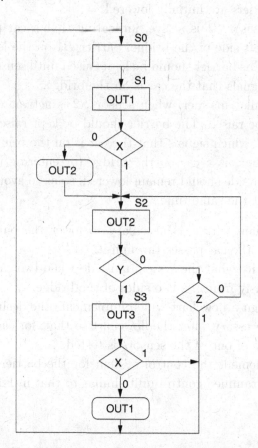

(a) Using the implementation method with one flip-flop per state, design the circuit.

(b) Obtain the equivalent state diagram.

7.15 It is intended to design a sequential circuit which guarantees exclusive access to a bridge where only one car at a time can pass. There are six sensors, three on each side of the bridge, and two barriers preventing access to a car when they are lowered, as shown below. The figure assumes right-hand drive.

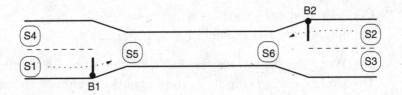

The objective is for the system to function in the following manner:

- The barriers are initially lowered.
- When sensor $S1$ is active, indicating that a car pretends to enter on the left side of the bridge, barrier $B1$ on the left side should be raised. The barrier should be kept raised until sensor $S5$ is actuated, which signals that the car is on the bridge.
- In a similar manner, when sensor $S2$ is activated, the barrier $B2$ should be raised. The barrier should be kept raised until sensor $S6$ is active, which signals that the car is on the bridge.
- When there is a car on the bridge (or entering it), the barrier of the other side should remain lowered, so as to avoid two cars on the bridge at the same time.

(a) Explain why it is necessary to lower the barrier immediately after the car passes through it.

(b) Specify what the system must do when two cars arrive simultaneously from the two sides of the bridge.

(c) Design a flowchart which implements the desired functionality.

(d) If necessary, alter the flowchart so that, for each state, only the value of one of the sensors is tested.

(e) Implement the control system for the barriers, using a micro-programmed control unit similar to that in Figure 7.40.

7.16 Consider the following flowchart:

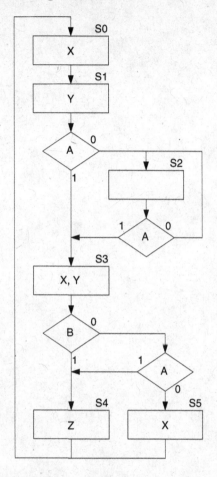

(a) Synthesise the circuit which corresponds to the flowchart, using the classical synthesis method.

(b) Repeat the previous paragraph, using the method of one flip-flop per state.

(c) Explain why this flowchart cannot be directly implemented with a unit similar to that in Figure 7.40.

Chapter 8

Register Transfers and Datapaths

The techniques for designing both combinational and sequential digital circuits presented in the previous chapters make possible the implementation of systems of small and medium complexity. The level of detail to which these techniques are applied is too high to use them in the design of large-sized circuits. Thus, when developing systems with a more complex functionality, we need a higher level of abstraction, to hide many details and make the problem manageable.

A real system with a minimum of complexity has, in fact, a large number of states. Its description needs an extensive state diagram or flowchart which, besides lacking clarity, entails considerable difficulty in its implementation. Moreover, approaching a system in this way does not enable the designer to take advantage of existing basic models such as multiplexers, registers, counters and arithmetic circuits, for example. This is why it is common to structure a digital system into two parts: a *datapath* and a *control circuit*. The first is essentially composed of modules of the type mentioned previously, which store the data for a problem and define a set of possible operations on them. The second provides support to the system algorithm, controlling the first so that it executes the necessary actions in the appropriate order, and basically consists of a state machine. Of course, this control unit has a much more reduced number of states than the overall number of states of the system, since the registers, counters and other sequential elements also contribute to defining the overall state of the system. Section 8.2 describes the design of digital systems using these two components.

This approach presupposes that a higher processing complexity normally requires various clock cycles to be completed. In fact, operations above a certain level of complexity may imply a specific logic circuit with a dimension that makes its practical implementation unaffordable. These operations are therefore divided into a sequence of simpler operations easily implemented in hardware. The datapath is the circuit which performs these simple operations, and the control unit is the circuit which sequences them so as to achieve the complete operation. Hardware description languages have been developed to clearly describe the implementation algorithm for complex operations using basic datapath operations. Section 8.3 presents a simple example of this type of language that we will use in the rest of this book.

Although one may design datapaths for a specific purpose, in many cases devices which provide a set of common arithmetic and logic operations are used, called arithmetic logic units, or ALU. Section 8.4 describes the example of an ALU that we will use in the P3 processor, studied in Chapter 12.

8.1   Levels of Abstraction

The approach employed in this chapter for the design of circuits involves raising the level of abstraction in describing logic circuits. The design of complex systems requires different *levels of abstraction*, with the design starting in the most abstract, and then successively descending to more concrete levels as discussed in Section 4.1. This approach involving levels of abstraction makes the design of complex systems possible when a direct approach would be too difficult.

To give a general idea of this process and a better context for the design methods analysed in this book, we will describe next the different levels of abstraction typically considered in the design of complex logic circuits. Figure 8.1 represents these levels of abstraction, with the levels ordered from top to bottom, going from the most abstract to the most concrete. In other words, in this ordering, the level of detail in the description of the system increases from top to bottom.

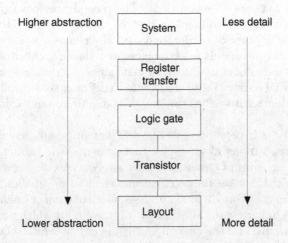

Fig. 8.1   Different levels of abstraction in the design of complex logic systems.

The design starts at the *system level* with general overall analyses about the design, in particular regarding the number of subsystems in which the system should be divided, the type of subsystems and the way in which they are interconnected. It finishes at the *layout level* with a level of detail where each electronic device and the path of each electric circuit interconnection is defined so that it can be manufactured.

At each level of abstraction, the analysis is carried out individually on the modules defined at the level immediately above. In this way, the design is successively divided into smaller modules, enabling the level of detail to be increased, and so always maintaining a manageable problem at each level. It is this process of "divide and conquer" that leads to the success of this concept of levels of abstraction.

Furthermore, at a given level of abstraction, it is possible to develop the design without needing information about lower levels. This characteristic hides the implementation details, allowing the designer to concentrate on achieving the best possible solution at each level.

Until the previous chapter, we focused all our analysis on circuits described at the *logic gate level*. That is the intermediate level of abstraction, as we can see from the hierarchy in Figure 8.1. We have mentioned that the implementation of logic gates is carried out using transistors which, as we can see in the figure, is the level of abstraction immediately below. However, to define the logic gate design, it was never necessary to know the transistor circuits that implement the logic gates except in very limited situations involving incomplete devices described in Section 3.1.6.

After obtaining a specification at the gate level, the next step is to convert these devices into transistors and make the electrical connections. For a given circuit manufacturing technology, each logic gate corresponds to an electrical schematic of interconnected transistors. However, besides this mapping, it is necessary to carry out the sizing of the transistors so as to ensure, for example, certain delay times and energy consumption.

Although it is possible to implement digital systems with discrete elements, it is increasingly common to build digital systems with integrated circuits, often designed on purpose. In this case, the final step is to convert this description at the *transistor level*, which is essentially a description of an electric circuit, to masks used directly in the manufacture of integrated circuits. This is called the *layout level*. These masks define areas where some types of elements or other substances are deposited to form the final circuit. For example, the interconnections are usually implemented by metal lines, and there may be various layers of these lines and a mask corresponding to each layer. In the case of CMOS technology, referred to in Section 3.1.1, the transistors are formed by crossing a polysilicon line with a line of substrate doping, corresponding to two more different masks. Typically, in passing from the transistor level to the layout level, the aim is to choose the path of each line so as to minimise the total area occupied by the circuit. These two levels of abstraction, as well as the system level, fall outside the scope of this book and will therefore not be further discussed.

This chapter presents the *register transfer level*, the level immediately above the logic gate level. Using the philosophy of levels of abstraction, we will use modules of higher complexity, but without detailing their internal structure. For example, we will directly use adders, without the concern about the implementation of these adders with logic gates.

For most of the design and optimisation operations at each level of abstraction, the designer may resort to synthesis tools for computer aided design. From a description of the circuit at a given level, these tools automatically generate the corresponding circuit in a lower level of abstraction, optimising it, while taking into account a set of parameters which the designer can specify. The area of logic synthesis algorithms is an area of intense research activity, but it is also a topic which falls outside the scope of this book.

8.2　Separation between Datapath and Control Circuit

Any digital system may be built from scratch, with flip-flops and discrete logic gates, using the design techniques for synchronous circuits presented in previous chapters. However, as discussed in the previous section, this approach has major limitations. For example, any of the methods to generate combinational circuits described in Section 2.3 is impractical when the number of input variables is high.

Digital systems are, therefore, normally structured into two main units, the *datapath*, sometimes called *data circuit* or *processing unit*, and the *control unit* or *control circuit*, as shown in Figure 8.2. The datapath is made up of regular, interconnected modules to store and process the useful information in the system. As shown in the figure, the circuit receives the inputs to be processed, that is, the external operands or data and calculates the result. The control unit is responsible for generating the control signals that sequence the elementary operations of the datapath so that the system can

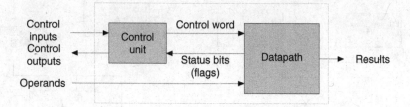

Fig. 8.2   Structure of a digital system in terms of datapath and control unit.

implement complex operations. The set of control signals which connect the control unit to the datapath is called *control word*. The sequence of control signals generated by the control unit may depend on the results of the calculations supplied by the datapath. The control unit receives this information through *status bits*, also called *flags* when the status bits are stored in a register, the operation of which we will discuss later. The control unit can also receive external information directly, such as, for example, an external signal which indicates when to start the operation or which operation is to be carried out. In general, there are control outputs to indicate externally the state of the operation, such as, for example, the signal which indicates the end of the operation.

Naturally, during the clock cycles necessary for the processing of a complex operation, temporary values for intermediate calculations will have to be stored in registers in the datapath. Section 6.7 shows methods for interconnecting registers and processing modules.

In general, we assume that the clock signal of the control unit and the datapath are the same, that is, that the two are synchronised.

8.2.1   *Motivation Example*

To illustrate this process of separation of a complex operation into a sequence of simpler operations, let us consider the case of the multiplication of two non-signed integers. Section 5.3 discussed the logic implementation of multipliers, referring the fact they are complex modules which require complex hardware.

Figure 8.3(a) shows the direct implementation for a multiplication operation $P = A \times B$ using a combinational multiplier. An alternative to this circuit is implementing the multiplication through successive additions, adding A times the value of B. Thus, instead of a multiplier module, only an adder will be necessary, a significantly simpler module. Figure 8.3(b) shows the datapath for this alternative implementation.

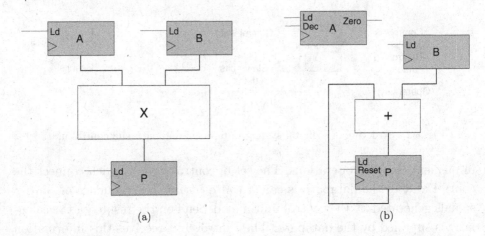

Fig. 8.3   Multiplier circuits: (a) combinational block and (b) successive additions.

The price to pay for the simplification of the circuit hardware is the need for an additional control module capable of implementing the following sequence of operations:

(1) set register P at zero;
(2) if register A contains zero, the process ends;
(3) load the sum of P and B into P;
(4) decrement register A;
(5) return to 2.

To facilitate these operations, the registers have some additional functionalities. Thus, register A is, in fact, a down-counter, with a control input *Dec* enabling it to decrement, and a status output *Zero* which is active when this register contains the value 0. Also, register P has a control signal *Reset* that can set it to zero.

The control unit is a sequential circuit which generates the sequence of signals to implement the algorithm shown above. Figure 8.4 shows this algorithm in the form of a flowchart, assuming that registers A and B have been previously loaded with the operands. The inputs and outputs of the circuit are the control signals referred, as well as two other signals: the *start* input that serves to indicate when the operation should start and the *end* output that signals the end of the process. The signal *end* is useful, because the number of clock cycles necessary for this operation is variable. For each multiplication operation, the processing time is determined by the initial value of A and therefore it is important that the system can indicate the end of the processing externally.

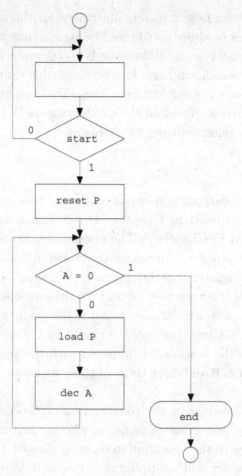

Fig. 8.4 Flowchart which describes the control unit for the operation of multiplication by successive additions.

It is possible to apply any of the sequential circuit design techniques presented in Section 7.5 to the flowchart in Figure 8.4. The following sections will describe a language used to describe the basic operations of the datapath, making easier the specification of a sequential circuit for implementing a complex operation.

This example shows how to reduce the complexity of the circuit to be implemented, by translating complex operations into a sequence of simpler operations. Therefore there is a compromise that the designer can explore, between the complexity of the datapath and the time (measured in clock cycles) that the operation takes. In general, the simpler the available operations are, the less hardware is necessary for the datapath, but in turn, the sequence of operations is longer, and a higher total execution time is needed.

The example shown here is merely illustrative. Although in practice combinational multiplier modules may indeed be avoided due to their complexity, there are more efficient sequential methods to compute the product of two numbers than the one shown here. Furthermore, this example discusses two possible alternatives, one combinational, the other sequential. In many cases, the operations are so complex that the consideration of a pure combinational model is out of the question from the outset.

8.2.2   *Datapath*

The construction of datapaths uses combinational modules of medium complexity, like those studied in Chapters 4 and 5, and registers (including counters), presented in Chapter 6. The operations carried out by the combinational modules process information contained in registers, and store the result in the same register, another register, or even in a memory location. For example, if a special purpose system requires an operation such as the calculation of $D = (A + B) \times C$, one possible datapath will simply be that shown in Figure 8.5. Given the way the circuit in Figure 8.5 is designed, in all the clock cycles the register D is updated with the value $(A + B) \times C$, in which the values of A, B and C are those of these registers at the start of each clock cycle.

There is some freedom in the construction of the datapath. First, the designer can choose from a set of modules, whether arithmetic, logic or others, in accordance with the operation to be implemented.The previous example assumed that adder and multiplier modules and registers were available.

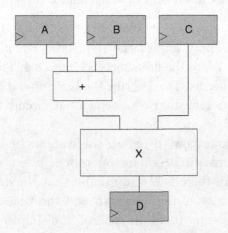

Fig. 8.5   Datapath to implement the operation $D = (A + B) \times C$.

However, new specific modules may also be constructed, using the design techniques from Chapters 2 and 6.

Second, in many cases, it is possible to make compromises between the complexity of the datapath and the complexity of the control unit. In these cases, it is necessary to strike a balance between the quantity of hardware necessary for the circuit and its performance. In the case of the previous example, to save hardware, instead of using a multiplier module, it is possible to opt for implementing the multiplication by successive additions, as was discussed in the previous section. This option needs that a temporary register is added to the datapath. In this new register, the value of C would be added k times, with k the value of the sum A + B. The obvious disadvantage is that the operation which would previously take a single clock cycle now needs k cycles for the multiplication, plus one cycle for the first addition. The complexity of the control unit increases since it now has to manage the number of times that the addition for the implementation of the multiplication is carried out.

Another point to consider in the design of the datapath is connected to the maximum frequency possible for the clock signal. As we mentioned in Section 7.5, for the system to function correctly, the clock period will always have to be greater than the largest delay in the logic between two datapath registers. For the example of Figure 8.5, $T_{\text{CLK}} > t_{\text{adder}} + t_{\text{multiplier}} + t_{\text{register}}$. Therefore, even if there are very simple operations in the system, the period of the clock will always be the maximum possible delay of an elementary operation. To reduce this delay, the modules can be interleaved with registers, as shown in Figure 8.6, where register T temporarily stores the result of the addition. In this case, the operation D = (A + B) × C takes two clock cycles. The first cycle to calculate the sum T = A + B and the second one to obtain the product D = T × C. The clock cycle may now be reduced to $T_{CLK} > \max(t_{\text{adder}} + t_{\text{register}}, t_{\text{multiplier}} + t_{\text{register}}) = t_{\text{multiplier}} + t_{\text{register}}$. Note that this optimisation may have a significant impact on system performance since this clock cycle reduction influences all the basic system operations. We will analyse this matter further in Chapter 15.

After choosing the modules in the datapath, the possible operations on the information stored in the registers at each clock cycle are therefore defined. These operations are called *microoperations* and determine how the control unit interacts with the datapath.

Further on in this chapter, we will present an example of a datapath built for a particular purpose (Section 8.3.2). However, there are datapaths with

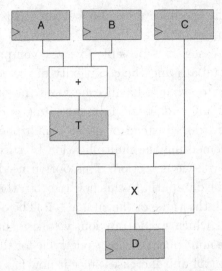

Fig. 8.6   Reduction of the clock period for the datapath implementing the operation $D = (A + B) \times C$.

no particular application defined at the outset, such as the datapaths for a general purpose processor in a computer. For these situations, the designer defines a set of microoperations which is sufficiently generic and powerful to accommodate a broad set of functionalities efficiently. This kind of datapaths is called *arithmetic logic unit* or *ALU*. We will exemplify the construction of an ALU at the end of this chapter.

8.2.3   *Control Unit*

The control unit is responsible for defining which of the microoperations to execute in the datapath in each clock cycle. The enabling of these microoperations is done through a set of control signals that drives the datapath, called a control word. Control units have two types of inputs. First, they have external inputs which control the overall operation of the system. Second, they have inputs coming from the datapath, the *status bits*. From these, the control unit has information about the result of a given operation and may set off different sequences of operations based on this information.

Considering, once more, the example in Section 8.2.1, as we can see in the flowchart of the control unit shown in Figure 8.4 this unit has two inputs, one external and one status bit from the datapath. The *start* signal is a control input which indicates when a new calculation should start. The signal $A = 0$ is an input coming from the datapath which informs the control unit if the result of the previous operation is 0, thus making the control unit able to decide which action to take next.

Besides the outputs which form the control word, the control units may also have external outputs which communicate with external entities to indicate the state of the system. An example is the *end* output in Figure 8.4. In this case, as the calculation time is not fixed, but rather dependent on the values of the operands, it is necessary that the system provides external information about the state of the calculation, particularly whether it has ended or not.

Having established the datapath, the designer must define the sequence of microoperations necessary to implement the intended functionality of the system. The design of the control unit is no more than the design of a sequential circuit, as was studied in Chapter 7. Its implementation may be carried out using any of the techniques shown in that chapter. However, the number of inputs (status bits and control inputs) and outputs (control word and external outputs) is usually very high. This is the reason why microprogrammed controllers, studied in Section 7.5.3 are the most commonly used technique for the design of control units.

8.3   Hardware Description Language

The specification of more complex systems needs a language capable of describing hardware with a level of abstraction higher than that of the Boolean functions or state diagrams so as to hide the details of the system and thus provide succinct descriptions. Languages of this type are called *hardware description languages.*

Although the level of abstraction may vary, this hardware description is generally at the register transfer level, where the designer defines which microoperations are carried out between registers at each clock cycle. The way to implement each microoperation with logic gates is not a concern at this point, we simply assume that the datapath can execute these microoperations.

There are various possible formats for hardware description languages. The one adopted in this book is very simple and only allows the specification of the microoperations which the system must implement. Other languages, such as *VHDL* and *Verilog*, have a level of description equal to a conventional programming language, but with the fundamental difference that they have to accommodate the fact that the hardware is inherently concurrent.

As such, hardware description languages define code blocks which describe an operation and which are therefore sequential, but the different blocks function in parallel.

8.3.1   *Register Transfer Language*

This section defines the simple hardware description language, at the register transfer level, used in the next chapters. In this language, the specification of a digital system uses a set of microoperations which define the desired functionality.

The transfer of information from one register to another, or more exactly the replication of that information, is designated in symbolic form by the following statement:

$$R2 \leftarrow R1.$$

This statement specifies a microoperation and means: R2 stores the content of R1. The value stored in R1 remains not altered. In block diagram terms, the previous microoperation corresponds to Figure 8.7.

If, in addition to this simple microoperation transfer, there is any processing, this is made explicit, for example, in $R1 \leftarrow R2 + R5$ or $R7 \leftarrow R5 \lor R4$. The block diagram of Figure 8.8 implements the first of these microoperations.

When two transfers take place simultaneously, microoperations can be grouped together separated by commas: $R3 \leftarrow R6 - R2, R9 \leftarrow R2 \times R4$. The corresponding block diagram is that of Figure 8.9.

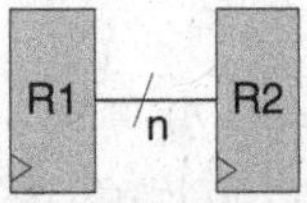

R1 —/n— R2

Fig. 8.7   Block diagram corresponding to the microoperation $R2 \leftarrow R1$.

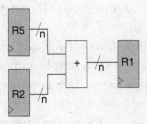

Fig. 8.8   Block diagram corresponding to the microoperation $R1 \leftarrow R2 + R5$.

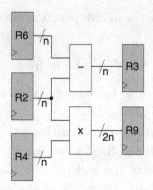

Fig. 8.9   Block diagram corresponding to the microoperations R3 ← R6 − R2, R9 ← R2 × R4

Fig. 8.10   Block diagram for the instruction $K1 : \text{R2} \leftarrow \text{R1}$.

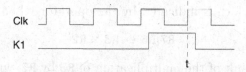

Fig. 8.11   Timing diagram which guarantees a single transfer from R1 to R2.

Besides registers, the operands of the microoperations may also be constant values or references to memory locations. The indication of a memory location is done using M[address], where address may either be a constant value or a register. Possible examples of microoperations are: R1 ← M[32d] ∨ R7 and M[R2] ← R2 ⊕ 55h.

In the way they are expressed, the microoperations presented until now are executed in every clock cycle. In a digital system, it is not normal that a register transfer, with or without processing, always takes place when a clock pulse occurs. To indicate that a particular operation should only take place under certain conditions, we use the format *condition: microoperation*. For example, an instruction such as $K1 : \text{R2} \leftarrow \text{R1}$ corresponds to the block diagram of Figure 8.10. For a single transfer, the line $K1$ has to remain at 1 only during one rising transition of the clock signal. An example of a situation of this type is shown in Figure 8.11, where the transfer only takes place at moment t.

The condition to enable the microoperation may be a general logic expression. For example,

$$X \cdot Y : R5 \leftarrow R0$$

means that at each clock cycle the content of R0 is transferred to R5 only if both the signals X and Y are at 1.

Sometimes it is useful to work not with all the bits stored in a register, but just with a subset of those bits. To indicate that a microoperation is only applied to part of the bits of the register, the bits concerned are indicated between parentheses following the name of the register. For example, if we intend to work only with bit 5 of register R2, this is indicated by R2(5). For a range of bits, the representation is of the type shown below

$$R3(15\text{--}8) \leftarrow R6(7\text{--}0)$$

which in this case indicates that the least significant byte of R6 is copied to the second least significant byte of R3. Of course, it is necessary to be careful and be consistent in the number of bits involved in a microoperation.

Furthermore, it may be necessary to concatenate various registers for a given operation, which is indicated by the operator «|». For example,

$$R7|R6 \leftarrow R3 \times R2$$

means that the result of the multiplication of R3 by R2, which, as previously mentioned, requires twice as many bits as the operands, will be stored in two registers, R7 and R6, where R7 will have the most significant part and R6 the least significant.

With this simple language, it is possible to describe datapaths with an arbitrary complexity. This description indicates which are the microoperations that can be executed in the datapath and under what conditions they occur. Given this description, the designer can implement the control unit, which generates the sequence of control signals necessary to implement an operation.

Note that this language does not completely define the implementation of the system. Often there is some freedom of choice since it is possible to consider different circuits that implement the same functionality. For example, consider the common case of a register which may be loaded from one of two sources:

$$T1 : R0 \leftarrow R1$$
$$\overline{T1} \cdot T2 : R0 \leftarrow R2.$$

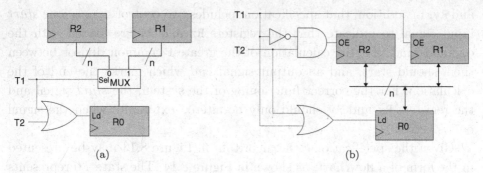

Fig. 8.12   Equivalent circuits to implement a transfer from two possible sources.

Greatest_Common_Divisor(X, Y)
1.   while (Y≠0){
2.   if X≥Y
3.   then X=X-Y
4.   else exchange X and Y
5.   }
6.   result in X

Fig. 8.13   Pseudocode for the algorithm to calculate the greatest common divisor.

As we discussed in Section 6.7, these registers can be connected through multiplexers or buses. Figures 8.12(a) and 8.12(b) represent these two situations as block diagrams. Note that interconnections using buses use less hardware than using multiplexers, but care has to be taken to ensure that the signals $T1$ and $T2$ are never simultaneously active.

8.3.2   *Example: Greatest Common Divisor*

To illustrate the concepts presented above, this section will provide and develop a complete example. Let us consider the design of a system to calculate the greatest common divisor for two positive n-bit positive integers. An algorithm known to implement this operation is shown in pseudocode in Figure 8.13.

In other words, this algorithm successively subtracts the smaller of the numbers from the larger until the result of the subtraction is 0. When this happens, the algorithm ends, and the result is the final value of the other operand. It is not a very efficient algorithm since, sometimes, it takes a long time to terminate, but it is simple to implement.

Let us assume that the specification of the system indicates that the operands X and Y are initially stored in two registers, designated as Rx and Ry. In addition, that specification includes two control signals, one *start* input signal to indicate that the registers Rx and Ry are loaded with the operands and that the calculation of the greatest common divisor between them should start, and an output signal *end* which marks the end of the calculation. For the correct functioning of the system, the *start* signal and the registers Rx and Ry should only be altered externally when the signal *end* is active.

Given the specifications, the algorithm in Figure 8.13 may be presented in the form of a flowchart, as shown in Figure 8.14. The state $T0$ represents a wait state, where nothing happens until the *start* signal is activated. In this state, the control output *end* is active. When the *start* input goes to

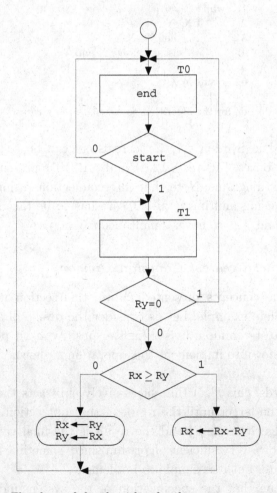

Fig. 8.14   Flowchart of the algorithm for the greatest common divisor.

1, the system advances to state $T1$, where all the processing is carried out. The system is maintained in this state while Ry does not reach zero, a situation where the calculation is terminated, with the system returning to $T0$. While at $T1$, the relative values of Rx and Ry are tested in each cycle and, according to the result of the test, their values are either exchanged, or Ry is subtracted from Rx. In this flowchart, the registers Rx and Ry are reused during the operation, since for each clock cycle there are no new values requiring different registers.

At this point, it is necessary to decide the functionalities the datapath should supply, that is, which microoperations will be available. For this example, the microoperations necessary are simple, so we opt to include them directly in the datapath. In general, however, this may not be the case, both because of the complexity of the operations or the possible use of a predefined datapath. In this case, it will be necessary to subdivide the operations into simpler suboperations supported in the microoperations of the datapath. Section 8.4.7 analyses this situation.

By considering the flowchart in Figure 8.14, the operations necessary are just the transfer of register values and subtraction. These indicate the need for registers with a load control signal, LDx and LDy, and a subtractor circuit.

Besides the operations, there are three conditions to be tested: *start* at 1, for which there is no need for any specific hardware; the value of the register Ry is 0; the value in Rx is greater than the value of Ry. For the second condition, we use a comparator with the constant 0. This module is simply a NOR gate with n inputs, connected to all the output bits of Ry. Most often we use a register for Ry which already includes this NOR gate and therefore with a status output, Zy, which indicates when the stored value is zero. For the third condition we use a n-bit comparator connected to Rx and Ry, with the signal xGy being its output.

Given the functionality of the datapath, the flowchart in Figure 8.14 may be translated into register transfer language as shown in Figure 8.15. In this figure, the signals $T0$ and $T1$ control the execution sequence of the remaining microoperations and will, therefore, be generated by the control unit.

As mentioned in the previous section, any of the microoperations for the lines in Figure 8.15 may occur at each clock cycle. What defines which of them in fact occur are the conditions indicated in the line. Since there is no condition in line 1, these operations are always evaluated. In this example, for proper operation, only one of the control unit signals, $T0$ and $T1$, should

1.		$xGy \leftarrow (\text{Rx} \geq \text{Ry}), Zy \leftarrow (\text{Ry} = 0)$
2.	$T0$:	$end \leftarrow 1$
3.	$T0 \cdot start$:	$T0 \leftarrow 0, T1 \leftarrow 1$
4.	$T1 \cdot Zy$:	$T0 \leftarrow 1, T1 \leftarrow 0$
5.	$T1 \cdot \overline{Zy} \cdot xGy$:	$\text{Rx} \leftarrow \text{Rx} - \text{Ry}$
6.	$T1 \cdot \overline{Zy} \cdot \overline{xGy}$:	$\text{Rx} \leftarrow \text{Ry}, \text{Ry} \leftarrow \text{Rx}$

Fig. 8.15   Description in register transfer language of the algorithm for calculating the greatest common divisor.

be active. With $T0 = 1$, only the operations in lines 2 and 3 can occur. With $T1 = 1$, only the operations in the last three lines can occur. However, it is easy to see that the conditions of these three lines, generated by the signals Zy and sGy, are mutually exclusive, such that in fact, only the microoperations of one of the three last lines in Figure 8.15 can occur at each clock cycle.

Examining this code line by line, we can see that the test signals Zy and sGy in line 1 are generated in every clock cycle. Line 2 indicates that the *end* signal remains active in state $T0$. Line 3 only occurs if the system is at state $T0$ and the *start* signal is active, thus passing control to state $T1$. Therefore, with the system in state $T0$ and the *start* line inactive, the system is kept in this state indefinitely, and nothing further happens. Line 4 corresponds to the detection that the register Ry has reached zero and the calculation has therefore finished. The corresponding action is to move to state $T0$, which in turn will make the output *end* active. Lines 5 and 6 may be active while performing the calculation, when the state is $T1$. Line 5 remains active when $\text{Rx} \geq \text{Ry}$, subtracting Ry from Rx. Line 6 is active when $\text{Rx} < \text{Ry}$, thus enabling the exchange of values in Ry and Rx.

Translating the register transfer level description in Figure 8.15 to a block diagram, Figure 8.16(a) shows the datapath for this problem. The signals LDx and LDy constitute the control word for the control unit, indicating in which clock cycles the registers are updated. The signals Zy and sGy are the status bits of the datapath and are inputs to the control unit. Note that the control of the multiplexer at the input of the register Rx connects directly to the output of the comparator since the signal LDx controls the loading of this register. While LDx is not active, it does not matter what the value in the Rx input is, and whenever it is active the output of the multiplexer will be the correct one.

The control of this datapath is indicated in Figure 8.16(b) and was obtained from the flowchart in Figure 8.14 by simple substitution of the operations by the control signals of the corresponding microoperations and

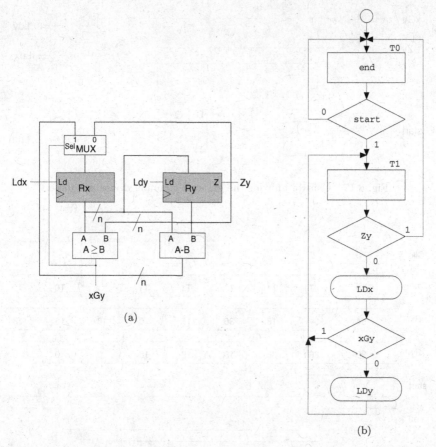

Fig. 8.16 (a) Datapath for the greatest common divisor example. (b) Flowchart of the control unit for the greatest common divisor taking into account the datapath in the left.

the tests made to the status bits. Therefore, the test $\mathtt{Ry} = 0$ corresponds to testing if $Zy = 1$ and $\mathtt{Rx} \geq \mathtt{Ry}$ to testing if $xGy = 1$. In turn, the operation $\mathtt{Rx} \leftarrow \mathtt{Rx} - \mathtt{Ry}$ is performed activating the LDx signal of the register $\mathtt{Rx}$, and for the exchanging of values between the registers, it is enough to activate both load signals LDx and LDy. Note that the selection of the value at the input for $\mathtt{Rx}$, $\mathtt{Rx} - \mathtt{Ry}$ or $\mathtt{Ry}$, is directly controlled in the datapath by the signal xGy.

This control unit is so simple that sophisticated techniques are not necessary for its construction. Using the technique for state machine synthesis of Section 7.5.1, it is enough to use a D-type flip-flop to store the state, and encode the states in the following way: 0 in the flip-flop corresponds to $T0$ in the control circuit, and 1 to $T1$. The synthesis of the logic is trivial, producing the circuit in Figure 8.17.

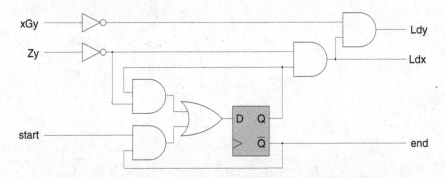

Fig. 8.17   Control unit for the greatest common divisor example.

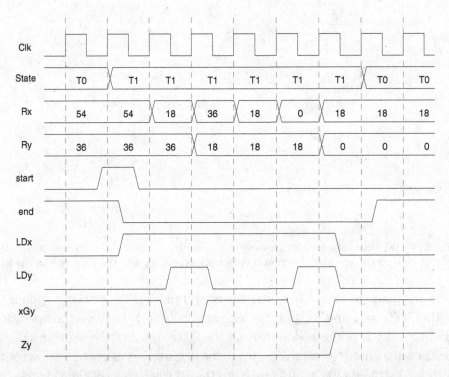

Fig. 8.18   Timing diagram for the calculation of the greatest common divisor between $X = 54$ and $Y = 36$.

The circuits in Figures 8.16(a) and 8.17 together, using the model in Figure 8.2, implement the intended functionality to calculate the greatest common divisor between two numbers. Figure 8.18 shows the operation of the circuits for the case when $X = 54$ and $Y = 36$, assuming that the registers are updated in the rising edge of the clock signal.

8.4 Arithmetic Logic Units

In the example presented above, we designed the datapath for a particular purpose. In fact, this is the most efficient approach to implement a digital system, because the datapath includes exactly the modules necessary for the microoperations defined, interconnected in an optimal manner. However, in many cases, that is not possible due to the required number of microoperations or their level of complexity.

In these cases, it is usual to design datapaths with basic functionalities, concerning both arithmetic and logic operations, linked to a set of general registers. The circuit which implements the operations is called an *arithmetic logic unit* or *ALU*. The number, type and complexity of the microoperations included in an ALU may vary considerably depending on the problem considered. Recall the principle mentioned in Section 8.2.2, which states that it is possible to simplify the datapath by transferring some complexity to the control unit. Hence, a sequence of microoperations available in a simple datapath can be made to replace more complex operations.

The ALU normally works with a register file (as in Section 6.7.3) to store the operands, results of operations and temporary values, which are necessary when a sequence of simple operations performs a complex operation. There can also be considerable variation regarding the number of registers available in the register file.

A datapath of this type is shown in Figure 8.19. Let us assume the more general case, in which the ALU accepts two operands and produces a single result. The control word contains information to select which two registers serve as operands and which destination register will store the result. The specification of the microoperation to be carried out by the ALU is also part of the control word. In turn, the ALU generates a set of status bits which, as previously mentioned, can be used by the control unit to take decisions that depend on the result of a microoperation.

8.4.1 *Structure of an ALU*

To illustrate these concepts, we will now design the ALU which we will use as the datapath for the processor P3, presented in Chapter 12. An ALU is a circuit that carries out basic arithmetic and logic operations. The first observation is that these two classes of operations do not have much in common. Therefore, we will consider separate units to implement each of these classes of operations, the *arithmetic unit* and the *logic unit*. Besides

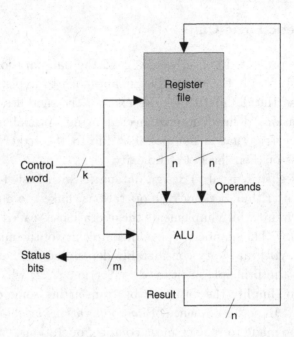

Fig. 8.19   Example of datapath with ALU plus register file.

these, a third unit is used to perform the shift to the right and to the left, a functionality similar to that of the shift registers presented in Section 6.5.3, but in this case implemented by purely combinational logic. We have decided to consider this *shift unit* separately since it corresponds to a functionality distinct from the other units. The operations carried out by the shift unit cannot be classified simply as arithmetic or logic operations, since, depending on the type of shift carried out, the operation may be considered as one type or the other, as we will see below.

Figure 8.20 shows the structure of the ALU under construction. This ALU has an architecture in which the three units mentioned work in parallel, with operands being available directly to each of them. Note that this option is one among other possibilities. A possible alternative, with advantages and disadvantages when compared to the one chosen, would be to place the shift unit at the output of the multiplexer, therefore in series with the arithmetic and logic units, which would enable the execution of more complex microoperations.

The microoperation carried out by either of these units is specified by the control word. The number of control bits required by each unit, p, q and r, depends on the number of operations available. This control word also controls the multiplexer at the output, which selects which of the units is

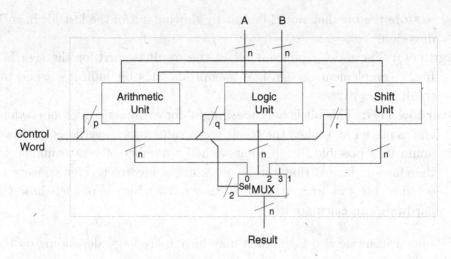

Fig. 8.20   Structure of the ALU.

the source of the result. Note that only the result of one unit is used. This means that the control bits of the three units may be shared, since it is only important to specify the control bits for the unit which will have its result selected at the output, the operation carried out by the other two units being irrelevant. Although it is not represented in the figure for simplicity, there exists also a multiplexer to select the status bits of the active unit.

8.4.2   *Flags*

As the ALU is a datapath with simple arithmetic and logic microoperations, the status bits passed to the control unit are also simple, and common to most of these microoperations. The status bits coming from an ALU and stored in a register are usually called flags, as already discussed. For the remaining of this book we will use preferently the term "flag". For the ALU under study, we have considered four flags, which are present in the overwhelming majority of ALUs:

Zero (Z): this bit is set to 1 when the result of the microoperation is 0. All ALU microoperations update the flag Z. Depending on the implementation, this bit may be generated by a NOR logic gate connected to all bits of the result.

Carry (C): This bit is used by arithmetic microoperations (such as addition and subtraction) to indicate that there is a carry bit beyond the most significant bit of the result. It is also used in shift microoperations to store the bit that would be lost by shifting out of the last bit in each direction.

Sign (N): The most significant bit of the result is used for the sign bit. In 2's complement or sign and magnitude, this bit indicates when the result is negative.

Overflow (O): This bit is only meaningful for arithmetic microoperations and is placed at 1 when the result has a value which overflows the maximum it is possible to represent with the number of bits available. It, therefore, indicates that the result value is incorrect. This concept of overflow bit was presented in Section 5.2.5 which explained how the hardware can calculate it.

Some arithmetic and logic units may have more flags, depending on the application in question. For example, in some cases it may be very useful to have a *parity bit* indicating that the number of bits at 1 in the result is even. The rule is normally that the ALU supplies information which is useful for the application and for which it is only possible, or substantially easier, to obtain directly through the hardware than through (micro)programming. For the ALU under study, we will consider only the four flags described above.

8.4.3 *Arithmetic Unit*

When one thinks of basic arithmetic operations, in the context of an *arithmetic unit*, it is natural to think of addition, subtraction, multiplication and division. Indeed, addition and subtraction are almost obligatory for arithmetic units. Multiplication, although very commonly used, is not always included because its hardware implementation is much more complicated, as we mentioned above. The implication of this option is that multiplication has to be implemented by a sequence of more elementary microoperations, such as we did before using successive additions, and therefore will take much longer to perform. The division is also not implemented directly by many arithmetic units since its implementation has the same order of complexity as multiplication and it is a much less utilised operation. Thus, the penalty that comes from its execution taking longer does not have the same weight on system performance.

Figure 8.21 shows an example of an arithmetic unit. Here, to simplify, we have decided not to include multiplication and division microoperations. An adder module is, therefore, the nucleus of this arithmetic unit which, with

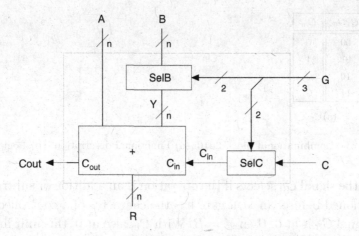

Fig. 8.21 Organisation of an arithmetic unit.

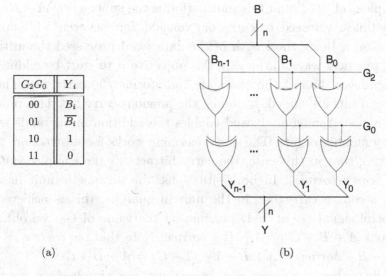

$G_2 G_0$	Y_i
00	B_i
01	$\overline{B_i}$
10	1
11	0

(a)   (b)

Fig. 8.22 Combinational block SelB: (a) Functional description. (b) Logic circuit.

the addition of simple combinational blocks which manipulate the operand B and the input of the carry signal, enable the adder to be used to execute an interesting set of microoperations.

As we discussed in Section 5.2.8, an adder can easily be used as a subtracter by applying 2's complement to one of the operands. This 2's complement may be obtained through bitwise logic complementation for this operand and by placing the input carry bit, C_{in}, at 1. The combinational blocks SelB and SelC, shown in Figures 8.22 and 8.23, respectively, have been defined in such a way that, with the control signals $G_1 = 0$ and

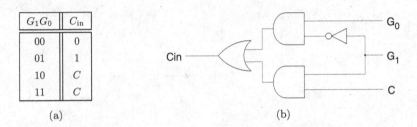

G_1G_0	C_{in}
00	0
01	1
10	C
11	C

(a)   (b)

Fig. 8.23   Combinational block SelC: (a) Functional description. (b) Logic circuit.

$G_2 = 0$, the signal G_0 selects if the operation is an addition or subtraction. As we mentioned before, an XOR gate has the character of a controlled inverter. If the signal G_0 is at 0, then $Y = B$. With C_{in} also at 0, this unit implements an addition. If the signal G_0 is at 1, then each bit of Y is the complement of the corresponding bit from B. As $C_{\text{in}} = 1$, then the unit sums A with the 2's complement of B, and this unit performs the subtraction $A - B$.

Sometimes, we need to carry out an addition between b-bit operands with $b > n$, n being the length of the data word processed the arithmetic unit. A practical way of achieving this objective is to start by adding the n least significant bits of the operands and storing the carry bit. Then the following n bits are added, including the previous carry bit. This procedure can be repeated indefinitely and enables the addition of operands with an arbitrary number of bits. The same reasoning works for subtraction, though considering that in this case, the carry bit acts as the complement of the *borrow* (*carry/borrow*). In both situations, the arithmetic unit has to be able to accept a carry bit. In the unit in analysis, this is achieved with the control signal G_1 at 1. Depending on the value of G_0, we obtain the operations $A + B + C$ or $A - B - borrow$. Note that, as $borrow = 1 - C$, then $A - B - borrow = A + \overline{B} + 1 - (1 - C) = A + \overline{B} + C$.

Finally, other very common operations are simple increments and decrements of an operand. To increment the operand A, just set the input corresponding to the operand B at 0 and the carry bit at 1 setting the control signals with the following configuration: $G_2 = 1$, $G_1 = 0$ and $G_0 = 1$. In a similar way, to decrement the operand A, we make the addition of A with $B = -1$ and $C_{\text{in}} = 0$. As the 2's complement of 1 is a value with all the bits at 1, the difference for this operation is the control signal $G_0 = 0$.

Table 8.1 summarises the possible microoperations implemented by the arithmetic unit shown in Figure 8.21, for each combination of the control inputs $G_2G_1G_0$. Note that the last two microoperations have not

Table 8.1   Set of microoperations for the arithmetic unit.

$G_2G_1G_0$	Y_i	C_{in}	Microoperation	
000	B_i	0	$R \leftarrow A + B$	sum
001	$\overline{B_i}$	1	$R \leftarrow A - B$	subtraction
010	B_i	C	$R \leftarrow A + B + C$	sum with carry bit
011	$\overline{B_i}$	C	$R \leftarrow A - B - \overline{C}$	subtraction with inverted carry
100	1	0	$R \leftarrow A - 1$	decrement
101	0	1	$R \leftarrow A + 1$	increment
110	1	C	$R \leftarrow A - \overline{C}$	decrement, if $C = 0$
111	0	C	$R \leftarrow A + C$	increment, if $C = 1$

been designed, but arise as secondary effects of the remaining operations. Although at first sight, they do not seem as useful as the six which were designed, they are available and can be used if necessary.

8.4.4   *Logic Unit*

The fundamental difference between the logic operations and the arithmetic operations is that the former are binary operations, and the latter operate on numerical values. Thus, for the logic operations, the bits are processed in an independent manner while for the arithmetic operations it is the set of the bits as a whole that has a meaning, according to the notation used in each case for the representation of numerical values. The *logic unit* executes the logic operations.

The microoperations available in a logic unit are applied individually to each bit of the input operands. For example, the microoperation $R \leftarrow A \wedge B$ represents a conjunction (application of the AND operation) between each pair of bits in the same position of the operands A and B: $R \leftarrow A_{n-1} \wedge B_{n-1} | \cdots | A_1 \wedge B_1 | A_0 \wedge B_0$.

A logic unit can include any logic operation. For the ALU under consideration, we have considered the four microoperations NOT, AND, OR and XOR, corresponding to the most used two-variable logic functions. Figure 8.24 shows how these microoperations are implemented for a generic bit i. Naturally, the logic unit will need as many blocks equal to that in Figure 8.24 as the number of bits of the operands. The control signals H_0 and H_1 choose which of the microoperations has its result selected at the output. Table 8.2 shows the correspondence between the combination of these signals and the microoperation selected.

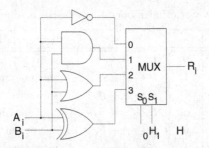

Fig. 8.24   Organisation of the logic unit.

Table 8.2   Set of microoperations of the logic unit.

$H_1 H_0$	Microoperation	
00	$R \leftarrow \overline{A}$	Complement
01	$R \leftarrow A \wedge B$	AND
10	$R \leftarrow A \vee B$	OR
11	$R \leftarrow A \oplus B$	Exclusive-OR

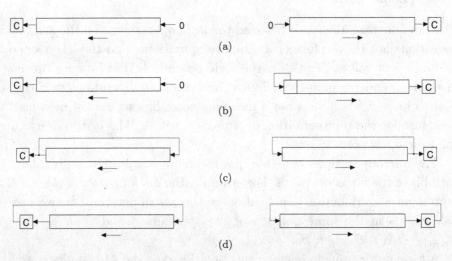

Fig. 8.25   Types of shift: (a) logic shift; (b) arithmetic shift; (c) rotation and (d) rotation with carry.

8.4.5   *Shift Unit*

The *shift unit* only accepts one input operand and enables all the bits of this operand to shift one position to the left or the right. There are various types of shifts possible, as indicated in Figure 8.25. We can see that, in any of the shift types, the carry bit field (C) receives the bit shifted out of the operand, the most significant bit of the operand in the case of shifts to the left, or the least significant bit in the case of shifts to the right.

Logic shift (Figure 8.25(a)): This is the simplest shift in which each bit passes to the next position, according to whether it is a left or a right shift. The carry flag (C) assumes the value of the bit which leaves the operand and the bit which enters is always 0. The flags carry (C), zero (Z) and sign (N) are updated. If the input operand is an unsigned number, a shift from a position to the left or the right is the same as an integer multiplication or division by 2, respectively.

Arithmetic shift (Figure 8.25(b)): This operation assumes that the operand is a signed number in 2's complement format. The goal is to maintain the rule for multiplication and division by 2, now with signed numbers. In the shift to the left, the movement of the bits is the same as for the logic shift. The difference is that, if the signal bit changes value, this means that the result has exceeded the capacity for the number of bits of the operand (multiplication by 2 cannot change the sign) and therefore the overflow flag (O) will be set to 1. In the shift to the right, the difference is also in the processing of the most significant bit, in this case the sign bit. As a division by 2 does not change the sign bit, this bit maintains the previous value. As it is an arithmetic operation, all the flags are updated.

Rotation (Figure 8.25(c)): In this microoperation, the movement of the bits is the same as for the logic shift, but the bit which enters has not always the value 0, rather a value equal to the bit which leaves the operand, thus closing the cycle. In a rotation to the left, the most significant bit goes into the least significant position. In a rotation to the right, the least significant bit goes into the most significant position. The flags carry (C), zero (Z) and sign (N) are updated.

Rotation with carry (Figure 8.25(d)): This type of rotation is the same as the previous one, with the difference that the rotation cycle includes the carry bit. The bit which enters is, therefore, the bit which was previously in the carry flag. Here the flags carry (C), zero (Z) and sign (N) are also updated.

Figure 8.26 shows a circuit which performs these shift microoperations. There are eight possible microoperations. Therefore three control signals are necessary, J_0, J_1 and J_2. J_0 indicates if the shift is to the right (0) or the left (1). For the intermediate bits of the operand, this is the only relevant

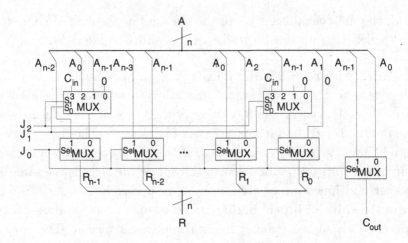

Fig. 8.26   Structure of the shift unit.

control signal, because it will simply go and get the bit with immediately greater or lower weight. In other words, the output bit i is equal to the input bit $i+1$ or $i-1$ according to whether J_0 is 0 or 1. J_0 is also the only control signal for the generation of the carry bit, which copies the most or least significant bit depending on whether the shift is to the left or the right, respectively.

Signals J_1 and J_2 define what is the type of shift to execute, which is achieved by control of the bit which enters, the most significant bit in the shifts to the right and the least significant bit in the shifts to the left.

In the case of a shift to the right, for a:

- logic shift: a 0 always enters;
- arithmetic shift: the bit is maintained since it is the sign bit;
- rotation: the least significant bit of the operand enters;
- rotation with carry: the carry bit enters.

In a similar way for a shift to the left:

- logic shift: a 0 always enters;
- arithmetic shift: a 0 always enters;
- rotation: the most significative bit of the operand enters;
- rotation with carry: the carry bit enters.

The microoperation carried out by the shift unit for each combination of control signals is listed in Table 8.3. The table also indicates the mnemonic for each microoperation.

Table 8.3   Possible microoperations in the shift unit.

$J_2 J_1 J_0$	Microoperation	
000	$R \leftarrow$ SHR A	logic right shift
001	$R \leftarrow$ SHL A	logic left shift
010	$R \leftarrow$ SHRA A	arithmetic right shift
011	$R \leftarrow$ SHLA A	arithmetic left shift
100	$R \leftarrow$ ROR A	rotate right
101	$R \leftarrow$ ROL A	rotate left
110	$R \leftarrow$ RORC A	rotate right with carry
111	$R \leftarrow$ ROLC A	rotate left with carry

8.4.6   *ALU Control Table*

Having established the operation of each of its internal units, we can define the overall functioning of the ALU shown in Figure 8.20. Thus, the arithmetic unit provides eight microoperations selected by the signals $G_2 G_1 G_0$, the logic unit offers four microoperations selected by the signals $H_1 H_0$ and the shift unit supplies eight microoperations selected by the signals $J_2 J_1 J_0$. Note that the multiplexer at the output of the ALU chooses the result of one of these units, and therefore for each microoperation, it is only necessary to ensure that the unit responsible for its execution has the correct control bits. That is, for each microoperation there is in fact only the concern to control one of these three units. This means that the control signals of these units can be shared, for example, in the following way: $G_0 = H_0 = J_0$, $G_1 = H_1 = J_1$ and $G_2 = J_2$. At the level of the ALU, the reference to these signals will be S_0, S_1 and S_2, respectively.

In addition to these three control signals, another two signals, S_3 and S_4, are necessary to control the selection signals for the multiplexer. By arbitrary choice, the combination 00 selects the arithmetic unit, the combination 01, the logic unit and the combination 10, the shift unit. The combination 11 remains available, and we opted to have this select the input A to provide a microoperation which merely copies an operand directly to the output. Table 8.4 lists the microoperations provided by this ALU and which is the control word that defines them.

The way the flags are updated depends on the active ALU unit. The flags zero (Z) and sign (N) are calculated in the same way for all the units, as defined in Section 8.4.2. The flag zero is computed by a NOR having as inputs all the bits of the result. In spite of not having much meaning for the logic microoperations, the sign bit is always available since it is equal to the most significant bit of the result.

Table 8.4   Table of ALU's microoperations.

$S_4S_3S_2S_1S_0$	Microoperation	
00000	$R \leftarrow A + B$	sum
00001	$R \leftarrow A - B$	subtraction
00011	$R \leftarrow A - B - \overline{C}$	subtraction with inverted carry bit
00100	$R \leftarrow A - 1$	decrement
00101	$R \leftarrow A + 1$	increment
00110	$R \leftarrow A - \overline{C}$	decrement, if $C = 0$
00111	$R \leftarrow A + C$	increment, if $C = 1$
01-00	$R \leftarrow \overline{A}$	complement
01-01	$R \leftarrow A \wedge B$	AND
01-10	$R \leftarrow A \vee B$	OR
01-11	$R \leftarrow A \oplus B$	exclusive-OR
10000	$R \leftarrow$ SHR A	logic right shift
10001	$R \leftarrow$ SHL A	logic left shift
10010	$R \leftarrow$ SHRA A	arithmetic right shift
10011	$R \leftarrow$ SHLA A	arithmetic left shift
10100	$R \leftarrow$ ROR A	rotate right
10101	$R \leftarrow$ ROL A	rotate left
10110	$R \leftarrow$ RORC A	rotate right with carry
10111	$R \leftarrow$ ROLC A	rotate left with carry
11- - -	$R \leftarrow A$	transfer

Arithmetic and shift units update the carry bit (C) but in different ways. In the case of the arithmetic unit, this bit is the output carry bit of the adder, the signal C_{out} in Figure 8.21. Section 8.4.5 defined the way of calculating this bit in the shift unit. Typically, this is the bit which leaves the operand, due to the shift operation.

Finally, the overflow bit (O) is only meaningful in the microoperations of the arithmetic unit and the arithmetic shift microoperations of the shift unit. Section 8.4.5 referred that the overflow bit in the shift unit assumes the value 1 when an arithmetic shift operation causes a change in the sign bit. For the arithmetic unit, this bit is calculated through an XOR of the two most significant carry bits of the adder in Figure 8.21, as explained in Chapter 5.

We assume that the values of the carry and overflow bits are not defined when the microoperation executed uses a unit in which they are not calculated. Of course, the transfer microoperation $R \leftarrow A$ is included here, since it does not use any of these units. In practice, one possibility, as good as any other, is to assume that these remain at zero.

The hardware necessary to generate these flags and their selection at the output of the ALU is not explicitly represented in the figures in this section, so as not to overload them.

8.4.7 *Example Revisited: Greatest Common Divisor*

Let us once again consider the example in Section 8.3.2, now showing how to implement the system which calculates the greatest common divisor between two operands using the ALU specified in this section as the datapath. Figure 8.27 shows the description of the system using only the microoperations available in the ALU. We have assumed here that the ALU has an associated register file with at least three registers, in which R1 and R2 initially have the input data, respectively X and Y, and R3 serves as a temporary register. The final result will be in R2.

We can see that this description is a little more complex than that of the original version in Figure 8.15. As mentioned above, when using a generic datapath, such as this ALU, as opposed to a datapath specifically designed for a given project, more microoperations are necessary to attain a given objective. In this particular case, in the original version, in the state $T1$ it was possible to make a comparison and also carry out a subtraction or an exchange of registers in the same cycle, depending on the result of this comparison. With the ALU, the comparison must be made first, and only in the following cycle can a new operation be carried out. In the code in Figure 8.27 a trivial optimisation was made, since as the comparison must be implemented through a subtraction, if the result is still positive, the subtraction is already done. Note that if the result is negative, the value of $R2$ has to be added to $R1$ to recover the initial value of $R1$. The other difference is that in the ALU it is not possible to perform an exchange of values between two registers. As such, three clock cycles and a temporary register are needed to carry out this operation.

1.		$T0$:	$end \leftarrow 1$
2.		$T0.start$:	$T0 \leftarrow 0, T1 \leftarrow 1$
3.		$T1$:	$R1 \leftarrow R1 - R2$
4.		$T1.Z$:	$T1 \leftarrow 0, T0 \leftarrow 1$
5.		$T1.N$:	$T1 \leftarrow 0, T2 \leftarrow 1$
6.		$T2$:	$R3 \leftarrow R1 + R2, T2 \leftarrow 0, T3 \leftarrow 1$
7.		$T3$:	$R1 \leftarrow R2, T3 \leftarrow 0, T4 \leftarrow 1$
8.		$T4$:	$R2 \leftarrow R3, T4 \leftarrow 0, T1 \leftarrow 1$

Fig. 8.27 Description at the register transfer level of the algorithm for calculating the greatest common divisor using a generic ALU.

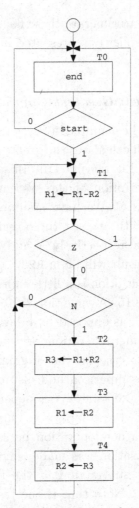

Fig. 8.28 Flowchart of the algorithm to determine the greatest common divisor using a generic ALU.

The sequence of operations to be executed is described in the flowchart in Figure 8.28. It is still a simple flowchart, such that any of the state machine design techniques is usable for the design of the control unit. A microprogrammed control has been utilised here (see Section 7.5.3).

Each microinstruction defines which microoperations will be performed in the datapath in the present cycle. It does that through the control word that will select the ALU operation, the two registers with the operands (*regA* and *regB*) and the destination register (*dest*). The ALU needs 5 bits for the choice of microoperation, as shown in Figure 8.20. Assuming only three registers in the register file (R1, R2 and R3), 2 bits are enough to select each of the registers for each operand and the register to store the result. In total, the control word will be made up of 11 bits:

10 9 8 7 6	5 4	3 2	1 0
ALU operation	reg A	reg B	dest

The number of states in the flowchart in Figure 8.28 is 5, which corresponds to the number of positions in the control ROM, implying that the number of bits for the control addresses will be 3. We can see in this flowchart that state $T1$ can have three different following states. Therefore, the microinstruction needs at least two following addresses (assuming that the third can be obtained by incrementing the CAR). Another consequence of this observation is that to decide among three addresses 2 bits are necessary for the choice of the following address to be loaded in the CAR. The jump conditions are: the control *start* signal at the state $T0$; the flags Z and N at $T1$; the following state at $T2$ and $T3$ (no jump); unconditional jump at $T4$. To cover these four hypotheses two control bits are necessary to select the jump condition. Finally, there has to be a bit for the control output *end*.

Adding the control word to the two Next State address fields for the CAR ($NS0$ and $NS1$), the 2 bits to select the jump condition (SEL) and the control output bit, we obtain the complete format for the microinstruction for the control unit:

19 18 17	16 15 14	13 12	11	10 9 8 7 6	5 4	3 2	1 0
NS0	NS1	SEL	end	ALU operation	reg A	reg B	dest

Figure 8.29 shows a microprogrammable controller adequate to the conditions of this problem. At the output of the control ROM there is the microinstruction with the control word that is sent directly to the datapath, with the fields $NS0$ and $NS1$, which store two possible next addresses for the CAR, and with the field SEL, which indicates which is the jump condition.

For this field it was arbitrarily chosen that:

00 — corresponds to an unconditional jump. The output of the multiplexer MUXS always has the value 00, a combination which selects the field $NS0$ of the microinstruction.

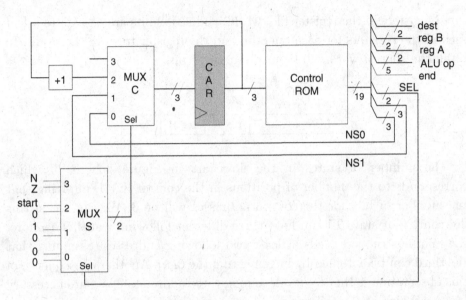

Fig. 8.29   Microprogrammed control unit for the maximum common divisor.

01 — corresponds to no jump. The CAR is incremented, because the MUXS always shows the value 10 at the output, which means that the input CAR + 1 is selected in the MUXC.

10 — corresponds to testing the *start* control input. When *start* = 0, the input $NS0$ is selected in the MUXC and, therefore, there is a jump. If *start* = 1, the CAR is incremented.

11 — corresponds to simultaneously testing the flags N and Z. If:

$NZ = 00$, the jump is carried out to the address in the field $NS0$,
$NZ = 01$, the jump is carried out to the address in the field $NS1$,
$NZ = 10$, there is no jump and the CAR is simply incremented,
$NZ = 11$, impossible combination.

We now need to define the microprogram which implements the flowchart in Figure 8.28 (the underlined positions indicate values which are, in fact, don't-cares):

Position ROM	NS0	NS1	SEL	*end*	op ALU	reg A	reg B	reg dest
0:	00	00	10	1	00000	00	00	00
1:	01	00	11	0	00001	01	10	01
2:	00	00	01	0	00000	01	10	11
3:	00	00	01	0	11000	10	00	01
4:	01	00	00	0	11000	11	00	10

In this microprogram there is a correspondence between the address location i of the control ROM and the index of the state Ti of the flowchart. Therefore:

Position 0: $end\leftarrow1$, $\overline{start}$: CAR$\leftarrow$ 0, $start$: CAR$\leftarrow$CAR+1

In this state, the control unit is constantly loading the CAR with 0, until the *start* input goes to 1, when it no longer loads the CAR and increments it. To do this, the field SEL must have the value 10 so as to enable the *start* signal to enter the multiplexer MUXS to be available for selection in the MUXC. While *start* is at 0, the multiplexer MUXC selects the input 0, field $NS0$ of the microinstruction which contains the address 0. If *start* goes to 1, then input 3 of the MUXC is selected. In this active waiting, the control output *end* is kept at 1, and the datapath does not carry out any operation, which is managed by specifying a non-existent register as the destination register, in this case 0.

Position 1: R1$\leftarrow$R1−R2, Z: CAR$\leftarrow$0, $\overline{Z}.\overline{N}$: CAR$\leftarrow$1, $\overline{Z}.N$: CAR$\leftarrow$ CAR+1

Here the ALU carries out the subtraction between R1 and R2, storing the result in $R1$. If the result is 0, the algorithm has terminated, and therefore the address 0 is loaded into the CAR through the field $NS1$ to return to the beginning (in the multiplexer MUXS input 3 is selected and in the MUXC input 1 is selected). While the result is positive (flag $N = 0$), the control unit is maintained at address 1 by loading the field $NS0$ in the CAR. If the result is negative, instead of subtracting, the values of R1 and R2 are exchanged. This is done beginning in address 2, that is, by incrementing the CAR. The test which determines which of these three following addresses is used is achieved by $SEL = 11$.

Position 2: R3$\leftarrow$R1+R2, CAR$\leftarrow$CAR+1

In this state, the value contained in R1 before the subtraction is placed in R3, adding R2 to it. The CAR is incremented by setting input 1 of the multiplexer MUXS.

Position 3: R1$\leftarrow$R2, CAR$\leftarrow$CAR+1

Here there is a simple transfer between registers, with the value of R2 copied to R1. Once again, the CAR is incremented.

Position 4: R2$\leftarrow$R3, CAR$\leftarrow$1

Finally, in this state, another simple transfer between registers is carried out, copying the value of R3 to R2, finishing the interchange of R1 and R2. An unconditional jump is executed to the state in address 1. This is achieved by selecting the input 0 of the multiplexer MUXS, forcing the selection of the field $NS0$ of the microinstruction.

8.5 Summary

This chapter focuses on the design of digital systems at the register transfer level of abstraction. This level of abstraction presupposes the existence of a module, the datapath, which supplies a set of elementary operations, and another module, the control unit, which, for each clock cycle, defines which operation is to be carried out by the datapath. In this way, complex systems can be implemented through sequences of elementary datapath operations. This design method does not lead to circuits as efficient as those developed at the logic gate level. However, by not going into such level of detail, it can be more easily applied in the development of circuits of greater complexity.

We briefly discuss the freedom there is in defining datapaths, noting that more complex datapaths, providing both a larger number of elementary operations but exhibiting greater complexity, reduce the number of clock cycles necessary for an operation. The compromise is, therefore, between the size of the circuit and its efficiency.

The control unit is nothing more than a sequential circuit. Chapter 7 analysed the design methods for this kind of circuits. Although any of the design methods studied in this chapter may be used, the control units typically have many input and output signals, such that expeditious design techniques are often used, particularly resorting to microprogrammed circuits (Section 7.5.3).

A paradigmatic case of this design method is the design of arithmetic and logic units. This chapter develops an ALU as a circuit to demonstrate the concepts presented. Although simple, it contains a set of typical operations for a generic processor. We will use this ALU in Chapter 12 in the construction of the P3 processor.

Exercises

8.1 Consider a system with three four-bit registers, R1, R2 and R3. Consider that the registers contain unsigned numbers. Initially, R1 has the value 5, R2 the value 3 and R3 the value 6.

Indicate the content of the registers after each of the following micro-operations:

(a) R1 ← R1 ∧ R3
(b) R2 ← R1 + R2
(c) R3 ← SHL R1

8.2 Design a four-bit arithmetic circuit with two selection variables $S1$ and $S0$ which can execute the following arithmetic operations:

$S1$	$S0$	$C_{in} = 0$	$C_{in} = 1$
0	0	$F = A + B$ (sum)	$F = A + B + 1$
0	1	$F = A$ (sum)	$F = A + 1$ (increment)
1	0	$F = \overline{B}$ (complement)	$F = \overline{B} + 1$ (change of sign)
1	1	$F = A + \overline{B}$	$F = A + \overline{B} + 1$ (subtraction)

8.3 Consider a system with three four-bit registers, AR, BR and CR, in which the following operations, in 2's complement, are possible:

$$X.\overline{S}: \quad CR \leftarrow AR + BR$$
$$Y.S: \quad CR \leftarrow AR - BR$$

Design a block diagram for the implementation of this system in hardware. Assume that it has available registers, **one** adder (with *carry-in* and *carry-out*) and all the simple logic gates needed. The inputs for AR and BR, as well as the control signals X, Y and S, enter externally. Do not worry about the loading of the AR and BR.

8.4 Consider the datapath in Figure 8.16(a), and assume that the modules have the following timing characteristics:

Module	Delay
Multiplexer (control to result)	2.5 ns
Multiplexer (data to result)	2.0 ns
Comparator	2.0 ns
Subtractor	3.0 ns
Registers (setup time)	1.0 ns
Registers (delay time)	1.5 ns

Determine the maximum operating frequency of this circuit.

8.5 Consider the datapath in Figure 8.16(a). Draw up a timing diagram similar to that in Figure 8.18, illustrating the waveforms of the relevant signals when the initial values of the registers are Rx = 36 and Ry = 48.

8.6 Design a control unit implemented with modules of medium complexity which implements the flowchart in Figure 8.4.

8.7 Consider a digital system with three registers: AR, BR and PR. Three flip-flops supply the control variables of the system: S is a flip-flop that is set at 1 by an external signal to start system operation; F and R are two flip-flops used to control the transfer operations when the system is operating. A fourth flip-flop D is set at 1 by the system when the operation is complete. The system operation is described by the following register transfer instructions:

$$S: \quad PR \leftarrow 0, S \leftarrow 0, D \leftarrow 0, F \leftarrow 1$$
$$F: \quad F \leftarrow 0, \text{ if (AR=0) then } (D \leftarrow 1) \text{ else } (R \leftarrow 1)$$
$$R: \quad PR \leftarrow PR + BR, AR \leftarrow AR - 1, R \leftarrow 0, F \leftarrow 1$$

(a) Show that the digital system described multiplies the content of the registers AR and BR and places the result in PR.

(b) Design a block diagram for its implementation in hardware. Include a start signal to set the flip-flop S at 1 and a completion signal from the flip-flop D.

8.8 Consider a system that has a set of registers connected to a bus, as shown in the following figure. All the registers are triggered on the positive edge, and the registers R2 and O have tri-state outputs. All the buses are four-bit buses.

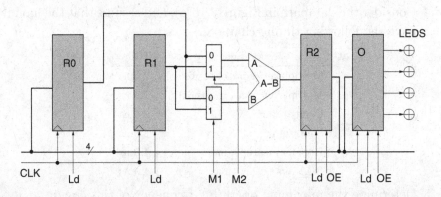

Execute the following sequence of operations: (1) Calculate R1-R0, placing the result in R2; (2) show the result in the LEDs connected to the register O; (3) load the result in register R0.

(a) Describe the register transfer operations and the respective micro-operations supported by this datapath.

(b) Describe the waveforms for all the control signals necessary for the implementation of this sequence of operations.

(c) Describe the state diagram which corresponds to the waveforms described in the previous item.

8.9 Consider the arithmetic unit in Figure 8.21. Indicate the values that the control variables G_2, G_1, G_0 should have so the unit implements the operation A-B, and determines the values at the points Y, C_{in}, C_{out} and R when A = 0155h and B = 0052h.

8.10 Consider the shift unit in Figure 8.26. Indicate the values that the control variables J_2, J_1, J_0 should have so the unit implements the operation that corresponds to a multiplication by 2 of a positive integer stored in register A, and determine the values of the signs R and C when A = 05A5h.

8.11 Suppose that we want to use the arithmetic logic unit in Figure 8.20, integrated into the datapath in Figure 8.19, to implement elementary operations on registers. Assume that the register file has three control inputs, 3 bits each, which specify the source registers RA and RB, and the destination register, RC. The arithmetic logic unit is controlled as shown in Table 8.4.

(a) Define the fields of the control word used to control the datapath.
(b) Indicate what the content of the control word is when each of the following operations is executed:

    (a) R1 ← R1 + 1
    (b) R3 ← R0 + R7
    (c) R7 ← ROR R1.

8.12 Suppose that we want to use the datapath in Figure 8.19 to implement a multiplier for 16-bit positive numbers. The goal is the result of the multiplication of register R1 by register R2 to be stored in registers R3 and R4, with the most significant component in R3. Consider that the register file has eight available registers.

(a) Design the flowchart for the control circuit.
(b) Implement this flowchart using a microprogrammed control unit.

8.13 Consider once again Problem 7.15 from Chapter 7. In the solution adopted in that chapter, it was necessary to close the gate when a car enters, to avoid the situation in which various cars could be circulating on the bridge in the same direction. For this to be possible, it was necessary to use the sensors $S5$ and $S6$. Design a circuit, using a counter and a control circuit, that controls access to the bridge in a secure manner, without using sensors $S5$ and $S6$. The idea is to count the number of cars which are located on the bridge (circulating in the same direction) and only raise the gate in the opposite direction when all the cars have left.

Chapter 9

Computer Architecture

Although we may design a digital system for any particular function from scratch, connecting registers and functional blocks, using the technique studied in Chapter 8, for reasons of flexibility it is preferable to have an adaptable and easily reprogrammable system, a computer. This chapter provides a summary of the development of computers and their internal organisation.

A computer is a digital system which is programmable through a sequence of instructions stored in memory. This sequence of instructions commands the computer to execute elementary data manipulation operations. The central processing unit, or processor, is a crucial element in a computer.

The processor, in itself, is a digital system made up of a datapath and a control circuit, like the systems studied in the previous chapter. It is flexible because these circuits are designed to execute a set of basic data manipulation operations that can be combined to carry out processing tasks of arbitrary complexity.

9.1 Historical Perspective

The idea of an information processing system which is reconfigurable through a program stored in some form of memory goes back to the beginning of the XIX century. *Charles Babbage* designed the first mechanical computer capable of automatically performing sequences of operations. This machine, known as the *difference engine*, used a technology entirely based on mechanical elements. The system could be programmed to construct mathematical tables, using instructions specified by the programmer.

The complexity of the mechanical systems necessary for implementing mathematical functions meant that more powerful computers could not be manufactured until the existence of technologies based on electronic circuits, although there had been plans for an even more powerful mechanical computer, called the *analytical engine.*

There were several attempts to construct electronic digital computers, but *ENIAC* is considered to be the first machine to actually work, which became operational in 1946 and could be programmed to calculate mathematical tables related to military applications. ENIAC used a technology based on electronic vacuum tubes and was programmed through a set of cables which, depending on whether they were connected or disconnected, specified the content of the program memory. The computation results were written on punched cards or an electrical typewriter.

ENIAC stored the program and the data in a memory which, for the time, operated at high speed. This concept of using memory to store both the program and the data is attributed to *John von Neumann*, who worked on the design. For this reason, this type of architecture, in which a single memory stores the data along with the programs, is called a *von Neumann architecture*. This architecture would dominate against the alternative of having two separated memories for the data and for the code, which is known as the *Harvard architecture*.

Other increasingly advanced computers, but still belonging to what is usually designated as the *first generation* of computers, would be designed and constructed, but the use of vacuum tubes imposed severe limitations on their reliability and size. These computers typically occupied a large-sized room and could only function continuously for a few hours, until one of the subsystems would stop working due to a fault on one of the tubes.

The use of transistors, invented in 1947, as the base technology would enable the development of the *second generation* of computers, which used magnetic disk technology to store information in a non-volatile way and worked with magnetic-core central memories.

The *third generation* of computers appeared with the advent of *integrated circuits*, in 1961, leading to a tremendous reduction in the size of computers and a subsequent increase in the number of logic gates which it was possible to pack within a given volume. One of the range of computers which achieved most success was the *IBM/360* family. With this family of computers, *IBM* introduced the concept of separating the definition of the instructions from the physical implementation of a computer, thus creating the first of a series of families which executed the same set of instructions in processors with different internal organisations. The introduction of this concept allowed for a much greater reuse of the programming effort, since a program encoded for one computer of a given family could now be executed by other computers of the same family.

The advance of technology and the creation of the integrated circuit with very large scale integration (*VLSI*), enabled the creation of processors entirely contained in a single integrated circuit, which would lower the price of a computer facilitating its use as a personal computer. These processors, made from a single integrated circuit, are called *microprocessors*. The first processor available in a single integrated circuit was the *Intel 4004*, and the first personal computer was based on the *8080* microprocessor from the same manufacturer. But the most important step for the dissemination of this type of computer was the definition by IBM of the standard model for *personal computers*, or PC, based on the *8088* processor. The success of this family of computers, based on various microprocessors of this Intel family, such as 80286, 80386, 80486, Pentium (I, II, III and IV) and Core (1, 2, i3, i5 and i7), is well known. As the technology evolved, other types of personal computer became also popular, the *MacBooks*, from *Apple*, deserving a special mention.

9.2 Types of Computers

Although the majority of current computers follow the von Neumann architecture, the application area of each particular machine determines many of their particular implementation characteristics, and we can consider that there are four broad classes of computers: personal computers, servers, mobile devices, and embedded systems.

Personal computers, which can be *desktop computers* or *laptop computers*, are the type of computer that the average person more commonly has in mind and would naturally associate with the definition of what a computer is. Over time, this class of computers has been optimised for the type of applications used by people in offices or at home, such as word processing, sound, images, video and games. These applications require a set of data input and output devices which have become familiar. Examples of data input devices are the keyboard and the mouse, and of data output devices, the monitor and the printer, although there are many other possible devices. An important factor to take into account in the design of personal computers is cost, followed by performance. In laptops, power consumption is also a very relevant factor.

Another type of computer is the *server*, which is used to process large quantities of data. Typically, these servers are installed in isolated rooms, with suitable environmental conditions. Large rooms with many servers, called *data centres*, have strict temperature and humidity controls, security controls at the physical access level and redundant and emergency power supply systems, etc. Computers of this type do not normally have a user sitting in front of them. Ultimately, it would be enough to have a network card as a data input and output device to enable the transfer of data between that computer and any other connected to the network. However, sometimes these computers have a keyboard and monitor to allow the local configuration of the server. For this class of machines, as a general rule, the price is not a decisive factor, being relegated to the background when compared to the important performance metrics for the main application being executed on the server.

The third class of computers we consider are mobile devices, such as smartphones and mobile pads. Although they could also be considered embedded systems, they are so common these days that they deserve a class for themselves. These computers communicate with the external world mainly through a touch sensitive screen, but also through radiowave based network interfaces. They can run many different programs, usually called *apps*. One of these apps is the phone app, enabling them to also be used as phones.

The fourth class of computers are *embedded systems*, which, as the name indicates, are computers embedded in other systems, which they control and monitor. Despite being perhaps the type of computer that goes most unnoticed, because they are hidden, it is estimated that 95% of existing computers are of this type. These systems exist in simple mobile phones, cars, planes, TVs and electrical appliances in general. These computers are characterised by having specific data input and output devices for the application for which they are intended.

Figure 9.1 outlines the interaction between the computer — digital system, and the real world — analogue system. Although this figure is in a general way applicable to any computer, it is more associated with the type of operation of an embedded system. Indeed, embedded systems often need to collect data about different physical reality parameters, so there is a large range of sensors with which the systems have to interact. The interface of personal computers and servers with the external world is carried out through devices specially constructed for this purpose, and over which there is, therefore, more control. Examples here are the keyboard as a sensor element and the monitor as an actuator element.

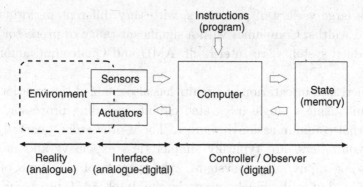

Fig. 9.1 Interaction between a computer and analogue reality.

9.3 Types of Processors

Nowadays, in the personal computer class, Intel processors clearly dominate. As mentioned above, the Intel 8088 processor was selected by IBM when building its first PC, which established itself as the standard architecture. To maintain compatibility at the software level, new generations of personal computers compatible with the IBM PC have always used new versions of Intel processors or compatible processors such as the ones manufactured by *AMD*. Some years ago IBM decided to end its activity in the area of personal computers, having sold its operation to *Lenovo*, but evidently many other companies manufacture personal computers compatible with this standard.

Although with a smaller market share in the personal computer market, the strongest alternative architecture is that of Apple which used in the beginning *Motorola* processors of the 680X0 family and then switched to the *PowerPC* family (a processor developed jointly by IBM and Apple itself). However, even Apple has opted to change to Intel processors and, at the time of this writing, uses the Intel Core family of processors in all their laptops.

Unlike the case of personal computers, in the server and embedded systems markets there is a large variety of different processors. In the server class, performance is a critical factor. These processors need a significant capacity to exploit parallelism in executing instructions and, sometimes using a wider data word. Examples of these processors are the Intel's Itanium family, the IBM Power architecture and the ARM-V8 architecture.

In the embedded and mobile systems market, the most important parameters are the price and power consumption of the processors. In this class, there is a large variety of processors, with very different performance and data word widths. Companies with a significant range of processor variants for embedded systems are Intel itself, AMD and Qualcomm, among many others.

The increased integration of circuits has also enabled the creation of computers built using a single integrated circuit, including processor, memory and external communication resources. These processors, generally known as *microcontrollers*, are typically simpler, less expensive and more flexible regarding input/output systems. An example of this type of circuit, already old, but still widely used, is the Intel *8051* processor and its sequels.

Another type of dedicated processors are *digital signal processors*, DSP, which are designed to be extremely efficient in signal processing applications, and are currently used in systems for telecommunications, such as telephones and televisions. Many companies that produce low power CPUs also produce special purpose digital signal processors.

9.4 Internal Organisation of a Computer

As was mentioned above, the computer is a digital system programmable through a sequence of instructions stored in memory that specify the sequence of data manipulation operations to execute.

Each instruction uniquely specifies which operation has to be carried out and over which operands. For example, a given instruction may specify that the addition of the value in memory location 10FAh and the content of register R3 should be computed and stored in the same memory location, 10FAh.

The unit which processes the sequence of instructions is the *processor* or *central processing unit*, abbreviated to *CPU*. The central processing units can execute a set of instructions which, although varying considerably from one computer to another, have a certain number of common characteristics. The CPU is made up of combinational circuits, which enable arithmetic and logic operations, and by registers that store the operands and the results of those operations.

In modern computers, the sequence of instructions to be executed is stored in memory. Assuming the von Neumann architecture, this memory also serves to store the data, both input into the program as well as that resulting from its execution.

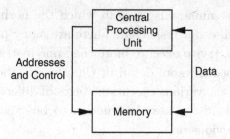

Fig. 9.2 Interconnection of the central processing unit with the memory.

Instructions are stored sequentially in memory and, most of the time, are executed in the order by which they are placed. However, there are also instructions which alter the execution order. For example, a given instruction may specify that the next instruction to be executed is the instruction stored in the memory location AAF0h.

The memory is connected to the central processing unit using two buses, as described in Figure 9.2.

Schematically, the execution of an instruction stored in memory involves the following stages:

- The CPU sends the address of the next instruction to be executed to the memory and receives a memory word which contains the encoding of the instruction to be executed.
- The CPU decodes the instruction, identifying the operands and the type of operation.
- The CPU makes one or more memory accesses to load the operands specified by the instruction into the internal registers.
- When it has all the operands, the CPU executes the operation specified by the instruction.
- After obtaining the result, the CPU writes this to memory, if this is necessary, or to an internal register.

This description is a description of the general operating principle, which might not apply directly to modern processors, which are very complex and use some different techniques to accelerate their processing speed. There are, however, some alternatives to this simple organisation, which are relevant to mention at this stage and are typically used in commercial processors.

First, it is not always true that each memory location is sufficient to store an entire instruction or each operand. Sometimes, it is necessary to make various accesses to memory to load an instruction or an operand.

Second, there are numerous cases in which the normal operational flow described above is also not respected. There are many processors which, for reasons of efficiency, try to execute more than one instruction in parallel. In these cases, described in more detail in Chapter 15, the central processing unit may interleave the various execution stages of different instructions, and may, for example, load the next instruction to be executed before writing the result of the previous one.

Another significant alteration to the organisation described above is not using a single memory to store the data and the program. It is common, especially in microcontrollers, to use the Harvard architecture described above, that is, use two different memories, one for the data and another for the program. In some cases, this is a consequence of the program being fixed and stored in non-volatile memory, while the data is stored in read-write memory.

9.5   Internal Structure of a Processor

Generically, a processor has the typical structure of the digital systems studied in the previous chapter: it is made up of a processing unit and a control unit, as shown in Figure 9.3. In turn, the processing unit has a structure made up essentially of an arithmetic logic unit, where the calculations necessary to execute the instructions are carried out, and by a register file, which stores the operands and the results of those calculations.

As mentioned, a processor sequentially executes instructions stored in memory. Several clock cycles are usually necessary to complete an

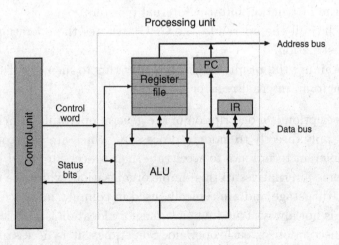

Fig. 9.3   Internal structure of a processor.

instruction. The control unit is responsible for generating the sequence of control words which define the desired functionality for each instruction. Therefore, at each clock cycle, the control word determines, among other things, the operation carried out by the ALU, the registers which will serve as operands for this operation and the register which will store the result. In the other direction, the processing unit sends the control unit a set of bits which provide some indication of the results of the operations executed by the ALU. This information is necessary, because, in many cases, the sequence of operations generated by the control unit is dependent on the result of previous operations.

There are two registers of particular importance in a processor, highlighted in Figure 9.3. One of them is the *program counter*, PC or, sometimes, *instruction pointer*. As the name suggests, the PC register is responsible for storing information about which program instruction is under execution at any given moment. Since these instructions are in memory, the content is the memory address of the next instruction to be executed.

The second register is the *instruction register, IR*, whose function is to store the instruction being executed by the processor. The control unit uses the content of this register to determine the sequence of operations that the processing unit has to carry out to implement the execution of that instruction. This connection is not shown in Figure 9.3 so as not to complicate it.

As we saw above, the initial execution stage of an instruction in a processor consists of reading the memory location defined by the program counter (placing the value of PC on the address bus of the system) and loading the value read in the instruction register (loading the value in the data bus to the IR register). After this operation, the program counter is incremented so that, when the present instruction finalises its execution, the next instruction in memory will be read (unless it is a jump which itself alters the PC register, as we will see).

Chapter 12 analyses in detail the internal structure of a simple processor implementing the high-level description presented in this section.

9.6 External Interaction

The central processing unit and the memory, shown in Figure 9.2, are the nucleus of a computer, but, by themselves, cannot perform any useful function. The computer uses various peripheral devices to communicate with users, such as keyboards, mouses, monitors and printers. It also uses disks and magnetic tapes, to store data permanently, and network interfaces to communicate with other computers.

These devices connect to *input/output ports* or *IO ports*. The input and output ports control these devices using a *protocol* which varies from device to device. A protocol is a set of rules enabling the correct information transfer between different entities.

From the CPU, the input/output ports are accessed, both for reading and for writing, in a way similar to that of memory. Conceptually, each input/output port is assigned one or more addresses, which are used by the CPU when it wishes to read data from that port or write data to it. Figure 9.4 shows that the CPU, the memory and the input/output ports are typically packaged into a single physical unit so that they can communicate through short, high-speed buses.

The distinction between memory access and input/output port access is achieved both through the address used and by the configuration of the control lines, as will be seen in Chapter 14.

The operation that each input/output port carries out on the data depends on the device that is attached to it. For example, an input/output port which corresponds to a serial port sends the data received to a serial line. The device connected to the port, then interprets the data on the line, as it understands the series protocol. In turn, the data sent by the mouse

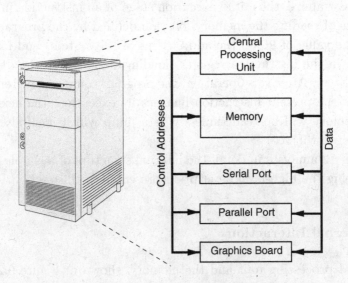

Fig. 9.4 Processor, memory and input/output ports.

through the serial line is read from the input/output port by the CPU when it accesses the corresponding port.

Other input/output ports handle data in a different way. A parallel port may be used to communicate with a parallel printer, through a set of lines. Other ports communicate with more complex devices, such as graphic cards and disk controllers. A graphics card interprets the data received as commands to draw points on the monitor and generate the video signal which appears there as the corresponding image, while the disk controller writes the data received onto specific locations of the magnetic disk or reads the data stored in the locations specified by the CPU. In practice, for reasons of performance and system modularity, there are various alternatives for reading and writing data in input/output ports, which we will be study in detail in Chapter 14. Figure 9.5 describes how the external peripherals connect to the computer. Note that, although the peripherals sometimes connect to the central unit through cables, there are various peripherals which are physically inside the same unit housing the CPU. In general, magnetic disks and compact disc readers are inside the unit containing the central processing unit, although they are peripherals connected in the same way as external devices like a mouse, a keyboard or a printer.

More recently, there are a lot of connections using radio waves, namely GSM, Wi-Fi, Bluetooth and others. However, for the computer, these links behave just like the others, as the input/output ports connect to radio devices that mask the physical link to the system.

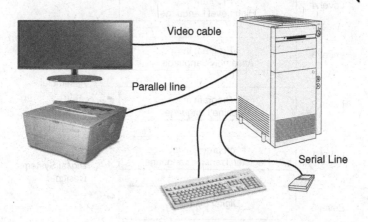

Fig. 9.5 Computer and peripherals.

9.7 Computer Abstraction Levels

Usually, users interact with the computer at a very high level of abstraction. Most computer users do not know, nor wish to know, any detail about its internal organisation or its architecture. Typically, a computer user runs an application, such as an editor, a word processor or a spreadsheet. These applications have as an objective making computers accessible to users who neither know, nor wish to know, how to program, and, through the use of the most recent interaction technologies with the user, have indeed managed to make the use of computers accessible to all.

However, a computer is, indeed, a programmable digital system and, as such, it can be utilised, programmed or configured at several levels of abstraction. Figure 9.6 shows the different *levels of abstraction* at which the user or the designer can view a computer.

We already mentioned the application level. Users who utilise computers at this level interact with an application, typically making use of metaphors from real life, such as folders, desktops, sheets, etc.

In most cases, this application was programmed using a *high-level language* such as Java, C or Python. It is the responsibility of programmers to interpret the specifications which define the functioning applications and write the code in high-level language to implement them.

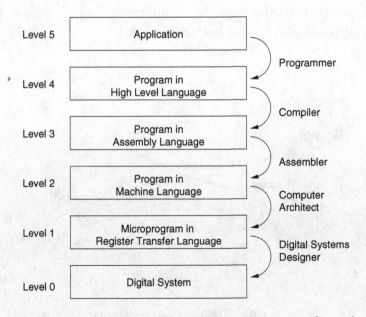

Fig. 9.6   Levels of abstraction at which a computer may be used.

The computer does not execute this high-level code directly. It must be translated by another program, called a *compiler*, into a much simpler language, the *assembly language*. This language only enables very simple operations to be specified, such as an addition of two memory positions or copying the contents of one register to another.

Despite its simplicity, assembly language is still not directly executed by the processor. It is necessary to translate it into *machine language* which is executed directly by the processor. This machine language is stored in memory and represents a program which the processor can run. The translation of assembly language into machine language is implemented by another program, the *assembler*.

There are still lower levels of abstraction than machine language. The instruction bits of a machine language program are not directly used to control the registers and datapaths of the processor. In most cases, each instruction in machine language corresponds to several elementary operations involving data manipulation and transfer between registers. These actions, defined by the designers of the processor, constitute the *microprogram*.

Finally, having defined the micro-operations which have to be supported by the hardware, the digital system which implements them has to be designed. This design is typically carried out by engineers specialised in digital system design, who may or may not be the same as those who develop and define the processor at a higher level of abstraction.

This simplified description of the operation of a computer omits various aspects of greater or lesser importance, although there is one which cannot be ignored, even in a superficial description such as this one. Almost all computers execute various programs, both simultaneously and sequentially. The execution of the various programs is controlled by a special program, the computer *operating system*. The operating system is itself a program, which schedules and manages the various tasks that the processor has to execute. The study of operating systems is in itself worthy of a whole book, and this matter will not be dealt with in any depth in this context. However, from a simplistic point of view, the operating system is a program which distributes processor time among the various tasks that it has to carry out. These tasks include not only the execution of applications but also responding to requests by peripheral devices, the management of the memory system and the management of resources shared among the various applications and users.

Conceptually, a processor may be utilised or programmed at any of the levels higher than level 0. This level is traditionally fixed and unalterable. However, there are recent technologies which allow for the reconfiguration of the connections between the digital components so as to alter their operation. Programming or using a computer at higher levels of abstraction typically requires less effort by the user or programmer, but the use of lower levels of abstraction can lead to greater speed and efficiency during execution.

9.8   Computer Components

We dedicate the following chapters to the study of computer architecture. We will start by analysing the operation of the central processing units, in the perspective of the assembly language programmer. To do this, Chapter 10 describes the way in which a typical central processing unit is programmed at this level, using for this purpose a hypothetical microprocessor, the P3 processor.[1] The P3 processor is similar to commercial processors, exhibiting many of their characteristics, though avoiding the idiosyncrasies inherent in these.

After presenting the assembly language of this processor, Chapter 11 describes the way in which assembly instructions are translated into machine language and techniques for programming in assembly, therefore dealing with levels 2 and 3 in Figure 9.6.

We made the option to use a non-commercial processor to illustrate the operation of the central processing units, but we are aware that this is an option that has advantages and disadvantages. The most significant disadvantage is that the reader cannot obtain the added value of the in-depth learning of a real processor, which could be very useful in the future. The authors believe that this disadvantage is more than compensated for by the pedagogic advantages of not having to deal with the complexities inherent to the use of a commercial processor during the learning process, many of them motivated by purely historical reasons.

We have therefore chosen to define this processor by using an approach in which the criteria of performance, realism or elegance take on a secondary position, as opposed to the criteria of pedagogic clarity and simplicity.

---

[1]P3 = PPP = Petite Pedagogic Processor.

In the opinion of the authors, this option justifies itself by the final result obtained, a processor which is clear and easy to program with an architecture of considerable regularity, which has enabled the learning process to be significantly simplified.

A central processing unit, such as the P3 processor, is a complex digital system which, although designed using the techniques described in previous chapters, deserves a more detailed study. Therefore, the internal structure of the P3 processor, that is, its *microarchitecture*, is described in Chapter 12, and this chapter is used not only to describe this processor in particular but also to present some techniques for processor design which a large number of systems use. This chapter, therefore, covers levels 0 and 1 of Figure 9.6.

Chapter 13 describes how the memory system of a modern processor is structured. Indeed, the description given above is an oversimplification of the memory system of a modern computer.

Chapter 14 describes in some detail how the central processing unit is interconnected with the peripherals and the methods and communication protocols which are most popular. It also describes, in a necessarily brief manner, some peripherals which are particularly important, such as disks and keyboards.

Finally, Chapter 15 serves as a brief introduction to more advanced topics in the area of computer architecture. This chapter will cover other relevant topics for computer performance, such as *pipelining*, philosophies related to *CISC*, complex instruction set computer, and *RISC*, reduced instruction set computer, as well as various techniques necessary to the design of current processors.

9.9 Summary

This chapter presents the concept of a computer as a programmable digital system and briefly introduces the historical evolution of computers.

It provides a high-level description of computer architecture listing its various components, amongst which are necessarily the central processing unit (CPU or processor), the memory and the input/output ports connected to the peripheral devices.

Finally, the chapter mentions the various levels of abstraction at which a computer can be viewed, levels which go from the application level up to the level of data transfer between the registers of a digital system.

Exercises

9.1 Moore's law, based on an empirical observation of past data regarding technological evolution, says that the number of devices in an integrated circuit doubles every 18 months. By consulting available data on the Internet for central processing units, draw a graph showing the development of the number of transistors from the year of introduction of the processor onwards. Alternatively, use the data available in Table 15.1.

9.2 Indicate three peripheral devices connected to your personal computer and identify which protocol or standard they use to communicate with the central processing unit.

9.3 Describe the differences between a von Neumann architecture and a Harvard architecture.

9.4 Estimate the volume and weight of a vacuum tube processor which has the same number of devices as a Pentium IV processor. Consider only the weight and the volume occupied by the active devices (vacuum tubes *vs.* transistors), assuming that a valve occupies around 50 cm^3 and weighs around 50 g.

Chapter 10

Instruction Set Architectures

This chapter studies some possible alternatives for the *instruction set architecture* or *ISA* of a processor. The choice of the instructions to be included in the instruction set for a processor represents a complex problem, which depends also on the features and the technology to be used. Specialised design teams, the instruction set architects, solve this issue after carrying out an analysis of the existing alternatives and the limitations imposed by the specifications.

The first part of the chapter analyses assembly instructions in general terms. The next section starts with a simple presentation of what assembly language is and its relationship with machine code. Section 10.2 discusses the different types of assembly instructions and the information fields that each type must include so that the processor can execute them correctly. Many assembly instructions need parameters, and Section 10.3 lists the most usual ways of specifying them. Section 10.4 considers the binary encoding of the instruction fields, analysing the advantages and disadvantages of the different possible formats for assembly instructions. The instructions and events which can alter the execution flow of an assembly program are studied in Section 10.5.

The second part of the chapter concerns a specific case study, where we build an instruction set for the P3 processor, which in the rest of the text is used as the main example. The P3 processor is a 16-bit microprogrammed processor solely designed for educational purposes, but which exhibits many of the characteristics of simple commercial processors. Section 10.6 describes the instruction set architecture of the P3, and Section 10.7 presents the encoding of the different types of instructions. Finally, Section 10.8 presents an assembler for the P3.

10.1 Programming Languages

As we saw in the previous chapter, a computer can be programmed using languages with very differing levels of abstraction. The lowest level of abstraction considered in this chapter is *machine language*. Each machine

Table 10.1   Machine language instructions for the P3 processor.

Address		Value	
Base 2	Base 16	Base 2	Base 16
0001000000000000	1000	1010111001110000	AE70
0001000000000001	1001	0000000001000000	0040
0001000000000010	1002	1000011001110000	8670
0001000000000011	1003	0000000010110000	00B0
0001000000000100	1004	1000011001110000	8670
0001000000000101	1005	0000000010110001	00B1
0001000000000110	1006	0100000000000001	4001
0001000000000111	1007	1010110001110000	AC70
0001000000001000	1008	1111000000000000	F000

language instruction is made up of a set of bits, directly interpretable by the processor. Take, for example, the sequence of machine language instructions for the P3 processor shown in Table 10.1, which adds three integers stored in the memory locations N1 = 0040h, N2 = 00B0h, N3 = 00B1h, and stores the complement of the result in the position N4 = F000h. This sequence of bits does not appear to have any meaning for a programmer, even though it specifies the operations to be carried out in an unambiguous manner. Indeed, a machine language program has the disadvantage that humans find it very hard to understand. For this reason, programming directly in machine language requires great use of memory and consultation of documents by programmers, which makes it very inefficient regarding the programmer time it requires.

Assembly language is at the level of abstraction immediately above. Each instruction in this language corresponds to a machine language instruction, but, instead of being specified as a set of zeros and ones, it is described using *mnemonics* and *symbolic names*. For example, the assembly instruction to add two numbers stored in the R1 and R2 registers and to deposit the resulting number in R1 is ADD R1,R2. For the programmer, it is much easier to memorise this instruction than its equivalent in machine language, which in the case of P3, is 1000011001000010b, or, 8642h. The program described in machine language in Table 10.1 corresponds to the program in assembly in the second column of Table 10.2.

Generally, in addition to the use of mnemonics for the instructions, assembly languages enable the definition of symbolic names for memory addresses, numerical constants and alphanumeric constants. This example directly uses the intended addresses, but it is possible to define symbolic names N1, N2, N3 and N4 to represent the values N1 = 0040h, N2 = 00B0h, N3 = 00B1h

Table 10.2   Correspondence between assembly and machine instructions.

Address	Assembly Code	Machine Code
1000h	MOV R1, M[0040h]	AE70
1001h		0040
1002h	ADD R1, M[00B0h]	8670
1003h		00B0
1004h	ADD R1, M[00B1h]	8670
1005h		00B1
1006h	NEG R1	4001
1007h	MOV M[F000h], R1	AC70
1008h		F000

Program 10.1.   Assembly program that adds three numbers located in memory.

```
ORIG    1000h
N1      EQU     0040h
N2      EQU     00B0h
N3      EQU     00B1h
N4      EQU     F000h

        MOV     R1, M[N1]
        ADD     R1, M[N2]
        ADD     R1, M[N3]
        NEG     R1
        MOV     M[N4], R1
```

and N4 = F000h using the assembly *directive* EQU. In the previous example, the program starts at address 1000h, which is specified in assembly using the directive ORIG. With the aid of these directives, the sequence of assembly instructions in Program 10.1 corresponds exactly to the sequence of machine instructions in Table 10.1.

Through analysis and comparison between the code in Program 10.1 and the machine instructions in Table 10.1, it is clear that, although both describe the same sequence of instructions, the code in assembly is much more understandable and easier to edit, debug and modify. Note that each instruction can correspond to one or more memory words, depending on its type and its operands. Directives are not translated directly into machine language instructions, but in some cases can still cause the occupation of one or more memory locations.

When programming in assembly, the programmer must, as if programming in machine language, have detailed knowledge of the architecture and the resources of the processor, since assembly instructions only make sense for that particular processor. Although similar to each other, assembly languages are different from processor to processor.

The translation of a program written in assembly to a program written in machine language is a fairly straightforward process since each assembly instruction corresponds to one, and only one, instruction in machine language. A programmer can make this translation manually, but usually, a program called *assembler* does the job. The assembler accepts a program written in assembly and generates a program in machine language, processing the directives and translating the instructions written in the source file. Section 10.8 describes in detail the operation of an assembler for the P3 processor.

As we saw in the previous chapter, programming a computer can be carried out using higher levels of abstraction that use high-level languages, which are, in most cases, processor independent. Examples are the languages *C*, *Python* and *Java*. Programs written in these languages have to be translated into assembly language and then into machine language, before processor execution. This translation process is much more elaborate than the one made by the assembler previously mentioned and is carried out by programs called *compilers*. In general, each instruction of a high-level program corresponds to various assembly instructions. In some cases, a high-level language can be interpreted directly by a program, the *interpreter*. In this case, there is no need for compilation, but this leads to a program execution which is considerably slower. *LISP* and *Scheme* are languages usually compiled, but which are often interpreted as there are very effective interpreters. Java is also executed in the interpreted mode, although the original program is, in this case, translated into an intermediate language which is close to a machine language (notwithstanding, critical parts of the code are automatically compiled to machine code at runtime).

10.2   Assembly Instructions

Since there is a direct correspondence between an *assembly instruction* and a *machine language instruction*, from now on we will use the term "instruction" to designate both. Normally the context is sufficient to indicate if this is a reference to a machine language instruction or an assembly instruction.

Each instruction is a combination of bits stored in memory which uniquely specifies a sequence of transfer operations between registers, to be executed by the processor. The execution of the instructions of a program follows the order in which they are listed in memory unless this execution sequence changes, either because of a control instruction or because the processor receives an external request and has to alter the instruction execution order. There are three main *classes of instructions*:

- *Data transfer instructions* move information from one location (register, memory address or input/output port) to another, without altering the original information.
- *Data manipulation instructions* apply an arithmetic or logic operator to the operand or operands, specified by their location, and store the result in the specified location.
- *Control instructions* can alter the normal sequence of instructions and define which is the next instruction to be executed.

Data transfer instructions are used to copy or save data. They are used to copy values to registers or memory address for future manipulation, to create various types of data structures, like arrays and lists, and also to carry out input and output operations.

In the P3 processor, the simplest data transfer instruction is the MOV instruction. For example, the instruction MOV R1,M[0040h] copies the content of memory address 0040h to register R1.

Data manipulation instructions are those that actually perform useful operations in a program. All processors support basic arithmetic instructions such as addition and subtraction. All processors also support basic logic operations, such as conjunction and disjunction, and shift operations. Many processors also execute more complex arithmetic operations such as multiplication, division and other mathematical functions, on integers or real numbers.

These instructions typically include instructions such as ADD, SUB, INC, MULT, AND, OR and XOR. For example, in the P3 processor, the instruction ADD R1,M[00B0h] adds the content of register R1 to the value in the memory address 00B0h and stores the result in register R1.

A special register, the *program counter*, defines the instruction to be executed, following the sequence in the program. Most processors call this register PC. This register contains the memory address of the next instruction that the processor executes. Transfer and data manipulation instructions normally increment the program counter to the value corresponding to the memory address where the following instruction starts in the normal sequence of execution, so that this instruction is the next one that is executed.

Control instructions can alter the instruction execution order, unconditionally or, alternatively, only if the previous operation produces a result which satisfies certain conditions. More specifically, the control instructions can specify the address of the next instruction to be executed, by altering the PC, the program counter register. Section 10.5 studies these instructions in more detail. With this type of instruction it is possible to take decisions based on the results of previous calculations or external events, and so they are essential for the correct operation of any program.

An example of a control instruction in the P3 processor is the instruction JMP (jump). For example JMP 00CCh makes the instruction in memory location 00CCh the next instruction that the processor executes.

The combination of bits which corresponds to each instruction uniquely encodes the operations to be executed, the operands and the location to store the result. Each instruction must, therefore, contain three components in its structure:

- The *operation code* (or *opcode*) which specifies the operation to execute. For example, in the P3 processor, the code to add two numbers is represented by the combination of bits 100001b.
- The specification of the operands to which the operation should be applied to. For example, when adding register R1 to register R2 in a processor with eight registers, it is possible to use 6 bits $(3 + 3)$ to represent the two operands, which would correspond to the sequence 001010b. The number of operands for each instruction varies with its type and the processor. In this aspect, there are processors with different approaches, from the ones where the instructions do not have explicit operands (all the operands are stored in pre-established locations) to processors where the instructions take one, two or three operands.
- Specification of the location of the operands (register or memory) where to store the result of the operation. For example, to store the results in register R1 in a processor with eight registers, the sequence of bits 001 can be used to specify register R1.

For example, in the P3 processor, the instruction ADD R1,M[N2], in the example in Section 10.1, is encoded in two 16-bit words. The first word contains the operation code (100001b) in the most significant bits. In the three least significant bits, it also contains the number of the register which should be used as the first operand and as the destination for the result (001b). The other bits specify, using an encoding which is explained in

Section 10.7.3, that the second operand is in the memory address stored in the second word of this instruction. Therefore, this instruction is encoded with the words 8670h and 00B0h, which correspond to the binary values 1000011001110000b and 0000000010110000b.

In practice, the specification of operands and the location of the result can be more complex as the data manipulation instructions and the transfer instructions operate on values originating in one of the following possible positions:

- internal registers of the processor;
- the instruction itself, which specifies a constant value;
- memory locations;
- input/output ports.

More complex forms of encoding make it possible to specify any of these locations flexibly. Section 10.7 describes the encoding mechanism for the P3 processor instructions.

Many commercial processors can execute more complex instructions. For example, the 8086 processor has an instruction which copies a certain number of memory positions from one memory location to another memory location. An instruction of this type requires at least three operands: two to specify the origin and destination addresses, and one to define the number of memory positions to copy.

Often one or more operands are fixed and predefined for instructions like this, to avoid the need to encode all the operands in the instruction. This addressing, called *implicit addressing mode*, is also used in simpler but very commonly used instructions, such as stack manipulation instructions, described in Section 10.3.5. There are also processors, called *stack processors*, where all the operands are in a stack, and all the arithmetic operations operate on the two operands stored on top of the stack. These operands are therefore implicitly specified. In other machines, one of the operands is always a particular register, known as the *accumulator*, so that an arithmetic operation only needs to have one explicitly defined operand.

10.3   Specification of Operands

There are four possible sources for the operands of an instruction: internal registers of the processor, the instruction itself which specifies a constant, a location in memory and input/output ports.

10.3.1   *Internal Registers*

The use of operands in registers is advantageous for two reasons. First, access to data stored in internal registers is much faster than access to data in memory. Second, there are fewer internal registers than memory locations, so fewer bits need to be used to specify a register than a memory location. Therefore, instructions that use just registers need fewer bits for their encoding, occupy less memory and are fetched and executed more quickly.

There are various ways to organise internal registers. In their simplest form, they are simply a set of registers, with the same functionality, structured in a register file like the one specified in Section 6.7.3, and identified by their number. The P3 processor has its registers organised in this way.

Other processors have more complex organisations. There can be registers with specific functions, which are always used for certain operations. Some processors have a special register called the *accumulator*, which stores the result of operations and is also frequently used to specify the address in a memory access. Complex processors, such as the Intel x86 family, have various registers with specific functions, such as handling character strings in memory and memory management.

Even simple processors with a very regular organisation, often have two registers for specific utilisations, which may not be directly accessible to the programmer. These two registers are the *program counter* (PC), with its functionality described in more detail in Section 10.5 and the *stack pointer* (SP), which we will discuss in Section 10.3.5.

10.3.2   *Constants Specified in the Instruction*

Almost all processors can execute instructions in which one or more operands are constant values, specified in the instruction. For example, the instruction ADD R1,0005h adds the value 5, a value specified in the instruction, to the content of register R1.

Although this method may appear as efficient, or even more efficient, than the use of a register to store the value, in many cases, that is not true. Indeed, specifying a constant in the instruction often involves the use of one more memory word to encode the instruction storing the constant.

Therefore, to load this value, it is normally necessary to carry out an extra access to memory,[1] which can be slower than the access to an internal register. In this way, the use of the constant specified in the instruction is equivalent, regarding speed, to the access to an operand stored in memory.

10.3.3 *Memory and Input/Output Ports*

There are two possible ways of accessing data from input/output ports. One philosophy, adopted in many processor families, consists in using a set of instructions intended only for data input and output. This solution, equivalent to having independent input/outputs from the memory system (*independent IO*) was adopted in many processors and, particularly, in the Intel x86 family. In this case, there is a distinct address space for input/output operations. Access to a given input/output port is specified by placing a value in the processor address bits (or in part of them) and controlling one or more additional lines which specify that the operation is an input or output operation and not a memory access.

Alternatively, it is possible to consider that the *input/output ports are mapped to the memory space* of the processor, with the data available in the ports handled through the same operations which handle memory data. This solution reduces the complexity of the instruction set, with the main disadvantage being that it reduces the addressable memory space of the processor. When this solution is adopted, the reading of data from an input port proceeds as if accessing a particular memory location, while writing data to output ports is executed as if handling a write operation in certain memory locations. It is up to the devices external to the processor to be able to distinguish, from the correct decoding of the addresses, accesses made to input/output ports and accesses made to memory. The reduced complexity of the instruction set will correspond to greater sophistication of the memory system architecture, as we will study in Chapter 13. When this solution is adopted, the input/output instructions may use all forms of available addressing modes, with the ports handled by the programmer as if they were memory positions. This approach also has the additional advantage of being able to process data directly from (or to) input/output ports.

---

[1] The loading of the constant may be faster if the specification of the instruction does not require an extra word to specify the constant.

Memory mapped input/output is the solution we adopted for the P3 processor, where all input and output port accesses are carried out using data transfer operations.

The access to operands in memory or input/output ports requires the indication of the address of the memory word, or the port desired. This can be achieved in several ways. The different alternatives to specifying the location of an operand, i.e., the possible addressing modes, are studied in detail in the next section.

10.3.4   *Addressing Modes*

The choice of the *addressing modes* supported by a processor has a major impact on its internal structure and the flexibility of the instruction set. Let us consider a memory access where the content of the register RX, the value of a word W or both, are used to specify the location of the operand. There are different ways of using the value of RX and W to define the value of the operand or its location. If the operand is in a memory location, its address is called the *effective address*. Table 10.3 summarises some commonly used addressing modes.

In *register addressing mode*, the operand is the value stored in an internal register. This addressing mode is efficient, since, as we mentioned before, obtaining an operand from a register is more efficient than obtaining an operand from memory.

In *register indirect addressing mode*, the content of the specified register indicates the effective memory address where the data is located, in the case of a read operation, or where to store the data, in a write operation.

In *immediate addressing mode*, the value of the operand is encoded in the actual instruction, which uses additional memory words where necessary.

Table 10.3   Main addressing modes used.

Addressing Mode	Operation
Register	op $\leftarrow$ RX
Register indirect	op $\leftarrow$ M[RX]
Immediate	op $\leftarrow$ W
Direct	op $\leftarrow$ M[W]
Indexed	op $\leftarrow$ M[RX+W]
Relative	op $\leftarrow$ M[PC+W]
Based	op $\leftarrow$ M[SP+W]
Indirect	op $\leftarrow$ M[M[W]]
Double register indirect	op $\leftarrow$ M[M[RX]]
Implicit	

This addressing mode can only be used to read operands since its use to define the location of the result of an operation implies a write to the memory area where the machine code is, which would alter the code. Although this is possible, it is highly dangerous and is never used.

In *indexed addressing mode*, the content of the register indicated in the instruction, RX, is added to a value encoded in the actual instruction to obtain the effective address to be used by the operation to read the operand, store the result in the memory, or both.

In *direct addressing mode*, the effective memory address to be used by the instruction to read the operand and/or store the result is specified in the actual instruction.

The *relative addressing mode* and the *based addressing mode* are particular cases of indexed addressing, where the RX register is PC or SP. In relative addressing, the RX register is the program counter, PC, and in the based addressing mode, the RX register is the pointer to the stack, SP.

The following two modes in Table 10.3 are less used and only supported by a small number of processors. In *indirect addressing mode*, the value specified in the instruction indicates the memory location which stores the effective address. In *double register indirect addressing mode*, the content of the register points, in a similar way, the memory location which stores the effective address of the operand. These two addressing modes, therefore, require two memory accesses, one to get the effective address and the other to obtain the operand (or store the result), and so they are considerably less used than the others described above.

In the *implicit addressing mode*, various registers not specified in the instruction are used to define the position of the operands. Since the particular use made of this addressing mode varies according to the instruction using it, it is not possible to systematise its application in the same way as we have done for the other addressing modes mentioned above.

The instructions of the P3 processor can specify operands using any of the options in Table 10.3, except for the indirect and double register indirect modes, which are not supported by this processor. However, in the P3 processor, only one of the operands can use one of the more complex modes, while the other operand has to use the register addressing mode, an option which is very common in commercial processors.

Different commercial processors show different philosophies concerning the addressing modes they support and the way the address of the operands of the instruction is obtained from the data encoded in the instruction.

In particular, the use of the concept of segmented memory, used, for example, in the Intel processors, implies the existence of registers which are implicit in the addressing process.

10.3.5 *Use of Stacks*

A widely used option to access and store operands in memory employs a *stack*. A stack is a contiguous set of memory locations whose access is under the control of a register called *stack pointer*, generally referred as SP. These memory positions can only be accessed in sequence, one by one, from the top of the stack, both to place a value (a push operation) or to remove a value (a pop operation). The stack contents goes from the bottom, which is a fixed memory position defined initially, to the top, which changes when executing a push or a pop. Care must be taken for never exceeding the bottom position when placing and removing data involving the stack. In some processors, the base of the stack is specifically defined, and accesses beyond that limit are prevented, but in others, such as the P3, this verification is not carried out by the processor hardware. The simplest form of use only allows access to the value stored on top of the stack, which corresponds to the last value placed there. Given this, it is possible to store a value on top of the stack using the instruction PUSH (or similar) or to recover the value on top of the stack through the instruction POP (or similar).

When a new value is stored in the stack, the value of the SP register is incremented and when a value is removed from the stack, the value of the pointer is decremented, as shown in Figure 10.1. In this way, the value of the stack pointer always indicates the memory location which represents the top of the stack. Consider the sequence of operations illustrated in this

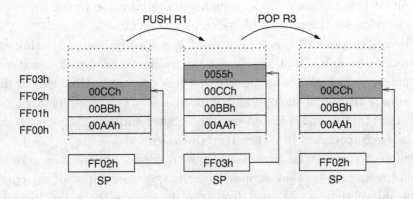

Fig. 10.1 Example of use of the processor stack.

figure. Initially, register R1 has the value 0055h and the stack pointer (SP) the value FF02h. After the instruction PUSH R1, the value of the SP register is incremented to FF03h, which is the memory location where the last value placed in the stack is stored. The instruction POP R3 results in loading R3 with the value found on top of the stack (0055h) and decrementing the value of the SP register. Note that, although not shown in the figure, the value of memory location FF03h keeps the value 0055h after the POP operation. However, from a logical point of view, this value is no longer in the stack, and so is not represented.

There are numerous applications for the stack of the processor. One of the most common uses the stack as a temporary space to store register values when the program needs them for other operations. In this way, the programmer can decide to place the contents of registers R1, R2 and R3 on the stack, to free these registers for some operation. When it is complete, the values can be popped from the stack, in reverse order, to restore the original values in the registers.

Another common application for the stack is passing parameters for subroutines. Section 10.5.2 provides a detailed description of this application.

Given that the stack has numerous applications, some processors may have several stacks that may or may not be accessible to the programmer. In this case, there is more than one stack pointer register.

Although the usage mechanism of a stack is very simple, it is necessary to take some precautions for it to be correctly used and not interfere with the correct operation of the processor.

First, the stack must use an area of memory not used by any other program or subroutine. To ensure this exclusive use, the programmer must consider the initialisation of the stack pointer carefully. The initial value of SP defines implicitly the base of the stack. The memory area used goes from the base to the top of the stack. Under normal usage conditions, the programmer must guarantee that the top of the stack will never reach the areas reserved for the code or the data. It is also necessary to ensure that there is a data removal operation from the top of the stack for each data insertion operation in it. If there is no such correspondence, the stack pointer value will increase (or decrease) without stopping, and write operations will corrupt memory areas reserved for other usages.

Also note that the logic of operation of the PUSH and POP do not change if the stack increases in the reverse direction to that shown in Figure 10.1, that is, if the processor decrements the SP register when placing a value on the stack, instead of incrementing it. In a similar way, the value of the SP register may be altered before or after the actual memory write. In the first case, the SP register points to the first free position, and in the second case, it points to the value on top of the stack.

In the P3 processor, the value of the SP register is decremented after a PUSH operation. This decrement is carried out after writing the value, such that the SP register always points to the next free position.

10.3.6   *Types of Operands*

Unlike in high-level programming languages, there are no data types in assembly language. References to data in assembly instructions always point to a set of bits, and it is the way the program uses this set of bits that assigns meaning to it.

For example, the instruction MOV R1,M[N1] from Program 10.1 loads the value 0040h in R1. You cannot assign a meaning to this value just by inspecting this instruction. However, this value had a precise meaning for the programmer when developing the program. This interpretation can be deduced from the context, that is, by the manner this value is manipulated in the instructions before and afterwards. Comments are also a good tool to provide that kind of information.

Possible meanings for the value 0040h are:

Set of bits: The 16 bits which make up the value 0040h have no relation to each other. They represent 16 binary variables which may take two values, 0 or 1, and in this case, their value is 0000000001000000b. In general, logic instructions are used to manipulate this value.

Integer value: Most commonly, this value is the representation of an integer value in unsigned natural binary or 2's complement representation, to be manipulated by arithmetic instructions. In this case, 0040h represents the value 64 in decimal.

Real value represented in fixed-point: As noted in Section 5.4, an integer is a particular case of fixed point representation, where the point is immediate to the right of the least significant bit. When putting the point in any other position, we alter the numeric value, but, by being careful in the way referred to in Section 5.4.2, it is possible to use arithmetic instructions for its processing. For example, by putting 2 bits to the right of the point, 0040h represents the value 16.0 in decimal.

Real value in floating-point: This case is more complex and requires a specialised set of assembly instructions to manipulate it. Nowadays, almost all processors use the standard format for the mantissa and the exponent (as in Section 5.5). This format requires a minimum of 32 bits, such that the value 0040h, using only 16 bits, does not have a valid meaning.

Code word: The value may correspond to a word of a code. The most usual case will be the representation of characters using ASCII code or ISO-8859, as defined in Section 1.3.4. The value 0040h represents the character «@».

Compression of different types: Sometimes, to save on space, a value may be the result of the compression of two, or more, variables, possibly with different types. A classic example is the representation of characters. The ISO-8859 code is an eight-bit code; therefore using a 16-bit value to represent a character in this code means a waste of 50% of space. Thus, it is typical to compress two characters into one 16-bit value. The value 0040h has the character «@» (40h) in the least significant byte and the character NUL (00h) in the rest of the word. The same happens for numerical values. For example, 0040h may represent two eight-bit values, the value 64 in the least significant half of the word and the value 0 in the upper half. As mentioned, any combination of variable types is possible. The disadvantage of this compression process is that, before manipulating values, it is necessary to carry out their decompression, which creates some overhead.

10.4 Instruction Encoding

Each assembly instruction is represented by a set of bits that specifies the operation and its operands, including the respective addressing mode. There is some freedom in terms of the number of operands and their addressing modes that the representation may accommodate, which defines a compromise between the bit-size of an instruction and the flexibility of the assembly language (which may impact the number of instructions of a program).

To analyse the different possibilities of *instructions encoding* for a processor, let us consider a processor with the following configuration:

- Registers: the processor has eight internal 16-bit registers, numbered 0 to 7.

- Memory: the processor accesses 2^{16} words, which means that each memory access needs a 16-bit address. This corresponds to a total addressing capacity of 64K 16-bit words or 128K byte.
- Import/output ports: the input/output ports are mapped in memory space and are accessed through normal data transfer instructions.
- Instructions: the instruction set contains 40 instructions.

Suppose that, for this hypothetical processor, each two operand instruction can have any of the possible locations as origin and destination, and let us analyse what the impact of this option has on the encoding of the instructions. We can, therefore, derive how many bits are necessary to encode each instruction:

- Operation code: since there are forty different instructions, 6 bits will be required to encode the operation to be carried out.
- Operands: each one of the operands can be specified, using one of the four first addressing modes specified in Table 10.3, hence 2 bits can be used to indicate which addressing mode. For some addressing modes, it is necessary to specify a register and a memory address.

With these options, and if uniform encoding for all the instructions is wanted, this results in the encoding shown in Figure 10.2.

The advantage of a uniform format of this type is clear since this approach provides total flexibility in the specification of operands, which can be at any location. Note, however, that this encoding requires a total of 69 bits for each instruction, which means that each instruction occupies five memory words, that is, 10 byte.

Let us consider, for example, Program 10.2, which, using instructions of this hypothetical processor, adds the content of the memory locations N1, N2 and N3, and stores the result, complemented, in memory location N4. Note that although this program only contains three instructions, the corresponding machine code uses 15 memory words.

Regarding performance, this option turns out to be disadvantageous, since as machine language programs occupy more memory than is necessary,

Code	Result			Operand 1			Operand 2		
	Mode	Reg.	Addr.	Mode	Reg.	Addr.	Mode	Reg.	Addr.
6	2	3	16	2	3	16	2	3	16

Fig. 10.2 Encoding of an instruction with three operands specified with any of the four permitted addressing modes.

Program 10.2 Assembly program that adds three numbers in memory, for a processor accepting complex addressing modes for all the operands.

```
ADD   R1, M[N1], M[N2]
ADD   R1, R1, M[N3]
NEG   M[N4], R1
```

Code	Direction	Mode	Reg.	Reg.	Addr.
6	1	2	3	3	16

Fig. 10.3 Encoding of an instruction in which one of the operands has to be addressed using a register.

they also become slower. Indeed, the greater flexibility of the permitted addressing modes is counterbalanced by the time it takes to load from memory and to execute one instruction.

It is, therefore, advantageous to restrict the number of operands and the permitted addressing modes, or, at least, have instructions with more limited addressing modes. The commonly adopted restriction consists in forcing the result of the operation to be stored in the same location as the first operand. Although this entails the destruction of the value stored in this operand, this restriction considerably reduces the number of bits necessary to encode each instruction.

Additionally, it is possible to force at least one of the operands to be available in a register. Again, this helps to reduce the number of bits necessary to encode the instruction, although it entails a considerable restriction on the type of performable operations.

With these restrictions, it is possible to use a more compact format to represent each instruction. It is necessary to use one direction bit indicating which of the first or the second operand use the unrestricted addressing mode. For example, the instruction ADD M[R1+N1],R2 has the value of this bit equal to 1 to indicate that the generic addressing mode is applied to the first operand and, consequently, to the location of the result.

With this approach, it is now possible to use the format described in Figure 10.3. Each instruction now only uses two memory words. However, it is no longer possible to represent an instruction like ADD R1,M[N1],M[N2]. However, it is possible to represent all the instructions used in the example on page 420, resulting in Program 10.3 occupying only ten memory words to carry out the same task, against 15 in the previous version.

In practice, it is usually necessary to use more than one format to encode instructions. Therefore, an instruction in which the two operands

Program 10.3   Assembly program that adds three numbers in memory, for a processor accepting complex addressing modes only for one operand.

```
MOV   R1, M[N1]
ADD   R1, M[N2]
ADD   R1, M[N3]
NEG   R1
MOV   M[N4], R1
```

Code	Reg.	Reg.	Reg.
6	3	3	3

Fig. 10.4   Encoding of an instruction with three operands in registers.

Code	Reg.	Addr.
6	3	16

Fig. 10.5   Encoding of LOAD and STORE instructions.

are registers can be encoded in a single memory word, while an instruction which uses an indexed or immediate addressing mode (among others) may need two memory words. In these cases, the value of a bit or combination of bits in the first word specifies the addressing mode and whether there is a second word.

In some processors, where one of the fundamental aims is that the most common instructions are encoded as uniformly as possible in a small space, although losing flexibility, all the arithmetic and logic operations must be carried out between registers. In this case, all memory accesses are done using specific data transfer operations (often named LOAD and STORE), and therefore the architecture of these processors is referred to as *load/store architecture*.

In a processor of this type, instructions which specify arithmetic operations may use the format in Figure 10.4, and so it is possible to encode instructions such as ADD R1,R2,R3 in a single memory word (more on this in Section 15.2).

The LOAD and STORE instructions need to use another format, shown in Figure 10.5, given that they specify only one register, but need to specify an address.

The greater efficiency to encode arithmetic and logic instructions in load/store architectures has a high cost, since they need to load all the operands in registers (using LOAD instructions, or similar) before

Program 10.4 Assembly program that adds three numbers in memory, for a processor of the type load/store.

```
LOAD    R1, M[N1]
LOAD    R2, M[N2]
LOAD    R3, M[N3]
ADD     R4, R1, R2
ADD     R4, R4, R3
NEG     R4, R4
STORE   M[N4], R4
```

carrying out any operation. In the same way, when it is necessary to store the result in memory, it is explicitly necessary to execute a STORE operation.

In a processor of this type, the task of adding the three memory locations and complementing the result, used as an example above, could be implemented by Program 10.4.

Given that the LOAD and STORE instructions use two memory words, while the arithmetic operations use only one, this code occupies 11 memory words.

As we can see from these examples, the choice of philosophy to adopt for encoding instructions involves many restrictions and tradeoffs and normally has a considerable impact on the final performance of the processor. In Section 10.7 we will study in detail the instruction encoding formats for the P3 processor.

10.5 Program Control Instructions

Processors execute instructions stored in consecutive memory addresses sequentially unless this execution flow is interrupted under two conditions: the execution of a control instruction or when an interrupt is serviced.

10.5.1 *Jump Instructions*

The simplest control instructions are *unconditional jumps*, designated in assembly language by JUMP or BRANCH. Unconditional jumps specify the address of the next instruction to execute, changing the value on the PC. In assembly language, this address is often defined by using a symbolic name. Therefore, for example, the P3 processor instruction sequence shown in Program 10.5 represents an infinite loop which continually increments the value of register R1.

Program 10.5.   Example of utilisation of the unconditional jump.

```
Label1:  INC   R1
         BR    Label1
```

Program 10.6.   Example of utilisation of the conditional jump.

```
         DEC   R1
         BR.Z  Label
         MOV   R1, 55AAh
Label:   ADD   R2,R1
```

10.5.1.1   *Conditional jumps*

In many cases, it is necessary to transfer control only when meeting a given condition. For example, consider that the program needs to leave a cycle when the value stored in a given register that is being decremented reaches the value 0. In these cases *conditional jump* instructions are used. For example, in the P3 processor, the instruction BR.Z Label transfers control to the instruction with the label Label, only if the last arithmetic or logic operation executed produced the result 0.

The code extract shown in Program 10.6 shows the use of conditional jump instructions.

The execution of instruction DEC decrements the value of R1. If the value that results from this operation is equal to 0, the instruction BR.Z Label transfers control to the instruction with label Label. If not, the following instruction is executed. In this case, it is the instruction which loads register R1 with the value 55AAh.

It is common to make the jump condition depend on the last operation carried out since this avoids the need to specify the location of the value to be tested. Thus, it is necessary to store the flags of the processor in a register which keeps the value of the conditions which can be tested by control instructions. This register is the *status register* (SR). The stored status bits are called *flags*. In principle, each condition corresponds to a flag. The conditions which can be tested by instructions of this type include the following:

- **Zero** (Z): this condition is true if the result of the last operation was zero.
- **Negative** (N): this condition is true if the result of the last operation was negative.
- **Carry** (C): this condition is true if the result of the last arithmetic operation resulted in a carry.

Program 10.7. Effects of instruction SUB in the values of the flags.

```
        MOV    R1, 0003h
        SUB    R1, 0004h
        BR.Z   Labl1
        BR.N   Labl2
Labl1:  NOP
Labl2:  NOP
```

- **Overflow** (O): this condition is true if the result of the last operation exceeded the representation capacity of the processor.
- **Positive** (P): this condition is true if the result of the last operation was strictly positive.

As an example, consider the sequence of instructions in Program 10.7. The instruction SUB R1,0004h stores the result, -1, in the same register R1. This operation activates the negative flag, N, since the value obtained has the most significant bit at 1. At the same time, it places the flags Z, P and O at 0, since the result is not zero, is not positive, and did not cause a non-representable value. Note that the carry bit, C, is also placed at 0, since, as we noted in Section 8.4.3, in a subtraction C represents the complement of the borrow bit.

In this way, the instruction BR.Z Labl1 will not transfer control to the instruction with the label Labl1 since the flag Z is inactive. Now the instruction BR.N Labl2 will transfer control to the instruction with the label Labl2, given that the flag N is active. Note that only data manipulation instructions involving the arithmetic and logic unit (Section 8.4) alter the values of the flags.

Many processors also allow jump conditions which test various flags of the processor, in addition to those we have mentioned. For example, testing if the result of an operation was even, or if a given internal processor condition is met.

10.5.1.2 *Absolute jumps and relative jumps*

There are two possible ways of specifying the jump address. The first option is to specify this address in an *absolute jump*, directly providing an address in memory which contains the next instruction to be executed. The second option is to use a *relative jump*, where the constant in the instruction is added to the PC. When using this possibility, fewer bits are often used than those necessary to describe an arbitrary memory address, since jump destinations are often memory positions relatively close to the address of the jump instruction.

The advantage of the first approach is to enable any memory address to be specified, independently of whether it is close to the jump instruction or not. The second approach, besides saving space when encoding instructions, allows the program to be *relocatable*. This means that the program continues to operate even if it is copied to memory positions other than where it was initially located.

In practice, many processors support both specifying methods, with the assembler choosing in a way which is transparent to the programmer, what type of jump results from the encoding of a given instruction.

In the P3 processor, there are two types of jump instructions. The BR instruction is a relative jump, and the specified value is added to the content of the PC. The JMP instruction specifies an absolute jump, and the specified value is the destination address to load into the PC register.

Note that, from the programmer's point of view, these two instructions are practically indistinguishable, since the assembler has the responsibility of encoding the instruction. However, in certain particular cases, there may be an interest in using one of the jump types, especially in cases when it is of interest to relocate machine code, without using the assembler.

10.5.2 *Subroutine Calls*

A well-structured program is typically made up of program blocks which carry out a clearly defined role and that may be reused many times in a program. In assembly, this modular program structure is achieved through the use of subroutines.

A *subroutine*, sometimes called abbreviatedly *routine* or *procedure*, is called through a CALL instruction, which, like a JMP, transfers control to the initial instruction of the subroutine. Additionally, however, the CALL instruction stores the address where the subroutine was called so that when it is finished, it is possible to continue with the instruction following the CALL. A subroutine ends with a return instruction (RET or RETURN), which transfers control to where the CALL was made.

Although different processors adopt different alternatives, a very common solution is to store the return address on top of the stack. In this way, the return instruction simply has to restore the program counter to the value on top of the stack, for the normal execution sequence to be re-established. Other processors use more complex mechanisms to improve performance, but

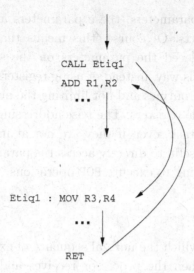

```
                    CALL Etiq1
                    ADD R1,R2
                    ...




         Etiq1 : MOV R3,R4

                    ...

                    RET
```

Fig. 10.6   Illustration of the subroutine call process.

a study of these alternatives lies outside the scope of this book. Figure 10.6 shows the instruction execution sequence during the subroutine call and return from a subroutine which takes place in the P3 processor.

In this example, the CALL Lab11 instruction transfers control to the instruction with the label Lab11, loading this value into the PC register. The address value of the instruction ADD R1,R2, which is the instruction following the CALL instruction, is placed on top of the stack and the value of the SP register is decremented to point to the next memory location.[2] After executing all the subroutine instructions, the execution of the RET loads the PC with the return address that is on top of the stack and updates the SP. For correct operation, it is important that the RET instruction finds the stack in the same state as it was when the subroutine was called, so that the return address is correctly retrieved. During the subroutine execution the number of PUSH and POP instructions must, thus, be the same.

The subroutines may use *parameters*, the values of which are defined by the main program when calling the subroutine. Passing parameters to subroutines may be carried out in different ways, and we will analyse this in more detail in Section 11.1.4. A common way to pass parameters is the stack of the processor. In this case, the convention is that if a subroutine accepts

---

[2]In the P3 processor, the processor stack is inverted, with the value of the stack pointer decremented when a PUSH instruction is executed.

a certain number of parameters, these parameters are on top of the stack when the routine starts. Of course, this means that the program calling the subroutine has placed the parameters on the stack before calling it. Passing parameters this way, instead of using registers, has the advantage of enabling recursive subroutines and not limiting the number of parameters to the number of available registers. The base addressing mode provides access to the values in the stack, even if they are not at its top. This addressing mode is particularly useful to directly access the parameters of a subroutine, without explicitly having to execute POP operations.

10.5.3 *Interrupts*

Another situation in which the normal sequence of execution of instructions is altered happens when the processor receives and answers an *interrupt request*.

In many systems, the processor has to react to external events, which signal the need to carry out some specific processing or input/output operation. For example, a peripheral device may wish to indicate to the processor that a key was pressed or the reception of a word at a serial port.

An alternative to the use of the interruption system is to ensure that the processor regularly checks the value of an input/output line or lines. This periodic sampling is called polling. The use of this strategy implies a considerable overhead for the processor since it is necessary to test repeatedly the existence of data to read in one or more input/output ports at time intervals which cannot be too long, as discussed in Section 14.6.1.

For this reason, the overwhelming majority of processors allow an external device to signal, in some way, that the program should be interrupted and that the control should pass to a piece of software called *interrupt handler*. In complex systems, there is a device, the *interrupt controller*, that centralises requests from various sources, encodes them, and sends them to the processor, according to its priorities.

Although the exact mechanism through which the interrupts are signalled, identified and handled varies from processor to processor, the following high-level description applies to most commercial processors and also to the P3.

First, each processor has one or more *interrupt lines*, which are activated by external devices. The number of lines does not, however, correspond to the total number of sources of possible interruptions, which is frequently much higher. This situation is possible because, after having received an indication that the processor will serve the interrupt, the device uses one of the external buses to identify which interrupt was activated. In this way it is possible, for example, to use only one interrupt line and eight data bus lines to signal 256 different interrupt types.

After receiving the interrupt and the number which identifies it, the processor accesses a table that indicates the subroutine address which must be used to handle that particular request. Execution control is therefore transferred to this subroutine, after saving the content of the program counter and other information about the state of the processor. This information must include the value of the flags of the processor, but may also include the value of other internal registers, the content of which may be destroyed by the interrupt subroutine. Saving this information is necessary so that execution can continue, without alterations, with the instruction that follows the one being executed when the interrupt was received, after the interrupt handling routine terminates.

Note that, unlike subroutine calls, external interrupts can occur at any moment, without the programmer's prediction. Therefore, they may arise, for example, between the execution of an arithmetic instruction and the conditional jump instruction testing the result of that instruction. This unpredictability is the reason why it is necessary to save the status register before the execution of the interrupt routine.

In the P3 processor, as with most other processors, the programmer may activate a flag to prevent the handling of interrupts. This may be necessary for program segments where the occurrence of an interrupt may cause an undesirable behaviour.

There are numerous variations on this mode of operation and various operating details which vary from processor to processor, but the general operating principle is common to all of them. The interrupt mechanism for the P3 processor will be studied in more detail when describing the instructions which control their handling.

One existing functionality in many processors consists of providing an instruction (for example, INT or TRAP) which accepts an argument (the interrupt number) which causes the processor to behave as if it had received an interrupt with that number. Although a subroutine call instruction may in principle substitute this instruction, certain differences in the operating details are sufficient to justify its existence as a separate instruction. This type of instruction is also useful at the *debugging* stage of a program, where the interrupt routines may be used to analyse the value of various registers and internal variables which may not be accessible in another way.

In general, interrupts may have three distinct origins. They may be external, caused by hardware or they may be internal, triggered by a TRAP instruction. In processors more complex than the P3, they may result from the detection of *exceptions* by the hardware, such as an incorrect memory access or execution of a division by zero.

10.6   Instruction Set for the P3 Processor

The P3 processor has 16 internal registers, R0 to R15, of which only eight (R0 to R7) may be used directly by assembly instructions. The P3 processor is a 16-bit processor, which means that it manipulates 16 bits of data in each operation.

In this processor both the data registers and the memory are also organised into 16-bit words, so a data transfer operation always handles a 16-bit value. In other processors, the number of bits transferred in data handling operations and memory accesses is not always equal to the number of bits of the registers. For example, on the Intel 8088 processor, the internal registers are 16 bits, but the memory transfers are made in blocks of 8 bits, to simplify the organisation of the external memory. In most cases, however, a N-bit processor can transfer and handle data in blocks of N bits, both internally and externally.

In the P3 processor, R0 is a fictitious register that always contains the value 0. This artifice is very useful, since programs use the constant 0 often, and access to a register is quicker than access to a constant stored in memory. R8 to R15 have specific utilisations that we will study in Chapter 12. These registers perform specific functions, and cannot be directly manipulated by general assembly instructions. Two of these registers, the PC and SP, are available to the programmer when using memory accesses carried out with relative and base addressing modes. The programmer has access to the registers R1 to R7 for general use. There is also the status register (SR) which stores the flags of the processor.

The P3 processor provides all the instructions for data transfer, handling and control which are common to simple commercial processors. These instructions can be classified into the following classes:

- Arithmetic instructions: instructions which apply an arithmetic operator to the operand or operands. Examples of arithmetic operations with two operands are addition, subtraction and multiplication. Arithmetic operations of one operand include the increment and decrement operations.

- Logic instructions: instructions which apply a logic operator to the operand or operands. Examples of logic operations for two operands are disjunction and conjunction, while the Boolean complement is a logic operation with only one operand.

- Shift instructions: instructions which apply a shift operation to one register. The shifts can be to the right, to the left, circular or not, arithmetic or logic.

- Control instructions: instructions which control the instruction sequence executed by the processor, possibly based on the result of previous operations.

- Transfer instructions: instructions which copy or move data from one location to another.

- Generic instructions: grouped in this category are a set of instructions which execute various operations about the state of the processor, which will be analysed in more detail later.

Table 10.4 contain the mnemonics for the instructions available in the P3 processor.

10.6.1 *Arithmetic Instructions*

The P3 processor provides the arithmetic operations described in Table 10.5.

All the arithmetic instructions available act on 16-bit operands, which, when they represent signed numbers, are represented in 2's complement notation. In all operations, except multiplication and division, the result is also 16-bit wide, and it is stored in the location of the first operand, destroying

Table 10.4 P3 processor instruction set.

Arithmetic	Logic	Shift	Control	Transfer	Generic
NEG	COM	SHR	BR	MOV	NOP
INC	AND	SHL	BR.cond	MVBH	ENI
DEC	OR	SHRA	JMP	MVBL	DSI
ADD	XOR	SHLA	JMP.cond	XCH	STC
ADDC	TEST	ROR	CALL	PUSH	CLC
SUB		ROL	CALL.cond	POP	CMC
SUBB		RORC	RET		
CMP		ROLC	RETN		
MUL			RTI		
DIV			INT		

Table 10.5 Arithmetic instructions for the P3 processor.

Instruction	Mnemonic	Example	
Arithmetic complement	NEG	NEG	R1
Increment	INC	INC	M[R2]
Decrement	DEC	DEC	M[R3+A5A5h]
Add	ADD	ADD	R3, M[R5+4]
Add with carry	ADDC	ADDC	R3, M[R6]
Subtract	SUB	SUB	R3, M[R5+4]
Subtract with borrow	SUBB	SUBB	R1, R2
Compare	CMP	CMP	R1, R2
Multiply	MUL	MUL	R3, R4
Divide	DIV	DIV	R3, R4

the previous value. For example, the instruction ADD R1,R2 executes the operation R1 ← R1 + R2.

In the case of multiplication, the result naturally has 32 bits and is stored in the locations which were used to specify the operands, with the most significant part stored in the location of the first operand. In the case of division, the result is stored in the location of the first operand and the remainder in the location of the second operands. This design option means that the operands of multiplication and division cannot be of the immediate type. Furthermore, the algorithm used for these operations means that the result only makes sense when the operands are unsigned numbers. For the same reasons, the two operands cannot be the same operand, which means that an instruction MUL R1,R1, if used, will result in an incorrect value.

To simplify arithmetic operations with operands of more than 16 bits, add and subtraction operations with carry are also available. The carry bit, C, is a flag generated by the arithmetic logic unit, and its value is set to 1 when there is a carry in an arithmetic or shift operation.

An addition with carry operation, such as ADDC R1,R2, calculates the result of R1+R2+C, where C is the value stored in the carry bit. In a similar way, subtraction with borrow, SUBB R1,R2, calculates R1-R2-(1-C).

To illustrate the functioning of these operations, consider a simplified case involving the addition of two eight-bit unsigned numbers, but using only four-bit registers and using a four-bit arithmetic logic unit. More specifically, consider the addition of 00101111b, stored in registers R1 and R2 and 00110011b, stored in registers R3 and R4.

When we add 1111b to 0011b, the result is 10010b, which does not fit in a four-bit register. The most significant bit corresponds to the value of the carry bit, and it is used for the next addition or subtraction instruction with

Program 10.8. Program to sum two 32-bit numbers.

```
ADD    R2, R4
ADDC   R1, R3
```

Program 10.9 Program to determine the first memory position with a value equal to the value of R1.

```
        MOV    R2, -1
Loop:   INC    R2
        CMP    R1, M[R2]
        BR.NZ  Loop
```

the carry bit. Now, when adding 0010b, 0011b and the carry bit, we obtain 0110b, and the final correct value of 01100010b.

Therefore, in the P3 processor, the instruction sequence in Program 10.8 correctly calculates the addition of two 32-bit values stored, respectively, in the registers R1, R2 and R3, R4, with the result stored in the register pair R1 and R2.

There are also unary arithmetic instructions. The instruction NEG calculates the arithmetic complement of its operand, while the instructions INC and DEC respectively increment and decrement their operand.

Finally, the compare instruction CMP carries out a subtraction, but without storing the result. This instruction is useful when updating the flags of the processor without altering any of the operands involved. For example, the piece of code described in Program 10.9 determines and stores in R2 the address of the first memory location which contains a value equal to that of register R1.

The operands of all instructions, except multiplication and division, may be unsigned integers or signed integers in 2's complement representation. The interpretation of results only depends on the programmer, given that the flag O (overflow) only has a meaning if the operands are interpreted as signed numbers.

All arithmetic instructions alter the value of the flags of the processor, particularly the Z, N, C and O flags, which indicate, respectively, if the result was zero, if it was negative, if it created a carry, and if it created a value greater than what the processor can represent with 16 bits.

10.6.2 *Logic Instructions*

Table 10.6 describes the logic instructions of the P3 processor. The first three logic instructions apply conjunction, disjunction and exclusive disjunction

Table 10.6   Logic instructions for the P3 processor.

Instruction	Mnemonic	Example
Conjunction	AND	AND R1, M[R3]
Disjunction	OR	OR R1, 00FFh
Exclusive disjunction	XOR	XOR M[R1], R2
Logic complement	COM	COM M[R2+4]
Test	TEST	TEST R5, M[R4]

Table 10.7   Shift instructions for the P3 processor.

Instruction	Mnemonic	Example
Logic shift right	SHR	SHR R1, 4
Logic shift left	SHL	SHL M[R1], 2
Arithmetic shift right	SHRA	SHRA M[R1], 2
Arithmetic shift left	SHLA	SHLA M[R2], 4
Rotate right	ROR	ROR R4, 15
Rotate left	ROL	ROL R4, 1
Rotate right with carry	RORC	RORC R4, 15
Rotate left with carry	ROLC	ROLC R2, 15

operations, respectively, to their operands. These operations are executed bitwise, with the result stored in the location of the first operand. The logic instruction COM calculates the bitwise complement of its single operand. Finally, the instruction TEST applies the conjunction operator to its two operands, not storing the result, but altering the value of the flags.

The logic operations alter the value of the flags Z and N but leave the flags C and O unaltered. Indeed, a logic operation never generates a carry, and an overflow has no meaning, so these flags are not updated.

10.6.3   Shift Instructions

Table 10.7 lists the shift instructions available in this processor. Section 8.4.5 has a more detailed explanation of the operation of the shift instructions.

For all these instructions, shift right means a shift in the direction of the least significant bit. These instructions have two operands. The first has to be a register or memory location, which is the object of the shift, while the second is a positive constant, which specifies the number of bits to shift in the first operand. This constant can take a value between 1 and 15. In all shift operations, the carry bit C assumes the value of the last bit that leaves the register.

The instructions SHR and SHL shift their operand right or left, respectively. In the SHR operation, the most significant bit assumes the value 0. The same happens to the least significant bit in the SHL operation.

The arithmetic shift right is similar to the logic shift, except in the value assumed by the most significant bit. In the arithmetic shift, the value of this bit after the shift is equal to its value before the shift. The difference between logic and arithmetic shifts is important when they operate over signed numbers. Indeed, an arithmetic shift right of one bit has the effect of dividing the operand by 2, whether it is positive or negative. On the contrary, the logic shift right does not correspond to a division by 2 when applied to a negative number. Logic and arithmetic shifts left are equivalent regarding the result, but alter the flags in a different way. The first is considered a logic operation, therefore updating only the flags Z, N and C, while the second, as an arithmetic operation, updates all the flags.

The rotate operations ROR and ROL represent circular shifts, where the bits leaving the register are reinserted at the other end. Rotation with carry operation applies a rotation to the operand bits plus the carry bit. Therefore, in a rotation to the right, the carry bit is inserted into the high part of the operand, and the carry bit assumes the value of the least significant bit that is leaving the operand. In a rotation to the left the opposite occurs. These operations affect the flags Z, N and C.

10.6.4 *Control Instructions*

Table 10.8 describes the control instructions available in this processor.

The unconditional jump instruction JMP Label transfers control of execution to the instruction stored in the position Label. This instruction loads the program counter with the specified value. A symbolic name may be used

Table 10.8   Control instructions for the P3 processor.

Instruction	Mnemonic	Example	
Relative unconditional jump	BR	BR	Pos1
Relative conditional jump	BR.cond	BR.cond	Loop
Absolute unconditional jump	JMP	JMP	M[R3+1]
Absolute conditional jump	JMP.cond	JMP.cond	Rout1
Unconditional subroutine call	CALL	CALL	Routin1
Conditional subroutine call	CALL.cond	CALL.cond	Rout2
Subroutine return	RET	RET	
Subroutine return with N parameters	RETN	RETN	4
Interrupt	INT	INT	55
Return from interrupt	RTI	RTI	

Table 10.9   Jump conditions for the P3 processor.

Condition	Mnemonics	Description
Zero	Z	Last operation produced zero result
Non-zero	NZ	Last operation produced non-zero result
Carry	C	Last operation generated carry
Non-carry	NC	Last operation did not generate carry
Negative	N	Last operation produced negative result
Non-negative	NN	Last operation produced non-negative result
Overflow	O	Last operation produced overflow
Non-overflow	NO	Last operation did not produce overflow
Positive	P	Last operation produced positive result
Non-positive	NP	Last operation produced non-positive result
Interrupt	I	There is a requesting interrupt
Non-interrupt	NI	There is no requesting interrupt

to specify the destination address, although it is possible to use any numerical constant or even an operand specified with any of the addressing modes supported by the processor.

The conditional jump instruction `JMP.cond Label` transfers control to the specified instruction, but only when the condition `cond` is true. All conditions described in Table 10.9 generate specific conditional jumps.

A conditional test always refers to the result of the last operation which affected the flags. That operation can be an arithmetic, logic or shift operation, though it can also be an instruction of another type, such as a `CMC` (complement the carry flag). For example, the instruction `BR.Z Dest` transfers control to the instruction at address `Dest` only if the last operation which altered the status register produced a zero result.

The `C` condition tests the result stored in the carry bit. The `N` condition tests whether the last result was negative, which in 2's complement representation is equivalent to testing if the most significant bit of the result is 1. The condition `P` tests if the result is strictly positive. Finally, a test for the `O` condition (overflow) produces a true result if the last arithmetic operation produced a result which, interpreted as a signed integer, cannot be adequately represented by the processor.

The bits which define the conditions are the flags, stored in the state register of the processor which, however, is not directly accessible to the programmer.

Subroutine call instructions transfer control to the specified program position, but only after storing the content of the program counter in the stack. Thus, the `RET` instruction can return control to the instruction following the `CALL` instruction, copying the value stored on top of the stack back to the program counter. For this mechanism to function correctly, it is important that, inside each routine, the number of push operations is equal to the number of pop operations.

It is common to use the stack to pass parameters to a routine. Therefore, there is also the instruction RETN, which, in addition to restoring the value in the program counter, updates the stack pointer, so that the passed parameters are removed from the top of the processor stack. Therefore, for example, the instruction RETN 3 takes three values from the processor stack and can be used to return from a routine which has three parameters passed through the stack. The instruction RETN 0 is equivalent to the instruction RET.

Note that the processor does not physically transfer these parameters anywhere. The effect of "removal" is obtained by the adjustment of the SP, excluding the memory positions with the parameters from the stack.

The instruction INT Intnum behaves in a similar way to a subroutine call since it transfers control to a program instruction linked to the interrupt specified by Intnum. Execution of this instruction has the same effect as receiving the interrupt Intnum. As we saw in Section 10.5.3, the processor prepares the return by storing in the stack not only the value of the program counter but also the status register with the flags. This action allows the return from interrupt instruction (RTI) to restore the state of the processor completely,[3] recovering the value of the program counter and the state register of the processor. This instruction should always and exclusively be used in interrupt routines, which can be called either through the instruction INT or the processor interrupt mechanism.

The control instructions do not alter the flags of the processor, unlike the arithmetic, logic and shift instructions studied in the previous sections.

10.6.5 *Data Transfer Instructions*

With these instructions, it is possible to copy words or bytes between memory locations or processor registers. Processor stack manipulation instructions are also considered transfer instructions. The P3 processor has the data transfer instructions described in Table 10.10.

---

[3]Regarding the value of the program counter and the status register. The interrupt routine may have altered the value of other registers, but that is the full responsibility of the programmer to restore.

Table 10.10   Data transfer instructions for the P3 processor.

Instruction	Mnemonic	Example
Copy the content	MOV	MOV R1, M[R2]
Copy least significant byte	MVBL	MVBL M[Pos1], R3
Copy most significant byte	MVBH	MVBL R3, R4
Exchange the contents	XCH	XCH R1, M[R2]
Place on the stack	PUSH	PUSH R1
Remove from the stack	POP	POP M[R5+4]

The most basic data transfer instruction is the instruction MOV POS1, POS2 which copies the word stored in POS2 to POS1. The instruction MVBH POS1, POS2 copies the most significant byte at location POS2 to the most significant byte at POS1, leaving the least significant byte unaltered. The instruction MVBL works similarly for the least significant byte. The instruction XCH exchanges the content of two specified locations.

Finally, the instructions PUSH and POP are used to manipulate the stack. More specifically, the instruction PUSH Val places the specified value in the memory location pointed to by the SP register then decrements the value of the SP. The instruction POP Loc starts by incrementing the value of the SP register and then stores the value of the memory location pointed to by the SP in Loc (which may be a register or memory location).

These data transfer instructions do not alter the value of the flags since their function is to copy data from one place to another. If it is necessary to update the value of the flags in function of one operand subject of a transfer, a logic or arithmetic instruction which operates on the copied value must be used. Typically, this would be the instruction CMP or TEST.

10.6.6   *Other Instructions*

The P3 processor also has a few more instructions, described in Table 10.11, that handle various aspects of processor operation. None of these instructions has operands.

The instruction ENI instructs the processor to accept interrupts from that moment on. The instruction DSI stops the processor from servicing interrupts. Both instructions act by modifying the value of a flag, the E bit, which acts as an interrupt enable.

Other instructions which directly change the value of flags in the status register are the instructions STC, CLC and CMC, which respectively set, clear and complement the carry bit of the processor, C.

Table 10.11   Other instructions for the P3 processor.

Instruction	Mnemonics
Enable interrupts	ENI
Disable interrupts	DSI
Set carry bit	STC
Clear carry bit	CLC
Complement carry bit	CMC
No operation	NOP

Program 10.10   Sum of ten consecutive memory locations, starting at the position Start.

```
        MOV     R1, 9
        MOV     R2, R0              ; Clear register R2
Loop:   ADD     R2, M[Start+R1]
        DEC     R1
        BR.NN   Loop                ; Continues if R1>=0
```

Finally, the instruction NOP does not execute any operation and does not alter the flags of the processor. It may be used to fill parts of the program temporarily to complete later, but it is not normally used, except to introduce short delays into programs.

10.6.7   *Examples of Use*

Let us consider, as an example, programming the P3 processor to add integers in ten consecutive memory locations, starting at the position Start. The section of code in Program 10.10 executes this operation.

Initialising the register R1 with the value 9 and iterating until that register reaches a negative value, this program adds all the memory locations from M[Start] to M[Start +9], starting with the highest memory locations.

Alternatively, it would be possible to use a counter to control the number of words to add. The programmer may create a loop where the values are successively added and simultaneously incrementing the counter until it reaches the limit, what causes the program to exit the loop. In this case, the code will be that ·shown in Program 10.11. where R1 serves as the counter.

The instruction CMP R1,10 updates the flags of the processor, as if executing a subtraction. Therefore, when R1 reaches the value 10, the flag Z will be at 1, and the loop terminates.

Program 10.11.   Sum of 10 consecutive memory locations, incrementing a counter.

```
        MOV     R1, R0
        MOV     R2, R0              ; Clear register R2
Loop:   ADD     R2, M[Start+R1]
        INC     R1
        CMP     R1, 10              ; Compare R1 with 10
        BR.NZ   Loop                ; Continues if R1-10 <> 0
```

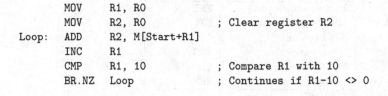

Fig. 10.7   General format for the P3 processor instructions.

10.7   Instruction Format for the P3 Processor

The encoding of the P3 processor instructions needs one or two memory words. The second memory word is the address of a memory location or an immediate operand when the addressing mode requires it, namely in the immediate and indexed addressing. In the figures representing the format of the various instructions in this section, W stands for the word with the address or the immediate constant.

Figure 10.7 describes the general instruction format for the P3 processor instruction. In this figure and the following ones, the fields marked with a question mark may or may not be present in a given instruction.

The six first bits (bits 15 to 10) of the first word of each instruction specify the *operation code* of the instruction (the opcode). The complete list of the opcodes for the P3 processor is shown in Table 10.12.

The instructions which do not have operands or parameters only use the field which specifies the operation code. In the instructions which have one operand, there is an M field with 2 bits, which defines the *addressing mode* used, as shown in Table 10.13.

In the operations which have two operands, the M field also specifies the addressing mode of one of the operands. The other operand needs to be a register.

The description of the operands includes other fields besides the M field which specify the operands and parameters for each instruction, in a way that we will explain below. This specification varies according to the type of operation, according to the values of the first 3 bits of the opcode.

Table 10.12 Operation codes for the P3 processor.

Mnemonic	Opcode	Mnemonic	Opcode
NOP	000000	CMP	100000
ENI	000001	ADD	100001
DSI	000010	ADDC	100010
STC	000011	SUB	100011
CLC	000100	SUBB	100100
CMC	000101	MUL	100101
RET	000110	DIV	100110
RTI	000111	TEST	100111
INT	001000	AND	101000
RETN	001001	OR	101001
NEG	010000	XOR	101010
INC	010001	MOV	101011
DEC	010010	MVBH	101100
COM	010011	MVBL	101101
PUSH	010100	XCH	101110
POP	010101	JMP	110000
SHR	011000	JMP.cond	110001
SHL	011001	CALL	110010
SHRA	011010	CALL.cond	110011
SHLA	011011	BR	111000
ROR	011100	BR.cond	111001
ROL	011101		
RORC	011110		
ROLC	011111		

Table 10.13 P3 processor addressing modes.

M	Addressing Mode	Operation
00	Register	op = RX
01	Register indirect	op = M[RX]
10	Immediate	op = W
11	Indexed, direct, relative or based	op = M[RX+W]

10.7.1 *Instructions with No Operands*

The instructions NOP, ENI, DSI, STC, CLC, CMC, RET and RTI, do not use any operand and are encoded as shown in Figure 10.8. The positions defined with X have a different value for each one of these instructions, according to the values described in Table 10.12. These instructions do not use the ten least significant bits, and their value has no meaning.

The instructions INT and RETN accept one parameter as an argument, which has to be an integer between 0 and 1023. This argument is encoded in the *ARG* field, as shown in Figure 10.9.

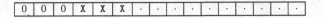

Fig. 10.8   Encoding of instructions without operands.

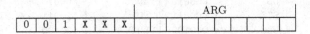

Fig. 10.9   Encoding of instructions with one parameter.

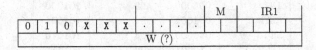

Fig. 10.10   Encoding of instructions with one operand.

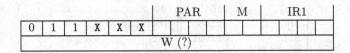

Fig. 10.11   Encoding of instructions with one operand and one parameter.

10.7.2   *Instructions with One Operand*

The instructions NEG, INC, DEC, COM, PUSH and POP have one operand. For the first four instructions, this operand simultaneously specifies the origin of the data and the destination for the result. For the PUSH instruction, the operand determines the value to write in the stack. For the POP instruction, the operand indicates where to transfer the value on top of the stack. In any of the cases, the operand may be defined using any of the addressing modes described in Section 10.3.4. The 2 bits of the M field, specify the addressing mode, as shown in Table 10.13 and the structure in Figure 10.10.

The value of the $IR1$ field, with 4 bits, is used to specify the register RX according to the addressing mode. This field enables the encoding of any value between 0 and 7 for the general registers, and also, in relative and base addressing modes, two other values to specify PC and SP. There is no use for the remaining 4 bits.

The instructions SHR, SHL, SHRA, SHLA, ROR, ROL, RORC and ROLC accept one parameter besides the operand. This parameter can be an integer from 1 to 15, and it is encoded in the bits 6 to 9 of the instruction (field PAR), as shown in Figure 10.11.

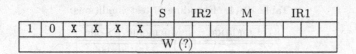

Fig. 10.12   Encoding of instructions with two operands.

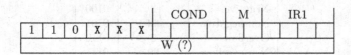

Fig. 10.13   Encoding of absolute jump instructions.

10.7.3   *Instructions with Two Operands*

The instructions CMP, ADD, ADDC, SUB, SUBB, MUL, DIV, TEST, AND, OR, XOR, MOV, MVBL, MVBH and XCH use two operands. The first operand specifies simultaneously, one of the source operands and the location for the result. These instructions are encoded as shown in Figure 10.12.

Since, as discussed in Section 10.4, the ability to use an arbitrary addressing mode for both operands would require instructions which are too long, in this processor one of the operands must use register addressing. Therefore, the value of the M serves to specify the addressing mode of only one of the operands. If the value of S is 0, fields $IR1$ and M, define the first operand, and $IR2$ is used to access the second operand. If the value of S is 1, $IR1$ specifies (according to M) what the second operand is, and $IR2$ is used to specify the first operand.

In either case, the register to which the addressing mode specified by the field M is applied is the register specified in the $IR1$ field of the instruction register.

10.7.4   *Control Instructions*

The control instructions JMP, JMP.cond, CALL and CALL.cond are encoded according to the scheme shown in Figure 10.13.

The M and $IR1$ fields have the same encoding rules as in the instructions with one operand. The $COND$ field, when necessary, is encoded according to Table 10.14.

The encoding of control instructions BR and BR.cond corresponds to the scheme in Figure 10.14. The value of the $OFFSET$ field specifies the value to add to the PC. An $OFFSET$ value equal to 0 is equivalent to the NOP instruction.

Table 10.14   Encoding of test conditions.

Condition	Mnemonic	Code
Zero	Z	0000
Non-zero	NZ	0001
Carry	C	0010
Non-carry	NC	0011
Negative	N	0100
Non-negative	NN	0101
Overflow	O	0110
Non-overflow	NO	0111
Positive	P	1000
Non-positive	NP	1001
Interrupt	I	1010
Non-interrupt	NI	1011

Fig. 10.14   Encoding of relative jump instructions.

As discussed in Section 10.5.1, these instructions have the advantage of always occupying just one memory location. The limitation is that, as the *OFFSET* field only has 6 bits, relative jumps are only possible up to 32 memory locations before and 31 memory locations after the current position of the PC. Note that the *OFFSET* field is an integer in 2's complement representation.

10.7.5   *Encoding Examples*

As an example, let us consider the instruction JMP.NZ R3 which jumps to the memory location pointed to by R3 if the last result in the arithmetic and logic unit was not 0. Encoding of this instruction is obtained noting that:

- the opcode is 110001 (Table 10.12);
- the addressing mode is by register, which means that the value of the *M* field is 00;
- the value of the *IR*1 field is 0011b, to specify the R3 register;
- the value of the *COND* field is 0001b, according to Table 10.14.

This information means that this is a one-word instruction, whose encoding is obtained by concatenating the values determined above, that is, 1100010001000011b, which is equivalent to C443h.

Now let us consider the instruction ADD R1,M[R7+00A0h], slightly more complex, which has two operands and uses a different addressing mode. To encode this instruction, we must consider that:

- The opcode for the instruction ADD is 100001b. Note that the value of the two most significant bits is 10b, which indicates that it is an instruction with two operands.
- This instruction has two operands, the first of which is addressed by register (R1) while the second is obtained through the use of indexed addressing from the values in register R7 and the constant 00A0h. Thus:
  - The value of the M field is 11b, to indicate indexed addressing mode.
  - The value of the S field is 1, defining the second operand as the one using the addressing mode specified by M.
  - The value of the $IR1$ field, which, in this case, specifies the second operand, is 0111b, since the register used is R7.
  - The value of the $IR2$ field is 001b, specifying the register used in the definition of the first operand.
- The value of the W field, in the second word of the instruction, will be 00A0h.

This instruction is therefore encoded using two memory words, which contain the values 100001 1 001 11 0111b and 0000000010100000b, that is, 8677h and 00A0h. Further examples of encoding can be seen in the example in Section 10.1, which contains the machine language code of the P3 and the corresponding assembly code.

10.8 An Assembler for the P3 Processor

Although there is a direct correspondence between an assembly instruction and the machine language instruction, the manual translation of a program written in assembly to a sequence of bits which make up the machine language is a tiresome and error-prone process.

For this reason, programmers use a tool, an *assembler*, a program which translates an assembly language program to a machine language program. Besides translating the mnemonics of the instructions and the values of the arguments in the operands, the assembler enables the programmer to use symbolic names instead of constants, which simplifies the programming task and makes assembly programs more legible.

The first, and perhaps the most important, characteristic of an assembler is the fact that it enables the programmer to use mnemonics for the instructions and symbolic names for the addresses of these instructions. The use of mnemonics is clearly advantageous, as it avoids the memorisation of opcodes. The use of symbolic names for the addresses also considerably simplifies the task of the programmer, who, when specifying a control instruction, may use a label which is the symbolic name of the address of the instruction to be executed next. If this possibility did not exist, the real address of the instruction would have to be used which, often, is still not known, and which, in any event, is subject to frequent alteration in the future, as the program is being developed, debugged and maintained.

As an example, let us consider the section of assembly code shown in Program 10.12. This section of code identifies the first memory position where the content is equal to the content of register R1, starting at position start=0F00h.

This section of code uses the ORIG and EQU directives. The ORIG directive defines the memory address where the machine code of the program begins, and the EQU directive defines the constant start as having the value 0F00h. This constant may be used later in any position where it is necessary to use the value 0F00h. Constant definitions should come at the start of the program to facilitate their alteration if needed. Names of constants make the reading of the code easier as they are more intelligible than a numerical value. Besides this, if there is a need to change the value of the constant, just change it in the definition, and all the code is automatically updated. For this reason, the programmer should not spread constants or constant definitions

Program 10.12 Assembly program that identifies the first memory position where the content is equal to the content of register R1.

```
            ORIG   0A00h
start       EQU    0F00h

; Search:   Localizes the first memory position
;           with a content equal to the content of R1
; Inputs:   R1 - Value to search
; Outputs:  R2 - Address of the result

Search:     MOV    R2, start    ; Initialize R2
LSearch:    CMP    R1, M[R2]    ; Compare the values
            BR.Z   EndProc      ; Terminate if found
            INC    R2           ; Increment pointer
            BR     LSearch      ; Next iteration
EndProc:    RET                 ; R2 contains de result
```

Table 10.15   Machine language for program `Search`.

Address	Machine Instruction		Assembly	
0A00h	1010111010100000b	AEA0h	MOV	R2, start
0A01h	0000111100000000b	0F00h		
0A02h	1000001001010010b	8252h	CMP	R1,M[R2]
0A03h	1110010000000010b	E402h	BR.Z	EndProc
0A04h	0100010000000010b	4402h	INC	R2
0A05h	1110000000111100b	E03Ch	BR	LSearch
0A06h	0001100000000000b	1800h	RET	

throughout the program. It is a good practice to make the definitions of these constants at the beginning of the program or the respective module.

Comments were also used to document the program. The comment starts with the character «;», which instructs the assembler to ignore all the text which follows on that line when translating the assembly code.

Note that the ORIG and EQU directives are not assembly instructions. Analysing Table 10.15, which contains the machine code resulting from the assembly code in Program 10.12, we can see that those directives did not generate machine instructions. The result of the directives is only visible when analysing the first machine instructions generated (Table 10.15), where it can be seen that this instruction is equivalent to the assembly instruction MOV R2,0F00h and is at memory location 0A00h. The ORIG directive determined the address of the instruction and the EQU directive defined the value 0F00h as one of the operands. Constants can be used as operands of instructions as well as to specify memory addresses.

Second, note that the programmer used symbolic names for the three instruction addresses, the labels Search, LSearch and EndProc. Two of these labels were used in the program, in the instructions with mnemonics BR.Z and BR. In this way, the programmer does not have to deal with the numerical value of the addresses of the instructions to where it is intended to transfer control. The label Search, on the other hand, is not used inside the subroutine but may be used later by another subroutine wishing to use this code. The call to the Search subroutine may be performed by the CALL Search instruction, and it is not necessary for the programmer to know the numeric address of this routine.

The assembler of the P3 processor accepts various directives (also known as *pseudo-instructions*), described in Table 10.16.

Besides the directives ORIG and EQU, already used, the assembler of the P3 processor accepts three other directives, whose utilisation is exemplified in Program 10.13.

Table 10.16   Assembler directives for the P3 processor.

ORIG	Specifies the origin address for the code which follows
EQU	Defines the value of a constant
WORD	Reserves a memory location for a variable
STR	Stores a character string in memory
TAB	Reserves memory locations

Program 10.13.   Example of use of directives.

```
Abc      WORD    0055h
Xyz      WORD    0011h
Text1    STR     'Hel','lo'
Table1   TAB     3
```

Table 10.17 Content of the memory locations, according to the directives in Program 10.13.

Address	Instruction
0000h	0055h
0001h	0011h
0002h	0048h
0003h	0065h
0004h	006Ch
0005h	006Ch
0006h	006Fh
0007h	0000h
0008h	0000h
0009h	0000h

The directive WORD reserves a memory location to contain a variable, which may be referenced later using a symbolic name. It also allows the initialisation of this memory location. In the example above, it reserves a memory location for the variable Abc, and initialises it at 0055h. It also reserves a memory location for the variable Xyz, initialised at 0011h.

The STR directive stores a character string in memory. In the case above, five memory locations are reserved and filled by the ASCII values of the character string *Hello*. The symbolic name Text1 is defined with the value of the address of the memory location where the string starts. The third argument of this directive consists of a list of elements, separated by commas, where each element may be a character string, starting and ending with the symbol « ' », or a numerical constant. The string characters are substituted by their ASCII values, and concatenated with each other (or with numerical arguments, if that is the case), and the result is stored in memory.

Finally, the TAB directive reserves memory locations, initialised at 0, which may be used to store a table, the start of which can be referenced by a symbolic name. In the example above, three memory locations are stored and the symbolic name Table1 defined.

If we assume that the directives above appear at the start of the program, preceded by the directive ORIG 0000h, the first ten memory locations will be filled according to Table 10.17. The constants Abc, Xyz, Text1 and Table1 will represent the values 0000h, 0001h, 0002h and 0007h, respectively. These constants may be used in another context to reference the respective addresses.

10.9 Summary

This chapter studies some of the possible alternatives for the instruction set architecture of processors and presents the instruction set for the didactic processor P3 that we use in this book as an example. This instruction set, typical of simple second generation processors, includes control, transfer and data handling instructions. The chapter also describes the assembly language of the P3 processor, which simplifies its programming, using a set of mnemonics instead of machine language.

We also study how the assembly language is translated into machine language, describing how each instruction is encoded.

Exercises

10.1 Consider that register R1 initially has the value 10110010b. Indicate the values obtained by applying each of the following instructions to this register:

    (a) SHL
    (b) SHR
    (c) ROL
    (d) ROR
    (e) SHLA
    (f) SHRA

10.2 Consider the following values for the P3 processor registers:

R1	93BAh	R6	CF03h
R2	CC00h	R7	8441h
R3	18AFh	PC	0707h
R4	0034h	SP	F105h
R5	6BEEh	SR	0004h

Indicate the new value, in hexadecimal, for the registers altered by the execution of each of the following instructions:

(a) SUB R2, 105d
(b) RORC R1, 2
(c) CALL.NZ BEEFh

10.3 Suppose that the value of the SP register is initially 00E0h. Indicate what the content of this register is and the content of the stack after executing the following code:

```
1. ORIG    0000h    start
2. start:  PUSH     10h
4.         PUSH     R0
3.         CALL     0C00h
```

10.4 It is known that the top of the stack contains the value 0344h and that the SP register contains 00E3h. A subroutine call instruction, which uses immediate addressing, is at memory location 01A3h. The content of memory location 01A4h is 2232h. What are the contents of the PC and SP registers:

(a) Before the CALL instruction is loaded into memory.
(b) After executing the CALL instruction.
(c) After returning from the procedure called by the CALL instruction.

10.5 Indicate the value of the registers R1 and R2 after the execution of the following P3 assembly program:

```
1. ORIG    0000h    start
2. start:  MOV      R2, 100h
3.         MOV      R1, 0
4. loop:   ADD      R1, R2
5.         DEC      R2
6. end:    JMP.NZ   loop
```

10.6 Consider the following program:

```
; main program
1. ORIG    0000h    start
2. start:  ENI
3.         MOV  R1, 1
4.         MOV  R2, 2
```

```
5.          MOV  R3, 3
6.          CMP  R2, R3
7. end:     JMP  end
; interrupt service routine
8. intr:    POP  R1
9.          PUSH R2
10.         MOV  R2, 1
11.         MOV  R3, 2
12.         SUB  R3, R2
13.         POP  R2
14.         PUSH R1
15.         RTI
```

Indicate and justify the value of R1, R2, R3 and the value of all the flags after running the program, assuming that an interrupt occurred during the execution of the CMP instruction in line 6.

10.7 Suppose that there is a 32-bit number stored in the registers R1 and R2, with the most significant component in R1. Indicate the sequence of instructions to be executed for this number to be incremented by 1 unit.

10.8 Indicate the addressing mode used for each of the operands in the following instructions:

  (a) SUB R1, R2
  (b) ADD R5, M[R3]
  (c) XOR M[R3+0101h], R2
  (d) SHRA R3, 4
  (e) JMP.NZ 04F5h
  (f) PUSH M[R3+5555h]

10.9 Describe how the instructions to the previous question are encoded in the P3 processor.

10.10 Describe the content stored in memory as a result of the following assembly code:

```
ORIG 0000h    ;start
x1   WORD   5A5Ah
c1   EQU    1515h
     MOV    R1, M[x1]
     ADD    R1, c1
     MOV    M[x1], R2
```

10.11 Suggest three instructions which have the same effect as the NOP instruction. Note that these instructions should occupy the same space in memory and have exactly the same effect on the processor status as the NOP instruction.

Chapter 11

Programming in Assembly Language

The previous chapter introduced the concept of assembly language and, in particular, the set of assembly instructions for the P3 processor. We will now consider briefly some design techniques for the development of programs based on these instructions. Assembly language is much more limited than high-level languages, particularly regarding the parameters accepted by the instructions. Because of this, developing programs in this language is more challenging and tends to be a slower process. The use of assembly programming methods is therefore of major importance.

We will start, in Section 11.1, with the translation of constructions from a high-level program language to assembly language. This approach makes possible to introduce assembly programming in a gradual manner using simple and well-defined functionalities. /

Section 11.2 discusses programming methods which, if followed, can make the development of assembly programs more reliable and fast. Section 11.3 presents examples of illustrative routines for the practice of assembly programming. Section 11.4 shows a complete example of a specific project.

11.1 Translation of High-level Language Constructs to Assembly

This section analyses the translation of program segments described in a high-level language into assembly language of the P3 processor with the objective of presenting assembly programming. This exercise uses the *C language*, as it provides for easier translation. The presentation which follows will only focus on direct translation and not consider any optimisation characteristic of a compiler.

11.1.1   *Variables*

Any program in an imperative language like the C language, however simple
it may be, requires the use of *variables* to maintain data and the context
of operations which are being carried out. In many high-level languages,
there must be a declaration of each variable before its use (languages which
do not require this, do so through an implicitly declaration the first time
the variable is used). Declaring a variable makes the compiler reserve space
for the data that this variable will store, and the size of the space reserved
depends on the declared type of the variable.

This space can be reserved in memory or in a set of processor registers.
As we saw in the previous chapter, it is preferable to use registers as they can
be accessed more quickly. However, the space available in registers is very
limited, and so, if there are many variables, they must be stored in memory.
The variables in memory are, typically, placed consecutively in the order of
their declaration, and the compiler may carry out some rearrangement, so as
to optimise the use of space. We will now briefly analyse the ways to reserve
space for variables in memory in assembly programming.

11.1.1.1   *Simple types*

For simple data types, a sufficient number of memory locations is reserved to
store the number of bits that make up this data type. For example, the data
type *short int* in C occupies 16 bits. As each data word (usually defined as
the width of a register, or a memory location) in the P3 processor is 16 bits
wide, exactly one position will be necessary to store each `short int` type
variable. Thus the statement in C,

```
short int Total;
```

is equivalent to the P3 pseudo-assembly instruction:

```
Total  WORD  0
```

Note that, when the declaration does not initialise the variables, only
global and static variables are initialised to zero, in most C compilers. The
following declaration in C carries out an initialisation:

```
#define INIT_TOTAL 10
short int Total = INIT_TOTAL;
```

which corresponds to the following P3 assembly code:

```
INIT_TOTAL  EQU   10
Total       WORD  INIT_TOTAL
```

If the data type has a smaller number of bits than one data word, one memory location will also be reserved for it. As we will see, the remaining space can be used to store another variable.

For example, the *char* data type uses 8 bits in C. If we have the declaration:

```
char Mask;
```

it will correspond in P3 assembly to:

```
Mask WORD 0
```

This solution does, of course, entail a significant waste of space, since only half of a word is used in a useful way. To minimise this waste, it is possible to pack several variables within the same data word. To illustrate this situation, consider the following declarations in C:

```
char Start;
short int Root;
char End;
```

A direct translation to assembly would be:

```
Start   WORD  0
Root    WORD  0
End     WORD  0
```

In this case, and whether or not they occur in consecutive declarations, it is possible to place the variables **Start** and **End** in the same memory location:

```
End_Start WORD  0
Root      WORD  0
```

where one of the variables will occupy the eight upper bits of the memory location, and the other the eight lower bits, for example:

15	14	13	12	11	10	9	8	7	6	5	4	3	2	1	0
End								Start							

The advantage is, of course, the use of less memory words. However, this solution does have the disadvantage of making it harder to manipulate the variables **Start** and **End**. Suppose we wish to increase the value of the variable **Start** by one unit. If this variable occupies the bits with least weight, as illustrated above, there is the danger that this increment can cause a carry which will alter the value of **End**. It is, therefore, necessary to make this increment in a temporary location (typically, a register), which will involve copying the eight least significant bits to this location, carrying out the operation and copying the result back to the eight least significant bits of the memory location without affecting the most significant bits:

```
MOV  R1, M[End_Start]    ; copy to the register
INC  R1                  ; increment in the register
MVBL M[End_Start], R1    ; only the LSB is altered
```

If the variable **Start** is in the position of greater weight

15	14	13	12	11	10	9	8	7	6	5	4	3	2	1	0
Start								End							

it will have to be shifted 8 bits to the right, before the increment operation, and 8 bits to the left, after the operation:

```
MOV  R1, M[Start_End]    ; copy to the register
SHRA R1, 8               ; Start is in the LSB and End is lost
INC  R1                  ; the value is incremented
SHLA R1, 8               ; Start is moved back to the MSB
MVBH M[Start_End], R1    ; it is stored altering only the MSB
```

Another possibility is to move the value of the increment 8 bits to the left, and transforming the increment of 1 unit into an increment of 256 units:

```
MOV R1, 100000000b       ; value of the increment shifted 8 bits
ADD M[Start_End], R1     ; increment
```

Note that this problem is typical of arithmetic instructions, and does not arise for logic manipulation instructions.

Indeed, both of these solutions for memory organisation are used in practice. In situations where performance is critical, the first is solution used, causing the program to occupy more memory space. In circumstances where performance is not so critical, the second solution is used to save memory.

In any case, in the previous example, the solution

```
Start_RootH   WORD  0
RootL_End     WORD  0
```

is never used, since the three variables become all harder to manipulate particularly the manipulation of the variable Root. For this reason, variables with a width equal to or greater than the data word are always *aligned*, that is, they start on the far right and never in the middle of a memory location.

When the data type has a width greater than the width of the data word, it is, of course, necessary to reserve more than one memory location for each variable. For example, in the C language, the type *long int* has 32 bits and so requires two memory locations of 16 bits for each variable. Thus the declaration

```
long int Sum;
```

can be translated into P3 assembly as

```
SumH  WORD  0
SumL  WORD  0
```

which means that the first memory position receives the half of the variable Sum with the greatest weight, and the half with the least weight stays in the second memory location. The reverse sequence is also possible:

```
SumL  WORD  0
SumH  WORD  0
```

There are no relative advantages between these two alternatives and, in practice, some systems use one, and other systems use the other. The first of these two options for memory allocation for data has the name *big-endian* (the greatest weight part in the lowest addresses), and the second, *little-endian* (the smallest weight part in the lowest addresses). In byte-addressed computers, the problem is similar and occurs at the level of the order of the bytes in a 16-bit word. The existence of these two formats sometimes creates problems when data is transferred between systems.

Of course, operations on variables occupying more than one memory location become more complex, because it is necessary to manipulate each part of the variable separately. However, there is no alternative to this organisation. Later in this chapter we will consider, in a little more detail, the issue of manipulating data with a width greater than the system data word.

Finally, let us consider the floating-point data type. The C language supports two of these, the *float* and the *double*, which correspond to the two IEEE standard formats described in Section 5.5. Only the size of the types is relevant when declaring variables, in this case, 32 and 64 bits, respectively, which implies the use of two and four memory locations, respectively, for the P3 processor. Once again the issue of little-endian versus big-endian representation must be considered. For example, assuming a little-endian representation, the declarations

```
float Temperature;
double Pressure;
```

will be equivalent to the following, in the P3 assembly

```
Temperature0    WORD  0
Temperature1    WORD  0
Pressure0       WORD  0
Pressure1       WORD  0
Pressure2       WORD  0
Pressure3       WORD  0
```

11.1.1.2 *Compound types*

High-level languages allow the construction of compound data types. Consider, for example, the definition of a type which stores the coordinates of a point on a plane, and the value of a particular parameter at that point. In the C language, a possible definition for this compound type is

```
typedef struct {
    short int X;
    short int Y;
    char Par;
} Plane;
```

For every instance of a variable of this type, it is made a reservation of a set of memory locations where the fields of the compound type are placed in a predefined order. Assembly does not have the ability to construct compound types, so it is necessary to explicitly reserve space for every instance of a variable. As such, the declaration for the variable Point

```
Plane Point;
```

in the P3 assembly will correspond to

```
Point  TAB  3
```

In the C language, access to each of the fields is carried out through `Point.X`, `Point.Y` or `Point.Par`. In assembly, this access is made using the indexed addressing mode, which requires calculating the offset from the start of the type for each field. In this example, field X has offset 0, field Y has offset 1, and the field Par, offset 2. Therefore, the operation

```
Point.X = Point.Y;
```

in assembly will be

```
MOV  R3, Point     ; R3 has the 1st address, field X
MOV  R4, M[R3+1]   ; R4 has the value of field Y
MOV  M[R3], R4     ; copies field Y to the field X
```

11.1.1.3 *Arrays*

Array elements are also typically placed sequentially in memory. Thus,

```
short int Vector[N_ELEMENTS];
```

in the P3 assembly will simply be

```
Vector  TAB  N_ELEMENTS
```

Access to an element of an array, `Vector[i]`, will be carried out in assembly by the indexed addressing mode, `M[R3+i]` (assuming that R3 contains the array address of the array origin, `Vector`).

Array declarations with initialisation use the pseudo-instruction STR. Thus,

```
short int Sequence[] = {0,1,2,3,4,5};
```

in assembly language will be

```
Sequence  STR  0,1,2,3,4,5
```

Note that a *string* is a particular case of an array in which its elements represent characters in a given code, for example, in ASCII.

In these examples, the data type has the same width as the data word. If the width of the type is less than that of the data word, once again there are two possibilities: either some waste of memory is accepted, or each memory location packs various elements of the array. In the first option, by placing each element of the array in a separate memory location, the performance is optimised. In the second alternative, the space occupied is minimised, at the cost of performance.

In the case where the data type of the array has a width greater than the data word, each element of the array will occupy several memory locations.

For example:

```
long int L[10];
```

in the P3 assembly will correspond to

```
L  TAB  20
```

(Here, we avoided the declaration of the constant and directly used the constant value to accentuate that the number of positions reserved is double the number of elements in the array). This situation is shown in Figure 11.1, in which it is considered that the first memory location attributed to L is 1000h.

The important point is that, in this situation, to access a position i in the array, it is necessary to use a displacement $i \times n$ in assembly, where n is the number of memory locations that each element of the array occupies. For the previous example, $n = 2$.

Multidimensional arrays are normally treated as arrays of unidimensional arrays. Therefore, the declaration

```
short int A[Row][Col];
```

reserves Row arrays of Col elements, with each of the Row arrays placed sequentially in memory. In assembly this declaration will therefore be

```
A  TAB  RowCol
```

in which RowCol has the value Row×Col. Figure 11.2 represents this situation in memory, where Row = 3 and Col = 5.

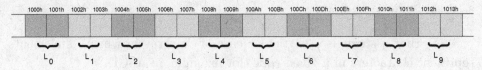

Fig. 11.1 Memory representation of an array with 10 entries, in which each entry occupies two memory locations.

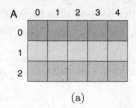

(a)

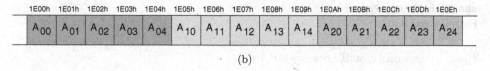

(b)

Fig. 11.2 Representation in memory of a three row by five column array: (a) two-dimensional array and (b) arrangement in memory.

Access to an element of this array, A[i][j], involves having to jump over i arrays of Col elements, until reaching the intended array and then advancing j positions in that array, that is, $i \times$ Col $+ j$. Assuming that the value of i is in R1 and the value of j in R2, in assembly this will be:

```
MOV R7, Col      ; gives the base of the array
MUL R1, R7       ; advances to the intended line
ADD R7, R2       ; positions in the column of that line
MOV R6, M[A+R7]  ; reads the intended element
```

This reasoning can easily be extended to arrays with three or more dimensions.

11.1.1.4 *Pointers*

Variables of the *pointer* type in the C language do not store data, but rather addresses of memory locations, and can function as a reference to data in memory. Of course, it is necessary to reserve space in memory to store the value of the pointer. In assembly language, a pointer is treated like any other type of variable, although it is frequently used along with indexed and indirect register addressing. Thus the declaration

```
List *Element;
```

in the P3 assembly corresponds to

```
Element  WORD  0
```

since the addresses in the P3 are 16 bits, that is, the same size of the data word.

Note that these declarations do not create space for the actual data, only for a pointer to that data. In C, this space can be reserved by a call to the routine `malloc()`.

As an example, let us consider the initialisations in the following C program extract:

```
short int Var, *Point;
Point = malloc(1);
```

that, in assembly, will correspond to

```
Data    WORD  0
Var     WORD  0
Point   WORD  Data
```

(`Data` represents the memory location reserved for the call to `malloc(1)`).

Assuming that the `R1` register contains the variable P, the following lines of C code and assembly are equivalent:

```
P = *Point;    ⟺    MOV R1,M[Data]
P = Point;     ⟺    MOV R1,M[Point]    ⟺    MOV R1,Data
P = &Point;    ⟺    MOV R1,Point
P = Var;       ⟺    MOV R1,M[Var]
P = &Var;      ⟺    MOV R1,Var
```

(note: `P = *Var;` is an invalid instruction.)

Note that the array type variables defined above, **Vector** and **Sequence** are also pointers. The difference is that these are fixed references while pointers can be changed.

11.1.1.5   *Variables in registers*

As mentioned, variables may occupy memory or registers. Normally, it is the compiler that makes the selection of the variables which stay in registers to optimise their use. However, in many languages, such as the C language, it is possible to indicate which variables should remain in registers. For example, in C the declaration:

```
register short int Accumulator;
```

indicates that a register should be reserved to keep the variable **Accumulator**. Since, in C, the **short int** type has 16 bits, in the case of the P3 processor, this declaration will imply that during the lifetime of the variable

`Accumulator`, one register will be reserved to hold its value. This reservation is made, provided that there are still registers available, otherwise, the `register` indication will be ignored, and the variable will go to a memory location. For variable types with a lesser number of bits, for example, if it were a `char` (8 bits), the behaviour would be the same. For types with a width that is greater, for instance, `long int` (32 bits), it will be necessary to reserve more than one register.

Note that the previous declaration in C does not have any correspondence in assembly code. It only implies, as was stated, that one register is reserved, for example, `R1`, which in a given area of code is designated to hold the value of this variable.

11.1.2 *Data Manipulation*

The translation of data handling operations from a high-level language to assembly is relatively direct. There are, however, two points which require some attention. The first point is that, typically, assembly instructions only allow two operands. Thus, complex expressions in a high-level language must be arranged as a sequence of assembly instructions. The second point can be more complicated and is related to the adjustment of the width of the data types of the operands to the width of the processor registers.

Consider the following expression in the C language:

`Q = (R + S - T) / 4;`

and let us analyse the translation of this expression into assembly.

11.1.2.1 *Same width for variables and data word*

Let us first consider the simplest case in which all the variables reside in memory and are of a short int type, hence, with the same width as the data word. In this case, it is only necessary to unpack the expression, taking into account operator priorities. The equivalent programming extract in the P3 assembly is listed in Program 11.1:

Some points regarding this assembly code:

- The division by four is made by an arithmetic (to keep the sign bit) shift of two places to the right. This strategy is possible as the constant in the divisor is a power of 2. When this is the case in a multiplication or division, this operation should always be substituted by a shift to the left or right, respectively. Besides the vast difference in efficiency, using the

Program 11.1   Assembly program extract to calculate Q = (R + S - T) / 4 with the same width for variables and the data word.

```
Q   WORD  0
R   WORD  0
S   WORD  0
T   WORD  0
    ...
    MOV   R1, M[R]   ; obtain R
    ADD   R1, M[S]   ; add S
    SUB   R1, M[T]   ; subtract T
    SHRA  R1, 2      ; divide by 4 (shifting right two positions)
    MOV   M[Q], R1   ; store the result
```

instructions MUL or DIV has the additional disadvantage of requiring the constant first to be copied to a register.

• For this assembly code to be equivalent to the C code, the memory location corresponding to the variable Q must receive the result stored in register R1. If this variable is subject to further processing, the programmer may delay this transfer until R1 has the final value of Q, as it is easier to keep processing Q by keeping it in a register.

• Overflow situations have been ignored since this is the behaviour of the program in C. The behaviour of the program extracts above is, therefore, equivalent even in these situations.

11.1.2.2   *Width of variables narrower than the data word*

Let us now analyse the case of the translation of the same expression, but now considering that the variable type is **char**, a type of data with a width narrower that the data word. As discussed above, in this situation it is possible to compact two variables into each memory location.

We begin with the case with no compaction, that is, each memory location contains one of the variables in the eight least significant bits. For this situation, the assembly program shown above works with minimal changes shown in Program 11.2. In ADD and SUB operations, the eight least significant bits only depend on the eight least significant bits of the operands. The only operation where this is not true is the shift operation to the right, SHRA since two of the bits with an immediately greater weight will enter the two positions to the left. If the eight most significant bits of R1 have not been properly prepared, they may have some content resulting from a previous operation. These unpredictable bits will enter to the left, and the right shift will not behave as a division. Therefore, the former assembly program will only operate correctly for the non-compacted **char** type if we ensure from the outset that the ADD and SUB operations do not generate a carry beyond the eighth bit. In this case, the eight most significant bits will all be either 0 or 1, depending on whether the result was positive or negative, respectively, in which case the shift to the right works correctly. As the most common situation is that there is no such guarantee, it is necessary to change the program so that the 8 bits of greatest weight, after the subtraction operation, comply with the sign extension (see Section 5.2.3) of the value in the eight least significant bits (Program 11.2):

Let us now consider compacted variables in memory. As an example, let us consider the following organisation of variables:

15	14	13	12	11	10	9	8	7	6	5	4	3	2	1	0
R								Q							
T								S							

As was discussed above, this packaging saves a lot of space, but requires some extra care in processing the variables as shown in Program 11.3.

Note that the compacted memory locations are first read to a register. The operation involving the variable in the lowest weight part can be carried out immediately. For the operation with the other variable, it is necessary to shift that same register eight positions to the right. Finally, note that the result is saved with the MVBL instruction, which copies only the part corresponding to the variable Q.

Program 11.2 Assembly program extract to calculate Q = (R + S - T) / 4 with the width of the variables narrower than the data word with non-compacted variables.

```
Q           WORD  0
R           WORD  0
S           WORD  0
T           WORD  0
            ...
            MOV   R1, M[R]     ; obtain R
            ADD   R1, M[S]     ; add S
            SUB   R1, M[T]     ; subtract T
            TEST  R1, 0080h    ; test the sign
            BR.Z  Pos          ; if negative
            OR    R1, FF00h    ; MSBs all set to 1
            BR    DoDiv        ; if positive
Pos:        AND   R1, 00FFh    ; MSBs all set to 0
DoDiv:      SHRA  R1, 2        ; divide by 4 (shifting two positions)
            MOV   M[Q], R1     ; store the result
```

Program 11.3 Assembly program extract to calculate Q = (R + S - T) / 4 with the width of the variables narrower than the data word with compacted variables.

```
RQ        WORD   0
TS        WORD   0
          . . .
          MOV    R1, M[RQ]   ; obtain the RQ package
          SHRA   R1, 8       ; R1 with the value of R in the lower part
          MOV    R2, M[TS]   ; obtain the TS package
          ADD    R1, R2      ; R1 with the sum R+S in the lower part
                             ; the higher part does not have meaning
          SHRA   R2, 8       ; R2 with the value of T in the lower part
          SUB    R1, R2      ; R1 with R+S-T in the lower part
                             ; the higher part does not have meaning
          TEST   R1, 0080h   ; test the sign
          BR.Z   Pos         ; if negative
          OR     R1, FF00h   ; MSBs all set to 1
          BR     DoDiv       ; if positive
Pos:      AND    R1, 00FFh   ; MSBs all set to 0
DoDiv:    SHRA   R1, 2       ; divide by 4 (shifting two positions)
          MVBL   M[RQ], R1   ; store the result
```

11.1.2.3 *Width of variables wider than the data word*

Let us finally consider in Program 11.4 the case of variables with a size greater than a data word. As an example, let us consider that the variables are of a long int type. In this case, each variable will occupy two memory locations. Let us also assume that their organisation is little-endian, which means that the part of the lowest weight of the variables is in the lowest memory locations (the treatment of the big-endian case is similar).

Note that for the addition and subtraction instructions, the operation is first carried out on the lowest part of the operands, since operations between the highest parts have to take into account the carry bit generated in processing the lowest part. This dependence would also be true in the case that a shift to the left was used. However, in this case, the operation is a shift to the right, and this operation must first be carried out on the highest part. Just as above, the SHRA instruction is necessary so that the shift keeps the sign bit. However, the bits which leave to the right of this shift must propagate to the highest part of the bits with least weight. This influence is possible through the use of the carry bit. However, as it is only possible to store one bit each time, this implies using a bitwise shift as many times as needed. The instruction RORC (rotate right with carry) is used to place the carry bit to the left of the lowest part.

Program 11.4 Assembly program extract to calculate Q = (R + S - T) / 4 with the width of the variables wider than the data word.

```
QL   WORD   0
QH   WORD   0
RL   WORD   0
RH   WORD   0
SL   WORD   0
SH   WORD   0
TL   WORD   0
TH   WORD   0
     ...
     MOV    R1, M[RL]    ; get the part of least weight of R
     ADD    R1, M[SL]    ; addition of the 16 bits of least weight R+S
     MOV    R2, M[RH]    ; get the part of greatest weight of R
     ADDC   R2, M[SH]    ; addition of the 16 bits of greatest weight of R+S
                         ; with carry
     SUB    R1, M[TL]    ; subtraction of the 16 bits of least weight
     SUBB   R2, M[TH]    ; subtraction of greatest weight with carry
     SHRA   R2, 1        ; division by 2 of the part of greatest weight
     RORC   R1, 1        ; division by 2 of the part of least weight
     SHRA   R2, 1        ; division by 2 of the part of greatest weight
     RORC   R1, 1        ; division by 2 of the part of least weight
     MOV    M[QL], R1    ; store the part of least weight of the result
     MOV    M[QH], R2    ; store the part of greatest weight of the result
```

Note that this approach is directly extensible to variable types with any number of bits which are multiples of the width of the register word.

11.1.2.4 *Floating-point data types*

If the variables involved in the expression in C are a type with floating-point representation, float or double, the translation to the P3 assembly is significantly more complicated. Section 5.5 presented the arithmetic operations on floating-point operands. It is not difficult to understand that to carry out any of these operations with the P3 instruction set, an assembly routine with some complexity is necessary.

Nowadays, general-purpose processors include hardware support to perform directly floating-point operations. Their set of instructions includes, thus, dedicated assembly instructions for manipulating floating-point operands. For example, the sum of two float values may be carried out by the ADDF instruction, and for two double values, by the instruction ADDD. The translation of the expression in C to the assembly of these processors is direct. Note that in floating-point operations it is not possible to substitute the division by 2^n by a shift to the right of n bits.

For simpler processors which do not have support in hardware, as is the case with the P3, compilers use mathematical libraries which include subroutines for each floating-point operation. Therefore, the translation of one of these operations in C is carried out by a call to the appropriate subroutine.

11.1.3   *Control Structures*

Control instructions in the C language include the simple decision, *if-else* and various forms of loops, *for*, *while* and *do-while*.

The format of the **if-else** decision is:

```
if (condition)
    code-then
else
    code-else
```

If the result of the *condition* is different from zero, then the *code-then* is executed. If the result of the *condition* is zero, the *code-else* is executed. Expressed this way, the translation to assembly is trivial:

```
        generate condition
        CMP     condition, R0
        JMP.Z   Else
        code-then
        JMP     Next
Else:   code-else
Next:   ...
```

However, the *condition* is typically an equality or inequality, the result of which in C is a 1, if true, or a 0, if false. It is therefore not very efficient to encode the condition in assembly in a way in which the result is 0 or 1, to then test this value. For example, let us consider

```
if (a > MAXIMUM)
    b = LIMIT;
else
    a = a + 1;
```

and that the registers R1 and R2 contain the variables a and b, respectively. Using the translation above, and assuming that R7 contains the result of the condition, it gives:

```
        CMP    R1, MAXIMUM   ;\
        MOV    R7, R0        ; \ Generate the condition
        BR.NP  Least         ; /
        INC    R7            ;/
Least:  CMP    R7, R0        ; Test the condition
        BR.Z   Else
        MOV    R2, LIMIT     ; Code Then
        BR     Next
Else:   INC    R1            ; Code Else
Next:   ...
```

In the generic case in which there is no explicit use of the value of the condition (in the program above, stored in R7), this assembly program can be simplified to:

```
        CMP    R1, MAXIMUM
        BR.NP  Else
        MOV    R2, LIMIT     ; Code Then
        BR     Next
Else:   INC    R1            ; Code Else
Next:   ...
```

The various versions of the loops are very similar regarding the basic functioning and are carried out using an **if-else** test, the result of which determines the code to execute: the code of the body of the loop or the code that follows the loop. The simplest case is perhaps the **do-while**, the format of which is:

```
do {
      body-of-the-loop
}     while(condition);
```

The program continues looping and executing the *body-of-the-loop*, until the *condition* has the value zero. The translation to assembly is:

```
Loop:   body-of-the-loop
        ...
        generate condition
        CMP      condition, R0
        BR.NZ    Loop
        ...
```

The remarks above on simplifying the generation of the *condition* also apply of course to this and the other versions of loops.

As an example, let us consider:

```
do {
      a = a + 1;
      a = 2 * a;
}     while(a < MAXIMUM);
```

and where the variable a is in register R1. A possible implementation in the P3 assembly is

```
Loop:  INC  R1           ; body of the loop
       SHL  R1, 1         ; body of the loop
       CMP  R1, MAXIMUM   ; generate condition
       BR.N Loop
       ...
```

The case of the while loop is similar to the do-while loop, with the difference that the test is carried out before starting the loop, and the loop finishes with a jump to this test

```
while   (condition) {
        body-of-the-loop
}
```

which, in the P3 assembly is:

```
Loop:   generate condition
        CMP     condition, R0
        BR.Z    Next
        body-of-the-loop
        BR      Loop
Next:   ...
```

The for loops are, in turn, similar to the while loops, but include the additional possibility of initialising and updating variables which are used to control the number of times to repeat the loop. The general format of the for loop is

```
for(initialization; condition; updating) {
        body-of-the-loop
}
```

In assembly this will be:

```
        initialization
Loop:   generate condition
        CMP     condition, R0
        BR.Z    Next
        body-of-the-loop
        updating
        BR      Loop
Next:   ...
```

To illustrate the translation of this type of loop, let us consider the following program extract in C:

```
for(i = 0; i < N_CAR; i++){
    word[i] &= UPPERCASE;
}
```

Assuming that the variable i is stored in the register **R3**, the translation to the P3 assembly will be

```
        MOV     R3, R0          ; initialization
Loop:   CMP     R3, N_CAR       ; generate the condition
        BR.NN   Next
        MOV     R7, UPPERCASE   ; body of the loop
        AND     M[R3+word], R7  ; body of the loop
        INC     R3              ; updating
        BR      Loop
Next: ...
```

We assume that **R7** is available to serve as a temporary variable, which is necessary as it is not possible to have two constants in the **AND** instruction. Note also that the initialisation of **R7** may be done a single time outside the loop.

11.1.4 *Subroutine Calls*

The translation of a call to a simple subroutine is trivial since it only involves using the **CALL** instruction. As an example, let us consider a subroutine which places a global **test** variable at zero:

```
void setZero(){
    test = 0;
}
    ...
```

```
setZero();
    ...
```

Assuming that the **test** variable is in memory, the corresponding code in assembly is simply:

```
setZero:    MOV   M[test], RO
            RET
            ...
            CALL  setZero
            ...
```

However, subroutine calls often presume *parameter passing* to that routine and the *parameter return* from that routine. The passage of parameters may use:

- registers
- memory locations
- the stack

11.1.4.1 *Parameter passing using registers*

Parameter passing and return through registers consists in using a set of registers when calling the subroutine, which will have the values that it needs for its execution and will have the values generated by the routine upon exit. The call to the subroutine, therefore, implies loading those registers previously with the corresponding values. Before returning, the routine loads the corresponding registers with the values it shall return.

To illustrate this case, let us consider[1]:

```
short int average(short int A, short int B){
    return (A + B) / 2;
}
...
result = average(55, 34);
...
```

---

[1]The use of the type **short int** in the following examples makes possible the simplification of the assembly code because of the easy mapping to registers and memory positions on P3. This simplification does not limit in any way the generality of the method and makes the essential points more clear.

Program 11.5.   Subroutine average (parameters passed by registers).

```
average:  MOV    R3, R1           ; get the value of A
          ADD    R3, R2           ; add it to B
          SHRA   R3, 1            ; divide by 2
          RET                     ; and return from the routine
          ...
          MOV    R1, 55           ; A is passed through R1
          MOV    R2, 34           ; B is passed through R2
          CALL   average          ; call the routine
          MOV    M[result], R3    ; get and place the result
          ...
```

The subroutine **average** has two input parameters and one return value. Let us consider that the registers R1 and R2 have been reserved for passing the values A and B, respectively, and also that register R3 will have the return value. Although it is not important, let us assume that the variable **result** is in memory. Program 11.5 shows the translation to assembly.

11.1.4.2   *Parameter passing using the memory*

The limitation for register parameter passing is that there are a reduced number of registers and many will normally be used for specific purposes within the program. Given this, the number of registers available may be less than necessary to pass the parameters and return values from the routine to call.

An obvious alternative is to use memory locations for this purpose. For each routine, the memory locations reserved for each parameter and each return value are defined, and their use is then the same as in register passing. The advantage is that the number of memory locations available for this purpose is far higher than the number of registers.

Returning to the previous example, this involves reserving three memory locations, two for the parameters A and B and one for the return value, AVE; the assembly extract is listed in Program 11.6.

As can be seen, one disadvantage of using memory locations when compared to registers is the incompatibility of addressing modes. In particular, loading constants to a memory location implies a greater number of assembly instructions, leading to longer and slower programs.

11.1.4.3   *Parameter passing using the stack*

Either of the two above alternatives has the limitation that the reference for the input and output parameters is always the same for each routine call.

Program 11.6.   Subroutine average (parameters passed by memory).

```
A           WORD   0
B           WORD   0
AVE         WORD   0
            . . .
average:    MOV    R7, M[A]        ; get the value of A
            ADD    R7, M[B]        ; add the value of B
            SHRA   R7, 1           ; divide by 2
            MOV    M[AVE], R7      ; put the result in memory
            RET                    ; and return it
            . . .
            MOV    R1, 55          ; put the value of A
            MOV    M[A], R1        ; in the memory to be read by the routine
            MOV    R1, 34          ; put the value of B in the
            MOV    M[B], R1        ; memory to be read by the routine
            CALL   average         ; call the routine
            MOV    R1, M[AVE]      ; get the result
            MOV    M[result], R1   ; and put it in place
            . . .
```

This problem is especially significant in the case of recursive routines, that is, routines which include direct or indirect calls to themselves. In this case, defining the parameters for the internal call to the routine will override the value of its input parameters which may still be needed ahead.

An example of a possible recursive routine is calculating the factorial of a number. In C this will be

```
short int factorial(short int N){
    short int resul;
    if(N == 0)
        resul = 1;
    else
        resul = N * factorial(N - 1);
    return resul;
}
```

In translating this to assembly, let us consider the case of register parameter passing (the problem is the same using memory locations for parameter passing). R1 is the register which passes the value of N and R2 the register which has the return value, so one solution in assembly is shown in Program 11.7

The problem with this solution is that passing the parameter N before the new CALL instruction will alter the value of R1 and R2, and the context of the current call to the factorial routine will be lost!

Program 11.7. Subroutine factorial (non-functional).

```
factorial:  CMP     R1, R0       ; Is N zero?
            BR.NZ   callDecN     ; if it is
            MOV     R2, 1        ; result = 1
            RET                  ; and return
callDecN:   MOV     R2, R1       ; if it is not, store
            DEC     R1           ; and decrement the value
            CALL    factorial    ; and call the routine again
            ...                  ; what will create a problem...
```

It is only possible to resolve the situation if each instance of a call to a routine manipulates different occurrences of the parameters on entry and exit. An elegant way of achieving this is to use the stack. However, this has to be carried out with some care, since the call and return instructions for the routine, CALL and RET, also use the stack, to store the return address.

This approach involves placing the input parameters in the stack in a previously established order before calling the routine. Note that space must be reserved in the stack for the output parameters before calling the subroutine. The reason for this procedure is that the instruction to return from the routine, RET, is expecting to find the return address at the top of the stack. Therefore, the space in the stack for the output parameters should be reserved a priori. For reasons which will become clearer later on, it is advantageous for the output parameters to be the first to be placed on the stack.

Returning to the example of the **factorial** routine, a possible version of this in assembly, reserving space for the return value on the stack before placing the number N, will be explained in Program 11.8.

After executing the routine, the result will be at the top of the stack. For example, to calculate the factorial of 2 and store it in register R7,

```
PUSH  R0           ; space for the result
PUSH  2            ; passing the value
CALL  factorial
POP   R7           ; placing the result
```

Figure 11.3 helps to understand the functioning of this routine, illustrating the state of the stack in some of the execution stages. Column (a) of this figure reflects the state of the stack after the CALL to the factorial routine, which assumes that the instruction POP R7, the first instruction after the CALL, is at address 01B7h (in this figure, let us consider that the memory locations not used contain the value A5A5h). The input value, 2, is two positions below in the stack and as such, with an address increased twice

Program 11.8.   Subroutine factorial.

```
factorial:  CMP    M[SP+2], R0   ; Is N zero?
            BR.NZ  callDecN      ; if it is the
            MOV    R1, 1         ; output value is 1
            MOV    M[SP+3], R1   ; and is stored on the stack
            RETN   1             ; free input parameter and return
callDecN:   MOV    R1, M[SP+2]   ; N is not 0, get N
            DEC    R1            ; decrement N
            PUSH   R0            ; reserve space for the result
            PUSH   R1            ; place input parameter
            CALL   factorial
            POP    R1            ; get result
            MOV    R2, M[SP+2]   ; get N
            MUL    R1, R2        ; multiply: R2 gets the lowest part
            MOV    M[SP+3], R2   ; place result
            RETN   1             ; free input parameter and return
```

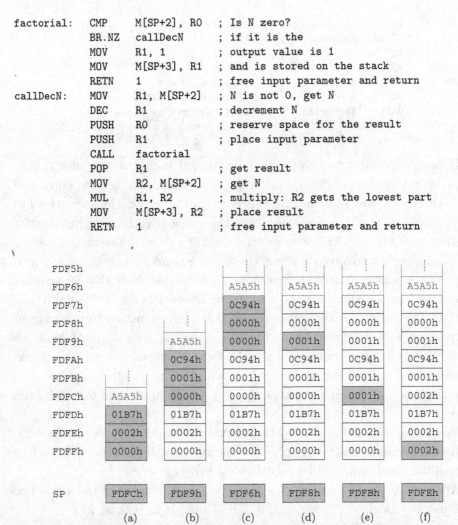

Fig. 11.3   State of the stack during the different phases of calculation of the factorial: (a) after the initial routine call; (b) after the first recursive call; (c) after the second recursive call; (d) after the return from the second recursive call; (e) after the return from the first recursive call and (f) after the return from the routine.

compared to the value of the SP. This value is initially 2, and this is the situation when the jump to the callDecN label is carried out. In this case, it is necessary to once again call the routine itself with the input parameter decremented. Column (b) of Figure 11.3 shows the state of the stack on entry to the routine after this call, assuming that the return address, corresponding to the instruction POP R1, is 0C94H. This situation is repeated one more time, with column (c) in the figure showing the contents of the stack on entry to the routine in this third call. Note that, at this point, there are three active calls to the `factorial` routine. However, each of these calls works on a set of parameters at different positions of the stack, so there are no conflicts.

In this call, the input parameter is now 0, such that the jump in the second line of the routine does not happen, and the recursion terminates here. Instead of this, the value 1 is placed in the stack position corresponding to the output parameter from the stack. The instruction `RETN 1` is used to remove[2] from the stack, not only the return address but also the corresponding position for the input parameter of the routine. Column (d) of Figure 11.3 shows the situation of the stack immediately after carrying out this instruction.

The return takes the processor to the instruction `POP R1`, which obtains the result from the stack. This is multiplied by the input value of this call to the routine, and the result is placed on the stack ($1 = 1 \times 1$), and the routine is exited, once again removing the input parameter from the stack with the instruction `RETN 1`. This situation is shown in column (e) of Figure 11.3.

The actions described in the previous paragraph are repeated, once more, with column (f) of Figure 11.3 showing the situation of the stack after the complete execution of the `factorial` routine. The final result is at the top of the stack, from where the instruction `POP R7` retrieves it.

The use of the stack is an elegant way of passing parameters to routines that efficiently solves the case of recursive routines. Due to the intense use of the stack, this manipulation also requires additional care, particularly in determining the position of each variable regarding the stack pointer location. One disadvantage of this method of parameter passing comparing with the passage through registers is that it involves memory reads and writes, which, as has already been mentioned, requires a greater access time.

11.2   Programming Techniques in Assembly

This section will discuss good practices for creating programs in assembly language. These techniques will allow for a more effective development and maintenance of software written in assembly.

---

[2]As the figure shows, the "removal" from the stack does not mean to erase from memory. This "removal" is obtained simply with additional increments of the stack pointer SP.

11.2.1 *Structured Programming*

As with any other programming language, the use of *structured programming* techniques is essential to carry out a programming project successfully. However, the use of the modular structure in an assembly program is perhaps even more important than in high-level languages, for two reasons. First, assembly language requires more instructions to carry out an operation than a high-level language, which makes programs considerably longer. Second, the legibility of a program written in assembly is considerably less than that of a program in a high level language, given the greater restrictions imposed on the program format and the use of variable names.

It is therefore important to avoid the temptation to start programming too early, without going through a phase of defining the program structure. This definition, possible both using flowcharting, pseudo-code or both, is the most important part of any assembly programming project and should be the part of greater time investment. If this time is not used here, the detailed programming phase and debugging will almost certainly be more extensive with the project taking more time overall.

The program structure definition phase enables the definition and clear understanding of the problem and its division into simpler problems, without worrying about details related to the programming language.

The use of subroutines is directly related to the program structure. Each block (or module) defined in the program structuring phase will correspond to one or more subroutines. Each subroutine should clearly describe:

- its functionality;
- the input and output parameters;
- the registers and memory positions changed by the subroutine.

With a suitable program structure, each subroutine can, and should, be developed and tested independently of the rest of the code. This procedure will enable the construction of the final program, obtained by connecting the subroutines, to be carried out with relative simplicity and speed, since most of the programming errors will have already been detected in the testing phase for each block. On the other hand, one should always avoid joining multiple subroutines which have still not been tested, with the aim of debugging the program as a whole. Errors are extremely hard to identify and resolve at this stage, even if they are relatively simple if analysed at the level of the subroutine.

. The correct approach for the structuring of programs is to divide a problem into a set of simpler problems. The aim is for this division to create independent problems, with a well-defined functionality and interface (that is, the set of input and output data) so that each one of these can be resolved by itself. Unless it is a simple problem, it is normal that the blocks obtained in this first division also have a high-level of complexity. In this case, the same technique of subdividing into simpler problems can be applied to each one of them, and so on, until each of the problems is so simple that its implementation in assembly is clear.

11.2.2 *Comments*

Given the difficult readability of a program in assembly, the use of comments that describe the functioning of the subroutines and the structure of important parts of them is essential. Each subroutine should, therefore, have a header which suitably documents each of the three points identified above. The header of the routine should also describe the type of parameters involved, and the order to pass them in the case of stack passing. The header should function as a manual for using the routine.

Also, code sections of greater complexity, or with a less obvious functionality, should be commented locally. Often, tricks used by the programmer may appear obvious at the time of programming, but can be nearly indecipherable, not only to another person who reviews the code but also, the next day, to the programmer him or herself! Believe us!

11.2.3 *Constants*

The use of numerical constants embedded in the code makes its maintenance and subsequent alteration more difficult, besides being the source of possible errors which are difficult to identify. The methodology which should be adopted is to define all the values of numerical constants at the start of the program using the EQU directive.

This practice gives some meaning to numerical values, and in this way helps to read and interpret the code. For example, while the following section of code

```
MOV   R2, FFFFh
MOV   M[FFFCh], R2
```

is difficult to interpret, the substitution of numerical values by constants with suitable names, such as those below,

```
INITIALIZE_TEXT_WINDOW   EQU   FFFFh
CONTROL_PORT_TEXT        EQU   FFFCh
                         ...
                         MOV   R2, INITIALIZE_TEXT_WINDOW
                         MOV   M[CONTROL_PORT_TEXT], R2
```

makes the functionality of the code much more explicit.

A second, and perhaps more important, reason has to do with associating values for constants. Let us take an example which defines a memory space as a certain number of memory locations, which for illustrative purposes can be assumed to be 100. The correct solution is to specify

```
MAX_DIM_MEMORY EQU 100
```

and use this constant in the code, whenever it is desired to test this limit. If for any reason, it is later decided to alter the number of memory locations, for example, to 500, it is sufficient to change this constant in the EQU declaration.

If the value 100 is explicitly used by the code to test the memory limit, besides making the code more obscure, as we have seen, the alteration of this limit from 100 to 500 is much more challenging. It is not only necessary to run through the code looking for this value 100, but it is also needed to carefully analyse the code, so as to evaluate if each instance of the value 100 is about the memory limit or some other different quantity.

The use of explicit names for the constants and the code can, in many cases, make comments unnecessary. The choice of adequate names, not only for constants but also for variables, routines and labels, is a precious help in debugging and maintaining code.

11.2.4 *Formatting Code*

Since programming in assembly is usually done using a file editor which does not have any specific support for programming in this environment, it is useful to use a format which improves the legibility of the program. Assembly code is generally written in four columns: labels, assembly instruction mnemonics, operands and comments.

11.3 Programming Examples

We will now show two non-trivial examples of programming in assembly with the aim of illustrating some of the characteristics of this programming language.

11.3.1 *List Manipulation*

In many situations, it is necessary to use dynamic data structures. The case of a *linked list*, such as that shown in Figure 11.4, is one of the simplest examples of dynamic structures.

In a list of this type, each element has two fields: the data field and a pointer to the next element in the list. In addition to the elements which make up the list, a pointer to the beginning of it is necessary.

In the example analysed in this section, we assume that the data field is made up of a 16-bit integer, and therefore occupies only one memory location. As already mentioned, the P3 processor uses 16-bit addresses, so the pointer field also occupies a single memory location. Each element of the list is therefore made up of two consecutive memory locations, in which it is assumed that the first (lowest address) contains the data field, and the second, the next element pointer.

Of course, each element of the list may be in any memory location. Figure 11.5(a) shows a possible arrangement in memory of the list shown in Figure 11.4, with the pointer indicating the start at memory location E000h. A usual convention is the use of the value 0 to represent an invalid pointer, used to indicate the end of the list (an obvious consequence is that it is not possible to use the memory address 0000h for any element of the list).

A typical routine in manipulating lists involves inserting an element in a given position. Let us suppose that we wish to make a subroutine **insertAfter** which receives three parameters: the pointer to the start of the list; the address of the element to be inserted and the value of the element after which it is intended to include the new element. We assume that the element to be inserted has the same two fields as the other elements

Fig. 11.4 Example of linked list.

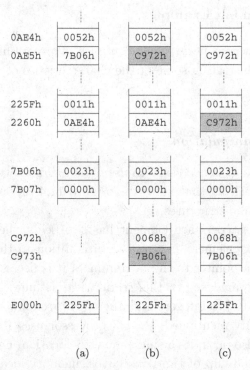

	(a)	(b)	(c)
0AE4h	0052h	0052h	0052h
0AE5h	7B06h	C972h	C972h
225Fh	0011h	0011h	0011h
2260h	0AE4h	0AE4h	C972h
7B06h	0023h	0023h	0023h
7B07h	0000h	0000h	0000h
C972h		0068h	0068h
C973h		7B06h	7B06h
E000h	225Fh	225Fh	225Fh

Fig. 11.5   Possible arrangement in memory of the list considered as an example: (a) initial list, as in Figure 11.4; (b) list after inserting an element, as in Figure 11.6 and (c) list after removing an element, as in Figure 11.7.

of the list. Although the use of any of the parameter passing methods discussed above is possible, for reasons of simplicity, we assume here that these three parameters use register passing, respectively, using the registers R1, R2 and R3.

The operation of this routine is simple. Let us start at the beginning of the list and advance until we find the element after which the insertion will be made. Once this element is found, copy its pointer to the next element to the same field of the new element, and alter this value to point to the address of the new element. When the element searched for does not exist in the list, we place the new element at the end of the list. In assembly, this routine is listed in Program 11.9.

The first lines of the routine, lines 1 to 5, deal with the special case of the empty list, a situation where the element to include becomes the only one of the list. It is therefore enough to place the pointer to the first element pointing to the new (and only) element (line 3), and the next element pointer field of the new element, with the value 0 (line 4) indicating the end of the list.

Program 11.9.   Routine to insert an element in a list.

```
 1.   insertAfter:  CMP     M[R1], R0     ; empty list?
 2.                 BR.NZ   startSearch   ; if yes,
 3.                 MOV     M[R1], R2     ; place the 1st element
 4.                 MOV     M[R2+1], R0   ;
 5.                 RET                   ; and return
 6.   startSearch:  MOV     R4, M[R1]     ; address of the 1st element
 7.   nextInsert:   CMP     M[R4], R3     ; verify if it is the one searched
 8.                 BR.Z    foundInsert   ; it is
 9.                 CMP     M[R4+1], R0   ; end of the list?
10.                 BR.Z    foundInsert
11.                 MOV     R4, M[R4+1]   ; next on the list
12.                 BR      nextInsert
13.   foundInsert:  MOV     R5, M[R4+1]   ; pointer to the next
14.                 MOV     M[R2+1], R5   ; copy to new
15.                 MOV     M[R4+1], R2   ; point to the new
16.                 RET
```

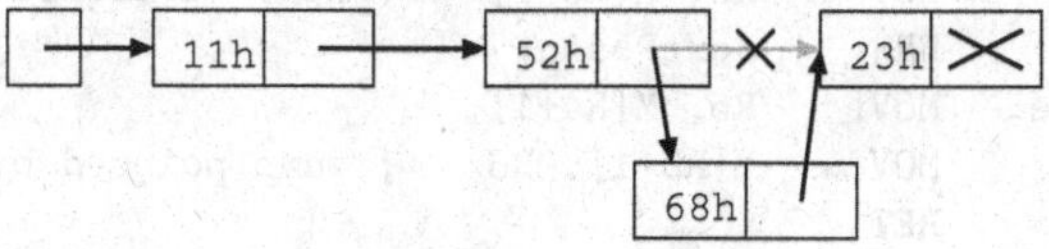

Fig. 11.6   Insertion in the list of the value **68h** after the value **52h**.

Line 6 serves to initialise the pointer that will go through the list. Lines 7 to 12 are the main loop of the routine. The test to see if the searched element has been found is carried out in lines 7 and 8, and the test to see if the end of the list has been reached, in lines 9 and 10. In either of these cases, the loop is exited to insert the new element in the next position of the row. Line 11 moves to the next element of the list. Lines 13 to 15 make the insertion of the new element.

To illustrate what happens in the memory, let us consider the insertion in the list in Figure 11.4 of a new element with the value 68h between the value 52h and 23h, as shown in Figure 11.6. Let us also suppose that this new element is in memory locations C972h and C973h. In this case, the program calls the routine **insertAfter** with R1 = E000h (pointer to the start of the list), R2 = C972h (address of the element to insert) and R3 = 52h (value of the element after which the insertion should be made). Figure 11.5(b) shows the situation regarding memory locations after the insertion of this element.

Consider now the case of another typical operation, that of removing a certain element from the list. Let us now present a possible implementation

Program 11.10.   Routine to remove an element from a list.

```
1.   removeElem:    CMP     M[R1], R0       ; empty list?
2.                  BR.Z    endRemove       ; if yes, do nothing and leave
3.                  MOV     R4, M[R1]       ; address of the 1st element
4.   nextRemove:    CMP     M[R4], R2       ; element found?
5.                  BR.Z    foundRemove
6.                  CMP     M[R4+1], R0     ; end of the list?
7.                  BR.Z    endRemove       ; if yes, do nothing
8.                  MOV     R4, M[R4+1]     ; next on the list
9.                  BR      nextRemove
10.  foundRemove:   CMP     M[R1], R4       ; first on the list?
11.                 BR.NZ   halfRemove
12.                 MOV     R5, M[R4+1]     ; remove 1st from the list
13.                 MOV     M[R1], R5
14.                 RET
15.  halfRemove:    MOV     R5, M[R1]       ; address of the 1st element
16.  nextPosAnt:    CMP     M[R5+1], R4
17.                 BR.Z    posAntRemove    ; previous position?
18.                 MOV     R5, M[R5+1]     ; next on the list
19.                 BR      nextPosAnt
20.  posAntRemove:  MOV     R6, M[R4+1]
21.                 MOV     M[R5+1], R6     ; jump pointed by R4
22.  endRemove:     RET
```

of this routine, removeElem. This routine has two arguments: the pointer to the start of the list and the value of the element to remove. Once again let us consider the case of register parameter passing, in this case, using the registers R1 and R2, respectively. The routine does not alter the list if the specified element is not found. The assembly code is listed in Program 11.10.

The first test to be made, in lines 1 and 2, is whether the list is empty, in which case there is an exit without carrying out any operation. Then, there is the search loop for the element to be removed, in lines 4 to 9. The routine exits this loop, either after reaching the end of the list, in which case a jump is made, as before, directly to the end of the routine without doing anything, or because the element searched for, has been found, with register R4 pointing to it. The CMP instruction in line 10 tests if the element to remove is the first of the list. In this situation, it is necessary to update the pointer to the start of the list to the previous second element or to 0 if there are no more elements. Lines 12 to 14, deal with this two situations, with both dealt with in the same way. If it is not the first element on the list, it is necessary to search the list again looking for the element immediately before the one to be removed. This task is carried out in lines 16 to 19 where it is now guaranteed that the element searched for will be found before the

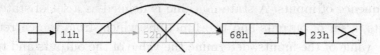

Fig. 11.7   Removal of element 52h from the list.

end of the list. Once found, one must copy the next pointer in the removed element to the next pointer in the previous element on the list.

Once again, to illustrate memory alterations, let us consider removing the element 52h from the list, as is shown in Figure 11.7. To do this, the routine removeElem should be called with the values R1 = E000h (pointer to the start of the list) and R2 = 52h (value of the element to be removed). The situation in memory after the removal of this element in the list is shown in Figure 11.5(c).

Note that the element that has just been removed from the list, and the memory position that it occupied, are lost, in the sense that there is no way of accessing them, originating a waste of memory positions. This space should be recuperated in some way so that in the future it can be reused for new elements in the list. This process is called *dynamic memory management*. Operating systems normally provide services that reserve or free memory locations (in the C language, the available routines are malloc and free, respectively). In simpler systems where there is no operating system, the program must do this management. This consists in keeping a list of free locations, accessed by the first location on the list. Obtaining a location consists in removing the first from the list. Releasing a location involves inserting it as the first element of the list. Sometimes, for reasons of efficiency, this solution is used even in systems which have an operating system, since a call to the operating system services always involves some penalty in execution time.

11.3.2   *State Machine*

Let us now consider the implementation of a state machine in assembly. The description and implementation of state machines in hardware were analysed in Chapter 7. It is often necessary, typically in control systems, to implement state machines in software. This section presents a very general method for achieving this.

As we saw in Chapter 7, what characterises state machines is that they have a set of states, and the state in which the machine is in at any moment determines its behaviour. The state keeps relevant information about the past sequence of inputs. A state machine is defined as a set of states, a set of inputs, a set of outputs and two functions which, from the current state and the value of the inputs, determine the value of the outputs and the next state.

The implementation shown here is based on the definition of the following tables in memory:

- a table with the routines which the machine executes for each current state;
- a table with the next state for each combination of inputs and current state;
- for each output, a table with the value of that output for each combination of inputs and current state.

With these tables, the body of the main routine of the state machine makes a call to the routine whose reference is obtained by reading the first table, then calculates the outputs and the next state, which, in turn, corresponds to successive readings of the remaining tables. Let us assume for the example presented here that:

- the current state of the machine is stored in register R7;
- `tabRoutines` is the first address of the table which contains the references to the routines to be executed in each state;
- `tabNxtSta` is the address where the table which contains the next state starts;
- `tabOutput1` is the address where the table which contains the value of the first output starts (here with the generic name `Output1`).

The following section of code illustrates this implementation:

```
1.    loopME:     CALL M[R7+tabRoutines]     ; processing state
2.                CALL calcIndex             ; R6 gets the index
3.                MOV  R7, M[R6+tabNxtSta]   ; following state
4.                MOV  R5, M[R6+tabOutput1]  ; first output value
5.                MOV  M[OUTPUT1], R5        ; send output port
                  ...
                  BR   loopME
```

Line 1 calls the routine with the processing corresponding to the current state. Sometimes, it may not be possible to reserve a register to store the current state, in which case, it will be stored in a memory location. In line 2 a routine `calcIndex` is called, which calculates the access index to the remaining tables, which is here defined as being returned in the register R6. This index is a function of the current state and the value of each input. Updating the machine state is carried out in line 3. Lines 4 and 5 generate the output Output1 of the machine, in which the register R5 is used as a temporary register due to the incompatibility of the addressing mode. These two lines should be replicated for each state machine output.

To implement this generic structure for a specific case, let us consider the flowchart in Figure 11.8, which specifies a variation of the handshake protocol from the receiver side (Chapter 14 will analyse this protocol in more detail). This state machine has four states (*A*, *B*, *C* and *D*), two inputs (*Ready* and *Error*) and one output (*Ack*).

State *A* represents the idle state, where the machine is waiting for the sender to signal, activating the input *Ready*, that a new value is available to be read at the data port. When *Ready* becomes active, the machine evolves to state *B*, where it carries out a reading of the value of that port. It then

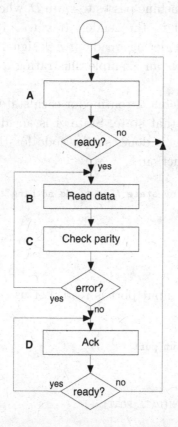

Fig. 11.8 Flowchart of the state machine to implement in software,

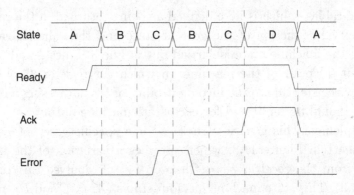

Fig. 11.9   Timing diagram to illustrate the operation of the handshake protocol.

transitions to state C, in which there is a test to see if there was an error in receiving the input value by checking the parity of this value. If the parity test fails, it returns to state B to try a new reading of the data input port. If it passes the test, the machine passes to state D, where the correct reception of the data is signalled to the sender. It stays in that state waiting for confirmation that the sender has read our Ack signal, by disabling the *Ready* signal. Figure 11.9 shows an example illustrating a possible evolution over time for this protocol.

The first step is to define a routine for each state, which implements the intended operation for that state. State A is an idle state, waiting for an event, in which nothing is done, so the code for the respective routine is simply the return instruction:

```
; StateA:  the function of state A is to do nothing...
; Inputs:
; Outputs:
; Effects:
StateA:    RET
```

In state B the data input port is read. Let us consider that the data is returned in register R1:

```
; StateB:  read data input port.
; Inputs:  -
; Outputs: R1
; Effects: -
StateB:    MOV      R1, M[DATA_PORT]
           RET
```

The purpose of state C is to confirm the validity of the data, testing the *parity* of the value just read. This simple error control technique, which will be studied in detail in Chapter 14, consists of adding an extra bit to the data, so that the total number of bits at 1 in the transmitted word is always even (or always odd). In this example, let us assume the first case, which means that the value read from the data input port should always have an even number of bits at one (which, unsurprisingly, is given the name of even parity). However, if an odd number of bits at one is detected, this is because there has been some error in reading the value or in the transmission process. Calculating the parity may be carried out by the following routine, which will shift the value read, one position to the right, and complementing the value of a temporary register whenever the bit that leaves is one. An even number of bits implies that the temporary register value is equal to the initial value, that is, 0. At the end, the variable **Error** is updated with the result:

```
; StateC:    calculate parity.
; Inputs:    R1
; Outputs:   M[Error]
; Effects:   alter R2 and R3}
StateC:     MOV      R2, R0        ; initialize R2
            MOV      R3, R1        ; do not alter input value
loopC:      CMP      R3, R0        ; finish when R3 is 0
            BR.Z     finishedC
            SHR      R3, 1         ; get the bit to the right
            BR.NC    loopC         ; if this is 1, complement R2
            COM      R2            ; an even number of complements
            BR       loopC         ; leave R2 at 0
finishedC:  MOV      M[Error], R2  ; store result
            RET
```

Finally, the state D is limited to writing the confirmation of the value received, in the output port:

```
; StateD:    write the value 1 in the output control port.
; Inputs:    -
; Outputs:   -
; Effects:   -
StateD:     PUSH     1
            POP      M[PORT_ACK]
            RET
```

By associating, in order, the indexes from 0 to 3 to the states A to D, respectively, the table of routines for each state is defined in the following way:

```
tabRoutines STR StateA, StateB, StateC, StateD
```

Once the operation per state has been implemented, it remains to define the tables which generate the following state and the primary outputs from the current state and the primary inputs. The content of these tables derives from the state transition table which describes the operation of the machine. Table 11.1 shows the state transition table for the example under study.

The tables for the implementation in software are easily obtained from the respective column. Thus, the next state table, using the indexes from 0 to 3 attributed above to the states, is defined by the following instruction:

```
TabNxtSta  STR  0, 0, 1, 1, 2, 2, 2, 2, 3, 1, 3, 1, 0, 0, 3, 3
```

Similarly, the table for the single primary output, *Ack*, is:

```
TabOutput  STR  0, 0, 0, 0, 0, 0, 0, 0, 0, 0, 0, 0, 1, 1, 1, 1
```

Table 11.1   Content of the state transition table of the machine to implement in software.

Inputs		Current	Next	Outputs
(*Ready*	*Error*)	State	State	*Ack*
0	0	A	A	0
0	1	A	A	0
1	0	A	B	0
1	1	A	B	0
0	0	B	C	0
0	1	B	C	0
1	0	B	C	0
1	1	B	C	0
0	0	C	D	0
0	1	C	B	0
1	0	C	D	0
1	1	C	B	0
0	0	D	A	1
0	1	D	A	1
1	0	D	D	1
1	1	D	D	1

Program 11.11 Routine that calculates the index for the following state tables and primary outputs from the values of the current state and primary inputs.

```
;                 calcIndex: calculates the index for the following
;                 state tables and primary outputs from the
;                 values of the current state and primary inputs
; Inputs:    R7 - Current state
;                 M[Error] - value of the input Error
;                 M[Ready] - value of the input Ready
; Outputs:   R5 - index to read for the tables
; Effects:   alter register R1
calcIndex:   MOV   R5, R7          ; get the base
             SHL   R5, 2           ; place the index in the first of the
                                   ; lines corresponding to that state
             MOV   R1, M[Error]    ; read the input Error and
             OR    R5, R1          ; correct the index
             MOV   R1, M[Ready]    ; read the input Ready,
             SHL   R1, 1           ; position and
             OR    R5, R1          ; correct the index
             RET
```

Now the routine `calcIndex` is needed, which determines the index of the position which should be read from the tables from the value of the current state and each of the inputs. For the example under consideration, a possible implementation is listed in Program 11.11.

To illustrate the operation of the access to the tables, let us consider that the current state is C and the inputs have the value $Error = 1$ and $Ready = 0$. The index corresponding to the state C is 2, therefore the return from the `calcIndex` routine is R5 = 9. The position 9 of the table `TabNxtSta` has the value 1, which means that the state machine will evolve to state B, as is intended. Position 9 of the table `tabOutput` has the value 0, which will be the value that the primary output Ack will take.

11.4   Complete Illustrative Example

We will now develop an assembly program to illustrate the methods described above. The program to be developed has to copy the text from an input port and write it to the output port with the first letter of all the words in uppercase and the others in lowercase. In this text, the only word separator is the space, and the character «@» indicates the end of the text.

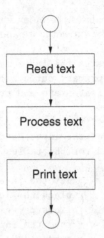

Fig. 11.10　Flowchart for the main program.

The first phase consists in defining the overall structure of the program. In a first approach, the program may be divided into three blocks, which correspond to the blocks of the flowchart in Figure 11.10.

This flowchart, although simple, specifies that in the first phase the text is read from the input port and written to memory; in a second step, the processing of the text in memory takes place; and, finally, the modified text is written to the output port. In this phase, we also specify that the subroutine which reads the text returns the number of characters read, to use in the following modules. The three steps indicated in the figure are not so simple that their realisation is obvious, and we need to refine each of those blocks.

The flowchart in Figure 11.11 describes the block which reads the text.

The subroutine in Program 11.12 implements in the P3 assembly the flowchart in Figure 11.11.

This subroutine reads the text, character by character, and writes it to memory, testing each character for the equality with the value indicating the end of the text and verifying if the maximum size for the text has been reached.[3] With this level of detail, it is then easy to transpose the

---

[3]In this simple solution to the problem it is not returned any indication if the reading of the characters terminates because the character @ is found or because the maximum number of characters is reached.

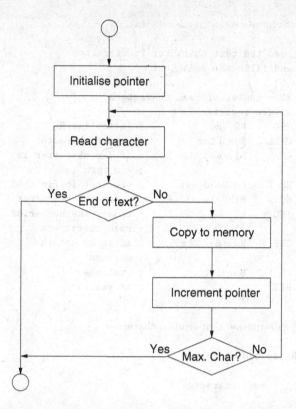

Fig. 11.11 Flowchart for the subroutine to read the characters.

flowchart to assembly language and create the corresponding subroutine, described in Program 11.12. Note that the program does not use numerical constants, but rather constants that the program header will define. In this case, the constants are: end_txt, the character code which indicates the end of the text; Text, first memory location reserved for the text; and max_char, the maximum number of characters for the text.

A character is read by the subroutine in Program 11.13. This subroutine waits until there is a character in the input port, and then returns it. We assume here that reading the control port returns 0 if no new character is present since the last reading of the input port. The input port corresponds to the keyboard.

It is now necessary to specify the block which processes the text. A possible flowchart for this block is shown in Figure 11.12.

Program 11.12.   Subroutine that reads the text.

```
; ReadText:     read the text character by character
;               and fills the zone text
; Inputs:
; Outputs:      R2 - number of read characters
; Efects:       alters register R1
ReadText:       MOV     R2, R0            ; initialize R2
ReadLoop:       CALL    ReadChar         ; read a character
                CMP     R1, end_text     ; if the character is
                                         ; end_text
                BR.Z    EndReadText      ; the text is finished
                MOV     M[R2+Text], R1   ; store the character
                INC     R2               ; update the number of
                                         ; read characters
                CMP     R2, max_char     ; if it is not the
                                         ; maximum
                BR.NZ   ReadLoop         ; continue
EndReadText:    RET                      ; if yes, end
```

Program 11.13.   Sub-routine that reads a character.

```
; ReadChar:   Reads one character
; Inputs:
; Outputs:    R1 - read character
; Effects:
ReadChar:       CMP     R0, M[control]
                BR.Z    ReadChar         ; Idle loop
                MOV     R1, M[in_port]   ; Read the character
                RET
```

This block advances character by character in memory, converting each letter that follows a space into an uppercase letter until it has processed the number of characters read. The conversion of lowercase to uppercase uses the operation AND for the character with the DFh mask. In ASCII, the code for the lowercase and uppercase of a given letter only differs in the sixth bit, which is, respectively, 1 for lowercase and 0 for uppercase. For example the letter «a» is represented in ASCII by 61h and the letter «A» is represented by 41h.

The inverse operation is done with the OR operation. The alteration of the value of the sixth bit is carried out with the help of the mask, which will only has the sixth bit set at 1. Note that it is not necessary to check if each character is uppercase or lowercase. Depending on its position in the word the right case is imposed.

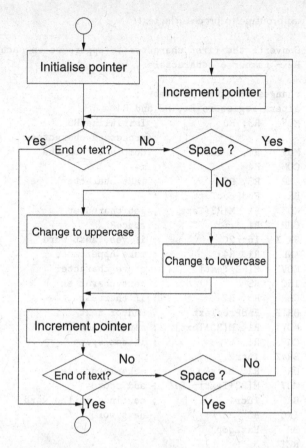

Fig. 11.12 Flowchart of the processing text block.

We have now achieved a sufficiently simple representation to be able to write the assembler code for this subroutine, described in Program 11.14.

Note that there is a correspondence between the flowchart and the code.

Finally, it is necessary to specify the text printing block. Figure 11.13 shows a possible flowchart for this block.

Given the simplicity of this block, we may do an immediate translation into assembly language, which results in the code shown in Program 11.15.

The main program, described in Program 11.16, corresponds to the flowchart in Figure 11.10 and will simply be a sequence of calls to the subroutines already defined, preceded by the necessary directives, which specify the program origin and the values of the constants and variables used in the program and subroutines.

Program 11.14.   Subroutine to process the text.

```
; ProcText:   Converts the first character to uppercase in each word
; Inputs:     R2 - number of characters
; Outputs:
; Effects:    changes the text in memory;
;             alters registers R1, R3 and R4
ProcText:      MOV   R3, R0            ; Initialize R3
                                       ; processed characters
               MOV   R4, mask          ; Complement of the
               COM   R4                ; mask
ExtLoop:       CMP   R3, R2            ; last character?
               BR.Z  EndProcText
               MOV   R1, M[R3+Text]    ; get character
               CMP   R1,' '            ; space?
               BR.Z  Incr2             ; if yes, next word
               AND   R1, R4            ; make uppercase
               MOV   M[R3+Text], R1    ; store character
Incr1:         INC   R3                ; next character
               CMP   R3, R2            ; if there is..
               BR.Z  EndProcText       ; End of text
               MOV   R1, M[R3+Text]    ; new character
               CMP   R1,' '            ; if not space
               BR.Z  Incr2
               OR    R1, mask          ; make lowercase
               MOV   M[R3+Text], R1    ; and store
               BR    Incr1             ; continue in the word
Incr2:         INC   R3                ; next word
               BR    ExtLoop
EndProcText:   RET
```

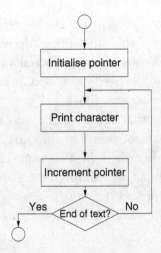

Fig. 11.13   Flowchart of the block for writing the text.

Program 11.15. Subroutine for writing the modified text.

```
; Print:    Prints the text in the output port.
; Inputs:   R1 - start of text
;           R2 - number of characters in the text
; Outputs:
; Effects:  alters registers R3 and R4

Print:      MOV    R3, R0              ; Initialize R3
PrntLoop:   MOV    R4, M[R1]
            MOV    M[out_port], R4   ; write character
            INC    R1
            INC    R3
            CMP    R3, R2             ; checks for the end
            BR.NZ  PrntLoop
            RET
```

Program 11.16. Main program.

```
            ; Constant definition
end_text    EQU    '@'
control     EQU    FFFDh
max_char    EQU    100h
in_port     EQU    FFFFh
out_port    EQU    FFFEh
mask        EQU    0020h

            ; Variable definition
            ORIG   8000h
Text        TAB    max_char

            ORIG   0000h
Start:      MOV    R1, F000h
            MOV    SP, R1        ; Initializes the stack
            CALL   ReadText
            CALL   ProcText
            MOV    R1, Text      ; Parameter to Print
            CALL   Print
            BR     Start
```

11.5 Summary

This chapter provides a quick introduction to programming in assembly language. Like any other language, there are some general rules that must be used, both to comply with the syntax of the language and for clarity of the resulting program. Assembly language, due to its close connection with the hardware of the computer, presents a greater level of detail and some particular characteristics. The set of rules and recommendations presented in this chapter can help in making the development process simpler and error free.

As such, the chapter starts by describing the direct translation of constructions in the C language into the P3 assembly. Although this process is usually carried out by a compiler which executes a complex set of optimisations on the code, this exercise gives an idea of the creation of executable code from a program written in the C language. More importantly, the C language allows for an unambiguous specification of the intended functionality of a program in assembly. This discussion also includes some considerations about data organisation in memory.

The next step then describes how general programming techniques can be applied to assembly programming and shows some concrete examples of assembly routines to resolve specific problems.

The chapter concludes with a complete example of a program in assembly, developed using the techniques described.

Exercises

11.1 Consider the following declaration of variables in C:

```
long int a1 = -8;
short int a2 = 15;
long int a3 = 65537;
```

Describe the content of the memory locations occupied by these variables, assuming that P3 uses big endian representation. Assume that a **short** occupies two bytes and that a **long** occupies four bytes.

11.2 Describe how to translate the following declarations in C into assembly directives for the P3 processor:

```
short int months[] = {31,28,31,30,31,30,31,31,30,31,30,31};
long int month1, month2;
short week[7];
```

11.3 Develop an assembly routine for the P3 processor which prints the content of a memory area in a text window. Each memory location appears on a separate line, and its content should be shown in binary. The passage of input parameters is by registers: R1 contains the address of the memory area, and R2, the number of memory locations to print. For this problem and the following, start by designing a flowchart which describes the intended function and then write the routine in assembly language.

11.4 Develop an assembly routine for the P3 processor which returns the number of bits at 1 in the words of a given memory area. Assume that the method to pass the input parameters which specify the memory area is the same as in the previous problem. Design a flowchart which carries out the intended function and write the routine in assembly language.

11.5 Develop a routine that, using Euclide's algorithm, calculates the largest common divisor between two integers, passed as arguments on the stack.

11.6 Consider a vector of numbers in consecutive memory locations, the end of which is indicated by the value 0. Develop a routine which increments each of the odd numbers of the vector by one unit. Consider that the start address of the vector passes to the routine on the stack and that the result should stay in the same memory locations as the initial vector.

11.7 Develop a routine which substitutes all the occurrences of the letter «A» (uppercase) in a text in memory by «ALPHA». The address of the start of the text is passed on the stack, and the character «#» marks the end of the text.

Assume that you can use auxiliary memory space, but that this space is not sufficient to contain all the text. The final text should remain stored in memory, starting at the same memory location as the original text.

11.8 Develop an assembly routine for the P3 processor which removes an element from a simple linked list. The data structure of each element of this list contains only one integer value and a pointer to the next element. These two fields are in consecutive memory locations, in that order. The end of the list is indicated by the pointer having the value 0.

The parameters to the routine are the address of the first element of the list, and the value of the element to delete, which pass on the stack. The routine should return the value 1 in the register R3, if the operation is successful, and 0 if the searched element is not present.

11.9 Develop a routine which transforms all the words of the text in memory into uppercase. The start address is passed on the stack and the end of the text marked by the character «$». Assume that there are only alphanumeric characters and spaces, which could be consecutive.

11.10 Develop a routine that sorts a vector of 16-bit integer numbers into ascending order. The routine receives the memory location of the first element of the list and the number of numbers of the list as parameters placed on the stack, in that order.

11.11 Develop a routine that calculates the transposition of an array represented in consecutive memory locations by lines. The routine receives the following parameters placed on the stack in the order indicated:

- address of the resulting array;
- address of the array of origin;
- the number of lines of the array of origin;
- the number of columns of the array of origin.

11.12 Develop a routine in the P3 assembly which accepts a positive integer passed on the stack and writes a list of all the prime numbers not greater than that number at the terminal.

11.13 Consider the state machine from Problem 7.3 in Chapter 7. Using the methods described in Section 11.3.2, design a state machine encoded in the P3 assembly which reads the input at bit 0 of an input port and writes the output at bit 0 of an output port.

11.14 Develop a program which implements a simple calculating machine in reverse Polish notation. The calculator should operate as follows:

- When the user introduces an integer, the value entered should be placed at the top of the machine stack.
- When the user enters one of the four arithmetic operations, the machine should calculate the result of that operation applied to the two positions at the top of the stack, remove those values from the stack, place the result at the top of the stack, and print that same result at the output.

For example, if the input data was

```
12
13
+
5
*
```

the machine should print

```
25
125
```

11.15 Develop a routine which multiplies two numbers represented in floating-point single precision, according to the IEEE 754 standard, as referenced in Section 5.5.3. The two numbers are passed in the four positions at the top of the stack, and the result should be on the register pair R1, R2.

Chapter 12

Internal Structure of a Processor

The instruction set architecture of the P3 processor was described in Chapter 10. The instruction set architecture defines the visible interface for the programmer, specifying the instructions which are available, as well as the internal registers, the memory access modes and other important characteristics of the processor.

For a given instruction set architecture there are many possible implementations for the structure of the processor. The numerous possible implementations result from a large number of choices which are available to the digital systems designer and involve different compromises between the number of clock cycles necessary to execute each instruction, the maximum clock frequency possible for the system and the area occupied in silicon for the physical implementation of the processor.

This chapter provides a detailed description of a possible implementation of the P3 processor, as well as the various compromises which are inherent to the choices made, focusing, when considered opportune, on the most obvious alternatives and reasons for why they have been put aside in favour of the described implementation.

Like any complex circuit, it is useful to analyse the P3 processor by separately considering two principal components separately, as discussed in Chapter 8, namely the datapath and the control circuit.

The datapath has all the logic modules used to store and process user data, and operates on data organised into bytes and words. The datapath includes the register file, the arithmetic and logic unit, the access circuits to memory and input/output ports and also, the internal connection buses.

The control circuit generates the signals which control the datapath, so that it performs the sequence of operations necessary to load and execute each assembly instruction, taking into consideration the state of the datapath.

517

12.1   Datapath

The datapath for the P3 processor, as laid out in Figure 12.1, has five main components: the register file, the arithmetic and logic unit, the instruction register, (IR), the status register (SR) and, finally, the data interconnection and multiplexing circuits. These components are interconnected by a number of buses.

The register file, whose internal structure was described in Section 6.7.3, contains 16 registers, R0 to R15, with 16 bits each, and is accessed through two read ports (ports A and B) and a write port (port D). Some of these registers are special-purpose registers, as for example the program counter, PC, and the stack pointer, SP, the use of which was described in the previous chapters.

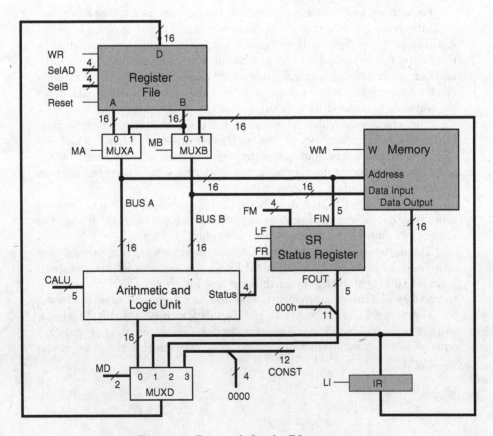

Fig. 12.1   Datapath for the P3 processor.

The arithmetic logic unit, described in detail in Section 8.4, is used to carry out arithmetic and logic operations on the operands, supplied by the register file.

The instruction register, IR, which is not part of the register file, is a special use register which, as we will see, serves to hold the instruction being executed. This register does not need to be accessed directly by the datapath. However, all of its bits are used by the control unit. Assembly instructions for the P3 are encoded in a number of fields defined by the general format shown in Figure 10.7.

The status register, SR, groups the various *flags* of the processor, connected to the datapath through two five-bit buses which enable read and write operations to this register.

The memory access circuits are made up of the address bus and two data buses, one for writing, the other for reading. The address bus is connected to port A of the register file, while the data bus for writing to memory is connected to port B. The data bus used for reading the memory is connected to the write port D of the register file. These connections allow a read operation from memory to the register file, through the control of ports A and D of the register file, or a write operation to memory through control of ports A and B.

The computation performed by the datapath is controlled by the control word, with the operation of each of the blocks described in detail in the following sections.

12.1.1 *Register File*

The register file was studied in Section 6.7.3 and is used almost unchanged in the datapath of the processor. The only alteration is that in this case the register R0 is not alterable and always takes the value 0. The benefits of this option will be discussed below. The write control signal, *WR*, is generated by the control unit, as well as the values in the four-bit buses *SelAD* and *SelB*. The *SelAD* value specifies the register that has its content placed in port A and, at the same time, where the value present in port D is written to, if the *WR* signal is active. The *SelB* value specifies the register that has its content placed in port B.

To have a more flexible control over the arithmetic logic unit, register R0 always contains the value 0. This option allows 0 to be selected as one of the operands and carry out various operations which would require a more complex arithmetic logic unit, otherwise. In practice, register R0 is not an

Table 12.1   Register file.

Register	Description
R0	Constant 0
R1	General purpose register
R2	General purpose register
R3	General purpose register
R4	General purpose register
R5	General purpose register
R6	General purpose register
R7	General purpose register
R8	Restricted use register
R9	Restricted use register
R10	Restricted use register
R11	Source data (SD)
R12	Effective address (EA)
R13	Result data (RD)
R14	Stack pointer (SP)
R15	Program counter (PC)

actual register, since it is implemented by connecting lines from the bus directly to the logic level 0, through tri-state buffers.

Except for register R0, all the other registers may be used to store values. However, some of the registers have predefined functions, listed in Table 12.1. Note that registers which are intended for specific functions have an index greater than 7. This option prevents the program encoded at the assembly level from having access to these and disturbing the normal operation of the processor, since, at the assembly level, the programmer may only access registers with indexes between 0 and 7.

Special purpose registers include R14 and R15. Register R14 is the stack pointer register (SP). It is this register which is used to address memory when executing an operation which directly (POP or PUSH) or indirectly (CALL, INT, RET, RETN and RTI) manipulates the stack of the processor.

Register R15 stores the value of the program counter, PC, which, after executing each instruction, always points to the next instruction that the processor will execute.

Altering the value of either of these registers outside their intended use will strongly interfere with the normal operation of the processor. Therefore, their use for any other operations should always be avoided.

Registers R11 to R13 are also used for specific purposes, but their meaning will only become clear when we analyse the way that the assembly instructions are executed, in Section 12.3.

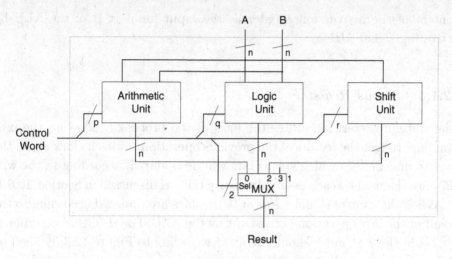

Fig. 12.2 Structure of the arithmetic logic unit.

12.1.2 *Arithmetic Logic Unit*

The arithmetic logic unit (ALU) used by this processor is the one studied in Section 8.4, which is shown once again in Figure 12.2.

The ALU is managed by five control bits forming the control field $CALU$. The value of these 5 bits specifies, as defined in Table 8.1, which operation the ALU executes on the two operands in its input. These two operands come, usually, from ports A and B of the register file.

The four status bits generated by the ALU are connected to the status register, whose detailed operation is studied in Section 12.1.4.

12.1.3 *Instruction Register*

The instruction register, IR, is directly connected to the data read bus connected to the memory and is used to store the code of the assembly instruction being executed.

As was described in Section 10.4, the 16 bits of this register encode which operation to execute and on which operands it should be applied. Most of the time, this register is not used in the datapath, except in the first stage of processing an instruction, where the instruction register is loaded from memory. The loading of this register is controlled by the value of the LI signal, generated by the control unit.

For certain operations, it is necessary to read one or more fields of the instruction register to the datapath. It is, therefore, possible to select the content of the instruction register as the input for port B of the ALU by activating signal MB.

12.1.4 *Status Register*

The status register, SR, stores the flags of the processor, allowing the programmer to test the results of the previous operation. At each clock cycle, the control unit defines which status bits will be updated, according to the way they are changed by each assembly instruction, as discussed in Section 10.6.1.

When the control signal LF is at 0, the flags are updated according to the result of the last operation carried out by the ALU. For this, the corresponding bit in the FM mask should be at 1, according to Figure 12.3, defined by the control unit and not visible by the programmer at the assembly level.

When the value of LF is at 1, the status register is loaded with the value from $BUS\ A$, through the input FIN bus. Independently of the value of the control signals, the status register may be loaded into the register file, through port D, using the output $FOUT$ bus.

There are 2 bits that reflect the result of the ALU operation updated in all the clock cycles, called *microstatus bits*. The two microstatus bits are z and c.

Figure 12.4 describes the internal schematics of the status register. The operation of the status register is controlled by signals activated by the control unit and by the four status bits ZR, CR, NR, OR, generated by the arithmetic logic unit.

In addition to the Z, C, N and O bits, the meaning of which was described in Section 10.6.4, there is also bit E. This bit controls whether the processor responds to interrupts (as discussed in Section 10.5.3). The value stored in bit E does not come from the ALU, but rather through the FIN input. Note that the signal P, used in conditional jumps, does not correspond to one bit in the status register. This bit is generated from the values of bits Z and N through the logic represented in the figure.

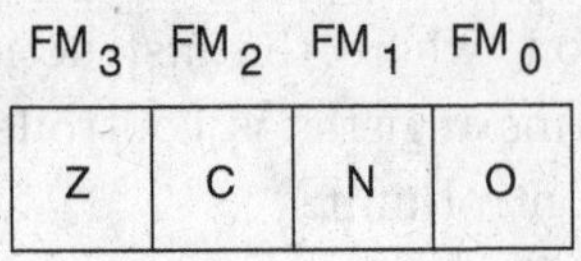

$$FM_3 \quad FM_2 \quad FM_1 \quad FM_0$$

Z	C	N	O

Fig. 12.3   Bits of the FM mask which controls the updating of the status bits.

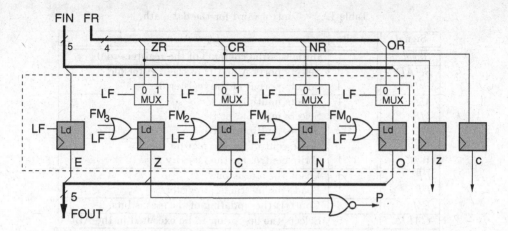

Fig. 12.4 Internal schematics of the status register and the two microstatus bits.

12.1.5 *Interconnection Buses*

The two read ports of the register file feed the arithmetic logic unit through the multiplexers MUXA and MUXB, which drive respectively the buses *BUS A* and *BUS B*.

During an access to the memory, *BUS A* contains the address to be accessed. For a write operation (*WM* signal at 1), the value in the *BUS B* bus specifies the value to be written. For a read operation (*WM* signal at 0), multiplexer MUXD selects the value returned from the memory, setting *MD* at 01. In this case, the value read from memory is written to the register specified by the *SelAD* control signal, provided that the write signal in the register file, *WR*, is activated.

12.1.6 *Datapath Control*

The operation performed by the datapath is defined through the control word, as shown in Table 12.2. Each of the signals described in this table controls the operation of one of the datapath elements, as specified in the previous sections.

To understand better the operation of this datapath, let us now consider some examples which illustrate the transfer operations between registers made possible by this design.

Let us suppose that we want to add the content of register R3 to the content of register R7 and place the result in register R3, updating the values of the status bits C and Z. What values should the control signals for the datapath take?

Table 12.2   Control word for the datapath.

Signal	# bits	Operation
Reset	1	Initialises the contents of the registers to 0
SelAD	4	Selects ports A and D of the register file
SelB	4	Selects port B of the register file
MA	1	Selects multiplexer A
MB	1	Selects multiplexer B
MD	2	Selects multiplexer D
WR	1	Write control for the register file
WM	1	Write control for the memory
LF	1	Loads the status bits
LI	1	Loads the instruction register
FM	4	Controls the updating of the status bits
CALU	5	Selects the operation to be executed in the ALU
CONST	12	Constant numerical value

First, so that the register file places the registers R3 and R7 in ports A and B, the signals *SelAD* and *SelB* must have the values 0011 and 0111, respectively. Moreover, since we intend to have a write in the register file, the value of the *WR* signal should be 1.

In order for the values present in ports A and B of the register file to reach the inputs of the logic and arithmetic unit, the value of the signals *MA* and *MB* must be 0.

The value of the *CALU* signal controls the operation of the ALU. Using Table 8.1, we can see that *CALU* should have the value 00000 so that an add operation is carried out. For the status bits to be updated with the values defined by this operation, the *LF* signal should have the value 0, and the *FM* signal should have the value 1100 (according to Figure 12.3).

Finally, for the write port of the register file can receive the output value of the arithmetic logic unit, it is necessary to control *MD* such that multiplexer MUXD selects the value at its input 0, which is achieved by placing *MD* at 00.

It now remains to set the value of the signals not yet defined, to avoid the execution of unintended operations. Since we do not intend to write to memory nor in the instruction register, the signals *WM* and *LI* must have the value 0. The unused constant field may take any value since it has no effect.

It can be concluded that the microoperation R3←R3+R7 is carried out if the control signals have the values of the second column in Table 12.3.

As a second example, let us now suppose we want to address the memory using the content of register R5 and store the value in this memory

Table 12.3   Signals which define the execution of the microoperations R3←R3+R7 (column 2) and R3←M[R5] (column 3).

Signal	R3 ← R3+R7	R3 ← M[R5]
Reset	0	0
SelAD	0011	0011
SelB	0111	0101
MA	0	1
MB	0	x
MD	00	01
WR	1	1
WM	0	0
LF	0	0
LI	0	0
FM	1100	0000
CALU	00000	xxxxx
CONST	xxxxxxxxxxxx	xxxxxxxxxxxx

position in register R3, without modifying the content of any of the other registers.

In these conditions it will be necessary to force *SelB* to 0101 and *SelAD* to 0011, while activating the signal *WR*. Multiplexer MUXA must select input 1, hence the value of the *MA* signal should be 1. To carry out a memory read and direct the value read to port D of the register file, the *WM* signal must be 0 and the *MD* signal takes the value 01.

So that neither the instruction register nor the status register are written to, the signals *LF* and *LI* must have the value 0. The *FM* signal should also have all its bits at 0.

In this example, as in most cases, the values of some of the signals are irrelevant, since they control parts of the datapath which are neither read nor written. That is the case with the control signals *CALU*, *MB* and *CONST*, which can take any value without affecting the operation of the circuit.

The third column in Table 12.3 describes the values which the signals must take to execute the microoperation R3←M[R5].

12.2   Control Unit

The signals that control the datapath are generated by a microprogrammed control unit, described in this section. As we saw in Section 7.5.3, the use of a microprogrammed control unit allows greater flexibility, and also a more

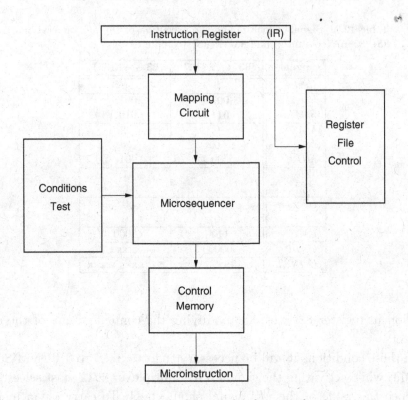

Fig. 12.5　General schematic for the control unit.

structured organisation than the one obtained when the control unit is made by synthesising a state machine using SSI circuits (flip-flops, gates) or MSI circuits (registers, counters).

Figure 12.5 describes the general structure of the control unit of the P3 processor. The heart of the control unit is the microsequencer, which controls the order of execution of the microinstructions stored in the control memory. The microinstructions specify the value of the signals used to control the datapath, the microsequencer itself and various aspects of the operation of other modules present in Figure 12.5.

The operation of the microsequencer is controlled by the conditions test unit and by the mapping unit, in addition to the control signals generated directly by the microinstructions. The conditions test unit works with the status bits of the processor and also other internal bits of the control unit.

The control of the register file is performed by a dedicated circuit, controlled by bits coming directly from the instruction register and the microinstruction register.

12.2.1 *Microinstruction Format*

Both the datapath and parts of the control circuit itself are controlled by a set of signals that make up the microinstruction. In a microprogrammed unit like this, the microinstructions which make up the microprogram are stored in the control memory, addressed through the CAR register.

One possible option is to select a microinstruction which has one bit for each of the control signals it needs to generate. However, this option is not always the most suitable, since not all combinations of control signals are always necessary or useful.

For example, for the circuit in Figure 12.1, the value of the $CALU$ signal is not relevant when loading the value of the constant using the $CONST$ control signal.

In this implementation, we took the option to use two microinstruction formats, distinguished by the value of the most significant bit of the microinstructions, F. Figure 12.6 describes the two possible formats for the microinstructions.

The format with $F=0$ corresponds to microinstructions which essentially control the datapath, while the format corresponding to $F=1$ is primarily intended for controlling the control unit, particularly the conditions test unit and the microsequencer.

Many other options would have been possible, from a single format, where all the control signals were always available, to a solution where there were more than two microinstruction formats. The first alternative would require a microinstruction with 50 bits yet not much faster since it is rarely necessary to control all the processor units at the same time. The use of an alternative with more microinstruction formats could, in fact, reduce the number of bits in the microinstructions, but would imply a significant reduction in execution speed, as there would then be too many signals which could not be simultaneously controlled.

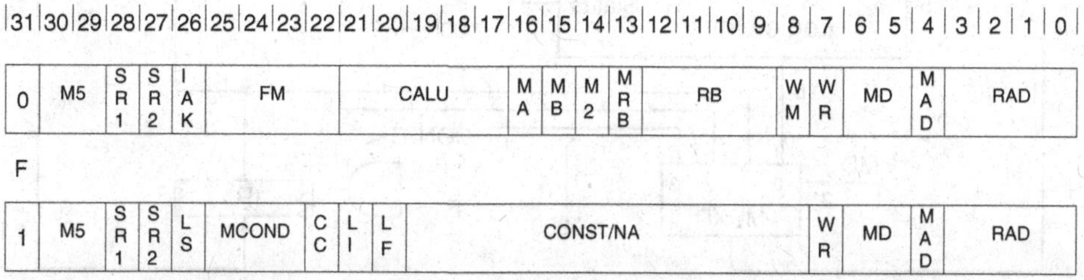

31	30	29	28	27	26	25	24	23	22	21	20	19	18	17	16	15	14	13	12	11	10	9	8	7	6	5	4	3	2	1	0

F

0	M5	SR1	SR2	IAK	FM	CALU	MA	MB	M2	MRB	RB	WM	WR	MD	MAD	RAD

1	M5	SR1	SR2	LS	MCOND	CC	LI	LF	CONST/NA	WR	MD	MAD	RAD

Fig. 12.6 Microinstruction format.

In the solution adopted, some signals are present in both microinstruction formats, for example, the WR signal, which controls writing to the register file. These signals can be enabled both through microinstructions of type 0 ($F = 0$) as well as microinstructions of type 1 ($F = 1$).

Other signals are present only in one of the microinstruction types, such as the signal which controls writing to memory, WM. These signals may only be enabled in microinstructions of that type and remain disabled for all others. Therefore, in the datapath in Figure 12.1, signals which appear in only one of the microinstruction formats result from the logic product of the signal F, complemented or not, with the value of the respective bits from the microinstruction.

The datapath, modified to explicitly include the logic gates addressing this issue, is shown in Figure 12.7. Note that the added logic implies that the control of the multiplexer MUXA and the write to memory signal are enabled only in instructions of type 0, given that the signals which control

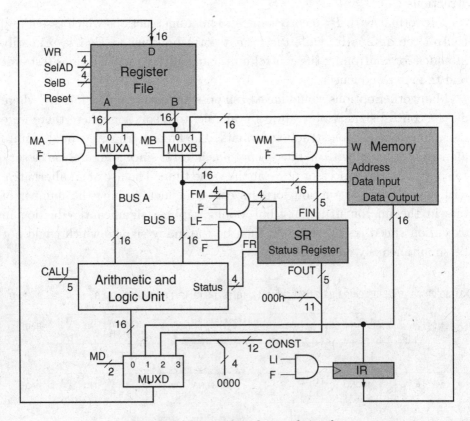

Fig. 12.7   Datapath and control signals.

the datapath are the logic product of the original signals, *MA* and *WM* respectively, with the complement of bit *F*. In the same way, the 4 bits of the *FM* signal should be enabled only when $F = 0$, which can be achieved with four AND gates, in the figure represented only by one of these applied to the 4 bits from the bus.

The signals for loading the instruction register and loading the status register, which are only generated by the control unit in microinstructions of type 1, are masked analogously, with the logic product made with the bit *F*

The same rule applies to the signals which control various parts of the control unit itself.

When the control unit generates a given signal only in the format $F = 1$, a logic product is made with the signal *F*, whereas when that signal only exists in the format $F = 0$, the product involves the complement of the signal *F*, that is, $\overline{F}$.

In some cases, it is possible to spare this logic if the signal acts on parts of the circuit which do not have any effect due to the value of other control signals. For example, the control signal *MB*, which controls the multiplexer MUXB, is only enabled in the microinstruction format where $F = 0$. As such, although there should be an AND gate to make the logic product of the signal *MB* with the complement of *F*, this gate is actually useless. In fact, a careful analysis of the datapath in Figure 12.1 shows that when $F = 1$, there is no control either on the arithmetic logic unit or on the write to memory signal, which is necessarily disabled. Thus, the value held in bus *B* is never used. Hence it is not necessary to control the multiplexer MUXB, saving one logic gate.

12.2.2 *Microsequencer*

The microsequencer is at the centre of the control unit and generates the sequence of addresses for the microinstructions which must be executed. According to the control signals, the microsequencer can do one of the following operations in each clock cycle:

- Increment the address of the microinstruction to be executed or jump to an address specified in the microinstruction, according to the value of the *COND* signal, generated by the conditions test unit.
- Return from a microroutine.
- Jump to one of the addresses supplied by the mapping unit.

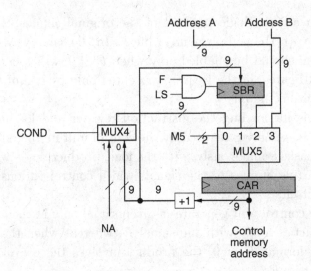

Fig. 12.8   Schematic for the microsequencer.

Figure 12.8 shows the structure of the microsequencer. The microsequencer uses two registers. The CAR register (Control Address Register) holds the address of the control memory containing the microinstruction currently being executed. This register has the same role for a microprogram as the program counter has for an assembly program and may also be referred to as the *microprogram counter*. The SBR (subroutine return register) stores the microprogram address to where control will be transferred to after terminating the execution of a microroutine. Since there is only one register to store the return address, it is only possible to use one level of microroutines, which means that one microroutine cannot call another one or itself recursively.

It is important to emphasise that there is no relation between a microroutine and a subroutine defined at the assembly level.

The operation of the microsequencer is under control of the 2 bits of the $M5$ signal which controls the loading of the CAR register, in the following way:

- $M5 = 00$: CAR is incremented if $COND$ is 0, and is loaded with the value of NA (standing for next address, the control memory address where to jump) if $COND$ is 1, thus allowing the execution of conditional jumps within microprograms.
- $M5 = 01$: CAR is loaded with the value contained in SBR, resulting in the execution of a return from a microroutine.

- $M5 = 10$: CAR is loaded with the value specified in *Address A* from the mapping unit.
- $M5 = 11$: CAR is loaded with the value specified in *Address B* from the mapping unit.

Most of the microinstructions are executed sequentially. Hence, after executing a microinstruction, the CAR register is incremented so that it points to the next position of the control memory. This behaviour is achieved by placing the value of $M5$ at 00 in the microinstruction, and controlling the conditions test block so that the value of *COND* is 0. To execute a conditional jump in the microprogram, the value of $M5$ must be 00, and the conditions test unit needs to select the intended jump condition.

The possibility of loading the CAR register with the content of the SBR register makes possible the usage of microroutines. When calling a microroutine, the LS signal must be enabled, and the CAR register is loaded with the NA value, which specifies the address of the microroutine to be called. As the LS signal is only present in microinstructions when $F = 1$, the signal for loading the SBR register must be disabled when $F = 0$. The activation of this signal means that the SBR register assumes the value of CAR+1, which represents the address of the first microinstruction to execute when the microroutine terminates. The return from the microroutine is executed by selecting $M5 = 01$, which forces the loading of the CAR register with the return address.

The content of the CAR register can also assume the values *Address A* (assigning $M5 = 10$) or *Address B* (assigning $M5 = 11$), generated by the mapping unit, whose purpose will be studied in Section 12.2.4.

12.2.3 *Conditions Test*

The conditions test unit, presented in Figure 12.9, has the function of selecting which condition is tested by the microsequencer when it executes a jump microinstruction or a call to a microroutine, whether conditional or not.

This unit has one single output bit, signal *COND*, which indicates to the microsequencer if a jump will be executed or not, as described in the previous section.

The conditions test unit is essentially made up of two multiplexers and some auxiliary logic gates. The multiplexer, MUXCOND, controlled by the *MCOND* field of the microinstruction, enables the selection of one of the

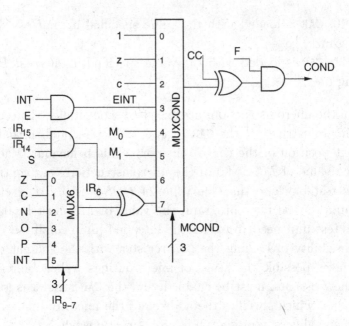

Fig. 12.9   Conditions test unit.

following bits:

- The constant 1, which enables the microsequencer to increment or execute an unconditional jump, depending on the value of the CC (Complement Condition) signal.
- Bits z and c of the status register. These bits are also known as microstatus bits. Bit z is at 1 if the last operation in the ALU generated the result zero, while bit c is at 1 if the last operation in the ALU produced a carry.
- The logic product of the bit E of the status register with the INT signal (this signal marks the presence of an interrupt) indicating if an interrupt which is present will be handled.
- The bits of field M of the instruction register, which encode the addressing mode of the assembly instruction which is being executed.
- Bit S of the instruction register, masked by the expression $IR_{15}\overline{IR_{14}}$, which for instructions with two operands indicates to which operand the addressing mode of the instruction is applied.
- One of the bits of the status register, plus the signals P and INT, chosen according to the value of bits 7 to 9 of the instruction register.

Input 7 of the multiplexer MUXCOND is controlled by the output of the multiplexer MUX6. Since bits 7 to 9 of the instruction register specify which condition is tested in a given instruction, as shown in Figure 10.13, and in accordance with Table 10.14, it is possible to select which condition is tested by the microsequencer.

An analysis of Table 10.14 shows that bits 7 to 9 of the instruction register select which condition, while bit 6 indicates if the condition must be complemented. The connection of the multiplexer MUX6, as shown in the figure, and the use of an XOR gate, which functions as a controlled inverter, enables the right condition to be available for selection at input 7 of the multiplexer MUXCOND. This architecture makes possible that the test for the condition specified in the instruction is performed with a single microinstruction, instead of carrying out various tests to the values of the status bits and the value of bits 6 to 9 of the instruction register.

When the microsequencer has to execute the instructions sequentially, the $COND$ output must be 0. This is achieved by placing the value 000 in the $MCOND$ field of the microinstruction and the value 1 in the CC field of the microinstruction.

When the microsequencer must execute an unconditional jump, the value 1 is placed in the $COND$ output, by placing 000 in $MCOND$ and 0 in CC.

Finally, when the microsequencer has to execute a jump on the condition that a given bit takes a given value, the multiplexer MUXCOND selects the intended bit, while the CC signal specifies if the condition is to be complemented or not.

Both the conditional and the unconditional jumps may only be executed by the microsequencer when the microinstruction is of type $F = 1$, given that the fields $COND$, CC and the jump address NA are only available in this format.

If the microinstruction is of type 0, the value of $COND$ is set to 0, and the microsequencer always increments the microprogram counter.

12.2.4 *Mapping Unit*

The P3 mapping unit is used to quickly generate the addresses of the microroutines called during the execution of instructions. Indeed, in various steps of the execution of an assembly instruction, it becomes necessary to jump to a microroutine or a microcode segment, according to the value in a given field of the instruction register.

For example, the value contained in the six most significant bits of the instruction register represents the instruction code and defines the operation to execute. This value is used in the decoding stage of an assembly instruction, to generate the control memory address which corresponds to the microinstructions which implement the assembly instruction.

In another stage of the instruction execution, it is necessary to jump to a given microcode address, according to the addressing mode used, and specified in field M of the instruction register.

The mapping unit is used in various stages of the execution of an instruction. In the P3 processor, this execution consists of the following steps:

(1) loading of the instruction register;
(2) decoding of the operation code and loading of the operands;
(3) execution of the microprogram which implements the instruction;
(4) writing the result;
(5) testing for interrupt requests.

With this sequence of operations, it is necessary to decode the operation code to know which operands to load and what is the address of the microprogram memory containing the microinstructions to execute. Given that the microsequencer can only test the value of one bit at a time, selected by the conditions test unit, and that the operation code has 6 bits, the choice of the microroutine using this mechanism would require six microinstructions just to determine the address of the microroutine to be carried out. More microinstructions would be necessary to decide which microroutines should be called to perform the reading of the operands and the writing of the result, which would be very inefficient.

The mapping unit, outlined in Figure 12.10, enables the transfer of control to be carried out in a single microinstruction. This transfer uses two mapping memories, which are addressed by the operation code, the addressing mode and the value of the direction bit in the instruction register.

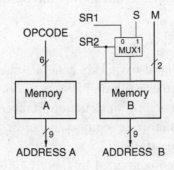

Fig. 12.10   Mapping unit.

The mapping unit can generate two addresses, either one of which may be selected by the microsequencer as the next microinstruction address to be executed (see Figure 12.8).

Memory A is directly addressed by the operation code (*OPCODE* field of the assembly instruction) and stores a table which contains the addresses of the microroutines which execute the operations between registers which implement each of the instructions.

The address lines of the mapping memory B are controlled by the value of the $SR1$ and $SR2$ bits of the microinstruction and also by the value of bits M and S of the instruction register. According to the values of the $SR1$ and $SR2$ bits, this memory generates the address of the microroutines for loading operands and writing the result.

Consequently, through the control of the $SR1$ and $SR2$ bits, it is possible to generate four different addresses. These addresses are used to specify various read and write microroutines, as listed in Table 12.4.

Therefore, if we wish mapping memory B to manage the address of the microroutine for reading one operand, the microinstruction sets $SR2$ and $SR1$ at 00. In this case, the value of S is irrelevant, given that this field has no meaning when the instruction uses a single operand. If we require the address of the microroutine to read two operands, it is sufficient to force $SR2$ to 1, as with this condition the value of S is used to address the memory, through multiplexer MUX1.

For the control circuit to operate according to what is intended, memory B should be loaded with the addresses of the microroutines corresponding to each of the intended operations, according to that shown in Figure 12.11.

To analyse the functioning of the mapping unit, let us suppose that you want to transfer the control to the first microinstruction which implements the assembly instruction stored in the instruction register. The address of this microinstruction is stored in mapping memory A, which is addressed by the six most significant bits (*OPCODE* field) of the instruction register.

Table 12.4   Operation of mapping memory B.

SR2	SR1	S	Selected address
0	0	—	Microroutine for reading one operand
0	1	—	Microroutine for writing the result
1	—	0	Microroutine for reading two operands for $S = 0$
1	—	1	Microroutine for reading two operands for $S = 1$

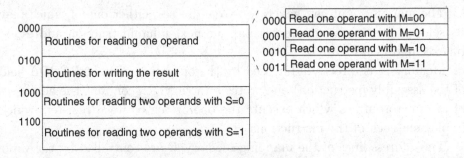

Fig. 12.11   Contents of mapping memory B.

We need to ensure that this value is loaded into the CAR register on the next clock edge. By analysing Figure 12.8, we can see that the control signal $M5$ should take the value 10, so that multiplexer MUX5 selects the value generated by the mapping memory A, as the next value of the CAR register.

The control of mapping memory B is slightly more intricate but also easy to understand. Let us assume that we want to transfer control to the sequence of microinstructions which loads one operand. By analysing Table 12.4, we can see that it is necessary to set the control bits $SR2$ and $SR1$ at 00 so that the mapping memory B generates the address of that microroutine. Give that the value of field M of the instruction register directly addresses this memory, it now suffices to set signal $M5$ to 11, so that the next microinstruction to execute is the intended one.

12.2.5 *Register File Control*

The control unit handles the register file through the control circuit described in Figure 12.12. By controlling the value of the MRB signal, available in the microinstruction, the control unit chooses if the address from port B of the register file is equal to RB (specified in the microinstruction) or equal to the values specified in the instruction register. The situation is identical for the control of the ports A and D of the register file, only this time the MAD signal controls the choice.

When the instruction register directly specifies the address of port B, the value of the control signal $M2$ chooses which of the instruction register fields, $IR1$ or $IR2$, defines this address.

In the case of ports A and D, this choice is made by logic that uses the values of the S bit and the most significant bit of the operation code. This logic chooses the value of WBR as being equal to $IR1$ or $IR2$, according

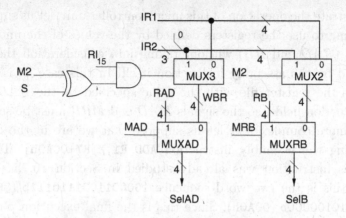

Fig. 12.12   Control circuit for the register file.

Table 12.5   Control of multiplexer MUX3.

IR_{15}	S	$M2$	WBR
0	—	—	$IR1$
1	0	0	$IR1$
1	0	1	$IR2$
1	1	0	$IR2$
1	1	1	$IR1$

Table 12.6   Value selected by the MUX3 multiplexer.

$M2$	Value selected
0	Register used for the first or single operand
1	Register used by the second operand, if present

to Table 12.5. Despite the apparent complexity of this table, its use is very simple and is described in Table 12.6.

The logic shown in Figure 12.12 results from the flexibility in coding the addressing modes and the involved registers in each instruction. In instructions with two operands, the field which contains the register to which the addressing mode is applied can be $IR1$ or $IR2$, according to the value of S. These instructions all have the most significant bit of the instruction register at 1, as described in Section 10.7.3. All instructions which have the most significant bit of the instruction register at 0 write the result in the register specified by the $IR1$ field, and this is carried out by the AND gate in the figure.

To illustrate the operation of this microcontroller unit, let us suppose that we are going to use the registers defined by the values of the microinstruction fields (RAD and RB) without taking into consideration the registers determined by the assembly instruction itself. In this case, it is necessary to address the register file with the value specified by the RAD and RB microinstruction fields, so the signals MAD and MRB must be set at 1.

For a more complex use, let us suppose that we are in the final stage of executing the assembly instruction ADD R1,M[R7+00A0h]. The encoding of this instruction was already studied in Section 10.7.5, where we saw that this is the two word sequence 1000011001110111b (8677h) and 0000000010100000b (00A0h). Since this is the final execution phase of the instruction, the result of the sum has already been calculated and, as we will see ahead, has been stored in register R13. We want to load this result into the destination register specified by the assembly instruction. As we saw in Section 10.7.5, the destination register is specified in the $IR2$ field of the instruction register. This is the case because, when encoding this instruction, the indexed addressing mode is applied to the second operand of the instruction, which is indicated by the value $S = 1$.

To execute this operation, it is first necessary to guarantee that the value in port B of the register file propagates to its write port. By analysing Figure 12.1 and Table 8.1, we can see that it is necessary to place the values in the microinstruction fields according to Table 12.7.

It is now necessary to control the circuit in Figure 12.12, so that the register used as the first operand for the assembly instruction is written with the result. The value of MRB must be 1, so that the RB field of the microinstruction can specify register R13. The value of MAD must be 0, so that the value selected by the MUXAD multiplexer is that coming from the MUX3 multiplexer.

Table 12.7   Signals which control the execution of the microoperation R1 ← R13.

Signal	Value
MB	0
MD	00
WR	1
WM	0
LF	0
LI	0
FM	0000
CULA	11XXX

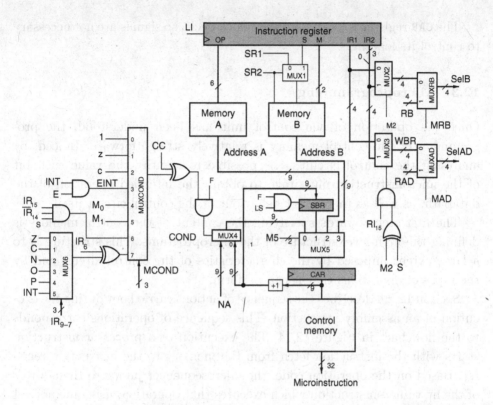

Fig. 12.13 Control circuit for the P3 processor.

Setting $M2$ at 0 provides suitable control for the MUX3 multiplexer, as described in Table 12.6. We can see that the value of the IR_{15} bit of the instruction register takes the appropriate value to control of the MUX3 multiplexer, 1 in this case.

12.2.6 *Control Circuit*

The complete control circuit for the P3 processor, described in Figure 12.13, results from connecting the various blocks described in the previous sections.

Note that control of the MUX5 multiplexer enables the selection, as the next address for the microinstruction to be executed, of either what is indicated by the MUX4 multiplexer, controlled by the conditions test unit, the content of the SBR register, or any of the addresses specified by the mapping unit.

The LI signal enables the load of the instruction register, which is shown in this figure as well as in Figure 12.1 that represents the datapath.

The CAR register is loaded at every clock cycle, so signals are not necessary to control its loading.

12.3   Microprogramming

Once the operation of the control unit has been understood, the programming of the control memory is relatively straightforward. Indeed, by analysing the control circuit, it is possible to identify the value each bit of the microinstruction must take to obtain the intended operation of the datapath, as well as the correct behaviour of the control circuit itself.

The first step towards specifying the content of the control memory is defining the high-level structure of the microprograms. This structure is to a large extent imposed by the characteristics of the control circuit and by the types of operations that it can perform.

Section 12.2.4 describes the sequence of actions carried out during the execution of an assembly instruction. This sequence of operations corresponds to the flowchart in Figure 12.14. The execution of a processor instruction starts with the instruction fetch from the memory to the instruction register. Based on the operation code, the microsequencer jumps to the address of the first microinstruction which executes that operation, using memory A of the mapping circuit to do this.

For instructions which have one or two operands, execution continues with the loading of these operands. This loading is carried out by calling a microroutine, the address of which is supplied by memory B of the mapping circuit. The next stage consists in executing the instruction itself, using a sequence of microinstructions which are specific for each instruction.

After executing the instruction, control is transferred to the microcode section which writes the result, in the cases where the instruction requires this operation.[1] Memory B of the mapping circuit is used once again since the microroutine for writing the result varies according to the addressing mode used in the instruction.

Finally, after writing the result (or after the execution phase, for instructions which do not require this step), control is transferred to a sequence of microinstructions which verify if there is a pending interrupt. If this is the case, control is transferred to the microroutine which handles the interrupt.

---

[1]Some instructions do not generate any result, such as JMP, TEST and CMP. Hence this step is bypassed.

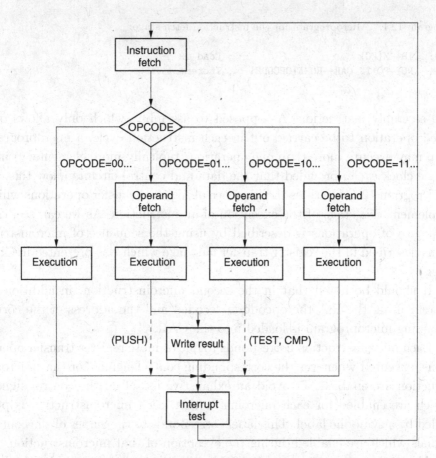

Fig. 12.14   Flowchart of the execution of an assembly instruction.

Note that if the instruction executed is the instruction *INT*, there is no need to check if there are pending interrupts since *INT* disables the bit of the status register which allows servicing the interrupts.

12.3.1 *Instruction Fetch*

As we saw above, the first stage of the execution of an instruction is the *instruction fetch*, *IF*. In this phase, it is necessary to load the instruction register, IR, with the content of the memory location pointed to by the program counter, PC. Then the value of the program counter must be incremented so that it points to the next position in the memory. This position may be the second word of the instruction just loaded to IR or the next instruction to be executed. The last operation consists of transferring control to the microprogram segment which carries out the operations necessary for executing

Program 12.1.   Microprogram for the instruction fetch stage.

```
IF0:   IR←M[PC]                    ; Load IR
IF1:   PC←PC+1, CAR←ROMA[OPCODE]   ; Increment PC
```

the assembly instruction. As opposed to assembly, which only allows one fixed operation to be carried out in each instruction cycle, a microprogram step may execute more than one operation (typically more elementary) in a single clock cycle, provided that the data and control circuits allow this.

Program 12.1 describes the sequence of register transfer operations which implement this stage of the execution of an instruction. As we can see, this sequence of operations is described by using the sequence of microinstructions described in the register transfer language which was presented in Chapter 8.

It should be noted that in the second microinstruction, in addition to incrementing the PC, the opcode is decoded and the address of the corresponding microprogram is loaded into the CAR.

Each microinstruction corresponds to one or more register transfer operations, executed whenever the corresponding control signals for that microinstruction are enabled. To avoid an exhaustive list of all the control signals which are enabled for each microinstruction, each microinstruction is preceded by a symbolic label. This label corresponds to the values of the control signals which are enabled during the execution of that microinstruction.

Although each microinstruction is described as a set of transfers of values between registers, the programming of the control memory is carried out by a sequence of zeroes and ones which specify the value of each microinstruction, according to the format described in Figure 12.6. The values of each bit of the microinstruction are defined to trigger the transfers between the specified registers.

The transformation of the microprogram, described at the register transfer level, into the combination of bits which properly controls the circuits of the processor may be carried out manually or with the help of a program, which in this case is called a *microassembler*. In practice, and given that programming at this level requires deep knowledge of the signals and circuits involved, a microassembler is considerably less useful than that of an assembler, so this transformation is frequently carried out manually.

In this case, the operation of the microroutines is illustrated using register transfer language, and Section 12.3.6 studies the translation process between the microinstruction and the microcode in binary format.

12.3.2   *Operand Fetch*

The next stage of the execution of an instruction consists of the *operand fetch*, or *OF*, according to the number of operands and their addressing mode. The microroutine to be called depends on the assembly instruction under execution, although the procedure is similar for all of them. As was described in Figure 12.10 of Section 12.2.4, the mapping memory B contains the address of the microroutines for reading operands, both for the cases where there is only one operand and for the cases where there are two operands.

Hence, an assembly instruction which needs only one operand calls the corresponding microroutine using memory B of the mapping unit, with the $SR1$ and $SR2$ control bits at 0. An instruction which needs two operands must address memory B of the mapping unit with the $SR2$ signal at 1. In this case, the second address bit of this memory is bit S of the instruction register, according to the circuit in Figure 12.10.

To communicate easily between themselves, the various execution steps of an assembly instruction regularly use temporary registers, according to the following convention and Table 12.1.

- Register EA (R12) is used to store the *effective address* of an operand, whenever this operand comes from memory or is written there.
- The value of the first operand is stored in register RD (R13). After the calculations, the result of the operation will be stored in that same register.
- The value of the second operand is stored in register SD (R11), whenever the instruction uses two operands.

Given this, the instructions for operand fetch must operate so as to leave the value of the first or only operand in the result data register, RD (R13). The address of the operand will be stored in register EA (R12). In some addressing modes (for example, in the immediate mode), the address of the operand is not necessary and, in these cases, register EA is not loaded. When instructions have two operands, the second operand must be in register SD (R11).

We can now examine the microroutines for operand fetching, starting with those which only load one operand. According to the addressing mode, the operand may be in various locations:

- Register mode: the operand is in a register. It must be copied from that register to register RD. There is no need to update register EA.

- Register indirect mode: the operand is in a memory location defined by the contents of a register. The value of that register must be copied to register EA, and the value of the memory position pointed to by this register must be copied to register RD.
- Immediate mode: the operand is in the instruction itself, or, more exactly, in the memory location pointed to by the program counter, which was already incremented in the microinstruction with the IF1 label. This memory location must be copied to register RD, and there is no need to update register EA.
- Indexed mode: the operand is in a memory location, the address of which is the result of adding the content of a register with the value of the memory location pointed to by the program counter. This address must be loaded into register EA, and the content of the memory position pointed by EA must be copied to register RD.

In all cases, the register to which the addressing mode is applied is the register specified in the *IR*1 field of the instruction register.

After executing the microinstructions which fetch the operand, control is returned to the code which called the operand fetch microroutine.

It is now simple to specify the microprograms for each of the operand fetch microroutines described in Program 12.2. The most complex of these microroutines is that dealing with fetching operands using the indexed mode, where it is necessary to sum the word W to the value of the register specified in *IR*1 and address the memory with the resulting value.

Program 12.2.   Microroutines for fetching one operand.

```
                                 ;Register mode
F1R0:     RD←R[IR1], CAR←SBR     ; Copy operand


                                 ;Register indirect mode
F1RI0:    EA←R[IR1]              ; Copy effective address
F1RI1:    RD←M[EA], CAR←SBR      ; Load operand


                                 ;Immediate mode
F1IM0:    RD←M[PC]               ; Load operand
F1IM1:    PC←PC+1, CAR←SBR       ; Increment PC


                                 ;Indexed mode
F1IN0:    EA←M[PC]               ; Load constant W
F1IN1:    PC←PC+1                ; Increment PC
F1IN2:    EA←EA+R[IR1]           ; Compute effective address
F1IN3:    RD←M[EA], CAR←SBR      ; Load operand
```

The microroutines for fetching two operands work in a similar way to those fetching one operand. However, in this case, the value of bit S of the instruction register indicates if the addressing mode applies to the first operand or the second operand. When the addressing mode refers to the first operand, it is also applied to the destination of the operation, since the first operand simultaneously specifies one of the operands and the destination for the result. In both cases, the register to which the addressing mode is applied is the register specified in the $IR1$ field of the instruction register. The other operand, specified by the $IR2$ field of the instruction register, is always a register.

The first set of microroutines, described in Program 12.3, is used when the value of S is 0. In this case, the addressing mode is applied to the first operand, such as, for example, in the instruction ADD M[R1+30],R3. The procedure to be adopted is similar to that which was used in the instructions with one operand, and, like before, there are four distinct cases: register, indirect, immediate and indexed addressing modes. The difference consists essentially in copying the value of the second operand to SD, so that the instructions have the two operands available in the registers RD and SD. Where relevant, register EA should, as before, receive the value of the address where the first operand is located. This value will be used later by the microcode for writing the result, as described in Program 12.8.

Program 12.3. Microroutines for fetching two operands for $S = 0$.

```
                                    ;Register mode
F2R0:    RD←R[IR1]                  ; Copy first operand
F2R1:    SD←R[IR2], CAR←SBR         ; Copy second operand


                                    ;Register indirect mode
F2RI0:   EA←R[IR1]                  ; Copy effective address
F2RI1:   RD←M[EA]                   ; Load first operand
F2RI2:   SD←R[IR2], CAR←SBR         ; Copy second operand


                                    ;Immediate mode
F2IM0:   RD←M[PC]                   ; Load first operand
F2IM1:   PC←PC+1                    ; Increment PC
F2IM2:   SD←R[IR2], CAR←SBR         ; Copy second operand


                                    ;Indexed mode
F2IN0:   EA←M[PC]                   ; Load constant W
F2IN1:   PC←PC+1                    ; Increment PC
F2IN2:   EA←EA+R[IR1]               ; Compute effective address
F2IN3:   RD←M[EA]                   ; Load first operand
F2IN4:   SD←R[IR2], CAR←SBR         ; Copy second operand
```

Program 12.4.   Microroutines for fetching two operands for $S = 1$.

```
                        ;Register mode
F2RS0:    SD←R[IR1]     ; Copy second operand
F2RS1:    RD←R[IR2], CAR←SBR  ; Copy first operand

                        ;Register indirect mode
F2RIS0:   EA←R[IR1]     ; Copy effective address
F2RIS1:   SD←M[EA]      ; Load second operand
F2RIS2:   RD←R[IR2], CAR←SBR  ; Copy first operand

                        ;Immediate mode
F2IMS0:   SD←M[PC]      ; Load second operand
F2IMS1:   PC←PC+1       ; Increment PC
F2IMS2:   RD←R[IR2], CAR←SBR  ; Copy first operand

                        ;Indexed mode
F2INS0:   EA←M[PC]      ; Load constant W
F2INS1:   PC←PC+1       ; Increment PC
F2INS2:   EA←EA+R[IR1]  ; Compute effective address
F2INS3:   SD←M[EA]      ; Load second operand
F2INS4:   RD←R[IR2], CAR←SBR  ; Copy first operand
```

When the value of the S bit of the instruction register is 1, the procedure is somewhat different. In this case, the addressing mode is applied to the second operand, such as, for example, in the instruction ADD R3,M[R4+30]. In this case, it is necessary to exchange the role of the RD and SD registers, and there is no need to store the address of the operand in register EA. Note that the addressing mode is still applied to the register specified in $IR1$, but, in this case, the $IR1$ field encodes the second operand and not the first one. Program 12.4 describes these microroutines.

12.3.3   *Execution of Instructions*

After the operand fetch microroutines, the processor can operate on the data, according to the operation specified in the instruction code field, and so enter the actual *execution stage*.

Since the operands are already available in the RD and SD registers, the operation itself is in most of the cases, relatively simple. We illustrate the execution of instructions using some representative examples.

As an example of an arithmetic instruction, let us consider the instruction ADD, shown in Program 12.5. After calling the microroutine that does the operand fetch, resorting to the mapping unit, this instruction must add the

Program 12.5.   Microprogram for the execution stage of the instruction ADD.

```
ADD0:   CAR←ROMB[1|S|M], SBR←CAR+1           ; Fetch operand
ADD1:   RD←RD+SD, FM←Fh, CAR←ROMB[0|1|M]     ; Addition
```

Program 12.6.   Microprogram for the execution stage of the instruction PUSH.

```
PUSH0:   CAR←ROMB[0|0|M], SBR←CAR+1    ; Fetch operand
PUSH1:   M[SP]←RD, SP←SP-1             ; Write to stack
PUSH2:   CAR←IH0                       ; Jump to IH
```

content of the RD and SD registers and leave the result in the RD register. It also updates the bits of the status register, by using the bits of the *FM* field.

Note that the first microinstruction corresponds to a call of one of the microroutines described in the previous section. The actual routine called is selected by the ROM B under control of the bits SR1, SR2, S and M in the IR register.

After having stored the result in the RD register, control is transferred to the write back microroutine. Since the address of these microroutines is stored in positions 4 to 7 of memory B (see Table 12.4) of the mapping unit, this transfer is made by loading the CAR register with the content of this memory, addressed with the most significant bits ($SR2$ and $SR1$) set to 01.

Given the simplicity of the ADD operation, the execution of the instruction itself can be summarised as the operation RD ← RD+SD and as the updating of the status bits. The other two microoperations are the calls to the microroutines for operand fetch and write back.

A slightly more complex example is that of the PUSH instruction, described in Program 12.6. This instruction must store its operand in the memory location pointed to by the SP register and then decrement this register. This instruction does not have to write the result in its operand since its value should not be altered. In this way, control is transferred directly to the microroutine for handling interrupts.

The control instructions are programmed using the same structure. However, in this case, these instructions act directly on the value of the PC register. For example, the microprogram which executes the CALL instruction is shown in Program 12.7.

Program 12.7.   Microprogram for the execution stage of the instruction CALL.

```
CALL0:   CAR←ROMB[0|0|M], SBR←CAR+1`   ; Fetch address
CALL1:   M[SP]←PC, SP←SP-1            ; Push PC
CALL2:   PC←RD                        ; Load PC
CALL3:   CAR←IH0                      ; Jump to IH
```

Program 12.8.   Write back microroutine.

```
WBR0:   R[WBR]←RD      ; Write to register
WBR1:   CAR←IH0        ; Interrupt handling

WBM0:   S: CAR←WBR0    ; Write to register if S=1
WBM1:   M[EA]←RD       ; Write to memory
WBM2:   CAR←IH0        ; Interrupt handling
```

12.3.4   *Write Back*

After executing the instruction, it is necessary to write the result either in the register file or memory, according to the addressing mode used. This phase is called the *write back* stage or *WB* in short. The write back microroutines (Program 12.8) receive the result in the RD register and write it in the location specified by bits M and S of the instruction register.

If bit S is 1, the write is always in a register. The address of this register is directly specified by the control unit for the register file, described in Figure 12.12. If bit S is 0 and the addressing mode is indirect ($M = 01$) or indexed ($M = 11$), the value is written in the memory location pointed to by the EA register. Since there are only two write back microroutines, the table corresponding to mapping memory B must be constructed so that the inputs corresponding to the indexed and register indirect mapping modes, point to the microcode with a WBM0 label. The entry in this table that corresponds to the immediate addressing mode is never used since this addressing mode cannot be used to specify the destination of an operation.

In the case where the first operand is specified using the register addressing mode, the write back is simpler, involving just copying the content of the RD register to the register specified in the assembly instruction. The address of this register is directly selected by the control circuit for the register file, according to Figure 12.12.

12.3.5 *Testing for Interrupts*

The final stage of the execution of an instruction is the test for the existence of pending interrupts and *interrupt handling, IH*. The issue of interrupts was presented in Section 10.5.3 and will be analysed in more detail in Chapter 14.

In this interrupt handling stage, the microcontroller verifies if the *EINT* signal is set, meaning that there is a peripheral which has generated an interrupt on the external *INT* interrupt line and that the bit which marks availability to attend interrupts, the status bit E, is enabled. If not, control passes to the first microinstruction of the microroutine for instruction fetching, *IF*0, which will start the execution of the next instruction.

Note that it is possible to carry out the first line of Program 12.9 in a single microinstruction. The register transfer operation is always executed, while the loading of the CAR register depends on the test for the complement of the *EINT* signal being true.

If interrupt handling is required, the status bit register and the program counter will be stored on the stack. The status register bit which indicates the availability of the processor to handle interrupts is disabled by loading the status register with the value 0 (note that the status bits have already been saved and that their value is irrelevant inside the routine handling the interrupt). Finally, the *IAK* bit is activated, indicating externally that the handling of the last generated interrupt is going to start.

In response to the activation of this signal, the interrupt controller must place the interrupt vector on the data bus, identifying the peripheral responsible for the interrupt. The routines for handling the interrupts for each peripheral of the system, to where the processor must pass control of the

Program 12.9. Microroutine for interrupt handling.

```
IH0:   R8←SR, EINT.CAR←IF0        ; Copy SR
IH1:   M[SP]←R8, SP←SP-1          ; Save SR to the stack
IH2:   M[SP]←PC, SP←SP-1, IAK←1   ; Save PC to the stack
IH3:   R9←INTVECT                 ; Read interrupt vector
IH4:   R8←0200h                   ; Interrupt table base
IH5:   R9←R9-R8                   ; Entry in interrupt table
IH6:   PC←M[R9]                   ; Address for interrupt routine
IH7:   RE←R0, CAR←IF0             ; Disable interrupts
```

execution after a peripheral interrupt, have their addresses stored in an *interrupt table* starting at address FE00h. The interrupt vector serves as an index to this table. Therefore, this value is added to FE00h to obtain the memory position containing the address to load into the program counter (note that $INTVECT + \text{FE00h} = INTVECT - \text{0200h}$ and this strategy is preferable because, unlike FE00h, the value 0200h can be represented in the 12-bit field $CONST$). Finally, control is transferred to the first microinstruction of the microroutine for instruction fetching which, in this case, will execute the first instruction of the interrupt subroutine.

12.3.6   *Generating the Microcode*

Having defined the structure of the microprograms and knowing the details of each of the blocks, it now remains to define the value of the bits for each microinstruction. Let us consider the first microinstruction to execute during the instruction fetching phase as an example:

```
IF0:   IR←M[PC]    ; Load IR
```

First, it is necessary to identify the type of microinstruction which permits the required transfers between the indicated registers. This case involves loading the instruction register with the value of the memory location pointed to by the program counter. The signal which controls the instruction fetch, LI, is only available in the format $F = 1$, which immediately defines the type of microinstruction to use.

By analysing the datapath in Figure 12.1, we can see that to carry out the intended operation, it is necessary to ensure that:

(1) port A of the register file receives the number of the register which stores the PC, that is, $15d = 1111b$;
(2) the multiplexer MUXA selects the input 0, placing the value of the PC on the address bus of the memory;
(3) the LI signal is active;
(4) the control signals for writing in memory and the register file are disabled;
(5) the signal which controls writing to the status register, LF, is disabled;
(6) the signal which controls writing to the SBR register, LS, is disabled.

Since we are using format 1 for the microinstruction, this automatically forces the intended values for the signals which control the writing into memory and the multiplexer MUXA.

By analysing the control circuit, in Figure 12.13, we can see that it is necessary to ensure that:

(1) The CAR register is incremented. To do this, it is necessary:
- to control the multiplexer MUX5 with the value 00;
- set the control of the multiplexer MUX4 at 0, selecting input 0 of the multiplexer MUXCOND and setting the CC signal at 1, so that $CCOND$ is 0.

(2) The multiplexer MUXAD selects RAD for its input, which takes the value 1111b since it is intended that this value is in $SelAD$.

Thus, for this microinstruction the following values must be defined:

$F = 1$ $M5 = 00$
$MCOND = 000$ $CC = 1$
$LI = 1$ $LF = 0$
$LS = 0$ $WR = 0$
$MAD = 1$ $RAD = 1111$

These values define the microinstruction shown in Figure 12.15, where the values which are not relevant have been left blank. By deciding to set at 0 the non-relevant values, we obtain the value that the bits must have for this microinstruction: 8060001Fh.

A slightly more complex example allows us to illustrate the use of a microinstruction of the type $F = 0$ and the use of mapping memories. Let us, therefore, consider the microinstruction:

IF1: PC←PC+1, CAR←ROMA[OPCODE]

In the datapath, it is necessary to control the arithmetic unit, so that it carries out an increment. This means making $CALU$ equal to 00101 and selecting the PC in port A of the register file. It is also necessary to select input 0 of the multiplexer MUXA and input 0 of the multiplexer MUXD. Finally, we need to enable the write signal WR for the registers and ensure that all the write signals for the other registers are disabled.

31	30 29 28 27 26	25	24	23	22 21 20	19	18	17 16 15 14 13 12 11 10 9 8	7	6 5	4	3 2 1 0
1	M5	SR1	SR2	LS	MCOND	CC	LI	LF	CONST/NA	WR	MD	MAD	RAD
1	00			0	000	1	1	0		0		1	1111

Fig. 12.15 Encoding for microinstruction IR←M[PC].

| 31 | 30 | 29 | 28 | 27 | 26 | 25 | 24 | 23 | 22 | 21 | 20 | 19 | 18 | 17 | 16 | 15 | 14 | 13 | 12 | 11 | 10 | 9 | 8 | 7 | 6 | 5 | 4 | 3 | 2 | 1 | 0 |

0	M5	S R 1	S R 2	I A K	FM	CULA	M A	M B	M 2	M R B	RB	W M	W R	MD	M A D	RAD

0	10			0	0000	00101	0					0	1	00	1	1111

Fig. 12.16　Encoding for microinstruction `PC ← PC+1, CAR ← ROMA[OPCODE]`.

In the control unit, it is necessary to select the value 1111 for the *SelAD* signal, as well as force $M5$ to 10, so that the output of mapping memory A is selected. It is also necessary to ensure that the *IAK* signal remains at 0.

These considerations lead to the definition of the values of the bits described in Figure 12.16. As before, deciding to fill with the value 0 the non-defined fields gives a final value of `400A009Fh` for this microinstruction.

12.4　Summary

This chapter describes the internal structure of the P3 processor, a 16-bit microprogrammed processor, whose instruction set is studied in Chapter 10.

The two most important components of this processor are the datapath and the control unit. The datapath consists of a register file and an arithmetic and logic unit, already studied in previous chapters, as well as the instruction and status registers and the various connection buses. The control unit is based on a microsequencer which generates the sequence of signals which control the operation of the datapath. The microsequencer uses a conditions test unit, a mapping unit and a unit which controls the register file.

The final part of the chapter is dedicated to the study of how the microprograms which control the operation of this microprocessor are defined and how to implement each of its instructions.

Exercises

12.1 To reduce the size of the microinstruction, two different formats were defined for it, each one with a subset of the control signals, although some of these signals are present in the two formats. However, this option means that some operations cannot be carried out in parallel, and so require two microinstructions. Consider that to implement all the instructions of the P3, x complete microinstructions would be necessary, that is, with all the control signals. With two simpler formats having been defined, calculate what is the maximum number, as a function of x, of microinstruction duplications which allow a reduction in the control memory.

12.2 Suppose that the width of the microinstruction is being reconsidered.

(a) State which signal you would select to include in each one of the two formats of the microinstruction if the width is increased by 1 bit.

(b) And if it was increased to 2 more bits?

12.3 For the P3 processor, say which microoperations are carried out by the following microinstructions and, for each of them, indicate an equivalent microinstruction in the opposite format, or justify why that is impossible:

(a) 80000000h
(b) D39FFFF0h
(c) 183FFED9h
(d) B84000F9h

12.4 Discuss the possibility of using more than two different formats for the microinstructions. What would be the width of the microinstruction? How would you organise the control signals?

12.5 For the following microoperations, which are intended to be carried out in parallel in a single clock cycle, indicate a microinstruction that can achieve this or justify why that is not possible:

(a) CAR←ROMA[OPCODE], LI←M[R3], R5←2F6h
(b) CAR←CAR+1, M[SP]←PC, SP←SP-1, IAK←1
(c) CAR←CAR+1, SR←0, IR←M[R2], R1←0
(d) CAR←CAR+1, SBR←CAR+1, M[R7]←0

12.6 It is intended to implement the instruction

MVS

for the P3 processor, which copies text at the start of the address indicated in register R1 to the addresses starting in R2, with the number of memory locations to be copied indicated by register R3. Register R4 specifies the increment for locations R1 and R2, normally +1, to increment, and -1, to decrement. The pseudocode for this instruction is:

```
for(i = 0; i < R3; i++) {
    M[R2] = M[R1];
    R1 = R1 + R4;
    R2 = R2 + R4;
}
```

(a) Suggest an opcode for this instruction.
(b) What is the addressing mode for register R1 used in this instruction?
(c) Indicate the binary representation of the instruction MVS (use X to indicate bits which may take any value).
(d) Write a microprogram in register transfer language for the execution phase of this instruction.
(e) Translate this microprogram into binary microinstructions.

12.7 It is intended to implement the following instruction for the P3 processor

TAS op1

which tests if the value of op1 is 0 or not, updating the status bit Zero (the status bit Zero is set to 1 if op1 = 0, and set to 0 otherwise). Also, and in any case, after executing this instruction op1 should contain the value 1. The behaviour for the other status bits is not defined, and so may be altered.

(a) Suggest an opcode for this instruction.
(b) Indicate the binary representation of the instruction TAS M[PC+F03Dh] (use «X» to indicate bits which may take on any value).
(c) Write a microprogram in register transfer language for the execution phase of this instruction.
(d) Translate this microprogram into binary microinstructions.

12.8 It is intended to implement the following instruction for the P3 processor

LOOP op1,op2

which decrements the value of the operand op1 and, if it has not reached zero, jumps to the address specified by op2. If op1 has reached zero, this jump is not executed, and, instead, the instruction at the following address is executed.

(a) Suggest an opcode for this instruction.

(b) Indicate the representation in memory of the instruction LOOP R7,M[R5+94ABh] (use «X» to indicate bits which may take on any value).

(c) Write a microprogram in register transfer language for the execution phase of this instruction.

(d) Translate this microprogram into binary microinstructions.

12.9 It is intended to implement the following instruction for the P3 processor

RETC op1

which, if the carry flag is at 1, returns from the routine and, if not, makes a relative jump adding op1 to the PC (the flags should remain unaltered). In pseudocode:

if(carry)
  RET
else
  PC←PC+op1

(a) Suggest an opcode for this instruction.

(b) Indicate the representation in memory of the instruction RETC M[R2+0B28h] (use X´to indicate bits which may take on any value).

(c) Write a microprogram in register transfer language for the execution phase of this instruction.

(d) Translate this microprogram into binary microinstructions.

Chapter 13

Memory Systems

In previous chapters, we examined the operation of a processor, modelling the memory as a set of registers, each of which individually addressable. This simplistic view does not correspond to reality, except in very simple systems, but it allowed us to describe the operation of the processor without taking into account the complexities of the memory system. In particular, any current computer, whether an embedded system, a personal computer, a server or a portable device, uses numerous devices for data storage. These devices belong to two major classes: primary memory and secondary memory.

The *primary memory*, more frequently known as *main memory*, built with integrated circuits, has a shorter access time, but is more expensive (per bit), and has a smaller capacity than the secondary memory. Besides that, it does not have the capability to hold data when the system is not powered.

Secondary memory, also known as *auxiliary memory*, uses devices based on magnetic (disks and magnetic tape) or optical (CD-ROM and DVD) technology and is slower, but has a lower cost per bit, a greater capacity and the possibility of holding stored data even when the computer is not powered. More recently *flash memories* started to be used in *solid-state drives* (*SSD*) to substitute magnetic disks. Secondary memory may be used by the processor when executing programs, through the use of the virtual memory system. The secondary memory is also used to store data in file systems. This organisation of secondary storage will not be studied in this chapter since it implies knowledge of operating systems which goes beyond the scope of an introductory book.

This chapter will analyse the memory system of a computer, starting in Section 13.1 with the organisation of its main memory, which, in some simple systems, is the only form of data storage. More complex systems have additional components, arranged in an hierarchic structure (see Section 13.2) and will be studied in the following sections. In particular in Section 13.3, we will study *cache* systems, which aim at speeding up access to the primary storage, and Section 13.4 will focus in virtual memory systems, which make possible the transparent use of secondary storage as if it was main memory, by the processor.

13.1   Organisation of Memory Systems

Chapter 6 analysed how to organise a set of registers into memory modules. A memory module is built as a set of registers (of one or more bits) and a decoding system which enables the selection of one and only one of the registers for read and write operations. It may be a single integrated circuit or a module combining several integrated circuits. These registers are usually made up of devices with a behaviour similar to that of the level enabled latches studied in Section 6.2.

The main memory of a computer, in its simplest form, consists of a set (or bank) of memory modules, organised so as to be visible by the processor as a set of locations where it can write or read data. In practice, the organisation of the memory system may be relatively complex, given that the address space controls the access to several memory devices, and also to the input/output system in some processors, such as the P3.

The following section describes how the memory of the computer is constructed by connecting various modules and how different types of memories may be interconnected, so as to share the addressing space of the processor.

13.1.1   *Memory Banks*

Normally, it is not possible to find a single integrated memory circuit which, just by itself, satisfies the needs of a given computational system. It is, therefore, necessary to use various interconnected memory modules, in order to offer the desired functionality and capacity, interconnected in a *memory bank*.

Commercial memory modules, integrated circuits or aggregates of integrated circuits, in addition to their address lines, have one or more lines which enable that module to be selected, called *CS* (chip select) or *CE* (chip enable). When this signal is not active, the data outputs of the memory module are in a high impedance state, and it is not possible to access the memory. These lines allow various memory modules to be connected in a very simple way to create memories with varying capacities and configurations.

Figure 13.1 shows the interconnections made available by a simple memory module, with a *CS* selection input. The address lines can select one of

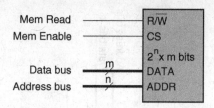

Fig. 13.1   Block diagram for a memory module with $2^n \times m$ bits.

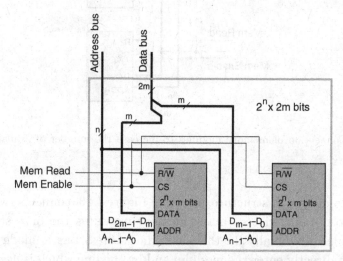

Fig. 13.2   Connection of memory modules to increase the number of bits in each memory location.

the memory locations of the module, and the data lines connect to the processor data bus. The $R/\overline{W}$ input selects the intended mode of operation. When the line is at 1, the memory is in reading mode and places in the data lines the content of the location specified in the addressing lines. When the line is at 0, the memory is placed in write mode and writes the value in the data lines to the specified location. Memory modules of this type may be interconnected so as to create a variety of memory configurations.

There are essentially two types of memory module interconnection: one which increases the number of bits for each memory word and another which increases the number of memory words.

The first type of connection, shown in Figure 13.2, makes it possible to interconnect different memory modules, to obtain words wider than the ones available individually in each memory module. In this type of connection, the words accessed in each module are concatenated to form a wider word.

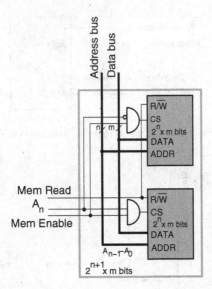

Fig. 13.3   Connection of memory modules to increase the number of available memory locations.

The second type of structure, shown in Figure 13.3, connects two memory modules to obtain twice as many memory words as the ones supplied by each module individually. In this case, the address bus is made up of the lines which directly enter the modules and by the line which is used to select which of the modules is active (A_n in the figure).

The above interconnection methods may be combined, to obtain a memory system with the desired characteristics.

This process can be shown more clearly with an example. Let us suppose that there are memory modules available with 16 Kbyte (that is, 2^{14} memory locations each with 8 bits) and that we want to build a memory system with 64 Kbyte, organised into 2^{16} memory locations of 8 bits each. In this case, the interconnection of four modules, as shown in Figure 13.4, provides the desired functionality.

Note that this is an interconnection of the same type as the one in Figure 13.3 where the data lines are interconnected, and the decoder is used to select which of the memory modules should respond to a given address. This interconnection of the data lines is only possible because the functioning of the decoder guarantees from the outset that only one of the memory circuits is enabled for each memory access. In this case, the 2 bits which control the decoder join the 14 address bits directly connected to the memories, into a bus of 16 address lines.

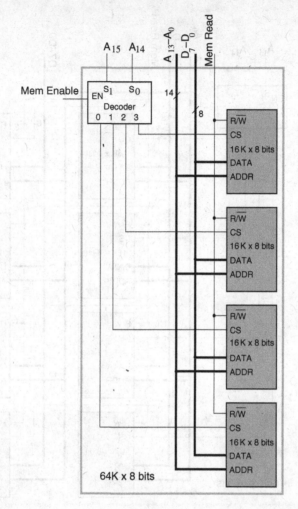

Fig. 13.4 Diagram for a 64 Kbyte memory, built with four modules of 16 Kbyte each.

Figure 13.5 shows the interconnections necessary to combine eight memory modules of the same type used in the previous example, to obtain a 128 Kbyte memory, organised into 64 Kword of 16 bits each. As in the previous example, there are 16 address lines with 14 of them directly connected to each of the memory modules and the other two connecting to the decoder.

13.1.2 *Memory Maps*

The previous section analysed how various memory modules may be interconnected to form a memory of the desired size. This section will study the

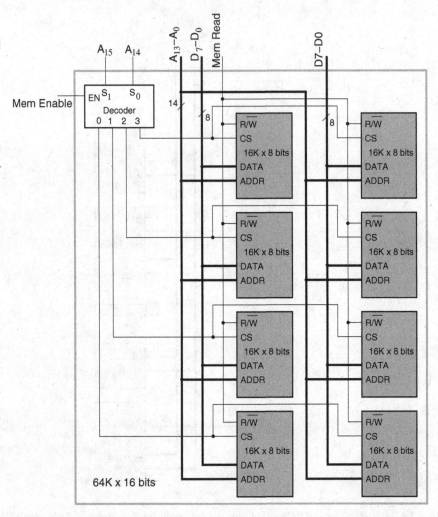

Fig. 13.5   Diagram for a 128 Kbyte memory, organised into 64 Kword of two bytes each.

way that memories are connected to the processor, to provide the designer with the desired addressing space in the location needed.

Let us consider a very simple situation, where we want to use the memory module in Figure 13.4 to provide 64 Kbyte addressing space in a processor which has 20 address bits and an eight-bit data bus. Although the memory can have a complex internal structure, the processor sees it in a way similar to the simple module in Figure 13.1, in this case with 16 address lines and eight data lines.

Since the processor has a total addressing space of 2^{20} byte, from 00000h to FFFFFh (greater than the capacity of the memory module), the designer

Fig. 13.6 Memory map of the processor addressing space of 2^{20} byte, but with only 64 Kbyte of RAM memory installed between locations F0000h and FFFFFh.

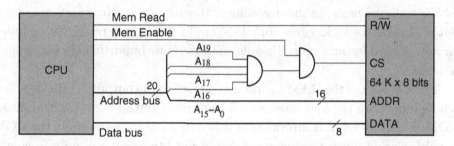

Fig. 13.7 Circuit corresponding to the memory map in Figure 13.6.

first has to decide the *addressing space* which will correspond to the memory. Let us assume the option of locating the 2^{16} memory words in the positions F0000h to FFFFFh that is, at the top of the addressing space that can be used by the processor.

The correspondence necessary to be carried out between memory addresses and modules is called the *memory map*. This map is often illustrated graphically, as is the case in Figure 13.6, which corresponds to this example.

Figure 13.7 shows a decoding circuit that makes the memory accessible only in this addressing space zone. The logic gate used causes that only addresses which have the four most significant bits at 1 enable the memory operation.

Usually, the memory maps of a processor are more complex, and isolated logic gates are not used, but rather decoders, or ROMs acting as complex decoders, to select individual memory modules.

When designing the circuit which decodes the addresses and generates the control signals for the memory modules, it is necessary to ensure that:

(1) Each memory module is selected when the address corresponds to a memory location stored in that module, and there is a memory access operation.
(2) The bits which are used to address the words inside the module are appropriately connected to the corresponding lines of the address bus.

Let us take the example of a system based on the same processor of the previous example, where we want to implement the memory map shown in Figure 13.8.

In this memory map, there is a ROM memory of 32 Kbyte in the lower part of the memory space and two non-contiguous areas of RAM, both of 64 Kbyte. Implementing the decoding of this memory system may be carried out with discrete logic gates, but this would result in a relatively complex circuit. A simpler and more flexible solution is to build this circuit around a decoder.

The *CS* lines of the RAM memories connect to the outputs of the decoder, whose inputs are the four most significant bits of the address. Control of the ROM is slightly more complex since it is necessary to ensure that the ROM is only selected when the five most significant bits are 0 and only in a read operation. Figure 13.9 shows the implementation of the decoding circuit corresponding to the memory map in Figure 13.8.

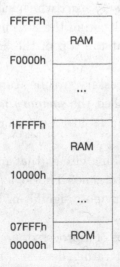

Fig. 13.8   Memory map of a processor with RAM and ROM.

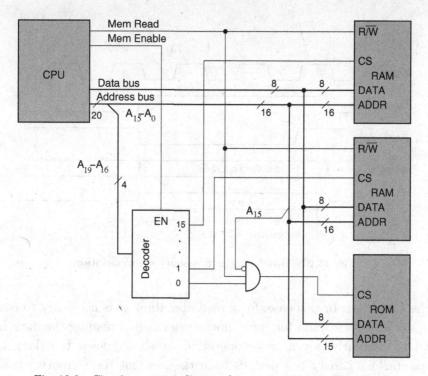

Fig. 13.9 Circuit corresponding to the memory map in Figure 13.8.

13.1.3 *Generation of Control Signals*

Until now, we have assumed that a memory module, when selected and in read mode, places the value of the desired memory locations at its output. In practice, the operation of the memory is slightly more complicated, because of the various operational speeds of the processor and the control bus.

Indeed, although a processor can operate with clock cycles in the order of 1 ns, memory access times vary, according to the types of memory, between a few nanoseconds, for static RAM, and tens of nanoseconds, for greater capacity dynamic RAM. This difference means that a memory module normally cannot make the data available within a processor clock cycle, and therefore requires a data transfer protocol.

The simplest way to ensure that the data is read or written correctly is to design the system so that the processor waits enough time for the read or write operation to conclude successfully.

Let us, for example, consider that a processor which works at 100 MHz (which corresponds to a clock cycle of 10 ns) has to communicate with a memory which has an access time of 25 ns, measured from the enabling

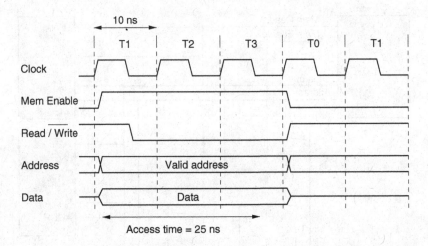

Fig. 13.10 Waveforms for a memory write operation.

of the CS signal. In this case, for a read operation, it is necessary to ensure that the processor waits for three clock cycles before reading the data from the bus. Similarly, for a write operation, it should keep the data valid on the bus for three clock periods from the moment the memory has been selected.

Figure 13.10 shows the waveforms for a write operation in a system with this configuration. After triggering the signal which selects the respective memory module, the data should remain valid in the bus for three processor clock cycles.

The read operation behaves similarly. In this case, the data only is assuredly valid on the bus after a time equal to the memory access time has elapsed, therefore the processor can read the data only at the end of the third clock cycle.

The waveforms in Figures 13.10 and 13.11 show the accesses carried out by a processor on static memories, which typically only have CS and $R/\overline{W}$ control lines. The reality of the modern computer is, however, much more sophisticated.

On the one hand, the memories used as primary storage are usually dynamic memories, whose control is significantly more complicated than the control of static memories. These memories are cheaper (per bit) and have various access modes, which provide features such as rapid transfer of data blocks. A detailed study of the control of dynamic memories is outside the scope of an introductory textbook, and so this matter is not developed here.

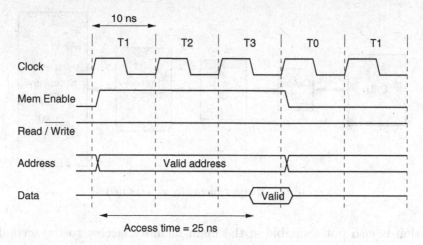

Fig. 13.11 Waveforms for a memory read operation.

On the other hand, processor access is not carried out on a simple memory, but on a memory hierarchy, which Section 13.2 will describe.

13.2 Memory Hierarchy

For reasons related to system performance, analysed in this section, the memory of a computer normally has various levels, as shown in Figure 13.12.

In what respects processor performance, the ideal situation is having the largest possible quantity of memory available operating at the fastest possible speed. However, as the cost per bit increases with operation speed, the commonly adopted solution involves the use of various types of memory, with different sizes and access speeds. The memory system is structured so that the most commonly used data and instructions in a program are in the fastest and smaller memories, while the least frequently accessed are in the slowest and larger memories.

A simple *memory hierarchy* will be analysed next, where there is only one *cache* level, one large capacity main memory, and secondary storage, which supports virtual memory. In general, there may be various cache levels, but this does not alter the operating mechanism.

When access to a memory location takes place, both for reading or for writing, the system starts by checking if it is available in the fastest memory, which is known as the *cache*. If this location is not available in the cache, the main memory, which is generally dynamic RAM, is checked. If the

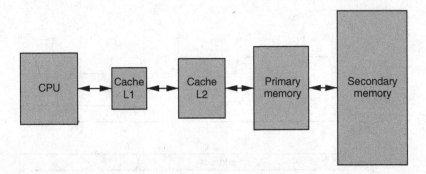

Fig. 13.12   Memory hierarchy in a computer.

location is also not available in the main memory, access to the secondary storage is carried out, Secondary storage is larger and slower than main memory, and uses in general, magnetic disks or, more recently solid-state drives.

If the memory system is well structured, this hierarchical system is only slightly slower, on average, than a memory system where all the memory operates at the speed of the cache. The total cost, however, is much smaller, since the slower memories have a cost per bit much lower than the fastest memories.

The possibility to come close to the original objective of a very large and very fast memory, by investing only a fraction of the amount that would be necessary for all the memory to be fast is a consequence of a fact observed in practically all programs, which is known as the *principle of locality*. This principle formalises the empirical verification that the memory accesses made by a processor are strongly correlated regarding its addresses and not uniformly distributed throughout the available memory. There are two types of locality:

- *Temporal locality*: if there is access to a particular memory address, it is highly likely that there will be a new access to that same address shortly.
- *Spatial locality*: if there is access to a particular memory address, it is highly likely that there will be a new access to another address close to this.

The temporal locality may be used to accelerate accesses to data and instructions by keeping memory locations that were used most recently in the fastest memories. Indeed, a very significant fraction of the execution time of a program is spent on cycles of a relatively small-sized program length, where the same instructions are repeatedly executed, and the same variables re-used, for example:

```
for(i=0; i < 100; i++)
   a[i] = 0.0;
```

The spatial locality may be used for the same purpose, copying to the fastest memories, locations which are spatially close to those which were recently used. The spatial locality of data results from the use of data structures, such as vectors, as illustrated above, where the values are sequentially accessed. Spatial locality in the instructions results from the way a processor operates, by essentially executing instructions located sequentially in the memory.

The two types of locality potentiate the use of caches, with the aim of reducing processor access times to the primary storage. Most current computers also use a memory management system known as virtual memory, which uses the principle of locality to allow programs to use a quantity of memory greater than that which physically exists in the computer.

The combination of these two techniques, caches and virtual memory, means that the central processing unit sees that a very fast memory is virtually available with a capacity much greater than the physical memory that the computer has. These two important techniques will be studied in detail in Sections 13.3 and 13.4, respectively.

13.2.1 *Caches*

The function of a *cache* in a memory system is to make possible most memory accesses to be carried out more quickly than what is possible by directly using the main memory of the computer. This concept of a small and fast memory can be generalised to include multiple levels of cache, as described in Figure 13.12. The cache levels closest to the processor are faster but have lower capacity. The outermost levels are progressively slower but have greater capacity.

The main memory of a computer usually consists of dynamic memories, with access times within the range of $60 - 70$ ns. Cache memories often share the same integrated circuit as the processor and therefore have access times compatible with the speed of the processor. Modern processors commonly have more than one cache level inside the chip, and may or may not have supplementary external caches. These caches may have access times in the order of the length of the clock cycle of the processor, which, with present-day technology, is less than 1 ns.

In a read operation, the function of the cache is to make data and instructions available within the shortest possible time when accessing the main memory. In a write operation, the cache should be accessed quickly to store data, with this data being written to the main memory later.

Since the cache has a smaller size than the main memory, only a small part of the total memory content is present in the cache at any given moment. Therefore, sometimes an access finds the intended address in the cache, and sometimes it does not, situations which are respectively called *hit* and *miss*. To maximise the number of hits, it is necessary to frequently substitute data and instructions in the cache by other data which have been accessed more recently.

To quantify the acceleration that the use of a cache may bring, let us consider a simplified example of a computer system that only has one cache level and a main memory.

Let us consider that a given processor operates at 500 MHz, accesses the data memory at each instruction and each instruction takes four clock cycles for its execution. In these conditions, the processor accesses the data memory[1] every 8 ns.

Let us assume that main memory has an average access time of 70 ns, while the cache, implemented with a technology similar to that of the processor, makes the data available in 2 ns, which corresponds to the processor clock period. Let us also assume that, in this system, memory accesses have a pattern such that 95% of accesses made to memory reach positions already in cache or, in other words, the cache has a *hit rate* of 95%. An alternative definition is the *miss rate*. Of course, the sum of these two rates is 100%, therefore, in this example, the miss rate will be 5%.

In these conditions, it is possible to calculate the number of clock cycles it takes on average to execute each instruction in this system, and in a similar system but without a cache.

The execution of each instruction takes four clock cycles, one cycle of which is memory access. The average time for memory access is, thus, given by

$$\overline{T}_{\mathrm{mem}} = 2 + 0.05 \times 70 = 5.5 \text{ ns.} \qquad (13.1)$$

---

[1] We will ignore for now the fact that the processor needs to access instructions, which are also stored in memory.

The average number of clock cycles per instruction executed by the processor is therefore $3 + 5.5/2.0$, that is, 5.75 (this performance measure is known as CPI, cycles per instruction). So, this processor executes an instruction every 5.75 clock cycles, that is, every 11.5 ns. This processor, therefore, executes 87 millions of instructions per second (or 87 *MIPS*).

Without cache, each memory access would have to be carried out using the main memory. Thus, to execute each instruction, the processor would take $3 + 70/2.0$ clock cycles, that is, 38 clock cycles. The processor would, therefore, execute only 13.2 MIPS, which means it would be about seven times slower.

This example shows the importance of caches to computer system performance and demonstrates how the inclusion of a small, fast memory between the processor and the main memory significantly increases the speed of instruction execution.

These analyses have not focused on the critical aspect of the size of the caches, but only their speed. The size of the caches is, however, critical for a good memory system operation. The value of the hit rate shows indirectly the impact of the size of the caches. When designing a cache for a memory system, it is necessary to consider two essential factors:

- the speed of the cache, which determines the maximum operation speed of the system;
- the size of the cache, which determines the hit rate of the same, and subsequently, the number of main memory accesses.

The best solution comes from a trade-off between these two factors.

For the processor studied in Chapter 12, we assumed that it was possible to execute a memory access in each clock cycle. Therefore, the memory represented in Figure 12.1, for a typical architecture, represents the most internal cache of the processor, which was assumed to have an access time no greater than that of the processor clock cycle.

The control lines necessary for the interface with the *cache controller* were omitted for clarity when describing the processor. Of these, the most important is the *READY* signal, which is tested for each cache read. This signal, generated by the cache controller, indicates that the read is complete and that the desired data is available on the data bus. When the data is not present in the cache, the processor waits before carrying out the processing. In the particular case of the architecture studied in Chapter 12, the processor continues to execute the same microinstruction until the *READY* signal is enabled. The use of a *READY* line is necessary for using caches since an access takes much longer when data is not available and reading from the main memory is needed.

In a write operation, the situation is a little simpler. In this case, the processor may immediately continue, provided that it is possible to store the data in the cache or the controller has a register available to store the data temporarily. This is generally the case, although the details of the operation of the controller may be complex. Section 13.3.4 studies this subject in greater detail.

13.2.2   Virtual Memory

A virtual addressing space is defined with a typical size considerably greater than the main memory so that the processor does not have an addressing space limited to the amount of memory installed in the system. In this way, all CPU processing is carried out using *virtual addresses*, as opposed to *physical addresses* which access the main memory and the cache.

Whenever the processor makes a memory access, the address placed on the address bus is, therefore, a virtual address. The effective access to memory needs first the translation of this virtual address to a physical address. This task is carried out by a specialised unit in the computer, the *MMU*, *Memory Management Unit*. Therefore, the sequence of operations for memory access will be[2]:

(1) the CPU places the virtual address it wants to access on the address bus;
(2) the MMU translates this address into a physical address;
(3) a cache access is carried out to test if this physical address is in the cache; if it is found in the cache, the read or write access terminates here;
(4) if not, access to the main memory is carried out.

Of course, as the virtual space is much greater than the physical space, not all the virtual memory locations will have a corresponding physical address. In this case, it is not possible for the MMU to translate them, and it is necessary to access the disk, which stores the virtual addressing space which does not fit in main memory. This disk access transfers the data corresponding to the virtual addresses accessed, to the main memory. In fact, one way of

---

[2]In certain systems, the cache operates directly with virtual addresses, a situation where points 2 and 3 are reversed.

looking at this system is thinking of the main memory as a cache for the virtual addressing space, with the observations made in the previous section therefore also valid.

The disk access time, in the order of tenths of milliseconds, is much greater than the access time to the main memory which, as we have seen, is in the order of tenths of nanoseconds. There is thus a factor of 1 million in the difference between the access times to main and secondary storage. Thus, whenever a given virtual address is not in main memory, there is a significant penalty concerning the processor performance. Fortunately, this impact is reduced since, due to the principles of temporal and spatial locality, the miss rate in accesses to virtual memory locations is very low. A typical value for the miss rate is in the order of 0.0001%, that is, only one in every 1 million accesses is not found in main memory.

Consider the values used in Expression (13.1). The access times to the memory and the cache of 70 ns and 2 ns, respectively, and a cache hit rate of 95%. Assume also that access to the disk takes 10 ms (or 10^7 ns), with a miss rate for virtual addresses of 0.0001% (or 10^{-6}). The memory access time becomes[3]:

$$\overline{T}_{\text{mem}} = 2 + 0.05 \times (70 + 0.000001 \times 10^7) = 6.0 \text{ ns} \qquad (13.2)$$

Therefore, 95% of the times, the access continues to be resolved by the cache. Of the remaining 5% of cases, when it is necessary to access the main memory, in 99.9999% of the cases, access is only made to the main memory, and in only 0.0001% of cases is it necessary to access the disk. As we can see, the great penalty involved in accessing the disk is reduced due to the low number of accesses to it.

In any event, whenever a miss occurs, the CPU does not generally remain blocked waiting for the data from the disk, which could mean the waste of millions of clock cycles. In present-day computers, there are usually several *processes* executing concurrently. This means that although at each instance only one of these processes is active, there is a set of other processes awaiting their turn. The processing time is therefore divided between these different processes under the control of the operating system. If the active process has a virtual address miss, this process is blocked, and one of the waiting processes is selected and put in execution. This way,

---

[3]To simplify, we ignore the time to translate the virtual to physical addresses by the MMU.

the loading of information from the disk occurs during the useful execution of another process, thus significantly reducing the waste of processing time.

13.3   Organisation of Cache Systems

As we saw above, there are two types of access locality: temporal locality and spatial locality. To take advantage of temporal locality, the cache should store data which has been recently accessed. To take advantage of spatial locality, the cache should store data which has addresses close to recently accessed data.

The various alternatives for cache architecture employ different solutions to be able to take the best advantage of each of these access characteristics. To make the discussion which follows clearer, let as assume a system with a memory hierarchy which consists of only two levels: a first level, the cache, and a second level, the main memory. In practice, the following level may not correspond to the main memory, but only to a second cache level. However, this does not affect the behaviour of the first cache level, which will be analysed next. The secondary storage will also be ignored for now, and it is assumed that all the addresses are physical addresses.

There are essentially four degrees of freedom which affect the choice of architecture for a cache system.

The first is the way to map the addressing space of the main memory to the more reduced cache addressing space. Since the cache necessarily has fewer locations than the memory, there is the need to define a process through which each main memory location can be mapped to a cache location.

The second aspect has to do with the size of the *cache blocks*, in order to make the best possible use of the spatial locality for data accesses. A cache block represents the minimum quantity of bytes loaded from the main memory to the cache when it is necessary to retrieve data from memory.

The third aspect is the method that is used to substitute data in the cache, so as to maximise the potential of temporal locality.

The fourth aspect is related to the processing of write operations. A write operation is fundamentally different from a read operation, because the processor can continue the execution of a program without waiting for the termination of a write operation, and because it affects data in main memory which can be accessed by other devices.

Fig. 13.13 Tag and index fields.

13.3.1 *Cache Data Mapping*

In general, the mapping of a larger-sized addressing space (which corresponds to the main memory) to a smaller addressing space (the cache) only has to consider a subset of the address bits.

A 32-bit address should, therefore, be seen as divided into two parts: the *index* and the *tag*. Figure 13.13 shows the partition of a 32-bit address into two parts, for a cache that provides 1024 positions. These positions are addressed by the index bits, hence the field index has 10 bits. The size of the tag depends on the maximum size of available memory and corresponds to the remaining 22 bits, because the total addressing space is 2^{32} byte, as mentioned above.

When reading the contents of a given address, the subset of bits which corresponds to the index is used to address the cache. This cache location stores the value that is found stored in the targeted memory location.

However, because a number of different addresses in memory will correspond to the same cache location, it is important to distinguish if the stored data in this cache location corresponds to the data in the intended memory location. This verification is made by storing not only the data in the cache but also the tag field of the address corresponding to the data which is present.

When a cache access is made using only the index bits, it is enough to compare the tag field of the memory location which we want to access with the tag stored in the cache. If they are equal, the content of that cache location is the intended content. Figure 13.14 shows in a simplified way the operating mechanism of a cache of this type.

If the tags are different, the data in the cache is not the intended data, and it will be necessary to read the main memory to obtain the correct data. Since, due to temporal locality, this data is likely to be used shortly, the data must be sent not only to the processor but also to this cache location and the tag value updated.

This type of mapping, which is called *direct mapping*, is not the only possibility of mapping the total addressing space to a more limited set of cache locations.

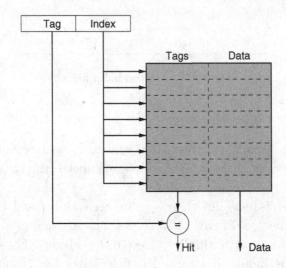

Fig. 13.14   Operating schematic for a direct mapping cache.

Direct mapping caches are the most simple. However, they are the most restrictive since, as each memory location may only be in a given location of the cache, performance will be poor if the program consecutively accesses two memory locations which, unfortunately, map to the same cache location.

An alternative to direct mapping caches is the use of *fully associative* caches. The best option to increase cache flexibility is that the contents of a given memory location might use any cache location. This consideration gives rise to the associative cache idea. In this case, the address is interpreted entirely as a tag, and there is no index field. The identification of the correct cache location results from the comparison of the tags. If there is a cache location that contains a tag with a value equal to the tag of the address being accessed, then that cache location contains the intended value.

Associative memories are used to implement these caches, and their operation is different from more conventional memories. In an associative memory, the value used to address the memory does not correspond to a location address, but rather to the content of a memory location. Each location in the associative memories contains not only data but also a tag. The address placed at the input of an associative memory is simultaneously compared with the tags of all the memory locations, making the data available which correspond to the location where the tag coincides with the value used to address the memory. Figure 13.15 shows the internal structure of a fully associative memory.

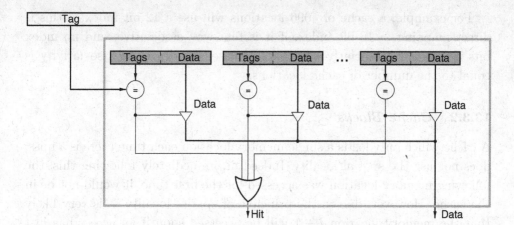

Fig. 13.15   Structure of a fully associative memory.

Despite being more flexible, these caches are slower and more complex than direct mapping ones, due to the need to carry out a simultaneous comparison of all the memory locations with the address tag. For this reason, larger caches are not usually fully associative. However, it is possible to obtain many of the advantages of fully associative mapping maintaining the speed of access and the cost of a direct mapping cache.

A *set-associative mapping cache* consists of a set of direct mapping caches, addressed in parallel. They are all simultaneously accessed with the address index field, but only the one with the correct tag makes its data available. If there are n direct mapping caches in parallel, a given memory location may be mapped to any one of the n caches, in the position which corresponds to the value of the index. This type of cache is called an *n-way associative mapping cache*.

These three types of caches can be seen as all belonging to the same type, only varying in the degree of associativity. In a direct mapping cache, the degree of associativity is 1. In a fully associative cache, the degree of associativity is M, where M is the number of cache positions. The address has two fields, the size of which varies with the size of the caches and the degree of associativity. In particular, the number of bits in the index is equal to $\log_2 \frac{M}{n}$, where M is the size of the cache, and n, the degree of associativity.

In caches which have various degrees of associativity, writing new data in the cache has to be preceded by choice of the cache to contain this data. Indeed, any of the caches can be chosen depending on the decision regarding the replacement policy, which is the object of study in Section 13.3.3.

For example, a cache of 4096 locations will use a 12-bit index, if this is direct mapping, a 10-bit index, if it is four-way associative, and no index bits if it is fully associative. In this last case, the degree of associativity is equal to the number of cache locations.

13.3.2   Cache Blocks

A cache which only loads a single memory location each time there is a miss, does not use the spatial locality. Indeed, if, immediately following this, the following memory location was accessed for the first time, it would not be in the cache. However, due to the principle of spatial locality, it is very likely that the memory location $i + 1$ will be accessed soon if an access has just been made to memory location i.

Caches make use of this feature of access patterns by mapping blocks of consecutive memory locations, and not individual positions. These sets of memory locations, the size of which varies from cache to cache, are called *cache blocks* or *cache lines*. The use of cache blocks also results in a greater efficiency in accessing main memory which typically have access mechanisms which are quicker for sets of consecutive locations.

When a cache works with blocks, which is the most common situation, the address is structured into three parts: the tag, the index and the *offset* within the block. The offset field has a sufficient number of bits to address an individual location inside a block and is used to select which of the block locations is addressed by the processor.

As previously, the index bits are used to select which of the blocks should contain the intended memory locations. The number of blocks in the cache is equal to the size of the cache divided by the size of each block. The number of bits in the index, therefore, becomes equal to $\log_2 \frac{M}{nB}$, where B is the size of each block, and, just like before, M is the size of the cache and n the degree of associativity. A cache with the same size as in the previous example, with 4096 locations, which uses blocks of 16 locations, will use only an eight-bit index if it is a direct mapping cache. Indeed, the 4096 locations correspond to 256 blocks of 16 locations each, with each of the blocks addressed by the eight-bit index field. Figure 13.16 shows the division of the address into the tag, index and offset fields for this example.

Figure 13.17 presents the correspondence between the locations of a main memory of 64 Mbyte and the blocks of a cache with these characteristics.

Note that the size of the tags does not change with the size of blocks in the cache. The number of bits in the index is lower when the block is larger

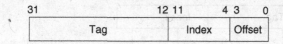

Fig. 13.16   Tag, index and offset fields for the example in the text.

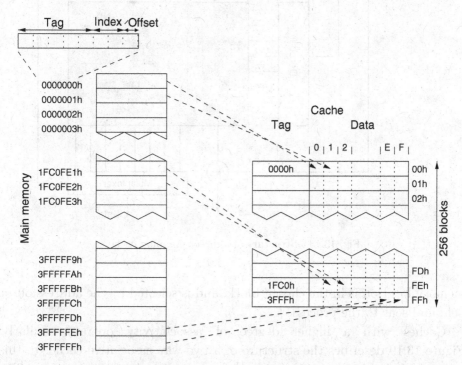

Fig. 13.17   Example of mapping of a memory of 64 Mbyte for a direct mapping cache of 4 Kbyte with 16-byte blocks.

(fewer lines in the cache), but the bits removed from the index are used as extra address bits for the cache block. However, only one tag is needed for each set of B cache locations, which means there is a smaller penalty for the need to store the tags, in addition to the data itself.

It is now possible to understand the internal structure of a direct mapping cache, shown in Figure 13.18. The cache consists of a set of blocks, each of which contains various memory locations and a set of bits which store the tag which corresponds to this block.

The address bits are used differently, according to the field to which they belong. In a first phase, the index bits are used to address, through a decoder, the cache block which may contain the data. In a second phase, the tag stored along with the selected block is compared with the tag of the intended address. If this comparison gives a positive result, the intended

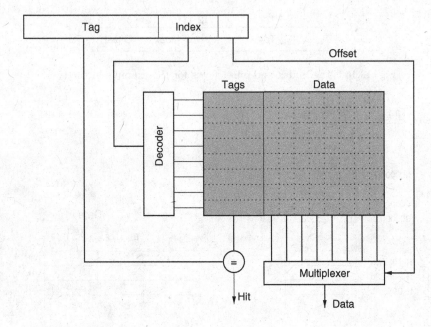

Fig. 13.18   Structure of a direct mapping cache.

memory location is in the chosen block, and is selected by the address offset field and sent to the processor.

Caches with a higher degree of associativity operate similarly. Figure 13.19 describes the structure of a two-way associative cache. In this case, the index bits select two blocks, one from each of the two sets. The comparison with the tags proceeds in parallel for each of the tags in the locations specified by the index field. Only one of these comparisons can give a positive result since the cache management ensures that one memory location is never simultaneously present in more than one cache location. The use of tri-state buffers simplifies the logic which chooses which of the ways should send the data to the cache. Without tri-state logic, it is necessary to use an encoder, the output of which controls a multiplexer which selects the way that should be enabled, as shown in Figure 13.19.

13.3.3   *Replacement Policies*

In the case of direct mapping caches, there is no need to make any decision when a given memory location is not present in the cache. Indeed, since one wants to store the most recently accessed data in the cache, it is necessary to substitute the data in the cache whenever there is a miss. Since the intended

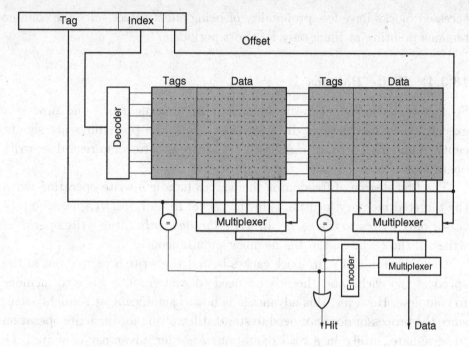

Fig. 13.19 Structure of a cache with two associativity ways.

data can only go to one cache location, the content of that position will have to be substituted.

In caches which have two or more ways, it is necessary to decide which of the ways will store the new data, as this implies removing data which is already in the cache. In general, the best solution consists in substituting the data that has not been accessed for the longest time, since, according to the principle of temporal locality, this is the least likely to be used shortly. This *replacement policy* is called *LRU*, for Least Recently Used. However, in caches with a high degree of associativity, this policy is challenging to implement in hardware, since it would require keeping note of the time each of the memory blocks was accessed and a way to quickly determine which way was the one without access for a longer time.

There are various alternatives to solve this problem. One possibility, which in practice produces good results, is to select one of the ways containing the block to be substituted, in a random manner. Another very effective solution, although slightly more complex, is to have a module-n counter per cache line (where n is the associativity level of the cache). When a block is accessed in set i, if the value of the counter in the respective line is i, the counter is incremented. When we need to replace a block in a line, the set corresponding to the value of the counter is used. In this way, frequently accessed blocks have less probability of being substituted, since the counter remains pointing at them only for short periods.

13.3.4 *Write Policies*

So far we have analysed the behaviour of a cache when the processor executes read instructions. In write operations, the procedures are significantly different. There are essentially two degrees of freedom regarding write operations.

The first degree of freedom is the way to handle a write operation when the targeted memory location is in the cache. In *write-back* caches, the processor only writes to the cache. In *write-through* caches, the write operation writes in the cache and in the memory simultaneously.

One advantage of write-back caches is that the write is carried out at the speed of the cache and there is no need to wait for the write to memory to complete. However, this advantage is not as significant as it might seem, since the processor does not need to stand still waiting for the write operation to terminate, unlike in a read operation. Another advantage of write-back caches is that it is possible to reduce the traffic on the bus caused by writes to memory since two writes to the same cache location do not lead to separate writes to memory. However, this advantage has a related disadvantage when it is necessary to substitute the cache block since it is then necessary to update the memory with the altered data in the cache. This operation can significantly delay the read operation which causes the substitution of the block, or, alternatively, make the structure of the cache considerably more complicated.

The second degree of freedom is related to the action to take when there is a write to a block which is not in the cache. The policy could be to copy the block from memory to the cache (*write-allocate*), or, conversely, writing the data directly to memory, without copying the block to the cache.

Usually, write-back caches are of the write-allocate type, while many of the write-through caches are of the no-write-allocate type. However, other options are possible, and it is necessary to analyse the impact on the performance of each of the options, given the profile of a typical program.

13.3.5 *Control Bits*

In a cache block, besides the data itself and the tag, there must also be a set of cache *control bits* which hold various types of information.

In the case of write-back caches, one of these bits is the *dirty bit*. This bit indicates if the data in this cache block has been altered and should be written to memory when that cache block is needed for other data.

Another control bit in all caches is the *valid bit*, which indicates if the data in that cache location is valid or not. There are various reasons why the data may no longer be valid. The computer may be starting to execute a program, a situation where all data is invalid. There may be other devices which alter memory locations, a situation where the cache copy is invalid. In operating systems which can execute more than one process at a time (*multitasking systems*), the cache blocks may also be marked as invalid when there is a change of context.

There may be other control bits which control the operation of the cache in other respects. For example, there may be control bits used by the replacement policy and bits which implement memory protection mechanisms. The number and function of those bits vary from system to system.

13.4   Virtual Memory

Caches are the part of the memory hierarchy closest to the processor and have the primary objective of accelerating data access speed by the processor. At the other end of the hierarchy is the *secondary memory*, typically made of magnetic disks or solid-state drives, which has the function of increasing the size of the memory seen by the processor in addition to the capacity of the main memory installed in the computer.

The main memory and the magnetic disk or solid-state drives are very different devices. However, in many systems, the physical location of the data that a program is using is transparent to the processor (and to the programmer). A processor may access data stored in an addressing space which is much greater than the available main memory. The provision of this *virtual addressing space*, beyond the main memory physically available, is possible through a mechanism that supports the use of *virtual addresses*.

When a system makes virtual memory available, all memory accesses carried out by the processor are made using virtual addresses. These systems provide a *memory management unit* or MMU, which translates a virtual address to a *physical memory address* if the virtual address corresponds to a memory location. If the virtual address corresponds to a location which, at that moment, is not in memory and only stored on disk, the system will search for that memory location on the disk and copy it to the main memory.

To facilitate this translation of addresses, and to optimise data transfer involving secondary storage, the virtual and physical addresses are divided into contiguous address groups called *pages*. The size of the page, equal in virtual and physical spaces, is commonly much greater than the capacity of a cache block since the data transfer between secondary and main memory incurs a much higher penalty than the transfer between main memory and the cache. The size of the virtual memory page usually varies between 1 Kbyte and 16 Kbyte, depending on the system.

Whenever access to a virtual address is carried out, the MMU verifies if the page corresponding to that address is in memory or not. If it is not, there has been a *page fault*, and the page is loaded from the disk into memory. The loading of the page, made by a routine of the operating system, may take several milliseconds, a time sufficient to execute millions of instructions in a modern processor. Therefore, the processor is free for other tasks, such as running other programs (in *multitasking systems*) or attending to pending interrupt requests.

The process of translating virtual addresses to physical addresses uses various physical and logic structures. The most important are the *page tables* and the *TLB* discussed in the next sections.

13.4.1　*Page Tables*

A given virtual address specifies a location in the virtual addressing space. As with caches, this address may be divided into several fields. Virtual memory addresses have two fields, the *page number* and the *offset* within the page.

The physical address may also be seen as divided into these two fields. Since the physical and virtual pages have the same size, the offset within the page in the physical address is equal to the one in the virtual address. The page number, on the contrary, may require a different number of bits, since the sizes of the physical and virtual addressing spaces are very different.

As such, the translation of virtual addresses to physical addresses mainly consists of translating the number of the virtual page to a physical page number.

13.4.1.1　*Flat page table*

The simplest translation scheme uses a table (see Figure 13.20) with as many entries as the number of virtual pages. Each entry in this table stores

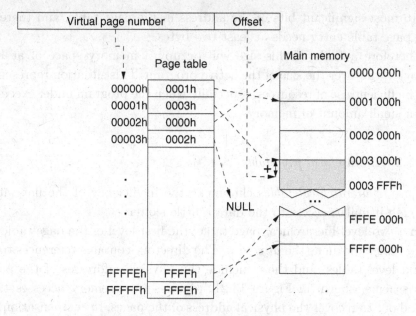

Fig. 13.20 Table to translate virtual addresses.

a *page table entry* or *PTE*, which includes information on the physical address of the page, and information necessary to locate the searched page on disk, possibly through the use of auxiliary tables.

When accessing a virtual memory page, the table is consulted to verify if the page exists in physical memory. If so, the physical address is constructed by concatenating the corresponding entry in the table with the offset within the page. If not, there is a page fault, and an operating system subroutine is called to copy the page to the main memory.

This simple scheme operates well, but only when the virtual addressing space is not too large. Consider a system which provides a virtual addressing space of 2^{32} byte and has a physical memory of 256 Mbyte (2^{28}), as an example. Let us also assume that the size of the pages is 4 Kbyte (2^{12}). This system offers a total of 2^{20} ($2^{32}/2^{12}$) virtual pages, which means that the page table has 2^{20} entries, independently of the amount of virtual memory used by a program.

Each entry in the page table must have sufficient space to identify which of the pages in physical memory corresponds to a virtual page. The physical memory has a capacity for 2^{16} pages ($2^{28}/2^{12}$). For simplicity, let us assume that all the pages are aligned in memory, which means that the first address of each page has the last 12 bits set at 0. In this case, we just need to store the 16 most significant bits of the address in the page table, and therefore each page table entry needs at least two bytes.

Therefore a table of this size will occupy a memory space of at least 2 Mbyte, whatever the size of the active program. This situation represents a very inefficient use of resources, especially when the program under execution uses a small amount of memory.

13.4.1.2 *Hierarchical page table*

The use of *hierarchical tables* eliminates the inefficiency of the flat tables, although it makes access to the data a little slower.

In a two-level hierarchical page table, the first level of the page table is a single table, known as the *directory*. The directory contains references to the second level tables, and these include the physical addresses of the pages. This scheme, shown in Figure 13.21, requires two memory accesses to be carried out to recover the physical address of the pages. In compensation, the second level tables only need to be present when the corresponding memory pages are being used.

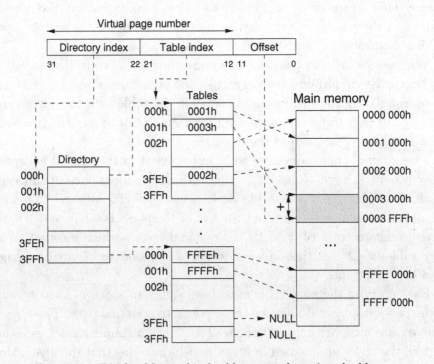

Fig. 13.21   Two level hierarchical table to translate virtual addresses.

Let us reconsider the previous example. In a flat table, the page table for any program will, as we have seen, occupy 2 Mbyte. In the case of a hierarchical table, the virtual address bits of the page will be divided into two groups of 10 bits each. The first ten most significant bits address the first level table, where the (physical) addresses of the second level tables are stored. The ten least significant bits of the virtual page number address the location within these secondary tables. Each of these tables will have 2^{10} entries, each of which with its page table entry which, as was seen above, will occupy at least two bytes for the physical page number.

To illustrate the advantage of hierarchical tables, let us consider a program which uses only 6 Mbyte, contiguous in virtual memory, from the address 00000000h. This program will only use $6 \times 2^{20}/2^{12} = 1{,}5 \times 2^{10}$ memory pages. The addresses of all these pages are found in the first two tables of the second level. It is only necessary, thus, to store the level 1 table (the directory) and two level 2 tables, occupying a total of $3 \times 2^{10} \times 2$ byte, that is, 6 Kbyte, instead of the 2 Mbyte necessary when using a flat page table.

The concept of hierarchical page tables may be generalised to hierarchical tables with more levels, which makes possible large-sized virtual addressing spaces. In this case, the directory operates as previously, while the last level continues to keep the physical addresses of the pages. The intermediate levels allow access to the following level tables. In general, three levels of tables are sufficient for all systems, independently of the size of the virtual and physical memory of the system, although there are architectures which already offer the use of four table levels for future implementations.

As a general rule, except for the directory, the page tables have the same size as a page. This scheme allows translation tables which are not active, to be stored on the disk such as data and code pages, and therefore reduce the fraction of memory occupied by translation tables.

There are also systems which use other forms of page table mapping, known as *inverted tables*. However, this technique has not been extensively used recently, and will not be studied in this text.

13.4.2 *Replacement Policy*

Just as with the design of caches, there are various options to take when designing a virtual memory system. Those options are related to the questions studied in the design of cache systems: *replacement policies*, protection mechanisms, and maintaining consistency between memory and disk for write operations.

The management of these mechanisms is usually the responsibility of the operating system. Whenever there is an access which does not find the desired page in main memory, that is, whenever there is a page fault, an operating system routine is called which copies that page from the disk to a given area of the main memory. This operation often implies copying the page previously located in that given area to disk.

Since copying a page between disk and memory is a lengthy process, it is worth using a much more sophisticated page replacement policy than that used for caches. The fact that this decision is a responsibility of the operating system, therefore performed by software, allows to maintain, for each memory page, detailed information about the most recent accesses, and decide which page should be substituted using a more elaborate algorithm. In particular, it is possible to use the *LRU* algorithm, which sends the least recently used page to disk, a method which cannot normally be used to manage cache block replacement.

The continued intensive use of an amount of virtual memory much greater than that available in main memory leads to a situation where it is necessary to continually send memory pages to disk and vice-versa, which is known as *thrashing*. In this situation, the computer continues to execute the intended program but spends most of the time (sometimes more than 99% of the time) managing the virtual memory system, leading to an apparent system block. This situation should be avoided.

13.4.3   *Write Policy*

Due also to the high disk access time, a virtual memory system with a write-through *write policy* is not typically achievable. Therefore, all writes are made to main memory, in an approach similar to the *write-back write-allocate* approach for caches. This policy implies the existence of a bit in the page table entries of the translation tables which indicates if this page has been altered in memory or not, also designated here as the *dirty bit*.

When substituting a given page, it is necessary to test this bit. If it is at 0, this means that the page remains unaltered since copied to the main memory. In this case, the copy on disk continues valid, meaning that we can write another page in the same location in memory. If, on the contrary, this bit is at 1, then, before writing a new page, it is necessary to copy the modified page to disk.

13.4.4 *Control Bits*

Besides the physical address of the page, the page table entries include a set of bits which indicate various properties of the page. Although the additional information stored varies from system to system, the following bits are typically always present:

- A bit which indicates if the physical address is valid. If it is not, this means that the page is on the disk and will have to be loaded into the main memory.
- A bit which indicates if there is any change in the page since it is in memory, which implies it should be copied to the disk when it is substituted.
- Protection bits, which indicate if the page is accessible for write, read and execution, in user mode.
- Protection bits, which indicate if the page is accessible for write, read and execution, in system mode.
- A bit which indicates that the page was recently accessed.

There may be other fields associated with each memory page which are used by the operating system for specific operations.

Note the parallelism which exists between the information stored in virtual memory pages and cache blocks. In both cases, a faster memory works as temporary storage for a larger but slower memory and, in both cases, it is necessary to store information to determine which data should be substituted or copied to the slower memory.

13.4.5 *Translation Lookaside Buffers*

If each access to memory went through a translation process involving accesses to various page table levels, the impact on system performance would be too large, making access to memory in a virtual memory system three or four times slower than in a system without virtual memory.

A small cache called a *Translation Lookaside Buffer, TLB* is used to overcome this difficulty, supplying the processor with the physical address corresponding to a given virtual page. Given that each page corresponds to a large number of memory locations, even a small cache will have a very high hit rate, since the number of different pages used in a given program section is usually small, due to the principle of locality.

The existence of this cache allows to avoid, in most of the translations, the access to the page tables that are necessarily slower.

13.4.6   *Interconnection of Virtual Memory with the Caches*

In general, the virtual memory system coexists with the caches, and the loading of data from a given address effectively triggers two processes: the search for this data in one of the caches and the translation of the virtual addresses to physical addresses.

There are essentially two possible ways of interconnecting the cache system with the virtual memory system. The first alternative addresses the caches with virtual addresses while the second option uses physical addresses.

In the first case, the addresses sent to the caches are the addresses issued by the processor, before any translation process. This alternative has the advantage of making data access faster since it is not necessary any translation before addressing the caches. Since the caches contain the data which corresponds to a given virtual address, their contents have to be invalidated whenever there is an alteration in virtual memory mapping, for example, when the process which is being executed changes.

In the second case, the virtual address is, firstly, translated to a physical address, which is used to address the caches. Access to the caches is slower than in the previous case but, in compensation, there is a more direct mapping between the data found in the cache and the data found in memory. If the memory pages are aligned in page-sized multiple addresses, the bits corresponding to the offset within the page do not change in the translation process. The sums necessary in the translation schemes are, therefore, implemented as concatenations of the bits returned by the TLB and the offset bits. Figure 13.22 shows the interconnection between the TLB and a physically addressed cache, in a situation where the pages are aligned in the memory.

Since the first access phase to a cache which is not fully associative uses only the index bits to choose the block where the data is, access to the cache can start before the table index has been translated by the TLB. This just requires that the number of index bits and offset bits used by the cache are not greater than the number of bits necessary to specify the offset within each virtual memory page. Figure 13.23 shows, in a very simplified way, the scheme of the complete memory system of a 32-bit processor, with virtual memory, TLB and a physically addressed cache.

In this example, the processor has a virtual addressing space of 4 Gbyte (2^{32} byte) with 4 Kbyte pages. The page address is sent to a direct mapping

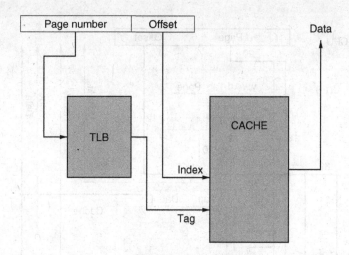

Fig. 13.22   Interconnection between the TLB and the cache.

TLB with 16 inputs, which sends the physical address of the page to a 4 Kbyte cache. This address is separated into four components: 20 bits ($A_{31} - A_{12}$) for the tag, 8 bits ($A_{11} - A_4$) for the index and 2 bits ($A_3 - A_2$) for the offset within the block. The two least significant bits (A_1 and A_0) are only used to select the byte within the word, which was not considered in this schematic. As the number of bits necessary to specify the offset within each page is 12, and the pages are aligned in memory, the selection of the cache block can be initiated (using address lines A_{11} to A_4) even before the TLB translates the address of the virtual page to a physical page. If the data is present in the cache, it is sent directly to the processor. If not, the main memory controller verifies that the *HIT* line has not been activated, and triggers an access to the 64 Mbyte main memory. This access is made by activating the control lines of the dynamic memories and the respective address lines and columns. The main memory in this example is made out of *DIMM, Dual In-line Memory Modules.*

This very simplified schematic does not show the circuits used for the write operations in the data cache and in the TLB, nor the various control signals necessary to control the dynamic memories. The reader may, however, note that the complexity of the memory system rivals that of the processor itself. In real systems, the complexity is even greater when there are various levels of caches, different caches for addresses and data, complex architectures for main memory and interconnection of the data buses with input/output devices.

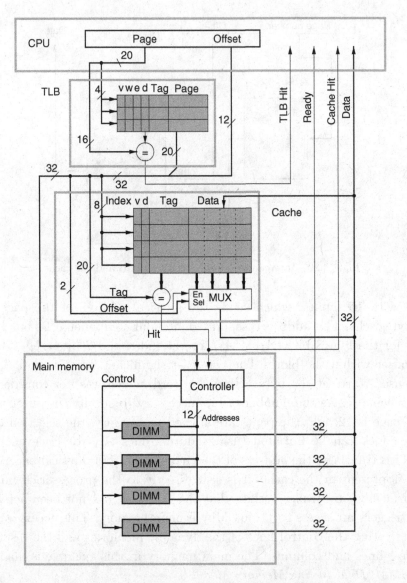

Fig. 13.23   Memory system of a 32-bit processor.

13.5   Summary

This chapter studies the various components of the memory system of a typical processor.

It describes the way the the main memory is made up of simple modules which are interconnected to enable the construction of the desired memory structure. Each of these modules corresponds to a given part of the memory visible to the processor. The logic organisation of the modules can be described by the memory map of the processor.

It also describes the way that memories of various speeds and capacities are interconnected within a memory hierarchy, with the fastest memories, of a lower capacity, being accessed first, so as to reduce the average memory access time.

Finally, this chapter describes virtual memory systems, which enable the use of secondary storage to extend the usable addressing space beyond that which is possible by using only the main physical memory installed.

Exercises

13.1 Consider that you have 16 Kbyte memory modules available, identical to those used in Figure 13.4. Design a 64 Kbyte memory system organised into 32 Kword of 16 bits each.

13.2 Sometimes, it is possible to save on decoding circuits when the memory map is relatively sparse, that is when using only a small part of the memory space. For the memory map in the previous problem, simplify the decoding circuits by using only the bits that are strictly necessary.

13.3 Using 64 Kbyte RAM memories and 16 Kbyte ROM memories, design the memory circuits which correspond to the following memory map:

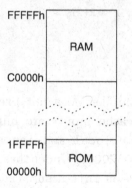

13.4 Consider that a 300 MHz processor uses a memory with a read access time of 12 ns. Sketch the waveforms for this system in a similar manner to those in Figure 13.11.

13.5 Consider a processor with an addressing space of 64 Kword which uses a direct mapping cache which interprets the address bits according to the following scheme:

15	14	13	12	11	10	9	8	7	6	5	4	3	2	1	0
Tag								Index						Block	

(a) What is the data capacity of this cache?

(b) Keeping the capacity of the cache, but making it with degree of associativity two, what are the alterations in how the address is interpreted?

13.6 Consider a CPU with an internal cache, with a degree of associativity two, with a size of 16 Kbyte and with 32-byte blocks. The cache uses write-back and write-allocate strategies. Assume as well that the cache is used in a system with an addressing space of 2^{32} byte, where each byte is individually addressable.

Analyse the performance of this cache when executing the following code segment programmed in C:

```
static int local[1024];

int init_n_sum (char inp[])
{
  register int k, sum=0;
  for (k = 0; k < 1024; k = k+2)
    local[k] = inp[k];

  for (k = 0; k < 512; k = k+2)
    sum += local[k];

  return sum;
}
```

Assume that the compiler does not execute any optimisations to the code, that the cache inputs are initially invalid and that the base addresses of the local and inp addresses are, respectively, 0x00100000 and 0x000E0000. Under these conditions, and during the execution of the function init_n_sum, calculate:

(a) the number of bytes transferred from the main memory to the CPU/cache block;

(b) the number of bytes transferred from the CPU/cache block to the main memory.

13.7 Repeat the previous problem, but now for a cache which uses write-through and no-write-allocate strategies.

13.8 Consider a 512-byte cache with a degree of associativity two and 32-byte blocks. This cache forms part of a system which can address 2^{32} byte, and each byte can be individually addressed.

(a) Describe which address bits are used to address the cache block and which bits are used to address within the block.

(b) Determine the size of the tags stored in the cache.

13.9 Using *comparators*, *decoders*, *registers*, *multiplexers* and *tri-state buffers* as basic blocks, make a sketch of the cache circuits for the previous problem which are involved in read operations. In this description, consider that the registers have a single control input, EN, and they have outputs at high impedance when they are not selected. Indicate the width, in bits, of each line of data or addresses used, but ignore any circuits necessary for writing data to the cache. The figure below shows examples of blocks that can be used.

13.10 Consider the virtual memory system of a 32-bit processor in which the maximum physical memory available is 64 Mbyte, byte-to-byte addressable. In this system, each page has a size of 2 Kbyte, and each entry in the page tables takes up four bytes. What is the size of the virtual addressing space in this system and what is the size of a flat page table which supports this translation process?

13.11 Suppose that the system in the previous question uses a 2-level hierarchical table, in which each table occupies exactly one page. Briefly, describe the steps and data structures involved in the process of translating virtual addresses to physical addresses. Explain which address bits are used during each translation step.

13.12 Consider a system which uses the following scheme for memory addressing, with words of one byte:

Virtual address:

Virtual page	Offset

31   12 11   0

Physical address:

Physical page	Offset

29   12 11   0

(a) Indicate and justify what the size of the virtual addressing space and the physical addressing space is.

(b) Indicate and justify what the size of each page is.

(c) Suppose that the system uses a TLB with an access time of one clock cycle with a 98% hit-rate. Knowing that one access to main memory takes on average two clock cycles, determine the average number of clock cycles spent for each data access executed by the processor.

Chapter 14

Inputs, Outputs and Communications

The previous chapters defined two of the main components of the computer, the central processing unit and the memory system. Although all the processing is carried out between these two units, this would be of reduced usefulness if there was not some way of interacting with the external world which would firstly allow the introduction of the data to be processed and, secondly, make results accessible.

In early computers, this interface was rudimentary. Inputs were specified by switches which defined their value bit by bit, and the result was visualised in lamps which also indicated their value at the bit level. Since then there has been considerable evolution not only in human-machine interfaces but also in interfaces between different machines. The development of new forms of interaction with computers and other digital devices is a subject of increasingly intense research.

The term *peripheral* is frequently used generically to designate the input and output devices of a computer. With the advance of technology, the complexity of peripherals has systematically increased to the point where it is sometimes difficult to make a clear distinction between peripherals and processing units. The current concept of peripheral, ranges from relatively simple units, such as a keyboard or a mouse, up to very complex units, which themselves provide significant computational power, such as monitors, hard disks or touch screen interfaces. The interaction mechanisms for each peripheral are very diverse and are responsible for a significant part of the complexity of current operating systems. Some peripherals, such as hard disks, have very tight response time requirements since they send data at very high speeds to the central processing unit. Others, such as a keyboard, have much less demanding requirements, and the processor can execute many millions of operations between each interaction with the device. Note that disks may be considered part of the memory system but, considering the way they interact physically with the processors, they are also considered peripherals.

At the introductory level which is the goal of this text, we assume a simplified form of interaction, in which access to the different peripherals has the same access protocol as the access to a memory location (Section 6.8).

Since the protocol is the same, it does not matter to the processor whether it is accessing a memory location or a peripheral, and this makes it possible to map the different peripherals into the memory space of the processor (Section 14.1). This simplification implies the presence of an interface circuit in each peripheral which converts information coming from the device to the protocol used for memory access.

This simplified form of interaction is representative of real situations, although there are various additional complications which are only possible to deal with in a more advanced study of specific architectures.

This chapter starts by discussing aspects of the input/output architecture in Section 14.1. The operation of some of the most well known simple peripherals is described in Section 14.2. It will then present in Sections 14.3 and 14.4 the different forms of communication between the computer and these devices. The interruption system is discussed in Section 14.5. Finally, in Section 14.6 it will consider different ways to transfer information with peripherals at different transmission rates.

14.1 Input/Output Architecture

The central processing units typically operate at frequencies in the order of GHz, executing many hundreds of millions of instructions per second. In contrast, different peripherals operate at very different speeds but typically at lower speeds, with access times ranging from hundreds of milliseconds to microseconds, in the case of more demanding peripherals.

It is, therefore, necessary to adapt the system operation to these very different processing speeds. Several techniques have been developed which enable the various devices to communicate with each other, without uselessly wasting processor cycles, or having devices waiting for each other.

The organisation of the *input/output* system of a computer is an aspect of central importance in defining its architecture. As was mentioned above, the design of computers around a system of buses enable the processor to exchange information with the memory and all the system peripherals. Figure 14.1 shows this overall architecture.

The processor uses the *address bus* to specify the memory location or peripheral with which it wants to interact. In many cases (but not all), this is a unidirectional bus, always controlled by the processor. We will come back to this aspect later.

The *data bus* allows the transfer of data between the processor and the memory or the peripherals. This is a bidirectional bus, where the processor may be the origin of the data when we want to write data to memory or

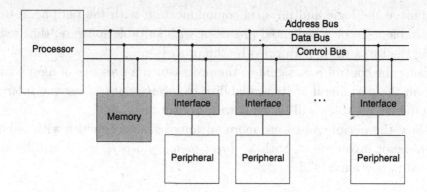

Fig. 14.1   General representation of the architecture of a computer.

transfer it to output peripherals, or the destination for data originating in the memory or input peripherals.

The *control bus* includes all the lines which manage and coordinate transfers. This bus has lines which can indicate the direction of the transfer, synchronise the transfer, specify the size of the data to be transferred, determine if the data transfer involves memory or peripherals, signal any attention requests from the peripherals and other control functions. The choice of the lines actually used is determined by the overall architecture options for the system.

14.1.1   *Interfaces*

Most peripherals connect to the processor through a module which can take different levels of complexity, known as the *interface*. The interface exists to isolate the processor from the particularities of the peripheral. Among the functions required for the interface, at this stage the following may be mentioned:

- Implement the necessary adaptations from a physical point of view, particularly regarding the voltages and currents involved in the communication between the processor and the peripherals, as well as the physical connectors necessary.
- Hide the speeds of the peripherals from the processor. Those are typically lower than that of the processor.
- Decode the addresses present on the address bus to identify a data transfer involving the peripheral to which it is connected.
- Control the peripheral when there can be various operating modes.

- Manage the logic and physical communication with the peripheral using suitable logic or a dedicated processor with suitable software, thus reducing the tasks to be performed by the processor.
- Using the control bus, signal to the processor the presence of data coming from the peripheral or its availability to receive data, using the *interrupt system*. This topic will be dealt with in Section 14.6.2.
- Allow the peripheral to use more advanced transfer modes with reduced processor involvement, such as *direct memory access*, which will be analysed in Section 14.6.3.

Figure 14.2 shows the conceptual structure of an interface.

In the case of unidirectional peripherals, such as a printer, or a mouse, the interface has a register where the processor writes the data to be sent to the peripheral or where it reads the data coming from the peripheral. As is evident, in bidirectional peripherals, such as a modem, there should be two registers, one where the processor writes the data to send to the peripheral and the other where the processor reads the data received. These registers, the simplest input/output unit addressable by the processor, are called *ports*.

The fact that the data is written to the ports and read from them, instead of on the peripheral itself, allows the operation to be carried out at the speed used by the processor. If in fact, reading or writing was performed by directly involving the peripheral, the processor would have to carry out its read or write cycle with the timing allowed by the peripheral,

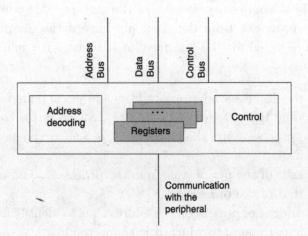

Fig. 14.2   General representation of the architecture of an interface.

typically a few orders of magnitude below the possible rate of transfer in internal buses.

As well as *data ports*, that is, the ports for transferring data, many interfaces have some other ports. In some of these ports, the processor can write control information to configure certain aspects of the operation of the interface, the peripheral or the communication with it. In other ports, the processor can read information about the status of the peripheral, its connection or the actual interface. These are, respectively, *control ports* and *status ports*.

Each of these ports has, of course, specific addresses. Conceptually, the address decoding module is responsible for identifying the presence on the address bus of an address corresponding to each of the registers in the interface so that the port selected is written to or read according to the action specified in the control bus. In practice, interfaces only decode the least significant bits of the address bus needed to address the various internal ports of the interface, whether these are data, control or status ports. These ports normally have successive addresses. As is the case with decoding memory addresses, part of the decoding is carried out externally to the interfaces and is common to all of them.

The control module for the interface coordinates its various actions, with emphasis on peripheral communication management and, where this is important, in transfers implying the interrupt system (Section 14.6.2) or direct memory access (Section 14.6.3).

14.1.2 *Port Addressing Types*

As mentioned previously, addressing is a function divided between an addressing decoding block external to the interfaces, often shared with the memory decoding, and some decoding internal to the interface. Figure 14.3 shows this type of structure.

Note that the decoding is mainly carried out by a decoding circuit external to the interface, which activates an enable line of the decoder inside the interface. In this way, it is possible for the interface only to be active for a given range of addresses. Internally, to address each of the n ports, there is a second decoding circuit which decodes i address bits, where $n = 2^i$. These bits commonly correspond to the least significant bits of the address bus. Figure 14.3 shows an interface with n ports, showing port 0 and port $n - 1$, with the first being an output port, and the second, an input port.

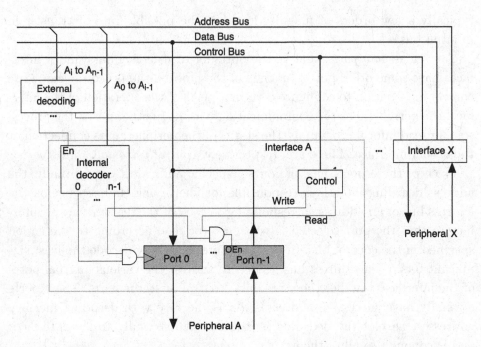

Fig. 14.3   Decoding addresses to access the ports of an interface.

There are three basic choices about the way to organise the addressing for the peripheral interface ports:

- to use separate buses for input/output and memory access;
- to use the same bus and the same addressing space for input/output and the memory access;
- to use the same bus, but different addressing spaces for input/output and the memory access.

The first option consists in using separate buses for input/output and the memory, therefore avoiding any conflict between these two types of operations. Until now we have assumed that the peripheral interfaces share the address, data and control buses with the memory. This option is not strictly necessary. In fact, it would even be conceptually interesting to consider a second set of buses for the input/output interfaces physically separate from the memory buses. This option would make possible to increase the performance of the computer, since, at the same time as communication with a peripheral takes place, it would be possible to maintain memory accesses, both to transfer data, as well as to read instructions. However, for this option to be useful, it would require a new conception of the processor, which would have a parallel processing capacity which would greatly complicate its architecture. That is not a solution frequently used. Another option, however, the use of a processor dedicated only to input/output transfers allows the same concept to be carried out in a more practical way, increasing the overall performance. This type of architecture will be referred to in a little more detail in Section 14.6.4.

The other two options only use one set of buses, differing in the way this set of buses is used.

The second option views the input/output addresses and the memory locations in a unified manner. Many architectures, as is also the case with the P3, assume the existence of a single addressing space which, just as with the buses, is shared by memory and peripherals. In this type of architecture, there will be addresses attributed to memory locations and other addresses assigned to ports. As was mentioned in Section 10.3.3, this involves an architecture with *memory mapped* ports. In architectures of this type, port addressing is carried out by placing the respective address on the address bus and enabling a line on the control bus which indicates the direction of the transfer. This line is usually a read/write line $RD/\overline{WR}$, which is at 1, when the goal is to read a port, and at 0, when the goal is to carry out a write.

Regarding the instruction set for this type of processor, there is no need for specific *input/output instructions*, since all transfers are similar to those involving memory locations. Therefore, the whole instruction set which enables access to memory is used for input/output.

This architecture has the disadvantage of requiring a set of addresses for input and output ports to be reserved in the memory addressing space. Besides the subsequent reduction in the size of available memory, this sometimes requires less elegant solutions, to prevent some addresses attributed to ports to provoke unwanted access to memory locations simultaneously.

The third option consists of using separate addressing spaces for the memory and the input/output ports, while still sharing the same buses. This option requires the control bus to supply information indicating if each address is a memory or a port address. The obvious solution is a line which distinguishes the two types of access. A line of this type can take the value 1 when memory access is involved and the value 0 when access to ports is involved. A proper designation is $MEM/\overline{IO}$, for example. An alternative solution is the use of separate read and write lines for memory and input/output ports. So there could be lines with designations such as *MEMREAD*, *IOREAD*, *MEMWRITE* and *IOWRITE*. This type of architecture is referred to as *independent input/output*, or separate input/output. In this type of architecture, the instruction set has to include explicit *input/output instructions*. Those instructions, when executed, lead to the enabling of the appropriate lines or the adequate level of the $MEM/\overline{IO}$ line so that the transfer involves ports and not memory. Typically, those instructions are more limited in their operation than memory access instructions and are sometimes limited to one data input and one data output instruction.

14.2 Peripherals

The following sections describe the basic operation of some of the most important peripherals for general-purpose computers, such as personal computers or portable computers. Note that, despite the importance, these have on the computers that most people deal with on a daily basis, there are many other systems which do not even have these peripherals. This is the case with the embedded systems present in many electrical appliances or portable devices. In these, data input and output uses specific peripherals integrated into the system they control.

14.2.1 *Keyboards*

The *keyboard* is the most widely used data input peripheral in computers for general use, such that it is normal for some computers not to start if they do not detect a keyboard connected. Figure 14.4 shows the internal design of a keyboard.

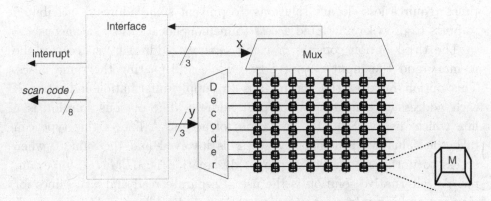

Fig. 14.4 Internal design of a keyboard.

A matrix of rows and columns of electrical interconnections forms the core of a keyboard. At each cross between a row and a column, a switch is placed corresponding to a key. Pressing that key closes a circuit between the row and the column involved.

Detecting the pressed keys is carried out by scanning the rows and the columns. To perform the reading of this matrix by scanning, the interface circuit of the keyboard includes a controller which contains two counters. As the figure shows, one of the counters, y, carries out the scanning of the rows, setting one, and only one, to the logic value 1. For each count of the counter y, the second counter, x, scans the columns, reading their value. Detecting a column set at 1 means that the key in position (x, y) of the matrix is pressed. From these coordinates, the control uniquely identifies the key.

The keyboard controller has some other functions. One of them is to take care of a particular problem associated with mechanical switches. When closing a switch, before the value on the line becomes stable at the new electrical level, there is a signal oscillation caused by mechanical vibrations of the contacts, which may wrongly be interpreted as the key being repeatedly pressed and released. The controller filters out these instabilities, waiting a reasonable time following a change in the state of the key to validate its final status. This operation is called *debounce*.

Only the changes to the status of the keys are sent to the CPU to reduce the amount of information transmitted. For example, when pressing the key «M», the code M_pressed is sent to the processor. When the key is released, the code M_released is sent. These codes are designated *make code* and *break code*, respectively. This operation also applies to *silent keys*, such as the keys *shift* and *control*. The controller has to keep the current state of all keys in a local memory to detect a change of state in the key. This architecture makes possible to press two or more keys, transmitting to the CPU the order in which they have been pressed (and released).

The codes referred have the designation of *scan codes*. Linked to the keyboard (as with any other peripheral) there is a program called the *device driver*, responsible for supplying an interface for the peripheral at the software level. For the keyboard, the device driver converts the (x, y) coordinates to a given *scan code*. It is this operation which enables a keyboard with a fixed layout of keys to have different arrangements of symbols and, therefore, efficiently adapt to different languages or even alphabets. For example, the symbol «ç» on the Portuguese keyboard is the same key as the symbol «:»

on the UK keyboard. The device driver can link that key to the corresponding scan code for the language correspondent to the configuration of the system.

Another aspect of *scan codes* is that they do not indicate whether the letter pressed by the user is uppercase or lowercase. The device driver will have to check if the `make code` of a character occurs between a `pressed_shift` and a `released_shift`. If so, then the letter is uppercase; otherwise it is lowercase. Converting `scan codes` to ASCII or any other code is usually the responsibility of the application.

Whenever there is a change in the status of a key, the keyboard controller sends an interrupt to the CPU, indicating that it has data to send. Sometimes the CPU is busy with other activities and cannot give immediate attention. To avoid the loss of data, the keyboard controller has a *buffer* capable of storing a sequence of keyboard events. This solution does not completely solve the problem since this buffer normally has a reduced capacity. When the CPU takes a little longer to read the keyboard data, the buffer can fill, and then the controller must discard all subsequent events. It is common for the keyboard controller to issue a *beep* to warn the user that these keys are being ignored.

14.2.2   *Monitors*

With a relevance similar to that of the keyboard, the *monitor* is usually the principal data output peripheral. The interface between the monitor and the CPU is carried out through a *graphics card*. Figure 14.5 shows a simplified diagram of the internal organisation of the graphics card and its connection to a monitor.

Most graphics cards have two operating modes programmable by the CPU, *text mode* and *graphics mode*. As far as the CPU is concerned, the monitor is a matrix of rows and columns for both operating modes. For

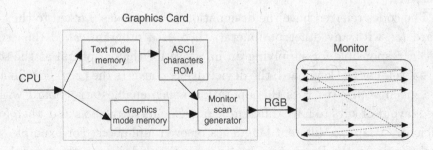

Fig. 14.5   Internal diagram of a graphics card and its connection to a monitor.

text mode, the components of this matrix are ASCII characters. In graphics mode, the elements are points on the screen, the smaller elements handled by the graphics card. Each of these points is called a *pixel*.

The first monitors only operated in text mode and were called *alphanumeric monitors*. Nowadays, text mode exists not only to maintain compatibility with older models and software, but also to serve as the simplest common denominator that any system can recognise, thus avoiding potential incompatibility problems between different graphical interfaces. In text mode, to place a character on the screen, it is sufficient to send its ASCII code to the graphics card. The *cursor* position, a reference (line, column) kept by the graphics card, determines the place where this character will appear on the screen. In typical operation, there is an increment in the value of the column of the cursor for each written character, building in this way, the sequence of characters in the line. When the value of the column exceeds the maximum number of columns, then the value for the line of the cursor is incremented, and the value of the column is set to zero so that the next character appears at the beginning of the following line. When exceeding the maximum number of lines of the screen, the whole text on the monitor scrolls up a line, the line at the top of the screen disappears, and a new line appears at the bottom. ASCII code includes some commands to control the cursor for alphanumeric monitors since these were the ones available when this code was defined. For example:

- «BS» (backspace) Makes the cursor go back one position, that is, decrease the column value.
- «LF» (linefeed) Moves the cursor to the next line, that is, increments the line value. The column maintains its value.
- «CR» (carriage return) Places the cursor at the start of the line, that is, sets the column value to zero. The line maintains its value.

To make use of modern graphics monitors possible, graphics cards, when in text mode, use a ROM to obtain the description of the characters in pixels. In graphics mode, the CPU defines point by point, that is, pixel by pixel, what should appear on the screen. The *graphics resolution* for the monitor is the total number of pixels on the screen, equal to the product of the number of lines and the number of columns. In old black-and-white (or monochrome) monitors, one bit per position (line, column) is enough to indicate if the respective pixel is on (white) or off (black). For colour monitors, it is necessary to specify for each pixel which colour it should take. Therefore, for each position (line, column) a value is specified to indicate an entry within a *colourmap*. The number of bits necessary for each pixel, therefore, depends on the size of this colourmap. For example, if the colourmap has 256 entries, each pixel needs 8 bits to specify it. The size of the colourmap determines the maximum number of different colours possible. However, each application can define the entries in the colourmap, so that different applications can use different colourmaps.

The graphics card keeps the state of each pixel within an internal memory. The capacity of this memory determines the maximum resolution of the graphics card. For example for the resolution of 1280×1024 (1280 columns by 1024 lines) with a palette of 256 colours (8 bits), it is necessary that the graphics card has a memory capacity of at least $1280 \times 1024 \times 8$ bits, that is, 1.25 Mbyte. To have a greater quantity of colours with this memory, it will be necessary to reduce the resolution. Supposing we want to increase the size of the colourmap to 64k colours (16 bits), it is not possible to use for example the resolution of 1024×768, since that would require $1024 \times 768 \times 16$ bits, that is, 1.5 Mbyte. It would, therefore, be necessary to opt for a lower resolution as, for example, 800×600, which corresponds to a memory of $800 \times 600 \times 16$ bits, that is, 0.9 Mbyte. Currently, the resolution of a typical monitor can be as high as 3840×2160 pixels with about 16 Million colours, which means that each pixel is coded by 24 bits. The memory necessary for this resolution is in the order of 23 Mbyte. But there are monitors considerably more powerful.

The CPU defines the colour for each pixel and writes this in the corresponding graphics memory location. To make the programmer's task easier, there are graphics libraries which supply high-level routines to define complex objects for the monitor. These routines are system specific.

The connection between the graphics card and monitor depends on the type of monitor. Nowadays monitors use flat screens using thin film transistors liquid crystal displays (TFT-LCD), plasma, organic light-emitting diodes (OLED) or some more exotic technologies. Cathode Ray Tube (CRT) displays are almost not used anymore. Nowadays almost only colour monitors are used. In these monitors, each pixel is composed of three monochrome pixels corresponding to the three basic colours, red, green and blue. The electronics associated with the screen technology controls the luminosity of each one of the pixels, and so, it is possible to define a different value for each of the three basic colours for each pixel. In this way, it is possible in principle to specify any colour of a broad palette.

The graphics card sequentially reads the internal memory locations and sends the values of the red, green and blue components for each pixel to write on the screen. These signals have the name RGB, after the three basic colours Red, Green and Blue respectively. In general, the intensity of each of these basic colours is defined by a byte. For this reason, the use of a colourmap with 2^{24} entries is called *true colour*, since it uniquely identifies every possible colour for the monitor.

So that users do not notice the scanning, the screen should be fully written at least 24 times a second.[1] If not, the user has the sensation that the monitor is flickering. This requirement implies a higher bandwidth between the graphics card and the monitor since it is necessary to send three bytes to each pixel 24 times a second. For example, for a 1280×1024 resolution, 90 Mbyte/s are transferred. Current monitors use a much higher data rate to achieve a smoother evolution of the image on the screen.

14.2.3 *Magnetic Disks and Solid-state Drives*

Finally, this section will analyse the operation of the *hard disk drive* (*HDD*), a data input and output peripheral. This peripheral is also ubiquitous in general-purpose computers. Its primary use is for permanently storing data, since the values in the registers of the processor, in the cache or main memory are lost when the power supply is disconnected. In addition to this function, disks were already studied, in Chapter 13, as the highest level element in the memory hierarchy. These two functions are both controlled by the operating system. The first is under control of the *file system*, and the second of the memory system. Therefore, the storage space of the disks is normally divided into at least two *partitions*, one for the file system, and another for the memory system or swap space. There may be more partitions since operating systems support more than one partition for each of these functions. Nowadays HDD are being substituted by *solid-state drives* (*SSD*) with the same general functionality but much higher speed.

Figure 14.6 shows a diagram of the internal organisation of a hard disk. A hard disk is in fact made up of a concentric stack of magnetic disks. These disks are permanently rotating at a constant high speed. Each of these disks is organised into *tracks*, as shown in the figure. The tracks also have the name *cylinders*, meaning, in fact, the set of tracks with the same radius for all the

---

[1]Currently the refresh rate of monitors is usually 60 frames/s.

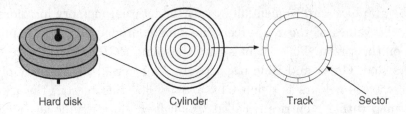

Hard disk　　　Cylinder　　　Track　　Sector

Fig. 14.6　Diagram of the internal organisation of a hard disk.

disks. Each of these disks has a magnetic head which can move radially and therefore position itself at any of the tracks on that disk. Each track, in turn, is divided into *sectors*, which are the minimum information elements on the disk. The SSD does not have any moving parts and is constituted by memory integrated circuits using a technology called *flash memory* which behaves like traditional memory but is non-volatile, meaning that the content is not lost when power is disconnected. It is also slower than static or dynamic RAM, but that is not relevant when used as a substitute for the HDD. Still, SSD devices are much faster than magnetic hard disk drives.

When the operating system accesses the disk, for reading or writing, it does so in sets of one, or more, sectors. Each sector has a unique reference, which is used by the operating system. Magnetic disk drives include an internal controller to provide an interface between the CPU and the mechanical part of the disk. From the reference specified by the CPU, the disk controller determines which of the cylinders contains the intended sector, and on which tracks of this cylinder this sector is located. The controller moves the head of this cylinder so as to place it over this track and waits until the sector in question passes below the magnetic head, at which point it is read or written.

There are therefore three components involved in a disk sector access time:

- The *seek time*, which is the time the magnetic head takes to reach the track where the sector is. Although the distances are short and the magnetic heads are very light, and therefore take very little time to move to the right track, the seek time is nevertheless an important component in the total time involved in disk access. A typical maximum value for this time for present-day disks is 8 ms, corresponding to the largest head trajectory. Of course, this figure on average will be lower and close to half of this.

- The *rotational latency* of the hard disk, which is the time it takes from the moment the magnetic head is in position until the intended sector passes below it. A typical value nowadays for the rotational speed of a hard disk is 10,000 rotations per minute. Thus, a full rotation of the cylinder takes 6 ms. As it has to wait for half a turn on average, so that the right sector passes below the head, the average rotational latency will be 3 ms.
- The *access time*, which is the time it takes to read or write a sector. To estimate the access time, it is necessary to know the number of sectors per track. For a typical value of 64 sectors per track, and assuming the same 10,000 rotations per minute, the read/write access time will be 6 ms/64 = 0.09 ms.

According to the values shown, we can conclude that the average access time for a disk sector is close to 7.1 ms. Two observations are pertinent regarding this value. First, when compared with the main memory access time, which is currently less than 100 ns, the access to the disk is around 100,000 times slower! Therefore, disk accesses severely degrade system performance and should be minimised.

The second observation is that the access time is negligible, given the seek and rotational times. For this reason, it would be desirable to increase sector size. There is, however, a compromise here because although there is a gain in efficiency, there could be a significant waste of space if the sectors were very long since when it is desired to store small quantities of information, the rest of the sector would be wasted. Typical values for sector length are currently between 512 byte and 4 Kbyte.

One way to increase disk access efficiency is to keep the data logically structured into continuous sectors wherever possible. To do this, many operating systems enable disk *defragmentation*, which is nothing more than placing the files in consecutively placed sectors. In this way, the seek and rotational time for access to all sectors of a file only occurs once.

The access time to SSDs is much shorter and is not dependent on localisation inside the device, and so it is more uniform than in HDDs. Access times to information stored in SSDs ranges currently from 25 μs to 100 μs compared with values in the order of 5000 μs to 10,000 μs in magnetic disk drives. This fact is changing the way to organise the memory system, and new operating systems begin taking advantage of this.

Note that data access is not directly carried out by the CPU since this would require a very high bandwidth. For example, if the size of the sector is

1 Kbyte, then reading it generates 1 Kbyte/0.09 ms = 11 Mbyte/s. Therefore, the disk controller has a buffer used to copy the sectors and only after this will they be read by the CPU, at an adequate transfer rate. The process is similar in the case of write operations. The sector coming from the processor is first transferred to this buffer and only when this process is complete, is it copied to the disk.

14.3   Parallel Communication

As we saw, communication between the processor and the peripheral interfaces is carried out through the computer buses. It is a case of parallel communication, involving several bits simultaneously, typically a computer word or, in some architectures or interfaces, a byte.

There is also communication between the interface and the peripheral, and this communication can use a parallel or a serial mode. In Section 14.4, we will study *serial communication*. This section analyses *parallel communication*.

The width of the processor word is frequently different from the width of the information communicated between the interface and the peripheral. In many cases, for example, the interface bus connecting the interface and the peripheral assumes the transfer of a byte, and the internal bus may have 16 bits, as is the case with the P3, or up to 64 bits, as happens in many commercially available microprocessors. This circumstance does not create any problems. For output peripherals, the interface just ignores the bits that cannot be transmitted, and the program has to take into account that the information should be formatted accordingly. For input peripherals, the interface does not activate the lines with no data. The bus treats the non-enabled lines using a default value. In the same way, the program has to take into account that the valid input information occupies a subset of the bits of the input word.

The complexity of the communication between the interface and the peripheral depends on the actual complexity of the peripheral and the level of functionality requested from the interface. A particular aspect to bear in mind is the grade of *synchronisation* necessary between the interface and the peripheral. At this level, synchronisation allows for the coordination of the information transfer, thus ensuring that the entity receiving information also receives a signal, which indicates that the entity sending the information has made it available on the interconnection bus. It may be further necessary to ensure that the entity which started the communication, sending information, receives an explicit confirmation of the reception.

In very simple peripherals, no synchronisation is necessary between the interface and the peripheral. Other types of output peripherals need to receive some signal to indicate that the interface has data to send. Also, for input peripherals, the interface has to accept signalling from the peripheral indicating that it is sending data to the interface. In more complex peripherals, it is necessary to fully synchronise communication between the interface and the peripheral, so as to ensure that the communication takes place correctly.

Furthermore, communication between the processor and the interface may also require some level of synchronisation.

The examples presented below will provide an overview of interfaces with different complexities. This study is not intended to be exhaustive, but rather to illustrate certain types of problems and standard solutions available for these problems.

14.3.1 *Interfaces without Synchronisation*

The first example refers to an elementary type of peripheral with no need for synchronisation. It involves an input peripheral made up of a set of switches and an output peripheral constituted by a set of light-emitting diodes (LEDs). Both the switches and the LEDs provide for basic communication between the user of the system and the processor.

Data input is carried out through a data input instruction directed at the port connected to the switches. The program may, for example, be executing a cycle which includes that instruction, and in each cycle, it has to take into account the status of each or some of the switches.

In this case, there is no need for any synchronisation, and not even for an input register. A set of tri-state buffers which implement the electrical interface between the switches and the computer bus plays the role of the input port. Figure 14.7 shows the structure of an interface of this type. Note that this simple interface does not take care of debouncing the switches (see Section 14.2.1).

In this interface, given its simplicity, there is no need for any internal address decoding, since there is only one port. When a read of the port is executed, the values assumed by the switches are directly introduced into the data bus through the tri-state buffers.

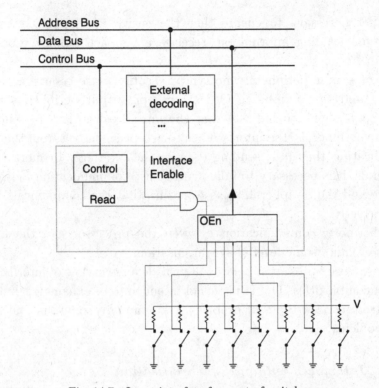

Fig. 14.7   Input interface for a set of switches.

Although it is conceptually possible to design interfaces with output ports without registers, this is not normally a useful option. The output port would take the value sent to it only during one processor write cycle, which is normally not enough.

Figure 14.8 shows an output interface which enables the processor to write a byte to a register. The information stored in the register is displayed in a group of LEDs, each bit controlling one of the LEDs. Once again, the simplicity of the interface dispenses the need for internal address decoding.

14.3.2   *Data Strobing and Handshaking*

14.3.2.1   *Strobe synchronisation*

Let us now consider an interface connected to a *digital-to-analogue* (*D/A*) *converter* and an *analogue-to-digital* (*A/D*) *converter*. A device of the first type allows you to convert a sequence of words with binary values into an analogue signal. An obvious application is generating audio in a computer. It is an output device. In turn, an analogue-to-digital converter converts an

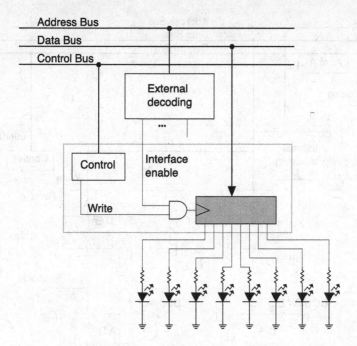

Fig. 14.8   Output interface for a set of LEDs.

analogue signal, which is variable over time, into a set of numeric values which represent it. An obvious application is the interface to a microphone, an input device.

In both cases it is necessary to transfer binary numerical values at a regular pace in both directions of communication between the processor and the peripheral, through the interface. The processor may take care of the regular generation of the data to transfer to the peripheral, with the help of an interrupt system and a timer, as we will see below. In the case of input data the periodic generation of data can be attributed to the peripheral itself. Figure 14.9 shows one possible interface and its connection to the two converters. In this example, the generation of periodic signals for the analogue-to-digital converter is carried out locally by the peripheral.

This interface has a D latch which generates a pulse, usually called *strobe* in this context, whenever the processor writes a word in the interface register. This strobe is timed by the clock on the control bus and is controlled by the write line in the register. In this way, whenever there is a write (in the internal address 0, corresponding to the output register), the D/A converter is warned, through the $DOUTVAL$ line, which signals that there is new data for the converter.

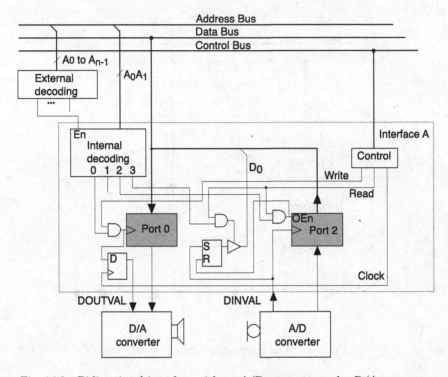

Fig. 14.9   Bidirectional interface with an A/D converter and a D/A converter.

Conversely, whenever the A/D converter generates new data, it places it on the input bus of the interface and updates the *DINVAL* line with a strobe. This strobe loads the data in the input register of the interface and also sets a latch that may be read by the processor (with the internal address 3). The processor can poll the status of the latch to see if there is new data in the input register. If there is, the processor reads it (by enabling the internal address 2), and this simultaneously resets the latch which indicates the availability of data. This synchronisation option used between the interface and the processor, through a one-bit status register with internal address 3, is not the only one. As we will discuss later, the latch output could have been used to activate the processor interrupt line directly.

In real interfaces there are of course more complex state machines (which are naturally more secure), to ensure the synchronisation processes with the peripherals and the processor.

The exchange of signals between the interface and the D/A converter is shown in the timing diagram in Figure 14.10. At instant 1, the processor writes new data to the register. At instant 2, the fact is signalled to

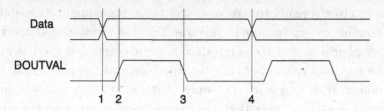

Fig. 14.10   Synchronisation by strobe.

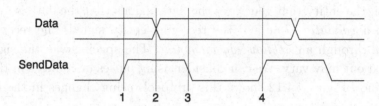

Fig. 14.11   Variant of synchronisation by strobe.

the peripheral. At 3, the signal activated in instant 2 is turned off and the peripheral returns to waiting for new data. The peripheral should, at this phase, have already stored the word present in the bus. At instant 4, the cycle restarts. This form of synchronisation is normally designated as *strobe synchronisation*.

The way the communication between the A/D converter and the interface is synchronised is similar. An alternative way would be to choose to synchronise the communication by the processor which is the recipient of data, in this situation. The protocol would be slightly different because the strobe would function not as a confirmation of the presence of data, but as a request for it to be sent. Figure 14.11 shows this variation. Now at instant 1, the recipient of the data asks for new data. At instant 2, the data source places it on the bus. At instant 3, the receiving entity has assumed that the data is present and has stored it. Finally, at instant 4, the cycle restarts.

14.3.2.2   *Handshake protocols*

There are various forms of synchronisation between the interface and the peripheral. In the ways described up to now, it is implicit in the interfaces some knowledge about timings of the communicating devices since there is no explicit confirmation by them of a successful communication. This situation means that it is the responsibility of the entity generating the data to know that the receiver is ready to receive new data. In some applications, however, it is impossible to synchronise in this way, because the timing characteristics of the peripheral to which the interface may be connected are not known.

In the communication between the interface and the peripheral, to solve this problem, it is necessary, not only that the sending entity signals the presence of data, but also that the receiver indicates that the data was accepted. This need leads to a type of communication protocol between the interface and the peripheral which is known as a _handshake protocol_. In this protocol, the entity that generates the data signals that the data is available through a _validation line_ and the receiving entity signals the reception of the data through an _acknowledgement line_. The specific way the signalling is carried out may vary. We can consider using pulses or changes in the level of the lines. Figure 14.12 shows this protocol, using changes in the level of the lines.

In the figure, the data to be sent is placed on the bus at the instant 1, and this produces a change in level of the _DATVAL_ line at the instant marked 2. The receiving entity recognises their reception at instant 3, inverting the level of the _ACK_ line. It is assumed that the data is no longer valid and stable from the instant marked 4. In the instants 5 to 7, the process of sending new data is repeated. The level of the lines linked to the protocol, in this case, has no meaning in itself and it is only the transitions that transmit information. As was already mentioned, the signalling can be done by pulses instead of level changing, and that happens frequently.

A more interesting option is a protocol which ensures a double synchronisation. In the simple handshake protocol, the entity generating the data receives confirmation that the receiving entity has, in fact, received the data. The double-handshake protocol also signals to the receiving entity that the sending entity has received that confirmation. This procedure constitutes

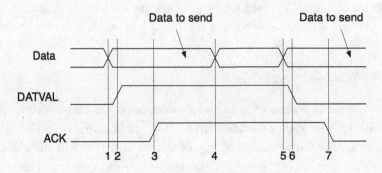

Fig. 14.12 Example of a handshake protocol.

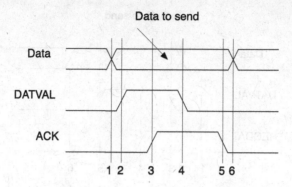

Fig. 14.13   Example of a double-handshake protocol.

a *double-handshake protocol*, and Figure 14.13 shows one of its possible variations.

In the figure, the data is made available at 1, and making $DATVAL$ line active at instant 2 signals this. The receiving entity can now read and record the data, responding by making the ACK line active at the instant marked 3. The issuing entity may, from now on, disable the $DATVAL$ line (instant 4), and so indicate to the receiver that it has received its confirmation. The receiver responds at instant 5, disabling the ACK line, terminating the cycle and resetting to the initial situation. In the figure, the data was removed by the issuing entity at instant 6, but it could have been removed at any moment from instant 4, for consistency with the meaning of the name of the $DATVAL$ line, or maintained until the occurrence of a new cycle.

Note that in this type of protocol there is no need for either of the entities involved to know the timing characteristics of the other. In fact, if, for example, an interface connects the processor to a slow peripheral, this only means that the cycle is longer than it would be with a fast peripheral. If this involved data output, it would be the $DATVAL$ line which would stay active for a longer time, with the interface waiting for the enabling of the ACK signal and, probably later, it would be necessary to wait again for its disabling. If it involved an input interface, it would be the $DATVAL$ line that would be slow. In either case, the cycle would be long, but the data would be exchanged safely.

In the handshake protocols shown, the initiative to start a data transfer is on the side of the issuing entity. There is nothing to prevent the designing of an alternative in which the receiving entity takes the initiative. In the case of a double-handshake, for example, a situation of this type is shown in Figure 14.14.

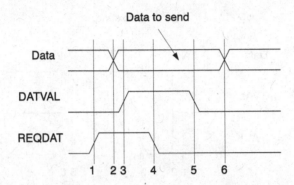

Fig. 14.14   Example of a double-handshake protocol initiated by the receiving unit.

In the figure, the receiving entity starts the cycle at the instant 1, requesting data from the issuing entity, by enabling the *REQDAT* line. The issuing entity places valid data on the bus at instant 2 and makes the *DATVAL* line active at the instant marked 3, informing the receiver that there is valid data on the bus. Instant 4 corresponds to the instant when the receiving entity finishes reading the data and informs the issuer that it no longer needs the presence of the data. The issuing entity confirms this at instant 5, disabling the line which indicated that data was valid. From this point onwards, the issuer may remove the data from the bus at any time. In the example, the data was changed at instant 6.

Of course, the internal structure of interfaces capable of communicating according to these protocols is more complex than the architectures previously presented. With the knowledge obtained in the previous chapters, however, the reader should be able to design any of them.

In this type of interface, it is normal to make a status register available. The processor can read this register to know in which phase the transfer is and to be able to know, in case of an output transfer, if it can send more data to the interface or, in the case of an input transfer, if there is data ready in the interface. As with the case previously studied, it is possible for the system to use interrupts to signal the processor that it must interact with the interface.

14.3.3   *Synchronous Interfaces*

In the interface architectures presented so far, we have assumed that there is no clocked transfer between the interface and the peripheral, which leads to the need for a synchronisation process. This is the general case when a computer interacts with a peripheral over an asynchronous interface, but it is not the only possibility. Alternatively, a communication protocol can be designed in which there is a common clock for the interface and the peripheral. This type of communication is naturally called *synchronous parallel* communication.

For the peripherals, synchronous parallel communication raises the same kind of problems that exist in the internal buses of processors, although the clock is usually slower. In any case, some interfaces of this type allow various peripherals to share the same interface, reinforcing the common aspects of the two bus types.

An important aspect to take into account in this class of interface is that the interface interconnects two buses, the internal bus of the computer and the connection bus to the peripherals, and these normally have clocks at different frequencies. These issues lead to greater internal complexity for this type of interface, compared with the simple interfaces described above. It is not within the scope of this book to explore this subject in more detail.

14.4 Serial Communications

The previous section analysed the structure of input and output interfaces and protocols assuming that the communication between the interface and the peripheral takes place in parallel, that is, the transfer of all the bits of a byte or a word is simultaneous. This section analyses the other type of communication using a bit-by-bit transfer of information, and which is therefore designated as *serial communication*.

The advantages of this type of communication over parallel communication are the following:

- It takes fewer wires to establish the connection, in this way economising something but also having cables which are mechanically more flexible and take up less space.
- There are no synchronisation problems between the signals from the various lines of parallel communication, which may be a problem at high speed with significant distances.
- It is more economically viable to have communications at greater distances as fewer lines are needed, each requiring electric drivers with high power, sensitivity and cost.
- Use of serial communication enables the use of connections through communication networks (initially through telephone lines), which would be more complex to use with parallel interfaces.

- Serial communication facilitates the use of local communication networks enabling the relatively easy sharing of a physical communication channel among several equipments.
- This type of communication also enhances the use of wireless communication channels, for reasons similar to those already mentioned.

The interfaces designed for serial communication are structured around a shift register. For output interfaces, the register is a register with parallel loading and serial output. In the case of input interfaces, on the other hand, this involves a serial input register with parallel output. The interface structure is more complex than what is needed for parallel communications, but these registers can support the need to compatibilise serial communication with a peripheral with parallel communication with the processor through the data bus.

Serial communication has the advantage, as has been suggested above, of facilitating the connection between two processors through input/output interfaces and serial lines. Although such connection is conceivable with parallel communication interfaces, the use of serial communication greatly facilitates this task.

As for the communication directions between two entities communicating in series, whether an interface and a peripheral or two computers, there are three possible types. When the communication is only carried out in one direction, for example, from an interface to an output peripheral, this is called *simplex communication*. It is not common nowadays, except in very specific applications. *Half-duplex communication*, in turn, is carried out in both directions, but not simultaneously, that is, with entity A sending data to entity B and, later, with entity B sending data to entity A. In this case, there is never simultaneous communication in both directions. Half-duplex communications involving general-purpose computers do not occur very often, this type of communication is common in control and automation applications. Finally, when two entities allow the simultaneous exchange of communication in both directions, this is called *full-duplex communication*. Nowadays this is the most common. Note that full-duplex communication, from a logical point of view, may be physically supported by simplex communications, such as happens, for example, in communications between a processor and a terminal (including monitor and keyboard) or with a modem.

As in the case of parallel communication, serial communication requires synchronisation between the two entities exchanging information with each other. There are two essential ways of doing this. In synchronous communication, in addition to transmitting the successive information bits, the clock signal is also transferred, by some means. In asynchronous communication, however, no clock signal is transmitted, and certain assumptions have to be assumed by both entities involved, regarding the timing characteristics of the transmitted signal.

14.4.1 *Asynchronous Communication*

Asynchronous communication is the form of serial communication that has the lowest level of complexity and historically was the first to be used. As we have mentioned, in asynchronous communication between two entities, the clock is not transmitted. The required synchronisation depends on the existence of clocks on the sender's and receiver's sides with frequencies that are as close as possible. If both entities have almost the same clock frequency, the receiver, using the local clock, will sample the line level in successive intervals, separated by the bit length. However, as both clocks are not exactly equal, after some bits, there is the risk that one of the bits received will not be read or will be read twice. To avoid this, in asynchronous communication bits are sent in short bursts. It is usual to send one character at a time or, when the information is not textual, one byte.

As successive sequences of bits are transmitted, it becomes necessary to have a second synchronisation level, which consists in the receiver identifying when a new sequence has started. While the former may be designated as *bit synchronisation*, this new way may be designated as *character* or *byte synchronisation*.

A classic approach to byte synchronisation is shown in Figure 14.15.

The transmission line remains at a certain level, the *standby level* when not transmitting data. Normally level H, the high voltage level, is chosen. When there is data for transmission (in this example, one byte), the

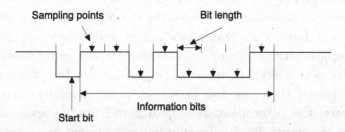

Fig. 14.15   Example of sending a byte in asynchronous communication.

transmission must start with the line changing to the level opposite to the standby level for the length of one bit. This interval is called the *start bit*, it signals the start of a new byte, but it does not belong to the set of information bits to transmit. Upon receiving this start bit, that is, on verifying the transition of the standby level to its opposite, the receiving entity calculates the instants corresponding to the middle of the bits transmitted and, at those moments, samples and reads the line level. In this way, the receiver obtains the successive values of the bits transmitted. In the example in the figure, the byte 10001011 is received, under the assumption that the least significant bits of the byte are the firsts to transmit.

For this to work, the line will have to stay in the standby level for a minimum time between each pair of bytes or characters to prepare the receiver for the next start bit. This interval usually corresponds to the length of 1 to 2 bits. There is, therefore, a guarantee that even if the last bit transmitted is a 0, there will be an interval with a minimum duration during which the line is in standby, which enables the receiver to detect the next start bit. The bit times which make up this interval are called *stop bits*.

Also, the likely occurrence of transmission errors led to adding to this system a mechanism to enable the detection of the possible existence these errors. A supplementary bit is used for this, indicating the parity of the set of bits. It is usual to designate this bit as the *parity bit*. During emission, the number of information bits at 1 is checked to see if it is even or odd and the value of the parity bit is determined. This operation is done to see if the parity for the complete set, including the parity bit, is of the desired type. For example, if the byte to transmit is 10001011, the parity of the 8 bits is even, since the number of bits at 1, is four. If we want even parity, the parity bit will be 0. If we want odd parity, this bit will be 1.

Parity will be rechecked during the reception. If there were no transmission errors, the parity tested at the receiving entity will be correct. If there is a change in one bit, the parity detection will indicate that there has been an error. In these circumstances, the receiving entity has the information that there has been a transmission error and, as a result, may trigger the appropriate actions, for example asking for the retransmission of the character or byte which has an error. Note, however, that this method has one limitation: if there are two errors or, more generally, an even number of errors, the determination of parity will not be sensitive to that. The use of the parity bit is generally left as optional in an asynchronous transmission.

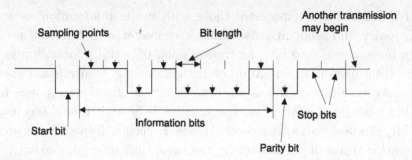

Fig. 14.16 Example of sending a byte in asynchronous communication with parity bit and two stop bits.

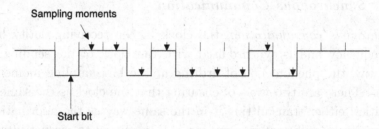

Fig. 14.17. Reception of a byte with a reception clock frequency slightly lower than that of the sender clock.

Figure 14.16 shows the structure of the information transmitted, including the parity bit (with even parity) and two stop bits.

If the reception clock was equal to that of the sender, the sampling of the bits would always be in the middle of the time interval corresponding to each bit. In reality, this is not what happens, since the clocks do not have exactly the same frequency. Let us, for example, consider what happens if the receiver clock is slightly slower than the sender clock as illustrated in Figure 14.17. Initially, the appearance of the start bit allows the reading to start by sampling the following bits. However, as the local clock is slower than the sender clock, each bit will be sampled a little later than the previous one until sampling skips one bit (a situation not shown in the figure). It can be seen from the figure that because of this effect, the number of bits transmitted each time has to be limited.

Not all the bits transmitted in asynchronous communication are useful information bits. In fact, the start bit, the parity bit and the interval known as stop bits are necessary for communication but do not carry useful information.

The *transmission speed* is usually measured in bits per second (bit/s) and refers to the number of bits transmitted per second. Note that all the bits transmitted are considered, those with useful information as well as start, parity and stop bits. Assuming a character of 8 bits, the use of a parity bit and one stop bit, the transmission of useful information is 8/11 of the transmission speed. Another designation for transmission speed is the *baud rate*, although this is not always correct. *Baud* corresponds to the simplest quantity of information transmitted. Whenever 1 baud is equivalent to 1 bit, the designation is correct. However, certain forms of transmitting information transmit various bits in the same time interval, making 1 baud correspond to various bits.

14.4.2   *Synchronous Communication*

In *synchronous communication*, the clock in the receiving entity has the same frequency and is synchronised with the clock of the sending entity. In this way, the phenomenon of drifting at the bit sampling moment does not exist. There are two ways of ensuring that the clock is the same in the two entities: either transmitting it in the same way as the information bits or, alternatively, sufficient information is transmitted to reconstitute at the receiver a clock synchronised with the transmitter.

The *Manchester code*, for example, imposes a voltage transition for each bit transmitted. If the bit is a one, the transition must be from 0 to 1. Conversely, if the bit is a 0, the transition must be from 1 to 0.[2] In this manner, if there are contiguous bits with the same value, the line level must change also between bits. Figure 14.18 shows an example of Manchester coding. Using this scheme it is possible to restore the clock at the receiving entity.

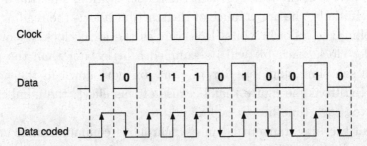

Fig. 14.18   Manchester coding of the sequence 10111010010.

---

[2]It is also possible to use the inverse convention.

Anyway, the presence of a synchronised clock does away with the need to segment the information into short length blocks, as is the case with asynchronous communication. In principle, information can now be transmitted on a continuous basis. Of course, this puts new demands on the interfaces and the level of priority that the processor gives to this communication. It must be ensured that a lack of data to transmit does not block the emitter and that the receiver does not lose information due to a delay on the reading by the processor from the interface.

There are, however, reasons to segment the information, although in larger-sized blocks than is usual in asynchronous communication. First, this results from the need to allow the processor to control communication, managing the quantity of information available to send or receive each time. Second, we must bear in mind that transmission errors do occur. Sending a long information block without segmenting it implies that a simple transmission error will compromise the entire block, leading to the need to retransmit it. On the other hand, blocks which are too small have the drawback of having low transmission yields, as we will see later. There is, therefore, a need to find an optimum size. The sizes currently used in standards range from a few hundred to some thousands of bits.

In current synchronous communication implementations, it is standard to transmit the clock continuously, even when there is no useful information to transmit. This situation raises the problem of discerning the absence of data from the transmission of useful data since the receiver is permanently sampling the line.

On the other hand, the development of this type of communication was essential in the implementation of computer networks. This implies that when a sequence of data is sent, there is the need to indicate what its destination is, that is, to which receiver the information is targeted, from a set of possible receivers.

For all the reasons mentioned, it was necessary to develop communication protocols which could support all the required functionalities. A brief introduction to this issue follows but consulting standard texts on data communications, or computer networks is mandatory to go more deeply into the matter.

Character-oriented protocols which were initially developed, assume that the information to be transmitted is made up of text characters. With the development of the need to send other types of information, bit-oriented protocols were developed and are currently the most used.

14.4.2.1 *Character oriented protocols*

Protocols of this nature are rarely used nowadays but are referred here as they were an important step that bridges the gap between asynchronous communication and present bit-oriented protocols. In this type of protocol, the useful information consists of text characters and possibly some control characters such as those contained in the Table 1.16 of the ASCII code presented in Section 1.3.4.

When there is no data, the «SYN» (synchronisation) character is continuously transmitted, which maintains the sending and the receiving entities synchronised. When there is data to be transmitted, which in the case of these protocols is usually text, the transmission is initiated by a header with information linked to the transmission control. The header begins with the «SOH» (Start Of Header) character. The text is, in turn, starts by the «STX» (Start of Text) character, and terminates with the «ETX» (End of Text) character. At the end of the information packet, there is a BCC (Block Check Character) character. «BCC» is not a regular character but rather a sequence of bits calculated to detect transmission errors. The information to be transmitted is segmented into blocks with a maximum defined length. Figure 14.19 shows the structure of an information packet in this type of protocol.

14.4.2.2 *Bit-oriented protocols*

In transmitting non-textual information in character oriented protocols, there is the problem of not being possible to transmit random bit configurations because they may correspond to control characters («STX», «SOH», etc.). In fact, only text or control characters can be transmitted. It is often the case that there is a need to send information that is not "characterisable", for example, programs. Bit-oriented protocols allow us to resolve this problem.

In *bit-oriented protocols*, the notion of character disappears. The information to transmit is a sequence of bits. When there is no useful information

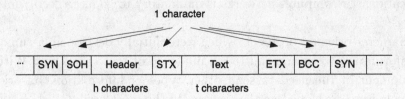

Fig. 14.19   Packet structure in a synchronous communication character-oriented protocol.

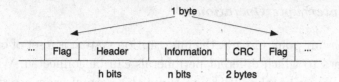

Fig. 14.20 Structure of a packet in a bit-oriented synchronous communication protocol.

to transfer, the sending entity continuously transmits a bit sequence, called the synchronous communication *flag* which, in many current protocols, is 01111110. When there is data to be transmitted, it starts with a header which has a fixed length, and after this, the data is transmitted. After the data, a *Cyclic Redundancy Check* (*CRC*) error block provides the necessary to detect transmission errors. After this packet, the emitter starts transmitting flags again. The appearance of the flag, therefore, marks the end of the data transmission. Figure 14.20 illustrates the structure of an information packet in this type of protocol.

There is a problem with this procedure. It concerns the possible appearance of the sequence 01111110, corresponding to the flag, in the middle of the information to be transmitted. If this sequence of bits is transmitted, the protocol assumes that the packet has finished. It was necessary to develop an additional procedure which is called *bit stuffing*: except for the flags, whenever the sender verifies that there are five successive bits at 1, it adds a 0, regardless of the value of the sixth bit. At the receiver, whenever five successive 1s occur, the next bit is checked. If it is a 0, it is removed. If it is 1, then the sequence is a flag, and the end of the packet is assumed.

If, for example, the sequence to be transmitted is

$$0101001101011111\overset{.}{1}111110110101$$

the sequence actually transmitted, due to bit stuffing, is

$$010100110101111\underline{1}0\underline{0}11111\underline{0}010110101$$

where the underlined 0 bits correspond to the inserted bits.

14.5   Interruption System

As mentioned previously, during normal processing the CPU has control over the system buses. Therefore, if any peripheral wants to read or write data, it does not have the autonomy to do so through these buses, and the CPU must manage that transfer. Thus, for the peripherals to request attention, most processors accept interrupts and have an *interruption system* to handle interrupts.

14.5.1 *Interrupts Operation*

From the circuit point of view, the interruption system is a set of one or more external lines to which different peripherals can be connected. When one of these lines is active, the CPU interrupts the normal sequence of program instructions and jumps to a dedicated routine called *interrupt service routine* to process the interrupt in question. This operation has already been dealt with in Section 10.5.3 for the particular case of the P3 processor.

The peripheral interface should keep the interrupt signal active until the CPU informs it that it will service the interrupt, usually through an *interrupt acknowledge* signal (in the case of the P3 processor in Chapter 12, the *IAK* signal). This signalling is necessary because the CPU may, for various reasons, take some time to respond to an interrupt signal. For example, the running programs may, for a period that should be small, disable interrupts (in the case of the P3, control of the status bit E makes this possible).

Another situation where an interrupt may take some time to service is when the CPU is dealing with an interrupt coming from another peripheral. As mentioned in Section 10.5.3, during the execution of an interrupt service routine, interrupts are automatically disabled, and this routine cannot be interrupted. Many processors minimise this problem by enabling higher priority peripherals to interrupt those interrupts with lower priority. The programmer may also enable interrupts inside an interrupt service routine.

The interrupt service routine is usually specific to the device which generated the interrupt. So, when the CPU receives an interrupt, it must have mechanisms to identify the device that originated that interrupt. A simple solution for this problem is for the CPU to provide a set of external independent interrupt lines, assigning one of those lines to each system peripheral. This solution may not be practical when the number of peripherals is high. The alternative is to use a single interrupt line (as is the case with the P3), but in this case, the CPU has to go through a process of identification of the interrupting peripheral. These alternatives are analysed in detail below. Note that it is possible for a processor to combine the two possibilities, with a set of interrupt lines where some peripherals may share one or more of them.

A problem which arises when there are several possible origins for the interrupts is the possibility of different peripherals simultaneously generating interrupts, posing the question of which of these interrupts should be handled first. It is necessary, therefore, to define an order of priorities when dealing with interrupts. Normally, the quickest devices (for example, the disk) have greater priority than the slowest (for example, the keyboard), which, as we have seen above (see Section 14.2), are typically those that interface with the user.

This order of priority results from the fact that the quickest devices demand lower response times because they need their information to be read or written quickly, so they can be ready for the next data, which comes at a high rate. In turn, the devices which interact with the user normally have a data generating rhythm which, when compared with the processing speed of the CPU, is very low. Therefore, even if the CPU takes a few million clock cycles to respond to an interrupt, the danger of data loss is minimal.

The way in which the processing of these priorities is handled depends on how to identify the interrupts and this will be discussed in the following sections.

14.5.2 *Independent Interrupt Lines*

Conceptually the simplest solution to identify the device generating an interrupt is, as we have mentioned, for the processor to make individual interrupt lines available. Given these conditions, it is enough to connect the interrupt line for each peripheral to one of the interrupt lines of the processor, as shown in Figure 14.21.

Each interrupt line will be associated with the address of the interrupt service routine. This address can be fixed and set at the outset. For example, the interrupt for the *Int*0 line in Figure 14.21 might always jump to address 0000h; the one for the line *Int*1 might jump to the address 0010h, etc. Therefore, address 0000h should contain the start of the interrupt service routine for the peripheral connected to line *Int*0. In Figure 14.21 this would be the service routine for disk interrupts.

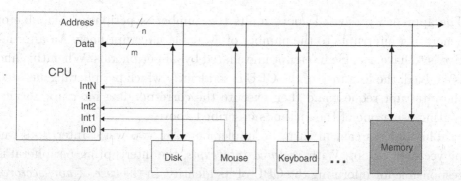

Fig. 14.21 Diagram of processor and peripherals connected with individual interrupt lines.

A more flexible alternative, which is also more common, is to use an *interrupt handler table*. This table is located in a fixed area in memory and has as many entries as processor interrupt lines. Each entry is linked to one of the interrupt lines and contains the address of the start of the service routine for the peripheral connected to this line. It is possible to define the content of this table through software, which thus provides more flexibility in the placement of the interrupt service routines in memory.

As an example, and returning to Figure 14.21, let us consider that the processor has 16 interrupt lines, from $N = 0$ to $N = 15$. In this case, the table of interrupt routines will take up 16 memory locations, with each position linked to the interrupt line index. Let us also consider that, for this CPU, it was established that this table starts at address 5000h. If there is an interrupt on the interrupt line i, the execution of the service routine starts from the value stored in memory location 5000h $+ i$, that is, the transfer PC $\leftarrow$ M[5000h $+ i$] will be made.

With such an organisation of independent interrupt lines, a fixed priority for these interrupt lines must be defined from the outset. For example, one possibility is to give greater priority to the interrupt lines with a lower index. In this way, if there is more than one interrupt at the same time, the one with a lower index will be serviced first. The rest will remain pending and will be serviced after the execution of that interrupt routine. This operation is possible thanks to the automatic disable of interrupts when starting an interrupt processing routine. Therefore, as noted above, the fastest devices should be connected to the interrupt lines with a lower index. For Figure 14.21, given the way the peripherals connect to the interrupt lines, the disk will be the device with greatest priority, followed by the mouse.

14.5.3   *Shared Interrupt Line*

The approach presented above limits the number of peripherals capable of generating interrupts to the number of available interrupt lines. An alternative is to have a single interrupt line shared by all peripherals. When this line is enabled, the first task of the CPU is to identify which peripheral generated the interrupt request and then execute the corresponding interrupt service routine using one of the methods described above.

This process can, in turn, be implemented in two ways. Interrupts can be vectored or not. With *vectored interrupts*, the interrupting peripheral is responsible for informing the CPU of its identity. In the case of *non-vectored interrupts*, also called *polled interrupts*, the CPU has to scan the peripherals until it identifies the source of the interruption, effectively polling them. Let us now analyse these two alternatives.

14.5.3.1 *Non-vectored interrupts*

As we have seen, a single interrupt line with non-vectored interrupts requires the CPU to have a software process to identify the peripheral that has requested its attention. The way to do this is to read the status register on the interface of each of the peripherals in sequence until finding one that is ready to transfer information. This procedure is called *polling* and is shown in Figure 14.22.

Therefore, in the case of non-vectored interrupts, the interrupt routine is unique, and Figure 14.22 presents the flowchart for its initial phase. However,

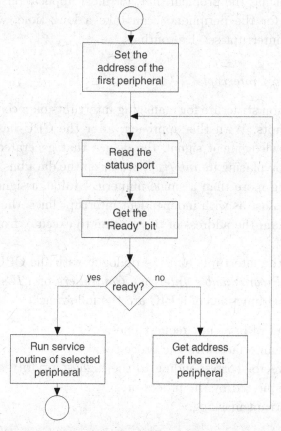

Fig. 14.22 Flowchart of the initial phase of the interrupt routine for non-vectored interrupts which identifies the peripheral to be serviced.

once the interrupting peripheral is identified, control passes to a specific interrupt service routine for that peripheral.

In this method for interrupt handling, the way priorities are defined is through the order in which the peripherals are tested. It is easy to see that if there has been more than one peripheral generating an interrupt, the one tested first will be serviced first. In fact, at that moment, the processor does not even realise that there are more peripherals requiring its attention. Once the processor completed the service to the first peripheral, if the interrupt line will continue to be active, there will be a new call to the interrupt handling routine and this time, if no new interruptions of a higher priority have arrived in the meantime, the lower priority peripheral will be attended. The test order is thus equal to the priority order of the peripherals.

This approach is simple and flexible because control is on the software side. However, it has the problem that, for most applications, it is too slow. The test cycle for the peripherals can take a long time, which is highly undesirable for interrupt service routines.

14.5.3.2   *Vectored interrupts*

The most common structure for managing interrupts on a computer is using vectored interrupts. With this approach, after the CPU has activated the interrupt acknowledgement signal, the device that generated the interrupt identifies itself by placing its *interrupt vector* on the data bus. This interrupt vector is nothing more than a single numerical value, assigned to each system peripheral. Just as with independent interrupt lines, the CPU uses this identifier to obtain the address of the routine to execute, from an interrupt handler table.

To manage the interrupts and the dialogue with the CPU, some special circuits called *Programmable Interrupt Controllers* or *PICs* are frequently used. The typical functions of a PIC are the following:

- accepting a set of interrupt request lines;
- managing the interface with the processor;
- providing a vector corresponding to the highest priority active interruption, when requested by the processor;
- enabling interrupt masking.

A possible internal structure for a PIC with eight interrupt lines is shown in Figure 14.23.

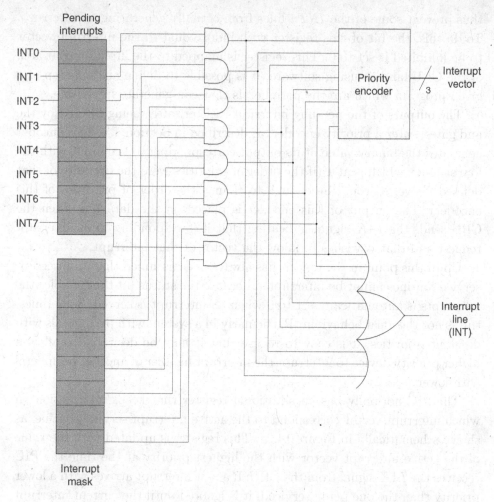

Fig. 14.23   Internal organisation diagram for an interrupt controller.

The *INTn* lines are the lines coming from the interfaces of the peripherals, where *n* defines the vector for the peripheral connected to it. Each value of *n* has a line priority associated with it. For example, let us assume that a lower value of *n* is linked to a higher priority for the line. In this situation, the higher priority peripherals should connect to the lower index lines.

The levels of all interrupt lines are stored in the register that keeps the pending interrupts. In its simplest form, an OR gate between all the outputs of this register would be enough to generate the signal *INT* for the CPU. However, the PIC generally allows interrupt masking to be carried out. An *interrupt mask* register is available which enables interrupts to be filtered and thus prevent some of the *INTn* lines from actually generating an interrupt. To do this, the bit of this register with index equal to the interrupt vector to be inhibited is set to 0. This register is mapped to the input/output area of the CPU, and so using software, it is possible to define at each step of a given program which are the peripherals that can generate interrupts.

The outputs of the pending interrupt register, after being filtered by the and gates, enter a priority encoder, as described in Section 4.3. This encoder generates the binary value at its output corresponding to the input with the lowest index which is at 1 (if the order of priorities were the opposite of that defined above, it would be enough to change the order of priorities of this encoder). The output of this encoder is placed on the data bus when the CPU sends the *IAK* signal indicating that it is responding to an interrupt request and that it wishes to know the vector of that interrupt.

Up to this point in the text, it has always been assumed that an interrupt service routine cannot be interrupted because the status bit that enables the interrupts is automatically set to 0 when an interrupt is served. Sometimes, this is not the ideal behaviour. Particularly in a system with peripherals with different priorities, it is easy to realise that it may be desirable to allow a higher priority device to interrupt the interrupt handler of another peripheral with lower priority.

The PIC normally has an additional register that keeps information on which interrupt vector correspond to the active interrupt serving routine, as shown schematically in Figure 14.24. This register is updated with the value of the active interrupt vector with the highest priority at the time the PIC receives the *IAK* signal from the CPU. If a new interrupt arrives with a lower priority than the one being serviced, it is ignored until the current interrupt handling has terminated. If the priority is higher, then the interrupt line *INT* for the CPU is immediately re-activated.

For this process to work correctly, the CPU has to behave differently than what has been defined in the P3 processor of Chapter 12, in two aspects:

(1) The status bit E that allows the servicing or not of new interrupts should not be automatically set at zero when entering an interrupt service routine. Alternatively, it is possible to maintain the same behaviour as in Chapter 12 as long as the first instruction of each interrupt service routine is an ENI.

(2) The CPU must warn the PIC at the end of the interrupt routine so that it can clear the corresponding entry in the register that keeps information on active interrupts.

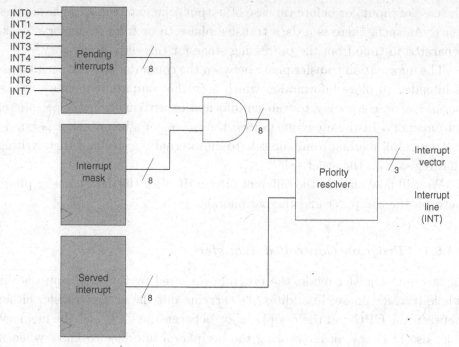

Fig. 14.24 Diagram of the internal organisation of an interrupt controller registering information on the vector to be served.

There are, of course, alternatives to the PIC model presented here. In particular, it is possible to execute this mode of operation in distributed ways.

A simple example is the *daisy chain* system, where the highest priority peripheral always receives the interrupt confirmation signal, *IAK*. If it did not generate the interrupt, it could send the *IAK* to the second highest priority, and so on until it reaches the device that generated the interrupt. The first device that receives the *IAK* signal and that has generated an interrupt (there may be more than one peripheral with a pending interrupt) executes the transfer operations for which it was programmed. When these operations are completed, the device disables the interrupt request, and system operation proceeds normally.

14.6 Data Transfer Modes

The processing of data coming from (or intended for) peripherals is not normally performed immediately at the time of the transfer. What normally happens is that this data is processed with the data in memory after (in the case of input) or before (in case of output) the *data transfer phase* takes place. As such, there is a data transfer phase to or from a memory block, separated in time from the processing stage for this data in memory.

The information transfer phase between the computer and the peripherals is intended to place information which is in the computer's memory to the peripheral or, conversely, to transfer information arriving from the peripheral into memory. In these circumstances, the processor's involvement is purely instrumental, reading from one side to an internal register and then writing that register on the other side.[3]

We will now analyse the different alternatives for the data transfer phase between the computer and the peripherals.

14.6.1   *Program Controlled Transfer*

In this data transfer mode, the program executed by the CPU controls the whole transfer phase. In addition to carrying out the actual transfer either between the CPU and the peripheral or between the CPU and the memory, it is also in charge of monitoring the peripheral interface to know when it can send data or when new data is ready to be read.

Consider the need to transfer a block of information from memory to a peripheral, for example. The processor must execute a loop that allows it to continually test the status port of the peripheral interface to analyse if it is ready to receive data. When this happens, it has to read from a memory location one word or byte of the block and place it on a register. This data is transferred to the data port of the peripheral interface, reinitiating the loop until completing the transfer of all the information.

This process is also called polling, although it is a different type of polling than that presented in Section 14.5.3. In the situation described there, it is known that there was a peripheral ready to transfer information, and the purpose of polling is to identify which one. Here, the processor uses polling in the context of a busy waiting, in which the CPU remains in a loop until the peripheral involved in the transfer is ready.

A flowchart of such a procedure is shown in Figure 14.25. A reverse transfer will involve a similar strategy, in which the wait loop tests whether the peripheral has data ready to be sent to memory.

---

[3]As we will see in Section 14.6.3 it is even possible that this transfer occurs without intervention of the processor.

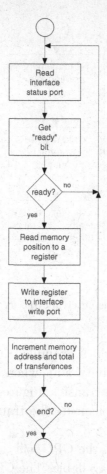

Fig. 14.25   Flowchart of a software data transfer control program.

This transfer method is the simplest approach regarding hardware since everything is solved through software. The major disadvantage is of course that the transfer completely monopolises the CPU with this task, which is usually a lengthy one. In many cases, the CPU will be in the wait loop most of the time testing whether the peripheral is available once again.

14.6.2   *Interrupt Controlled Transfer*

A more optimised way to perform data transfer is to use the processor interrupt system described in Section 14.5. In this case, the transfer of information is carried out by the CPU, but it no longer has to stay in a loop reading the interface status bit and waiting for it to indicate that it is possible to carry out a new transfer. Instead, when the peripheral is again available, its interface sets an active signal that causes a processor interrupt.

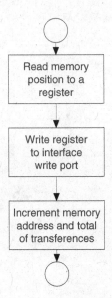

Fig. 14.26   Flowchart showing the interrupt service routine for an interrupted data transfer.

In the context of the previous example, this transfer mode enables the processor to execute any activity and, when interrupted, to run the routine that carries out the data transfer. Figure 14.26 shows the structure of the routine. This routine implements the transferring of data between the memory and the peripheral.

With this implementation, the CPU will no longer waste cycles waiting for the peripheral to become available. The CPU does, however, have some of its processing time dedicated to the transfer, but this is useful time, in the sense that the data is being copied.

Also, this implementation enables multiple transfers to take place concurrently with different peripherals. In the previous situation, this was not possible because the CPU was dedicated to the transfer of one block with one peripheral, not paying attention to anything else, such as other peripherals.[4] With interrupt controlled transfers, after starting the transfer of a block to a given peripheral, the CPU is free to initiate another transfer involving another peripheral, concurrently.

One problem that may arise is the CPU not responding immediately to the peripheral interrupt if it has been interrupted by another one a short

---

[4]Obviously the cycle of the processor can sequentially poll two or more peripherals instead of just one, but this remains not very flexible and the waste of processor cycles remains.

time previously and, therefore, is still handling that transfer. Each device normally has a *time-out*. If that time is exceeded, the resulting behaviour is specific to each device, from aborting communication generating an error code, to those that carry out a new attempt to communicate (until reaching a maximum number of attempts), to ignoring this transfer error and passing immediately to the following data. Interfaces are usually capable of buffering some data, such that, when transfer becomes possible, the buffer may be emptied.

Because the interrupt service routines used in data transfer are very simple (as in Figure 14.26) and involve a very short execution time, this is not usually a serious problem. Also, as previously discussed, the fastest peripherals have generally a higher priority and consequently are less affected by this possibility. Therefore, even in the event of a conflict, the response times for an interrupt do not normally exceed the maximum response times of the devices.

14.6.3 *Direct Memory Access*

As we saw, in the case of interrupt controlled transfer, the CPU has been relieved of the task of testing the availability of peripherals for a new transfer and can focus on other tasks, with its attention only being diverted from time to time to carry out the transfer of a data word. But even this transfer uses the CPU only because it cannot be implemented directly from the memory to the peripheral or vice versa, since the CPU is only performing the task of getting the word from one of the places and putting it in the other.

The purpose of *DMA* (direct memory access) transfers is exactly that of making possible this transfer without interference from the CPU. In addition to freeing the CPU from the data transfer process, a second advantage of using DMA is allowing the CPU not to become the bottleneck for transfers with high-speed peripherals.

A *DMA controller* is, therefore, a circuit that takes control of the system buses whenever a transfer is necessary and coordinates the transfer of data between the main memory and a peripheral or vice versa.

During the data transfer, the CPU may not access the buses that connect to the main memory and the peripherals, so it cannot access memory either to fetch a new instruction or to read or write data. However, this does not prevent the CPU from continuing to execute an instruction, as long as this does not involve accessing the buses.

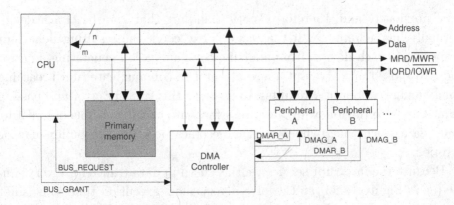

Fig. 14.27   System architecture with a DMA controller.

In systems with cache memories, the impact of DMA transfers can be substantially lower. During a DMA transfer, the CPU can continue to access the cache hierarchy as usual, because DMA transfers only involve the main memory. Thus, as long as the CPU can get the instructions and data it needs from the caches, it can continue its normal execution. If a fault occurs in the cache, then the processor does indeed lock up and waits until it can access the buses again.

Before taking control of the system buses, however, the DMA controller must ask the CPU for it and wait for the processor to grant its request. This process uses two lines, which may be called *BUS_REQUEST* and *BUS_GRANT*.

Therefore, when the DMA controller wishes to make a transfer, it sets the *BUS_REQUEST* signal active. The processor, if it is performing a read or write cycle, terminates the cycle and then releases the buses, setting them at a high impedance state, and makes the *BUS_GRANT* line active. The DMA controller carries out the transfer and then disables the *BUS_REQUEST* line, returning control of the buses to the processor.

14.6.3.1   *DMA architecture*

The operation can be understood better by considering Figure 14.27 in which the cache hierarchy is not shown to avoid making the figure unnecessarily complicated. The sequence of operations for a DMA transfer is as follows:

(1) The CPU executes a program, processing instructions and performing memory writes and reads.

(2) Peripheral A, for example, has a data word that must be transferred to memory. The interface of this peripheral activates the $DMAR\_A$ line, asking the DMA controller for authorisation for the operation.

(3) The DMA controller, for its part, activates the $BUS\_REQUEST$ line and waits for authorisation from the CPU.

(4) When possible, the CPU frees the buses, leaving them at high impedance and sets the BUS_GRANT line active.

(5) The DMA controller places the address of the memory location to be written on the address bus, sets the $RD/\overline{MW}$ line at 0, initiating a write-to-memory cycle, and activates the $DMAG\_A$ line, thus indicating the authorisation for the transfer to the peripheral.

(6) Upon receiving the authorisation, the peripheral places the data on the data bus and makes the $DMAG\_A$ line inactive.

(7) The controller disables the address bus (respecting the memory write or read timings), and the various lines it had enabled ($RD/\overline{MW}$, $BUS\_REQUEST$ and $DMAG\_A$).

(8) The CPU removes the BUS_GRANT line and continues with its regular activity.

Note that both the $BUS\_REQUEST/BUS\_GRANT$ signals and the $DMAR\_A/DMAG\_A$ signals follow a double-handshake protocol.

14.6.3.2 *The DMA controller*

During a DMA cycle, the DMA controller operates as the bus master, but for the rest of the time, it operates as a slave. In particular, before performing DMA cycles it must be programmed by the CPU so as to know the memory addresses involved with data transfer, how much information to transfer and the DMA type.

For this programming to be possible, the DMA controller has a set of internal registers that can be written to or read by the CPU. The common internal structure of a DMA controller is described in Figure 14.28.

At the start of a DMA transfer, the processor addresses the internal registers of the controller to program the type and direction of transfers in the control register, the address of the start of the memory area involved in the transfer and the number of accesses to be carried out. The processor will also have to program the relevant peripheral interfaces. From here on, the processor is no longer involved in the transfer process. When the programmed

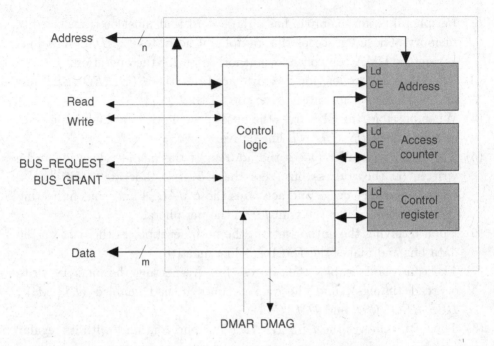

Fig. 14.28   Internal structure of a DMA controller.

transfer finishes, the DMA controller may interrupt the processor to signal the end of the process.

Whenever a peripheral wants to carry out a transfer, it activates the signal *DMAR* (DMA Request) line. The controller, as we have seen, requests control of the buses through the *BUS_REQUEST* line. When this control is granted by the processor via the *BUS_GRANT* line, a transfer of a byte or a word is performed managed by the DMA controller.

After this transfer, the controller:

(1) withdraws the *BUS_REQUEST*;
(2) increments the address register, to point to the next memory location;
(3) decrements the access counter;
(4) when the access counter reaches zero, it activates the interrupt line to warn the processor that the requested transfer has finished.

The figure shows a controller with a DMA channel, but many commercial controllers have more than one channel. In that case, only the modules specific to each channel are replicated, and the control must manage priorities in accessing the various peripherals to manage competing requests.

14.6.3.3 *Types of DMA*

There are various aspects that can define the characteristics of DMA. A DMA transfer can be:

- from memory to peripheral;
- from peripheral to memory;

or with some additional complexity and different procedures:

- from memory to memory;
- from peripheral to peripheral.

Transfers such as the ones described previously are of the *simultaneous* type. In this type of DMA, in a transfer from peripheral to memory, for example, the reading of the peripheral and the writing of memory are carried out simultaneously, using the data bus.

Sequential-type transfers require the DMA controller to sequentially read the word to be transferred from its source to an internal controller register and to immediately write it at its destination.

The first type is faster, and the controller is less complex than in sequential type. With the second type, however, it is possible to transfer information between two peripherals, or between two memory areas.

DMA transfers use three different modes: *word mode*, *burst mode* and *block mode*.

In word transfer mode, each DMA cycle transfers one word, after which bus control is returned to the CPU, as shown in the flowchart in Figure 14.29.

In burst transfer mode, a DMA cycle is used to transfer one word, after which, if more words are ready to be transmitted, a new transfer occurs immediately. Bus control is only returned to the CPU when there is no more data to transmit. This behaviour is shown in the flowchart in Figure 14.30.

In block transfer, when a transfer starts, the DMA controller remains in control of the buses until all the words for which it has been programmed have been transferred, regardless of whether the peripheral is ready or not ready between each pair of words. This mode is used to transfer data to and from fast peripherals. Figure 14.31 describes this transfer mode.

14.6.4 *Transfer Using an Input/Output Processor*

DMA transfers make it possible to free the CPU from the process of copying data from peripherals to memory or vice versa. An input/output processor

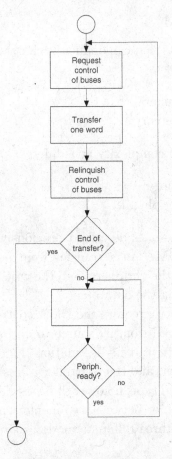

Fig. 14.29   DMA word transfer flowchart.

has the same goal, with the added flexibility of being a programmable processor.

The interconnection of an input/output processor is shown in Figure 14.32.

As we can see in the figure, all the system peripherals communicate with the input/output processor. This processor connects to the system memory buses, but in normal operation, these are controlled by the main CPU. As the DMA controller, the input/output processor can only use these buses after requesting authorisation to do so, and having it granted, by the CPU.

The additional advantage of the input/output processor is that, like a generic processor, it runs programs. The set of assembly instructions these processors execute can be smaller than that of the main processor in a computer system, but they normally have specific instructions for reading and

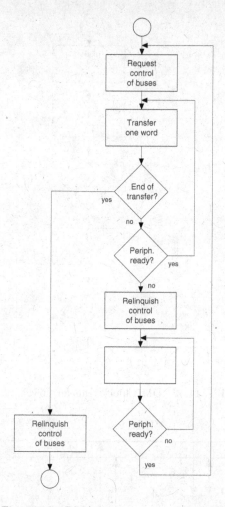

Fig. 14.30   DMA burst transfer flowchart.

writing data from different sources. Thus, this processor can not only transfer information from a peripheral to memory, or vice versa, but it can itself perform some processing of this information namely the control and recovery of transmission errors, further reducing the weight of the input/output system on the CPU. Input/output processors usually have some private memory to avoid loading the system buses with unnecessary traffic.

As the DMA controller, the input/output processor usually operates as a slave of the CPU. In addition to the input/output processor having to request authorisation to access the buses with the memory, it is the CPU that at the outset defines which program the input/output processor should execute to control the transfer of a given peripheral.

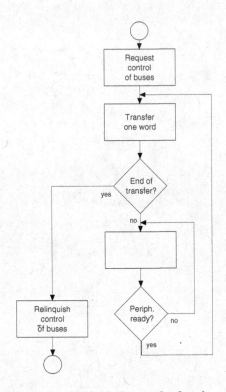

Fig. 14.31   DMA block transfer flowchart.

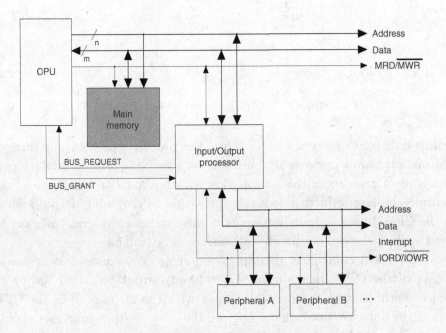

Fig. 14.32   Interconnection of an input/output processor.

14.7 Summary

This chapter presents the main concepts of the input/output system for generic computers. As this is a vast topic, with many variants, and constantly developing, the study focuses on the essential aspects of its architecture.

It begins by highlighting the diversity of peripherals that can be connected to a computer. Instead of the processor adapting to the specifics of each device, it uses interface circuits which provide a communication protocol with the processor which is equal to the existing protocol with the memory. These circuits are responsible for establishing communication with the peripherals and for converting the data into formats compatible with those of the processor. In communication with peripherals, serial and parallel communication are discussed, in their synchronous and asynchronous forms.

The chapter then discusses how a peripheral requests attention from the processor, whenever it has data available for sending or receiving. Here, the system of interrupts and the operation of interrupt controllers is studied.

Finally, the chapter analyses the different modes of information transfer. The chapter considers whether the processor is kept dedicated to that transfer or if it only pays attention to that when the peripheral requests it to do so, or even whether the control is left to external devices, such as a DMA controller or an input/output processor.

Exercises

14.1 Indicate an example of a transmission error that:

(a) has a problem with strobe synchronisation but is resolved with handshake synchronisation;

(b) has a problem with a handshake protocol but is resolved with a double handshake protocol.

14.2 Consider the following timing diagram regarding the transmission of information through asynchronous serial communication with eight-bit data. The least significant bit is sent first, and a stop bit is used.

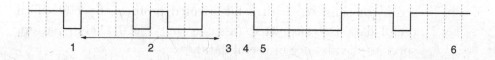

(a) Indicate what corresponds to:

Bit 1

Set of bits 2

Bit 3

Bit 4

Bit 5

Status of line 6.

(b) Specify, in hexadecimal, the information being transmitted.

14.3 Consider a 9,600 baud serial line, in which the characters are encoded with 8 bits, with odd parity and with a stop bit.

(a) How many characters are transmitted per second?

(b) Draw the timing diagram corresponding to the consecutive transmission of the ASCII characters «1» and «9» (ASCII code 31h and 39h, respectively). Assume that the least significant bit is transmitted first.

(c) Using the same conditions as (2), draw a timing diagram at the receiver in which a transmission error is detected in the second character.

(d) Using the same conditions as (2), draw a timing diagram at the receiver where the transmission arrives with errors in the second character, but the parity detection cannot detect this (and so the receiver mistakenly assumes the transmission as correct).

14.4 Consider the following timing diagram at the receiver, regarding the transmission of information through asynchronous serial communication. In this transmission, the least significant bit of an eight-bit value is sent first, and one stop bit and an even parity are used:

(a) Indicate the values received, in hexadecimal, and check if there has been a transmission error. Justify your answer.

(b) Why is the number of bits between the start bit and the stop bit necessarily low in the asynchronous serial transmission?

(c) Now assume that the above diagram corresponds to a synchronous series transmission, with a bit-oriented protocol. Specify which useful data is transmitted (assume that the 01111110 pattern specifies the absence of useful data).

14.5 Assume that you want to connect a peripheral to a computer through a parallel cable, with a transmission rate of 1G words per second. Determine the maximum length difference of each cable line as a function of distance so as to ensure that the bits in the receiver have at most a half-time phase-out (i.e., each word has at least half a cycle of all overlapping). Assume the value of 2×10^8 m/s for the propagation speed of the electrical signals on the copper lines.

14.6 Consider a processor with an address space of 32 Kword ($A_{n-1} \ldots A_0$, with A_0 being the line of least weight). However, only 8 K memory words are installed, in the lowest part of the address space. There are two peripherals, X and Y, mapped in memory, respectively, at addresses 7FF0h and 7FFAh. A status register is available in these peripheral's interfaces which, in particular, has a bit which is at 1 when the peripheral wishes to transfer information to the processor.

(a) How many lines does the address bus have?

(b) Draw the decoding logic for the X peripheral using elementary gates (that is, the logic to generate the chip select signal, CS).

(c) Draw the decoding logic for the memory circuit (chip select signal, CS) for the memory.

(d) Assume that the processor uses non-vectored interrupts and that peripheral X has a higher priority than Y. Describe the interrupt operation routine, to identify which peripheral asked for attention.

14.7 Consider a system with five devices, each one accessed through two ports, one control, and another status, mapped in memory at addresses from FF50h to FF59h. Also, consider that each status port has a bit it Ready that indicates that the device has information to send. The mapping for each device, address of each port and location of the Ready bit, is as follows:

Device	Control port	Status port	Bit *Ready*
1	FF50h	FF51h	3
2	FF52h	FF53h	0
3	FF54h	FF55h	2
4	FF56h	FF57h	5
5	FF58h	FF59h	7

Using P3 assembly, write a routine that polls these devices and calls the corresponding routine when it detects that the *Ready* bit is set to 1.

14.8 Using the P3 processor assembly language, program an interrupt routine, associated to the *Int0* interrupt, to set the *Carry* status bit to zero.

14.9 Specify and justify what is the effect of the occurrence of the *Int0* interrupt at any time during the execution of the following program section:

```
          XOR     R1, R1
          MOV     R2, FFFFh
          SHL     R2, 1
          ENI
loop1:    ROLC    r1, 1
          CMP     R1, 80h
          JMP.NZ  loop1
```

14.10 Consider the following program in P3 processor assembly:

```
1.   start:   ENI
2.            MOV    R1, 1Fh
3.            PUSH   R1
4.            CALL   int0
5.   end:     JMP    end
6.   int0:    RTI
```

(a) Specify which transfer is being obtained through lines 5 and 6, in register transfer language. Justify.

(b) Using a similar approach, state the sequence of assembly instructions needed to carry out the opposite operation to that of (a).

14.11 Consider the following interrupt processing routine:

```
ServInt:   MOV    R1,Here
           XCH    M[SP+1],R1
           RTI
Here:      CLC
Jump:      JMP    R1
```

(a) Specify and justify what the functionality of this routine is.

(b) This routine does not always behave in the same way. Describe the situation in which the behaviour is different from normal. Suggest a solution to this problem.

(c) Specify the start-up steps required for the `ServInt` routine to be linked (i.e., to become the interrupt service routine) to the interrupt with interrupt vector 14.

14.12 Let us assume that, erroneously, an interrupt processing routine ends with `RETN 1` instead of `RTI`. State and justify all the implications of this error.

14.13 The goal is to implement a routine that counts the number of different values sent by a device. Whenever the device has a new value available, it generates an interrupt. The routine should compare this value with all the values previously sent and increment the counter if it is the first time this value was read. Consider a basic version of the system where there is no interrupt controller.

(a) Write the service routine for the interrupts of this device.
(b) Now assume that there is a second device in the system that requires very short response times. Confirm if your solution for (a) can accommodate the restrictions of this new device and, if not, suggest a new solution.
(c) How does an interrupt controller help solve this problem?

Chapter 15

Advanced Computer Architecture Topics

The previous chapters considered the fundamental concepts of computer architecture from a perspective of increasing system complexity.

After analysing the binary number system and elementary logic gates, we studied combinational circuits and increasingly sophisticated sequential circuits. Chapter 12 began the study of computer architectures. That chapter presents a possible internal structure for an implementation of the P3 processor instruction set, based on a microprogrammed control unit and in a datapath which included a register file, an arithmetic logic unit and the main memory as building blocks. Chapters 13 and 14, are devoted to the study of memory and input/output systems, external modules connected to the central processing unit, which are an integral part of a computer.

The constant technological development and the major economic importance of computers in current society have led computers, in general, and central processing units, in particular, to use ever more elaborate techniques to attain increased performances which enable them to execute programs faster, which in turn are also increasingly complex.

The development of technology has made possible increasingly higher levels of integration of logic gates with increasingly shorter clock cycles. As an example, Table 15.1 lists some essential characteristics of Intel central processing units and shows the ever increasing number of transistors and decreasing clock period. At the date of writing this book, the latest manufactured processors use thousands of millions of transistors and operate at frequencies above 3 GHz. The most complex dynamic memory modules have more than four billion transistors.

The possibility of using more and more transistors made possible the use of increasingly sophisticated architectures for the central processing units, memories and peripherals. The detailed study of more advanced structures is outside the scope of this book, and the topic is so complex that it cannot be dealt with in a complete manner from one single source. But it is important that the reader has an idea of the fundamental concepts that allow sustaining this permanent revolution. This goal is the purpose of this chapter.

Table 15.1   Evolution of the complexity and clock frequency of some Intel processors.

Processor	Date of Introduction	Word Length	Physical Cores	Number of Transistors	Clock Frequency
4004	1971	4	1	2 300	740 kHz
8080	1974	8	1	6 000	2 MHz
8086	1978	16	1	29 000	5 − 10 MHz
80286	1982	16	1	134 000	8 MHz
80386	1985	32	1	275 000	16 − 33 MHz
80486	1989	32	1	1 200 000	16 − 100 MHz
Pentium	1993	32	1	3 100 000	60 − 66 MHz
Pentium II	1997	32	1	7 500 000	233 − 450 MHz
Pentium III	1999	32	1	9 500 000	0.45 − 1.4 GHz
Pentium IV	2000	32	1	42 000 000	1.3 − 3.8 GHz
Core 2	2006	64	1	291 000 000	1.1 − 3.33 GHz
Core i3	2010	64	2	624 000 000	1.2 − 3.7 GHz
Core i7	2008	64	4	781 000 000	2.6 − 3.6 GHz
Xeon	2009	64	4	781 000 000	2.4 − 3.33 GHz
Core i7-5557U	2015	64	2	1 300 000 000	3.1 − 3.4 GHz
Core i7 Haswell-E	2014	64	8	2 600 000 000	3.0 − 3.5 GHz
Xeon Platinum 8180	2017	64	28		2.5 − 3.8 GHz

15.1   Microprocessor Performance

The comparison of the *performance* factor between two processors with different sets of instructions is a complex task because the number of instructions executed is not a good indicator of overall speed. In fact, a program compiled for a (more powerful) set of instructions may require a much smaller number of instructions than the same program compiled for a set of simpler instructions. On the other hand, powerful instructions may be slower to execute than simpler ones.

Nevertheless, an often used indicator is the number of instructions per second (more usually, Million Instructions Per Second), or *MIPS*. The Intel 4004 processor executed around 0.06 MIPS while more modern processors have performances greater than 300,000 MIPS, which means that they are more than 5,000,000 times faster. However, the complexity of the instructions of modern processors is much higher, which means that a current processor is much more than tens of million times faster regarding overall performance than the 4004. One of the reasons for this is that each instruction of the 4004 operates with only 4-bit data, while modern processor instructions operate with data that is 32 or 64 bit wide. Another reason is that modern processors provide intrinsically more powerful operations than the 4004.

This simplistic comparison, based on the number of instructions executed per second, should never be used to precisely compare the performance of two different processors in a given task. In fact, the most useful method is to measure what is the execution time for the task or set of tasks under representative experimental conditions.

The architecture used in Chapter 12, which uses a few thousand logic gates and less than 10,000 transistors, has a performance that grows linearly with the clock frequency of the processor if we assume that the speed of the memory also increases at the same rate. However, that architecture cannot easily benefit from the possibilities afforded by a large number of transistors and therefore logic gates.

The ability to achieve performances which are many orders of magnitude greater involves the use of more sophisticated architectures that allow to execute more powerful instructions in a faster way.

Essential to understand these structures is first to know what the limiting factors for the performance of processors are, and then to understand how, exploiting the parallelism inherent in the programs, accelerations of various orders of magnitude become possible.

15.1.1 *Limiting Performance Factors*

The amount of time a computer takes to execute a program is given by $n \times c/f$, where:

- f is the computers clock frequency;
- c is the number of clock cycles that each instruction, on average, takes to execute;
- n is the number of instructions which have to be executed.

The first variable, the *clock frequency*, affects the execution time in an obvious and direct manner. However, a higher frequency does not guarantee better performance, because it may cause an (indirect) increase in the second factor, the number of clock cycles which each instruction takes, on average, to execute. As we will see in this chapter, the clock speed of the processor and the number of cycles it takes to execute a given instruction are closely related.

The second variable is the average number of clock cycles that each instruction takes to execute, or cycles per instruction, *CPI*. With a simple architecture, such as that defined in Chapter 12, the average number of clock cycles per instruction depends on the number of microinstructions that is necessary to execute each instruction. Table 15.2 describes the number of cycles per instruction for some P3 processor instructions.

Table 15.2   Number of clock cycles necessary to execute some typical
P3 processor instructions.

Instruction	Number of Cycles
NOP	4
MOV R1,40h	10
ADD R3,M[R2]	11
DEC R2	8
BR NZ,L1	13 (if taken)
BR NZ,L1	4 (if not taken)
MOV M[R1],R2	11
CALL 0200h	11
ADD M[R3+0100h],R1	13
SHR M[R4+0100h],15	59

As this table shows, there are instructions which take a substantial number of clock cycles to be executed, although they correspond to relatively simple operations. The average number of cycles per instruction depends on the program that the processor is running since it is calculated taking into account the number of times it is necessary to execute each instruction.

The third variable, the number of instructions to complete, depends itself on two factors: the code generation process (and its level of optimisation) and the processor instruction set.

The code generation process depends on many issues which are outside the scope of this book and particularly of the programming language used to write the program and the compiler used (if the language is not assembly).

Within the field of the architecture itself, the instruction set is the factor which most affects the number of instructions necessary to execute a given task. For this reason, the design of the instruction set architecture (ISA) is a complex undertaking, carried out by teams which study the effect of each instruction on the complexity of the processor and its efficiency. Section 15.1.2 studies some of the possible options in a very simplified way. This task is carried out in cooperation with the team that develops the compilers and other development tools, in order to make the most of the processor's potential.

Modern processors achieve much greater performances than those possible to attain with simple architectures such as that studied in Chapter 12. The ability to execute instructions much more quickly is managed by optimising the three factors mentioned, namely:

- increasing the clock frequency of the processor;
- reducing the number of clock cycles per instruction (CPI);
- decreasing the number of instructions necessary to execute a task.

Modern computer architectures manage high values for the operating clock frequency and low values for the CPI, using technological advances that enable faster logic gates to be built and exploiting the parallelism inherent in executing programs.

The technological changes which have enabled the use of ever faster logic gates are very important, but an in-depth study of the related technologies used in modern processors would far exceed the scope of this book. Readers interested in this material should first familiarise themselves with basic concepts of physics and digital electronics, and then carry out a more in-depth study of the technologies involved in the design of complex electronic systems, from transistors to advanced integrated circuits interconnection technologies.

Increasing the operating clock frequency by exploiting the parallelism inherent in each program is especially interesting in the context of computer architecture, and this chapter focuses on this matter. This increase in frequency is achieved in part by reducing the number of calculations necessary to execute in each clock cycle. Section 15.3 describes how the use of *pipelines* makes possible to reach this goal and exploit the parallelism that is present in all computer programs.

However, before considering in detail how the pipelines operate and understanding how they make possible to achieve these goals, it is necessary to figure out the various compromises present when designing instruction set architectures, and the various possible approaches to this problem.

15.1.2 *CISC and RISC Computers*

As mentioned, exploiting the *parallelism* inherent in programs is one of the fundamental aspects of modern computer architecture. Indeed, accelerating processing can in large part be achieved by executing the various operations which make up each instruction in parallel or, more frequently, executing several instructions in parallel.

For readers familiarised with the assembly language of a processor (for example, the P3 processor), it may not be evident that there is considerable parallelism in the program, that is, that there are a large number of operations which can be executed in parallel. Analysing a concrete example will allow us to better understand how programs inherently contain operations which can be executed simultaneously. For example, let us consider Program 15.1, which was studied in Chapter 10. This program adds ten consecutive memory locations, starting at the address Start.

Program 15.1   Program in the P3 assembly that adds ten consecutive memory locations.

```
        MOV     R1,9
        MOV     R2,R0               ; Clears register R2
Loop:   ADD     R2,M[Start+R1]
        DEC     R1
        BR.NN   Loop                ; Continue if R1>=0
```

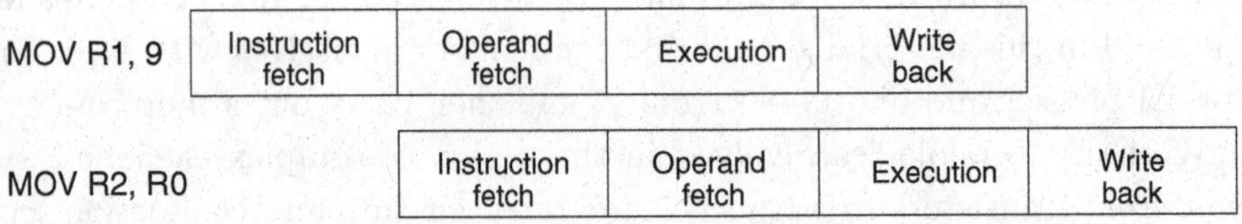

MOV R1, 9	Instruction fetch	Operand fetch	Execution	Write back			
MOV R2, R0			Instruction fetch	Operand fetch	Execution	Write back	

Fig. 15.1   Overlapping of the various operation stages of two instructions.

It is easy to see that the first and second instruction of this small program do not depend on each other, and may indeed be carried out in parallel. One reason why the P3 processor executes them sequentially is the fact that both instructions need to use resources which cannot be shared, such as the register file and the arithmetic logic unit, in addition to other components in the datapath.

Assuming it is not an objective to duplicate all these units, the parallelisation is considerably more complex. However, a closer analysis shows that, if there were circuits dedicated to the various instruction stages, it would be possible to execute these two instructions in a more efficient manner, by overlapping several stages, as shown in Figure 15.1.

This mechanism of overlapping the various operation stages is called *pipelining* and allows to accelerate the instruction execution rate significantly. However, its use requires a profound change in the structure of the processor, both regarding the set of instructions that it can execute, as well as the architecture of the datapath circuit and the control unit.

In order to make it possible to design the new architecture, it is necessary to understand how the overlapping of operations shown in Figure 15.1 can be achieved. Analysing the problem we can see that the datapath with the global structure presented in Figure 15.2 can carry out the different operation stages with the overlapping indicated in Figure 15.1. The first *stage* of the pipeline of the data circuit accesses the memory and passes the content of the instruction register to the second stage.

The second stage decodes the instruction and carries out the operand fetch, transferring the operands to the third stage and the operation code

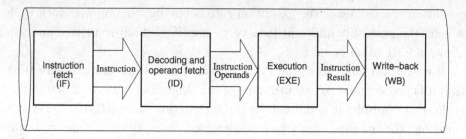

Fig. 15.2   General structure of a 4-stage pipeline.

which has to be executed on them. The third stage performs the operation defined by the opcode on these operands and passes the result to the fourth stage, which writes it back to the location specified by the instruction.

This operation has conceptual similarities with a pipeline (or pipe), where products are fed into one end, before the first products that were introduced leave at the other end. Just as a real pipeline, it is important to keep the pipe full, in order to use the available capacity in the best manner. In the pipeline, there is a sequence of data processing stages as in Figure 15.2 each executing a step of an instruction.

This scheme, which is conceptually very simple, does however raise some difficulties. The first is that there should not be any resources shared by the various stages, so that they can operate independently and without interference. The second difficulty is related to the execution times of each stage. In fact, if each stage has the same execution time, the instructions cross the circuit from left to right in a synchronised manner. However, if each stage has different execution times, there is a need to synchronise the various stages so that an instruction is only transferred to the following stage when it is available. This greatly complicates the operation of the circuit, and is not desirable. The third difficulty arises due to the data dependence in consecutive instructions. This problem will be considered in Section 15.3.4. The last challenge has to do with the loss of sequential execution of instructions, either through a jump instruction (Section 15.3.5), or due to the occurrence of an interruption (subject not addressed in this text).

Maximum acceleration is achieved when each stage is executed in exactly one clock cycle and there are no shared resources between stages. In these conditions, the instructions flow through the pipeline, at the speed of one stage per clock cycle. It is easy to see that, in this situation, although each instruction takes four clock cycles to be executed, the overlapping of various execution stages means the execution rate is one instruction per clock cycle, which (theoretically, and still in a very simplified manner in this analysis) allows a CPI value equal to 1.

However, an analysis of the P3 processor instructions immediately shows that it is problematic to execute some of the stages in Figure 15.2 in one clock cycle. For example, it is difficult in the instruction ADD M[R3+0100h],R1 to carry out the operands fetch in a single clock cycle, since in order to obtain the first operand it is necessary to add the value 0100h to the register R3 and access the memory using the result as the address. Trying to carry out these two operations in a single clock cycle would require a very large clock period, therefore losing a large part of the possible acceleration achieved with the pipeline.

On the other hand, when the operands are both in registers, as for example in the instruction ADD R1,R2, it is possible to access both the operands and make them available for the following stage in a single clock cycle.

There is, therefore, a compromise between the complexity of the possible instructions in a processor and the speed at which they can be executed. On the one hand, a set of more powerful instructions, with more flexible addressing modes and the ability to execute complex operations, leads to a particular task being performed using fewer instructions. On the other hand, some instructions take more clock cycles to run than others not so powerful, and the exploitation of parallelism allowed by pipelining and other more sophisticated techniques is more difficult in this case.

In a simplified and very schematic manner, processors can be classified into one of two categories, according to their instruction set: *CISC* (Complex Instruction Set Computers) or *RISC* (Reduced Instruction Set Computers).

CISC processors have complex instruction sets and addressing modes, which enable compact programs, encodable using a more reduced number of instructions. The P3 processor, although it does not have a very wide instruction set, has certain specific characteristics of CISC processors, including the various addressing modes, the existence of instructions which take many clock cycles to execute, and the non-uniformity of instruction formats, due to the need to encode many different instructions. Other CISC processors include even more sophisticated addressing modes, complex operations on character strings and tables in memory, and operations over various types of operands.

RISC processors, in turn, opt for more reduced instruction sets with simpler instructions. Given the greater simplicity of their instructions, the execution time necessary for each instruction is less. This latter option often results in faster processors since many of the CISC-type processor instructions and addressing modes are rarely used, but they contribute to a greater hardware complexity with a consequent reduction in operating frequency.

RISC processor instruction sets are typically characterised by having simpler addressing modes, by imposing restrictions on the type of operands that can be used in arithmetic and logic instructions and by not having complex instructions, which involve repetitions of operations (such as operations on character strings).

In their most simple and radical version, RISC processors have only three types of instructions:

- arithmetic and logic instructions, which operate on registers;
- data transfer instructions between memory and registers;
- control instructions.

These architectures, also known as *load-store* architectures, in reference to the two single instructions that can access memory, are an interesting study case, and will serve as the basis for the P4 processor (abbreviation for the petite pedagogic pipeline processor) which will be considered next.

It should be mentioned that, despite the difficulties, some CISC processors successfully manage to carry out pipeline execution. A notable case is the Intel Pentium 4. This processor has CISC characteristics to maintain compatibility with the x86 family instruction set. However, the architects of this processor managed to implement a pipeline execution unit.

15.2 The P4 Processor

In this section, the objective is to define a processor with a smaller set of instructions than the P3, designed in such a way that it is possible to execute each of the stages of each instruction in only one clock cycle. Adopting this instruction set, in line with the RISC philosophy, will allow changing the datapath so that it is possible to apply the pipelining concept and increase the speed with which the processor executes programs.

15.2.1 *Addressing Modes*

As we have seen, one of the features that most strongly influences the complexity of the instructions is the variety of addressing forms supported. Since the intention is to be able to have the operands available in only one clock cycle, the P4 processor will only perform arithmetic and logic operations on operands in the registers.

All memory accesses use, therefore, the LOAD and STOR instructions, which can be used to copy an operand from memory to a register, or from a register to memory. The most complex addressing modes are obtained indirectly through composite operations. In practice, this option turns out to have relatively little impact on the programmer, who usually uses a high-level language. Translating the memory accesses for a set of processor instructions is the responsibility of the compiler.

15.2.2   *P4 Processor Instruction Set*

Just like the P3 processor, the P4 processor provides basic instructions for data transfer, data manipulation and control. Like those of the P3, these instructions can be classified into the following classes:

- Arithmetic instructions: they apply an arithmetic operator to the operands, which are necessarily registers.
- Logic instructions: they apply a logic operator to the operand or operands, located in registers.
- Shift instructions: they shift or rotate the content of a register one bit to the left or the right.
- Control instructions: they control the sequencing of instructions executed by the processor.
- Data transfer instructions: they copy data from memory to a register, from a register to memory, or between registers.

Table 15.3 describes the mnemonics for the instructions available on the P4 processor.

Table 15.3   Instruction set for the P4 processor.

Arithmetic	Logic	Shift	Control	Transfer	Generic
NEG	COM	SHR	BR	MOV	NOP
INC	AND	SHL	BR.cond	MVI	STC
DEC	OR	SHRA	JMP	MVIH	CLC
ADD	XOR	SHLA	JMP.cond	MVIL	CMC
ADDC	TEST	ROR	JAL	LOAD	
SUB		ROL	JAL.cond	STOR	
SUBB		RORC			
CMP		ROLC			

On first analysis, and comparing with Table 10.4, which lists the mnemonics for the instructions available in the P3, this shows great similarities, which may lead to the erroneous conclusion that the adoption of a RISC philosophy does not imply major changes in the instruction set. However, that is not true, and it is necessary to examine each group of instructions in detail to understand the reason.

The following sections describe each of the instruction groups and their encoding. This encoding takes into account that the instruction formats in a RISC processor must make it possible to easily decode the information relating to the *operation code* and operands. Ideally, this decoding should be carried out in just one clock cycle to allow sufficient information to be passed to the next pipeline stages to start the operand fetch stage immediately.

Thus, instruction formats that involve variable-length instructions such as those used in the P3 processor must be avoided, since they make the decoding process of the instruction more complex. It is also preferable to use the most uniform formats possible for the different types of instruction. However, this requirement is sometimes difficult to comply with, since there is a limited number of bits available to encode the instructions.

15.2.2.1 *Arithmetic and logic instructions*

The set of arithmetic and logic instructions shown is very similar to those in Table 10.4. There are, however, significant differences, which are a direct consequence of adopting a RISC philosophy for the P4 processor.

Comparing Table 15.3 with Table 10.4 it is possible to verify that the MUL and DIV instructions are missing from the P4 processor. This change is necessary because these instructions are executed in the P3 using successive additions or subtractions or both, controlled by microprograms. Since the execution phase of the instruction itself is now intended to use only one clock cycle in the P4 processor, this approach cannot be used. It would, therefore, be necessary to use an arithmetic logic unit that would perform integer multiplication and division operations in only one clock cycle. The design of such a unit, although possible, is complicated and goes beyond the scope of an introductory text. Also, a combinational multiplier or divider would always be much slower than the used adder. This alternate design would impose an upper limit on the clock frequency which is much lower than it would be possible to achieve not using the MUL and DIV instructions.

Since the relative occurrence of the MUL and DIV instructions in a typical program is very low, the reduction of the frequency implied by the inclusion

Format I

15	14	13	12	11	10	9	8	7	6	5	4	3	2	1	0
1	0		RC			OPCODE					RA			RB	

Fig. 15.3   Format of the logic and arithmetic instructions for the P4 processor.

of the MUL and DIV instructions would probably result in a slower processor that would execute most programs more slowly, despite being more complex. Not including the MUL and DIV instructions implies the creation of routines that enable multiplication and division to be carried out by combining more elementary instructions.

The logic instructions for the P4 processor are the same as those for the P3 processor since all of them are easily executed in one clock cycle.

The arithmetic and logic instructions of the P4 processor are encoded according to the format in Figure 15.3. Note that three operands are encoded: two operands containing the data sources and one operand where to store the result. Regarding P4 processor assembly, this translates into instructions where three operands are specified. The convention adopted for the P4 is that the first operand is the destination register, and the latter two, the source registers. For example, the instruction ADD R3,R4,R6 adds the contents of registers R4 and R6 and stores the result in register R3.

For the sake of decoding efficiency, the opcodes can be chosen to coincide with the operation codes of the arithmetic logic unit (Table 8.4). In cases where the same operation can be obtained by leaving some unspecified bits, the combination of all these bits is arbitrarily set to zero.

The numerical values for the operation codes of the logic and arithmetic instructions are therefore those shown in Table 15.4. Here, we consider three groups of instructions. The first group contains the instructions that directly map to the Table 8.4 format.

For example, the instruction ADD R1,R2,R3 will correspond to machine code 8813h:

Format I

15	14	13	12	11	10	9	8	7	6	5	4	3	2	1	0
1	0		001			00000					010			011	

The instructions in the second group, with DEC, INC and COM, are one-operand instructions. Their encoding is carried out by specifying that operand in the RA and RC fields and choosing an arbitrary value for the

Table 15.4   Operation codes for the logic and arithmetic instructions of the P4 processor (Format I).

Mnemonic	OPCODE
ADD	00000
SUB	00001
ADDC	00010
SUBB	00011
AND	01001
OR	01010
XOR	01011
DEC	00100
INC	00101
COM	01000
CMP	00001
NEG	00001
TEST	01001

ignored RB field. For example, the instruction COM R5 will be encoded as AA28h:

Format I

15	14	13 12 11	10 9 8 7 6	5 4 3	2 1 0
1	0	101	01000	101	000

The third group contains the instructions CMP, NEG and TEST. Careful observation reveals that the operation codes of these instructions repeat codes which are in the upper part of the table. Indeed, the machine code generated by the assembler is the same for these instructions and for the instructions at the top of the table that affect the status register in the same way. For example, the encoding of the CMP instruction is the same as a subtraction instruction that does not write the result anywhere, by choosing register R0 as the destination register. The instruction CMP R4,R7 corresponds to machine code 8067h:

Format I

15	14	13 12 11	10 9 8 7 6	5 4 3	2 1 0
1	0	000	00001	100	111

15.2.2.2   *Shift instructions*

The shift instructions for the P4 processor have the same mnemonics as those for the P3 processor, but they work very differently. Shift instructions for the P3 processor can move the contents of a register several bit positions in a single instruction which does not happen in the P4 processor. The number of bits to shift in P3 instructions is specified by an additional instruction parameter, which is used by the microprogram to count the number of times the one-bit shift allowed by the circuits is applied to the data.

With a RISC processor, which does not use a microprogram, it is not possible to use this solution. One possible approach to the problem is to use combinational circuits that can shift the input value of several bits in a single cycle (known as *barrel shifters*). However, this type of circuit is complicated and is not used in the P4 processor. In this case, we considered that the additional functionality allowed by these circuits does not compensate for the increased complexity of the processor, and the need to deal in more detail with the construction of these specific circuits. Therefore, the shift instructions for the P4 processor only allow making one-bit shifts on the operands in the direction specified by the operation code.

The encoding of the shift instructions for the P4 processor follows the format in Figure 15.3. The respective operation codes are also obtained from the operation codes of the arithmetic logic unit, resulting in Table 15.5. As instructions with one operand, the RA and RC fields keep the operand register identification, and the encoding does not consider the RB field.

15.2.2.3   *Control instructions*

The changes in the P3 and P4 processor control instructions processor are more visible and deserve a more detailed explanation.

The BR and JMP instructions work in the same way as in the P3 processor, and therefore do not merit any special attention.

Table 15.5   Operation codes for the shift instructions of the P4 processor (Format I).

Mnemonic	OPCODE
SHR	10000
SHL	10001
SHRA	10010
SHLA	10011
ROR	10100
ROL	10101
RORC	10110
ROLC	10111

However, the disappearance of the CALL instruction and its replacement by the JAL instruction should be noted. Although the instructions have similar objectives, this different notation reflects significant differences in operation.

In the P3 processor, the CALL instruction, in addition to transferring control to the address specified in its argument, stores the content of the program counter in the stack so that it is possible to return later to the address following that of the CALL instruction. The execution of a CALL in a RISC processor with a simple pipeline such as the P4 processor raises problems which are difficult to solve since the manipulation of the stack cannot be carried out efficiently in parallel with the change in the content of the program counter. The reasons for this limitation will be clear when we analyse the pipeline structure of the P4 processor in Section 15.3. This issue causes many RISC processors not to provide stack manipulation operations explicitly and to keep the return address in a register when a call to a subroutine is executed.

The JAL instruction works exactly this way. The JAL addr instruction transfers control to the instruction with address addr and stores the return address in the R7 register. It is the programmers' responsibility to save the contents of the R7 register, if they intended to use it or make other calls to subroutines. In this case, there exists no RET instruction, since the same functionality is achieved with the JMP R7 or with an equivalent instruction if the return value has been copied to another register.

The control instructions for the P4 processor are encoded according to one of the two formats in Figure 15.4. For all formats, the OP field specifies which of the control instructions is encoded, following Table 15.6.

Format II, used for the BR instructions, enables an eight-bit displacement to be specified, which represents a signed number, between -128 and $+127$.

Format II

15	14	13	12	11	10	9	8	7	6	5	4	3	2	1	0
0	0	0	X	Cond				Destination							

Format III

15	14	13	12	11	10	9	8	7	6	5	4	3	2	1	0
0	0	1	OP	Cond				X					RB		

Fig. 15.4   Format of the control instructions for the P4 processor.

Table 15.6   Formats and operation codes for the P4 processor control instructions.

Format	Mnemonic	OPCODE
II	BR	X
III	JMP	0
	JAL	1

Table 15.7   Encoding of the test conditions.

Condition	Mnemonic	OPCODE
Zero	Z	0000
Non-zero	NZ	0001
Carry	C	0010
Non-carry	NC	0011
Negative	N	0100
Non-negative	NN	0101
Overflow	O	0110
Non-overflow	NO	0111
Positive	P	1000
Non-positive	NP	1001
True		1111

Format III, used for JMP and JAL instructions, enables a jump to any memory location, specified by a register. Of course, this register should have been preloaded, typically using data transfer instructions.

In both formats, the jump conditions are coded in the *Cond* field, following Table 15.7 which is virtually identical to Table 10.14, the only change being the introduction of a True condition, which enables the encoding of unconditional jumps, using the same format for conditional jumps.

15.2.2.4   *Data transfer instructions*

There are several types of data transfer instructions in the P4 processor. Data transfer from, and to memory, are carried out, respectively by the LOAD and STOR instructions, which accept two registers as an argument. One register specifies the memory address, and the other the destination (in the LOAD instruction) or the source (in the STOR instruction) for the data.

The transfer of values between registers is carried out with the instruction MOV, while the loading of constants uses the instructions MVI, MVIL and MVIH. In these instructions the constant has only 8 bits as can be seen in Format IV in Figure 15.5. MVIL and MVIH instructions load the constant respectively

Format IV

15	14	13	12	11	10	9	8	7	6	5	4	3	2	1	0
0	1		RC			OPCODE				X				RB	

Format V

15	14	13	12	11	10	9	8	7	6	5	4	3	2	1	0
1	1		RC			OPCODE					Constant				

Fig. 15.5 Format of the data transfer instructions for the P4 processor.

Table 15.8 Operation codes for the logic and arithmetic instructions of the P4 processor.

Format	Mnemonic	OPCODE
IV	MOV	000
	LOAD	010
	STOR	011
V	MVI	000
	MVIH	010
	MVIL	011

in the least significant bits and in the most significant bits of the register. MVI performs a signal extension on the constant to 16 bits, and stores the result it in the register.

Figure 15.5 and Table 15.8 present the formats and opcodes for these instructions.

15.2.2.5 *Other instructions*

The other P4 processor instructions are similar to those of the P3 processor, although it does not have the control instructions for interrupts (ENI and DSI) since this version of the P4 processor does not consider the interrupt mechanism. Indeed, handling interrupts is considerably more challenging in processors with a pipeline, and it is not easy to cover this matter in an introductory text. The problem has to do with the fact that it is necessary to execute various instructions present in the pipeline at the same time when an interrupt occurs. This process can be very complex, mainly since some of these interrupts have to be dealt with immediately. For the same reasons, the INT and RTI instructions are also not present.

The detailed study of how to handle interrupts in processors with a pipeline should occur in the context of a more advanced computer architecture course and text.

15.3　The P4 Processor Pipeline

The basic idea underlying RISC processor design, which conditions the available set of instructions, is to make possible a faster execution of simpler instructions, sacrificing some more elaborate instructions, used more rarely.

The fact that all the instructions are encoded simply and uniformly and require approximately the same number of operations allows the overlapping of various phases of execution of a sequence of instructions in the different stages of a pipeline. This section analyses the circuits used for the several execution steps of an instruction and then the interconnection of these stages within the pipeline. The datapath of the P4, which is organised according to the structure of Figure 15.2, will thus be detailed.

The four stages of the pipeline of this processor correspond to the four first execution phases of an instruction, as was studied in Chapter 12:

(1) instruction fetch;
(2) decoding of the operation code and operand fetch;
(3) instruction execution;
(4) write-back.

As mentioned, in processors with pipelines, the handling of interrupts is much more complex than in microprogrammed processors. For this reason, the architecture that will be studied does not consider the interrupt handling mechanisms in detail, and this phase of the execution of instructions is not mapped to any stage of the pipeline.

15.3.1　*Stages in the P4 Processor Pipeline*

We assume in the following description of the P4 processor pipeline that there are two independent caches, the instruction cache and the data cache.

15.3.1.1　*Instruction fetch*

The first phase of an instruction processing is the instruction fetch, from the memory location specified by the program counter. The program counter in this processor is a dedicated register (which is not part of the register file). In each clock cycle, this register can be incremented or loaded through the parallel input.

The content of the program counter is used to address the instruction memory and obtain the intended instruction. The circuit required for this stage of the instruction processing is shown in Figure 15.6.

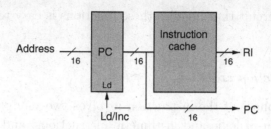

Fig. 15.6   Instruction fetch circuit.

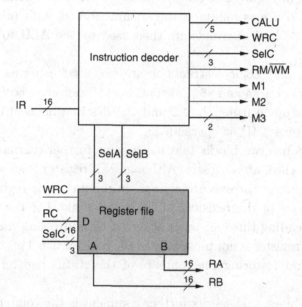

Fig. 15.7   Operand fetch circuit.

15.3.1.2   *Decoding of the operation code and operand fetch*

The circuit for the second phase of the instruction execution, the operand fetch, is shown in Figure 15.7.

The combinational circuit shown in Figure 15.7 decodes the opcode of the instruction, identifies the registers involved in it, and addresses the register file, obtaining the operands necessary for executing the instruction. It also decodes the destination register, and activates the *WRC* line, if the instruction has to write to the register file. For reasons that will become clear when all the stages are interconnected, both the number of the destination register and the *WRC* line do not connect directly to the register file. This happens because writing to the register file will only occur at the fourth stage of the pipeline. Given the simple and regular way the instructions are encoded, the combinational circuit that handles these functions is easy to design and not very complex.

15.3.1.3 *Instruction execution*

The execution phase of the instruction involves two modules, one assigned for the execution of logic and arithmetic instructions, and another for the execution of accesses to memory.

The circuit in Figure 15.8 selects (using the MUX1 and MUX2 multiplexers) the operands to use as inputs in the arithmetic logic unit (already studied in Chapter 8). These operands are then used by the ALU to calculate the desired result.

Arithmetic and Logic instructions are executed using as operands the contents of registers RA and RB. Calculation of the effective address in control instructions is made using the PC and the destination field of the control instruction (Format II) as operands.

Figure 15.8 has two blocks that merit some further comments.

The first is the status register. Although this register is shown separately, and as belonging to the execution stage, in practice, this register should be accessible as one of the registers in the register file. For the P4 processor, loading and reading this register is achieved by addressing the R15 register, although this register is not physically in the register file. This option enables backing up and restoring the contents of the status register when this is required.

The other block that merits further comment is the combinational block marked with the letters *SE*, for Sign Extension. This block accepts an

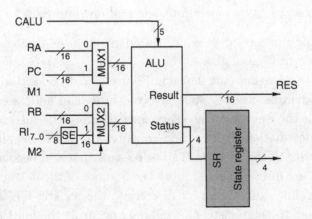

Fig. 15.8   Circuit for executing arithmetic, logic, shift and control instructions.

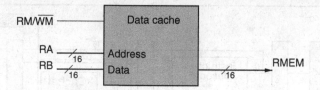

Fig. 15.9   Circuit for executing memory access instructions.

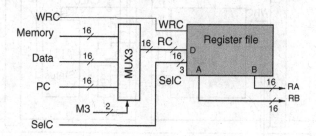

Fig. 15.10   Write-back circuit.

eight-bit value and outputs a 16-bit value using the rules of sign extension so that both positive and negative eight-bit numbers are correctly represented in a 16-bit number.

The circuit in Figure 15.9 supports the execution of the memory access instructions. Since all memory accesses have the address specified by the content of a register, the execution of this type of instruction is very simple, since it is enough to access the data memory with the address obtained from the previous stage.

15.3.1.4   *Write-back*

The fourth processing phase for instructions corresponds to the write-back and is executed by the circuit in Figure 15.10. This circuit selects the value that should be written to the register file using the MUX3 multiplexer and writes this value in the register file. The values of the write control variable and the register where to write are passed to this stage by the previous ones.

Note that the register file is the same used in the second stage, which is shown here again, just to make the description clear.

Each of these circuits, individually, is very simple and further description is not needed. Their interconnection, using buses and a microprogrammed control unit, would lead to a processor similar to the P3, although with smaller capacities due to the more limited instruction set. The potential of this approach only becomes explicit when these blocks are interconnected

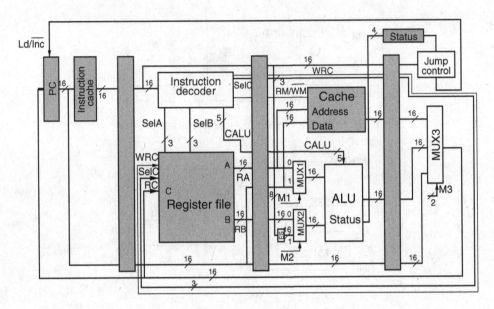

Fig. 15.11   P4 processor pipeline.

to operate simultaneously on four instructions, each at a different execution phase. This interconnection of the modules described above in a pipeline, using registers between the stages will achieve the intended potential.

15.3.2   *P4 Processor Complete Pipeline*

Figure 15.11 shows how the various stages of the P4 processor pipeline are interconnected.

The advantage of such organisation arises from the fact that at each moment four instructions are executed simultaneously. Consider, for example, the section of assembly code in Program 15.2. Figure 15.12 shows the situation of the first four instructions of this code in the pipeline.

Program 15.2   Code that adds two values located in registers and writes-back the result.

```
MVI    R1,00A0h
MVI    R2,00B0h
MVIL   R3,5Ah
MVIH   R3,FFh
ADD    R4,R1,R2
STOR   M[R3],R4
```

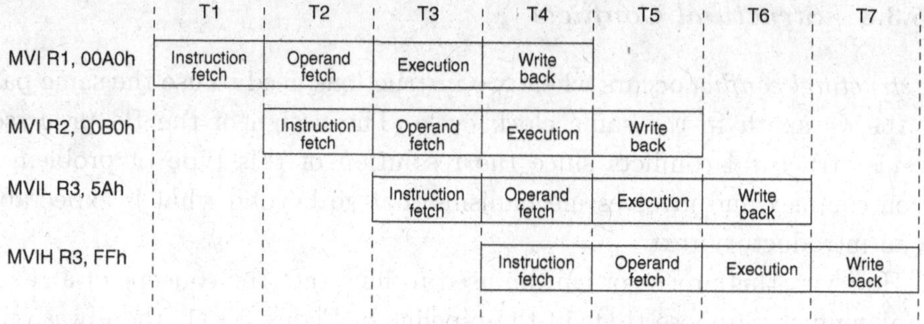

	T1	T2	T3	T4	T5	T6	T7
MVI R1, 00A0h	Instruction fetch	Operand fetch	Execution	Write back			
MVI R2, 00B0h		Instruction fetch	Operand fetch	Execution	Write back		
MVIL R3, 5Ah			Instruction fetch	Operand fetch	Execution	Write back	
MVIH R3, FFh				Instruction fetch	Operand fetch	Execution	Write back

Fig. 15.12   Execution of the first four instructions from Program 15.2 in the P4 processor pipeline.

In the $T1$ time frame in the figure, the first instruction (`MVI R1,00A0h`) is loaded, occupying the first stage of the pipeline, which carries out the instruction fetch. In the $T2$ time frame, this instruction passes to the second stage (decoding the instruction and operand fetch), while the instruction `MVI R2,00B0h` is fetched using the first stage circuits. In the following cycles, the instructions progress through the pipeline, advancing one stage in each clock cycle.

By analysing this figure, we can see that only one clock cycle separates the moments when each of these instructions ends.

Therefore, although each of these instructions takes four clock cycles for its execution, the P4 processor executes them at the rate of one instruction per clock cycle.

To maintain this instruction execution rate and be able to execute an instruction in each clock cycle, some conditions must be respected.

First, it is necessary that two instructions that are under execution in the pipeline do not have to use the same part of the datapath simultaneously. Section 15.3.3 briefly analyses this problem which, while not occurring in the P4 processor, occurs in more complex processors.

Second, it is necessary that two consecutive instructions do not have data dependencies between them, that is, that the second instruction does not need the result of the first to proceed. When there is a dependency, this means there is a data conflict. This situation will be studied in Section 15.3.4.

Third, it is necessary to always know the next instruction to be executed. This does not happen when a jump instruction is in the pipeline, changing the normal sequence of instruction execution. This situation will be studied in Section 15.3.5.

15.3.3   *Structural Conflicts*

A *structural conflict* occurs when two instructions need to use the same part of the datapath in the same clock cycle. The design of the P4 processor avoids structural conflicts since the resolution of this type of problem is often complex and involves mechanisms that go beyond what is expectable in an introductory text.

However, this processor can be used to illustrate the concept of a structural conflict. Suppose that, in the pipeline of Figure 15.11, there was only one cache, which stored both instructions and data. This situation means, in practice, that the two caches presented above, would correspond to just one physical memory. In these conditions, there would be a structural conflict, whenever an instruction of the type memory access is at the third stage of the pipeline since the instruction in the first phase (instruction fetch) at that time needs to use the same physical structure (cache). Both instructions would need in this case to use the same resource simultaneously.

The resolution of this situation makes necessary to delay the instruction in the first stage of the pipeline until the memory access instruction terminates its access to the cache. The pipeline control circuits should analyse the operation code of the instruction on the third stage. When this code indicates that the instruction is a memory access instruction, it is necessary to delay access to the cache that takes place on the first stage of the pipeline.

Of course, for the third and the first stage of the pipeline to share access to the cache, it would be necessary to use multiplexers that would enable addressing of the cache both by the contents of the program counter and the value obtained by the arithmetic logic unit. Also, the result returned by the cache should be able to be forwarded to both the first and the third pipeline register.

To avoid these additional complexities, it was decided to opt for two separate caches, one for code, addressed by the program counter, and one for data, addressed by the output of the arithmetic logic unit. This solution allows describing the operation of the pipeline more simply since it is possible to simultaneously access a part of the memory in the first stage and another part of the memory in the third stage. However, this approach can also pose complex problems, especially when considering the situation where the same memory block can be loaded simultaneously in the two caches. In these conditions, a problem of coherence of images occurs in the caches, a problem that needs a solution that surpasses what the objectives of this book are. However, in many cases, it is possible to assume that the same memory block does not contain both data and code, which means that the same memory block is not simultaneously loaded into both caches.

In more elaborate pipelines, it is possible to have much more complex structural conflicts. For example, various instructions may need to use a multiplier or an arithmetic logic unit. However, the P4 processor pipeline has been designed to avoid all structural conflicts so that no more time will be devoted here to this type of conflict. Mechanisms for bypassing or resolving structural conflicts will once again be considered in Section 15.5, although in a necessarily brief manner.

15.3.4 *Data Conflicts*

While it is possible to avoid structural conflicts by carefully designing the pipeline, the presence of data conflicts is commonly unavoidable since, over time, in any pipeline, there is an overlap of more than one instruction. Data conflicts occur when there is an instruction that uses results calculated by a previous instruction, still being processed at one of the stages of the pipeline.

Consider, for example, the section of assembly code in Program 15.3. Let us consider the execution of the pipeline for these operations, as shown in Figure 15.13. We can see that the value of R1, which is written in the register file only at the end of the $T4$ interval, is necessary at the start of that same interval when the third instruction carries out the operand fetch. Also, the value of R2, which is written in the register file only at the end of the $T5$ interval, is needed at the beginning of the $T4$ interval.

Program 15.3. Code that originates data conflicts in the pipeline.

```
MVI   R1,A0h
MVI   R2,B0h
ADD   R4,R1,R2
```

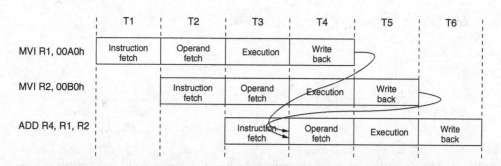

Fig. 15.13   Data conflicts in the pipeline.

If the processor executes instructions without considering this conflict, the result obtained will be incorrect, since the values that will be used by the ADD R4,R1,R2 instruction will be the values previously stored in the registers R1 and R2, and not the values calculated by the two previous instructions.

There are two possible solutions to this problem. The first, conceptually simpler, consists of identifying the conditions under which the situation occurs, and inserting NOP instructions in sufficient number so that the data are correctly written to the register file when the instruction which uses them starts the operand fetch phase. This inclusion of NOP instructions is commonly referred as *stall* insertion.

In the present case, we can immediately see that inserting two NOP statements before the ADD R4,R1,R2 instruction (Program 15.4) avoids the data conflict caused by this particular sequence of instructions. The resulting code, although executed more slowly, obtains the intended results, as can be seen in Figure 15.14.

Program 15.4.   Resolution of the data conflict through stall insertion.

```
MVI   R1,00A0h
MVI   R2,00B0h
NOP
NOP
ADD   R4,R1,R2
```

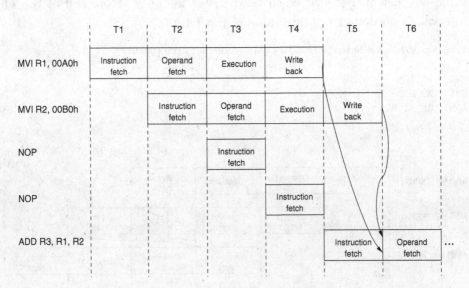

Fig. 15.14   Resolution of the data conflicts by inserting stalls (NOP instructions) in the pipeline.

Of course, it is impractical for the programmer to have to worry about inserting these additional instructions when programming in assembly. However, it is possible to release the programmer from this task, as long as the assembler (or the compiler) inserts NOP instructions whenever necessary. More commonly, there are dedicated circuits in the processor that detect the existence of a conflict and introduce a NOP instruction.

However, there is a second and more effective solution to this problem, outlined in Figure 15.15.

As shown, the value of R1 is known at the end of the period $T3$ and only must be present at the arithmetic logic unit input at the beginning of the $T5$ period. By introducing two multiplexers, MUX4 and MUX5 (Figure 15.16),

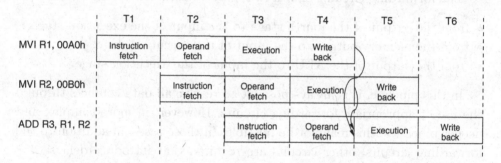

Fig. 15.15 Sending of data between stages (forwarding).

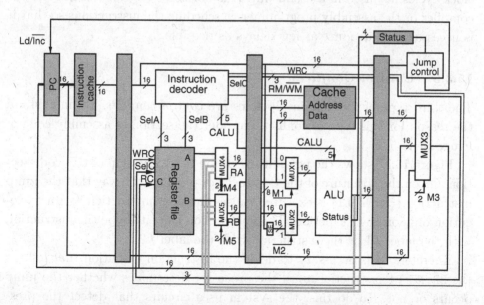

Fig. 15.16 Forwarding circuits in the P4 processor.

it is possible to make the correct value that is in the fourth stage, available in time at the input of the execution stage of the pipeline. In the same way, the value of R2 is available at the output of the execution stage and can also be sent to the input of the execution stage.

These circuits are referred to as *data forwarding* circuits, since the data is sent forward in time, anticipating the delivery of the data to the pipeline stage where they are needed. It is now necessary to control two additional multiplexers with signals $M4$ and $M5$. The control circuit of these two multiplexers should analyse the instruction registers, in the various stages of the pipeline and activate the respective forwarding circuits where necessary.

The forwarding circuits, shown in Figure 15.16, allow to send data:

- from the output of the fourth stage to the input of the execution stage;
- from the memory output to the input of the execution stage;
- from the output of the ALU to the input of the execution stage.

In this pipeline, it is always possible to resolve all data conflicts through the use of appropriate forwarding circuits. However, in more complex and deeper pipelines, this may not be possible. In those cases, in addition to the forwarding circuits, other circuits are required that introduce delays (NOP instructions) into the pipeline. In those cases, there will always be a few clock cycles not used in a useful way. It is normally the responsibility of the compiler or the assembly programmer to schedule the instructions so that it is necessary to introduce as few delays as possible.

15.3.5   *Control Conflicts*

The third type of conflicts in pipelines are *control conflicts*. To understand the reason for this type of conflict, consider the section of assembly code in Program 15.5.

Figure 15.17 shows the pipeline execution of an iteration of this code section. Given the structure of the P4 processor pipeline, the way that the jump instruction (BR.NZ L1) is executed causes the next instruction to start execution only on the $T7$ period. This instruction can either be the instruction with the label $L1$ or the instruction with the label $L2$.

Therefore, it is necessary to delay the instruction execution that follows the BR.NZ L1 instruction until the processor determines whether the jump occurs or not. To do this, the system uses circuits that detect the presence of a control instruction in the pipeline. They also introduce the NOP

Program 15.5   P4 assembly program to add the first 64 memory positions and write the result in the memory position pointed by **R1**.

```
        MVI     R2,40h
        MVI     R3,00h
L1:     LOAD    R4,M[R2]
        ADD     R3,R3,R4
        DEC     R2
        BR.NZ   L1
L2:     STOR    M[R1],R3
```

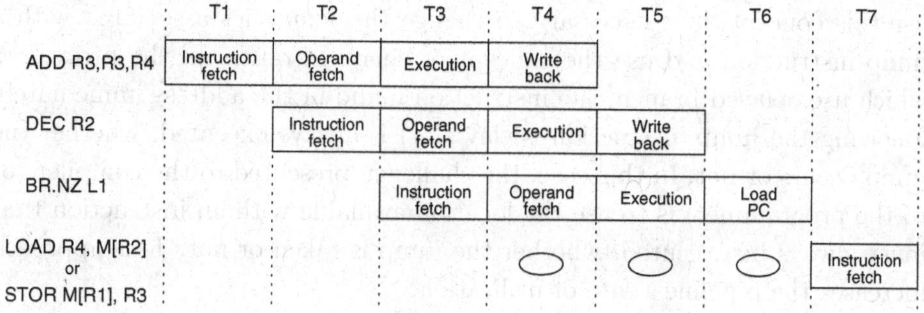

Fig. 15.17   Pipeline execution of the code in Program 15.5.

instructions necessary for the control instruction to finish before fetching the next instruction to execute.

Since much of a program's execution time is spent in loops, introducing delays of this type, whenever executing a jump instruction, has a very large impact on processor performance. The deeper the processor pipeline is, the bigger the impact, which means that this situation represents a significant limitation in the design of faster processors.

For this reason, various solutions to this problem have been adopted, which are intended to prevent the pipeline from being left unused for a significant fraction of the time. There are essentially three ways to mitigate the impact of control conflicts:

- use the dead periods that follow a jump instruction;
- determine earlier in the execution cycle if the jump will or will not happen;
- try to predict the result of the execution of the jump instruction.

The first approach is conceptually the simplest one and consists in trying to use the dead times that follow a jump instruction, before knowing the address of the next instruction to be executed. A simple (but ineffective) approach is to assume that the jump will not be made and continue to fetch the instructions that follow. If the jump must be done (contrary to what was anticipated), the execution of those instructions will be interrupted, to avoid writing the results or changing any status bit. It is also possible to use the opposite approach, which consists of predicting that the jump will be done, but the implementation, in this case, is more complex, since it is necessary to immediately determine the jump address to be able to carry out the correct instruction fetch.

It is also possible to use the dead times using a method common to various RISC processors, which is to use the concept of *delayed branch*. To use this concept, it is necessary to change the semantics associated with a jump instruction and use the concept of delayed branch. In the processors which use delayed branch, the instruction found in the address immediately following the jump instruction (delay slot) is always executed, whether the jump occurs or not. In this case, the challenge presented to the compiler (or to the programmer) is to use the location available with an instruction that must always be executed, whether the jump is taken or not. This approach increases the pipeline's rate of utilisation.

In the example of the code in Program 15.5, if the processor used a delayed jump, it would be possible to use the location following the jump to execute the add instruction. The resulting program following this modification is Program 15.6.

It is possible to generalise the concept of delayed jump to execute more than one instruction after the jump. However, this generalisation is rarely used, given that it is challenging to fill the locations available after the jump in a useful manner. Consider, also, that the use of the delayed jump hinders the interpretation of programs, a difficulty which would increase with the use of more than one delay slot.

The second approach is often used together with the first, and consists of changing the pipeline in such a way that the result of the jump instruction is known earlier. This approach implies the use of additional circuits dedicated only to executing jump instructions.

Program 15.6 Program for a processor with delayed jump to add the first 64 memory positions and write the result in memory.

```
        MOV     R2,40h
        MOV     R3,00h
L1:     MOV     R4,M[R2]
        DEC     R2
        BR.NZ   L1
        ADD     R3,R3,R4    ; Delay slot
L2:     MOV     M[R1],R3
```

In the case of the P4 processor, there are two types of jump instruction which change the sequence of instructions to execute, and which can cause control conflicts. In the relative jumps (BR instructions), the displacement should be added to the content of the program counter. In the absolute jumps (JMP and JAL instructions), the program counter assumes the value of the specified register. In both cases, the new value of the program counter is present at the end of the second stage of the pipeline, provided that there are one additional adder and some supplementary routing circuits. These changes, shown in Figure 15.18, enable loading the program counter at the end of the second execution cycle of the jump instruction.

The execution of the code in Program 15.5 in this pipeline, shown in Figure 15.19, shows that this solution only wastes one clock cycle, instead of the three which were unused (Figure 15.17).

Solving the jump instructions in the second stage is also more effective if coupled with the use of the delayed jump. In this case, the execution of the code in Program 15.6 will not waste any clock cycles (Figure 15.20).

We assumed, therefore, that the P4 processor would use the pipeline in Figure 15.18 and the delayed jump technique, and the instruction following the jump instruction is always executed. Whenever it is not possible to fill

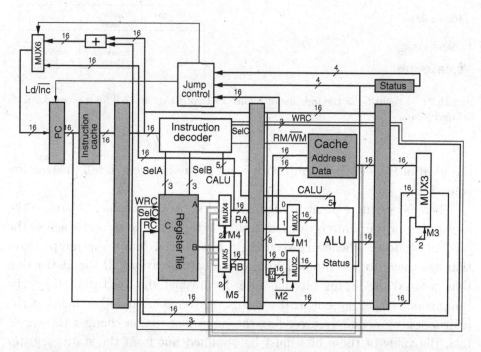

Fig. 15.18 Modified pipeline to accelerate the execution of jump instructions.

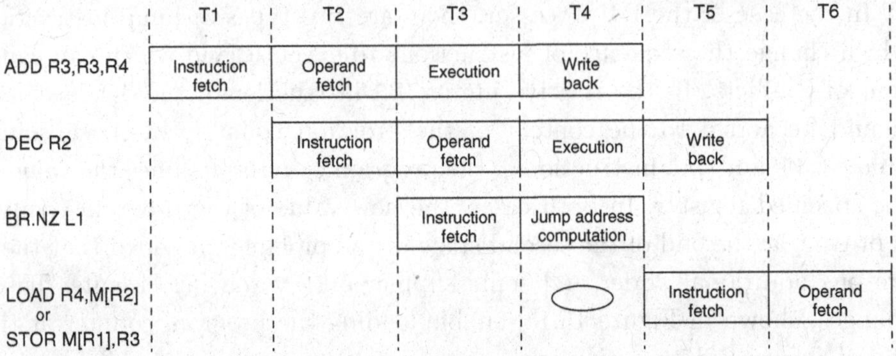

	T1	T2	T3	T4	T5	T6
ADD R3,R3,R4	Instruction fetch	Operand fetch	Execution	Write back		
DEC R2		Instruction fetch	Operand fetch	Execution	Write back	
BR.NZ L1			Instruction fetch	Jump address computation		
LOAD R4,M[R2] or STOR M[R1],R3					Instruction fetch	Operand fetch

Fig. 15.19   Execution in the pipeline of Figure 15.18 of Program 15.5.

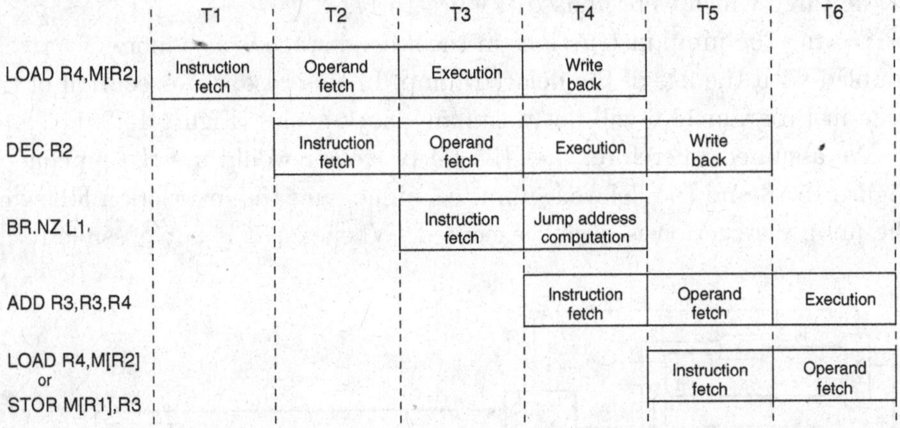

	T1	T2	T3	T4	T5	T6
LOAD R4,M[R2]	Instruction fetch	Operand fetch	Execution	Write back		
DEC R2		Instruction fetch	Operand fetch	Execution	Write back	
BR.NZ L1			Instruction fetch	Jump address computation		
ADD R3,R3,R4				Instruction fetch	Operand fetch	Execution
LOAD R4,M[R2] or STOR M[R1],R3					Instruction fetch	Operand fetch

Fig. 15.20   Execution in the pipeline of Figure 15.18 of Program 15.6 for a processor with delayed jump.

the location following a jump with a useful instruction, a NOP instruction is used.

There is one more point to highlight in Figure 15.18, which relates to the forwarding of the jump condition, from the third to the second stage of the pipeline. Indeed, whenever executing a conditional jump, the jump condition may have to be obtained from one of two locations. If the instruction that enabled the status bits has already finished the execution stage, the jump condition is present in the status register. On the other hand, if the instruction immediately preceding the jump instruction changes the status bits, the value of these bits must be obtained not from the status register (which is not yet updated), but directly from the output of the arithmetic logic unit. This approach in effect corresponds to forwarding the value of the status bits, as Figure 15.18 shows.

The jump control unit must analyse the instruction operation code that is on the third stage of the pipeline and decide which set of status bits should be used to specify the jump address.

15.4 Performance Comparison between P3 and P4

As discussed earlier, it is extremely difficult to compare the performance of two processors in an objective and universally valid way. The relative speeds of two processors vary with the executed program, and the quotient of the execution times can vary greatly according to the type of task.

This section compares the time it takes to run a particular program (Program 15.6) on P3 and P4 processors. The result of this comparison is not particularly significant as an overall indicator of the relative performance of these two processors since the relationship between run times would probably be radically different if the comparison were made using other programs. However, this can illustrate the advantages and disadvantages of RISC and CISC architectures, and analyse the impact of data and control conflicts on the processing speed of a pipeline processor.

To compare the execution speed of the two processors, it is necessary to calculate (or estimate) the values of the three performance parameters specified in Section 15.1.1:

- the processor frequency, f;
- the number of clock cycles per instruction, c;
- the total number of instructions that must be executed in each of the architectures, n.

The task that will be analysed is the Program 15.6, adding the contents of the first 64 memory locations and writing the result to a memory location. For the P4 processor, this program will be used as a reference. For the P3 processor, it makes sense to use a program that uses the richest instruction set of this processor in the most efficient manner. This program (Program 15.7) adds the first 64 memory locations, using fewer instructions than Program 15.6.

It is easy to calculate the total number of instructions executed and the total number of clock cycles that Program 15.7 takes to finish. The number of instructions is given by $1 + 1 + 64 \times 3 + 1$, that is, 195 instructions. Using the values from cycles, it is also possible to obtain the total number of clock

Program 15.7 Program for the P3 processor that adds the first 64 memory positions and writes the result in memory.

```
        MOV     R2,0040h
        MOV     R3,0000h
L1:     ADD     R3,M[R2]
        DEC     R2
        BR.NZ   L1
L2:     MOV     M[R1],R3
```

cycles spent:

$$t = 10 + 10 + 63 \times (11 + 8 + 13) + (11 + 8 + 4) + 11,$$

that is, $2\,070$ clock cycles. For this program, this results in c (CPI) equal to 10.6, which means that each instruction takes, on average, approximately 11 clock cycles to execute.

For the P4 processor, when executing Program 15.6, the number of instructions is given by $1 + 1 + 64 \times 4 + 1$, that is, 259 instructions. However, analysing the number of clock cycles necessary should be carried out with care. It is easy to see that, the use of the forwarding circuits in Figure 15.16, resolves all the data conflicts. In the same way, using the circuit to calculate the jumps in Figure 15.18 and the delayed jump, all the control conflicts are also resolved without it being necessary to introduce stalls in the pipeline. These two considerations allow us to immediately obtain the final CPI value for this processor which is 1. If we ignore the pipeline loading and emptying stages, the execution of this program takes exactly 259 clock cycles.

Given these numbers, we could conclude that the relationship between the execution times for this task in the P3 processor and the P4 processor is $2\,070/259 \approx 8$, which would mean that the P4 processor is about eight times faster. However, this analysis ignores the third factor, which is fundamental to the speed of a processor, which is the operating frequency.

Unfortunately, it is not possible here to carry out an analysis as precise as the one made for the number of instructions and the number of cycles per instruction. Indeed, the degree of abstraction with which the components of the two processors have been defined prevents us from having an exact estimate of the maximum frequency at which each of them can operate. This frequency does indeed depend on numerous factors, including the detailed structure of the units used, the speed of the gates, the delays caused by the interconnections and many other factors that are impossible to quantify without making a detailed design of the processors. Despite this limitation, it is possible to use artificial arbitrary values which are sufficiently realistic

Table 15.9   Estimated delays for each of the major circuit blocks.

Unit	Delay
Register file	5 ns
Cache	10 ns
Multiplexer	1 ns
ALU	5 ns
Adder	4 ns
Simple register	1 ns

to obtain a minimally correct estimate of the relation between the maximum operating frequencies of each of these processors.

As we saw in Chapter 6, the maximum operating frequency of a digital circuit is limited by the sum of the delays of all the gates in the longest path (considering the delays) between two registers enabled by the same clock signal. At the level of analysis of interest to us, it is not reasonable to analyse the delay times of each of the gates in the circuit in Figure 15.18, for the P4 processor, or Figure 12.7 for the P3 processor. Let us, on the contrary, consider delays (somewhat arbitrary, but realistic, in relative terms) for each of the blocks, according to Table 15.9.

Under these conditions, the longest path in the datapath in Figure 12.7 has a total delay of 17 ns, which leads to a maximum operating frequency of 58.8 Mhz for the P3 processor. For the pipeline in Figure 15.18, the critical path also goes through the data cache and has a total delay of 12 ns, which leads to a maximum operating frequency of 83.3 Mhz. These data mean that the P3 processor takes $1/f \times c \times n = 17$ ns$\times 10.6 \times 195 = 35.2$ μs to execute this section of code, while, in the case of the P4 processor, this value is approximately $1/f \times c \times n = 12ns\times 1 \times 259 = 3.1$ μs.

Therefore, we can see that the P4 processor executes this section of code around 11.3 times faster than the P3 processor. This acceleration was achieved without altering the basic operating units (register file, arithmetic logic unit, etc.), by simply interconnecting them to exploit the parallelism inherent in the instructions more efficiently.

15.5   Advanced Techniques for Exploiting Parallelism

The methods described in the previous sections represent only the first step towards exploiting the parallelism which is inherent in all programs.

At first glance, we may consider that all the parallelism inherent to the execution of instructions has already been explored by the use of the pipeline and that it is not possible to further accelerate program execution. However, this is far from reality. Much of the acceleration achieved (see Table 15.1) in the speed of current processors results from the use of more advanced techniques for exploiting parallelism.

In the context of an introductory book like this, it is impossible to describe, or even list, all the advanced techniques which have been developed to exploit to the maximum the parallelism inherent in programs. It is useful, however, to briefly describe the fundamental ideas underlying the most commonly used methods. Amongst these are the *superpipelining* techniques, *dynamic instruction scheduling*, *branch prediction* and *speculative execution*. Among the more aggressive architecture models are the *superscalar architectures* and the *Very Long Instruction Word* architectures. The following paragraphs describe these concepts briefly.

Analysis of the pipeline for the P4 processor shows that cache access limits the value of the clock period. In architectures which use superpipelining, access to more complex blocks, and involving greater access times, is carried out at several pipeline stages. For example, for a cache, it would be possible to break the access time into two stages: address decoding and data access. This process can be taken further, leading to pipelines with 10, 12 or more stages. Of course, in these pipelines, data and control conflicts become more problematic, since there is an increasing number of instructions under execution simultaneously.

The use of deeper pipelines, however, does not fully explore the parallelism inherent in many programs. Let us consider, for example, Program 15.8, which multiplies each position in a table by a constant.

This program could be implemented by the P3 assembly code in Program 15.9. The purpose of this program is to multiply by 1000 the

Program 15.8.   C program that multiplies 100 elements of the table a by 1000.

```
for(i=100; i>0; i=i-1)
  A[i] = 1000*A[i];
```

Program 15.9   Assembly program to multiply 100 positions of the table A by the constant 1000.

```
        MOV    R2,100
L1:     MOV    R3,M[R2]
        MUL    R3,1000
        MOV    M[R2],R3
        DEC    R2
        BR.NZ  L1
```

elements 1 to 100 of Table *A*. An analysis of this code shows that, in principle, the 100 multiplications can be carried out at the same time, as long as sufficient units are available and it is possible to fetch the elements from memory simultaneously. This possibility would ideally allow executing all of the code at the same time that it takes to perform one iteration of the program.

The use of superscalar processors allows approximating this optimal situation within limits. A superscalar processor has several operating units (which themselves use pipelines) that can be used in parallel. In each clock cycle, a superscalar processor starts executing a certain number (greater than one) of instructions, which are in the next memory locations of the program in execution. Resolution of data dependencies is similar to how they were solved in the P4 processor pipeline, using a mechanism similar to forwarding. However, as the data which is necessary for an instruction may become available at various locations (at the output of several operating modules), much more elaborate mechanisms are required to ensure sending the correct values to the units which need them, as soon as they are available. These dynamic instruction scheduling mechanisms are indispensable to obtain the maximum possible performance from the multiple operating units available.

Executing Program 15.9 on a superscalar processor would enable the simultaneous execution of instructions from several cycles of this section of code. This approach would lead to a CPI less than one, which is the minimum value that a processor with a single pipeline can achieve. A CPI value lower than one means that the processor executes more than one instruction in each clock cycle.

Increasing the number of instructions executed in each clock cycle extends the impact of control conflicts on processor performance since the latency inherent in solving jumps prevents knowing what is the next instructions to execute. For this reason, it is essential to use more sophisticated mechanisms to reduce the impact of control conflicts. Among the most effective methods is the branch prediction technique.

This technique is based on the fact that program behaviour involves very repetitive patterns in the sections of the code executed. For example, the jump in Program 15.9 is taken most of the time. Other jumps may be taken only a small fraction of the times the instruction is executed, while still others may or may not be taken alternatingly, but repetitively.

Through the use of an additional cache, accessed by the jump address, it is possible to predict, even if only roughly, whether a jump is to be taken or not. It is also possible to use more sophisticated mechanisms that address the cache, using not only the jump address but also the results of executions immediately preceding this instruction, which can increase the quality of the prediction. Based on the expected result, instruction execution can be started at the predicted address, taking into account that results cannot be written before confirmation of the actual result of the jump instruction. If the execution has a different result from that initially predicted, it is necessary to avoid that the instruction writes the result in registers or to memory.

Although in this way, it is possible to reduce the impact of control conflicts on the processor performance, this technique has limitations, since the branch prediction necessarily has limited precision. When a jump is predicted as taken and, after executing the instruction, the jump has not been taken, it is necessary to cancel all the instructions that started to be processed and restart the execution with the new address.

Processors that use speculative execution circumvent this problem by simultaneously starting instruction execution in the two possible addresses that follow a jump instruction. In this case, the result of one of the instruction sequences is necessarily useless but, in compensation, as soon as the result of the jump is known, processing continues without wasting any cycles. It is, therefore, possible to exchange hardware complexity for execution speed, although at increasing costs for ever smaller benefits.

The aggressive use of dynamic scheduling techniques or speculative execution or both of them results in circuits progressively becoming very complicated, which in practice represents a limitation to attaining very high clock frequencies. For this reason, an alternative that has also been followed in recent processors is based on the VLIW philosophy, which is positioned as an alternative to superscalar architectures. In this approach, each processor instruction is made up of a certain number of basic instructions (arithmetic operations, memory accesses, control instructions, etc.) which, by definition, can be executed simultaneously. It is the responsibility of the compiler to generate correct instructions, by compacting sub-instructions which are compatible with each other within a processor instruction. This way the compiler resolves any data conflicts which might exist. This approach provides an alternative to many of the complex forwarding and control circuits which are necessary for the superscalar approach to ensure correct resolution of data conflicts.

15.6   Summary

This chapter studies or mentions techniques to accelerate the execution of programs, by exploiting the parallelism inherent in programs.

The most fundamental of these techniques is based on the use of pipelining, which allows the overlapping of the various execution phases of an instruction. The use of pipelining causes the emergence of data conflicts and control conflicts, the impact of which can be mitigated or avoided through the use of forwarding. The application of these techniques makes possible to sketch the architecture of a RISC processor with a pipeline, the P4 processor, which is significantly more efficient than the P3 processor, and which uses approximately the same number of logic gates.

More advanced techniques exploiting parallelism used in recent processors are also briefly discussed. Some techniques are summarised, including jumping prediction and speculative code execution.

Exercises

15.1 Consider the following program for the P3 processor, at 300 Mhz, analysed in Chapter 10.

```
     ORIG      0000h start
     start:    MOV R2, 100h
               MOV R1, 0
     loop:     ADD R1, M[R2]
               DEC R2
     end:      JMP.NZ loop
```

Calculate:

(a) The total number of instructions executed.

(b) The average number of clock cycles per instruction (CPI).

(c) The total number of clock cycles this program takes to execute.

(d) The program execution time.

15.2 Recode the program from the previous exercise using P4 processor assembly, and recalculate the execution time, assuming that the clock frequency is now 500 MHz.

15.3 Give three reasons why the direct implementation of the instruction set for the P3 processor in the pipeline of the P4 processor would cause difficulties.

15.4 Show the coding in the P4 processor machine language for the following instructions:

(a) SUBB R3, R5, R6

(b) TEST R3, R6

(c) DEC R2

(d) SHLA R2

(e) JAL.Z R4, 64h

(f) STOR R3,M[R4]

(g) MVI R2, 32h

15.5 Translate into P4 processor assembly the Program 11.14.

15.6 Consider the following section of code, executed by the pipeline in Figure 15.11:

```
L1:    LOAD R1, M[R2]
       ADD R3, R4, R1
       STOR M[R5], R3
```

Sketch the execution time line for the instructions in this pipeline (similar to that in Figure 15.14), explicitly indicating the stalls.

15.7 Consider the case where a LOAD instruction is followed by a STOR instruction, where both reference data in the same register, as in the following example:

```
L1:    LOAD R1, M[R2]
       STOR M[R3], R1
```

(a) Assuming that the data circuit in Figure 15.11 is used, determine the number of clock periods necessary to delay the execution of the second instruction, so that the write operation in memory is executed correctly.

(b) Repeat the previous item but now considering that the datapath in Figure 15.16 is used.

15.8 Design the control circuits for the MUX1, MUX2 and MUX3 multiplexers in the pipeline of Figure 15.11.

15.9 Design the circuits that generate the control signals for the arithmetic logic unit ($CALU$), and the $RM/\overline{WM}$ and WRC.

15.10 Design the control circuits for the MUX4 and MUX5 multiplexers in the Figure 15.16 pipeline.

15.11 Design the jump control unit for Figure 15.18.

15.12 Consider the datapath in Figure 15.18, where forwarding circuits are used, and a dedicated unit for executing jumps, which uses the delayed jump technique. Consider the following section of code, which copies a number of locations, given by the content of R4, between two tables in memory:

```
        MVI R4, 64
    L1: LOAD R1, M[R2]
        STOR M[R3], R1
        INC R2
        INC R3
        DEC R4
        BR.NZ R4, L1
        NOP
```

(a) Calculate the number of clock cycles that this code takes to execute.

(b) Calculate the number of clock cycles when the branch delay slot is used to execute a useful instruction.

(c) Compare the number of clock cycles of lines (a) and (b) with those used by the P3 processor to perform the same task.

15.13 Consider the 5-stage pipeline shown in the figure below, of a processor which uses delayed jumps.

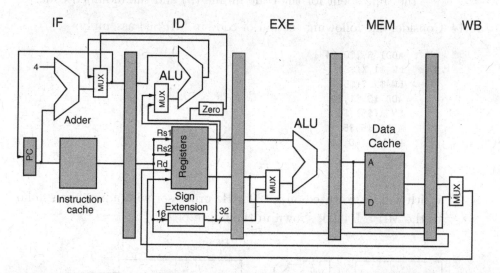

Consider also the following section of P4 processor assembly code:

```
L1:    LOAD R1,M[R2]
       ADD R1,R1,R3
       STOR M[R2],R1
       INC R2
       DEC R4
       BR.NZ R4,L1
       NOP
```

which adds the value contained in R3 to the first R4 locations of the table pointed to by R2.

(a) Indicate where wait cycles have to be inserted in the pipeline so that the code above executes correctly in a processor which does not have any forwarding circuits.

(b) Indicate where wait cycles have to be inserted in the pipeline so that the code above executes correctly, assuming that the processor has all the necessary forwarding circuits between the stages $MEM \rightarrow EXE$, $MEM \rightarrow ID$ and $EXE \rightarrow ID$.

(c) Assume that R4 initially contains the value 100d. Calculate the relationship between the execution time of the above code under the conditions of lines (a) and (b).

(d) Rewrite the code above, so that the execution is as fast as possible for the conditions in line (b). Calculate the relationship between the time spent for the code in line (b) and the modified code.

15.14 Consider the following section of code in MIPS64 assembly:

```
       ADDI $5,$0,64
L1:    LW $1,X($5)
       LW $2,Y($5)
       ADD $3,$1,$2
       SW X($5),$3
       ADDI $5,$5,-4
       BNE $5,$0,L1
       NOP
L2:
```

which will be executed on a 120 MHz processor with a pipeline similar to the MIPS R4400, shown in the figure below.

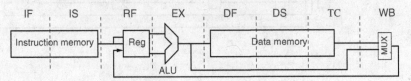

This processor uses the delayed jump technique. Instructions that do not access memory go directly to the write-back stage, and the jump address and conditions are known at the end of the EX stage. Also, the register file is transparent, which means that the value written to the register files is available at its output in the same clock cycle.

Calculate the number of cycles the code above takes to execute, assuming that all the forwarding circuits that are possible to use are present.

Appendix A

The P3 Processor

A.1 P3 Instruction Set

This section presents the P3 instruction set, specifying the knowledge necessary to program P3 at the assembly language level.

A.1.1 *Registers*

The P3 processor contains the following registers visible to the programmer:

R0-R7: general purpose registers. Register R0 can not be changed and always has the value 0.

  PC: program counter, contains the address of the next instruction to execute. It cannot be accessed directly with assembly instructions and only jump, call or int instructions may change its contents.

  SP: stack pointer, contains the address of the top of the stack. It is also used indirectly, and can only be manipulated directly (for initialisation) through the instruction MOV SP, R[1-7].

  SR: status register, a register which stores the status bits (flags) of the processor, described in the following section. There are also no instructions to manipulate this register directly.

A processor reset initialises all these registers to 0.

A.1.2 *Status Bits*

From the programmer's perspective, there are five status bits, or flags, on this processor. The status bits are stored in the five least significant bits of the SR register, with the remaining bits of this register containing 0.

The meaning of the status bits, from the lower to the higher order bit of the SR, is:

O: Overflow, indicates that the result of the last arithmetic operation exceeds the capacity of the destination operand. In other words, the result is not representable in two's complement with the number of bits available in the destination operand, so this therefore has an incorrect value.

N: Negative or sign, indicates that the result of the last operation was negative, which in two's complement is equivalent to saying that the most significant bit of the destination operand was at 1.

C: Carry, which indicates that the last operation generated a carry bit beyond the last position of the destination operand. It can also be modified by software through the instructions STC, CLC and CMC.

Z: Zero, which indicates that the result of the last operation was 0.

E: Enable interrupts, which allows or not to accept interrupts, depending on whether it is 1 or 0. This status bit is modified directly by software using the ENI and DSI instructions, to enable and disable interrupts, respectively. It is also automatically set to 0 while an interrupt is being served.

A.1.3   *Memory*

The addressable memory space is 64 Kwords (16-bit address bus), storing 16-bit words (width of the data bus). Access to a memory location can be carried out with any instruction, using the appropriate addressing mode.

This memory space is organised as follows:

    0000h-FDFFh: usable physical memory
    FE00h-FEFFh: interrupt vector table
    FF00h-FFFFh: input/output device ports

A.1.4   *Inputs/Outputs*

The input and output (I/O) devices are memory mapped. Memory addresses from FF00h are reserved for the I/O space. Therefore, any instruction can have access to any I/O device mapped in this upper memory space of the processor.

A.1.5 *Interrupts*

The normal execution of the processor may be interrupted by the triggering of an *INT* signal, connected to one of the external pins of the processor. After executing each instruction this signal is tested to check for any pending interrupt. If so, the processor will activate the *IAK* signal indicating to the device that it will start processing the interrupt. For the processor be able to identify which device needs attention, and so call the corresponding processing routine, the device should immediately place its interrupt vector on the data bus following the enabling of the IAK signal.

The addresses of the interrupt routines are located in the Interrupt Vector Table, a table with 256 entries stored in memory from the address FE00h. Thus, to carry out a call to the corresponding routine to process the interrupt, the value of the memory location M[FE00h+vector] is loaded into the program counter, PC, being *vector* the value read from the data bus.

The call to the routine to process the interrupt is preceded by placing the SR register in the stack and disabling the interrupt, by assigning E=0. It is the responsibility of the programmer to save any register which the interrupt routine may modify. The routine must terminate with the RTI instruction which, besides carrying out the return, restores the value of SR from the stack.

A.1.6 *Instruction Set*

The P3 processor instructions are listed in Table A.1, grouped by class. The instructions in the "Pseudo" column are not actual assembly instructions, since they do not generate binary code, but rather commands interpreted by the assembler to control the generation of code.

Table A.1   Instruction set for the P3 processor.

Pseudo	Arithmetic	Logical	Shift	Control	Transfer	Generic
ORIG	NEG	COM	SHR	BR	MOV	NOP
EQU	INC	AND	SHL	BR.cond	MVBH	ENI
WORD	DEC	OR	SHRA	JMP	MVBL	DSI
STR	ADD	OR	SHLA	JMP.cond	XCH	STC
TAB	ADDC	TEST	ROR	CALL	PUSH	CLC
	SUB		ROL	CALL.cond	POP	CMC
	SUBB		RORC	RET		
	CMP		ROLC	RETN		
	MUL			RTI		
	DIV			INT		

The condition *.cond* in conditional jump instructions (BR.*cond*, JMP.*cond* and CALL.*cond*) may be one of:

O, NO: overflow status bit
N, NN: negative status bit
C, NC: carry status bit
Z, NZ: zero status bit
I, NI: bit which indicates if there is a pending interrupt
P, NP: positive result ($P = \overline{Z} \wedge \overline{N}$).

These combinations allow each of these conditions to be tested and to make the jump if the condition is 1 or 0, respectively.

The arithmetic instructions assume operands in two's complement format. The exceptions to this rule are multiplication and division where operands are considered unsigned numbers. For these two operations, the programmer must be careful and handle the sign separately.

In this set, there are instructions with zero, one and two operands. For instructions with two operands, one has to be a register. The other operand may have various addressing modes, as explained below. For details of the operation of each instruction (the operation carried out and the updated status bits), please check the P3 manual available online at the companion site.

A.1.7   *Addressing Modes*

The operands in the assembly instructions can have seven addressing modes, as indicated below.

The meaning of the symbols used in this section is:

op: operand;
Rx: register Rx. The processor has eight registers visible to the programmer, so $0 \le x \le 7$, where R0 is always equal to 0;
W: constant with value W (16 bits);
M[y]: reference to the memory location with address y;
PC: program counter register;
SP: register pointing to the top of the stack (stack pointer).

Register Addressing $\boxed{op = Rx}$

The value of the operand is the content of the register Rx.

Indirect Register Addressing $\boxed{op = \text{M[Rx]}}$

The value of the operand is the content of the memory location, which address is stored in the register **Rx**.

Immediate Addressing $\boxed{op = \text{W}}$

The value of the operand is **W**. Of course, this mode is not possible as the destination operand.

Direct Addressing $\boxed{op = \text{M[W]}}$

The value of the operand is the content of the memory location with the address **W**.

Indexed Addressing $\boxed{op = \text{M[Rx+W]}}$

The value of the operand is the content of the memory location with the address resulting from the sum of **W** with the content of **Rx**, **Rx+W**. *Note*: the assembler does not accept the version **W+Rx**.

Relative Addressing $\boxed{op = \text{M[PC+W]}}$

The value of the operand is the content of the memory location with the address resulting from the sum of **W** with the content of **PC**, **PC+W**. *Note*: the assembler does not accept the version **W+PC**.

Based Addressing $\boxed{op = \text{M[SP+W]}}$

The value of the operand is the content of the memory location with the address resulting from the sum of **W** with the content of **SP**, **SP+W**. Note: the assembler does not accept the version **W+SP**.

When using these addressing modes, there are two restrictions:

- for instructions with two operands, one of them must use register addressing.
- immediate mode cannot apply to the destination operand, for obvious reasons.
- as in the instructions XCH, MUL and DIV both operands are a destination, they cannot use the immediate mode in either of the operands. Furthermore, for the MUL and DIV instructions, the two operands cannot be the

same due to processor architecture limitations which would cause, if used, losing part of the result.

A.2 P3 Implementation

As mentioned before, the P3 has been implemented in two ways, in hardware and as a simulator, with both made freely available on the companion website for the book.

The two implementations behave exactly the same to allow students to test their executables in the simulator and so be able to execute them in hardware without any modifications. We also ensured the same definition and operation of the available peripherals in the two implementations.

A.2.1 *Assembler*

The way to run the P3 assembler on a terminal is simply:

```
$ p3as <program-name>.as
```

The assembly file name must have the extension `.as`. If there are no assembly errors, the assembler generates two files:

`<program-name>.exe`: file with the binary code, ready to be executed in the p3sim simulator.
`<program-name>.lis`: file listing the values assigned to the references used in the assembly program.

As mentioned, this executable runs either in the hardware version, or the simulator version.

A.2.2 *Peripherals*

As the input/output addressing space is mapped in the memory addressing space, each access port of the different devices will have a corresponding memory location. These ports may be for reading, for writing or both reading and writing, depending on whether it is an input, output or bidirectional port, respectively. Writes to read-only ports are ignored. Reading write ports returns a value with all the bits at 1, that is, `FFFFh`.

Besides the memory-mapped peripherals, this implementation also includes a set of push buttons which can generate external interrupts.

The available devices will now be presented, along with their access ports and their operating mode.

A.2.2.1 *Interrupt buttons*

There are 15 push buttons available, each associated with a different interrupt vector, with a button index of 0 to 14. So, activating button i causes P3 to execute the interrupt routine associated with the vector i, naturally, provided that the interrupts are enabled (status bit E at 1) and bit i of the interrupt mask is at 1. Before the execution of the interrupt routine, the updated status register, SR and the program counter, PC, are placed on the stack and the program counter is loaded from the memory address M[FE00h+i].

A.2.2.2 *Input and output devices*

- Eight switches, address FFF9h: a read to this address allows a simultaneous read of the status of the set of the eight switches. Each switch corresponds to one bit, with the least significant bit corresponding to the switch to the right and the eighth bit corresponding to the switch to the left (the eight most significant bits are always at 0). A lowered switch sets the respective bit at 0 and a raised switch sets it at 1.
- LEDs, address FFF8h: set of 16 LEDs, the individual status of which, on or off, is defined by a write to this port. Each bit of the data word corresponds to one LED, with the LED on the right corresponding to the least significant bit and the other LEDs by each of the other bits, in order.
- Seven-segment display, addresses FFF0h, FFF1h, FFF2h and FFF3h: for each of these control ports, from right to left, there is a set of seven LEDs which form a display. The four least significant bits of the value written to the port determine the hexadecimal character (0 through F) which appears on the respective display.
- Liquid crystal display (LCD), addresses FFF4h and FFF5h: display with 16 columns and two lines of text. A write to port FFF5h echoes the character in extended ASCII code corresponding to the eight least significant bits of the written value. Port FFF4h is a control port, in which the different active bits trigger different operations, as indicated in Table A.2. The writing of the character does not change the position of the cursor, which implies that between each write it is necessary to update its position.
- Text window, addresses FFFCh through FFFFh: enables the text level interface, making possible reading characters from the keyboard and writing

Table A.2   Function for each bit of control port FFF4h.

Bit	Action
15	turn on or off the LCD;
5	clear the LCD;
4	place the cursor on line 0 or 1 (defines the next position to be written to);
3 a 0	places the cursor at the specified column;

characters to the monitor. Four ports are reserved for accessing this device:

Read port, address FFFFh: a read from this port returns the ASCII code of the character corresponding to the last key pressed to the text window. Therefore, if a key is pressed before reading the previous key causes this key to be lost. It is possible to test if there is some key to read through the status port. A read to this port without a key have been pressed returns the value 0.

Write port, address FFFEh: this port enables the writing of a character in the text window. The character with the ASCII code equal to the value written to this port is echoed in the window. This window has an internal cursor where the character is written to. Whenever a write happens, this cursor moves forward. It is possible to position the cursor at any point of the window through the control port.

Status port, address FFFDh: port which can be used to test if there is a character to read in the text window. If there is not, a read from this port returns 0. If a key has been pressed, this port returns 1. Reading a key through the read port resets the status port to 0.

Control port, address FFFCh: port which allows the positioning of the cursor in the text window, defining where to write the next character. This port needs an initialisation, writing the value FFFFh to it, before using the positioning commands.[1] Once initialised, the cursor may be positioned on a given line and column by writing a value to the port where the eight most significant bits indicate the line (between 0 and 23) and the eight least significant bits indicate the column (between 1 and 80):

15	14	13	12	11	10	9	8	7	6	5	4	3	2	1	0
Line								Column							

---

[1] A secondary effect of this initialisation is completely clearing the content of the window.

- Timer, addresses **FFF6h** and **FFF7h**: timer device which enables defining real-time intervals. There are two ports to control the timer:

  — Counting units, address **FFF6h**: a write to this address sets the number of counting units, each with a duration of 100 ms. For example, to obtain an interval of 1s, the value ten should be written to this address. A read to this address obtains the current counting value.

  — Control port, address **FFF7h**: this port can start or stop a count by respectively writing a 1 or a 0 in the least significant bit (the remaining bits are ignored). A read of the least significant bit of this address indicates the state of the timer, whether counting (1) or stopped (0).

  The common use of this device consists of writing the number of 100ms periods corresponding to the desired time interval to the port at **FFF6h**, followed by writing the value 1 to the port at **FFF7h**. The routine to handle the signalling of the end of this interval should be connected to interrupt vector 15.

- Interrupt mask, address **FFFAh**: this mask can enable or disable each of the 16 first interrupt vectors individually, defined by writing a binary pattern. For example, to allow the interrupts from the timer solely, the value **8000h** should be written to this address. A read from this address indicates the current situation of the mask.

Table A.3 summarises the set of input/output devices defined for this implementation of the P3.

A.2.3 *P3 Card*

The P3 hardware version was described in VHDL and implemented for a Xilinx Spartan 2E FPGA XC2S200E on a Digilent D2SB board. The system consists of the following Digilent modules:

- D2SB: the main module, with the FPGA programmed to implement the P3. In addition to the P3, this FPGA contains the components that control the loading of the executable program into the main memory and the loading of the mapping ROMs A and B, and of the Control ROM. These three ROMs are also included in this FPGA. One ROM on the board allows the FPGA to be automatically programmed as soon as the power is turned on.

708 *Computer Architecture: Digital Circuits to Microprocessors*

Table A.3 Summary of input and output devices.

Address	Device	Description	Action
FFF0h	Seven-segments display 0	Enables writing the seven-segments display more to the right. Only the four least significant bits written to the address are considered.	Write
FFF1h	Seven-segments display 1	Same as before for next display to the left.	Write
FFF2h	Seven-segments display 2	Same as before for next display to the left.	Write
FFF3h	Seven-segments display 3	Same as before for next display to the left.	Write
FFF4h	LCD	Enables sending control signals to the LCD.	Write
FFF5h	LCD	Enables writing on the LCD a character with the extended ASCII code written to the address.	Write
FFF6h	Timer	Counter value associated with the timer.	Read/Write
FFF7h	Timer	Starts or stops the timer.	Read/Write
FFF8h	LEDs	Enables turning on/off the LEDS corresponding to the value in binary written to the address. The LED on the right corresponds to the least significant bit.	Write
FFF9h	Switches	Enables reading the value specified by the position of the switches, using the eight least significant bits. The switch to the right corresponds to the least significant bit.	Read
FFFAh	Interrupt mask	Allows defining the enabled interrupt vectors, one for each bit of the mask.	Read/Write
FFFCh	Text window	Enables the cursor to be placed at any given position in the window.	Write
FFFDh	Text window	Enables the testing of whether a key has been pressed.	Read
FFFEh	Text window	Enables a character to be written in the window.	Write
FFFFh	Text window	Enables reading the last key pressed.	Read

- DIO5: input/output device module. This board contains: 16 push buttons (the one with the largest index is not currently used); 16 LEDs; 8 switches; four 7-segments displays; an LCD.
- MEM1C1: RAM module, for the P3 main memory.
- PIO1: module with a parallel port through which the program and the ROMs are loaded.

The complete P3 board is depicted in Figure A.1.

In addition to the card, and a parallel cable to connect it to the PC, the cp3 program is necessary to enable files from the PC to be loaded to the card. Loading an executable program to the card simply involves using:

```
$ cp3 <program-name>.exe
```

The development of the system makes possible to change the control unit ROMs easily, thus enabling the operation of the P3 assembly instructions to be modified or even to create new instructions. To load the A, B or Control ROMs, use the -A, -B or -C modifiers, respectively, in the cp3 program. The files to upload are text files, with one line per ROM position to change each of these lines with two integers: the address to change and the new content for the ROM.

Fig. A.1   P3 card.

A.2.4 *Simulator*

The simulator developed for the P3 simulates execution at the microprogram level and, as mentioned, it is fully compatible with the operation of the card.

This simulator has two key advantages. The first is to allow to test programs when the card is not available. This aspect allows programs to be developed using just a computer.

The second advantage of the simulator is to help debug programs. This task is very difficult to carry out on the card because there are no control or observation mechanisms when executing programs. The simulator allows execution instruction by instruction, or the setting of breakpoints in the code. Also, the simulator window indicates the contents of all the registers, updated every time the execution stops. Figure A.2 shows the main interface window for the P3 simulator.

As with the card, in the simulator it is possible to change the contents of the control unit's ROMs, to redefine the existing assembly instructions or to create new assembly instructions. The simulator allows step-by-step execution of the microinstructions and the visualisation of the internal registers, both in the control unit and in the register file, to carry out the debugging

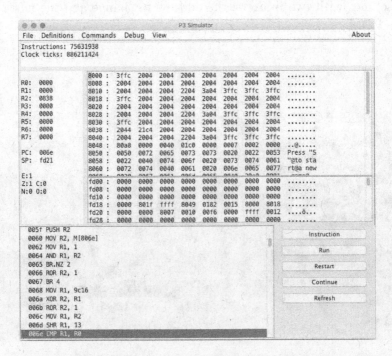

Fig. A.2   Main interface window for the P3 simulator.

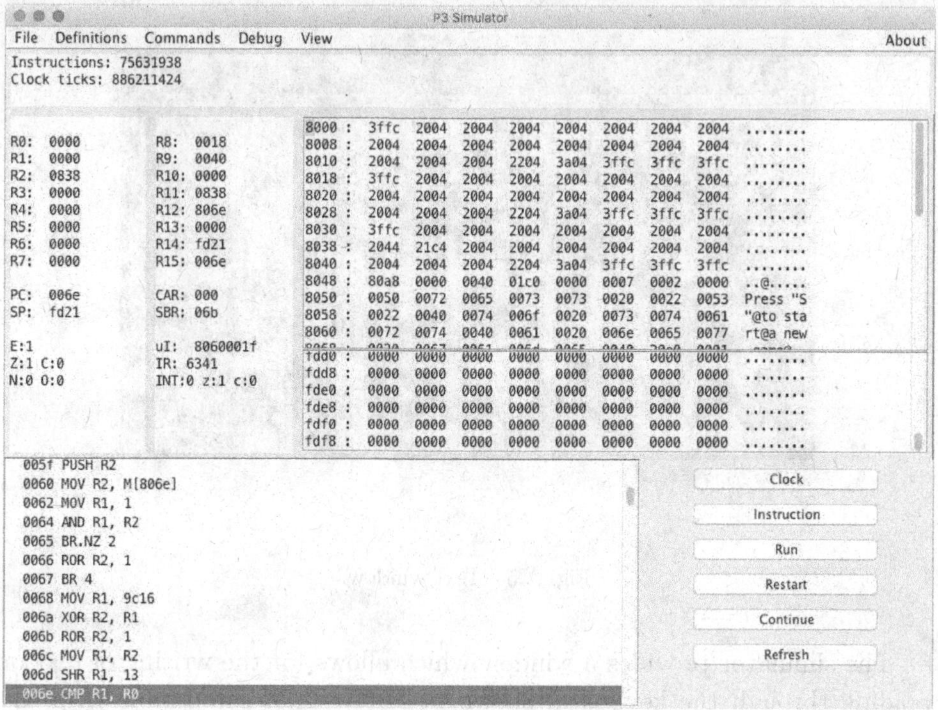

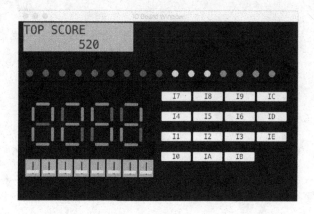

Fig. A.3   Interface window with additional information about the control unit.

Fig. A.4   Window with the P3 peripherals.

of the microprograms. The expanded interface containing this information is shown in Figure A.3.

The peripherals are available in a separate window, as shown in Figure A.4.

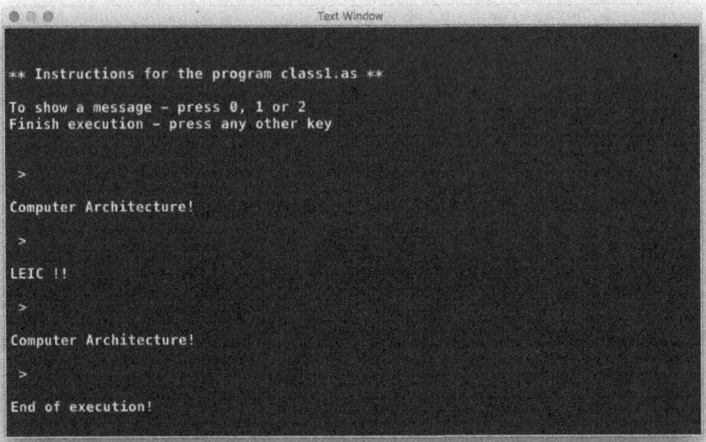

Fig. A.5   Text window.

The simulator provides a window which allows for the writing of text or reading through the keyboard, shown in Figure A.5, compatible with the card's interface to a keyboard and a monitor.

Index

Printed in the United States
By Bookmasters

Printed in the United States
By Bookmasters